WRITING JAPANESE MONSTERS

From the Files of
The Big Book of Japanese Giant Monster Movies

By John LeMay
Edited by Ted Johnson

BICEP BOOKS
Roswell, New Mexico, U.S.A.

BICEP BOOKS
Roswell, New Mexico, U.S.A.

© 2020 by John LeMay. All rights reserved.

ISBN: 978-1-7341546-6-5

The following is a critical analysis and textbook. It has not been approved, authorized, endorsed, licensed, sponsored or associated by any entity involved in creating or producing any tokusatsu film. The opinions expressed in this book are those of the author's and do not reflect the views or opinions of Toho International Co., Ltd. or any of its employees.

Toho International Co, Ltd. is the owner of all copyrights and trademarks in its related and respective films, characters and photographs. All of its rights are expressively reserved © 1943-2020 Toho Co., Ltd. and its related entities.

Godzilla is a Registered Trademark of Toho Co., Ltd. in Japan as are Anguirus, Rodan, Mothra, Varan, King Ghidorah, Ebirah, Kumonga, Kamacuras, Minilla, Gabara, Gorosaurus, Manda, Baragon, Hedorah, Gigan, Megalon, Jet Jaguar, Mechagodzilla, King Seesar, Titanosaurus, Biollante, Battra, Space Godzilla, Destroyah, Godzilla Junior, Orga, Megaguirus, and Monster X.

Kadokawa Daiei Studio Co., Ltd. is the owner of all copyrights and trademarks in its related and respective films, characters and photographs. All of its rights are expressively reserved.

Toei Studio Co., Ltd. is the owner of all copyrights and trademarks in its related and respective films, characters and photographs. All of its rights are expressively reserved.

All text © 2020 by John LeMay, All Rights Reserved.

No part of this book may be reproduced or transmitted in any form or by any means, electronic or mechanical, including photocopying or recording, without written permission from the publisher.

For Kyle Byrd, Matt Parmley, and Kevin Derendorf.

TABLE OF CONTENTS

Acknowledgments...v
Preface...6

1. Project "G": *Godzilla* (1954)...8
2. Put On Ice: Godzilla vs. the *Abominable Snowman* (1955)...17
3. Of Meganuron and Mysterians (1956-1957)...22
4. American Imports: *Varan* and *The Volcano Monsters* (1958-1959)...29
5. Tales of *Kuru Island*: *Gorgo's* Japanese Roots (1958-1961)...35
6. The Secret History of *Mothra* (1961)...41
7. The End of the World: *Gorath* and *The Last War* (1961-1962)...47
8. Beast Meets West: *King Kong vs. Godzilla* (1962)...51
9. Voice in the Night: *Matango* Sprouts (1963)...54
10. The Undersea Battleship vs. The Undersea Kingdom: *Atragon* (1963)...58
11. *Mothra vs. Godzilla*: Round One (1964)...65
12. Space Monsters: Dogora and King Ghidorah Attack (1964)...69
13. Frankenstein vs. Godzilla, Baragon, and the Giant Devilfish (1965)...78
14. The Birth of *Gamera* and *Daimajin* (1965-1966)...86
15. War of the Sea Monsters: Gaira, Ebirah, and Gezora (Almost) Attack (1966)...93
16. TV Monsters: *Ultra Q* and *Ultraman* (1966-1967)...100
17. The Big One: 1967 (1967)...104
18. Return of the TV Monsters: *Agon* and *Ultraseven* (1968)...114
19. Attack of the Killer Stock Footage from Outer Space: *Gamera vs. Viras* (1968)...119
20. The Dirty Dozen: The Original *Destroy All Monsters* (1968)...125
21. Tales from *Latitude Zero* (1969)...133
22. The Animated Origins of *All Monsters Attack* (1969)...139
23. *The Vampire Doll* and the Death of the Old Studio System (1970)...145

24. Pollution Monsters: Zigra vs. Hedorah (1971)...151
25. Dueling Drafts:
    The Development of *Godzilla vs. Gigan* (1972)...162
26. Attack of the Automatons (1973)...170
27. *Horror of the Wolf* (Guy) (1973)...178
28. *Japan Sinks!* (1973)...186
29. Enter the (Mechanical) Dragon (1974)...195
30. In the Wake of *Japan Sinks*:
    ESPY and *Catastrophe 1999* (1974)...205
31. Clash of the Titans: *Terror of Mechagodzilla* (1975)...210
32. *The Last Dinosaur*(s) (1977)...221
33. The Influence of *Star Wars* in Japan (1977-1984)...227
34. The Long Road to *The Return of Godzilla*
    (1978-1984)...233
35. "Wonder Lizard is Down for the Count"
    Godzilla 1985 (1985)...241
36. "Godzilla 2" and the Birth of Biollante (1989)...248
37. Big Screen *Ultra Q* (1990)...265
38. Back to the Futurians: Mothra and King Ghidorah Return
    (1990-1992)...268
39. Attack of the (Godzilla) Clones (1993-1994)...277
40. Rebirth of Gamera (1993-1995)...290
41. Long Live the King: Developing Destoroyah (1995)...295
42. Mothra Flies Solo (1996-1998)...303
43. Tri-Star's *Godzilla* (1998)...309
44. *Gamera 3*: Incomplete Screenplay (1999)...314
45. *Godzilla 2000*: (New) *Millennium* (1999)...321
46. Giant (Holy) Monsters All-Out Attack (2001)...327
47. Birth of the Kiryu Saga (2002)...333
48. From Rolisica With Love: *Godzilla X Mothra* (2003)...337
49. Don't Call it a Comeback:
    Godzilla Junior in *Final Wars*? (2004)...343
50. Legendary Monsters: *Godzilla* (2005-2014)...349

Appendix I: Script Development Dates ...355
Appendix II: Project Hierarchy...373
Appendix III: Toho Manga Adaptations...378
Appendix IV: Daiei Manga Adaptations...398

Bibliography...409
Index...414
About the Author...422

Acknowledgments

This book is built upon the shoulders of giants—and I am not talking about the monsters. I'm talking about the researchers who interviewed the directors, actors, and screenwriters behind these beloved films. Without them, this book would not have been possible. So, even though you didn't help directly, thank you David Milner, Stuart Galbraith IV, Steve Ryfle, Ed Godziszewski, Brett Homenick, August Ragone, Peter Brothers, Patrick Macias, Toho Kingdom, Totorom, J.D. Lees, and all the other researchers out there who have enriched our fandom with knowledge. And an especially big thank you to Ted Johnson, who edited this—our biggest project together yet!

PREFACE

Another trip to the well?" you might ask. Or perhaps, "Pouring old wine into new bottles again, are we?" While this book is certainly tangential to *The Big Book of Japanese Giant Monster Movies: The Lost Films*, this is not a case of old wine in new bottles. I will, however, confess that much of this material was intended for a revised and expanded second edition of said book. The idea for a separate book comprised of this new material came upon me as I was writing up an additional chapter on the development of 1963's *Atragon*, which is based upon a book dating all the way back to 1899. Tracking *Atragon*'s evolution from the novel to Shinichi Sekizawa's script was fascinating, but I eventually realized it was never a "lost film". I had also decided to compile bios for the many screenwriters for the 2nd Edition of *The Lost Films*. That was the impetus for a book about the writers and the writing process itself that had never been done. There have been English-language books devoted to Eiji Tsuburaya and Ishiro Honda, which encompassed the aspects of directing and special effects, so why not a book on the writers and the writing process?

While many fans are intrigued by the special effects techniques used to bring these monsters to life, I have always been more enamored with the creative aspect in the writer's room—how the films developed and changed over time. In many cases, the writer's original ideas were naturally much grander than the budgets and technology of the times could pull off. A lot more goes into the development process than just the scriptwriting phase. Take this quote from Heisei era producer Shogo Tomiyama for example:

> "First, Mr. Tanaka and I decide what kind of film we should make. Then, the screenwriter and I write the first draft of the script. After the director and the special effects director have read it and offered suggestions, the second draft is written solely by the screenwriter. While it is being written, pre-production sketches are drawn, locations are selected, and so on. After all of that has been completed, the third and final draft is written." [www.davmil.org/www.kaijuconversations.com/tomiya.htm]

Problems with budgets can necessitate certain scenes be cut or, in more drastic cases, cause the film to be scaled down to the point that only the concept remains. *Space Monster Dogora* was originally devoid of the cops and robbers aspect and was a global epic comparable to *Gorath* and *The Last War*. When that was deemed too expensive, Shinichi Sekizawa had to set the film solely in Japan and overhaul the characters, which is where Detective Kommei and the gangsters came in. Another factor that can tweak a film's development are demands that come from the producers. Henry G. Saperstein's determination to get a giant octopus into *Frankenstein vs. Baragon* necessitated an entirely new sequence to be written and shot after principal photography was already over. Ironically, the scene ended up in neither the Japanese nor the American versions of the film.

I have recently learned the answers to many nagging questions that have plagued more devoted tokusatsu fans. Want to know why publicity photos for *Godzilla vs. Megalon* show Godzilla munching on a telephone pole toothpick and brandishing a tree sword despite no such scenes in the finished film? I can tell you that not only were those scenes written by Jun Fukuda and filmed by Teruyoshi Nakano, but also who cut them out and why. Want to know the real reason Gorosaurus attacked Paris instead of Baragon in *Destroy All Monsters*? It may not be the reason you thought. And I know you're curious to learn just where it is Anguirus is hanging out at the beginning of *Godzilla vs. Mechagodzilla...* or is that just me and a few other overly obsessive fans?

In any case, I hope you enjoy another journey into the unknown realm of what could have been. A *Gamera vs. Guiron* without Space Gyaos. *All Monsters Attack* starring Megalon instead of Gabara. Magma and Ebirah in *Destroy All Monsters*. A giant halibut/flatfish monster instead of whatever Gappa is in *Gappa, the Triphibian Monster*. The possibilities in the imaginations of our favorite screenwriters were truly endless, and now their original visions—good and bad—can finally be revealed.

John LeMay,
Spring 2018

1.
PROJECT "G"
GODZILLA

As every die-hard fan knows, *Godzilla* came about from the cancellation of another Toho film. *In the Shadow of Glory* was a war film to be shot in Indonesia, though visas for the cast couldn't be secured and was canceled. Producer Tomoyuki Tanaka was flying back to Japan and looked down at the ocean depths below. He imagined a giant monster under the waves and his next project was born. Some people say this story is just a studio legend and Tanaka really thought up the idea at another time.

For certain, the concept called "Project G"—as in "Giant"—went through several different ideas during the creative process. Eiji Tsuburaya, whom Tanaka had taken the idea, imagined the monster as a giant octopus that would attack Japanese ships in the Indian Ocean.[1] Tsuburaya even went so far as to create two octopus maquettes.[2] However, Tanaka was set upon a reptilian dinosaur monster in lieu of the success of 1953's *The Beast from 20,000 Fathoms,* and his tentative title for the project was even *The Giant Monster from 20,000 Miles Under the Sea*. In the interest of secrecy, Toho President Iwao Mori insisted the super-secret film be referred to only as "Project G".

Tanaka next asked Tsuburaya to begin designing a dinosaur monster, and he not only did that but also submitted another effects-heavy story treatment with it.[3] Tanaka reportedly filed the treatment away for future use and then set out to find a writer talented enough to turn the giant monster story into something special. The producer eventually decided on acclaimed novelist Shigeru Kayama, whom he visited on May 1, 1954. Kayama recalled the pitch like this:

> "One day in early summer, producer Tanaka from Toho visited me and asked if I could write the original story of a certain movie. If someone chooses me to write an original story, that means it's not an ordinary story they are looking for. But when I first heard the concept that a monster came back to life because of the hydrogen bomb and goes on a rampage, it made me feel a little uneasy... However, as I

listened to the rough storyline from Mr. Tanaka, I became interested in it."[4]

Kayama signed onto the project on May 11th then retreated to an inn near Atami City where he worked on the treatment for the next two weeks.[5] As it turns out, Kayama had already written something similar in a short story entitled "Jira Monster" in 1952. In the story, a giant bipedal lizard monster that is immune to gunfire terrorizes a group of primitive people. From here, we can easily see Godzilla's roots on Oto Island. The resultant film treatment was 50 pages long and similar to the finished film with a few intriguing differences and frightening concepts. Godzilla's early scenes are certainly more creepy as he stalks ships in a dense fog before lighting them on fire. A survivor, blind from the ordeal, tells of a huge monster's head rising from the ocean. In another spooky scene, Godzilla comes ashore on Oto Island in the darkness unbeknownst to the natives. It is only when his dorsal fins light up that they spot him through the forest. Yet another scare occurs when Emiko drinks from a spring only to see Godzilla's face reflected on the surface.[6]

One axed scene would have harkened directly to *The Beast from 20,000 Fathoms*; the beam from a lighthouse shines onto a huge dark figure that has just risen from Tokyo Bay. The enormous dark form, naturally, turns out to be Godzilla, whom the light enrages and he attacks it. In another scene, Godzilla picks up a jeep full of people and peers in at them with curiosity. Godzilla also has a voracious appetite in this version, eating sheep and cattle—he even attacks a cargo ship full of wild animals. This element wasn't scrapped until very late in the production, and a scene was filmed but later discarded of Godzilla eating a cow on Oto Island (though references to missing cattle remain in the finished film). And, as in 2016's *Shin Godzilla*, the government is so shocked and befuddled by Godzilla that they do nothing to slow his journey to Japan. Only after the monster has caused damage and killed civilians do they finally take action.[7]

The most significant difference in this Godzilla is that he has floppy ears like an elephant—or Baragon, if you prefer. In this draft, Godzilla swipes helicopters from the sky with his tail. He also doesn't use his atomic ray much (simply a fiery breath in this version) and mostly uses it on Oto Island. Oddest of all, Godzilla doesn't completely decimate Tokyo like he does in the finished film. In this version, he comes ashore three times but only does moderate damage each time. Tokyo then lives in fear of the monster, but Serizawa kills him with the Oxygen Destroyer before the beast comes ashore to cause any more destruction. However, in this version, Serizawa has to lure Godzilla to him with an underwater spotlight to get him to a deeper part of Tokyo Bay, which would have made for a suspenseful scene.

In this draft, Emiko has an even more proactive role. In one scene, she and Ogata track a departing Godzilla in Tokyo Bay with a boat. In another scene, she must physically confront her father when he tries to sabotage the power plant powering the electric towers meant to deter Godzilla. At the last second, Emiko flips the switch herself and electrocutes Godzilla, though it has no effect. Dr. Yamane is a less sympathetic and much more peculiar character in this version. A recluse said to wear a cape[8] and only go out at night, he is an eccentric extremist when it comes to protecting Godzilla, whom he believes should be studied. At the story's end, Yamane sits in his room incredibly depressed at Godzilla's demise. Dr. Serizawa is a less-developed character and he isn't Emiko's fiancé/childhood betrothed. A scene where Ogata and Emiko were to fly over Tokyo Bay and drop a memorial wreath in its waters in Serizawa's honor is included in this script and was planned for the final film but was never shot.

Ishiro Honda was not the first director eyed for *Godzilla*. Senkichi Taniguchi, who had been slated to helm *In the Shadow of Glory*, immediately refused the project. That was when Tanaka brought in Honda. As Honda began taking over the project's creative aspects, he brought in screenwriter Takeo Murata to further flesh out Kayama's treatment, which Honda had apparently already re-written. In *Ishiro Honda: A Life in Film, From Godzilla to Kurosawa,* Murata is quoted as saying, "Honda told me that he would write first, so I gave the whole thing to him. Then I polished what he wrote."[9]

Murata locked himself away in a local inn just as Kayama did, though he did receive the occasional visit from Tanaka, Tsuburaya, and Kayama, dropping by from time to time to give their input. Finally, Honda came in for the final round and together, the two devised some rather interesting ideas. One such idea not present in the finished film is that Honda had the idea that Godzilla should be several species fused into one gigantic being—an idea coincidentally similar to 2016's super-controversial *Shin Godzilla*. One of Honda's final touches was changing Godzilla's ability to simply breathe fire to spitting an atomic-powered ray.[10]

Godzilla's design naturally came about due to the limitations and beliefs about dinosaurs at the time. Designer Teizo Toshimitsu said that it "was just a reptile, not a bit scary."[11] Tanaka, Mori, Honda, and Tsuburaya all put their heads together and had it redesigned. "How about making the scales more prominent? How about making the face a bit more ferocious?" were ideas the quartet batted around.[12] One early concept had Godzilla's head looking like a mushroom cloud itself and some earlier designs may have looked somewhat simian even though Kayama clearly intended Godzilla be a reptile.[13] Eventually, Godzilla became a bipedal dinosaur influenced by Tyrannosaurus Rex, Iguanodon, and Stegosaurus.[14]

The final draft has several additional scenes—some of which were shot and later cut—and some which may have never been shot at all. One of the ship disaster scenes has a creepier air to it as the *Bingo-Maru* shines a spotlight into the waters and spies what looks like an oil slick. The ship enters into the oily waters and that is when the ship bursts into flames. Since this oil slick is never explained, one can assume it was supposed to be a residue left by Godzilla like some reptiles leave behind in the water. Most of the additional scenes revolved around Oto Island. One showed the helicopter landing on the island with Hagiwara being surrounded by excited children as he exits looking for shipwreck survivors. Another had Emiko, Ogata, and Yamane coming off the boat and being introduced to the village magistrate, who takes them to a cemetery where victims of Godzilla's attack are buried. It is there that they first meet a tearful Shinkichi, which better-explained his leaving the island with the Yamane family later on.

The radioactive element of Godzilla is discovered by the characters earlier when Dr. Tanabe inspects the raft which carried Masaji (Shinkichi's brother) to the island. A scene later that night in Emiko and her father's tent would show the scientist still awake, troubled by the mystery of the radiation and the giant lifeform emitting it. The next morning had a precursor to Godzilla's reveal over the hill. As Emiko and Ogata take a stroll on the beach, Emiko spies a rock—in fact, the tip of Godzilla's tail—that seems to be moving and disappearing behind a hill. Godzilla's grand reveal, as stated earlier, would have shown him clutching a dead cow in his jaws. In addition to this, Godzilla's roar would have set the trees in front of him aflame.

There is a lengthy deleted scene involving all of the film's principal leads taking a car ride together into Tokyo after returning from Oto Island. In the scene we get to see Dr. Serizawa (there to greet them), Dr. Yamane, Emiko, and Ogata all interact with one another. It is the interactions between Ogata and Serizawa that are of most interest, as one has to wonder how Serizawa feels about Emiko and Ogata's relationship—or if he even knows about it. Ogata is said to sit in the front seat, while Emiko, Yamane, and Serizawa sit in the back (in Japan, unlike America, the more esteemed sit in the backseat rather than the front). From this scene, it is also implied that Yamane still looks at Serizawa as his future son-in-law. This scene was filmed and cut, likely for pacing reasons. Serizawa is in another interesting deleted scene when he is spied in the background as two Japanese men on a rainy street corner fearfully discuss Godzilla. Serizawa doesn't seem terribly concerned. Even more curious are production stills of Emiko with Serizawa minus his eye patch. Some scholars wonder if this was a flashback scene (before Serizawa lost his eye in the war) shot and later cut from the film.[15]

Another scene was written of Japanese citizens discussing Godzilla, and over the radio, they would hear that yet another tanker has sunk. This would have lead into the scene where the depth charges are dropped and from there, the story switched to a beer hall where people happily toasted to the news. In the corner, Dr. Yamane slowly gets up and leaves. After this, there are no known deleted scenes until the epilogue, wherein Emiko drops a wreathe into Tokyo Bay from a helicopter to honor Serizawa as the "Prayer for Peace" begins to reprise.

Overall, the finished film fares just fine without these scenes, though it would have been interesting to see some of them. As special effects can only take a film so far, it is partly the social commentary in the writing of *Godzilla* that has made it stick out as a seminal classic for the past 60 plus years. The early scenes meant to mirror the *Lucky Dragon No. 5* incident exemplify this.[16] The families asking about the missing ships' whereabouts were meant to be celluloid stand-ins for the real-life families of the Lucky Dragon crew. A scene on a train between several Japanese citizens says it best when one laments, "First atomic tuna, and now this," while another complains about finding a new shelter in reference to the WWII Tokyo air raids. The most powerful scene just might be one set during the destruction of Tokyo: a widow and her two children choose not to run from the monster as he approaches. Instead, they sit on the ground, the mother rocking her children as she says, "We'll be seeing father soon."[17] And then, to top it all off, is Dr. Serizawa's self-sacrifice; not wanting his invention to become the next weapon of mass destruction, he decides to end his own life with Godzilla's. It would be the first of many similar themes repeated in Ishiro Honda's films.

The publicity campaign designed for *Godzilla* by Toho president Iwao Mori was quite elaborate. One of the tent poles of the campaign was an 11-episode radio serial called *Kaiju Gojira*, which was broadcast on Saturdays during the summer. While listeners obviously couldn't see what the monster looked like, pictures of Godzilla were advertised everywhere, but the fact that the monster was a man in a suit was a closely-guarded secret. Shigeru Kayama's original version was even published as a novel (also called *Kaiju Gojira*) before the film came out to build anticipation. Sources say the printing was limited to 500 copies only and each had Kayama's hanko stamp on the inside. The book was 295 pages and published on October 25, 1954. Budgeted at ¥100 million, *Godzilla* was the most expensive Japanese film of all time. It was also a resounding success attracting 9,610,000 theatergoers, roughly 11% of Japan's entire population at the time. The film would go on to sell in markets across the world, and one of the longest-running film franchises in history was born.

Chapter Notes

[1] During the development of *Ultra Q*, writer Tetsuo Kinjo used the idea as a basis for an episode pitch for the series called "Vengeance of the Giant Octopus." It was produced as episode 23 "Fury of the South Seas" using the octopus prop from *Frankenstein vs. Baragon*.

[2] When Teruyoshi Nakano came to G-Fest XI in 2004, he gave a totally off-the-wall account of the making of *Godzilla* which could be attributed to a rushed translation of what he was saying in real time. Nakano would seem to imply that originally Eiji Tsuburaya and Tomoyuki Tanaka weren't just inspired by *King Kong*, but wanted to make a King Kong movie! The giant octopus existed as an opponent for Kong. As development progressed, Godzilla was then created to battle the octopus. Nakano is quoted in *G-Fan* as saying, "They were only going to give Godzilla a small part in the film. They were still thinking about this big octopus. Little Godzilla, big octopus is what they were thinking of." As stated already, the translation, which had to be done rapidly as Nakano spoke in real time, could be misunderstood. Furthermore, Nakano could have been misremembering. Furthermore, his first Toho job was *The Three Treasures* in 1959 and he didn't work on a special effects film until *King Kong vs. Godzilla*. Source: "Information Explosion: Teruyoshi Nakano talks of Godzilla past, present and future." *G-Fan* #71 (Spring 2005) pp.53-54.

[3] Two years earlier, Tsuburaya had come up with an idea entitled *The Ghostly Whale That Came from the Sea to Attack Tokyo* about a whale that walked upright to attack Tokyo. The 1952 re-release of *King Kong* had fired his imagination.

[4] Brothers, *Atomic Dreams and the Nuclear Nightmare* pp.23.

[5] According to Ed Godziszewski, Kayama's first story draft actually had Oto Island orphan Shinkichi as the protagonist. Shinkichi would come back from Oto Island with Ogata and get a job at his salvage company in addition to living with Dr. Yamane.

[6] This scene would later play out with the Tyrannosaurus in *The Last Dinosaur* (1977).

[7] Presumably, the government as portrayed within the original *Godzilla* treatment weren't as inept as the ones in *Shin-Godzilla*.

[8] Shiro Sano's cameo appearance as a cape-wearing assassin in *Godzilla: Final Wars* is believed to be a nod to this version of Dr. Yamane.

[9] Ryfle and Godziszewski, *Ishiro Honda*, pp.89.

[10] Though Honda added many of Godzilla's nuclear elements, in *Ishiro Honda: A Life in Film, From Godzilla to Kurosawa* Steve Ryfle and Ed Godziszewski say that an early draft of Kayama's story began with the *Lucky Dragon No. 5* returning to Japan.

[11] Ryfle and Godziszewski, *Ishiro Honda*, pp.89.

[12] Ibid.

[13] On the note of Kayama, some sources imply he named Godzilla, though studio lore says there was a burly Toho worker who went by the name of Gojira, a combination of the Japanese words "gorira" and "kujira", which mean "gorilla" and "whale."

[14] Paleontologists at the time hadn't yet come to the conclusion that dinosaurs like the Tyrannosaurus Rex walked parallel to the ground with their tails in the air in line with their bodies, not to mention the fact that to do this via suitmation would be very difficult. In fact, it was still impossible to accomplish for *Godzilla, Mothra and King Ghidorah: Giant Monsters All-Out Attack* (2001). There is also a still of Satsuma doing this pose in the suit on the set of *Godzilla vs. Space Godzilla* and it doesn't look good at all.

[15] Kodansha's 2018 book *Godzilla Special Effects Making Photograph Collection* says that these images are indeed meant to represent Emiko and Serizawa in their youth. However, the book is not clear if these were just photographs or deleted footage. The book does say the photographs were taken shortly after the two actors were cast. (pp.9)

[16] In March of that year, the fishing vessel *Lucky Dragon No.5* drifted into contaminated waters from the testing of the H-Bomb on Bikini Atoll resulting in the radiation poisoning of the crew. The death of the first crew member, Aikichi Kuboyama, and the contaminated tuna soon sparked an international incident between Japan and the U.S., who eventually paid a $2 million settlement to the families of the crew.

[17] Some viewers may notice that the children survive, but the mother dies.

PROFILE: SHIGERU KAYAMA

Shigeru Kayama was born July 1, 1904, in Tokyo. During his education, Kayama dropped out of the Hosei University Economics Department and began working for the government, entering into the Ministry of Finance to work in the Deposit Division. In 1940, Kayama also began working as a writer and poet for *Tanka Magazine*. His first story, 1946's "Orang Pendek's Revenge," was something of a precursor to Toho's 1955 *Abominable Snowman*, which he would write the treatment for. Kayama's second published novel, *Eerie Story*, won him the prestigious New Novelist Prize of 1947. After this, Kayama worked vigorously, also earning the Japan Detective Artist Club Award. In May of 1949, Kayama retired from the Ministry of Finance to write full time. In 1954, Tomoyuki Tanaka, a fan of Kayama's stories on strange creatures, came knocking on Kayama's doorstep to ask him to help refine ideas for a movie about a giant monster. To do so, Kayama more or less took inspiration from his own 1952 short story, "Jira Monster," about a bipedal lizard monster terrorizing primitive islanders. As such, Kayama qualifies as one of the original creators of Godzilla in a joint effort between himself, Tanaka, Eiji Tsuburaya, Ishiro Honda, and Akira Ifukube. Peter Brothers' *Atomic Dreams and the Nuclear Nightmare* features Eiji Tsuburaya's remarks on Kayama, saying, "My first impression of him was that he seemed like an agreeable, very good-mannered person and a remarkable human being. He had unruly hair, a gentle face, and friendly eyes hidden behind round glasses; he also had the ability to calm the hearts of those around him, so from our first meeting I was able to talk to him freely and comfortably." [Brothers, *Atomic Dreams*, pp.23] Kayama's version of *Godzilla* was even published as a novel, *Monster Godzilla*, by Iwatani Shoten before the film was released. Kayama was naturally asked to help write a sequel to *Godzilla* in 1955, though he was said to be somewhat consternated as how to bring the monster back to life (hence a second monster of the same species). Before *Godzilla Raids Again*, Kayama also came up with a treatment for *Abominable Snowman* (which began as "Project S"). *The Mysterians* was the last sci-fi film project Kayama worked on, and after the late 1950s, his story output greatly diminished. On February 7, 1975, Kayama died of heart failure.

Selected Filmography/Bibliography
"Revenge of Orang Pendek" (1947) (writer)
"The Fate of Orang Pendek" (1947) (writer)
Eerie Story [novel] (1947) (writer)
"El Dorado" (1948) (writer)
"Jira Monster" (1952) (writer)
Godzilla (1954) (writer)
Monster Godzilla [novel] (1954) (writer)
Godzilla Raids Again (1955) (writer)
Abominable Snowman (1955) (writer)
The Mysterians (1957) (writer)

2.
PUT ON ICE
GODZILLA VS. THE ABOMINABLE SNOWMAN

Before "Project G" had even come to completion, Toho was already planning their next monster movie in the form of "Project S"—to be about a giant snowman in the Himalayas.[1] Shigeru Kayama began writing a story for Toho, which was partially inspired by two of his first short stories, "Revenge of Orang Pendek" and "The Fate of Orang Pendek"—both published sometime between 1947 and 1948. The stories concerned a Japanese anthropologist discovering a race of ape men in the Sumatran rainforest based on the real-life cryptid of the same name. Kayama's treatment, also inspired by the legends of the Hibagon (a monster allegedly sighted in the mountains of Chugoku, the westernmost region of Honshū), was ready by October 16, 1954. The film was then announced for production in November of 1954 as *Snowman of the Alps*. Ironically, the snowman was put on ice after *Godzilla*'s huge success at the Japanese box office.

As *Godzilla* was raking in the dough, Toho president Iwao Mori was out of the country making a Japanese-Italian co-production of *Madame Butterfly*. When he returned to Tokyo, a party was held in his honor. While there, he approached Tomoyuki Tanaka to congratulate him on *Godzilla*'s success and also asked him to start work on a follow-up immediately. Like many sequels of the old studio system cranked out as quickly as possible,[2] the result was the slightly underwhelming *Godzilla's Counterattack/Godzilla Raids Again* released five months after *Godzilla* in late April of 1955.

The story's concept was quickly scratched together by *Godzilla* story writer Shigeru Kayama, who was reportedly anxious about how to bring back the dead Godzilla until he just decided to have another member of the same species show up. Sadly, not much is known of Kayama's treatment/story pitch, but whatever he came up with was again fleshed out by Takeo Murata. Also contributing to the script was Shigeaki Hidaka, whose only previous writing

 **INVISIBLE AVENGER**

RUSHED INTO PRODUCTION IN LATE 1954 AFTER THE SUCCESS OF *GODZILLA*, THIS JAPANESE TAKE ON THE INVISIBLE MAN WAS PITCHED BY A TOHO PRODUCTION DESIGNER NAMED TAKEO KITA. *INVISIBLE AVENGER'S* STORY PROPOSAL BY SHIGEAKI HIDAKA AND HIROSHI BEPPU WAS SUBMITTED ON OCTOBER 21ST AND BY THE 25TH, THE PRODUCTION WAS GREENLIT TO BE THE DECEMBER 1954 NEW YEAR'S RELEASE. ALTHOUGH THE SCRIPT'S DEVELOPMENTAL PROCESS WAS SHORT (THE FILM WOULD BEGIN SHOOTING IN NOVEMBER), THERE ARE SOME DIFFERENCES IN THE THREE DRAFTS. FOR INSTANCE, IN THE FIRST DRAFT, THE INVISIBLE MAN'S LOVE INTEREST, MICHIYO, WAS THE DAUGHTER OF A FLOWER SHOP OWNER RATHER THAN A NIGHTCLUB PERFORMER. ALSO, SHE AND THE INVISIBLE MAN'S BLOSSOMING ROMANCE WAS REPORTEDLY BETTER HANDLED IN THE FIRST TWO SCRIPTS AND WAS NOT AS ABRUPT AS IT WAS IN THE FINISHED FILM.

credit was Toho's *Invisible Avenger* (1954), a Japanese take on the classic Invisible Man tale released in late December of 1954.

This earliest version of *Godzilla Raids Again* was submitted on December 20, 1954. Most sources say it is mostly the same as the finished film, except Anguirus (then unnamed) could breathe fire. Also, his two-piece, flappy carapace was part of his intended design, not just a function of the suit. Everyone on the Toho lot was allowed to submit ideas for the new monster's name and Yoshio Tsuchiya (who, unable to appear in *Godzilla*, demanded a role in its sequel, ultimately playing defense force pilot Tajima[3]) remembers he suggested "Gyottosu".

A main theme in the story seemed to be how does the world defeat the new Godzilla without the Oxygen Destroyer. Takeo Murata also decided to utilize working-class heroes rather than scientists and military men for the new story. Murata had a desire to bring to life what would happen in the event of a monster attack in reality: looting and chaos. However, there simply wasn't enough time to film such scenes and the sequence with the escaped convicts was Murata's only vestige of the idea.

Together with Hidaka, Murata came up with what would become the series' signature concept: dueling monsters. Although the story structure is odd in that Godzilla's opponent is killed midway through the film, it still ranked as the first Japanese monster vs. monster film. The climax where humanity must defeat Godzilla once again is mostly well done and one can tell the writers were likely instructed to make sure Godzilla lived this time—or they knew better than to paint themselves into a corner again. This film wisely ended with Godzilla safely packed in ice for a future adventure.[4]

Storyboards showcase at least one scene that was radically different from the finished film. When Tsukioka and Kobayashi huddle around the campfire on Iwato Island, Godzilla can be seen sneaking up on the two men. They are startled by his presence only when he growls. Notably, Godzilla is not engaged in battle with Anguirus and chases the two men into the rocky chasm. The storyboards show Godzilla's hand reaching in to grab them until his fingertips hover over their heads. Another monster (still unnamed in the storyboards) charges Godzilla, saving the two men. The two monsters then tussle as in the finished film until they tumble into the ocean, spraying water all over Kobayashi and Tsukioka. The storyboards also confirm that Anguirus breathes fire. Also, the spikes on his head are more pronounced, extending to his cheekbones, making him similar to a Styracosaurus.

Later, the two monsters begin their Osaka battle in the water, splashing around in the shallow waves. Tsuburaya envisioned a rather unique shot of Godzilla crushing a tank. The first shot would be a low angle looking up as the monster's foot comes down. The following shot was envisioned above Godzilla's head looking down. Unfortunately, the scene was never filmed.

While a resounding success selling 8.3 million tickets, the film is often reported in retrospect as something of a critical disappointment (actually, Ishiro Honda noted that critics liked *Raids Again* MORE than *Godzilla* because it was a more traditionally-told Japanese movie!). Special effects cameraman Sadamasa Arikawa recalled, "Something was missing when we wrapped *Gojira no Gyakushu*. At the staff screening, people were talking about the first *Godzilla* movie."[5] Tanaka also admitted, "We didn't have much preparation time and it would be difficult for me to say the production was successful."[6]

With *Godzilla Raids Again* in the can, Honda and Tsuburaya were able to begin collaborating on *Abominable Snowman* again. Reportedly, the Snowman was initially much more frightening in design. Described as having fangs and being ten feet tall, Tsuburaya and Honda decided to make the beast more sympathetic as a way to better serve the story (an immobile prop of the Snowman looking as such was made for publicity stills to terrorize actress Akemi Negishi).

The snowman's tale is a tragic one. Though we are lead to believe he may have killed a man in a cabin early on, as the film draws to a close, we learn the snowman—the last of his kind—was just lonely and looking for company. Not only that, he even rescued an injured man from the snow and cared for him in his cave. The snowman's benevolent nature dissipates with the death of his son at the hands of some circus exploiters, necessitating that he be killed. The once gentle snowman kidnaps the female lead Machiko (played by *Godzilla's* Momoko Kochi) and takes her back to his cave (slightly hinted at for mating purposes in a misguided effort to continue his species). Like *Godzilla* and many other Ishiro Honda films, this story ends with a tragic death when a native girl, Chika, is pulled into a sulfur pit along with the snowman when he is shot. However, an alternate ending featured Chika accidentally being shot instead of the Snowman. Another deleted scene had the Snowman watching Chika bathe nude in a river. All around, Chika's character had a bigger role in earlier drafts.

The story is basically well written aside from setting the film up as a flashback. While this works well initially, building up the mystery, it makes for an awkwardly abrupt ending when the story returns to the present. In reality, the film should have ended with the characters mourning Chika's death instead of the awkward fade back to the present time where the movie began.[7]

Abominable Snowman was received well enough theatrically but is now a banned film due to its portrayal of the Anui native people who live in the mountains—a touchy subject in Japan. Today the film can only be viewed (legally, that is) in its U.S. version, titled *Half Human* released in 1957 with new footage starring John Carradine.

Chapter Notes

---

[1] Perhaps it was no coincidence that Dr. Yamane mentions the abominable snowman in *Godzilla* (1954).
[2] *Son of Kong* was released a mere nine months after the original *King Kong*.
[3] Speaking of Tsuchiya, he was Motoyoshi Oda's first choice for the lead, but Toho wanted Hiroshi Koizumi instead.
[4] The editor remembers reading an article stating that either Kayama or Murata felt so badly about killing Godzilla in the first movie, that they wanted the new Godzilla to live.
[5] Ryfle, *Japan's Favorite Mon-Star*, pp.65.
[6] Ibid.
[7] Peter H. Brothers theorizes that Honda wanted to end the film on the death of the snowman and perhaps Tomoyuki Tanaka insisted on a less downbeat ending by returning to the present.

PROFILE: TAKEO MURATA

Takeo Murata was born in Shinagawa on June 17, 1907. Though he attended the Japanese College of Literature, he dropped out. By April 1, 1934, he was working at the Nikkatsu Tamagawa shooting station where his brother-in-law, a movie supervisor, had got him a job as a screenwriter. In March of 1935, his brother-in-law established the "Tokyo Voice Film Manufacturing Co," where Murata served as an assistant director. In 1937, the company was integrated into Toho Movie Co. He was promoted to film director in 1941 on *Pray to the Earth*. During WWII, he was commissioned by the Army Airlines Headquarters and engaged in recording films regarding planes on the southern front lines. He even began a film called *Shield of the Great Sky* which went unreleased (it is unknown if it was only written or actually began shooting). In 1953, Murata was put in charge as screenwriter and director of Japan's first 3-D movie *Southern Sunday*. In 1954, he read the review script for Shigeru Kayama's "Project G" and began fleshing out the treatment into a full shooting script with director Ishiro Honda. Murata's success in writing *Godzilla* ironically seemed to spell the end of his directing career. From then on, Murata would primarily be a writer, working on the screenplays for Toho's next two monster movies in 1955: *Godzilla Raids Again* and *Abominable Snowman*. In between these two films and *Rodan* (1956), Murata wrote a few non-monster films, then capped off his feature film career with 1959's *Son Goku*—a little known (in the west) Toho adaptation of the Chinese epic *Journey to the West* with effects by Eiji Tsuburaya. Afterwards, Murata went to work writing the television series *Special Mobility Investigation Corps* (1961), a crime drama. In 1963, Eiji Tsuburaya invited Murata to participate in the planning for the special effects series *Woo* at the newly-established Tsuburaya Productions. Eventually, *Woo* would turn into *Ultra Q* and *Ultraman*. Murata passed away on July 19, 1994.

Selected Filmography
Pray to the Earth (1941) (director)
Girls Student Account (1941) (director)
Youthful Boss (1953) (director)
Southern Sunday (1953) (writer/director)
Godzilla (1954) (writer)
Godzilla Raids Again (1955) (writer)
Abominable Snowman (1955) (writer)
Rodan (1956) (writer)
Son Goku (1959) (writer)
Special Mobility Investigation Corps [TV series] (1961) (writer)
WoO [TV series] (1963) (writer) [unproduced, developed into *Ultraman* and *Bio Planet WoO* (2006)]

3.
OF MEGANURON AND MYSTERIANS

Toho's next monster film was initially to be another Godzilla sequel, though it came from the most unlikely of sources. In an interview, Ishiro Honda told David Milner, "During the 1950s and 1960s, the planning department would accept ideas from any of Toho's employees. *The H-Man* is a typical example. The idea for that film came from an almost completely unknown actor."[1] The small-time actor Honda spoke of was Hideo Unagami. Before he penned *The H-Man*, however, Unagami wrote what he hoped would be the third Godzilla film. The wild tale called *Bride of Godzilla?* was somewhat ahead of its time with Godzilla fighting a giant robot. It was also quite odd as said giant robot was a naked woman (probably naked in the Barbie doll sense, mind you) made in the image of its creator's ex-lover. Though written straightforwardly with many horror elements, in the end, Godzilla becomes infatuated with the Bride, who locks her arms around him and detonates a hidden atomic bomb in her body destroying them both.

Whether they asked for it or not, someone (likely Tomoyuki Tanaka) at Toho liked Unagami's idea to the point that three script drafts were written. There were even talks of filming the story in Tohoscope and color. Though this didn't pan out, one would be hard-pressed to argue that Unagami's story didn't influence Tanaka's decision to produce *Rodan*. A large portion of *Bride of Godzilla* revolves around a mysterious cavern discovered in a Kyushu mine full of prehistoric horrors. Among them are giant, bloodsucking insects (more akin to *The Return of Godzilla's* Shokilas than *Rodan's* Meganuron) and a giant Archaeopteryx. Though not a Pteranodon, the creature was a prehistoric bird and early concept designs and maquettes for Rodan show it as such an animal. The Archaeopteryx even engages in an aerial battle with jet fighters in *Bride of Godzilla*. Though its suspicious Unagami gets no writing credit on the film, the coincidence is too much. Unagami has a small role in *Rodan*, so perhaps it was a reward of sorts from Tanaka?

From what this author can surmise, Tomoyuki Tanaka approached Ken Kuronuma to begin a story that focused on the giant flying, prehistoric monster element of Unagami's script. Kuronuma, a horror novelist, used the Kyushu setting and giant murderous bugs, but also took inspiration from a deadly real-life U.F.O. sighting known as the "Mantell U.F.O. Encounter." It involved a 25-year-old Kentucky Air National Guard pilot, Captain Thomas F. Mantell, who on January 7, 1948, died while in pursuit of a U.F.O. This scene made it into the finished film where a jet fighter chases a "U.F.O." (actually Rodan) and crashes.

Kuronuma's treatment was called *The Birth of Rodan* (and was also published in *Boys Magazine* under that title). It is similar to the film except that Rodan is defeated with freeze bombs that immobilize him and he sinks to the bottom of the sea. Tanaka gave the treatment to Takeo Murata and newcomer Takeshi Kimura who would go on to become one of Toho's top scriptwriters thanks to this film. In their first full script draft, there is only one Rodan and the monster's feeding on livestock was more heavily emphasized. After Rodan attacks Fukuoka (and it is said to be a much less grand attack than in the finished film), the flying monster is attacked by the U.S. Air Force over Okinawa and severely wounded. When Rodan returns to Mt. Aso, Shigeru himself leads the efforts to dynamite the volcano to induce an eruption. However, the detonation doesn't cause the eruption as intended and only angers Rodan who plans to strike back against humanity. Miraculously, the volcano erupts anyway, consuming the wounded monster. Rodan's mate was introduced in the second draft which is mostly like the finished film.

In addition to the Rodan maquette (which appeared on the release poster) looking much like an Archaeopteryx, storyboards for Rodan showcase yet another alternate design. The giant bird monster presented in the storyboards has forearms and hands built into the wings, which are much more pronounced. Alternate versions of the finished scenes are also presented. For instance, storyboards show an exterior shot of a Meganuron lurking outside Kiyo's home (its eye can be seen through the bushes which its claw also protrudes through). A huge insect pincher pokes through Kiyo's door and that is all we see of the bug before Shigeru and Kiyo run away. Rodan's reveal came much earlier in the storyboards based on the numbering. The Meganuron chase (in abbreviated form) takes place from sections 23 to 36 before Shigeru becomes lost in the mine. Frame 38B shows scorpion-like Meganuron crawling atop a giant egg. It hatches in frame 38C. In the drawing, a huge pterodactyl head is eating a Meganuron and staring straight at Shigeru, very near its beak. Presumably, the scene cuts away here, and we learn Shigeru's fate later. The honeymooners' scene is also slightly different in the storyboards. The couple kisses passionately before Rodan comes to eat them (the monster's head can be seen in the drawing). The greatest "deleted scene" from the storyboards shows Rodan's POV from the air, sighting a train snaking its way across the ground. Rodan dives down and grabs a boxcar. What a wonderful scene that would have made.

Perhaps the biggest surprise from the storyboards is the reveal of a winged, adult Meganuron which would menace the heroes during the climax. The storyboard version of the climax appears to be the one from Kuronuma's early draft as men can be seen planting explosives within Mt. Aso. That is when the adult dragonfly comes to menace them. The design is itself oddly Rodan-like, as it features scales and a beak! The wings, however, are very much like a dragonfly's. Rodan's head appears to come out of a crevice and presumably eats it. The characters run away as the explosives detonate.

Filmed in color (though some sources say it was originally going to be in black and white), *Rodan* was another huge hit when released as the New Year's Blockbuster at the end of 1956. It's not hard to see why, as not only did *Rodan* have excellent effects work but another powerful story to back it up. This story's subtext revolves around man digging too deep into the earth's natural resources. The entertainment value stems from the film's mystery and horror elements. Surely audiences who saw a preview for a movie about a giant flying dinosaur were somewhat confused when the movie's first half revolved around murderous insects instead. One of the best of these early, mysterious scenes has three mining inspectors tied together on a rope that are pulled under waist-deep water one by one by an unseen force. The only escapee is tracked down by a giant shadow accompanied by a horrific ringing noise before he meets his fate. The culprits are later revealed as the Meganuron—inspired by both the big bugs of American movies like *Them!* and also Unagami's bloodsucking giant lice from *Bride of Godzilla?* In a horrific scene, Rodan begins to feed on the insects which had themselves been feeding off man. This idea came from Akira Kurosawa of all sources, who was said to have taken a cursory look at the script and offered this suggestion to his friend Ishiro Honda.[2]

One of the film's most poignant moments wasn't scripted at all and was the result of an accident. The scene occurs as Rodan and his mate are flying over the volcano and the female suddenly falls into the fire. What actually happened was the marionette's wires broke and it went plummeting to the volcano set. Tsuburaya kept the cameras rolling as the technicians tried to hoist the model up which inadvertently gave the impression that the female Rodan was struggling for her life in the fire. Honda and Tsuburaya liked the scene so much that they altered the script to reflect it. Even on-set accidents can change the course of a film's story or add a touching moment.

Toho's next big effects opus would be the sci-fi spectacle, *The Mysterians*. The story came from 39-year-old Jojiro Okami, who had been a test pilot in the Japanese Air Force. After this, Okami began writing stories, the first of which won acclaim in a mystery magazine in 1949. It's murky just how Okami met Tomoyuki Tanaka, but all information seems to indicate that Okami either met Tanaka's brother—or Tanaka met Okami's brother—and a meeting was set up to discuss Okami's sci-fi story *Earth Defense Forces* (the original Japanese title of *The Mysterians*). In the unpublished novel-length story by Okami, there were no monsters of any kind nor are the aliens interested in interbreeding with human women.

Tomoyuki Tanaka, who tried to help get Okami's novel published, liked what he saw in the story and handed it over to Shigeru Kayama for further refinement. It was Kayama's idea that the Mysterians wanted to mate with the earth women to repopulate their dying race. Tanaka did insist upon one change for certain: the inclusion of a monster. At first, the alien monster was to be a sort of proto-Baragon underground reptile monster. Ishiro Honda wanted to show the superiority of the Mysterians and so it became the giant, burrowing robot monster Mogera instead. As the drafts progressed, Mogera originally looked like a flesh and blood monster and it was only after its defeat that the characters realized that it was a machine all along.

Storyboards offer a more in-depth look at the attack by the monster. The creature's stature is smaller than that of Mogera from the film. One frame shows it being only a little taller than a semi-truck. Another frame shows the monster's hand reaching through a window to grab a man. Sketches also show the Mysterians to resemble male versions of the all-female Kilaaks from *Destroy All Monsters* (1968) and are lacking their signature helmets from the film.

There were other differences in early drafts too; instead of emerging from underground, the Mysterian Dome was supposed to emerge from a lake. The Mysterians were to have had an invisible laser that would shoot down planes when they flew too close to their territory at Mt. Fuji. Earlier drafts also portrayed the decision to form the multinational Earth Defense Forces as being more controversial in the eyes of the public. And—though nothing major—it's worth noting that Yoshio Tsuchiya himself improvised some of his lines as the Mysterian Leader, notably about mankind selling real estate on Mars and the moon.

Takeshi Kimura, hot off *Rodan*, turned in four versions of the script in total. Though it's unknown whose idea this was, it's interesting that even though the film is about an alien invasion, a strong anti-nuclear theme was still interjected into the storyline. The Mysterians explain that their homeworld was destroyed as the result of an atomic civil war. The aliens also mention that there is so much Strontium 90 in their bodies that most of their children are born with defects, which leads to their desire to breed with earth women.

Contrary to popular belief, the widescreen, color *Earth Defense Forces* was not a massive hit in Japan (it sold only 500,000 tickets), though it is very fondly remembered today. Notably, it was the favorite tokusatsu film of Koichi Kawakita, who created an update of Mogera for 1994's *Godzilla vs. Space Godzilla*. Kawakita also tried unsuccessfully to get a *Mysterians* remake made up until the early 2000s.

Chapter Notes

---

[1] www.davmil.org/www.kaijuconversations.com/honda.htm
[2] The Japanese Wikipedia page for *Rodan* makes this claim.

PROFILE: HIDEO UNAGAMI

Relatively little is known about *The H-Man* and *Bride of Godzilla?* writer Hideo Unagami. His real name was actually Jiro Ogawa, and he was born in 1912. He dropped out of Meiji University in 1932, and had plans to be an actor before WWII broke out. After the war, Ogawa (as Hideo Unagami) acted for Shochiku in *Comedy is Not Over* (1946) and left soon after to start his own theater company. He also ran for the 23rd General Assembly elections for the House of Representatives in April of 1947, but was defeated. While recuperating from a bad case of stomach ulcers in 1953, Unagami wrote a treatment for a film which roughly translated to "People Outside the Living Area" which sounded to be a drama rather than a sci-fi story. Unagami gave his treatment to Toho president Iwao Mori who never did make the script, but did give Mori a job in their acting department that fall. At some point after the release of *Godzilla Raids Again* (1955), Unagami wrote a sequel to that film and gave it to Mori. Though *Bride of Godzilla?* was never made, 1956 saw the release of *Rodan,* which contained elements from *Bride of Godzilla?* Oddly, Unagami received no writing credit on *Rodan* but had a bit part in the movie. [For those who wonder if perhaps Kimura simply had the same great idea as Unagami, recent Japanese books have begun to credit Unagami's *Bride of Godzilla?* script as helping to inspire *Rodan's* story.] The next year, Unagami appeared as one of the Mysterians in 1957. That same year, Tomoyuki Tanaka greenlit a script Unagami had written called *Beauty and the Liquid People* (U.S. title, *The H-Man*). Unagami's treatment was given to Takeshi Kimura for an overhaul which was completed on November 13th, 1957. Unfortunately, Unagami died of a heart attack the very next day. In the Japanese audio commentary for *Invasion of Astro-Monster*, Yoshio Tsuchiya began talking about *The Mysterians* and made the strange comment that, "One of the actors who played a Mysterian died of stress from the material of the costume." Perhaps Tsuchiya is saying Unagami had an allergic reaction to something made to construct the costume? In any case, it is sad Unagami didn't get to see his H-Man treatment brought to life. If he had, he likely would have written more treatments for Toho (he may even have written another Godzilla script, and the series could have turned out wildly different). As an actor, Unagami had only six acting credits comprising of *Comedy is Not Over* (1946), *Seven Samurai* (1954), *Madame White Snake* (1956), *Prisoner Ship* (1956), *Rodan* (1956) and *The Mysterians* (1957). So just remember, the next time you watch *The Mysterians*, one of the aliens wrote one of the most notorious unmade Godzilla films of all time, in addition to possibly inspiring elements of *Rodan*.

Selected Filmography
Comedy is Not Over (1946) (actor)
Seven Samurai (1954) (actor)
Bride of Godzilla? (1956) (writer)[unproduced]
Rodan (1956) (actor) [uncredited story work]
Madame White Snake (1956) (actor)
The Mysterians (1957) (actor)
Prisoner Ship (1956) (actor)
The H-Man (1958) (story)
Bride of Godzilla (1978) (story concept) [unproduced]

4.
AMERICAN IMPORTS
VARAN AND THE VOLCANO MONSTERS

In 1956, the American version of *Godzilla*—retitled *Godzilla, King of the Monsters!* —had become a huge hit. After the King Brothers' U.S. release of *Rodan* in 1957 was also a huge hit, it is no surprise that American film producers soon came knocking on Toho's door. The first was AB-PT (ABC Pictures), interested in *Godzilla Raids Again*. However, they were only interested in the monster footage and wanted to completely remove the Japanese cast in favor of an all American one.

The story was to be called *The Volcano Monsters* (strangely, it would seem the producers either feared using Godzilla's name or thought new monsters would fare better). This was orchestrated by Paul Schreibman, Harry Rybnick, Richard Kay and Edmund Goldman—all of whom had a hand in the Americanized *Godzilla, King of the Monsters!* Ib Melchior, the future writer of films such as *Reptilicus* (1961) and *The Angry Red Planet* (1959), wrote a script revolving around Caucasian characters. The film was even advertised in a May issue of *Variety* with a production start date set for June.

The story involved American scientists unearthing two dinosaurs in suspended animation from a Japanese volcano: a Tyrannosaurus (Godzilla) and an Ankylosaurus (Anguirus). The two beasts are transported to America, where they reawaken and destroy Chinatown in San Francisco. As in the original Toho film, the "Tyrannosaurus" kills the Ankylosaurus and heads for the Antarctic to "lay eggs." Toho, eager to get a foothold in the American marketplace, agreed to the idea and—although the script meshed well with the actual footage—Toho constructed new suits of Godzilla and Anguirus to fill in the gaps of *The Volcano Monsters* script. That same year, Toho had sent the young snowman suit to America so it could perform a similar role for new shots in *Abominable Snowman's* U.S. version, *Half Human*. No one knows what became of the new Anguirus and Godzilla suits once they made it to America. A color photograph of the American Godzilla suit has surfaced posing with the Phantom of the Opera though, but where exactly is unknown.

29

 **THE H-MAN**

IN 1957, TOHO FINALLY GREENLIT A SCRIPT BY ACTOR AND ASPIRING WRITER HIDEO UNAGAMI. THE STORY WAS ENTITLED *LIQUID MAN APPEARS*. SADLY, UNAGAMI DIED SOON AFTER AND TAKESHI KIMURA TOOK OVER WRITING DUTIES, TURNING THE STORY INTO 1958'S *BEAUTY AND THE LIQUID PEOPLE* (*THE H-MAN* IN THE U.S.). IN THE ORIGINAL DRAFT, KENJI SAHARA'S HEROIC CHARACTER MASUDA VOLUNTEERS TO TURN HIMSELF INTO AN H-MAN AS A MEANS OF BETTER UNDERSTANDING AND DEFEATING THE ENEMY. ALSO, THERE WAS NO FIERY CLIMAX AS IN THE FINISHED FILM. THE MOVIE WAS ORIGINALLY ENVISIONED AS BEING IN BLACK AND WHITE, BUT AFTER THE SUCCESS OF *RODAN* (1956) IN COLOR, IT WAS DECIDED TO FILM *THE H-MAN* IN COLOR AS WELL.

Ib Melchior remembered the production falling apart saying, "These three producers had a production/distribution deal with a company called AB-PT when, in July of 1957, that company closed down. Now, for whatever reasons that I have no idea why, they did not replace the production/distribution company, and *The Volcano Monsters* bit the dust."[1] Strangely, when *Godzilla Raids Again* was re-edited and dubbed into English for its eventual American release, Godzilla's name was still kept out of the new title, *Gigantis, the Fire Monster*. According to Schreibman, "We called it *Gigantis* because we didn't want it to be confused with *Godzilla*."

Ironically enough, it is thought that some of Melchior's ideas for *The Volcano Monsters* made their way into *Reptilicus*! In that film, miners discover a long-dead monster that regenerates from a frozen piece of flesh. Though a bit of a stretch, one could say the concept was similar to finding the dinosaurs in the volcano. The cast of characters are very similar with a military man, a professor and his daughters—one of whom the military man falls for (in *The Volcano Monsters*, it's the professor's female assistant). The scientist character even suffers a heart attack at one point, something else that happens in *The Volcano Monsters*. When Reptilicus approaches a lab developing a weapon against it, this is similar to a scene where the Tyrannosaurus was to approach a university lab where a weapon against it is being devised. Finally, *The Volcano Monsters* would have ended with another dinosaur claw emerging from the volcano. *Reptilicus* ends with the monster's severed foot regenerating on the ocean floor. Melchior himself said, "[*The Volcano Monsters*] was the usual story of a monster that gets loose and destroys a city, very much like *Reptilicus*."[2]

In 1958, Toho was approached about producing a four-part miniseries focusing on a giant monster for television in America, which an unnamed company (possibly still AB-PT despite reports of their demise in mid-1957) would purchase.[3] "*Rodan* had arrived in the U.S., and a request for another came from [America] to Toho. [Tomoyuki Tanaka] approached me, asking me to come up with something, anything," writer Ken Kuronuma remembered in an interview in the 1980s.[4] Kuronuma's comment would seem to imply Tanaka was rushed for time. The finished film, *Varan*, would also seem to imply this was the case. What Kuronuma more or less did was create a monster that walked on all fours like Anguirus, was also bipedal like Godzilla, and could fly like Rodan. Kuronuma's story treatment seems to be the same as the finished product outside of the naval battle at sea (which was added later) and the ending. In Kuronuma's version, rather than swallowing explosives, a jet fighter crashes into a fuel reserve at Haneda Airport and the explosion is big enough to kill Varan.

This treatment was then handed over to new writer Shinichi Sekizawa, writer and director of the Shintoho film *Fearful Attack of the Flying Saucers* (1956). "We told Sekizawa to keep it basic and simple," said Koji Kajita, Ishiro Honda's assistant director. Time was so rushed that only two drafts were written, the preparatory manuscript with red title lettering, and the decision draft with a green title. Both scripts were said to come in "four parts," or episodes. The beginning rocket launch scene was missing from the preliminary draft and added in the decision draft. In a nod to the fact that the genre was popular with children, Sekizawa scripted a scene where children play as though they are Varan, which was never filmed. There is also no introductory scene of Dr. Sugimoto explaining the butterflies, and instead, we find the two researchers already in the mountains looking for them. Sekizawa's ending also had balloons being used to carry the flares to Varan rather than dropping them from planes.

The development of *Giant Monster Varan: Monster of the Orient* (the original title) was excitedly reported on in the July 11, 1958 *Tokyo Chunichi Newspaper*. The paper reported how it was the first Japanese made-for-TV monster movie slated to air in America. Not only that, if it were successful, there would potentially be more made-for-TV monster movies from Toho. At some point, Toho decided to make this both a theatrical feature film *and* a TV movie for the American distributor or they decided to switch the film to

BATTLE IN OUTER SPACE

THE ORIGINAL TREATMENT WAS AGAIN CREATED BY JOJIRO OKAMI, CREATOR OF *THE MYSTERIANS*, AND CALLED *GREAT SPACE WAR* (*BATTLE IN OUTER SPACE* IN AMERICA). AS THE FINISHED FILM HAS CHARACTERS NAMED DR. ADACHI, DR. IMMERMAN, AND ETSUKO (THE SAME NAMES OF CHARACTERS THAT APPEAR PROMINENTLY IN *THE MYSTERIANS*), IT IS BELIEVED IN THE FIRST DRAFT THEY WERE TO BE THE EXACT SAME CHARACTERS AS THOSE FROM *THE MYSTERIANS* CARRIED OVER. APPARENTLY, THE FINAL SCRIPT JUST KEPT THE NAMES AND THEY ARE NOT MEANT TO BE THE SAME CHARACTERS. THE ORIGINAL DRAFT FOR THIS FILM INCLUDED A SCENE WHERE, ON THE MOON, THE EARTH DEFENSE FORCE BATTLES NATAL TANKS THAT RESEMBLE PILLBUGS. EARLY DESIGNS FOR THE NATALS WERE ALSO INSECTOID, AS THEY HAD SIX TENTACLE-LIKE ARMS AND ONLY ONE EYE. *TOHO SPECIAL EFFECTS MOVIE ULTIMATE COLLECTION* (2012) SAYS THAT IN THE SECOND DRAFT SCRIPT, A NATAL APPEARS DURING AN EARTH CONFERENCE MEETING AND HAS AN EPIDERMIS LIKE TREE BARK AND OTHER PLANT-LIKE ATTRIBUTES. IN THE FINAL FILM, THERE IS MENTION OF AN ATTACK ON A SHIP IN THE PANAMA CANAL WHEN IT IS PULLED FROM THE OCEAN AND DESTROYED. IN EARLY DRAFTS, IT WAS MEANT TO BE A FAIRLY MAJOR EFFECTS SCENE.

a theatrical version and that was that—interviews with staff imply that either theory is possible. Whatever Toho's primary plan was, the American company did eventually back out, necessitating the change to feature film and new scenes added to the script to pad it out to feature-length.

Added segments included early scenes regarding Dr. Sugimoto discussing the rare butterflies and also the struggles with the Iwaya villagers. New effects scenes were added which comprised of Varan's lengthy and somewhat pointless battle with the navy at sea. The opening narrated prologue promising the "most mysterious story ever told" was also a leftover from the TV version and likely wouldn't have been scripted for a feature. However, there are conflicting reports as to whether or not these scenes were added in for the feature version. *Tokusatsu Hihou* Vol. 8 has an article on *Varan's* 60th Anniversary. In it, the original scope of the four-part miniseries is detailed episode by episode. Part 1 ("Varan Appears") was to detail the search for the butterflies, Varan's first kill, the reporters coming to the village and would end with Varan emerging from the lake. Part 2 ("Varan Attacks") would encompass Varan's rampage on land and end with him taking off into the skies. Part 3 ("Varan Advances") would focus on the war with Varan at sea, and Part 4 ("Varan's Counterattack") would have the beast's death at Haneda Airport. If this is true, then the idea that those scenes were added for the movie is false. If anything, the TV version would have been longer than the finished feature film.[5]

Sadly, the finished film is among the blandest of Toho's monster movies, even if said monster sports one of the better designs of the Toho pantheon. Essentially, the film is a standard monster-on-the-loose story with a very boring ending (the monster swallows explosives and dies). It's actually rather appropriate that the film was written and produced by the Japanese for American audiences as its story structure has more in common with American monster movies than it did Japanese ones!

Varan never did make it to U.S. TV as planned, though it was released in America as *Varan, the Unbelievable* in 1962. In Japan, it was released in October of 1958 and was a critical and commercial disappointment. This is not surprising; though the effects were good, there is nothing to the story other than setting up Varan's rampages. This didn't sour Toho on Shinichi Sekizawa, though, who would go on to write some of the studio's biggest hits. It did, however, seem to sour the studio on giant monster films[6] and they instead opted to produce a semi-sequel to *The Mysterians* for 1959. The seeds for this production can be seen in comments made by Eiji Tsuburaya in publicity materials for *Varan*. Tsuburaya states, "The Dark Side of the Moon is still a mystery, and I would really like to make a film on that subject."[7]

Chapter Notes

[1] vantagepointinterviews.com/2017/05/18/the-imagination-of-ib-melchior-a-conversation-with-the-danish-monster-movie-maker/
[2] Ibid.
[3] It was a four part miniseries in its inception, but by the time production was over it was only a two part series comprising of "Varan Appears" and "Varan's Counterattack". A reconstruction of these two episodes can be found on the *Varan* DVDs from Toho and Media Blasters.
[4] Ryfle and Godziszewski, *Ishiro Honda*, pp.148-149/*Fantasy Literature* No.8 (1984).
[5] Actually, Toho did a partial reconstruction of their Varan TV series in two parts, each 27 minutes long. These two "episodes" do in fact contain extra scenes (audio only) exclusive to the TV version. The 54 minute "Special TV Version" of Varan can be found on both Toho and Media Blasters' DVD.
[6] A giant monster did appear in Toho's *The Three Treasures* (1959), but it was not a giant monster film.
[7] Brothers, "Moon with a View: The Making of 'The Great War in Space'. *G-Fan* #74 (Winter 2005) pp.30.

PROFILE: KEN KURONUMA

Takeshi "Ken" Kuronuma (real name Soda Michio) was born May 1, 1902, in Kanagawa. He graduated from the Tokyo Imperial University Faculty of Law and belonged to the Association of Japanese Literary Artists, the Association of Japanese Children's Literature, and even served as a director at the Japan Reasoning Association. Rather than turning to Shigeru Kayama for his next big monster movie after *Godzilla Raids Again*, Tomoyuki Tanaka instead turned to Ken Kuronuma to cook up a story. Tanaka presumably gave him a pitch on a flying prehistoric monster that comes from a cave in Kyushu (accompanied by giant insects) from ideas originating in Hideo Unagami's *Bride of Godzilla?* (1955) even though Unagami gets no credit on *Rodan*. Kuronuma took this idea and added in his own ideas inspired by a real life U.F.O. incident in America where a pilot lost his life in pursuit of a U.F.O. Next up, Tanaka asked Kuronuma for ideas for another monster film and he came up with *Varan*. Though some wonder if *Varan* sunk Kuronuma's career with further Toho monster films, Tanaka reportedly asked Kuronuma for the idea in a very rushed manner and it would be surprising if he held it against him (he didn't hold it against *Varan* screenwriter Shinichi Sekizawa who wrote steadily for the studio for many more years). In any case, *Varan* was Kuronuma's last Toho monster movie, and he subsequently kept to writing novels and short stories, though in 1960 he also wrote scripts for one of Japan's first science fiction series, *Undersea Man 8823*. The series ran for 26 episodes from January to June. In addition to writing the scripts for the series, he also helped to compose the music. In the 1970s, Kuronuma was the man who introduced Japan to the Prophecies of Nostradamus. Kuronuma stopped working in the late 1970s and died on July 5, 1985.

Selected Filmography/Bibliography
The Birth of Rodan (1956) (writer)
Rodan [feature film] (1956) (writer)
The Secret Story (1957) (writer)
Giant Monster Varan [feature film] (1958) (writer)
Undersea Man 8823 [TV series] (1960) (writer)
The Story of Ancient Continents (1963) (writer)
Prophecy and Strange Story (1964) (writer)
Monster Tale of the World-Mystery and Recording of Miracles (1964) (writer)
Eternity Monster Story (1965) (writer)
The Story of the Underground Kingdom (1966) (writer)
The Lost Ancient Continent of Lemuria (1967) (writer)
The Prophecy of the World (1970) (writer)
A Living Monster (1970) (writer)
Flying Saucer and Alien (1973) (writer)
Ancient Lost City (1976) (writer)

5.
TALES OF KURU ISLAND
GORGO'S JAPANESE ROOTS

In an era of stop motion monsters, 1961's *Gorgo* always stood out in the west because the monster was brought to life through the distinctly Japanese suitmation technique. Perhaps it shouldn't come as a surprise then that *Gorgo* actually has some roots in Japan. It all started with the King Brothers' very successful U.S. distribution of *Rodan*. As a result, they wanted to create their own giant monster. To do this, they first contacted Eugene Lourié, director of *The Beast from 20,000 Fathoms* (1953) and *The Giant Behemoth* (1959). Lourié wasn't exactly itching to make another such film, though he had made a promise to his daughter after her disappointment in *The Beast's* ending. She had apparently told her father, "You are bad, Daddy! You killed the big nice Beast!" Lourié told Paul Mandell of *Fantastic Films* that, "I knew that someday I would have to write a story in which the creature does not die—it just goes away!"

This story, co-written with Lourié's friend and collaborator Daniel James (under the name David Hyatt) was titled *Kuru Island* and is similar to *Gorgo* but with a huge difference in location: it is set in Japan and the South Pacific. Interviewer Mandell described the story as being set on "a fictitious atoll in the South Pacific where cultured pearls were the main export. After a tremendous storm and an underwater eruption, the baby creature surfaces and adheres [sic] to the island... The beast was to have been captured and brought to a Tokyo zoo for observation when the mother beast surfaces to rescue it." The only other details known about the script was that it had a reverence for nature, a few of the main characters would be pearl divers, and the opening volcanic eruption seen in *Gorgo* was also present in *Kuru Island*. Bill Cooke's *Gorgo* book also offers a similar synopsis: "...an oceanic earthquake unleashes a sea monster that is captured by a couple of pearl divers off said island and brought to the Tokyo Zoo for study. But in a surprising plot development, the creature's much-larger parent soon surfaces, trampling through the city in search for her stolen offspring."

Setting the story in Japan was a mandate from the King Brothers, whose production partner at the time was a mystery Japanese studio[1] that, to this day, has yet to be named. Lourié was keen on making a "poetic" non-violent monster film. He told Mandell, "I wanted the creature to confront human beings but there were no scenes of the military shooting at it and not being able to destroy it. That concept is really ridiculous... The creature was not supposed to destroy the town, and there were no stock shots planned of military intervention." The basis for Lourié's story was centered instead on motherly love over conflict with the military. He was sure the idea would appeal to the King Brothers, whom Lourié said, "I believe they had a bit of a mother complex."[2] However, later when it would come time to shoot, the King Brothers made sure to add in plenty of city destruction and military battles.

In April of 1959, the deal fell through with the mystery Japanese studio and the King Brothers were on their own. This also meant finding a new location to set the story. In an interview with Art Buchwald in his column on May 18, 1959, Maurice King told him, "We're going to destroy Paris like it's never been destroyed before. Frank's dying to because of the prices. But Paris has something. Tokyo's already been destroyed [on-screen and in real life], and so has Berlin. And King Kong wrecked New York." King said that, "In trying to find her baby, [the mother monster] wrecks the Eiffel Tower, the Arc de Triomphe, the Louvre, the Opera, the Grand Palais and two bridges on the Seine."[3] The Kings also told Buchwald that they almost made *Gorgo* in Australia, "but there are no monuments in Australia, and besides, who cares if a monster destroys Australia?"

Lourié pointed out a very important reason why the Paris setting was scrapped. The idea was for the monster to wade up the canals until it reached Paris—only Paris is 100 miles inland! In searching for a new location, London was the one finally slated for demolition. *Gorgo*'s eventual production turned out to be the biggest King Brothers film ever produced and was so troublesome it actually led to the delay/cancellation of 30 other King Brothers films! There were also several ambitious scripted scenes that were never filmed such as a scuffle with a giant octopus that may have been present in the *Kuru Island* script. The scene was to have Joe and Sam diving amongst a graveyard of Viking ships only to be pursued by a killer whale. As the duo hides out in one of the ships, they find it to be home to a giant octopus which naturally attacks them. After struggling in the grasp of the beast's tentacles, baby

Gorgo makes his entrance shrouded by a cloud of ink from the octopus:

BACK TO SCENE - ANOTHER ANGLE - THE TWO   59
as Joe charges in, CAMERA MOVING with him. Sam has dropped his flare, and it now lies a little distance below on the rocky bottom. As Joe comes in, another tentacle whips out for him, and now we can see the huge, dirty-green body of the thing and its great, staring, saucer-eyes. But Joe does not make the mistake of trying to avoid the tentacle. He fights only to keep his arms and gun free, and rides in with the snake-like arm, Intent only on getting in close enough for a killing shot. Sam by now is almost helpless. With a half-Imprisoned arm, he is trying to cut through a truck tire with a Jackknife. Another tentacle has coiled around Joe, but he drives in.

And now, straight between the eyes of the thing, he fires. There is a dull, muffled explosion (the exploding tip of the harpoon). The great octopus shudders violently, its color changes rapidly from the dirty-green to a reddish-brown, its tentacles loosen and become limp, and, as the two men struggle free, in its death agony, it emits a great, jetting cloud of black ink, all but obliterating the scene.
Joe and Sam pull back a little, close together.

CLOSE SHOT – JOE   60
his anxious face seen through his face plate, looking at Sam.

TWO SHOT   61
as Sam, exhausted, nevertheless gestures that he's okay. Now the two look around, looking upward through the murk, the killer whale not forgotten.

WHAT THEY SEE: 62
dimly through the darkly clouded waters, a shadow passing over. The whale has not forgotten them.

BACK TO SCENE   63
as Joe gestures caution. They are in no shape for another fight at the moment. From his belt, Joe gets another charge for the harpoon gun, loads it. Prom somewhat below, the flare glows dimly. Then suddenly there is a tremendous,

thrashing turmoil in the water above them. They look up quickly, SEE:

WHAT THEY SEE: 64
Through the murk and the wildly turbulent water, they can see only something fantastically big and vague, like a great thundercloud. The water is whipped to fury. Then all at once there is a great jetting gush of blood that crimsons the water all around, blotting out everything in a swirling red haze.

BACK TO SCENE 65
as the two cling to the rook formation, staring up-wards, staring at each other.

Other unfilmed scenes include baby Gorgo scuffling with a circus elephant and Ogra (the mother) destroying a lighthouse. Even though the film finished shooting in December of 1959, its release was delayed by nearly two years. The film ironically premiered in Tokyo on January 10, 1961, where it became a massive hit in Japan.

Lourié said of the finished *Gorgo* script (further tweaked by John Loring), "The story as originally conceived was far more poetic. But the King Brothers butchered the idea entirely." Lourie was so disappointed with the additions of graphic city destruction and military conflict that in later years, he even edited his own version of *Gorgo*! He told Mandell, "I recently acquired an old print of *Gorgo*...and made a 35-minute version by taking out all those unnecessary scenes. Everything was so much better." This cut was created during the year 1980 (or possibly sometime prior), but no one knows if it was ever shown in any official capacity.

And what of the mystery Japanese studio?[4] Japanese Magazine *Tokusatsu Hihou* put forth a very intriguing theory that the studio involved in *Kuru Island* was none other than Toho! This would make perfect sense as the King Brothers had very successfully distributed *Rodan* in 1957. Also, Toho was the only Japanese studio at that time known for giant monster movies. To take things even further, Ishiro Honda's first film, *The Blue Pearl* (1951), was about pearl divers; the main characters of *Kuru Island* were also pearl divers! Further proof that Toho was the mystery studio would seem to be in a Godzilla manga in which Godzilla's child (not Minilla) is stranded in Tokyo and is rescued by his father. The only problem with this manga is that it predates *Kuru Island*'s pre-production and was published in 1957.

The manga story is called "The Last Godzilla" and was written by Yoshiharu Hashimoto. It begins with an audience settling down in a theater to watch *Monster King Godzilla*.[5] As the movie progresses and Godzilla shows up onscreen, the head of the real Godzilla bursts through the movie screen.[6] The monster, in fact a juvenile Godzilla, crawls into the theater and chases out the patrons and then bursts out of the theater into the streets of the city. The nimble young kaiju climbs atop a building and the police begin to fire their guns at it. When it starts to breathe fire, the fire department shows up and pelts it with water. Off the coast, the adult Godzilla surfaces to retrieve his young and battles the military on his way into the city. Godzilla embraces his son atop the building and it climbs onto its father's back. Godzilla carries his child out of the city. The two Godzillas are next seen attacking a circus where animals run in fear and some are eaten. Many of the animals run loose through Tokyo as the U.S. military flies in from the skies. They launch a nuclear warhead at Godzilla in the heart of the city, but the monster catches it in midair. Godzilla then bites off part of the missile and throws the rest into the water.

The human aspect of the storyline is somewhat harder to follow, but it centers on a young couple, Masao and Emi, who are on a date in the theater when Godzilla shows up. Masao seems to have some sort of involvement with the government or gives them unsolicited advice. In one of the comic's more interesting scenes, a man arrives at the conference claiming to have yet another of the deceased Dr. Serizawa's heretofore unknown doomsday weapons—a type of poison gas. There appears to be a Kumayama-like, cigar-smoking villain of sorts who possibly has ideas of killing the Godzillas so that he can put their corpses on display. He tries to lure the monster to the beach with a deer (filled with poison) as bait. Masao tries to free the deer and gets in a scuffle with the bad guy's henchmen. Emi frees the deer just as Godzilla and his child arrive, but the monsters cause no harm and head out to sea into the sunrise.

The manga was published in Shonen Magazine's *Omoshiro Book* for the October 1957 issue. Today, it is also available in Kodansha's Godzilla DVD Collector Box Vol. 23 with *The Return of Godzilla*. Any possible connections between Toho (if they even were King Brothers' partners) and *Kuru Island* are purely speculation from this point on, but it's possible that Toho noticed similarities between Lourié's script and the 1957 manga, and perhaps they proposed making *Kuru Island* into a Godzilla film. This could have led to the split because Lourié, like Ray Harryhausen, was not a

Godzilla fan. Lourié said, "...although the locale was to have been Japan it had nothing to do with the Godzilla-type story construction. I wanted the creature to confront human beings, but there were no scenes of the military shooting at it." Although this comment is focused more so on Lourié's want for a gentler monster film, the way he is quick to distance himself from the Godzilla franchise could be telling. Furthermore, Lourié also disliked the Godzilla suit which he considered to be "clumsy" which was why he insisted the Gorgo suit be enhanced with hydraulics to move the eyes, ears and mouth.[7] On the other hand, perhaps Toho, who had just been burned by their deal with AB-PT falling through on *The Volcano Monsters* and *Varan*, cancelled the collaboration themselves.

Another possibility was that the Japanese studio was Nikkatsu. Though Nikkatsu more or less remade *Gorgo* in 1967 as *Gappa, the Triphibian Monster*, back in 1959, Nikkatsu wasn't known for special effects films—nor were they in 1967, which is why they brought in Toho's Akira Watanabe to handle the special effects. However, *Gappa* writers Gan Yamazaki and Ryuzo Nakanishi were quoted in *Monsters Are Attacking Tokyo* stating that they had never seen *Gorgo*.

Chapter Notes

[1] Bill Warren's *Keep Watching the Skies* even implies that most of the financing was to have come from this Japanese studio.
[2] Don Glut remembers his writing teacher, Irv Blacker, at USC who knew the King Brothers, believed *Gorgo* was in part inspired by *Beowulf*. However, this could have merely been Blacker's own opinion, and not anything actually gleaned from the King Brothers themselves.
[3] Actually, the King Brothers requested that Gorgo climb the Eiffel Tower, and Lourié made some drawings to that effect.
[4] The *Tokusatsu Hihou* article on the Gorgo connection also draws another interesting parallel with some of the names used in the finished *Gorgo*. The author of the article states, "At the beginning of the story is 'Nara Island', the sea spirit reminiscent of Gorgo is called 'Ogra.' Actually there is a place called Ogura Town, Nara Prefecture." *Tokusatsu Hihou* Vol. 6, pp.246-248.
[5] In 1957, Toho released *Godzilla, King of the Monsters!* in Japan under this title.
[6] The meta aspects of the manga also show up in the Japanese version of *King Kong vs. Godzilla* where, during Tako's rant that Godzilla is getting too much media exposure his secretary interjects, "There's even a movie!"
[7] It was actually Lourié's idea to go the suitmation route for the sake of expediency. The King Brothers had the zany idea to create their monster through a giant balloon which they would then pull through the actual city for filming!!!

6.
THE SECRET HISTORY OF
MOTHRA

In 1960, Toho President Iwao Mori had an ambitious idea to make a giant monster movie with female appeal to boost the box office receipts. Toho had taken a break from giant monsters since the disappointment of *Varan* in 1958.[1] Mori wanted a "third" Toho monster to join the ranks of Godzilla and Rodan, so he asked Tomoyuki Tanaka to produce a giant monster film "that women will also enjoy." Mori even suggested that the film feature a beautiful woman. Since he had good luck with novelists Shigeru Kayama in helping to create Godzilla, and Ken Kuronuma for Rodan, Tomoyuki Tanaka approached popular novelist (and successful scribe of radio dramas) Shinichiro Nakamura to come up with a female-friendly monster for Toho. Nakamura then brought in fellow writers Takehiko Fukunaga & Zenei "Yoshie" Hotta to collaborate with him.[2] The trio then individually wrote one portion of a complete story to combine them into a finished novel. The result was *The Luminous Fairies and Mothra*, published in *Weekly Asahi Extra* in January of 1961 as a sort of preview for Toho's upcoming monster movie.

The skeletal structure of the novelization is basically the same as the finished film; it has the same villain and trio of lead characters—except Michi is Chujo's assistant rather than Fukuda's photographer. Also, Chujo and Fukuda take separate trips to the island and it is Fukuda who figures out the legend of Infant Island. Though Mothra's mysterious history was never explained in the Showa Godzilla series, in the novelization it is fleshed out thoroughly, devoting a good deal of time to the lost civilization of Infant Island. The beginning of Infant Island is not unlike the Japanese creation myth, where a god creates the island then splits himself in two, creating a female god. Together, the two create Mothra's egg. When the female goddess becomes distressed, she tears herself apart and from her remains are born the four tiny fairies, here called the Ailenas. Fukuda is also present to watch Mothra hatch after Nelson abducts the four fairies and heads for Japan. This version addresses the post-World War II treaty between America and Japan through the fictional Rolisica

41

 **THE SECRET OF THE TELEGIAN**

THE SECOND ENTRY IN TOHO'S "TRANSFORMING HUMAN" SERIES, *THE SECRET OF THE TELEGIAN* (1960), WAS ORIGINALLY TO BE DIRECTED BY ISHIRO HONDA WHO REPORTEDLY HAD A HAND IN ITS DEVELOPMENT. DUE TO SCHEDULING CONFLICTS THAT BEGAN BECAUSE OF *THE THREE TREASURES* PUSHING BACK THE FILMING OF HONDA'S *BATTLE IN OUTER SPACE*, JUN FUKUDA DIRECTED THIS FILM IN HONDA'S PLACE. AS TO HOW DIFFERENT THE FILM WOULD HAVE BEEN HAD HONDA DIRECTED IT, WHO CAN SAY?

a little more strongly than the finished film does. In this version, Mothra chases Nelson to Rolisica, where he is assassinated by an angry member of the Rolisican public who knows Mothra is going to destroy their city because of the fairies. Like the finished film, Chujo and the main characters hand the fairies off to Mothra at an airfield. Strangely, they crawl into a compartment within Mothra's eye! The story takes an even wilder left turn when Mothra flies off to Antarctica. Part of the frozen continent floats up into the sky with Mothra and the fairies and it is stated that they will settle on a "negative earth,"[3] though they may return should Infant Island ever fall into danger.

Early pre-production art reflects this version of the story. The artwork shows the fairies appearing considerably larger on an Infant Island rife with huge, megalithic ruins. Mothra's egg even sits on a cliff above a huge temple not dissimilar to the Japanese Diet Building. In the concept art, Mothra is also very different from how she would appear onscreen; much more menacing-looking. Her larval stage resembles a centipede and her adult form is closer in line with Battra than the finished design.[4]

When it came time to write the script, Shinichi Sekizawa didn't follow the novel entirely. He mostly picked the aspects he liked and threw out the rest.[5] He removed one of the fairies, bringing the count down to three and renamed them the Pichi, though they are still 60 cm tall and luminescent. Furthermore, Sekizawa says they are aliens![6] One of these small fairies was to fall in love with one of the male characters and when she does so, she loses her telepathic ability. In this version, Infant Island is inhabited with gigantic plant life, and the expedition is thoroughly surprised to find the island populated with natives in spite of the radiation.[7] The natives warn the men to stay away from a certain area, which naturally prompts them to explore said area where they find one of the fairies. As in the finished film, a second secret expedition by

Caucasian Clark Nelson forcefully captures the fairies. Aside from the love story between one of the characters (it isn't stated if it revolves around Chujo or Fukuda) and one of the fairies, events basically play out as in the finished film except that Mothra spins her cocoon around the Diet Building and rather than a fictional city, Nelson actually takes the fairies to New York. It can be assumed Sekizawa did away with the fictional Rolisica for the real America! It's likely that it switched back to the fictional Rolisica when Columbia Pictures became involved with distribution.[8]

Fans will also be intrigued to know that Godzilla himself was mentioned in *The Luminous Fairies and Mothra* as well as the preparatory draft of the script. An onlooker was to note that Mothra is "even bigger than Godzilla." This indicates that Toho planned on a shared universe much earlier than anyone ever knew (or the character was referring to *Godzilla* the film)![9]

In the second draft, the number of fairies was cut down to two. This is likely due to Columbia Pictures signing a deal to distribute—and many sources say partly finance—the film sometime during this pre-production period.[10] Supposedly, it was they who secured the singing duo "The Peanuts" (Emi and Yumi Ito) who had a contract with Columbia Records, for the film.[11] Also, the plan seemed to be for a simultaneous release in Japan and America, though the American release didn't occur until the next year. Also, Mothra now spins her cocoon around the newly-constructed Tokyo Tower, in part because it was a new structure to destroy but also because destroying the Diet Building could be misconstrued as disrespectful.[12] It's also worth noting that in storyboards, there was a structure in Mothra's courtyard on Infant Island that greatly resembled the Diet Building. In all likelihood, this was intentional, and that's why Mothra was to seek out the structure originally. A new character, Chujo's younger brother Shinji who was absent from the first draft, was added to the story. Storyboards also show Mothra in battle with the Rolisican Air Force. In the finished film, Clark Nelson only listens to a radio report about how Mothra has overcome Rolisican Air Forces.

Though many fans initially believed the end attack on New Kirk City was concocted by Columbia only after Toho shot the infamous "original ending," this is not the case. In actuality, it was in the Toho/Columbia contract that Mothra needed to attack a western-looking city. And, as seen in the synopsis of both the novel and the treatment, Mothra's attack on a western city was always the plan. However, as scripting progressed, due to budget concerns, this ending was cut and replaced with a less expensive new ending

THE HUMAN VAPOR

THE THIRD ENTRY IN TOHO'S "TRANSFORMING HUMAN" SERIES, *THE HUMAN VAPOR*, WAS ALMOST DIRECTED BY JUN FUKUDA BEFORE ISHIRO HONDA BECAME AVAILABLE. EARLY VERSIONS OF THE SCRIPT ARE SIMILAR TO THE FINISHED FILM EXCEPT FOR ONE SCENE ISHIRO HONDA INSISTED BE CUT. IN THE SCENE, MIZUNO THE VAPOR MAN WAS TO HAVE MURDERED THE WIFE AND CHILD OF A POLICEMAN! STORYBOARDS ALSO SHOW A MUCH MORE DRAMATIC VERSION OF THE SCENE WHERE MIZUNO ESCAPES THE POLICE FROM A HIGH RISE BUILDING. IN THE STORYBOARDS, MIZUNO DRAMATICALLY JUMPS THROUGH THE GLASS. WE CUT TO AN EXTERIOR SHOT OF MIZUNO'S CLOTHES FLAPPING IN THE AIR AS HE DISSOLVES WHILE THE POLICE ARE SHOOTING AT HIM.

written by Ishiro Honda and Sekizawa. In it, Nelson has Shinji Chujo and the Shobijin both held hostage in his Cessna airplane. The heroes are in hot pursuit, causing them to be absent from Mothra's big reveal where she hatches from her cocoon. Mothra takes to the skies, knowing just where the Shobijin are, and brings Nelson's plane down in the Japanese Alps—specifically Takachiho Peak in Kyushu.[13] She then uses gusts of her wings to blow Nelson over the side of a cliff where he falls into a volcano.

At the start of shooting, Toho sent off a letter asking the permission of the American producers to change the ending. Ironically, the first scene scheduled for shooting was the ending itself, and Toho went on location to Kagoshima to shoot the scene before receiving a reply! Numerous publicity stills of this scene (shot on Mt. Kirishima, an active volcano) exist, although according to Honda, the footage was never developed. As it turned out, right when they returned from shooting, Columbia had denied Toho's request to shoot the new ending, as it was a breach of contract not to include the planned ending in a U.S.-style city. Honda said, "Unfortunately, the budget was stretched in creating the New Kirk City sets."[14] Also, New Kirk City originally had a different name, New Wagon City, until it was changed to Newark. Jerry Ito (the actor who portrayed Nelson) then informed Toho that there was a real city in America by that same name so it became New Kirk. In any case, New Kirk was a combination of New York, San Francisco and Los Angeles in design. In fact, Honda had hoped to do some on-location shooting in Los Angeles but this never panned out.

The creation of the huge New Kirk City set resulted in scaling back the Infant Island scenes, which was, as mentioned earlier, to be much grander with massive temples and megalithic ruins. What bothered Honda the most was the cutting of a scene that would have explained just how the Infant Islanders survive the radiation. Honda said, "When Koizumi goes into the cave, the important thing is the image of the mold. I got a microscopic photo of mold and asked our art department to reproduce it. There were all those mysterious ferns, with seven different colors, the big forest... but we couldn't create the atmosphere of the mold forest so well. That was disappointing, but it probably would have cost too much. I really wanted to... create this mysterious scene on an island that had been bombed. I actually wrote that scene."[15]

The book, *Mothra/Mothra vs. Godzilla Toho SPFX Series* lists some of the more minor differences between the first draft and the final one. It states that the rescue of the missing ship's crew was "simplified" from what it was originally though doesn't elaborate.[16] It also implies the vampiric plant would have been foreshadowed before it appeared somehow.

In the end, *Mothra* came out to a whopping ¥200 million budget. But it was worth it, for it sold 9,000,000 tickets. As Iwao Mori had hoped, the colorful fantasy appealed to both men and women alike and indeed, *Mothra* is much more of a fantasy than its grimmer kaiju eiga predecessors. Notably, it takes place in a less grounded, more fantastical world than what we saw in *Godzilla* or *Rodan*—which were very much set in the real Japan and had tragic endings. By Honda's own admission, the story was inspired by the more fantasy-like *King Kong* with the exotic island and a monster deity that clashes with civilization. However, Honda wanted to the movie to have a happy ending, unlike *King Kong*. Therefore, not only was Mothra a sympathetic figure, but she survived the movie as well. This was a wise decision on Toho's part, as Mothra would return in 1964's *Mothra vs. Godzilla*, where she would cement herself as one of the most popular monsters in the Toho stable. In fact, unlike her cohort Rodan, Mothra is the lone Toho monster to originate in a solo film, be incorporated into the Godzilla series and then branch off on its own again. The monster goddess headlined her own trilogy of films in the 1990s starting with *Rebirth of Mothra* (1996).

Chapter Notes

[1] Though it features the eight-headed dragon Orochi, 1959's *The Three Treasures* was not a kaiju movie per se.
[2] The main character's name Senichiro Fukuda, is a combination of the writers' names.
[3] If this idea was known to Kazuki Omori, or if it influenced him on the ending of 1992's *Godzilla vs. Mothra*, is unknown. In that film's epilogue, Mothra and the Cosmos fly into outer space on a mission to destroy a meteor that will strike earth in 1999.
[4] Stranger still, despite the original story having Mothra as an insect, during development of the first draft, Toho played with the idea of making Mothra bird-like or specifically a bird-like creature with human traits (perhaps this was meant to be evocative of an angel?).
[5] Ironically, his first draft for *Mothra* was entitled *The Giant Monster Thing* and years later, 1964's *Mothra vs. Godzilla* would be retitled *Godzilla vs. the Thing* in the U.S.
[6] *Mothra/Mothra vs. Godzilla Toho SPFX Movies* pp.86-87. Specifically it states, "Three beautiful small beauties came from other planets."
[7] The script notes state that there was an intent to have the natives as descendants of a lost tribe of Japanese.
[8] Actually, the *Mothra* program booklet writes that *Mothra* was, "contracted by Columbia Pictures International for worldwide distribution even before the shooting started."
[9] This was not unprecedented, as the manga "The Last Godzilla" (1957) mentions Rodan as existing in the same universe as Godzilla.
[10] The studio had just recently released *Battle in Outer Space* and *The H-Man* in America.
[11] This would make sense, as the casting of identical twins would mean all the fairies would need to match in appearance.
[12] By 1992, for *Godzilla vs. Mothra*, this attitude had changed and Mothra spins her cocoon on the Diet Building as originally planned.
[13] Storyboards tell a different story, and actually, the plane crashes before Mothra even comes out of her cocoon. Nelson then hides in a cave with his hostages while being pursued by the heroes.
[14] Ryfle and Godziszewski, *Ishiro Honda*, pp.178.
[15] Ibid.
[16] Storyboards show scenes of the men lost at sea and even washing up on the beach before being aided by the natives.

7.
THE END OF THE WORLD
GORATH AND THE LAST WAR

After *Mothra's* success, Toho produced two somber disaster films. First came *The Last War* and then *Gorath*. These films went through many revisions, particularly *The Last War* which saw six script drafts. *The Last War's* development is a complicated one and precedes a similar developmental process that would happen with 1973's *Submersion of Japan* when Toho and Daiei both planned to adapt the same novel. In this case, Toho and Toei both had their eye set on a World War III film.

In 1960, Tomoyuki Tanaka took note of a story entitled "The First 41 Hours of World War III" that had appeared in the *Weekly Shincho* and subsequently wanted to adapt it. The only problem was Toei Studios had already beat him to the punch in grabbing the film rights. It would seem that a script at Toho was written before it was known that Toei already had the rights. As it is, the first draft of *The Last War* is remarkably similar to Toei's *The Final War* (1960). If one watches both films side by side, it's fairly obvious that they were based upon the same source material. Both focus on the effects of World War III on the "little people." In the case of the finished *Last War*, we follow Tamura, played by Frankie Sakai, and his family that includes his sickly bedridden wife, his daughter Saeko (Yuriko Hoshi), and her fiancé Takano (Akira Takarada). The main character of Toei's film was a reporter, Masaaki, who had a girlfriend, Tomoko, who is a nurse who refuses to abandon her patient when Tokyo is bombed. The film also follows a musician who has a sickly wife who is mostly bedridden.

In Toho's first draft of *The Last War*, Saeko was also a nurse. The Tamura family would have also fled from Tokyo to escape the bomb rather than staying inside the city. Takano was to try and convince Saeko to leave with him, but she wouldn't abandon her patient just as in Toei's movie. Notably, Tamura's wife was also sickly and bedridden, an element that would stay in the finished film despite it being similar to the subplot in *The Final War*. The first draft also explicitly identified the U.S. and the Soviet Union as in Toei's film, but subsequent drafts would change the names to "the Federation" and "the Alliance" to make the movie easier to market internationally.

Toho's script was finished on July 29, 1960, written by Shinobu Hashimoto and Toshio Yasumi. The film was approved for production at the Toho National Branch Chairperson's Board of Directors' meeting on August 8th. Only a few days earlier, Toei had also had their shareholders meeting on the 6th, where they announced the production of their film, *The Final War*. The Mainichi Newspaper heard about the dueling projects and soon reported on the brewing competition between the two studios.

Toho called in several experts to help consult on the second draft of the script to make it as authentic as possible. The experts included Nori University professor Keijiro Irie, a prominent authority on international law as well as Toshio Shinzo, a member of the New Interview Study Team and an expert on the military. The second draft was finished by August 11th, only three days after Toho announced the film for production. However, this draft was still incredibly similar to Toei's, which claimed to have the blessing of the original author of "The First 41 Hours of World War III." Worried about the similarities, Tanaka quit trying to beat Toei's release date and had Yasumi and Hashimoto do a rewrite on the script to shake any similarities that could lead to legal action. Another problem arose when the original director, Hironobu Horikawa, balked at the number of effects sequences. In response to *Mothra*'s recent success, Toho considered the effects scenes to be very important. As a result, Toho turned to Shue Matsubayashi, known for his successful war films, as the new director.

On September 2nd, Toshio Yasumi and Shinobu Hashimoto turned in a third draft script, which Toho President Iwao Mori feared was still too close to Toei's version and decided to stop production on September 7th. However, the project wasn't dead just yet; Yasumi turned in a fourth and fifth draft of the script on his own at an unknown date in 1961. The sixth and final draft was turned in by Takeshi Kimura almost a year later on June 26, 1961, so that production could finally commence. Though Toei's film had already been released six months prior, Toho had the edge in that their film would not only feature far more effects scenes than Toei's but also be filmed in color.

Though not well-remembered today, *The Last War* is a superb anti-war film. It would actually seem that the many rewrites may have improved the story. As stated earlier, the original draft had the Tamura family fleeing Tokyo to go into the wilderness. The finished film has them deciding to stay in Tokyo for one last family meal and meet their doom. It remains the film's most potent scene as Tamura remains in a state of denial all through the dinner, reminding his sick wife to take her medicine even though it is pointless. Saeko pines for Takano, who is out to sea. Finally, Tamura has a breakdown and realizes all his hard work has been for nothing. Then the nukes fly, killing the main protagonists of the film except Takano out at sea. The film's final scenes feature a devastated Takano looking out to sea from his ship, knowing his wife is dead. It's some of Akira Takarada's finest acting. Thirteen years later, the family dynamic and basic outline from *The Last War* would be resurrected as *Prophecies of Nostradamus (Catastrophe 1999)* (1974).

Gorath came from another idea by Jojiro Okami, who had created outlines for *The Mysterians* and *Battle in Outer Space*.[1] In Okami's original story pitch, the giant asteroid was named Lagos (Toho decided to rename the asteroid when they discovered Lagos was the name of a city in Nigeria). The giant star Lagos was also scripted to absorb the surrounding stars and blow up all the asteroids between Jupiter and Mars. In Okami's treatment, rather than move the earth as in the final film, the Japanese elite escape earth as the planet is destroyed.

The idea to move the earth instead of escape it is evident in the first script draft's title: *Great Earth Modification*. Just like *The Mysterians*, what became *Gorath* didn't originally include any monsters in Okami's story pitch. Once again, Tanaka requested Takeshi Kimura add one. Initially, instead of the giant walrus Magma attacking the polar base, Kimura had a dinosaur-like monster attacking it. Honda didn't want to emulate Godzilla so it was changed to a walrus, though the reptilian element carried over to Magma's initial design, described as having scaly skin with a metallic luster. Even stranger, storyboards for *Gorath* seem to show a second monster. The image appears in *Godzilla and Toho-Tokusatsu Pictorial Sketch* and shows a reptilian monster with spines and scales, not unlike Manda, swimming in the ocean. This could be an early design for Magma. However, in the same storyboard section, Magma is drawn as it would appear on film as a giant walrus.[2] The storyboards seem to be showing the effects of the great polar jets melting the ice, the implication being this creature—whatever it is—is becoming active due to the jets. The storyboards also show that Tsuburaya had hopes of showing the affects of Gorath on the whole world as it passes—not just Japan. This is evidenced by a storyboard panel of one of the pyramids of Egypt submerged underwater.

In the end, the story didn't need a giant monster at all. As it is, Magma was badly shoehorned in. If Tanaka hoped this would help sell the film overseas, he was mistaken, as the American version removed the monster entirely. Monsters aside, *Gorath* could be described as a disaster film with *Mothra*'s fantasy element and *The Last War*'s downbeat mood. In fact, the depressing atmosphere is more akin to a disaster film from the 1970s with notable characters dying or becoming injured because of Gorath's approach. Akira Kubo's character Kanai suffers amnesia by getting too close to the star and does not regain his memory until it passes earth. Like many of Honda's films, *Gorath* shows a world where the nations put aside their differences to save the earth—an idea that Honda hoped would one day become a reality. For this reason, *Gorath* would turn out to be one of Honda's favorite tokusatsu films.

Chapter Notes

[1] Supposedly, his idea for *Gorath* was pitched all the way back in 1959.
[2] One storyboard showed a scene not in the film where Magma emerges from some icy water.

8.
BEAST MEETS WEST
KING KONG VS. GODZILLA

In a roundabout way, the Godzilla series owes its resurrection to the exact same monster that inspired its genesis: King Kong. In the late 1950s, the giant ape's creator Willis O'Brien had just authored a potential sequel entitled *King Kong vs. Frankenstein*, in which Kong would do battle with a Frankenstein-style monster stitched together by various African animals. Specifically, the story involved Frankenstein's grandson stitching together dead animals in Africa to create a monster he names Gingko (O'Brien would eventually retitle the script *King Kong vs. the Ginko*). Carl Denham has also rediscovered Kong (who didn't really die but was smuggled back home) on Skull Island. Denham then gets the bright idea to display Kong and the Ginko in San Francisco side by side and chaos ensues as Kong and the monster fight it out in the city. The story ended with both monsters tumbling from the Golden Gate Bridge and into the sea.

This idea was proposed by O'Brien to Daniel O'Shea, then president of RKO, which O'Brien may or may not have realized owned the rights to Kong.[1] O'Shea connected O'Brien to Universal-International producer John Beck who, in turn, took over O'Brien's idea and had George Worthington Yates rewrite *King Kong vs. the Ginko* into *King Kong vs. Prometheus*. In this version, the doctor who creates Prometheus isn't revealed to be a descendant of Frankenstein until later in the script as a surprise twist. He also has the ability to remote control the monster—or so he thinks. The intelligent creature actually pretends to follow the doctor's commands and then kills him once they reach San Francisco. King Kong, on display in San Francisco, then plays the hero in defeating the monster. Also, for some reason, Yates did away with the Carl Denham character in this draft.

Unable to find any studio interest in America for the film, Beck was directed to Toho in Japan by RKO Pictures (who had recently distributed *The Mysterians* in the U.S.). Toho was more than happy to helm the production but tossed out Frankenstein's monster in favor of Godzilla. As Toho's 30th Anniversary was looming, they had hoped to resurrect the monster and a bout with

51

King Kong would make things even better. Willis O'Brien was completely unaware of this development until he read about it in the newspapers!

Very little of O'Brien's ideas survived Shinichi Sekizawa's rewrite, though the underlying concept of monsters being used for publicity made it into to the final film. The character of Mr. Tako could be considered the film's Carl Denham-type character, who brings Kong to Japan oblivious to the jeopardy he is placing the nation in. Kong's heroic stature when fighting a more dangerous monster, in this case Godzilla, also carried over. The ape's curious new ability to generate lightning from his fingertips is thought to have been a power given to the Ginko in O'Brien's idea.[2]

Knowing that Toho would rewrite the film, RKO placed specific stipulations on them. These included insisting that at some point Kong abduct a maiden and climb a tall structure with her and also that Toho's Kong be designed differently from theirs. In the words of Toho suit designer Keizo Murase to Toho Kingdom, "We could get the rights to use the name King Kong but unfortunately, we were unable to get the rights for the likeness."[3]

RKO's guidelines for Kong wasn't the only problem Toho faced with the big ape. Beck had entered an agreement with Toho to split the costs of Kong's expensive licensing fee from RKO and at the last minute, left Toho holding the bag to pay for it entirely. Most of the film's budget ended up being eaten up by Kong's licensing fee, which totaled over $220,000. As a result, the special effects budget had to be reduced and one will notice Tsuburaya's effects on this film are not as elaborate as those in the previous year's *Mothra* or *Gorath* earlier the same year. Also, planned on-location filming in Sri Lanka had to be cancelled. Instead, nearby Oshima Island would play Faro Island in the film.

Shinichi Sekizawa also had stipulations placed on him from Toho, who instructed him to write the new Godzilla film with a light satiric tone. Trying to repeat the success of *Mothra*, which featured comedy star Frankie Sakai in the lead, Tadao Takashima and Yu Fujuki (a popular comedic duo in Toho's "salaryman" films) were cast in lead roles. In fact, this author would assume the roles were written specifically for the pair. This same case was likely true in the casting of Ichiro Arishima (the "Charlie Chaplin of Japan") as Mr. Tako.

The only known major difference in the first draft was that Kong's battle with the Odako (giant octopus) either took place in the water, began in the water, or extended into the water but was scaled down in the second draft. The scene where Kenji Sahara's character screams at Kong while the ape has carried Fumiko atop the Diet Building wasn't in the shooting script but thought up on the spot by director Ishiro Honda who felt the scene was missing Sahara's presence and called the actor to join the scene. Overall, aside from starting out as a film starring Frankenstein, *King Kong vs. Godzilla* would seem to have gone through very few revisions compared to the G-films that would follow.

How does the film's satiric tone fare? Actually, pretty well with Honda balancing the film's lighter and darker moments expertly. Scenes that worked out well from the comedic perspective included things like Mr. Tako bowing to an angry executive over the phone (a scene axed from the American version). There is also a scene where Tako's secretary makes mention of plans for a Godzilla movie! The pharmaceutical executives win the island natives over by giving them all cigarettes, including the children. Godzilla and Kong are surprisingly played for laughs, such as moments like when Kong blinks in amazement at the first time he sees Godzilla's atomic ray.[4] On the other end of the spectrum, scenes surrounding the submarine stranded in the Bering Sea evoke a great deal of suspense and mystery (handled much better in the Japanese cut). Fumiko's abduction by King Kong and Fujita's reaction are also very well done (again, in the Japanese version more so than the American re-edit). Whatever fans may now think of the film's comedic tones, audiences of the time loved it, making it the highest-grossing Godzilla film of all time.

Chapter Notes

[1] The legal rights to King Kong were not concrete as to who owned him at that time. Merian C. Cooper felt he owned Kong, while RKO felt they owned Kong exclusively. This legal debate would not be settled until the mid-1970s. Actually, legal action was filed against Toho by Merian C. Cooper regarding *King Kong vs. Godzilla*, though nothing ever came of it.
[2] Thanks to Jason Z. Weppler for pointing this out to me.
[3] www.tohokingdom.com/interviews/keizo_murase_12-2017.html
[4] These scenes made special effects department newbie Teruyoshi Nakano aghast when he read the script.

9.
VOICE IN THE NIGHT
MATANGO SPROUTS

In 1907, William Hope Hodgson (1877-1918) wrote a short story entitled "The Voice in the Night." It was one of many macabre stories by Hodgson, who shared similarities with H.P. Lovecraft, whom Hodgson was said to have influenced. However, only three of Hodgson's stories were ever put on film—three adapted for television and one for a feature film. The lone feature film was *Matango* by Toho in 1963, a loose adaptation of "The Voice in the Night."

"The Voice in the Night" was first published in *Blue Book* magazine in November 1907. The story opens with a man named George, one of several men working aboard a ship at sea near an uncharted northern Pacific island. On a dark and starless night, George is the first to hear the titular "Voice in the Night" come out of the fog. The voice belongs to a man in a rowboat who explains that he and his fiancé are stranded on a nearby island (the fiancé is still there). Though he requests food and water, he denies the ship's offer to rescue them. The man also goes to special care not to be seen by the crew. He takes the goods back to the island but later returns on his rowboat to the ship—again keeping his distance—to tell the men his cautionary tale.

After the sinking of their ship, the *Albatross*, the couple had drifted through a strange haze for several days on a raft. Finally, after four days, they came upon an island and landed in its lagoon. On the island, they found another shipwrecked vessel on land and decided to use it for shelter (sound familiar?). Onboard they found a "grey, lichenous fungus." The couple scraped the fungus away to make the ship habitable, but to their disappointment, it always grew back. Eventually, they left the ship, only to find the whole island infested with the fungus. The only clean spot they could find was a small white patch of fine sand. Soon, they began to grow the fungus on their skin themselves. Short on food, the woman gave in to temptation and ate one of the mushrooms and discovered it to be delicious. Soon after, the man encountered the first mushroom man on the island, a grotesque walking fungus with distorted arms. He then realized this was likely an occupant of the ship that had eaten the fungus! The monster's arm brushed his face, giving him an accidental taste of the fungus and a hunger for more. Not long after, he and his wife themselves turned into one of the fungal people of the island. This concluded the man's sad tale. As he rows away from the boat, the sunlight breaks through the fog momentarily exposing him to George, who says, "I thought of a sponge–a great, grey nodding sponge..."

The story was eyed by Alfred Hitchcock for one of his television programs, but initially was denied by the censors of the time. In fact, Hodgson's "The Voice in the Night" was published in Alfred Hitchcock's 1957 book, *Alfred Hitchcock Presents: Stories They Wouldn't Let Me Do on TV*. Only a year later, in 1958, the story was adapted as part of *Suspense*, an anthology TV series that Hitchcock had a hand in—though he did not direct this proto iteration of *Matango*. The hour-long segment was more faithful to the story than Toho's was, though no mushroom people are ever glimpsed. It was directed by Arthur Hiller, written by Stirling Silliphant, and starred Barbara Rush, James Donald, Patrick Macnee, and James Coburn.

Toho's version was adapted by Masami Fukushima (editor of *Sci-fi Magazine* in Japan) into *Matango*. Fukushima and Shinichi Hoshi then adapted it into either a treatment or script for Toho. Takeshi Kimura then took the reins and allegedly threw out most of Fukushima and Hoshi's new ideas—some think he was partially inspired by *Lord of the Flies* for his version. In the end, Kimura would reportedly consider *Matango* his best script.

According to Steve Ryfle and Ed Godziszewski in *Ishiro Honda: A Life in Film, From Godzilla to Kurosawa*, filming of this story was partially inspired by a real-life incident wherein some rich kids took their father's yacht out to sea and had to be rescued. Allegedly the first draft of *Matango* centered around more youthful, spoiled characters—this was Masami Fukushima's version. In Fukushima's story, it is clear that inhaling the spores can also turn one into a Mushroom Person (this is implied in the climax of the finished film as well).

Aside from the mushroom people themselves, the only other main idea to carry over from Hodgson's original story into the finished film is the shipwrecked vessel the characters call home. Also, one could suppose Akira Kubo and Miki Yashiro's characters were stand-ins for the sympathetic lovers in Hodgson's original. Furthermore, both versions utilize the plot device of being told in flashback, bookended by scenes set in the present. In this case, the film begins and ends with Kubo in a mental asylum. As for developments and changes during shooting, Kumi Mizuno's transformation scene was different. Originally, she was to sport the same keloid scars as the other Mushroom People, but Honda felt it would be more effective if instead, she became more beautiful—to heighten the temptation to eat the mushrooms.

According to actor Yoshio Tsuchiya, the film has an alternate ending where Akira Kubo's face is still normal. This is not meant to convey that he wasn't affected by the mushrooms, but to leave the picture on an ambiguous note where the audience wonders if Kubo's character is just crazy. And indeed, the book *Toho SPFX Movie Complete Works* states that the first draft ends with the face of Kubo's character being normal and unscarred.

Matango was not a hit at the Japanese box office and effectively marked the end of movies about human-sized monsters for Toho until the "Bloodthirsty Trilogy" of the 1970s.

PROFILE: MASAMI FUKUSHIMA

Born in Toyohara, Karafuto, on February 18, 1929, as Masami Katō, Masami Fukushima was one of Japan's best-known sci-fi writers. His father was a public official and in 1934, the family moved to Manchuria. They returned to Japan in 1937. Fukushima studied at Nihon University in 1945 and later moved to Meiji University in 1950. There, he majored in French literature (presumably he enjoyed the works of Jules Verne). In 1954, Fukushima began to study translation under Shunji Shimizu—this should come as no surprise since Fukushima would sometimes translate versions of English horror and sci-fi stories into Japanese for his magazine, *SF Magazine*. Fukushima began the magazine in 1959 and stayed with it for ten years, leaving in 1969. In addition to his work on the magazine, Fukushima also translated sci-fi greats such as Arthur C. Clarke and Isaac Asimov into Japanese. In the early 1960s, Fukushima and another writer, Shinichi Hoshi, adapted William Hope Hodgson's "The Voice in the Night" into Japanese and brought it to Tomoyuki Tanaka, who commissioned a treatment from the two men. The film version, called *Matango*, was released in 1963. Three years later, a book that Fukushima had written was adapted by Toei to become *Terror Beneath the Sea* (1966). Fukushima didn't return to the world of film until he ran into Tomoyuki Tanaka at the construction site of the Okinawan Expo in 1973. Tanaka asked Fukushima if he might pitch an idea for the next Godzilla movie. Fukushima proposed a mechanical monster (not Mechagodzilla, it was called Garugan) and co-wrote a script with Shinichi Sekizawa entitled *Giant Monsters Converge on Okinawa: Showdown in Cape Zanpa*. Eventually, the script turned into *Godzilla vs. Mechagodzilla*. Fukushima died at the young age of only 47 on April 9, 1976.

Selected Filmography
Matango (1963) (writer)
Terror Beneath the Seas (1966) (story)
Godzilla vs. Hedorah (1971) (consultant)
Giant Monsters Converge on Okinawa: Showdown in Cape Zanpa (1973) (writer) [unproduced, became *Godzilla vs. Mechagodzilla*]
Godzilla vs. Mechagodzilla (1974) (story)

10.
THE UNDERSEA BATTLESHIP VS. THE UNDERSEA KINGDOM: ATRAGON

Toho's 1963 classic *Atragon* was based upon a story written in 1899, *Undersea Battleship*, by 22-year-old Shunro Oshikawa.[1] The story follows a Japanese Captain Nemo of sorts, Captain Sakurai, an exiled navy commander with a hard, samurai ethic who is building a super submersible (called the "Thunderbolt Ship") with a drill in its bow. His goal: to make Japan a world superpower.

The original novel is set in the late 1890s and focuses on a young man named Yanagikawa, traveling back to Japan from Italy with the wife of a friend and her eight-year-old son. Their ship is sunk by pirates in the Suez Canal, and Yanagikawa makes sure to save his friend's son as the ship goes under. The two find an abandoned lifeboat and climb aboard, floating aimlessly for ten days before they make way to a tropical island. There, they are confronted by a gorilla in the jungle which is frightened off by two naval men. Yanagikawa recognizes one, Captain Sakurai, from a newspaper article stating that he vanished some months ago.

When Yanagikawa tells the captain he has a responsibility to return his friend's son to Japan, Captain Sakurai regretfully informs him it will be three years before he can do so. At the moment, he is on a secret mission to construct a super submarine that will establish the Empire of Japan as a major military force. The submarine's secret is that it runs on a special fuel created by the captain himself, and also has the ability to extract oxygen from seawater—meaning that the ship can stay submerged for prolonged periods of time. The captain takes the young boy under his wing, as it was his father's wish he return to Japan to begin military training.

Three years later, as promised, the Undersea Battleship (with a huge drill attached to the nose) is finished. Before Sakurai leaves, he tasks Yanagikawa and an officer with placing a marker atop the island claiming it in the name of the Japanese Empire. The men become stranded in the jungle after placing the marker, and Sakurai rescues them in a hot air balloon made from the silk curtains within the Undersea Battleship! Finally, the submarine goes on its test run. However, a tidal wave decimates the island's fuel reserve, and when the Undersea Battleship returns to the island, the men are all effectively stranded there.

It is debated whether or not to destroy the submarine, lest it fall into the hands of another country, or send someone out to get the ingredients for the special fuel. Yanagikawa volunteers to take the hot air balloon on a mission to reach India to get the needed elements. A storm blows him off course, however, and next, he is attacked by a huge bird that shreds the balloon. Yanagikawa crashes into the ocean where he is saved by a passing Japanese ocean liner. On it is none other than his friend and his wife, who survived the pirate attack. Yanagikawa tells them that their son lives and is on an island with a Japanese super submarine. The cruiser sails to the island where parents and son are reunited, the father thrilled his son has gotten an education from the legendary Captain Sakurai. On the return voyage, the cruiser is surrounded by eight pirate ships and all hope seems lost. Suddenly, one of the pirate ships mysteriously explodes. One by one, the Undersea Battleship sinks the marauders by ramming into them with its huge drill, saving the cruiser.

Obviously, the story is very much inspired by not only *20,000 Leagues Under the Sea* but also its sequel *Mysterious Island,* which prominently featured a hot air balloon and island base. Though this would have made for a fantastic film (it even had a monster of sorts—the giant bird), in the end it was wise that Toho turned it into something a bit more fantastical. Surprisingly, when Tomoyuki Tanaka instructed Shinichi Sekizawa to write a script based on the story, Sekizawa didn't even reread *Undersea Battleship*! Sekizawa instead decided the script would turn out better if he went with his childhood impressions of the story. Sekizawa said:

"I read *Undersea Warship* when I was a child, before the war, and I forgot the details of the story itself. Instead, I only remembered the strong impression of romance and epic scale. When I was told the title of the movie, that impression came back to me right away. In writing the story, my major goal was to retain that impression... That the rest of the details would change did not matter much. In addition, the producer wanted the story to be set after the war (WWII), so we had to change everything. Another consideration was that we couldn't make Japan as a military power at that

 **THE GREAT THIEF**

KNOWN AS *THE LOST WORLD OF SINBAD* IN THE U.S., TOHO'S 1963 TOSHIRO MIFUNE FANTASY FILM *SAMURAI PIRATE* (*THE GREAT THIEF* IN JAPAN) CONTAINED WITCHES AND WIZARDS, BUT NO GIANT MONSTERS. HOWEVER, STORYBOARDS SEEM TO SHOW HIDEYO AMAMOTO'S WITCH CHARACTER GRANNY GROWING TO GIGANTIC PROPORTIONS TO BATTLE TOSHIRO MIFUNE'S CHARACTER, LUZON/SINBAD. ALSO, THE GIANT KITE MIFUNE'S CHARACTER RIDES WAS ORIGINALLY SUPPOSED TO BE A BIRD DISGUISE.

time, so that's why all the staff agreed to come up with a new enemy."[2]

The idea to make their version of Captain Sakurai—in this case, Captain Jinguji—a post-WWII Japanese patriot makes for some fascinating ideas and conflicts within the story. For those no doubt wondering how the mythical Mu Empire became involved, it would seem Sekizawa's early story musings didn't involve them but utilized the real-life threat posed by the Soviet Union instead, chiefly because they were the enemy nation at the forefront in the original novel. This was deemed uncomfortable and risky from a political standpoint, so Sekizawa took inspiration from a short story, *The Undersea Kingdom*, by Shigeru Komatsuzaki—a Toho illustrator who designed the fantastic weaponry of *The Mysterians* and *Battle in Outer Space*. The story was serialized from October of 1954 through December of 1955 in *Omoshiro Book*. It followed the survivors of a plane crash at sea rescued by a nuclear submarine, the *Atomfish*, commanded by eccentric aristocrat Marquis Horne. The survivors soon become involved in thwarting the plot of an evil queen who rules the titular undersea kingdom. Komatsuzaki himself was possibly inspired by *Undersea Battleship*, which he created illustrations for all the way back in 1952 for *Omoshiro Book*.

To give life to their incarnation of the Mu Empire, Sekizawa heavily researched the works of James Churchward, specifically *The Lost Continent of Mu*. On Toho's commentary track for the *Atragon* DVD, First Assistant Director Koji Kajita said:

"Mr. Sekizawa himself told me this about James Churchward, a civilization researcher around 1921. He theorizes the sinking of Mu, the continent of Mu, or the Mu Empire sunk by earthquakes and volcanoes. And after it sunk, they took advantage of geothermal power, created the sun, and aimed to recapture the control of the earth's surface."

Sekizawa's first draft was given to Shigeru Komatsuzaki to begin work illustrating concept paintings for the film. Considering that Manda is presented in one of the paintings, albeit as a giant rattlesnake, it's presumable that Manda was in the first draft. There is some debate as to whether Manda was always in the script (for certain, a snake monster doesn't appear in *The Undersea Kingdom*) or whether the beast was added at Tomoyuki Tanaka's insistence a la Magma in 1962's *Gorath*. In any case, Manda's design was changed to resemble a Chinese Dragon due to 1964 being the Year of the Dragon, and this was Toho's New Year's Blockbuster.[3] Many of *Atragon*'s most memorable elements weren't added until the final draft, including the Mu attack launched from Mt. Fuji, the earthquake assault on Marunochi in Tokyo, and Atragon's[4] zero canon (which means it had to defeat Manda in a different way in early drafts). Sekizawa also hoped that Jinguji would be played by Toshiro Mifune, though he knew his hopes were in vain as Mifune was too expensive and tended to decline offers for giant monster films—*The Three Treasures* being the lone exception.[5]

Despite shying away from the antiquated roots of *Undersea Battleship*, the rendering of both Atragon and the base are similar to the novel on film. Take this following excerpt from the novel to see the similarities:

> "Following them and entering the dock yard, abruptly the view got much wider. There, inside a great tunnel of incredible width and length, I could see gigantic walls of seemingly carved stone surrounding us. There must have been 5 to 10 meters of the ship that was underwater... My heart raced, but soon I tried to observe the body. How could such a strange, heavily armored ship exist anywhere in the world? The length of the undersea battleship was a full 40 meters, it was 7 meters in width, and its shape was like a sharp javelin such as those which the barbarians of southern India used to kill great elephants or savage tigers in a single strike. Both ends formed an unusual, acute angle. On the deck was an oval bridge near the bow, and it had nothing but one single mass on the top."[6]

Ironically, Shinichi Sekizawa didn't picture the battleship like this at all. In his mind, since Jinguji and his men were piecing the ship together on a South Seas island, their resources would have obviously been limited. As a result, the ship would have been more along the lines of *Space Battleship Yamato*. In fact, this idea came from stories that Sekizawa picked up on during his time in WWII when he heard a tale of Japanese soldiers constructing a new airplane out of discarded parts of other planes.[7]

A late draft of the script had a more dramatic scene where Jinguji decides to finally attack the Mu Empire only to learn that Makoto is held prisoner there. Jinguji decides to attack even if it costs his daughter her life. Admiral Kosumi disagrees with him and an argument proceeds, which was cut by Honda, who wanted to focus the story more on the conflict with Mu. In *Toho SFX Movie Series Vol. 4* Honda said, "I wanted to concentrate of the larger scale problem of mankind versus the Mu and ignore the personal problems in that scene. If they talk about their personal problems, unless you express it really deeply, the audience won't be satisfied." The film was originally scheduled to show the Mu Empire also attacking New York, but there simply wasn't time due to a rushed shooting schedule. Another elaborate deleted scene is expressed in the film's storyboards and occurs as the characters arrive on Jinguji's island. As they drive through the vast wasteland in the jeep, they are consumed by a black dust cloud. The jeep almost drives into a huge pit, and Makoto nearly plunges inside until she is saved by Susumu. In his book, *Godzilla and My Movie Life*, Honda also expressed his regret in not being able to show more of the Mu Empire, "I wanted to show something like its towns or residential areas. Those kinds of things were a necessity, but we didn't have the budget." Assistant director Koji Kajita also explained that they deliberately wanted Mu to be a multinational country. "Because Mu spanned from Hawaii up north, to Fiji in the south all the way to the Easter Islands. It was a huge continent. So it's not strange to have all these different people," he said on the DVD audio commentary.

Though it had a rushed production shoot due to *Matango* falling behind schedule, *Undersea Battleship* was a huge success when released in December of 1963. The origin of Atragon's American name may have been something of a miscommunication. Toho titled the movie *Atoragon* for international distribution. "Atoragon" was a combination of the words "Atlantis" and "dragon"—the name many say was meant for Manda (whose name apparently means "ten thousand meter snake"). The theory goes that Toho felt the sea serpent would be the most marketable aspect of the film, so they named it after the dragon for international markets. When AIP dubbed the film into English, they (rather logically) decided that was the submarine's name instead. However, this rumor that Atoragon was the name meant for Manda is false, as the Japanese program booklet identifies the "super sub" as Atoragon in a special English language page. When released in the U.S. in 1965, many of the film's scenes dealing overtly with Japanese patriotism in the post-WWII era—a central theme in the film—were either removed or dubbed over with new dialogue.

Chapter Notes

[1] Author Oshikawa had four other of his works become films before this: *King of the Silver Mine* (Nikkatsu, 1913); *Island of New Japan* (Nikkatsu, 1926); *Master Fist* (Nikkatsu, 1927) and *Society of Oriental Chivalry* (Nikkatsu, 1927).
[2] Godziszewski, "*Atragon*: A Toho Classic Revisited." *G-Fan* #21 (May/June 1996), pp.19
[3] In *G-Fan* #22 Haruo Nakajima claims Manda was designed after one of the heads of Orochi from *The Three Treasures* (1959).
[4] Known as the Gohten in Japan.
[5] *The Three Treasures* is a retelling of the Japanese creation myth and the Yamato no Orochi is a part of that myth. Mifune could not very well fault the movie for being faithful to the myth could he?
[6] Godziszewski, "*Atragon*: A Toho Classic Revisited." *G-Fan* #21 (May/June 1996), pp.19.
[7] Sekizawa wrote a whole script based off this idea: 1966's *Zero Fighter*.

PROFILE: SHIGERU KOMATSUZAKI

One of the unsung heroes of Toho special effects films is Shigeru Komatsuzaki, a worker in Toho's art department who designed many of the marvelous mechs in Toho's films. Among Komatsuzaki's creations were the Markalites in *The Mysterians*, the Natal craft in *Battle in Outer Space*, and the Maser Tanks of *The War of the Gargantuas*. Komatsuzaki was born February 14, 1915, in Tokyo. Komatsuzaki began drawing military hardware for the mechanical journal *Kikaika* as a teenager, and his first published work was illustrating "Mystery of the White Fox" for *Otaru Shinbun* in 1938. Komatsuzaki studied physics and electronics and was assigned to the task of laser research during WWII! During this time, Komatsuzaki also aided in a project to construct a huge airborne bomber called the Fugaku which never got past the planning stages. This probably inspired elements of *The Flying Battleship*, a cancelled movie that eventually birthed the Tsuburaya TV series *Mighty Jack* (1968). Through his military background, Komatsuzaki had great insight into how fantastic technology worked. After WWII, Komatsuzaki began writing fantastic fiction such as "Second World" serialized in *Shōnen* from October of 1952 through January of 1955. A young adult tale like most of his fiction, this one concerned a teenager living in a prosperous future world while also reminiscing on his time as an orphan during WWII. In the late 1950s, he began designing for Toho sci-fi films and in 1963, Shinichi Sekizawa utilized elements of Komatsuzaki's story *The Undersea Kingdom* when writing *Atragon*, which Komatsuzaki also submitted designs for. The following year, a monster design by Komatsuzaki previously published in a 1961 magazine was chosen as the design for the titular monster in *Space Monster Dogora* (1964). In 1995, Komatsuzaki suffered a tragedy when his home burned down, destroying many of his original drawings. Despite the setback, Komatsuzaki continued to draw. Quite the eccentric, Komatsuzaki's pants were peppered with holes from cigarette ash burns in his later years! He continued to steadily give interviews up until his death at the age of 86 on December 7, 2001.

Selected Filmography
The Undersea Kingdom (novel) (1955) (writer)
The Mysterians (1957) (concept design)
Battle in Outer Space (1959) (concept design)
Matango (1963) (concept design)
Atragon (1963) (concept design)
Space Monster Dogora (1957) (concept design)

11.
MOTHRA VS. GODZILLA
ROUND ONE

After the immense success of *King Kong vs. Godzilla*, one thing was for certain: Toho wouldn't wait six years to produce another G-film. Toho's first idea was the somewhat unoriginal *Continuation: King Kong vs. Godzilla* by Shinichi Sekizawa. That script, however, would eventually evolve into what many fans consider to be the best of the Showa Godzilla sequels: *Mothra vs. Godzilla*. Elements fans will find familiar between the two is a monster used as an amusement park attraction by a greedy entrepreneur, plus a theme of human selfishness and greed throughout. In *Continuation: King Kong vs. Godzilla*, Kong has become the surrogate father of a Japanese baby recovered in a plane crash in the wilds of Africa. When the baby is rescued and taken to Japan, Kong comes looking for it. The baby and its new surrogate human parents are ordered to leave Japan, while at the same time no other country will offer them solace! Simultaneously, Godzilla's body (thought to be dead but really just unconscious from the previous film's bout) is dredged from the ocean to become an amusement park attraction. Godzilla is then revived to fight Kong, who has followed the baby to Kyushu. Naturally, the two titans have a rematch and both are swallowed up by Mt. Aso when it erupts.

Once it was decided to make Mothra Godzilla's next opponent instead, Sekizawa's first treatment acted as both a direct sequel to *Mothra* and also utilized ideas from the axed rematch with Kong. In *Ishiro Honda: A Life in Film, From Godzilla to Kurosawa*, Ed Godziszewski and Steve Ryfle wrote, "As originally conceived, Shinichi Sekizawa's screenplay picked up where *Mothra* ended, and Godzilla was to attack the fictional nation of Rolisica before heading to Japan."[1] In the first treatment, rather than Mothra's egg, Godzilla's lifeless body washes ashore after a typhoon, comatose since the end of *King Kong vs. Godzilla*—this element itself lifted from Sekizawa's *Continuation: King Kong vs. Godzilla* treatment. Like that story, an entrepreneur then exploits Godzilla. As this author doesn't actually know where Godzilla washes ashore, it is possible he washes ashore in Rolisica, where another greedy Clark Nelson type exploits the situation. Presumably, after Godzilla awakened he began attacking Rolisica. However, Godzilla may have washed ashore in Japan and attacked Rolisica for the climax instead.

Considering that the trio of main characters in the finished film comprises of a reporter, his photographer, and a scientist studying Mothra, one could almost presume that Sekizawa had ideas of bringing back Fukuda, Michi and Chujo—but this is just conjecture.[2] Whatever the case, Godzilla makes his way to Japan and the adult Mothra flies there to protect them in the climax—there are no twin larvae. To defeat Godzilla, Mothra was to spin a web around the monster and then drag him out to sea by his tail where she would dump him to await his next sequel.

Tracking Sekizawa's developmental process gets foggy from here. Obviously, at some point in the developmental process, Godzilla's unconscious body was swapped for Mothra's egg. This way, Mothra had a more natural tie to the story. As stated earlier, Sekizawa's theme about man's inhumanity to their fellow man (as emphasized in Junko's impassioned plea in the finished film) originated in *Continuation: King Kong vs. Godzilla*. As stated earlier, in that story, an infant whom Kong has grown attached is banned from Japan and then not allowed sanctuary in other countries. In this story, this theme is represented in Happy Enterprises' unwillingness to turn Mothra's egg back to its rightful owners, as well as the Infant Islanders refusal to aid Japan when Godzilla attacks.

Rather than Sakai and Junko, the focus in the first screenplay was more on Sakai's college friend, Hara, a zoologist, and Hara's mentor, Dr. Miura (eventually these two roles would be combined into the lone Professor Miura). The character of Torahata didn't exist at all and instead, there is only Kumayama. Presumably, in this first draft—though some imply it is also in the second—Godzilla somehow finds the time to go to Rolisica where he is confronted by the Frontier Missiles. Also, instead of the Lightning Control System, a set of high tension towers are constructed around Tokyo to keep the monster out until he develops an immunity to them.

A first draft was completed by Shinichi Sekizawa on December 31, 1963. By the next draft, the Rolisica attack scene was replaced with Godzilla sticking to Japan and walking through the Yokaichi Industrial Complex and Nagoya.[3] Godzilla's entrance was saved for later, surfacing in western Japan. Godzilla was to destroy

Hijemi Castle rather than Nagoya Castle and Godzilla would then trek through the Keihanshin area until he reaches the Tenyu River where a confrontation with the self-defense forces takes place.

In these early versions, Mothra doesn't come to Japan to rescue her egg herself because she doesn't want to start a conflict with Japan. When Sakai, Junko, and Miura go to Infant Island and are denied the aid they seek, they offer themselves as hostages. This gets the attention of Mothra, who agrees to help them and flies to Japan to battle Godzilla. It is still unclear at this point if the climactic battle is Godzilla and the adult Mothra only. It's possible that the battle ended with the adult Mothra defeating Godzilla, dying, and then the egg hatches and the larvae swim back to Infant Island with the Shobijin, but that's my own conjecture.

There are still differences of interest all the way up to the final draft. The rescuing of the children on Iwo Island doesn't exist and instead, Godzilla battles the two larvae along a beach. Before this happens, though, some suspense is added in having Godzilla chase Sakai and his friends across said beach. Godzilla's battle with the larvae was also meant to be intercut with the Infant Islanders dancing for their god's victory.

Rather than finding one of Godzilla's scales in the aftermath of the typhoon, Junko finds one of Godzilla's fangs, which she thinks is a bull's horn. Godzilla also becomes immune to electricity rather than melting the towers.[4] Overall, the dialogue sections of the script were cut down and simplified considerably. A scene was deleted that would have shown Miura sleeping in his hotel room and being awakened by the sounds of winds caused by Mothra's landing. The following hotel lobby scene was said to be shortened from there.

Also of note, Kodansha's novelization of *Mothra vs. Godzilla* offers an explanation of Mothra's origin, stating that Mothra evolved on Infant Island through many years of abnormal climate change. Whether this was in Sekizawa's script or not is unknown, but it is interesting considering Mothra's origins were also cut from *Mothra*. Honda once again wanted to portray Infant Island as being more scarred by nuclear radiation, but the art department didn't have the budget to comply with his ideas.[5]

Tsuburaya storyboarded some interesting battle techniques, one of which had Mothra standing on her hind legs to generate a wind attack. The brutal battle would also have had Mothra bite Godzilla on the shoulder, and concept art of this was even used on a lobby card. In some storyboards, Mothra is presented as being a tad smaller than Godzilla, and maneuvers included Godzilla throwing rocks at Mothra, head-butting her, and also wrapping both arms around her massive wings and squeezing her.

Many fans consider *Mothra vs. Godzilla* the gold standard of Godzilla sequels. This is, in large part, thanks to the engaging human storyline anchored by some very likable characters who are pitted against some very unlikeable villains. Couple this with near flawless (for the time) effects sequences and monster battles and it's no surprise that many fans hold the film in such high regard. Tonally, the film is a departure from *King Kong vs. Godzilla*'s satirical nature, even if the theme of rampant commercialism returns. Overall, one could say it strikes a rather fine balance between light fantasy and drama.

Perhaps most notable of all was the fact that this was the first of Toho's films to hint that all of their monster movies take place in the same universe.[6] When Mothra dies, it packs a punch considering that she too is a returning character.[7] The idea of an expanded universe would get taken to the next level in the following Godzilla film.

Chapter Notes

[1] Ryfle and Godziszewski, *Ishiro Honda*, pp.207.
[2] Considering the fact that Hiroshi Koizumi played Chujo and Professor Miura both, this isn't a bad theory.
[3] Godzilla doesn't actually attack either of these locations per se. He strolls through them (in the middle of downtown Nagoya, no less). At the complex, he blasts his ray when he's startled after his tail accidentally whacks into something and all the destruction in Nagoya is due to Godzilla's clumsiness, not any malicious intent on his part. This was a point Ishiro Honda wished to make with the film: that Godzilla does not fit into this world.
[4] In the series proper, this would eventually occur naturally, but not until 1971's *Godzilla vs. Hedorah*.
[5] This was also his same desire for *Mothra*, but once again, the budget wasn't enough to comply with his ideas.
[6] Toho had hinted at this fact in the manga "The Last Godzilla" which mentioned Rodan. It would seem early scripts for *Mothra* were to mention Godzilla, but these references were deleted in the final film.
[7] Given extra life in her death throes by Tsuburaya as he causes the Mothra marionette to expand and contract to show the goddess' dying breaths.

12.
SPACE MONSTERS
DOGORA AND KING GHIDORAH ATTACK

Toho had ideas of producing a space monster movie immediately after the successful release of *Gorath* in 1962. The simply-titled "Space Monster" was based on another story proposal by Jojiro Okami. As it turned out, it would be his last proposal for Toho and the story would sit for two years before being picked up again. As to the why, apparently, Toho wasn't entirely confident that they could bring the strange space cells to life at the time. Also, the monster's eventual on-screen design predates Okami's draft by a year. Surprisingly, the then-unnamed space monster was designed by Shigeru Komatsuzaki (an often uncredited Toho designer) in a 1961 issue of *Weekly Shonen Sunday*. Whether this was tied to Okami's story is unknown but it's likely someone saw the design, liked it, and asked Komatsuzaki if they could use it in the new film.

Space Monster Dogora was something of a last minute decision by Toho brass who wanted another effects picture released in the summer of 1964. As they had just released *Mothra vs. Godzilla*, it was still far too soon to release another G-film even though they would anyway as the New Year's Blockbuster at the end of 1964. Looking for a quick project, Toho dusted off Okami's *Space Monster* draft and pushed it into production. *Earth Martial Law*, a first draft title, was written by Shinichi Sekizawa. It's not known exactly when, but at some point, the script was given a major overhaul, scaling down the global destruction in favor of a light cops 'n' robbers caper film.

Elaborate storyboards (not to be confused with equally elaborate but misleading publicity stills) exist showing Okami's original vision.[1] Among them are a group of space monsters shown being born in the Van Allen radiation belt. They immediately do battle with rocketships called P-Boats (one of which is swallowed by the shapeshifting monster). Other storyboards show the space station model first used in *The Mysterians* being in a state of repair as it is attacked and destroyed by the monster. Radar guided ground-to-air missiles are launched at the space monsters to no avail. Next, the monsters attack jewelry stores in New York along Broadway. The monster even crashes a fancy dinner, as women react in horror to watching their jewelry vanish right off of their bodies.

The space monsters then go on a global tour of destruction, lifting a cruise ship out of the water. Subsequently, San Francisco's Golden Gate Bridge is uprooted by the monster. Coal mines in Russia fall under attack, and a freighter is sunk in the Pacific. The monster attacks the heart of Tokyo, lifts Tokyo Tower high into the air, attacks a bullet train, and even causes an atomic power plant to explode, killing thousands.[2] Using a carbon rod as bait, one of the space monsters is caught in a container (called a "giant mousetrap") and airlifted by helicopter for study. Scientists studying the "space mice" then deduce that beta rays are the answer to defeating the creatures. Powerful beta ray generator weapons are built and cause the monsters to convert into a new, inorganic substance. This substance is used as a new source of energy as the world begins to rebuild itself.

This concept was scaled down immensely for the sake of the budget by Honda and Sekizawa, who didn't consult with Okami at all, which was apparently unusual. "We just got his original story and took it from there," Honda said.[3] In Sekizawa's early drafts, Dogora makes its entrance in the skies above the Bering Sea—or possibly in the Bering Sea, this is unclear. Also, Dogora initially converts carbon into nitrogen and in this version, the jellyfish-like creature occasionally ventures into the sea. There are also many smaller, human-sized Dogoras as well. One would think the famous bridge scene—a highlight of the finished film—was in Okami's 1962 story since Wakato Bridge, the longest suspension bridge in the east at that time, was completed in 1962. Strangely enough, it was not and was added into the story by Sekizawa.

Space Monster Dogora arrived in theaters with very little fanfare in August of 1964. The main draw, rather than the monster, was action star Yosuke Natsuki. In an era where kaiju were becoming more and more humanized, as just a giant space jellyfish, Dogora seemingly lacked personality.[4] *Space Monster Dogora* is one of the few monster films where the "human scenes" wound up preferable to the monster scenes. The cat and mouse game between Detective Kommei (Yosuke Natsuki) and Mark Jackson (Robert Dunham [5]) is quite an entertaining development throughout the film. Shinichi Sekizawa should be commended for coming up with an entertaining human storyline when Okami's more elaborate concept was axed.

It would seem that Toho had no plans of returning Godzilla to the silver screen until the next year, likely in *Frankenstein vs. Godzilla*. In 1963, future *Star Trek* writer Jerry Sohl had cooked up a plot called *Godzilla vs. Frankenstein*. Through Henry G. Saperstein of United Productions of America (who had just sold *Mothra vs. Godzilla* in the United States), that story pitch eventually came to Toho in 1964. Upon receiving Sohl's *Godzilla vs. Frankenstein* treatment, they gave it to Takeshi Kimura for further elaboration.

As the title implies, *Frankenstein vs. Godzilla*[6] featured Godzilla fighting a giant version of the Frankenstein Monster. Toho's script was dated July of 1964, meaning it was likely being planned for a 1965 release date since Akira Kurosawa's forthcoming *Red Beard* was already slated to be the New Year's blockbuster for the end of 1964. However, as the year progressed, it was learned that *Red Beard* would not be ready in time (a standard occurrence with Kurosawa, who often took an entire day just to get one shot). A New Year's Blockbuster was a critical part of Toho's financial earnings and they needed a replacement fast. Rather than rush *Frankenstein vs. Godzilla* into production (that would likely have required too much approval from UPA since they were co-producers), Toho instead decided to cook up a new story entirely.

Tomoyuki Tanaka reportedly brought in a book of Greek mythology, pointed to the Hydra, and suggested they come up with something similar for Godzilla, Mothra, and Rodan to face off against.[7] One source (*Tokusatsu Hihou*) believes Tanaka was inspired by the giant three-headed dragon from the Russian film *The Sword and the Dragon* (1956).[8] To further the Russian connection, some even say the resultant King Ghidorah was meant to represent the threat of the Soviet Union (while others have said Red China). Whatever the monster may have been metaphorically, initially Sekizawa described the space monster as having the body of a lion, dragon-like heads (but with sharp beaks), and feathery wings. Outside of Ghidorah's odd design, draft #1 (dated August 27, 1964) of Sekizawa's script didn't have Princess Salno in it at all. Instead, the human plot revolved around Detective Shindo trying to take down a drug trafficking ring. In Princess Salno's place was a male member of the drug trafficking ring, Goro Aikawa, who would become possessed by the spirit of a long-dead Venusian. *Tokusatsu Hihou* Vol. 8 even goes so far as to imply that Yoshio Tsuchiya was eyed for the role.[9]

The scene with the "Space Disc Club" is in this version but instead of Naoko covering it, her editor (played by Kenji Sahara in the final film) is there instead. The Goro Aikawa character is also there for some reason. As they watch the meteor shower, Goro experiences a miraculous event, falling off the roof and waking up miles away at Kurobe Dam! Professor Murai, out to find the meteorite that crashed there, discovers Goro, now convinced that he is a Venusian prophet. This draft of the script noted that Murai was Naoko's lover, something only joked about in the finished film. Naturally, no one believes that Goro is a Venusian. Everyone except the "Space Disc Club," who take his wild claims to heart.[10] It would also seem that Goro remembers who he is, as opposed to Princess Salno who has no memory of being a princess or why she has fled to Japan. As in the finished film, Goro predicts Rodan's awakening from Mt. Aso and Godzilla's appearance at sea. However, Godzilla's entrance cushions his character in this draft; rather than entering the film by murdering everyone on an innocent cruise ship, he destroys a ship illegally transporting drugs at sea. Goro was initially one of the smugglers in that gang. The possessed gangster's explanation of King Ghidorah was also more detailed in this draft, explaining that Ghidorah had destroyed multiple planets in the past. Goro then explains that Ghidorah has been searching for a new world to destroy since it had wiped out Venus.

In this version, there is a subplot about the Cold War involving an extremist group known as the World Federation that wants to nuke King Ghidorah on Japanese soil. Goro says that while this may kill the monster, it will mean the end of all life on earth in the process. During this portion of the story, King Ghidorah would fly all the way to New York where he would destroy the Statue of Liberty.[11] This would encourage the U.S. to push for a nuclear strike on the monster. As King Ghidorah returns to Japan, it would next destroy the newly-completed Tokyo Monorail System. After another push from the U.S. base in Okinawa to utilize nuclear weapons, Goro makes one final plea. He tells the delegates that on Venus all they had to fight with was science but the earth has something that Venus didn't: Godzilla, Mothra, and Rodan. Together, they may be able to drive the monster away.

Halting the nuclear attack is contingent upon Mothra convincing Godzilla and Rodan to cooperate.[12] The battle was to play out more or less as in the finished film, but the epilogue was quite different. After Ghidorah leaves earth, there were to be shots of newspaper articles celebrating the occasion which would read "King Ghidorah Escapes to Space!" and "The Fear of the Dead Star Leaves!" As soon as this problem resolves, tension at the "15th Parallel at the Sarzan Peninsula" was to heat up again immediately, implying the world was back on the brink of self-created nuclear annihilation once again. And even though Godzilla and Rodan have just saved the world, the World Federation makes it clear they will take up countermeasures against the two monsters as soon as possible. At the story's end, the final shot was to be Godzilla and Rodan shrouded in mist at the foot of Mt. Fuji, their futures uncertain. Needless to say, this ending is rather bleak compared to the happy ending of the finished film.

In the second draft, Sekizawa was inspired by *Roman Holiday* (1953) to create the Princess Salno storyline and during pre-production, Kumi Mizuno was the intended choice for the new character. By the script's third draft, she had been replaced by Akiko Wakabayashi. Likewise, the role of Selgina assassin Malness was meant for Yoshio Tsuchiya, who was filming *Red Beard* and couldn't break away. The idea to dress Princess Salno in the fisherman's clothes wasn't in the script and came from Akiko Wakabayashi herself.

King Ghidorah, as designed by Akira Watanabe, evolved into a limbless monster colored in crimson red scales. Next, the monster's body changed to have blue scales with rainbow-colored wings. Photographic evidence exists showing a blue King Ghidorah suit in *Tokusatsu Hihou* Vol. 2 as well as in *The History of Keizo Murase Godzilla and Toho Monster Suits*! Teruyoshi Nakano mentioned that since the monster was "from Venus"[13] that the monster should be gold. Tsuburaya liked the idea and the three-headed monster became gold. Also, King Ghidorah's breath was originally meant to be fiery like a flame thrower, as evidenced in early publicity photos, but the effect was too hard to animate.[14]

Rumor has it the twin Mothras from the previous film were set to return, one still a larva and the other an adult—according to Eiji Tsuburaya in an interview with a French magazine. The wireworks of an adult Mothra, Rodan, and King Ghidorah all on one stage likely would have been staggering (Ghidorah alone required 22 wires to operate!), so the adult Mothra was cut. However, *Tokusatsu Hihou* has a lengthy write up on the first draft and says nothing about there being two Mothras.

Though some fans consider *Ghidorah, the Three-Headed Monster* inferior to *Mothra vs. Godzilla*, in the end, *Ghidorah* wound up being a great deal more fun. The script utilizes Toho's past continuity much like Marvel would in the 2000s. Here, we find a fantastic Japan where the Shobijin willingly perform on a live TV variety show, a Venusian spirit possessing a princess from a fictional Himalayan country, an alien monster crashing from outer space to Earth, and in the middle of it all, Godzilla and Rodan battling across Japan as though it was an everyday thing. Sekizawa balances the monster storylines wonderfully with the human plot and has them collide in fantastic fashion several times. The best example might be when

Godzilla and Rodan's battle inadvertently saves Princess Salno's life (one person who reportedly did not appreciate the film's many plot threads was Ishiro Honda, who thought it was all too much in addition to the comical monster congress scene).

Despite being the second Godzilla film that year, not to mention the third giant monster movie from Toho overall, *Ghidorah, the Three-Headed Monster* wound up being more successful than *Mothra vs. Godzilla*—likely due to being the New Year's Blockbuster, which is a more profitable time for movies.

Chapter Notes

[1] It's unknown if they were done in 1962 or 1964.
[2] It's unclear, but storyboard notes may also imply that Dogora recognizes humans as another form of edible carbon to consume.
[3] Ryfle and Godziszewski, *Ishiro Honda*, pp. 212.
[4] An early poster of *Space Monster Dogora* shows a totally different, cartoonish monster on the poster.
[5] Toho even considered a Mark Jackson spin-off film.
[6] Yes, Sohl called his version *Godzilla vs. Frankenstein* while Toho reversed it to *Frankenstein vs. Godzilla*.
[7] Though likely, it is unknown if Toho ever considered a simple *Godzilla vs. Rodan* movie.
[8] When *Mystery Science Theater 3000* aired *Sword and the Dragon*, the moment the dragon appeared, Crow shouted out "It's Ghidrah!"
[9] This is the second time Kurosawa kept Tsuchiya out of a Godzilla film
[10] As always, there seems to be more to the story that is lost in the translation of Japanese to English. It would seem in this story that it is hinted that the meteorite's arrival has awakened other people's long dormant Venusian power for prophecy. We even meet another potential Venusian in the first draft. It is none other than Rodan's first victim, the man who goes to retrieve the hat at Mt. Aso! As stated earlier, something is lost in translation here, but there is more to the Venusian aspect in Draft #1 than the final script.
[11] Pre-production art of the beast flying over Manhattan exists. Supposedly this idea remained up into the final draft. Perhaps not coincidentally, mockups of this nonexistent scene are present in the film's lobby cards.
[12] This is a fun, fascinating idea that further hits home the film's anti-nuclear theme that was watered down as the drafts evolved. Of course, the finished story is crowded enough as it is.
[13] Something he assumed but was not a part of the character's actual history; Venus is considered the "golden planet" in Japan.
[14] Though for some reason, these fire blasts were retained all the way up to stills for *Godzilla vs. Gigan*.

PROFILE: SHINICHI SEKIZAWA

Probably the most prolific of all the Godzilla writers, Shinichi Sekizawa was born June 2, 1921, in Kyoto. Sekizawa has roughly over 60 finished film/TV series screenplay credits, but even more if counting unmade projects like *Godzilla: Legend of the Asuka Fortress* (1985). Before deciding to take up a career in screenwriting, Sekizawa attended an animation school with famous manga artist and animator Osamu Tezuka. Before WWII, Sekizawa had his own serialized manga in a Kyoto newspaper. During the war, Sekizawa was mostly stationed on isolated Pacific islands where he would hear rumors of wild tales. One such rumor (that a group of Japanese soldiers had constructed an airplane out of discarded parts) would later inspire his 1966 film *Zero Fighter*. After the war, Sekizawa racked up three producing credits in a series focusing on outcast children in post-WWII Japan, the first of which was *Children of the Beehive* (1948). In fact, Sekizawa ghostwrote these films for famous director Hiroshi Shimizu. Sekizawa first began writing (credited) screenplays in 1949 and had written three in all before his first sci-fi screenwriting credit for Shintoho's *Fearful Attack of the Flying Saucers* (1956), which he also directed. Considered lost, not much is known of the film but photos of it have surfaced in Japanese magazines. Sekizawa began writing for Toho with 1957's *Tokyo Yoitoko*. Sekizawa's first kaiju eiga for the company was 1958's inauspicious *Giant Monster Varan*. Though it wasn't terribly popular, Sekizawa was still given writing duties on *Battle in Outer Space* the next year which was much better received. Sekizawa didn't cement himself as a bonafide talent until 1961's *Mothra* which became a runaway hit, followed by the even bigger hit that was *King Kong vs. Godzilla* (1962). Sandwiched between his sci-fi/kaiju epics were many other films, usually crime thrillers like the Toshiro Mifune film *The Last Gunfight* (1960) and *Blueprint of Murder* (1961). He even wrote a Tadao Takashima/Yu Fujuki comedy, *Ganba* (1961). Sekizawa also contributed materials to the original *Ultraman* series from 1966, writing the pilot as well as several Toei Dōga films such as *Gulliver's Travels Beyond the Moon* (1965) and *Jack and the Witch* (1967). Writing for Toei was a breach of contract, and Sekizawa could have gotten fired, but the writer was too important to Toho, who let the matter slide. This wasn't even the first time this had happened, as Sekizawa wrote the TV miniseries *Agon the Atomic Dragon* in 1964, which many sources claim Toho themselves stopped from airing! [Yet other sources say the miniseries never aired due to a lack of sponsorship until 1968.] Quite the eccentric, Sekizawa would show up to the Toho lot in a kimono instead of a suit and tie and his home was filled with model railroad sets. Sekizawa was also equally renowned in the field of song writing, and wrote many hits for Hibari Misora, the "Japanese Judy Garland." From 1967 forward, Sekizawa's credits were mostly genre-related apart from the 1970 TV miniseries *Dokushin no Scat*. Sekizawa was also very busy writing song lyrics in the 1970s, so much that he was unable to give Toho a full script for 1973's *Godzilla vs. Megalon*. As a result, Sekizawa's last real screen-writing credit was on *Godzilla vs. Gigan* though as stated earlier, he contributed stories for *Godzilla vs. Megalon*, *Godzilla vs. Mechagodzilla*, and also returned to write several unmade Godzilla scripts and treatments starting in 1978. In his later years, Sekizawa worked as a railroad photographer. He served as the first editor-in-chief of the magazine *Steam Locomotive*. In 1990, Sekizawa received the Purple Ribbon, a prestigious award. He died two years later on November 19, 1992. His last credit was as a songwriter for the TV series *Jirochô Sangokushi*. When David Milner asked Fumio Tanaka about Sekizawa, Tanaka replied, "Mr. Sekizawa was childish, but in a good sense. He also was very frank. He became rich not by writing screenplays, but instead by writing song lyrics." [www.davmil.org/www.kaiju-conversations.com/tanak.htm]

Selected Filmography
Children of the Beehive (1948) (co-producer)
Musume jûhachi usotsuki jidai (1949) (writer)
Buddha and the Children (1952) (co-producer/co-director)
Fearful Attack of the Flying Saucers (1956) (writer/director)
Varan (1958) (writer)
The Big Boss (1959) (writer)
Battle in Outer Space (1959) (writer)
The Last Gunfight (1960) (writer)
Take Aim at the Police Van (1960) (writer)
Blueprint of Murder (1961) (writer)
Mothra (1961) (writer)
Ganba (1961) (writer)
King Kong vs. Godzilla (1962) (writer)
Frankenstein vs. the Human Vapor (1963) (writer) [unproduced]
Continuation: King Kong vs. Godzilla (1963) (writer) [unproduced]
Attack Squadron (1963) (writer)
Samurai Pirate (1963) (writer)
Atragon (1963) (writer)
Mothra vs. Godzilla (1964) (writer)
Space Monster Dogora (1964) (writer)
Ghidorah, the Three-Headed Monster (1964) (writer)
Gulliver's Travels Beyond the Moon (1965) (writer)
Invasion of Astro-Monster (1965) (writer)
Ultraman [pilot episode] (1966) (writer)
Zero Fighter (1966) (co-writer)
Ebirah, Horror of the Deep (1966) (writer)
The Flying Battleship (1966) (writer) [unproduced]
The Killing Bottle (1967) (writer)
Jack and the Witch (1967) (writer)
Kaiju Booska [TV series] (1967) (writer)
Son of Godzilla (1967) (co-writer)
Agon the Atomic Dragon (1968) (writer/production manager)
Mighty Jack (1968) (writer)
Latitude Zero (1969) (writer)
All Monsters Attack (1969) (writer)
Dokushin No Scat [mini-series] (1970) (writer)
Godzilla vs. Gigan (1972) (writer)
Godzilla vs. Megalon (1973) (story)
Monsters Converge on Okinawa: Showdown in Cape Zanpa (1973) (story) [became *Godzilla vs. Mechagodzilla*]
The Anger of Godzilla (1978) (story) [unproduced]
Godzilla: Legend of the Asuka Fortress (1985) (writer) [unproduced]

13.
FRANKENSTEIN VS.
GODZILLA, BARAGON, AND THE GIANT DEVILFISH

At the onset of 1965, Toho found themselves in the middle of a shakeup regarding their planned U.S. co-production for *Frankenstein vs. Godzilla*. *Ghidorah, the Three-Headed Monster* had just changed Godzilla's status quo into that of a hero. Therefore, his villainous role in *Frankenstein vs. Godzilla* would no longer be a viable idea. However, rather than Toho, it was apparently the American camp who suggested a new Godzilla-like monster who eats people as a replacement villain.[1] Though some fans mistakenly believe that Baragon merely replaced Godzilla in the draft for *Frankenstein vs. Baragon*, this was not entirely the case.

The first treatment was written by Jerry Sohl, a future *Star Trek* writer. The 17-page treatment, titled *Godzilla vs. Frankenstein*, surfaced only recently and is similar to Toho's later script, *Frankenstein vs. Godzilla*. Sohl's story begins similarly to *Frankenstein vs. Baragon* during the final days of WWII. In a secret Nazi laboratory, multiple scientists (as opposed to the completed film's one) work on the still-beating heart of Frankenstein's Monster (there is no scene of a scientist wrecking his lab in despair when the heart is taken away). Events continue to play out as in *Frankenstein vs. Baragon*, with the Nazis giving the heart to the Japanese at sea. Here, the heart is still taken to Hiroshima but rather than a hospital, it is taken to a secret Japanese lab hidden within a cave on the outskirts of the city.

Sohl creates more buildup to the dropping of the bomb and even had a scene set on Tinian Island showing the U.S. army boarding the Enola Gay. On an observation plane to follow the Enola Gay is young James Bowen (Nick Adams' character in *Frankenstein vs. Baragon*)! This better explains Bowen's guilt regarding WWII and the dropping of the bomb. Perhaps the biggest element lost from Sohl's version is the way he portrays the monster's heart after the explosion. It is very much reminiscent of American horror films. Sohl wrote scenes where after the bomb has dropped, the heart slithers across the floor as it develops a fetus-like shape with arms and legs! Sohl's treatment would seem to confirm that the heart regenerated into the body whereas in the film, it is implied a starving orphan may have eaten it. Speaking of eating, there was also a bit written where the fetus-like heart grabs and devours a mouse!

We then jump into the future to meet Dr. James Bowen and Dr. Suehiko "Sue" Yoshi. The only significant difference is they also mention Godzilla was recently discovered hibernating in the Kurile Trench. The duo soon go picnicking in front of the secret cave lab from earlier in the story, meaning this is a progenitor of the scene where Bowen and Sueko find Frankenstein in a random cave in the final film. Sohl's description of the monster would seem to imply that he envisioned something similar to the Universal Frankenstein Monster: "...we see enough to know that the heart has grown/regenerated itself into the monster that once was and is again." Bowen, who in this version has an infatuation with the Frankenstein family, identifies the monster as Frankenstein right away.

Things continue to play out similarly to the finished film except Bowen never ponders cutting off a body part to see if it regenerates. Noticing the monster never seems to stop growing, he does restrict the monster's rations which is what entices it to escape. When the monster—impervious to the self-defense force's attacks—reaches only 12 feet in height, the Japanese government begins discussing reviving the much more destructive Godzilla to squash Frankenstein! A plan is hatched to guide Godzilla to Japan using sonar where he can literally squash the monster like a bug underfoot.[2]

Godzilla is indeed eventually led to Japan where he encounters Frankenstein, now 20 feet tall. Naturally, there is no fight and Frankenstein just runs away—which greatly irks Godzilla for some reason. When Frankenstein enters a populated area, Sue offers herself to him in an effort to get him to turn back—similar to a scene that plays out in *King Kong Escapes* (1967). Frankenstein picks up Sue and takes her into the woods.[3]

Frankenstein places Sue in a safe spot and then goes to forage for more food (Frankenstein's hunger is more emphasized in this treatment). At this point, Godzilla shows up to menace Sue and her screams bring Frankenstein (now more of a match for Godzilla's size) to the rescue. A battle ensues between the two monsters in the forest until it leads to the summit of an erupting volcano. Frankenstein falls inside the crater while the lava discharge knocks Godzilla backward until he tumbles down the volcano and into the sea.[4]

Takeshi Kimura's expansion of the treatment obviously retains Bowen and Sueko, but also adds the third scientist character, Kawaji. Kimura also makes one of the Japanese naval officers a central character, though this version of Kawai (played by Yoshio Tsuchiya in the finished film) is different from the one who appears in *Frankenstein vs. Baragon*. Here, Kawai is now a submarine captain, monitoring Godzilla, who is frozen inside an iceberg. And on that note, there is no implication that this is meant to retcon *King Kong vs. Godzilla* or the films that followed. The monster has somehow just found himself frozen yet again!

According to Ed Godziszewski, who had the script translated, the first 36 scenes of *Frankenstein vs. Godzilla* are more or less identical to those in *Frankenstein vs. Baragon* with only minor differences. The first difference is that Dr. Bowen has a somewhat colder demeanor than what we see in the film. Another scene featured the young Frankenstein breaking into a man's home to kill his dog. The child monster then escapes carrying the dog and runs in front of a passing train. Another deleted scene had a farmer discovering his entire vegetable field has been eaten by Frankenstein!

It is Sueko and Kawaji who go to Miyajima Island to pay their respects to a dead patient, not she and Bowen. Nor was Bowen at Sueko's apartment when Frankenstein was hit by a car in a previous scene. In fact, the romantic infatuation in this version seems to be between Kawaji and Sueko. The duo spy some boys starting a fire while at Miyajima Island. The boys inform the two that they are doing so to trap a strange boy inside a cave because he kills and eats local animals. A policeman arrives who wants to get the boy out by force but Sueko, who recognizes the boy, convinces him to let her try. Sueko peacefully coerces the boy out of the cave.

Kawai becomes involved as he is listening to a radio report on the strange boy being studied by Dr. Bowen on his ship. Later, he goes to visit Bowen and tells him his story from the war, just as in the finished film. Here, however, he also goes to see Frankenstein for himself with his own eyes.

In this version of the story, Kawaji, Bowen, and Sueko are all much less sympathetic to the monster. All three agree to amputate a piece of Frankenstein's body to see if it will grow back. Here however, they choose a finger over his whole hand. The operation is a success and the finger grows back, confirming their theory. In a scene that was perhaps too reminiscent of the same scene from *King Kong vs. Godzilla*, the monster king breaks free of the iceberg. The difference here is that he is rather sluggish for some reason.

Frankenstein's escape from custody is more similar to the version of the scene that appears in the U.S. version, *Frankenstein Conquers the World*, which is more lively and violent than the Japanese version. Ironically, Kimura's version has Frankenstein emerge from the hospital holding a police officer in each hand (in the U.S. version, he traps a policeman under some rubble while he does not in the Japanese original). And despite Teruyoshi Nakano's claim that UPA asked Toho to add in the scene where Frankenstein visits Sueko, it is present in this script too.[5] Here, Frankenstein even breaks her window and sticks his head into the apartment! Scenes of the military tracking Frankenstein in the forest are similar to the finished product with minor differences. We never see Frankenstein dig a trap for the boar which a tank falls into. Here, a tank falls into a trap that the military assumes was for them.

The story then progresses as in Sohl's treatment, with the idea pitched to entice Godzilla to battle Frankenstein. Godzilla is revived to the horror of Dr. Bowen and Kawai, who has to lead the reptile to Japan. Naturally, Bowen, Sueko, and Kawaji take a trip to see Frankenstein just as the two monsters are set to collide in the forest near Mt. Fuji. However, here the goal is merely to take a photograph of the monster before he is destroyed by Godzilla! In this version, Sueko sits in the car as Bowen and Kawaji wander outside and Frankenstein picks up the car and tips it over so that she falls into his hand!

Soon we get to the end battle, which starts when Godzilla tries to eat Sueko just like Baragon does! Ed Godziszewski sums up the end battle rather well in his *The Illustrated Encyclopedia of Godzilla,* where he writes, "The climactic battle is rather unremarkable, with Godzilla left to do little more than be pushed down or stumble as the ground regularly gives way under his feet."[6] Many of the battle maneuvers are also quite similar to those in the final film with Baragon, such as Frankenstein stuffing a rock in Godzilla's mouth at one point. When dislodged, Godzilla immediately fires his ray like Baragon. Frankenstein even judo-throws Godzilla as he does Baragon!

Instead of a forest fire, the battle of the giants here causes Mt. Fuji to erupt.[7] As all this happens, Bowen makes his way into the forest to rescue Sueko while the battle enters its final round. As in Sohl's treatment, the battle rages up the volcano until Frankenstein is destroyed in a lava flow and Godzilla tumbles into some rushing water nearby (so that he could star in more sequels).

Though a great title, overall, it was probably for the best that the script dropped Godzilla and evolved into *Frankenstein vs. Baragon* instead. The idea of the defense forces using Godzilla as a weapon is interesting but in the end, Frankenstein just doesn't pose a big enough threat to warrant the Japanese turning to such draconian measures for help. The method of monster disposal is unimaginative

 **INVASION OF ASTRO-MONSTER**

UNLIKE MANY G-FILMS OF THE 1960S, IT WOULD SEEM *INVASION OF ASTRO-MONSTER* WENT THROUGH VERY FEW REVISIONS. SUPPOSEDLY, ALL THREE OF SHINICHI SEKIZAWA'S SCRIPTS WERE VERY SIMILAR TO THE FINISHED FILM. THE MAIN DIFFERENCE IS THAT IN THE FIRST DRAFT, THE XIANS TRANSPORT GODZILLA AND RODAN TO PLANET X BY FREEZING THEM AND THEN ATTACHING ROCKETS TO THEIR BODIES. AN ASPECT OF THIS REMAINS ALL THE WAY INTO THE FINAL SHOOTING SCRIPT MENTIONING THAT GODZILLA AND RODAN HAVE ROCKETS INSTALLED TO THEIR BODIES TO HELP CARRY THEM TO PLANET X. ALSO, KING GHIDORAH WAS TO REPRISE HIS FIERY BIRTH FROM THE FIRST FILM WHEN INITIALLY CONFRONTING GODZILLA AND RODAN ON PLANET X. AND, AS IS OFTEN REPORTED, GODZILLA'S JUMPING SHIE IS NOWHERE TO BE FOUND. THAT IDEA WAS DREAMED UP ON SET—MUCH TO ISHIRO HONDA'S CHAGRIN—BY YOSHIO TSUCHIYA. THE ACTOR THOUGHT IT WOULD BE FUNNY IF GODZILLA IMITATED A POPULAR JAPANESE COMIC CHARACTER AT THE TIME AND EIJI TSUBURAYA AGREED (WHEN HONDA AND TOMOYUKI TANAKA BALKED AT THE IDEA, TSUBURAYA OVERRULED THEM WITH "THE KIDS'LL LIKE IT."). THIS WASN'T THE ONLY IDEA THE ACTOR IMPROVISED. TSUCHIYA ALSO CREATED HIS OWN ALIEN LANGUAGE FOR THE COMMANDER OF PLANET X! IN THE THIRD SCRIPT DRAFT, MENTION IS MADE OF KING GHIDORAH ATTACKING THE U.S. AND INTRIGUINGLY, THIS IS FOLLOWED BY A MISSING SCENE (SCENE 119 TO BE EXACT). PERHAPS DRAFTS 1 AND 2 FEATURED SCRIPTED U.S. DESTRUCTION SCENES THAT WERE CUT FOR BUDGETARY REASONS? ALSO, HONDA HAD HOPED THAT GLENN COULD ENCOUNTER HUNDREDS OF NAMIKAWA CLONES ON PLANET X, BUT THE BUDGET WOULDN'T ALLOW. COSTUME DESIGNS FOR THE FEMALE XIANS WERE ALSO VERY DIFFERENT, WITH STRANGE, FULL-BODY COVERINGS. THE A-CYCLE LIGHT RAY DOES APPEAR BUT IS UNNAMED. NO MENTION IS MADE OF MOTHRA IN THIS DRAFT, THOUGH IT'S POSSIBLE HER ABSENCE WAS ADDRESSED IN THE FIRST AND SECOND DRAFTS, SUBMITTED ON JULY 24TH AND AUGUST 23RD OF 1965, RESPECTIVELY. SAPERSTEIN ALSO ENCOURAGED TOHO TO CUT A PRESS CONFERENCE SCENE AT THE ONSET AND SHUFFLE IT INTO A LATER SPOT IN THE SCRIPT. HIS FEAR WAS THE TV VIEWERS WOULD CHANGE THE CHANNEL IF THE FILM STARTED WITH SUCH A SCENE AND OPTED TO CUT RIGHT TO THE ACTION. SEKIZAWA CLAIMED THAT THIS WAS THE LAST ENTRY IN THE SERIES HE FELT "TRULY PASSIONATE" ABOUT.

as well. Perhaps Henry Saperstein knew Godzilla was ill-suited for the story—not to mention that Saperstein was an unabashed fan of Godzilla the hero—as he said in *Monsters Are Attacking Tokyo*: "We felt the Frankenstein boy–monster character should have been the focal point and putting in another monster was a dilution."[8]

Frankenstein vs. Baragon is a fun film full of wonderful, wild ideas. No one in America would have ever dreamed up a story where Frankenstein grows to giant size and battles a floppy-eared, subterranean dinosaur. The switch to the villainous Baragon works well over Godzilla, as Baragon eats people and the heinous acts committed by the monster are blamed on poor Frankenstein. This creates an interesting scenario where a monster needs to have his name cleared of wrongdoing (a concept repeated in its semi-sequel, *The War of the Gargantuas*). The tragic hero, Frankenstein, defeats Baragon and possibly dies in the end, sinking into the ground with the dead monster—or dragged underwater by a giant octopus, depending on which ending one is watching.[9]

The U.S. producers threw a monkey wrench into production by requesting that a giant octopus be worked into the script. Takeshi Kimura (who had recently adopted the unisex pen name Kaoru Mabuchi to hide his identity) had no idea how to shoehorn the creature into the story and simply had it crawl out of the mountains once Frankenstein defeats Baragon.[10] The two wrestle about and fall into a nearby lake. The scene had to be shot after principal photography was already finished and to add insult to injury, the American producers decided to not even use the footage! In the fanzine "Monster Graffiti" Ishiro Honda said:

"The budget for the film came from America. Benedict's arrangement was to integrate a scene with an octopus at the end. The co-producers had seen Tsuburaya's spectacular scene with Kong and the Octopus in *King Kong versus Godzilla* (1962) and wanted something similar. We complained because we thought it would make little sense if somewhere in the mountains suddenly an octopus appears. We even flew to America to discuss with the people of Benedict Productions. Finally, we shot two Octopus scenes. One for *Furankenshutain tai Baragon* and the other for the next film *Furankenshutain no Kaiju - Sanda tai Gaira*."[11]

In any case, it was later agreed between Toho and UPA that there would be a Frankenstein sequel to utilize that same octopus prop. Saperstein either greatly enjoyed or thought that the American public greatly enjoyed Kong's battle with the octopus in *King Kong vs. Godzilla*. Either way, he felt that the film needed an octopus. Today such meddling from producers is still very common.[12]

After the successful co-production on *Frankenstein vs. Baragon*, Toho signed a contract with Henry G. Saperstein's UPA in the summer of 1965 to co-produce five films for both theater and television. According to U.S. sources, the five projects were three giant monster films (one of which was the already in-production *Invasion of Astro-Monster*), a spy thriller, a war movie, and a TV series. *Toho SPFX Film Ultimate Collection* lists the four remaining films (there was no TV series, only TV movies) after *Invasion of Astro-Monster* in English writing as follows: THE TWO FRANKENSTEINS, THE TWO MEN, THE BATTLE OF LEYT GULF, THE SPACE MONSTER.

Chapter Notes

[1] Ironically enough, Baragon had similarities to the original Godzilla. Shigeru Kayama and Takeo Murata's early drafts envisioned Godzilla with big, floppy ears.
[2] One could argue the government fears Frankenstein growing larger than Godzilla, so why not kill him sooner rather than later?
[3] In this same scene, as Bowen watches in horror, he wonders aloud that if Frankenstein were to be torn apart, would his body not regenerate into multiple Frankensteins? Eventually, this idea was used for *The War of the Gargantuas*.
[4] Fans have often criticized this ending on Toho's part, when in fact this was Sohl's idea.
[5] It's possible it was removed from the *Frankenstein vs. Baragon* script.
[6] Godziszewski, *Illustrated Encyclopedia of Godzilla*, pp.166.
[7] In Sohl's outline, no location is given, and Kimura apparently decided on Mt. Fuji.
[8] Galbraith, *Monsters Are Attacking Tokyo*, pp.102.
[9] In "Memories of Ishiro Honda" by Hajime Ishida in *Famous Monsters of Filmland* #269, Honda claimed that "five or six" variations on the ending including Baragon and the octopus were shot by Eiji Tsuburaya!
[10] It's possible Mabuchi didn't even write the scene and Honda or someone else came up with it.
[11] As found on a supplement to the Anolis DVD from Germany.
[12] That's not to say that this author doesn't enjoy what is surely one of the greatest deleted scenes in kaiju history though.

PROFILE: REUBEN BERCOVITCH

United Productions of America producer Reuben Bercovitch is something of an enigma as far as Godzilla fans are concerned. Fans will remember his name appearing on titles such as *Frankenstein vs. Baragon* (1965), *Invasion of Astro-Monster* (1965) and *The War of the Gargantuas* (1966) as both a writer and producer. Bercovitch was born July 18, 1923, and was predominantly a Los Angeles screenwriter where he still lives at the time of this writing. Bercovitch began writing screenplays for television on programs such as *The Richard Boone Show*, and in 1968 even wrote an episode of *Bonanza* and *The Virginian*. In the mid-1960s, Bercovitch produced and helped develop the stories for Toho's two Frankenstein films on behalf of UPA/Benedict Productions, though he only served as a producer on *Invasion of Astro-Monster*. Presumably, this relationship would have continued if not for a mishap in the development process of 1968's *Hell in the Pacific* (see Chapter 15). At one point, Bercovitch even headed the Motion Picture Department of Lorimar Productions that produced films such as 1975's erotic thriller *Out of Season*, which Bercovitch also wrote. As it turned out, this would be his last major feature film. In the 1970s, Bercovitch began a turn writing several acclaimed novels, the first of which, *Odette*, won him a PEN/Hemingway Award for Fiction in 1978. And yet, that same year Bercovitch returned to the world of Godzilla at the behest of Henry G. Saperstein when he penned two treatments, one of which was *Godzilla vs. Gargantua*. Presumably, this would have been a sequel to *The War of the Gargantuas* which Bercovitch had a hand in writing. Bercovitch's other script was *Godzilla vs. the Devil*, which in recent years has been proven to exist despite reports to the contrary. This author and Steve Ryfle have both at different times tried to contact Bercovitch over the phone to no avail. Somewhere, sitting in an attic likely rests the enigmatic treatments for both un-produced Godzilla films.

Selected Filmography
Checkmate [TV series] (1962) (writer)
The Richard Boone Show [TV series] (1964) (writer)
Frankenstein vs. Baragon (1965) (writer, producer)
Invasion of Astro-Monster (1965) (producer)
The War of the Gargantuas (1965) (writer, producer)
What's Up, Tiger Lily? (1966) (producer)
Hell in the Pacific (1968) (writer, producer)
Bonanza [TV series] (1968) (writer)
The Virginian [TV series] (1968) (writer)
Out of Season (1975) (writer, producer)
Godzilla vs. Gargantua (1978) (writer) [un-produced]
Godzilla vs. the Devil (1978) (writer) [un-produced]

14.
THE BIRTH OF
GAMERA AND DAIMAJIN

While Toho was occupied with Frankenstein, Daiei Motion Picture Company was busy cooking up their own monster to compete with Godzilla. Ironically, the inception of Godzilla's soon-to-be competitor was not unlike his own birth in the mind of Tomoyuki Tanaka a decade prior. Just as Toho used *Godzilla* to replace *In the Shadow of Glory*, Daiei had recently suffered a loss in unsuccessfully trying to film a story titled *Giant Horde Beast Nezura*.[1] The script, which had begun filming, was about giant rats running amok in Tokyo. It was cancelled due to the difficulty of using live rats (not to mention the fleas that had subsequently infested the studio). The studio was left with miniature sets and no monsters to destroy them.

On a flight to Tokyo, Masaichi Nagata, then president of Daiei, looked out the window and saw a cloud formation that reminded him of a flying turtle. Seeing Toho's success with Godzilla, Nagata insisted his screenwriters cook up a story about a flying turtle monster, which Daiei resident writer Niisan Takahashi did in record time.[2] Takahashi says in the Gamera DVD Box booklet that, "Yojiro Saito, who was working at Daiei at that time called me and said, 'Are you interested in monster movies and instant movies? Will you just send me an idea?'" Takahashi's first treatment, entitled *Giant Fire-Breathing Turtle Attacks Tokyo*,[3] was written very quickly. This version is similar to the finished story but was said to focus on an engaged couple as the two main characters. Director Noriaki Yuasa said, "I remember that the first planning meeting I attended ended around 10 a.m. and Mr. Takahashi had a synopsis written by noon."[4]

Rather than coming up with the plot first, Takahashi first put serious thought into how this turtle monster would fly and came up with the idea of jets shooting out of the leg holes in the turtle shell. Quite a few designs for the monster—eventually named Gamera—were considered as Noriaki Yuasa recounted, "[Akira] Inoue drew about 500 pre-production sketches, but his original design ended up being used."[5]

During the scripting process, Takahashi made a decision that would pay off immensely for Daiei when, on a hunch, he wrote a scene where Gamera saves a small boy to cater to children, whom he observed loved giant monster movies more than anyone. Takahashi claims he knew the film would be a hit that spawned a series even before it was released and joked, "There will be a boom of Niisan Takahashi next fiscal year!"[6] And indeed, against all odds, *Giant Monster Gamera*—released in November 1965—struck a chord with children and became a huge hit.

Aside from the child rescue scene, *Gamera* wasn't particularly innovative and has a typical monster-on-the-loose plot structure. That said, the military's ideas for dealing with the monster are certainly entertaining. First, they use freeze bombs to immobilize him, dynamite to knock him onto his back, and for the finale, they trap him inside the head of a rocket! From this non-lethal ending, it's easy to see that Daiei wanted to keep Gamera alive for sequels.

Niisan Takahashi's first sequel idea revolved around an alien invasion and was called *Giant Monster Gamera vs. the Ice Men from Outer Space*. It would have brought back Dr. Hidaka and the other two leads from *Gamera* as they witness the earth begin to slip into a new ice age induced by volcanic eruptions across the world. The eruptions turn out to be caused by ice-like aliens who also have a giant ice man in their arsenal. Luckily for humanity, Gamera escapes from the Z-Plan rocket and comes back to earth to save the day by squaring off with the ice giant.

From this axed project, two things survived. If one has ever wondered why a chameleon monster like Barugon would have a tongue that freezes objects, the answer is that Takahashi liked the idea of fire vs. ice as the theme of *Gamera*'s sequel. After all, since Gamera expelled fire, it would be interesting if his opponent fired ice. Apparently, Daiei also requested that Gamera fight another monster more similar to Godzilla, which led to the creation of Barugon[7] (who was a quadruped to avoid being *too* similar to Godzilla). However, Daiei executives were still intrigued enough by the ice giant from the aborted script to give it its own movie: *Daimajin*! The ice became stone, the story was set in feudal times (Daiei had a large number of pre-existing feudal era sets to use), and the stone samurai Majin was born.

Not much is known about the early drafts of *Gamera vs. Barugon*. Supposedly, Onodera's mistress was not in the first draft. One source says there were no references to the first film initially, while this same source also claims that originally the film had a more ambitious opening where the Z-Plan rocket crash lands on earth.[8] For certain, Masaichi Nagata and new director Shigeo Tanaka insisted there be no child characters this time around. The intent seemed to be to make an adult monster movie and allegedly, the native dancers in New Guinea were meant to appear topless! At least one scene that didn't make it into the film because of a mistake during filming had Barugon crossing a bridge full of explosives. "...At one point Barugon was supposed to cross a bridge, with a series of explosions going off behind him. But the explosives guy accidentally wired them in reverse, so they started going off in front of and under Barugon's feet!" Yuasa explained at G-Fest X in 2003. "We couldn't salvage anything from that shot," the director (who directed the special effects for *Gamera vs. Barugon*) explained.[9]

Due to its more mature tone, some rank *Gamera vs. Barugon* as the best of the Showa era. Like *Mothra vs. Godzilla*, Takahashi's theme would seem to be greed as exemplified through Onodera, the human villain. It's also undeniably fun watching the self-defense forces come up with new, creative ways to attack Barugon—and vice versa—throughout the film. It would seem that every time the defense forces think they have a way of defeating the monster, it either reveals a new power (like its deadly rainbow beam [10]) or something goes terribly wrong (Onodera stealing a diamond used to lure Barugon into a lake). Perhaps the story's only flaw is that Gamera seems like a guest star in his premiere sequel. In later entries, he would become better-integrated into the proceedings. Despite the fact that it alienated its burgeoning child fan base (Noriaki Yuasa has said that children were bored by the non-monster scenes and were running up and down aisles in the theaters), *Gamera vs. Barugon* was part of a hit double-bill with *Daimajin*—ensuring that both monsters would return for more sequels in the future.

Chapter Notes

[1] Because a Nezura rat suit was built, Daiei executives tried to get Noriaki Yuasa to consider it for use as one of Gamera's foes for several years—this according to Yuasa in an interview with David Milner.
[2] Another story says that producer Tomio Sagisu (*Spectreman, Ambassador Magma*) had come up with a jet propelled tortoise for his cancelled stop motion animation series called *STOP!* before *Gamera*. Years later, he accused Masaichi Nagata of stealing the idea for *Gamera*. Yet another conflicting story says that
[3] Another source called it *A Lowly Tortoise Flies in the Sky*.
[4] www.davmil.org/www.kaijuconversations.com/yuasa.htm
[5] Ibid.
[6] Gamera DVD booklet.
[7] As an interesting aside, Barugon's roar was actually Nezura's roar as created for the cancelled film.
[8] www.imdb.com/title/tt0060446/trivia?ref_=tt_trv_trv
[9] "Mr. Yuasa's G-Fest", *G-Fan* #65 (Nov/Dec 2003) pp.12.
[10] This is just the author's conjecture, but since the ice aliens in the original script were partially based upon the frost giants of Norse mythology, it's entirely possible they had a rainbow weapon ala the Rainbow Bridge of Norse myth.

PROFILE: NIISAN TAKAHASHI

Though it was Daiei president Masaichi Nagata who came up with a flying turtle that could breathe fire, screenwriter Niisan Takahashi considered himself the true creator of Gamera, and after Daiei's bankruptcy in 1971 fought them for the monster's rights. Takahashi was born on February 3, 1926, and his real name was Yukito Takahashi. In his lifetime, he wrote 44 scripts (possibly more) for television and movies, the first being *Girl in Ginza* (1955). From 1959 on (Takahashi seemed inactive in 1957 and 1958), he steadily wrote, predominantly for Daiei and Shochiku. Takahashi was even present to see some of the infamous filming of *Giant Horde Beast Nezura* in 1963. From that point forward—or at least for the next six years—Takahashi would spend most of his time writing Gamera films. Director Noriaki Yuasa spoke of his relationship working with Takahashi stating, "…once he got started, he worked very quickly. It took him much longer to come up with ideas for a screenplay than to actually write one. Once Mr. Takahashi finished a script, he would leave it completely in my hands. He never did any editing during production." [www.davmil.org/www.kaiju-conversations.com/yuasa.htm] Takahashi typically did three drafts, and the only changes requested by the studio were usually due to budgetary concerns. Yuasa and Takahashi didn't just collaborate on Gamera movies, but non-genre projects as well, such as 1964's *Clap Your Hands if You Are Happy*. "[It] was originally written by another screenwriter, but Daiei's executives thought that it was not very exciting. So they had Mr. Takahashi revise it," Yuasa said. [Ibid.] "I'm very proud because Mr. Takahashi always praised my work. He once said that no matter how fantastic his writing, I could create film footage from it. In addition, the Gamera movies were the only ones he worked on that he went to see." [Ibid.] Takahashi saw his greatest success with *Gamera vs. Gyaos* (1967) which was the highest-grossing monster movie of 1967—a year with stiff competition as it was the year of the legendary "Monster Boom" when every major Japanese studio set a kaiju loose. Supposedly, Ishiro Honda even sent Takahashi a congratulatory New Year's card for the occasion. Even between the Gamera films, Takahashi worked steadily, writing four to six movies in between each Gamera film. In 1970, Yuasa and Takahashi worked on the film *I Am Five Years Old* (1970), said to be based on a true story about a five-year-old boy who travelled on his own to Osaka to see his father. That same year, Takahashi's wife, a Christian, had serious brain surgery. The operation was successful but a second operation some time later killed her. At some point before this, Takahashi, a devout Buddhist, converted to Christianity as well. When Daiei officially declared bankruptcy in December 1971, Takahashi was set to begin working on *Gamera vs. Two-Headed Monster W*, but never got the chance to finish it. Takahashi moved into TV writing, notably a stint on Shintaro Katsu's *Zatoichi, the Blind Swordsman* (1974-1979). In 1980, when Tokuma Publishing decided to produce *Super Monster*, Takahashi and Yuasa both begrudgingly returned. "Mr. Takahashi and I never imagined that there would be a new Gamera series. That's why we decided to go ahead and kill Gamera," Yuasa said. [Ibid.] "I grieved for my son Gamera—it was a strange fate." [Galbraith, *Monsters Are Attacking Tokyo*, pp.114.] At some point after this, Takahashi began arguing with Tokuma/Daiei that he was the true creator of Gamera, not the company, and that he should have rights to the monster. Though the two never came to an agreement, Takahashi was consulted for the short film *Gamera vs. Giant Beast Garasharp* for the Gamera LD Box Set in 1991, and it is believed Daiei finally paid Takahashi some sort of small royalty package in later years—though not as much as he had hoped. Yuasa explained the situation like this, "When Daiei declared bankruptcy, it owed more money to him than to any other person. However, because the studio was in bankruptcy, it could not pay him. In addition, Mr. Takahashi had never joined the screenwriters' union, so he could not receive any money from its fund for uncollected wages. Mr. Takahashi eventually went to see Mr. Nagata, and received all rights to Gamera from him." [www.davmil.org/www.kaijuconversations.com/yuasa.htm] These rights, however, weren't strong enough to hold up in a court of law. Takahashi was greatly incensed in 1994 when not only was he not paid anything for Gamera's revival in *Gamera: Guardian of the Universe* (1995), but also for the fact that his own script, *Gamera vs. Phoenix*, was passed over entirely. Takahashi published the script as a novel the same year the film came out. This was his last truly published work. Yuasa reports that he and Takahashi lost contact in later years, and the director greatly regretted missing a phone call from Takahashi in the mid-1990s. Niisan Takahashi passed away on May 5, 2015, due to brainstem bleeding.

Selected Filmography
Girl in Ginza (1955) (writer)
The Wind-of-Youth Group Crosses the Mountain Pass (1961) (writer)
Clap Your Hands if You Are Happy (1964) (writer)
Gamera (1965) (writer)
Giant Monster Gamera vs. the Ice Men from Outer Space (1966) (writer) [unproduced]
Gamera vs. Barugon (1966) (writer)
Gamera vs. Gyaos (1967) (writer)
Zoku sex doctor no kiroku (1968) (writer)
Gamera vs. Viras (1968) (writer)
Gamera vs. Guiron (1969) (writer)
Gamera vs. Jiger (1970) (writer)
I Am Five Years Old (1970) (writer)
The Secret Ceremony (1971) (writer)
Gamera vs. Zigra (1971) (writer)
Seijuku (1971) (writer)
Thunder Mask [TV series] (1972) (writer)
Zatoichi, the Blind Swordsman [three episodes] (1974-1979) (writer)
Maya the Bee [TV series] (1975) (writer)
Little Lulu to chicchai nakama [TV series] (1976) (writer)
Ashita e Atakku! [TV series] (1979) (writer)
Super Monster (1980) (writer)
Huh! Bumbu [TV series] (1985) (writer)
Gamera vs. Giant Evil Beast Garasharp (1991) (writer/consultant)
Gamera vs. Phoenix (1991) (writer) [unproduced]
Gamera vs. Phoenix [novel] (1995) (writer)

15.
WAR OF THE SEA MONSTERS
GAIRA, EBIRAH, AND GEZORA (ALMOST) ATTACK

Always planned as a sequel to *Frankenstein vs. Baragon*, *The War of the Gargantuas* (Japanese title *Frankenstein's Monsters: Sanda vs. Gaira*) began as *The Two Frankensteins*.[1] The first draft of the script brought back the same leading trio of characters portrayed by Nick Adams, Kumi Mizuno and Tadao Takashima in the previous film. Unfortunately, Kumi Mizuno wound up being the only member of the original three to return in the finished film. As a result, all of the original characters are confusingly changed to become brand new characters similar to the old characters. The finished film contains many esoteric references to the previous movie. Notably in the Japanese version (where the Gargantuas are called Frankensteins), new lead Russ Tamblyn mentions how Frankenstein went missing at Mt. Fuji (in the International dub he says he died at Mt. Fuji).[2] The rather confusing implication seems to be that some of Frankenstein's cells grew into the hairy, ape-like baby Sanda seen in a flashback, who in turn escaped from Dr. Stewart's lab and grew into the adult Sanda seen throughout the film.[3]

Kaoru Mabuchi's inspiration for the story was the Japanese folktale "The Sea Boy and the Mountain Boy" to make up the backbone of the saga of the two Frankenstein brothers—one of which hails from the sea and the other from the mountains. And though they are called Frankensteins in the Japanese version, Henry G. Saperstein felt they looked nothing like Frankenstein and renamed them the Gargantuas. This must have been decided upon during production, because Toho's international version is entitled *The War of the Gargantuas*, even though the dubbed dialogue still calls them Frankensteins. Certain scenes were shot twice—one for the American version and again for the Japanese version—each with different dialogue.[4] Curiously, most of the alternate scenes revolve around the Maritime Safety Bureau's investigation into the sunken ship. In the U.S. version, Russ Tamblyn is present in these scenes, while in the Japanese version, he is not. Also, by his own admission, Tamblyn changed much of his own dialogue from what was originally in the script.[5] Kipp

Hamilton's infamous song and dance number is notably absent from both the Japanese and U.S. scripts—in its place a "missing scene." It was Saperstein's idea to have Gaira's giant hand come down and grab Hamilton. "I wanted kind of a King Kong-style sequence," Saperstein said.[6]

Originally, the aquatically-spawned Gaira was designed to be semi-similar to the *Creature from the Black Lagoon*, of which Eiji Tsuburaya was supposedly a huge fan. In another draft of the script, the good Frankenstein was white and the other was gray, the monsters did not have names in early drafts, and the famous Maser tanks did not appear at all. The original ending (as conceived by Honda when Kimura/Mabuchi lost confidence in the script and asked him to help write it) was to have Tokyo destroyed by the underwater volcano's eruption. Specifically, Ishiro Honda wished to have the lava from the undersea volcano wash ashore and immolate Tokyo (and possibly kill everyone in it, including our heroes). His idea was that mankind should be punished for trying to kill the monsters with explosive military force after being warned repeatedly not to do so. When Tomoyuki Tanaka said it would be too expensive to film, Honda suggested the use of stock footage from *The Last War* (1961), but the idea was still shot down. And before Hiroshi Sekita took over the role of Sanda, King Kong and King Ghidorah suit performer Shoichi Hirose was to play the part. Hirose's last-minute departure from the project angered Tsuburaya, who never worked with him again.[7]

In the end, *The War of the Gargantuas* is one of the best Japanese monster movies to exemplify that the monsters are characters that have moral dilemmas and stakes in the story rather than just mindless engines of destruction. Sanda, the brown Frankenstein/Gargantua, finally finds his long-lost sibling, Gaira the green Frankenstein/Gargantua, only to discover that he is evil. He must then decide to make an enemy out of his only brother to save humanity and the audience knows that a happy ending is not in the cards. The film also takes up the subject of nature vs. nurture. Sanda was raised by humanity while Gaira was left to his own devices and eats people. Today, the finished film is remembered fondly on both sides of the Pacific, even if its director was never enamored with it.

Toho and UPA had high hopes for one of their proposed war films, *The Two Men,* which turned into a project titled *Island of Fear.* Set in the South Pacific, it concerned a Japanese soldier and a U.S. soldier stranded together. The two must overcome their prejudices and the language barrier to survive. Toho considered it a high enough profile project to cast Toshiro Mifune. Eventually, this project turned into 1968's *Hell in the Pacific*. When Mifune found out he would be paid half of what Lee Marvin (who had just won a best actor Oscar for *Cat Ballou*) was offered, he walked, necessitating an American studio, ABC Films, to take over the expensive production entirely. "Along came ABC and Cinerama," Henry Saperstein said in *Filmfax* #45. "They wanted to get into the deal and guaranteed network play. I made a stupid mistake: I agreed to go along with them. They immediately became pigs and didn't want Toho in the deal as a partner." This killed off *The Battle of Leyt Gulf*, another war movie Toho planned to produce with UPA, and it may also have lead to the death of their next monster movie: *The Space Monster*.[8]

As it turns out, the simply-titled *The Space Monster* was an early incarnation of what became 1970's *Space Amoeba*, actually called *Giant Monster Assault*. It was turned in by Ei Ogawa on May 9, 1966. The script being written in May would seem to imply that it was a contender for the New Year's blockbuster that for the past two years belonged to Godzilla. Some Japanese webpages even attest that this was initially a Godzilla film, though that is false. Considering that *Operation Robinson Crusoe: King Kong vs. Ebirah* was in development at the same time, it would seem Toho may have planned to give Godzilla the year 1966 off.

Giant Monster Assault was an answer to the monster boom beginning to develop with *Ultra Q* (this script even references *Ultra Q*) that would explode further in the year 1967 when nearly every Japanese studio released a monster movie. Specifically, *Toho Special Effects Film Ultimate Collection* describes it as, "a monster movie in which the human race is in danger of extinction by a group of mysterious giant creatures, the alien Hydra, which came from space. Hydra induces crystal deformation and melting of polar waters. Half of the continents of the world drowns in the sea, and the battle of scientists exploring the weak points of monsters in a desperate situation will be drawn."[9]

The story is a much bigger version of *Space Amoeba* with the parasitic alien called Hydra inhabiting the body of a giant jellyfish-like monster called Dodora (NOT Dogora; despite the similarities the kanji are different). The alien invader (or possibly invaders plural, it's not clear) floods whole continents by melting the frozen poles. The exact opposite of the freezing-cold Gezora, Dodora was blazing hot—probably the cause of the melting poles. But like Gezora, Dodora and the Hydra aliens' weakness turns out to be ultrasound. It is also unclear whether Dodora is an earth monster made gigantic by Hydra or an already giant space monster. It's also not clear whether Dodora was the sole monster (determining the plural and the singular in Japanese texts is difficult for the layman). *Toho Special Effects: All Kaiju Illustrated Encyclopedia* compares Ogawa's original idea as having similarities to the 1959 TV special effects movie called *Giant Water Monster Gebora* as well. In early-to-mid 1970, Tomoyuki Tanaka would dust off *Giant Monster Assault* to produce *Space Amoeba* (see Chapter 23).

It seemed that the next Godzilla movie being considered was *Batman vs. Godzilla* by Shinichi Sekizawa—or rather that was the only Godzilla storyline being played with at the time. Nothing much is known of Sekizawa's draft aside from the fact that it was completed in November of 1965 (when they planned on producing it was a mystery). Presumably, this story was given to UPA and it eventually wound up in the hands of William Dozier, producer of TV's *Batman*, a few years later.[10]

By 1966, Toho had their sights set on bringing King Kong back to the silver screen. Their deal with RKO allowed them the use of King Kong for five years, an agreement that would be over in 1967. Why Toho waited so long to produce another Kong film is anyone's guess. The planned movie, *Operation Robinson Crusoe: King Kong vs. Ebirah*, was a co-production with Rankin/Bass, who was about to debut their animated program *The King Kong Show* in September of 1966.[11] According to *Toho Ultimate SPFX Movies*, Jun Fukuda was approached about an untitled U.S./Japanese King Kong co-production on April 21, 1966. Even before that in February of 1966, Toho's senior staff manager Makoto Fujimoto met with a movie theater owner in Kansai and spilled the secret that the New Year's season would see the release of a new King Kong movie.[12]

However, the Kong vehicle was not to be. Toho was dead-set on Jun Fukuda directing the live action and Eiji Tsuburaya's protégé, Sadamasa Arikawa, directing the special effects. Rankin/Bass was equally dead set on the creative team being Ishiro Honda and Eiji Tsuburaya. Toho refused to budge and Rankin/Bass dropped out. Toho liked the script so much that they just decided to drop Godzilla in place of Kong and made it as *Godzilla, Ebirah, Mothra: Big Duel in the South Seas* [13] (*Ebirah, Horror of the Deep* under Toho's international title and *Godzilla vs. the Sea Monster* for U.S. television) for their New Year's Blockbuster.

So far as anyone knows, *King Kong vs. Ebirah* had the same exact story as *Ebirah, Horror of the Deep*. What is somewhat questionable—if this was always an adaptation of *The King Kong*

Show—is whether or not it for certain had Mothra in it at the time (though the synopsis presented in *Encyclopedia of Godzilla [Mechagodzilla Edition]* includes Mothra alongside Kong). And as to why Mothra and Kong, relatively strange bedfellows, all things considered, were thrown together, Mothra had ranked as Toho's #1 most popular monster in a recent survey and so she was included in the story—as it turned out, it would be the adult Mothra's last film role for nearly 25 years.

Little was done to tweak the script and Godzilla even displays a Kong-inspired interest in Kumi Mizuno's character, Daiyo. It's even possible the electric shock to revive Kong was a nod to the big ape's love of electricity in *King Kong vs. Godzilla*, also written by Shinichi Sekizawa. The King Kong version of this script had quite a few similarities with *The King Kong Show*. A giant condor (who makes for a not-so-threatening opponent for Godzilla) appeared in two episodes of *The King Kong Show* (episode 5 "The Green Eyed Monster" and episode 41). Furthermore, in episode 7, "The Electric Circle," an evil scientist wants to turn Mondo Island (the primary setting of the series) into a nuclear missile base much like the Red Bamboo had done to Letchi Island.

As for the villain kaiju, though there were no giant shrimp on *The King Kong Show*, Ebirah would have been a menacing opponent for Kong with his sharp pinchers and aquatic advantage. For Godzilla, Ebirah makes for one of his least challenging opponents (especially coming off bouts with King Kong, Mothra, Rodan, and King Ghidorah twice). However, since the Ebirah suit had supposedly already been built, a new monster could not be created for the film. According to Teruyoshi Nakano, Godzilla was supposed to fight a giant octopus in this film. However, Nakano was likely confusing this film with an early version of *All Monsters Attack*[14] and furthermore, Nakano and Fukuda both acted as though they were unaware the film ever started out starring King Kong! Fukuda said, "Godzilla was in the first draft of the script that I saw. I don't know what the earlier drafts were like." Fukuda further elaborated that making the film "was like pouring two cups of water into one. I had to cut one sequence after another."[15] What these cut sequences entailed are unknown, but Godzilla's infamous helicopter spin of Ebirah which exists only in publicity photos was apparently planned for the film as storyboards exist of the scene.

It should also be noted that *Ebirah, Horror of the Deep* was subject to some major recasting after production had begun. Initially, 17-year-old Noriko Takahashi (who had played an island girl in an episode of *Ultra Q* earlier that year) was originally cast as Daiyo and at least one production still exists of her in costume. Takahashi became ill with appendicitis and had to bow out of production. Kumi Mizuno was brought in at the last second as her replacement and the rest is history.

Despite being confined to an island locale, in some ways *Ebirah, Horror of the Deep* is more exciting than *Invasion of Astro-Monster*. This is partly due to Jun Fukuda's direction (Fukuda was a seasoned action movie director in Japan) and Sekizawa's script built around a series of chase scenes between the shipwrecked survivors and the Red Bamboo. Author Stuart Galbraith IV offered the film a very high compliment when he suggested that one could remove the monster scenes and still have a solid, entertaining film! The film's climax does best *Invasion of Astro-Monster*'s, as it has an element of suspense severely lacking from the previous film. In this script, Godzilla must defeat Ebirah and Mothra must rescue the stranded Infant Islanders before Letchi Island is obliterated by a nuclear explosion. *Ebirah, Horror of the Deep* was still a success at the box office and managed to sell more than three million tickets. It would be the last Godzilla film to do so until the series was relaunched in 1984.

Rather than Ebirah, Godzilla's next big threat had already arrived and had been brought upon him by his own creator. Eiji Tsuburaya had plans to take monsters to the small screen. Though this idea would prove wildly successful, it would have unforeseen consequences for Godzilla...

Chapter Notes

[1] It was also called *Frankenstein's Sons*, then *The Frankenstein Brothers*, and after that *Duel of the Frankensteins*.
[2] This is also a continuity error for another reason as the climax of *Frankenstein vs. Baragon* took place at Mt. Shirane, a good four plus hours from Mt. Fuji. But, maybe Dr. Stewart is simply an unreliable narrator.
[3] In a way it's similar to the case of the three main characters in *Mothra vs. Godzilla* and *Ghidorah, the Three-Headed Monster* as Hiroshi Koizumi played Professor Miura in the former and Professor Murai in the latter—two separate characters with similar names played by the same actor. It is the same here, with the new story being an abstract follow-up to the previous.
[4] The Japanese script, published in a volume of *Tokusatsu Hihou*, even has alternate U.S. and Japanese scenes within the same script.
[5] Tamblyn told author Bill Warren that the original dialogue track was lost, and Tamblyn then had to redub his dialogue for the U.S. version without the script!
[6] Lees, "An Interview with Henry G-Saperstein", *G-Fan* #15 (May/Jun 1995), pp.46.
[7] Or so the story goes. If you think about it, it honestly makes no sense for Hirose to be cast as Sanda. Sanda is meant to be taller than Gaira and Hirose was around the same height as Nakajima. A more in-depth version of the story says that after making *Invasion of Astro-Monster*, hidden behind Ghidorah's chest twice in a row, Hirose got hired to play a "normal" role in a movie at another studio. Hirose boldly told Tsuburaya "I'm going to play a role where people get to see my face!" Of course, that irritated Tsuburaya to no end. The movie wound up never happening. It is thought that Hirose's final role in a Toho monster film was in *Ebirah, Horror of the Deep* as one of the escaping Infant Islanders (the fatter one) who is killed and devoured by Ebirah/Hiroshi Sekita. This may have been orchestrated by Tsuburaya as payback.
[8] It's possible that this was an alternate name for *Invasion of Astro-Monster*.
[9] *Toho Special Effects Movie Complete Works*, pp. 142.
[10] In the William Dozier papers can be found a real treatment entitled "Batman Meets Godzilla" written in the style of the TV series.
[11] *The King Kong Show* was created by Rankin/Bass for ABC TV, but was animated by Toei in Japan. They wanted to do a live action King Kong movie along with it.
[12] *Toho Special Effects Movie Complete Works*, pp.117.
[13] This title came from another script: *100 Shot/100 Killed: Big Duel in the South Seas*, a scrapped sequel to *100 Shot/100 Killed* (1965) which starred Akira Takarada as a James Bond-type character. Coincidentally, Jun Fukuda also directed *100 Shot, 100 Killed* which starred many members of *Ebirah, Horror of the Deep's* cast including Akihiko Hirata, Chotaro Togin, and Toru Ibuki.
[14] Specifically, in the original script for *All Monsters Attack* (1969), Godzilla was supposed to fight a giant octopus. Ishiro Honda axed the scene for budgetary reasons and decided to use stock footage of Godzilla's battle with Ebirah instead.
[15] www.davmil.org/www.kaijuconversations.com/fukuda.htm

16.
TV MONSTERS
ULTRA Q AND ULTRAMAN

In January of 1966, Tsuburaya Production's first television series *Ultra Q* premiered. Japanese monsters would never be the same and the introduction of kaiju to TV would change the game for cinematic monsters altogether.

The origins of *Ultra Q* date back to 1962 when Eiji Tsuburaya's son, Noboru, caught wind of a TV show pitch by producer Tomio Sagisu focusing around giant monsters. Eiji had similar ideas so Noboru urged him to begin work on their own series. Tetsuo Kinjo, Ken Kumagi, Shigeru Komatsuzaki, and a panel of sci-fi writers met in December of 1962 to discuss ideas for the potential series. Next, Sakyo Komatsu (future writer of *Submersion of Japan*) and Shinichi Hoshi came up with a concept that served not only as the springboard for *Ultra Q* but the roots of *Ultraman* as well.

Titled *Woo*,[1] the story focused on a cloud-like benevolent alien named Woo who is displeased with his own race's disinterest in other species. When the comet his race lives on is destroyed, he sets out to explore the universe and comes across earth where he meets Art Graphic Center photographer Joji Akita, his assistant Taro Dan (the comic relief character), and beautiful model Dorothy (hopefully to be played seventeen-year-old model Yoshimi Ukisu). Akita learns to communicate with Woo through his transistor radio after being showered by Woo's rays. Even though Woo is hunted by the self-defense forces who considers him a threat, the creature still defends earth from monsters and other threats. The series was to take place over thirteen episodes, the usual amount of most Japanese TV series. Though it is not known yet just how child-friendly this series would have been, main character Akita had a background in photographing nudes!

Fuji Television backed out of the project when Eiji Tsuburaya requested they buy him an Oxberry 1200 optical printer to do the series. Tokyo Broadcasting System (TBS for short) stepped in and agreed to do so but requested changes to the series. The next step in *Ultra Q*'s evolution was to do away with the Art Graphic Center and replace them with a scientific investigation team. With that in mind, writer Tetsuo Kinjo went back home to Okinawa to create a new series as TBS said *Woo* would be far too expensive. He returned with *Unbalance*, heavily influenced by *The Twilight Zone* and *The Outer Limits*, which would focus on a rebellion by nature against mankind's tampering with the environment.

His three story pitches notably included "Vengeance of the Giant Octopus" (based upon Eiji Tsuburaya's original idea for *Godzilla*), "Metamorphosis," and "Mammoth Flower." TBS approved of the pitch and the writers began to think about the main cast of characters. Initially, the lead was Jun Manjome, a 25-year-old car enthusiast who owned a flying supercar! Jun would pal around with his nineteen-year-old girlfriend Yuriko and teenaged sidekick Ippie "Tiger" Togawa. As their mentor would be 58-year-old Dr. Ichinotani, who initially was also to serve as a Rod Serling-type narrator to bookend the program.

The show would have began shooting for an April 1965 premiere date but when TBS was unable to sell the series to CBS Films, they postponed production and ordered an additional 13 episodes. The main request from TBS was that the next 13 episodes (or second season) focus more on monsters and less on Japanese culture to be more appealing internationally. Jun's supercar was dropped and the characters evolved into their final forms.

The project's name change came about due to the popular Ultra C maneuver at the 1964 Olympics used by Japanese athlete Yukio Endo. Consequently, the term "ultra" caught on in Japan after announcer Bunya Suzuki shouted it every time a Japanese athlete got high marks. TBS agreed "Ultra" should be part of the title and Eiji Tsuburaya decided it should be *Ultra Q*—for question or quest.

As *Ultra Q* was about to finish its run, a new series was created to take its place called *Scientific Investigation Agency Bemular*. This series focused on a heroic monster named Bemular—a name later given to Ultraman's first enemy monster. The series, created by Tetsuo Kinjo and Eiji Tsuburaya, would have followed the Scientific Investigation Agency as they investigated strange occurrences and received aid from the heroic giant Bemular who could grow to 164 feet tall when needed (alternating sources argue as to whether or not Bemular was an alien or an earth-based monster). The SIA would have been located in Paris, though the series would focus on the Japanese branch—headed by Captain Muramatsu. The captain was the only one who knew that tough 28-year-old Officer Sakomizu was the man who secretly transformed into the reptilian Bemular.

Masahiro Yamada completed a teleplay for the pilot entitled "The Birth of Bemular." Fans will notice that Bemular's design is rather evocative of Nikkatsu's monster Gappa. In the interest of being thorough, the design for Bemular was based upon a legendary crow creature called Karasu Tengu crossed with Garuda, a legendary bird-like creature of Hindu and Buddhist mythology.[2] After receiving the pitch for *Scientific Investigation Agency Bemular,* TBS producer Takashi Kakoi felt that a heroic monster fighting evil monsters was potentially confusing and asked for the heroic giant to be more discernable from his opponents. Tsuburaya and Kinjo created the humanoid, armored hero Redman. The first draft is basically similar to Ultraman, only the hero is still named Sakomizu of the SIA. Likewise, Redman's home planet has been completely destroyed, necessitating his coming to earth and merging with Sakomizu. To transform into Redman, Sakomizu would use the "Flashbeam" which would envelop him in light and transform him into the giant hero. Early designs of Redman were somewhat hostile-looking (Toru Narita designed both Bemular and Redman, who had horns at one point) so the design was softened until the concept evolved into *Ultraman* as we now know it.

After changing the title from *Redman* to *Ultraman,* the new series was the same as the finished one aside from a few last-minute changes. It was decided that giving Ultraman a weakness would add interest to the character. This is why the three-minute fight window and color timer were added. Also, the original cast was apparently larger before it was cut down to the five major members of the Science Patrol. Female member Fuji was the last to be added to the team during the *Redman* phase.[3]

In what proved to be a somewhat symbolic/prophetic episode, Ultraman kills a thinly-veiled Godzilla. Eiji Tsuburaya would somewhat brazenly haul old Toho monster suits and props to his company and use them for his shows. He had already cannibalized the Mosugoji costume from *Mothra vs. Godzilla* in the premiere episode of *Ultra Q.* King Kong, Baragon, Manda, and Magma also made their way into the show as new monsters Goro, Pagos, Kairyu, and Todola (he almost used the Mothra larva to make a new monster, but it didn't happen). This would cause resentment from Corporate Toho who only continued dealing with Tsuburaya because they wanted the money his name undoubtedly drew on their films.

At any rate, the Ultraman crew created the monster Jirass out of two old Godzilla costumes. The main body was the Mosugoji costume but the head belonged the Daisensogoji from *Invasion of Astro-Monster.* The effects craftsmen elected to hide the connection of the new head on another suit's body by placing a frill around the monster's neck. Near the end of the battle, Ultraman rips off Jirass' frill before killing him (though he does put it back onto the monster's corpse). As it would later turn out, the popularity of monsters on TV would severely hurt the Godzilla franchise. Ironically, the crew at Tsuburaya Productions had no clue of this ripple effect because they explicitly planned the episode to be "Ultraman vs. Godzilla".

Chapter Notes
---

[1] Years later, this concept name was resurrected by Tsuburaya Productions as *Bio Planet WoO* in 2006, where a tiny monster transforms into an Ultraman-like hero called Aikichi to battle evil monsters.
[2] Rumor has it this design was later sold to Nikkatsu who used it for *Gappa, the Triphibian Monster* (1967). It's also possible that they didn't buy it, and that Akira Watanabe simply gave it to them as he was the film's special effects director.
[3] In 1972, Tsuburaya Productions revived the concept name, though not the concept, to produce the TV series *Redman*.

17.
THE BIG ONE
1967

1967 was a banner year for the Japanese giant monster movie. That year, every major Japanese studio (plus one in Korea, working in association with Toei) released a monster movie. The previous year had seen one Godzilla and Gamera film each, *The War of the Gargantuas*, the Daimajin trilogy, and Toei's *Grand Duel in Magic*. Add in the debut of *Ultra Q* and *Ultraman* on television and a full monster boom was in effect. The Japanese government took notice of this and came up with a program that offered film loans to Japanese studios to make such movies for export. This is what finally brought holdouts Nikkatsu and Shochiku into the kaiju eiga fold.

The first—and most successful—release that year was Daiei's third Gamera film, *Gamera vs. Gyaos*. During *Gamera vs. Barugon's* theatrical run, Noriaki Yuasa noticed that the audience was comprised mostly of children. When the monsters were on screen they sat tight. When they were off-screen they ran wild or went to go buy candy. Daiei acknowledged to Noriaki Yuasa that he had been right about the series—Yuasa had always argued that Gamera films should be for children, though he had been sidelined from *Gamera vs. Barugon*'s human actors in favor of house director Shigeo Tanaka. Daiei placed Yuasa back in the main director's chair and instructed Niisan Takahashi to write the film with a prominent child character.

Since Toho had done a film about a giant Frankenstein, Daiei thought it would be a good idea to do a giant take on Dracula, so the early draft of the third Gamera film was entitled *Gamera vs. Vampire*. It was hoped that this "Dracula monster" would boost the film's international appeal. *Gamera vs. Vampire* is basically similar to the finished film but begins with U.S. and Soviet aircraft going missing over Mt. Fuji where an alarming amount of hikers are also disappearing. When a cow's half-eaten remains are discovered, it is concluded that it was eaten by a gigantic being and an investigation begins. Eventually, a huge vampire bat is revealed to be the culprit. The Japanese government learns that bright lights are the monster's weakness and they also create special bullets out of a moss that is deadly to the vampire. The only other significant difference in this version is that the young boy character is not saved from the man-eating monster by Gamera but by a man (presumably Kojiro Hongo's character in the finished film).

It is stated on the film's Japanese Wikipedia page that Gyaos' vast array of powers was influenced by *Mission Impossible* (1966), known in Japan as *Grand Spy Strategy*. Among Gyaos' many abilities is the power to emit a slicing ray known as the Supersonic Scalpel, a napalm powder that can put out Gamera's flames known as the Fire-Extinguishing Fluid (despite the fact it is obviously a gas), and the ability regenerate severed body parts. Naturally, there would be some scientific discussion on Gyaos' powers but interestingly, Yuasa said he hated the monster conference scenes in Toho movies and was very careful in terms of how he handled the conference scenes in this film.

Like many films that year, this one benefited from government funding, though its budget was still lesser than *Gamera vs. Barugon*'s. The finished film is regarded as one of the best Gamera entries; it's not entirely kid's stuff just yet. The film's main human storyline centers on an old village that opposes the creation of a highway in their vicinity. Child character Eiichi isn't the main star and shares the screen equally with superstar Kojiro Hongo. The previous film was strictly for adults and the fourth film was purely for kids. The balance between the child and adult characters seen here would never be repeated in the Showa era. The reputation of *Gamera vs. Gyaos* is not without good reason. The battles are quite creative and are easily the best of the entire series as Gamera battles Gyaos on land, in the air, and on the surface of the sea (the Japanese title was the extremely attention-catching *Giant Monster Mid-Air Battle: Gamera vs. Gyaos*). Niisan Takahashi claims that Ishiro Honda himself took note of the film's success, and sent Takahashi a New Year's greeting card that said Honda would like to work with Takahashi on a film one day.[1]

Next up on the monster merry-go-round was Shochiku, who produced *Space Monster Guilala*, eventually released to U.S. television by AIP as *The X From Outer Space*. Little has been revealed about the writing process, but the story started out simply as *Space Monster* and would have featured giant plants and Guilala, who was then called Monster Bug X. The next treatment was named *SF Space Monster* and introduced the concept of the Astro-Boat. The following draft was titled *SF Giant Space Monster* and Guilala was called "insect monster Demora." The final shooting draft was titled *Space Monster Guilala*—a name decided upon by Japanese children.

To set their entry apart from Toho and Daiei, Shochiku decided to set the first half of their movie entirely in outer space. This first portion serves mainly to show off the costly-looking sets. At one point, the ship's doctor becomes ill and it would seem the main reason this happens is so the main characters have an excuse to stop at the moon base. An interesting question is raised when a U.F.O. buzzes the AAB-Gamma and leaves the hull covered in spores (one of which develops into Guilala). However, the U.F.O.'s identity and purpose are never explained, though some chock this up to Japanese storytelling which is usually more concerned with posing interesting questions rather than answering them.

The biggest problem with the film's story is that Guilala itself is too bizarre to anchor the film around. Rather, the monster is too goofy-looking to generate any real suspense. By 1967, audiences had seen plenty of monster-on-the-loose films which is all *The X From Outer Space* really is. Simply put, the film's writing is painfully uninspired (despite having three writers working on it!) when compared to other kaiju films that same year. It's easy to see Shochiku simply made the film for government funding. Though it was the worst of the non-Toho/Daiei kaiju movies, it was remarkably the second highest-grossing monster movie of 1967! Perhaps the positive reception of *Gamera vs. Gyaos* helped the film at the box office.

Next on the kaiju roster was *Gappa, the Triphibian Monster* from Nikkatsu. Like almost every other film that year, it was written to take advantage of government loans. Co-writer Gan Yamazaki's comments in *Monsters Are Attacking Tokyo* are very enlightening and worth quoting in full:

"Nikkatsu was one of the major studios, but had never done a kaiju eiga. Godzilla had become a very successful series, and so Nikkatsu became interested. If the film could be successful overseas in the international market and thus get hard currency, Nikkatsu could get financing from the Japanese government as part of its protection program. And so the film was financed in this manner. It was funny that we were asked to write a big-budget monster movie to get government financing! The budget was ¥500 million (about $1.4 million)—10 times the average cost of a Nikkatsu film. The government paid for all of it! Of course, we had to pay it back, but the studio owned real estate – hotels, golf courses, and so on. Nikkatsu was in the red at the time, and they used all the money to pay back its debts instead of on the film! Suddenly, we had to make do with much less money, and this really pissed me off!"[2]

Before Yamazaki came on board, the studio had played around with four distinct concepts the previous year. These consisted of story pitches by Hideo Kodama and included *Monster Gigant* (a giant alien spider of sorts), *Giant Squid Akitiusu* (about a giant squid fighting the Nazis in WWII), *Monster Momonra* (a giant flying squirrel), and *Reigon: Devil of the Seabed*. Of the four, *Reigon: Devil of the Seabed* went furthest in development, with a story treatment by Shunichi Yukimuro and Ryuzo Nakanishi written wherein a giant stingray would surface from the sea to battle a giant iguana.
Nakanishi was next paired with Yamazaki to begin writing what would eventually become *Giant Beast Gappa*, released internationally as *Gappa, the Triphibian Monster* and to American TV by AIP as *Monster from a Prehistoric Planet*. In *Monsters Are Attacking Tokyo*, Nakanishi said, "I wrote *Gappa* as a kind of halibut/flatfish monster. But it would have cost too much."[3] Rather than a halibut monster, Nikkatsu had their eye on a design either sold or given to them by Tsuburaya Productions. The design was none other than the original winged, Garuda-like design for Ultraman when the concept was called *Science Investigation Agency: Bemular*.
Ironically, the film's final story had some similarities to its real-life inspiration (Nikkatsu's real estate debts) in that it partially revolved around real estate and company politics. An expedition explores a South Pacific island where they plan to collect exotic wildlife to be a part of a Japanese resort. Naturally, they find a baby monster egg and from here the story becomes evocative of *Gorgo*. Though *Gorgo* had been very popular in Japan, both writers denied ever having seen it when Stuart Galbraith asked them about the film! The story not only takes inspiration from *Gorgo* but several other popular Japanese monster films as well. One could argue the happy ending at the airport is like *Mothra*, and the satirical tone with the publishing magnate is similar to *King Kong vs. Godzilla*. Baby Gappa is even airlifted with balloons at one point! Naturally, like many films in this book, according to the screenwriters, the movie was originally more ambitious. "The story was really big, but during this process it began shrinking. They cut corners everywhere," Yamazaki said.[4]

Although derivative at times, *Gappa, the Triphibian Monster* is at least more original and innovative than Shochiku's Guilala story. "It's not very interesting just to have a big monster destroy things, so that's why we created the story of affection between the parents and baby monster," Yamazaki explained.[5] Though it was beaten in numbers at the box office by Shochiku's film earlier that year, *Gappa, the Triphibian Monster* has emerged as the more fondly remembered of the two in Japan.

Back at Toho, their first monster movie for that year was the King Kong feature they originally had intended to be their 1966 New Year's Blockbuster. Rankin/Bass tried to co-produce a Kong film with Toho again, this time successfully making *King Kong Escapes* (*King Kong's Counterattack* in Japan), which was based upon their animated *The King Kong Show*. The program revolved around the Bond family comprising of Professor Bond and his two children, Bobby and Susan. Along for the ride was Captain Englehorn, based on the character from the original 1933 *King Kong*. In the pilot episode, the family arrives on Mondo Island via Englehorn's boat. In the jungle, Bobby is attacked by a Tyrannosaurus Rex and is saved by Kong. From that point on, Kong acts as the family's protector. Ironically, the series was animated by Toho's competitor Toei in Japan and aired on American television on ABC from September of 1966 through 1969. As Toei was not known for monster movies, Rankin/Bass connected with Toho for their live-action version.

Though Kaoru Mabuchi gets credit on the script for *King Kong Escapes*, he was supplied with some sort of outline from Rankin/Bass to base his story upon this time. The plot comes from elements of *The King Kong Show*, namely the robotic Mechanikong and its creator Dr. Who. Portrayed as a bald, bespectacled midget[6] on the show, the not-so-good doctor was on several episodes and also created other robot opponents for Kong, including a robot sphynx. Additionally, this Dr. Who had a base in the arctic as well. It's also worth mentioning there was an episode where Dr. Who captures Kong by helicopter, and another where Who trapped the Bond family in a room with freezing walls. That said, the biggest departure in *King Kong Escapes* from *The King Kong Show* is the fact that the Bond family does not appear at all (though it can be presumed it's not a coincidence the female lead is named Susan).

Differences in early drafts were apparently fairly minor. Certainly, the Mondo Island sea serpent was absent from the first draft and Jiro was to save Susan atop Tokyo Tower without the aid of the military. One scene that was toned down was Gorosaurus's defeat, which Rankin/Bass and Toho President Iwao Mori both wanted to be bloodier.[7] Tsuburaya refused and had the monster foam at the mouth, perhaps to troll them for their bloodlust. Before this though, it was Eiji Tsuburaya's intent to build the new Kong suit based upon the look of the 1933 King Kong, but Rankin/Bass wanted this Kong to resemble his cartoon counterpart, so Tsuburaya was forced to deliver the look that's onscreen.

It is unknown how much free reign Mabuchi had when adapting Rankin/Bass's treatment but the script is one of his best, not to mention upbeat, stories ever (it plays out far more like one of Shinichi Sekizawa's scripts. Mabuchi's stories were generally cynical and brooding). The story clips along at a brisk, adventurous pace, and like all the best Toho monster movies does a good job of intertwining the human and monster storylines. The ending fares particularly well in this regard, where Jiro must rescue Susan who is stranded in Tokyo Tower as Kong battles his robotic double above her. The idea of a good Kong and a bad Kong is spectacular, especially considering that the bad Kong absconds with the female lead at one point. One could even presume that the battle atop Tokyo Tower was inspired by the end battle of *King Kong vs. the Ginko* where the two monsters fought while climbing the Golden Gate Bridge (though it might also have been inspired by the ending of the original 1933 film).

Though they obviously got no funding from the Japanese government, that same year, South Korea's Far East Entertainment and Toei produced *Great Monster Yongary*, released in Japan by Toei as *Daikaiju Yangari/Giant Monster Yongary* and to American TV by AIP as *Yongary, Monster from the Deep*. Toei also dealt with the international sales of the film. Though a Korean film, it was entirely inspired by those emanating from Japan. Yongary looks a lot like Godzilla with Gamera's head and Barugon's horn[8] and the costume is closer to those by the Gamera camp rather than the generally better-looking Toho stable of monsters. He breathes live fire like Gamera and fires a beam that can slice through metal like Gyaos. Near the end of the movie, he uses Barugon's roar occasionally. Like in the Gamera series there is a prominent child character, Icho, who cheers the monster on, as well as a groovy rendition of the Korean folk song, "Arirang." The Yongary suit was even built by Masao Yagi, designer of the Gamera costume. However, the film's director, Ki-duk Kim, was reportedly disappointed with what he got as he wanted a scarier-looking monster.

Writer Yun-sung Seo claims Yongary was originally a single-celled organism from outer space that became mutated by earth's nuclear testing. Whether he meant this was the film's original concept—or that it is Yongary's secret backstory in his own mind—is uncertain. None of it is in the final film, only that Yongary, who seems to be a prehistoric monster, exists and he is somehow awakened from underground in Korea by an atomic bomb blast in the Middle East. Another significant plot point was apparently lost in *Yongary*'s English translation by AIP. Though it appears Yongary dies one of the most disturbing deaths in kaiju eiga history, the surviving Korean version's dialogue for Icho's character tells a different story. In the scene, Icho confirms that Yongary is actually still alive and states he hopes that scientists can construct a rocket and shoot Yongary to another planet where he can live in peace—another idea clearly inspired by the ending of *Gamera* (1965). The final shot of the movie is such a rocket sending Yongary to galactic parts unknown—just like Gamera and Guilala before him—which plays with absolutely no context whatsoever in the American version.

Overall, the storyline of Korea's monster movie is too derivative of the Japanese ones to be of any real interest. Basically, Yongary shows up, begins destroying Korea, and is later defeated in a rather odd manner. In short, been there, done that. The movie was very successful in South Korea, but it is unknown how it fared at the Japanese box office.

Finally, for his end of year Godzilla blockbuster, Tomoyuki Tanaka decided to give Godzilla a child—an idea most Japanese sources say came from wanting to try something new. Director Jun Fukuda[9] said, "We wanted to take a new approach. So, we gave Godzilla a child. We thought that it would be a little strange if Godzilla had a daughter, so we instead gave him a son."[10]

Rather than Shinichi Sekizawa taking a crack at the first draft, Sekizawa's protégé, Kazue Shiba, wrote the script. Like Sekizawa, Shiba was a lyricist. She was also a woman, meaning it was Shiba who beat Yukiko Takayama's *Terror of Mechagodzilla* to the punch of the first-ever female-conceived Godzilla film. Shiba's only experience up to that point had been collaborating with Sekizawa on *Zero Fighter* (1966), a war movie based on stories Sekizawa heard during WWII while he was stationed on an island.

Shiba's script was entitled *Two Godzillas: Japan S.O.S* and has many elements familiar to *Son of Godzilla*. Like the finished story, this one too revolves around a weather control experiment on an island, here called "Godzilla Island." The character of Saeko is present and it is her father, Dr. Senjimori, who is in charge of the experiment, not Dr. Kusumi. Strangely, the baby Godzilla (called Godzilla Junior) doesn't get a hatching scene and just emerges from the ocean with his father.[11] The little tyke is a good deal tougher than Minilla—in one scene, he gets swallowed in a river of lava with his father! Godzilla Junior does not fire smoke rings, but has the ability to spit a regular atomic ray at all times—though the famous teaching scene does appear. Notably absent from the film are the giant insects. Instead, the only other enemy monsters are a batch of giant clams that Godzilla Junior battles at sea! The film's ending has the two Godzillas surfacing in Tokyo, where Junior clomps across a race track called Funabashi Circuit.[12] The day is saved when the weather experiment is used to create a tsunami that forces the two Godzillas deep into the Japan Trench—essentially making them the villains of the film! Tomoyuki Tanaka likely took issue with this in addition to the fact that the film didn't end with a monster battle, which audiences now expected. From here, Sekizawa was given Shiba's script to rewrite, confining all of the action to a deserted island as in the last film.[13] The character of Saeko was carried over from Shiba's story but became a jungle girl orphaned on the island long ago. Instead of her father, it is a new character, Dr. Kusumi, who creates a weather control device. As in Shiba's script, it is used to subdue the monsters via freezing.

As in the previous film, Sekizawa simply mutated existing life forms into giant-sized versions to serve as the monster opponents. They work rather well, as the story's focus is more on Godzilla and his son rather than the monster battles, which are just a bonus.[14] Godzilla's son is a rather odd if endearing creature with many fans stating that he looks like a cross between Godzilla and the Pillsbury Doughboy! Though a rather apt description because of the creature's fatty, smooth skin, there is actually a reason for this: Minilla was designed with smooth skin because he was never scarred by the H-Bomb blast like Godzilla was. Minilla's name isn't spoken on film and wasn't thought up until midway through shooting. The name means "Mini-Godzilla" shortened to Minilla— or Minira (Mini-Gojira) in Japan. However, the child monster is identified by name in the Japanese dialogue of his next appearance, *Destroy All Monsters*. Though disliked by many U.S. fans, Minilla is extremely popular in Japan.[15] In 2017, Minilla was listed as the fourth most popular non-Godzilla Toho monster by the Japanese (after, of course, Mothra, King Ghidorah, and Mechagodzilla).

Many scenes were shot but removed of Godzilla being mean or harsh to Minilla. One such scene shows Godzilla expecting the newborn Minilla to get up and walk after the Kamacuras have been defeated. Another featured Godzilla head-butting Minilla to make him stop following Saeko. Perhaps worst of all, after Kumonga is defeated, Godzilla pulls a "I never liked you anyway" thing on Minilla and ditches him in the snow while he flees the island. Once out in the ocean, Godzilla has a change of heart and goes back to the exhausted Minilla, who is being buried by the snow (Godzilla looks so ashamed when he returns). The sequence in the movie now more or less just cuts out the "Godzilla abandoning Minya" bit. It is unknown who was responsible for these bits being deleted, but it was possibly Tsuburaya since he would not have allowed time and resources to be wasted shooting such scenes if he was not okay with them in the first place. Footage from this sequence can be glimpsed in the film's Japanese trailer. More deleted footage included Minilla being able to fire his own type of atomic breath during his fight with Kamacuras. However, in the final film, the smoke rings and his Godzillian breath were utilized instead.

Though it sports the same director and island locale, *Son of Godzilla* is a different animal from *Ebirah, Horror of the Deep*. While the aforementioned film was structured around a series of chases, *Son of Godzilla* has a more relaxed pace. By comparison, it seems to be a film about relationships more so than action. Much of the first act focuses on the mystery surrounding the island, the gigantic egg, and the jungle girl Saeko. After the egg is broke open and reporter Goro Maki formally meets Saeko, the film's focus shifts to the relationship between her and Goro and Godzilla and his adopted son. Perhaps it's no surprise that this entry of the Godzilla series was aimed at the date crowd and double-billed with an entry in the popular *Young Guy* series. *Son of Godzilla* sold fewer tickets than its predecessor and many sources claim that this, along with the rise in popularity among TV monsters, persuaded Tomoyuki Tanaka to consider ending the series.

Chapter Notes

[1] This is why many years later in the early 90s, when Takahashi wrote *Gamera vs. Phoenix* he lobbied for Honda to direct the film.
[2] Galbraith, *Monsters Are Attacking Tokyo*, pp. 109-110.
[3] Ibid.
[4] Ibid.
[5] Ibid.
[6] For the film, this portrayal as a bald midget was never considered and reportedly the role was written for actor Hideyo Amamoto from the onset.
[7] At this point, Gorosaurus was just an unnamed, throwaway Tyrannosaurus and never intended to be a part of the greater pantheon of Toho monsters.
[8] There are photos of Yongary without the nasal horn, so perhaps it was a last minute addition? Or, perhaps it was meant to be assembled when shipped to South Korea?
[9] Ishiro Honda was signed on to direct the film when it was *Two Godzillas: Japan S.O.S.*, but when it turned into *Son of Godzilla* and he saw how Godzilla was going to be portrayed, Honda bailed.
[10] www.davmil.org/www.kaijuconversations.com/fukuda.htm
[11] One could argue that Minilla didn't get a hatching scene either. He was yanked out of his egg by the Kamacuras before he was done growing. This is why Minilla is deformed and why he never grows beyond what we see at the end of the movie.
[12] Ironically, Funabashi Circuit closed down in 1967 as *Son of Godzilla* was being filmed.
[13] It's unknown if Shiba actually collaborated with Sekizawa on the second draft or if he simply took her script and altered it. That said, *Son of Godzilla* has an unusual femininity to it that cannot be found in Sekizawa's other works, so perhaps she did.
[14] At least one battle maneuver was deleted, as Sadamasa Arikawa's storyboards showed the giant spider Kumonga crawling on top of Minilla during the final battle. Godzilla then blasts him off with his ray.
[15] For fans who think Minilla completely disappeared after 1969's *All Monsters Attack*, this is not the case. A new Minilla suit, possibly built initially just for publicity purposes, appeared as an evil clone of Minilla in an episode of *Go! Greenman* in 1973. This same Minilla suit was present to cheer Godzilla on during a live stage show to tie into the release of *Godzilla vs. Mechagodzilla* in 1974. And in canon with the films, Minilla is shown (via stock footage) living on Monster Island with Godzilla in 1972's *Godzilla vs. Gigan*.

18.
RETURN OF THE TV MONSTERS
AGON AND ULTRASEVEN

Back in 1964, Toho screenwriter Shinichi Sekizawa began working with Japan Radio Pictures to write *Giant Phantom Monster Agon* (aka *Agon the Atomic Dragon*). This monster TV series was originally much more ambitious than what was eventually produced. Rather than the four episodes that were completed, the series was initially supposed to encompass 26 episodes (or two 13-episode seasons). The show focused on a Godzilla-like dinosaur monster called Agon who feeds upon radioactivity. In the middle of the show's run, when mankind attacks Agon with nuclear weapons, the monster was supposed to further mutate and sprout wings!

Other storylines had interesting similarities to concepts both used and abandoned in future Godzilla scripts. One episode would have had Agon lured into an open volcano as in *The Return of Godzilla* (1984) and another would have had satellites attacking Agon from the sky.[1] At least one other known episode would have had Agon going to the North Pole and the series was slated to end with Agon being killed by a heat ray similar to the Maser cannons. When Toho got wind of the project, they argued the monster too closely resembled Godzilla, and the two studios did some negotiating and cut down the episode order to four (though a newspaper at the time said there would be five episodes). Ironically, had Agon debuted as a flying dragon (rather than metamorphosing midway into the series as planned), Toho would have had no argument. To top it off, Japan Radio Pictures went bankrupt and the series (filmed in 1964) wasn't aired until 1968.

Sekizawa utilizing the same crime aspect he incorporated into *Space Monster Dogora* and *Ghidorah, the Three-Headed Monster* gives away the fact that he wrote the script in 1964. In this case, he includes a subplot involving a couple of criminals smuggling drugs who are eventually caught by Detective Yamato. In addition to the detective, Sekizawa uses the rest of his usual character types for this script such as a reporter[2] who romances a female laboratory assistant. And naturally, said lab assistant's elderly scientist boss also features in the story.

The four episodes comprise of the reporter, Goro, teaming with Detective Yamato to research strange occurrences along the Japanese coast. A giant monster dubbed Agon (for "atomic dragon") emerges and attacks an atomic power plant. After learning that uranium can appease the monster, it is used to keep the beast sated underwater. However, two criminals disturb the monster's peace and it surfaces again, grabbing a fishing boat with the small boy Monta in its jaws. Using a uranium lure on the end of a rope attached to a helicopter, Agon finally drops the boat and Monta is able to be rescued. Agon is then poisoned by narcotics and staggers off into the ocean, his fate uncertain. *Agon the Atomic Dragon* aired with little fanfare over the course of four nights in January of 1968.

At this same time, *Ultraseven*, the sequel to *Ultraman*, was extremely popular on TV. Back when the series was being developed, TBS had wanted another season (or 13 episode block) of *Ultraman*. However, Tsuburaya Productions wanted to produce an all-new series. Initially more of a spiritual sequel than an in-continuity sequel, the first pitch was called *The Ultra Garrison*. The series was to be set in the year 1999 with the action revolving around astronauts in the space station Mother—earth's first line of defense against alien invaders. TBS made the stipulation that the series must focus on space and alien invaders because they were having great success with a line of space-themed programs at the time. Apparently, there was no giant hero in the first draft; rather, just a team of six humans (jointly part of the Solar System Mobile Police and the Special Investigation Team—together the Ultra Garrison) and their android helper John. At TBS's insistence, a superhero like Ultraman would be added into the next draft.

The next step in *Ultraseven's* evolution was *Ultra Eye*, influenced in part by Toho's *The Mysterians*. The new series would be set at least ten years in the future and revolve around the son of *Ultraman's* Hayata and Fuji, who was born in space. When this younger Ultraman couldn't make it to earth to help, earth-based monsters (ideally four in total, one of which would be a loyal, dog-like kaiju) would fight the alien invaders. As the development went on—to cut costs—these monsters were to be Red King, Antlar, and Peguila from *Ultraman* and *Ultra Q*. As development progressed, writer Tetsuo Kinjo looked back to the old *Woo* treatment and was inspired by the concept of a stranger (alien) in a strange land (earth). From there, the concept got closer to the finished *Ultraseven* with the creation of Dan Moroboshi, a clairvoyant half human-alien hybrid who has a human mother and a father from the Planet R. Moroboshi would search for his lost human mother and transform into Redman when needed.

The series quickly progressed into *Ultraseven* as we know it today, though there were still some slight differences. The Ultra Garrison, now called the Terrestrial Defense Force, was more elaborate, with six main members and 300 supporting members overall. The TDF was located in a vast, almost city-sized, underground base situated near Mt. Fuji. Also, the show as to be set in the year 1987. To design the hero—still not an in-canon "Ultraman"—production designer Toru Narita turned to the elaborate Mayan headdresses and incorporated it into his new design. This Ultraman was to be silver and blue, not silver and red, though they had to go with the silver/red color scheme to avoid problems with blue screen in the end.[3] The idea of reusing old monsters for Dan's capsule monsters was also dropped in favor of brand new creations. Finally, as the series concept was revised once more (scaling down the TDF into the Ultra Garrison), *Ultraseven* officially became tied to the previous series when the hero's backstory read that he was a cartographer from Nebula M78 (which had been mentioned as the home of Ultraman in the final episode of that series).

The finished series tackled a diverse set of issues, including war, genocide, racism, and oppression thanks to head writer Tetsuo Kinjo. Of all the Ultra series, *Ultraseven* became one of the most beloved and spawned a multitude of spinoffs and follow-up movies in the future.

Chapter Notes

[1] This concept was considered for *Godzilla vs. King Ghidorah* (1991) and abandoned.
[2] Sekizawa even recycles a gag from his *Mothra* script where the lead reporter is nicknamed "snapping turtle" because he never lets go of a story.
[3] Ironically, and probably intentionally, Ultraseven's son—who debuted in 2009's *Mega Monster Battle: Ultra Galaxy Legends - The Movie*—was silver and blue.

PROFILE: TETSUO KINJO

One of the leading series writers on *Ultra Q*, *Ultraman*, and *Ultraseven* was Tetsuo Kinjo, a protégé of Shinichi Sekizawa. Kinjo offered a unique perspective because he was from Okinawa, which was somewhat isolated from Japan at that time. Kinjo was born in Naha in July of 1938, meaning he was old enough to be cognizant of the bloody battle of Okinawa, where over 150,000 people died on both sides of the conflict combined. Because he was from Okinawa, he required a visa to travel to Tokyo to go study at Tanagawa University. It was at this time that he met Shinichi Sekizawa, who introduced him to Hajime Tsuburaya, which led to his connection to Tsuburaya Productions. Eiji Tsuburaya was impressed with Kinjo, who he had develop *Ultra Q* in its early phases. Struck by his talent for weaving social commentary into sci-fi stories, Tsuburaya promoted Kinjo to head writer on *Ultraman*. Naturally, this carried over into *Ultraseven*, which took Kinjo's experience in WWII-era Okinawa to the next level with even more serious stories. Minoru Nakano described it best in *Monsters Are Attacking Tokyo* stating, "Kinjo was Okinawan and had a very hard time in mainland Japan – it's just like England and Ireland – and this was reflected in several of his scripts for *Ultraseven* and others. Some of the scripts were very controversial, but Eiji Tsuburaya permitted them to be made, and it is this humanity I still respect." [Galbraith, Monsters Are Attacking Tokyo, pp.89] Also, one of the more popular *Ultraseven* foes, the robot monster King Joe was named after him. When the U.S. occupation of Okinawa ended in 1972, Kinjo decided to return home. By then, he had only written one episode of *Return of Ultraman* (1971), his last Ultra episode. Overall, he wrote 13 episodes of *Ultra Q*, 14 episodes of *Ultraman*, and 15 episodes of *Ultraseven*. In 1972, Kinjo teamed with fellow writer Kazuho Mitsuda to pen *Godzilla, Redmoon, Erabus, Halfon: No Man's Land of the Monsters*, a Toho-Tsuburaya collaboration to celebrate Tsuburaya Productions' 10th anniversary. The story featured the monster Redmoon rising from the moon's surface where it comes to earth and mates with earth-based monster Erabus. The two have a child and settle peacefully in Okinawa. A greedy entrepreneur kidnaps the baby monster and it dies during the capture. The angry parents go on a rampage and Godzilla intervenes to stop them. Unfortunately, the film was never made and if it had been, it would have served as Kinjo's final screenwriting credit. On February 26, 1976, Kinjo fell from his roof while doing repair work. The fall killed him and the great writer was dead at only 37 years old. Today, his home serves as the Tetsuo Kinjo Museum.

Selected Filmography
Ultra Q (1966) (writer)
    "Goro and Goroh"
    "The Gift From Space"
    "Mammoth Flower"
    "S.O.S. Mount Fuji"
    "Terror of the Sweet Honey"
    "Baron Spider"
    "Garadama"
    "Garamon Strikes Back"
    "The 1/8 Project"
    "Challenge from the Year 2020"
    "Metamorphosis"
    "Fury of the South Sea"
    "The Disappearance of Flight 206"
Ultraman (1966-1967) (writer)
    "Ultra Operation No.1"
    "The Blue Stone of Baraji"
    "The Lawless Monster Zone"
    "The Mysterious Dinosaur Base"
    "Oil S.O.S."
    "Brother from Another Planet"
    "Terror on Route 87"
    "The Prince of Monsters: Part 1"
    "The Prince of Monsters: Part 2"
    "The Challenge Into Subterra"
    "Phantom of the Snow Mountains"
    "The Forbidden Words"
    "The Little Hero"
    "Farewell, Ultraman"
Ultraseven (1967-1968) (writer)
    "The Invisible Challenger"
    "The Green Terror"
    "The Secret of the Lake"
    "Respond, Max"
    "Alien Prisoner 303"
    "The Targeted Town"
    "Fly to the Mountain of Evil"
    "The Ultra Garrison Goes West, Part 1"
    "The Ultra Garrison Goes West, Part 2"
    "Escape Space X"
    "Showdown at 140 Degrees Below Zero"
    "The Vanishing City"
    "Ambassador of the Nonmalt"
    "The Greatest Invasion in History Part 1"
    "The Greatest Invasion in History Part 2"
Return of Ultraman (1971) (writer)
    "Poison Gas Monster Appears"

19.
ATTACK OF THE KILLER STOCK FOOTAGE:
GAMERA VS. VIRAS

At Daiei, *Gamera vs. Gyaos* had gotten the attention of American International Pictures, causing them to want a hand in production of the next Gamera film. This did not mean, however, that they wanted to release it theatrically; it would still go straight to TV as *War of the Monsters* (*Gamera vs. Barugon*) and *Return of the Giant Monsters* (*Gamera vs. Gyaos*) had before it. To boost international appeal, AIP suggested adding an American boy. Reportedly, AIP told Daiei "the faces of Japanese children all look the same"![1] Noriaki Yuasa stated:

> "AIP's representative had seen all of the Gamera films, and said that he didn't think much of the performances of the Americans in Gamera. He also said that if we wanted to have success distributing Gamera movies in foreign markets, we should put American boys in them. So, a member of the International Division went to the American military bases in Japan and interviewed some of the children of the soldiers. I then conducted final interviews, and made a selection."[2]

As Daiei president Masaichi Nagata was an advisor to the Boy Scouts Association of Japan, he set up a deal between the studio and the Boy Scouts. It became a prerequisite that the Boy Scouts be included in Niisan Takahashi's script.[3] Planner Kazumasa Nakano also asked Takahashi to plot the film conservatively due to budget woes at the time. Supposedly, Takahashi's first script did see Gamera and Viras battle in a city and Viras gets thrown into a building just as he does on the poster. These ideas were subsequently cut and the end action is confined to a beach devoid of miniature buildings. The film was also the first to begin a trend of oversaturating monster films with stock footage. Whether or not this was Takahashi's idea is unknown, but in the pre-VHS era, it was actually an ingenious way to keep monsters on the screen. And being the pre-VHS era, children had not yet "over watched" these same scenes. As most of these scenes are flashbacks, they work well in the context of the story. Where they do not is when Gamera

119

 **GOKE, BODY SNATCHER FROM HELL**

ODDLY ENOUGH, SHOCHIKU'S ACCLAIMED 1968 HORROR MOVIE *GOKE, BODY SNATCHER FROM HELL* BEGAN LIFE AS A TV PROJECT TO BE FILMED WITH PUPPETS! THE SERIES (FROM P-PRODUCTIONS) WAS TO FOCUS ON BENEVOLENT ALIENS TRYING TO RECAPTURE AN ALIEN MONSTER THAT ESCAPED FROM THEM ON EARTH. IN THIS VERSION, GOKEMIDORO IS A FURRY MONSTER WITH MULTIPLE ARMS. THE CONCEPT WAS SOMEHOW ACQUIRED BY SHOCHIKU, WHICH TEAMED WITH P-PRODUCTIONS (WHO WOULD HANDLE THE SPECIAL EFFECTS) TO TURN THE CONCEPT INTO A MUCH MORE SERIOUS HORROR FILM. WRITER SUSUMU TAKAKU SUGGESTED TOEI'S HAJIME SATO AS DIRECTOR AND OFF THE FILM WENT. INITIALLY, SATO CAME UP WITH AN IDEA WHEREIN INVISIBLE ALIEN MONSTERS RAN AMUCK IN A MENTAL WARD UNTIL HE CAME UP WITH THE IDEA OF INSTEAD SETTING THE FILM IN AN AIRLINER THAT CRASHES. SATO WAS ALSO APPARENTLY INSPIRED BY THE PREDICTIONS OF NOSTRADAMUS, NOTING, "CREEPY FOUR-LINE POETRY BY NOSTRADAMUS PREDICTS THAT THE WORLD WILL END IN 1999. A TERRIBLE KING WILL COME DOWN FROM THE SKY. EYEWITNESSES OF FLYING SAUCERS ARE INCREASING. IS THE EARTH BEING TARGETED? I WOULD LIKE TO CREATE 24 HOURS OF THE DESTRUCTION OF EARTH BY DRIVING THE TYPHOON OF TEN PEOPLE REPRESENTING MODERN JAPAN INTO EXTREME CONDITIONS." [JAPANESE WIKIPEDIA PAGE FOR *VAMPIRE GOKE*] SOME SOURCES INDICATE THAT THE MULTI-ARMED GOKEMIDORO WAS CONSIDERED TO APPEAR IN THE FINISHED FILM AS A GIANT MONSTER, BUT WAS DROPPED. IMAGES OF THIS INCARNATION OF GOKE HAVE BEEN INCLUDED IN A SERIES OF JAPANESE TRADING CARDS FEATURING KAIJU AND ASSOCIATED CHARACTERS. ALSO, THOUGH HIDEO KO PORTRAYED GOKE FOR MOST OF THE FILM, EVENTUALLY THE ACTOR HAD A SCHEDULING PROBLEM AND HAD TO LEAVE, HENCE THE SCRIPT WAS CHANGED DURING SHOOTING AND HIS CHARACTER IS KILLED OFF EARLY AND THE ALIEN VAMPIRE HAS TO FIND A NEW HOST.

is placed under alien control and attacks Tokyo—black and white stock footage tinted sepia from *Gamera* (1965) inserted into the new color film.

Despite this grating flaw, there are plenty of good things about *Gamera vs. Viras*. The story cuts right to the action with Gamera engaging in an outer space battle with a uniquely-designed spaceship. With the threat established, the focus shifts back to earth and the story's two leads, rowdy boy scouts Masao and Jim. It is in this department where *Gamera vs. Viras* improves upon its predecessors. Whereas Toshio was a rather odd, unlikeable character in the first *Gamera* and Eiichi in *Gamera vs. Gyaos* was a bit too young to be relatable to anyone over eight, Masao and Jim are lively characters given valid functions in the story other than to represent the target demographics.

Noriaki Yuasa had said that the balance between monsters and child protagonists was what he had strived for from the onset but was just now getting the freedom to do. Takahashi, on the other hand, did not fully embrace this change. He felt giving the film adult appeal as he had done with *Gamera vs. Gyaos* gave his stories a larger margin for success and that aiming the films strictly at children limited the audience.

Yuasa also took note of how children cheered when Eiichi rode on Gamera's back in *Gamera vs. Gyaos* and wanted to devise another such scene, so the submarine race with Gamera was devised. Observing how much children loved the bloodletting in the previous film, more violence was devised for this one with Viras impaling Gamera's abdomen! Another reason for this scene was that at the time, it was thought *Viras* would be the final Gamera movie, so Yuasa decided to raise the stakes by having Gamera badly wounded in the fight. Yuasa also half-joked, "Perhaps there was a feeling of the staff's anger that the shooting was made with a cheap budget."[4] In any case, children in the theater screamed when they saw the scene. Viras was also the first Gamera monster to have its name decided upon by the people. Daiei offered a contest with *World WE Magazine* to name the new film's monster, a tradition that continued with subsequent sequels.

It's interesting to note the difference between Viras and the alien kaiju of Toho films. Unlike the brute muscle monsters utilized in Godzilla films, the Gamera movies featured alien monsters with intelligence who were the invaders themselves, very much like what was done in *Ultraseven*. As a result, *Gamera vs. Viras* has a satisfying twist up its sleeve when it came to the monster villain— something rarely done in kaiju films. Because of Masao and Jim's baseless speculations, we are led to believe Viras is nothing more than a space animal in a cage. While everyone in the audience knows the creature will eventually grow to giant size, the twist comes when the monster is not a caged animal but is, in fact, the leader of the invasion and the human aliens are merely his underlings! Then Viras declares to his subjects that to have victory, "I must take all of your lives." He then swiftly decapitates the men with one swipe of a lone tentacle!

The end result represented the favorite of Yuasa's Gamera movies, in large part because it was what Yuasa always wanted to make: a great children's adventure. Yuasa made the film under the impression it would be the final Gamera outing and even cried when he called a wrap on shooting. To his great surprise, after *Gamera vs. Viras* went on to be a huge success at the box office, Daiei asked him if he could begin producing two Gamera movies per year! He, of course, balked at the idea since one a year was difficult enough to make, but it insured that Gamera would continue as long as Daiei kept producing movies...

Chapter Notes

[1] Japanese Wikipedia page for *Gamera vs. Viras*.
[2] http://www.davmil.org/www.kaijuconversations.com/yuasa.htm
[3] This in particular irked Kojiro Hongo who had to run around in "short shorts" in what is noticeably his last starring role in a Gamera movie.
[4] Japanese Wikipedia page for *Gamera vs. Viras*.

20.
THE DIRTY DOZEN: THE ORIGINAL
DESTROY ALL MONSTERS

Thanks to the internet, it is widely believed now that *Destroy All Monsters* was created as the grand finale to the Godzilla series. However, the first draft of the script was turned in on November 22, 1967, before *Son of Godzilla* had even been released in December of that year! Furthermore, several sources attest that *Attack of the Marching Monsters* (the Japanese title of *Destroy All Monsters*) was announced alongside of *Son of Godzilla*, possibly as a competing project.[1] Toho's inspiration for their grand monster opus was probably the Monster Boom of 1967 in which Shochiku, Nikkatsu, Daiei and even Keuk-Dong Entertainment (with Toei's help) in South Korea produced giant monster movies and Toho felt they needed to up the ante to prove that they were still masters of the genre.[2]

On the other hand, many believe Tomoyuki Tanaka planned to end the series due to rising production costs and the advent of television drawing potential ticket buyers away from theaters. In the book *Godzilla Days*, Sadamasa Arikawa is quoted as saying, "They were going to end the Godzilla series then. Producer Tanaka figured that all the ideas had just run out."[3] However, the commentary track by assistant director Seiji Tani for *Destroy All Monsters*' Japanese DVD release denies that the film was ever meant to be the final Godzilla movie at the time.

Kaiju Chushingura [4] —the earliest version of what would eventually become *Destroy All Monsters*—was titled after the famed Japanese tale of 47 Ronin (the Kilaak aliens are named after that story's villains, the Kirakozukenosuke). Supposedly in this version, every monster suit in Toho's arsenal was to be included, even King Kong, Sanda, and Gaira.[5] In fact, in an interview with David Milner, Ishiro Honda even said, "The original idea was to show all of the monsters."[6] Of course, this statement is open to interpretation as to what "all of the monsters" really means.[7] In any case, this idea came directly from the Toho brass.

The first draft script, *Total Monster Attack Directive*, by Kaoru Mabuchi,[8] submitted on November 22, 1967, included a confirmed roster of Godzilla, King Ghidorah, Rodan, Varan,

Mothra (larva), Manda, Baragon, Kumonga, Ebirah, and Magma. Everything presumably plays out just as in the finished film except that Magma and Baragon guard the Kilaak base and Baragon actually attacks Paris.[9] Also in this version, Varan and Rodan work in tandem to attack King Ghidorah from the air during the final battle (presumably because these are the only two "good" monsters with the ability to fly). Ebirah would have most likely stuck to the water and it's presumable the scene of Godzilla destroying an ocean liner at sea in the finished film was meant for Ebirah. However, a Japanese website dedicated to tokusatsu scripts, cyberkids1954.com, seems to imply that Ebirah would have made it onto land for the final battle. The author of the website writes, "Apart from the smaller number of monsters, it is a very well-written script."[10]

How the second draft differed is unknown, but the monster roster of the third draft, submitted on January 9, 1968, is known to be Godzilla, Rodan, Mothra (larva), King Ghidorah, Baragon, Varan, Manda, Kumonga, and new additions Minilla and Anguirus. By this point, Ebirah and Magma were discarded... or were they?[11] There is a curiously written scene for the beginning of the end battle that says Godzilla leads a charge flanked by Rodan, Anguirus, and Mothra and behind them are Baragon and Manda, plus more monsters making for exactly a dozen earth monsters (who are never named in this script) against King Ghidorah![12]

The listed monsters only number six, and if one adds in Varan, Minilla, and Kumonga, that ups the number to nine. Naturally, one can speculate Gorosaurus was among the unnamed monsters, but he was a very last minute addition. As this script was post-1967, King Kong was no longer a candidate for consideration and was probably dropped by this time. The Gargantuas, or possibly just Sanda, were a possibility. Frankenstein, being free of copyright unlike King Kong, was another possibility, but still very unlikely. Second-rate kaiju like Kamacuras, the Mondo Island Sea Serpent, the Giant Condor, and the Giant Octopus were also possibly candidates, but probably never seriously considered due to the required wireworks. As it was, Kumonga and King Ghidorah alone were nightmares for the wireworks crews, so the Toho special effects men likely shot down any more heavily wire-operated monsters. [13] The likeliest candidate for one of the other mystery monsters was still giant walrus Magma; cyberkids1954.com features an excerpt from the third draft script that mentions the beast:

Scene#93 Security Headquarters/Liaison Conference
(between Director Sugiyama and Moonlight SY 3 Captain Katsuo Yamabe)
Director Sugiyama: At Izu all the hot springs are dried out, the same situation as in monster land.
Katsuo Yamabe: Is it also proof that it is Kilaak?
Director Sugiyama: I am checking the underground monsters at Amagi.
Katsuo Yamabe: Magma...

In the finished film, this line was naturally changed to Baragon and it's possible the mention of Magma (who guarded the base in one earlier version) was just a mistake. As mentioned earlier, Baragon was initially supposed to attack Paris but his ears [14] proved too difficult to manage (actually, the ears may have been in danger of being damaged) and the part was taken over by Gorosaurus towards the end of production. [15] However, there curiously do exist storyboards of Gorosaurus emerging from beneath the Arc de Triumph! Since his 1965 debut in *Frankenstein vs. Baragon*, the Baragon suit had been utilized by Tsuburaya Productions and converted into new monsters. They did this by removing Baragon's head and placing new heads on the body creating Pagos for *Ultra Q* and Neronga, Gabora, and Magular for *Ultraman*. After that, the suit was kept at Tsuburaya Studios until Toho requested it back for *Destroy All Monsters*. As to why Toho even bothered to repair the suit, chances are it was because Baragon was a very popular kaiju and toy sales of the beast were high.[16] A new head was created just so the monster could have a cameo, but the body of the suit couldn't be repaired because, supposedly, too much money had already been spent repairing King Ghidorah and Kumonga, in addition to creating new Godzilla and Anguirus suits (the only new costumes constructed for the film). Haruo Nakajima crawled into the Baragon suit for scenes on Monsterland that play in a Monsterland base monitor as well as the shot in the final moments.[17] As Baragon is still blamed for the attack in the finished film, one can assume that despite the storyboards, Gorosaurus's attack on Paris was a last minute change. Perhaps the storyboards were even drawn on set or maybe the writers and the artists were in disagreement over who should attack Paris.

Other mysteries concerning *Destroy All Monsters* include why recent creations Minilla and Gorosaurus, whose suits were in relatively usable condition, weren't included in the first draft (while not so noticeable in the film itself, in behind-the-scenes stills, Minilla's chest can be seen cracking apart).[18] Equally curious is why Sanda was axed, though supposedly, the third draft script featured Sanda hanging around Monsterland (likely glimpsed in a monitor early on), but he didn't partake in any of the action afterwards. Anguirus' inclusion is slightly more surprising since, at least in part, this film revolved around using existing monster suits. Naturally, the 1955 suit had now deteriorated so a new suit had to be constructed. The new suit would pay off for the studio in the 1970s when the dino-monster replaced Rodan as Godzilla's main battle ally.

The suit actors themselves had some rather interesting suggestions regarding the film. Notably, Haruo Nakajima wanted to bring back Godzilla's infamous "jumping shie" from *Invasion of Astro-Monster* into the ending of the film! Stills exist of Godzilla in said pose on the Mt. Fuji set. Ishiro Honda, who hated it the first time around, saw to it the shie didn't make it into the movie (since Eiji Tsuburaya wasn't there to overrule him this time). Likewise, Sadamasa Arikawa commented that each of the monster suit actors wanted a chance to show their monster being "cool" or "badass" so as "not to become unpopular in the sequel!"[19]

The film's manga adaptation could shed some light on early script concepts as well. At the beginning, Minilla can be seen holding up a giant shark he has caught. Manda's attack of London is shown and considering it is mentioned in the final film's newscast, chances are high the London sequence was meant to be filmed as well. Other notable differences include the Fire Dragon resembling an actual dragon. And naturally, Baragon destroys Paris. Most exciting of all, Manda wraps himself around King Ghidorah's wing during the final battle and Baragon and Varan also participate.

Another concept dropped to the wayside in one of the later scripts was that of lunar colonies and interbreeding the monsters—both Ishiro Honda's ideas. What these creations would have looked like was anyone's guess. Specifically, Honda said, "We then started thinking about undersea farming... You see, we imagined that undersea farming would be required to feed all of the monsters. I very much wanted to explore that idea but because of financial constraints, I was not allowed to do so. Only the idea of an island of monsters survived."[20] Another, even more in-depth quotation from Honda exists telling of his original hopes for *Destroy All Monsters*:

"[Kimura] and I... agreed it would be crazy to make each of the monsters just somehow appear. Eventually, we came up with an island on which all of the monsters had been collected for scientific study. We imagined that undersea farming would be required to feed all of the monsters... What would happen if that got developed on a super scale? I thought about the idea of a marine ranch... Scientifically, it would be what we now call aquaculture... From there, we started to develop the storyline. Initially, I had a lot more underwater scenes in the script. I was going to use special effects and set filming to depict them. But because of... financial as well as time constraints, what you ultimately see is what we were able to do, the bare minimum. In a way, those things [that I could not do] were the scenes I wanted to film the most. Back then, the notion of aquaculture and biotechnology was already there, and we knew that things were going in that direction in the future."[21]

In later years shortly before his death, Honda would reflect that the film had the same premise as *Jurassic Park* (the book, of course, as the movie didn't come out until after he'd died) and this included an unused idea of raising the new crossbred monsters on the island. These crossbred monsters wouldn't be due to forced mating of the monsters, but biotechnology!

As fun as it would have been to see some of the discarded monsters and ideas, overall fans should be thankful for the ambitious film they got. Upon watching *Destroy All Monsters*, with its bright colors and fast-paced action, it almost seems more like a Jun Fukuda film rather than an Ishiro Honda picture. Like *Ebirah, Horror of the Deep*, *Destroy All Monsters* goes from action scene to action scene rather breathlessly. As such, it is somewhat hard to connect to the film's main characters, who lack the charm of those that appear in *Invasion of Astro-Monster*. *Destroy All Monsters'* story more or less expands upon the former title's premise—aliens controlling the earth monsters and King Ghidorah—but with less interesting human characters. However, the film's main purpose was to showcase all of the Toho monsters in one grand extravaganza, which it certainly does. If it had been the final Godzilla movie as intended, it at least presents a happy ending where Godzilla and his chums live out the rest of their days in peace—presumably...[22]

Chapter Notes

[1] This is implied on the back cover of Kodansha's Godzilla All Movies DVD Collector's Box Vol. 15 *Son of Godzilla*. Notably, as is customary in Japanese, the titles are in separate brackets which state [*Son of Godzilla*] [*Attack of the Marching Monsters*] after mention of [*ESPY*] and [*The Flying Battleship*], both of which were put on hold.
[2] A 1966 Sonorama book called *Giant Monster Battle: 30 Monsters Rampage* toyed with the idea of a group of earth monsters (including obscure kaiju like Magma alongside Godzilla) battling space monsters including King Ghidorah, Dogora, and Mogera. So the seeds for this idea had been gestating for some time in someone's mind.
[3] Ryfle, *Japan's Favorite Mon-Star*, pp. 145-146.
[4] "The Treasury of Loyal Monster Retainers", a title which would hold little meaning to anyone outside Japan.
[5] Toho's rights to Kong would have expired January 1, 1968. Perhaps they felt that from a legal standpoint, if they began filming before that date Kong could be included. Or conversely, as stated earlier, some sources imply Toho had competing Godzilla projects in 1967 comprising of *Son of Godzilla* and *Attack of the Marching Monsters*. Perhaps Kong was considered only if this film was to be released in December of 1967? Fanaticized artwork of King Kong vs. King Ghidorah has appeared in at least one Sonorama book, and had he been included in the film this fantastic battle could have finally taken place. It would have also been interesting to see Kong team up with his old enemy Godzilla. Coincidentally, a European release of *Destroy All Monsters* renamed the film *The Heirs of King Kong* and features a giant ape on the poster.
[6] www.davmil.org/www.kaijuconversations.com/honda.htm
[7] Is an H-Man a monster, for instance? Is the Human Vapor a monster? Or *Matango's* mushroom people?
[8] Due to the adaptation of *Frankenstein vs. Godzilla* into *Frankenstein vs. Baragon*, this makes *Destroy All Monsters* Mabuchi's first Godzilla script.
[9] According to Wikizilla's translation of *Toho Special Effects Movie Complete Works*, Baragon was supposed to guard the base with Magma. Furthermore, according to Wikizilla's translation, Magma was also the one who was supposed to attack Paris and not Baragon, which is odd.
[10] www.cyberkids1954.com/toho_script.html
[11] Considering Ebirah had his claws ripped off in *Ebirah, Horror of the Deep* (1966) this was probably a wise decision for reasons of continuity, although Toho's publicity materials indicate that Ebirah can regenerate his lost limbs, which he would of course have again by *All Monsters Attack*. The same can be said of Magma who appears in *Gorath* (1962, though set in 1979/80) because the moon is destroyed in that film. In *Destroy All Monsters* (set in 1999), the moon plays a very prominent role. On the note of no moons, the moon is never seen throughout *The War in Space* (1977, set in 1988) leading some fans to speculate that it is a sequel to *Gorath*.
[12] Some interpret this as a dozen more monsters behind Baragon but this is too unlikely.
[13] Look carefully when Kumonga's onscreen and you'll see that very few shots feature all of the spider's legs moving at once, as they had in *Son of Godzilla*.

[14] Ironically there exists concept art from *Frankenstein vs. Baragon* showing Baragon's ears functioning as shields for his eyes when he travels underground.
[15] *All Toho Monster Large Picture Book* confirms that the ears were to blame on page 146.
[16] Baragon's head doesn't look new at all. It looks like a deteriorated version of the old '65 head. Also, the Baragon suit does not look bad enough to not be used. It's likely that Tsuburaya just didn't get the suit back to Toho in time for them to use it properly.
[17] The scene of Baragon arriving to the Mt. Fuji battlefield with Varan and Manda doesn't use a suit, but a smaller model, just like with the other two monsters.
[18] In Minilla's case it's entirely plausible that Ishiro Honda didn't want him in the film. Honda was at one time attached to *Son of Godzilla* and then bowed out—possibly due to the comical nature of Minilla and Godzilla. Another possibility is that Mabuchi's initial treatment was actually in consideration as a competing project to *Son of Godzilla*.
[19] Arikawa's talk of sequels is ironic as he is the one quoted as saying Toho planned to end the Godzilla series.
[20] www.davmil.org/www.kaijuconversations.com/honda.htm
[21] Ryfle and Godziszewski, *Ishiro Honda*, pp.245.
[22] Fans often argue whether the 1970s-era Godzilla films are prequels or sequels to *Destroy All Monsters*. Considering *Godzilla vs. Megalon* is set in the year 197X (later retconned to 1973 by Toho because of *Zone Fighter*), and elements from *Megalon* harken back to *Godzilla vs. Gigan*, which itself has an element that harkens back to *Godzilla vs. Hedorah* (which itself was meant to reflect Japan's problem with pollution at its time of release), that would make the 1999-set *Destroy All Monsters* still the last Showa Godzilla adventure. *Godzilla vs. Megalon* also definitely states that Monster Island, found in the South Pacific, is not the same location as Monsterland, found in the Ogasawara Island chain near Japan.

 **PROFILE: TAKESHI KIMURA/KAORU MABUCHI**
If Shinichi Sekizawa was king of the Godzilla scripts, Takeshi Kimura (later Kaoru Mabuchi) was unquestionably the king of Toho's sci-fi non-Godzilla scripts. Ishiro Honda summed up the differences between Kimura and Sekizawa best when he said, "Their styles were very different. If the story were very positive, or even childish, it would go to Mr. Sekizawa. If it were negative, or involved politics, it would go to Mr. Kimura. I really can't compare the two styles because they're so different." [www.davmil.org/www.kaiju-conversations.com/honda.htm] Kimura was born February 4, 1911, in Osaka Prefecture. Kimura was somewhat notorious for dropping out of Kansai University and then joining the Japanese Communist Party in 1930. He even spent 10 years in prison and also served as the chairman of the Saga Prefecture of Japan Communist Party. Yoshimitsu Banno spoke of his communist ties to Vantage Point Interviews, stating, "[Kimura] was a communist for quite a while. So during school and everything else, they'd have the songs that they sing, and they got very emotional. During those times, Mr. Tanaka would have him run errands; he'd be more of a gofer than anything else because he was hard to deal with. When he turned 40 years old, he quit communism, and they brought him to Tokyo, and he was a lot easier to work with. That's when they started to give more work to him." [vantagepointinterviews.com/2017/05/09/making-godzilla-fly-an-interview-with-godzilla-director-yoshimitsu-banno/] After Kimura withdrew from the communist party in 1950 and began studying with Toshio Yasumi, future writer of *The Three Treasures* (1959) and *The Last War* (1961)—which both writers worked on. Kimura's first filmed script was *Red Line Base* (1953). The next year he wrote one of Ishiro Honda's most famous pre-*Godzilla* films, *Farewell, Rabaul* (1954). Kimura made his big break when he collaborated with Takeo Murata on *Rodan* (1956) which was a huge hit. After this, but before the arrival of Shinichi Sekizawa, Kimura would be assigned to nearly all of Toho's effects films. Kimura's best work came from this period, notably his downbeat scripts for *The Last War* (1961), *Gorath* (1962), and *Matango* (1963), the latter of which Kimura considered to be his absolute favorite. Kimura's last significant genre film under his real name was *The Great Thief* (1963; *The Lost World of Sinbad* in the U.S.). In 1965, he apparently became ashamed of his script for *Frankenstein vs. Baragon* and started going under the name Kaoru Mabuchi. He felt this provided him more anonymity as Kaoru could be a male or female name. Future Toho producer Fumio Tanaka remembers meeting Kimura around this time, "I first met Mr. Kimura while I was working as an assistant producer. He was writing the screenplay for a film entitled *The Great Pirate* at the time. I think Tomoyuki Tanaka wanted Toshiro Mifune to play the pirate. When Mr. Tanaka read the script, he found it a little odd because there was no sea battle in it. That's why *The Great Pirate* wasn't made."

[www.davmil.org/www.kaiju-conversations.com/tanak.htm] (this is either *The Great Thief* or a heretofore unknown cancelled production, though the former is more likely and Fumio Tanaka may just be confused). Of Kimura, Fumio Tanaka also remarked, "Mr. Kimura liked me. I don't know why he did. One day, Mr. Kimura asked me to ask his daughter out on a date. I don't know if he wanted me to marry her or not." [Ibid.] In 1964, Mabuchi was finally tasked with writing his first Godzilla film for Ishiro Honda…which didn't end up being his first G-film after all since it was completed as *Frankenstein vs. Baragon*. Instead, *Destroy All Monsters* would end up being his first completed Godzilla script. Notably, in *Destroy All Monsters* and the previous year's *King Kong Escapes*, the stories are less downbeat and almost seem like Shinichi Sekizawa scripts. In 1971, Mabuchi was paired with newcomer Yoshimitsu Banno to pen *Godzilla vs. Hedoron* (the original title). Though one would think the two were a match made in heaven (as Banno wanted a gloomy film) this was not the case. Banno felt Mabuchi didn't put much effort into the script and even revealed, "I said to [Mabuchi], 'You're not really getting sincere about this. You're not working hard to make this thing work.' Gradually, as we worked together, and as I rewrote it for him, Mr. [Mabuchi] gradually got onboard and started writing better things." [vantagepointinterviews.com/2017/05/09/making-godzilla-fly-an-interview-with-godzilla-director-yoshimitsu-banno/] At another point, Mabuchi became angered when Banno added in a scene without consulting him, shouting, "If you write by yourself, I will go home!" As it turned out, this would be Mabuchi's last produced script and according to Banno, the script of the final *Godzilla vs. Hedorah* (1971) was written by himself, not Mabuchi. After the film was released, Tomoyuki Tanaka was more disappointed in Banno than he was Mabuchi and asked him to write a storyline based around the return of King Ghidorah, *Godzilla vs. the Space Monsters*. However, Tanaka also asked Shinichi Sekizawa to write a competing script and went with Sekizawa's instead, which became the basis of *Godzilla vs. Gigan* (1972). On May 3, 1987, Toshio Yasumi received a strange phone call from a man struggling to breathe. As it turned out, it was Kimura, who died from a throat obstruction at the age of 76 in his Tokyo apartment, which he had reportedly not left for months. Before he died, Kimura/Mabuchi apparently was suffering from a severe depression brought about by poor life choices. After dropping out of film following his loss to Sekizawa in 1972, Kimura became estranged from his wife and daughter. He had never been socially friendly with Ishiro Honda or anyone else for that matter and simply vanished until he was found dead just days before his 77th birthday. In an interview, Honda felt Kimura's isolation was—intentionally or not—of his own making. The director regretfully said, "Kimura did it to himself."

Selected Filmography
Red Line Base (1953) (writer)
Farewell, Rabaul (1954) (writer)
Rodan (1956) (writer)
The Mysterians (1957) (writer)
The H-Man (1958) (writer)
The Human Vapor (1960) (writer)
The Last War (1961) (writer)
Gorath (1962) (writer)
Matango (1963) (writer)
The Great Thief/The Lost World of Sinbad (1963) (writer)
Frankenstein vs. Godzilla (1964) (writer) [unproduced; developed into *Frankenstein vs. Baragon*]
Frankenstein vs. Baragon (1965) (writer)
The War of the Gargantuas (1966) (writer)
King Kong Escapes (1967) (writer)
Destroy All Monsters (1968) (writer)
Godzilla vs. Hedorah (1971) (writer)
Godzilla vs. the Space Monsters (1971) (writer) [unproduced]

21.
TALES FROM
LATITUDE ZERO

In 1967, Toho was struggling to get two ambitious projects off the ground. One was an adaptation of Sakyo Komatsu's manga *ESPY* and the other was *The Flying Battleship*—a spiritual sequel of sorts to *Atragon*. That same year, Toho executive Masami Fujimoto went to America where he met with Don Sharpe,[1] head of Ambassador Productions, about doing a series of co-produced special effects films. One of Sharpe's projects was a film adaptation of Ted Sherdeman's NBC radio serial *Latitude Zero*, which Sherdeman had been trying to get adapted into film for the past several years.[2] Considering the story revolved around fantastic submarines,[3] Toho decided to strike *The Flying Battleship* and produce *Latitude Zero* with Sharpe instead. The deal to split the budget on the $1 million epic was agreed upon between the two studios in June of 1968.

Ted Sherdeman's well-received radio serial was broadcast in 1941 by NBC. The first episode of *Latitude Zero* concerned three crew members of the old vessel "Hope," who discover a futuristic submarine after surviving a storm in the Bering Sea near the Arctic Circle. As in the film, the submarine (here called the Omega) was launched in 1805 and Captain Mackenzie is incredibly old despite his appearance. The plots of the other *Latitude Zero* episodes (there were 17 total) have been lost to the sands of time, though the first episode has been preserved somewhere. John Dunning, in his book *On the Air: The Encyclopedia of Old-Time Radio*, wrote "*Latitude Zero* was the first serious attempt to break the science fiction story out of the category of juvenile entertainment. It was remarkable in many ways, deserving of a better run than its one partial season. Almost everything known about the show comes from one surviving disc, the premiere episode."[4]

Author Vincent Terrace describes the first episode and the series premise very well in his book *Radio Programs, 1924–1984: A Catalog of More Than 1800 Shows*:

"While fishing off the coast of Alaska, the men of a boat called the Hope discover a submarine embedded on the beach of a remote island. The vessel has a smooth shell (no rivets or plates), the insignia of a horseshoe and appears to be over 250 feet long. After determining that the sub is not American, Japanese, or Russian, they hear an S.O.S. tapping coming from inside the sub. Brock Spencer, captain of the Hope, returns the code, asking for a way into the sub. A message is returned that instructs Brock to a secret hatchway under a six-inch gun. Brock and his shipmates Tibbs Canard and Bert Collins enter the sub to discover Capt. Craig MacKenzie and his bodyguard Simba, a six-foot, five-inch black man with incredible strength. They also learn that MacKenzie is an alien from a world beneath the sea called Latitude Zero and that the submarine, called the Omega (the horseshoe is its Greek symbol), was built in 1805. MacKenzie and Simba are capable of piloting the sub alone. They were transporting prisoners when an escape attempt was made that cost the prisoners their lives and wounded both Simba and MacKenzie. The sub beached itself; the fresh air let in by Brock and his men revived them. Brock, Tibbs, and Bert soon find their lives changed when MacKenzie asks for their help in returning to Latitude Zero. Serialized stories relate their adventures as they battle the enemies of the undersea world (in particular, the evil Lucretia)."[5]

This synopsis features only two characters from the film, Captain MacKenzie and Lucretia. Obviously, Simba—further described by John Dunning as "an enormous black man who cannot be harmed by gunshots"—is a version of the muscular Japanese Kubo in the film. MacKenzie was voiced by Lou Merrill, with Bruce Payne voicing Captain Brock Spencer, Jack Zoller as Tibbs Canard, Ed Max as Bert Wheeler, Charlie Lung as Simba, and Anne Stone as the villainous Lucretia.

The program's opening went as follows:

Voice: Longitude 180 degrees, 12 minutes.
Voice: Latitude Zero.
Voice: All hands at stations. Stand by for dive.
Announcer: The National Broadcasting Company presents—
Voice: Lat-i-tude Zerrrooooo.
Announcer: Latitude Zero. Adventure fans, tonight begins the first episode of the most exciting and fabulous adventure story you've ever heard, Latitude Zero, especially written for radio by Ted Sherdeman. A story of five men against the world;

heroic men with ideals and courage and strength to fight for them in Latitude Zero.

It closed with this announcement:

Announcer: Next week, same day, same station, don't miss the thrilling revelations of the mysterious Capt. MacKenzie, builder of the Omega, the strange submarine from the unknown port. You'll find thrills, action and adventure on the next installment of—
Voice: Lat-i-tude Zerrrooooo.
Announcer: Latitude Zero, especially written for radio by Ted Sherdeman, originates in Hollywood's Radio City. This is the National Broadcasting Company.

Time Magazine even did an article on the serial on June 23, 1941, writing,

"For the past fortnight, U.S. listeners coast-to-coast have been diverted by a killer-diller called *Latitude Zero* (8 p.m. E.D.S.T.), which makes its way out of NBC's Hollywood studios accompanied by the world's most bizarre barrage of sound effects. The script is written to match. The program dwells on the doings of one Captain Craig MacKenzie. Anxious to save civilization from its doom, the Captain operates an insular Shangri-La in the South Pacific. The Captain populates his island with all kinds of high-toned people, whom he transports to his hideaway at 'Latitude Zero' (i.e., somewhere on the Equator) in a submarine."

John Dunning also sang the serial's praises stating, "The imagery was extraordinary for a sustained adventure series at that time. There was a huge wind effect, emphasizing the puniness of their boat's engine."[6]

According to *Toho Special Effects Movie Complete Works*, the first draft script was quite different from the shooting script. It was said to be closer to the first episode, and also included giant carnivorous plants that ate the giant rats that appear in the film. The romance between Dr. Anne Barton and Dr. Jules Mason was also emphasized more. Pre production art also shows a long-snouted reptilian giant monster with tusks attacking MacKenzie at what is presumably a snowy version of Blood Rock. Also, Malik is drawn with an eye patch.[7] The submarine's name was changed from the Omega to the

 **MIGHTY JACK**

THE TSUBURAYA PRODUCTIONS TV SERIES *MIGHTY JACK* WAS BASED UPON AN UNFILMED SCREENPLAY, *THE FLYING BATTLESHIP*, WRITTEN BY SHINICHI SEKIZAWA WITH CONCEPTS BY SHIGERU KOMATSUZAKI. NOT WANTING TO LOSE THE PROJECT ENTIRELY, EIJI TSUBURAYA TRANSPLANTED THE CONCEPT OVER TO TSUBURAYA PRODUCTIONS FOR TELEVISION. SHINICHI SEKIZAWA WROTE SCRIPTS FOR THIS SERIES, WHICH EVOLVED INTO *MIGHTY JACK*. FUNDAMENTALLY, IT IS THE SAME AS *THE FLYING BATTLESHIP*, WITH A GROUP OF SPIES THAT BATTLE AN ORGANIZATION CALLED Q BENT ON GLOBAL CONQUEST. THEY DIDN'T BATTLE ALIENS AND MONSTERS AS WAS THE CASE IN NEARLY EVERY OTHER TOKUSATSU TV SERIES ON THE AIRWAVES AT THE TIME. THE SERIES STARTED AIRING ON APRIL 6, 1968, ON FUJI TV. THE FIRST 13 EPISODES WERE SERIOUS AND HAD AN HOUR RUNNING TIME BUT RECEIVED POOR RATINGS. THIS CAUSED FUJI TV TO REQUEST AN OVERHAUL OF THE CONCEPT, AND THE SECOND HALF OF THE SERIES FEATURED MONSTERS AND RAN ONLY 30 MINUTES. THIS VERSION OF THE SERIES LASTED 26 EPISODES, HAD BETTER RATINGS, AND RAN UNTIL DECEMBER 28, 1968.

Alpha because "Omega" was trademarked by the watch company! Blood Rock was called Zakum and Lucretia was able to turn into a vampire bat to attack Captain MacKenzie. The Black Shark was simply the Shark in the original, and in early drafts, the captain was male until the casting of actress Hikaru Kiroki.

The initial script was by Ted Sherdeman himself and then handed over to Shinichi Sekizawa when Toho agreed to co-produce the film. In the making-of featurette on the *Latitude Zero* DVD, Teruyoshi Nakano says that Sherdeman's script "just dragged on for such a long time. Sekizawa said it was all over the place... He couldn't believe what he was reading." There was constant friction between the American camp and the Japanese camp, especially between producer Don Sharpe and writer Warren Lewis regarding Toho. While Sherdeman was considered agreeable by the Toho staff, Lewis in particular grated on their nerves. Steve Ryfle and Ed Godziszewski humorously point out in their Ishiro Honda biography that one draft of Sekizawa's script contained a henchman for Malik named Warren. The character was caveman-like and was eventually dropped into a boiling vat of acid.

During the start of production, there were plans to film the movie in 70mm Panavision but the equipment wasn't available to Toho, so the format was switched back to Cinemascope. Dr. Okada was originally played by the esteemed Takamaru Sasaki (*Throne of Blood*, *The Sword of Doom*) but he became ill and was replaced by Tetsu Nakamura, necessitating Honda reshoot all scenes involving the character. To make matters worse, three weeks into filming, Sharpe announced he was bankrupt and that Toho would have to foot the entirety of the very expensive bill. Sharpe left the project though Lewis was allowed to stay as a creative consultant. Production was shut down for four days in November 1968 and then resumed. When this happened, Toho had to cut the budget down by $200,000 and it would be the special effects scenes that suffered the worst. In particular, this is the reason that Kroiga the griffin looks like a resident of the Island of Misfit Toys.[8]

During shooting, there were two major points of contention; the first involved the bath of immunity. At the time, the Motion Picture production code had just been lifted in America and Lewis wanted to take advantage by showing Lynda Haynes' breasts as she entered the bath. Ishiro Honda refused to film such a shot and this included the idea of an alternate version just for the American release. Instead, Honda showed Haynes in silhouette to make her appear naked, though she wasn't really. Haynes remembered this topical matter like so: "They wanted me to be nude when getting out of a bath scene... I was told, 'Well, in Japan, that's no big deal.' But I refused to do that, and they even put some kind of skin-colored foam rubber over my breasts to get me to do the scene – must have been a long shot."[9]

During the finale, MacKenzie was supposed to use Lucretia as a shield, but Lewis objected, saying it was unheroic. Instead, they went back to the way Sherdeman had originally written it. This iteration appears in the finished film with Malik accidentally stabbing Lucretia when MacKenzie pushes her away. The climactic battle between the Alpha and the Black Shark owes some of its maneuvers to Shinichi Sekizawa's cancelled script *The Flying Battleship*. During that story's climactic battle, the Super Noah emits magnetic silver flakes that attach themselves to the NOO warship, which then crashes into a wall just as the Black Shark does to the Alpha in *Latitude Zero*. Though Ted Sherdeman wrote the *Latitude Zero* script, Sekizawa also contributed ideas of his own and it's too coincidental that Sekizawa didn't incorporate that idea from *The Flying Battleship* into *Latitude Zero*.

The original epilogue went through several revisions. One would have seen reporter Perry Lawton return to the surface only to learn that fifty years had passed since he had traveled to Latitude Zero, making it the year 2020 (there would have been a scene where Captain MacKenzie explained, "One day in Latitude Zero is equivalent to 50 years on earth"). The next ending changed it to only five days passing for every day on the surface. In this ending, Lawton meets MacKenzie's grandson who tells him Craig MacKenzie went missing fifty years ago. There was yet another alternate ending planned, but only for the American version. It would have had Lawton showing slides of his adventure in Latitude Zero, which naturally turn out to be blank. In the back of the room, he spots a man who looks just like Captain MacKenzie. After the reporters leave, MacKenzie walks up to the projector and the slides miraculously show the undersea city of Latitude Zero. This less ambiguous unfilmed ending would have confirmed that Glenn MacKenzie is indeed the same Craig MacKenzie from Latitude Zero manipulating the situation. However, the script notes for the filmed ending explicitly state that Glenn is a descendant of Craig MacKenzie, though this goes unspoken in the film.

It's hard to determine just how *Latitude Zero* performed overall. Some sources claim that it had decent grosses for a Japanese film, but the huge budget kept it from being considered a success. Other sources say that it was not received well at all in Japan. Whatever the case, had the production not unraveled on Don Sharpe's end, this would have been the first of several co-productions between Ambassador Productions and Toho. It's presumable these could have included sequels to *Latitude Zero*.

Chapter Notes

[1] Not to be confused with Don Sharp, the English director of such British horror classics as *Rasputin the Mad Monk* and *The Face of Fu Manchu*.
[2] Before that, Sharpe and Sherdeman had also tried to make a *Latitude Zero* TV series in the late 1950's.
[3] Some rumors indicate Toho considered *Latitude Zero* to be an *Undersea Battleship/Atragon* sequel of sorts.
[4] Dunning, *On the Air: The Encyclopedia of Old-Time Radio*, pp.389.
[5] Terrace, *Radio Programs, 1924-1984: A Catalog of More Than 1800 Shows*, pp.193.
[6] Ibid.
[7] Inspired, perhaps by Adolfo Celi in *Thunderball*?
[8] Supposedly, a griffin creature appeared on an episode of the radio show.
[9] "Lovely Lady from Latitude Zero." *G-Fan* #82 (Winter 2008), pp.38-39.

22.
THE ANIMATED ORIGINS OF
ALL MONSTERS ATTACK

Big changes were on hand for Godzilla at Toho in 1969 as Tomoyuki Tanaka decided for the first time to aim the franchise solely at children. He intended to do this even before the production of *All Monsters Attack*—unquestionably the single most maligned entry in the Godzilla series among the fandom. The film's storyline is a result of the times and some of the film's pre-production is surprising.

If *Destroy All Monsters* was supposed to be the last Godzilla movie, why was *All Monsters Attack* produced? Despite its stellar reputation in fan circles, *Destroy All Monsters* was not as big a hit as Toho had expected with only about 100,000 admissions over *Son of Godzilla*. So why produce another movie? The answer is that Toho had no such plans; they were going to create a TV series instead.

In 1969, Toho announced 30 projects for production. A Godzilla movie was not among them. Toho's big effects opus would be the ill-fated *Latitude Zero*. Instead, while preparing *Latitude Zero*, Toho was getting ready to create the first ever animated Godzilla. *Toho SPFX Movies Complete Works*—a book which contains information about this project—makes no mention of Henry G. Saperstein or UPA, but identifies Toho's producing partner as the Los Angeles-based Filmation, producer of animated programs like *The Archie Show* (1968).[1] Toho and Filmation signed an agreement in April of 1968—bad timing considering the Japanese studio would also agree to co-produce *Latitude Zero* with Ambassador Productions later that June.

The cartoons would be designed for 30-minute time slots and would air both in America and Japan throughout 1969 and 1970. This was an ingenious idea and Toho was probably inspired by the success of the animated *The King Kong Show*. And just as the aforementioned animated series resulted in *King Kong Escapes*, there was even talk of co-producing a live-action tie-in movie with the series between Toho and Filmation. In his semi-autobiographical work, Lou Scheimer wrote, "We also made a deal with Toho to produce a live-action Godzilla movie and try to sell

139

an animated series for the 1969-1970 season. That never happened, though I don't remember why."[2] The project was formally announced in the June 17, 1968 issue of *Television Age* which wrote:

Taming Godzilla
It looks like *Godzilla* is going the way of *King Kong*. Hero (or is it heroine?) of seven Toho horror shows (the seventh Godzilla epic is now being made in Tokyo), the enormous saurian will be transformed into a benefactor of all mankind in a cartoon series to be made as a coproduction between Filmation in Hollywood and Toho, with Filmation doing the animation.
King Kong, the Lewis Milestone classic fable, suffered a not dissimilar sea change when the great gorilla was turned into friend of the good guys by Toei as hero of a cartoon for U.S. network tv. The Godzilla cartoon will be pitched for U.S. networks' '69 season.[3]

The cartoons would also be made available in 35mm prints so Toho could edit episodes into feature-length movies for theaters—possibly for their upcoming Toho Champion Matsuri Festivals. Things seemed to be set for Godzilla to enter a potentially new and exciting medium. And then *Latitude Zero* went south.

It's unknown when exactly *Latitude Zero* killed the animation project, but most Japanese sources feel it had something to do with it. Late October 1968 is when *Latitude Zero's* American investors bailed on the project but it's possible the decision was made when Toho looked at their earnings in August of 1969. At the time, they saw they were down 21% from last year, precisely down to ¥580 million (roughly $5,293,080) compared to ¥735 million ($6,707,610) the previous year when *Destroy All Monsters* was released. A Toho business consultation meeting held on September 9th decided that another kaiju picture was the way to go for their annual New Year's Blockbuster. One way or the other, Godzilla's animation career was brought to a halt in favor of a new live-action film. Since Toho's output wasn't returning expected results, and noticing that the stock footage-laden *Gamera vs. Viras* did good business in 1968, Tomoyuki Tanaka decided to keep costs down on the next Godzilla movie by having Shinichi Sekizawa plot the film as conservatively as possible. Ishiro Honda said, "The company wanted a lot of monsters, but they told us that they had no money."[4]

 **GAMERA VS. GUIRON**

IT WAS ANOTHER YEAR AND ANOTHER SUCCESSFUL GAMERA RELEASE FOR DAIEI BUT THE FINISHED FILM DIDN'T TURN OUT AS INITIALLY PLANNED. AN ENTIRE NEW MONSTER WAS CUT FROM THE PRODUCTION! INSTEAD OF SPACE GYAOS, THE FIRST DRAFT OF *GAMERA VS. GUIRON* FEATURED A BRAND NEW MONSTER CALLED MONGA. IT WAS REPORTEDLY TO BE A BLUE-FURRED, GIANT, FLYING SQUIRREL MONSTER. HOWEVER, PRE-PRODUCTION ART FROM *THE GAMERA CHRONICLES* SHOW PRELIMINARY DESIGNS OF A REPTILIAN MONSTER NOT DISSIMILAR TO VARAN BUT WITH BULL-LIKE HORNS ATOP ITS HEAD AND A MACE-LIKE SPIKED TAIL. WHEN A NEW MONSTER WAS DEEMED TOO PRICEY FOR THE BUDGET, MONGA WAS AXED AND THE OLD GYAOS COSTUME WAS DUSTED OFF AND PAINTED SILVER TO BECOME SPACE GYAOS. AIP EXERTED EVEN MORE INFLUENCE OVER THIS FILM'S STORYLINE, INSISTING IT HAVE MORE OF A SPACE-BASED FEEL THAN LAST TIME. IN OTHER WORDS, THEY REQUESTED THE OUTER SPACE ASPECT BE MORE THAN JUST INVADING ALIENS. THE IDEA TO SET THE WHOLE FILM ON ANOTHER PLANET WAS BOLD FROM BOTH A CREATIVE STANDPOINT AND A BUDGETARY ONE. THE MEXICO CITY OLYMPICS WERE WHAT INSPIRED GAMERA'S FAR OUT BATTLE MANEUVERS (THE TRAILER FOR THE FILM PROCLAIMS "SPACE IS THE ARENA FOR THE MONSTER OLYMPICS!") AND GAMERA DEFLECTING GUIRON'S NINJA STARS WAS A NOD TO DAIEI'S FAMED ZATOICHI SERIES. AS FOR GUIRON, THE MONSTER WAS DESIGNED AFTER SOMETHING CHILDREN SHOULDN'T PLAY WITH: KNIVES. THE MONSTER'S NAME WAS MEANT TO BE GUILLON ACCORDING TO YUASA AS THE NAME WAS DERIVED FROM "GUILLOTINE." AS IT TURNED OUT, GUIRON/GUILLON WAS ORIGINALLY TO BE A BIPEDAL MONSTER, BUT THE SUIT'S KNIFE HEAD WAS SO HEAVY, HE HAD TO BE PORTRAYED AS A QUADRUPED FOR MOST OF THE FILM!

Sekizawa's ingenious (financially speaking, that is) idea was to set the film in the daydreams of a young boy, which would allow for liberal use of stock footage.[5] However, it wasn't initially as high on stock footage and there would have been more original battles. New footage was written for Kumonga, Rodan, and the giant octopus/odako (who would battle Godzilla at sea) in addition to Godzilla, Minilla, and a new monster named Gabara.[6] As either an additional enemy monster or an alternative to Gabara, the "Monster Island Insect Monster" Megalon was set to debut![7] Megalon was shelved for later, and, for the sake of the budget and limited shooting time, Godzilla's battle with the Odako[8] was cut in favor of stock footage of his battle with Ebirah from *Ebirah, Horror of the Deep* (1966). The new Kumonga footage was likewise jettisoned in favor of footage from *Son of Godzilla*. And yet, interestingly, Honda did take the time to recreate a scene from *Son of Godzilla* where Godzilla teaches Minilla to breathe fire in a less stern manner. Apparently, this was done as a way to better create a parallel between Minilla and Godzilla with Ichiro and his father. Rodan, who was meant to chase Ichiro through the jungle, was replaced with Kamacuras. It's unknown why Kamacuras was deemed easier to work with over Rodan, though perhaps the wireworks involved had something to do with it.[9] Oddly, Rodan is one of the few monsters not to receive a stock footage cameo when he easily could have been shown, though Ichiro does drop his name to Inami. According to pre-production drawings done by Yasoyuke Inoue, there were plans for scenes involving Sanda, Gaira, and Mothra! Considering these were pre-production drawings, it's reasonable that this was new footage (why draw storyboards for stock footage?). Furthermore, this same concept art was shown at G-Fest XXVI in 2019 by Ed Godziszewski and Steve Ryfle during their *Godzilla's Revenge* 50th Anniversary panel. They show an adult Mothra, the Gargantuas, the odako, and Kamacuras along with Godzilla and Minilla.

At least one scene featuring the detectives was cut and another scene featuring Ichiro's father expressing his fear of debt collectors also went unfilmed. The plot regarding the bank heist was inspired by a sensationalized heist from 1968 and the child kidnapping plot was also taken direct from headlines of the times. Honda had desired for the film to end on the shot of Ichiro's mother crying, but this was rejected in favor of a happier parting shot. Some sources say that when Honda was allowed to re-edit this film for a digest VHS release in the 80s, he ended the movie as such, on the scene of Ichiro's mother crying.[10]

Gabara's name was originally Gebara and *Toho Special Effects Movie Complete Works* says that Sekizawa named the monster after revolutionary Che Guevara![11] Other sources say the name may have come from the German word for violence (gewalt). However, the Japanese word "geba" also means violence and is probably the more likely candidate. As many fans have often heard, Gabara is indeed meant to be a mutated toad as indicated in script notes. He also had this same origin for a guest appearance on Toho's *Go! Greenman* in 1973. Furthermore, Gabara is identified as a mutated toad in the film's manga adaptation.[12] It would seem someone had ideas of Gabara not only conducting electric shocks from his hands but also shooting electric beams from his fingertips. This is evidenced not only in touched up publicity stills but the manga adaptation as well.

Instead of *All Monsters Attack*'s monster scenes, it's actually Honda's scenes in the real world that stand out, especially the footage shot in the city of Kawasaki. The story is really about the neglect many Japanese children endured as "latchkey kids" during this time period rather than battling monsters. Notably, Ichiro and his father are never presented in the same shot together early in the film. Only in the epilogue are they glimpsed in the same frame, but still greatly distanced from one another. Ichiro's mother (also rarely glimpsed) is shown crying in her last scene because she knows that despite everything that's happened, nothing will change in their lives. The final scene where Ichiro—having learned courage from his visits to Monster Island and his spiritual guide, Minilla—confronts his neighborhood bully, Sanko/"Gabara." Ichiro overcomes his tormentor then goes on to either take over or become a member of his gang of miscreants! One could interpret this seemingly happy ending as either a thinly-veiled tragedy or victory. None of Ichiro's circumstances have changed, yet his attitude has. Ichiro is still distanced from his parents and now runs with the gang of boys who used to harass him (even if they are relatively harmless).

Disdained by many American fans, the Japanese take *All Monsters Attack* for what it is: a movie made for 10-year-olds, rather than some attempt at continuing the themes and ideas set about by the original *Godzilla* that American fans seem obsessed with.[13] Ironically enough, *All Monsters Attack* was even one of Honda's favorites and is very well-directed for a children's film.

Chapter Notes

[1] As always, translations make this difficult to discern but text in *Toho Special Effects Movie Complete Works* also mentions Tokyo Movie Animation (also known as Tokyo Movie Shinsha founded in 1964) as being involved.
[2] Scheimer, *Creating the Filmation Generation*, pp.61.
[3] G-Fan Kaiju Scrapbook, *G-Fan* #120 (Summer 2018), pp.66.
[4] Ryfle and Godziszewski, *Ishiro Honda*, pp.253.
[5] It's unclear if the stock footage was Tanaka's idea or Sekizawa's. Furthermore, this is entirely conjecture, but I feel there's a possibility some axed concepts from the Filmation Godzilla series could have leaked into *All Monsters Attack*. It's entirely possible that Minilla's ability to speak, change his size at will, and communicate with humans could have been a concept from the series. After all, what better bridge between the human and monster characters could there be than a talking Minilla?
[6] It's also surprising that no new footage was written for Gorosaurus as the monster fights Godzilla in the manga scene featuring Kumonga.
[7] This according to the back cover copy on Kodansha's Godzilla All DVD Collector's Box Vol. 19 *Godzilla vs. Megalon*.
[8] The odako prop already existed, so it was a matter of time constraints rather than the cost of creating a new marionette.
[9] Script notes show that it was Honda himself who cut Rodan and the odako, specifying that these scenes be replaced with stock footage.
[10] Neither I nor the editor have ever seen proof of this VHS release, however.
[11] A film about the revolutionary had recently came out that summer.
[12] More recently, fans have speculated Gabara is based upon an *oni*, or demon, due to his green skin and horns.
[13] That said, Hikari Takeda (aka Modstoon) remembers in *G-Fan* #22 that he and other children were disappointed with *All Monsters Attack*. "...everyone was expecting a new, exciting story to follow *Destroy All Monsters*. Everyone felt, 'We don't need a non-exciting kaiju eiga!'"

23.
THE VAMPIRE DOLL
AND THE DEATH OF THE OLD STUDIO SYSTEM

The Vampire Doll has the dubious distinction of being produced because Toho producer Fumio Tanaka eavesdropped on director Michio Yamamoto at a party. Yamamoto was explaining to another guest how he yearned to make a psychological thriller akin to the works of Alfred Hitchcock. Somehow in Tanaka's mind, this translated to a Hammer-esque Dracula movie. Hammer's Christopher Lee Dracula films were very popular in Japan and *Horror of Dracula* (there, titled *Vampire Dracula*) even included footage that had been cut by the British censors from the British version when it was released in Japan in 1958.

Three days after overhearing Yamamoto, Tanaka sent him horror novels and comics to review with instructions to make a vampire film. At first, Yamamoto refused the offer, disliking the idea of a vampire movie. Eventually, Yamamoto met Tanaka in the middle by adapting a story by Edgar Allan Poe—though he refused to throw Dracula into the mix. The Poe story was *The Facts in the Case of M. Valdemar*, which involved hypnotism to reanimate the dead. The resultant film would feature a vampire girl who was hypnotized at the moment of death by her father.

The Poe story wasn't the only influence on the film. The idea of a woman searching for her missing brother was taken from a TV movie, *Love Trap*, directed by Yamamoto during his television days in the 1960s. To flesh out the script, Yamamoto teamed with writer Ei Ogawa (who had also written Yamamoto's film *Resurrection of the Beast*). Relatively new writer Hiroshi Nagano also wrote with Ogawa and Yamamoto on *The Vampire Doll*. Reportedly, while watching a screening of *Horror of Dracula* for inspiration, Yamamoto noticed how Nagano jumped in his seat when the female vampire, Lucy, was burned by a crucifix.[1] Supposedly, this is what inspired Yamamoto to make his vampire female.

The developmental process for this film came about so quickly that it resulted in an unusually short script and the finished film runs only 70 minutes long. Very little changed from draft to draft, which is unusual. Ei Ogawa and Hiroshi Nagano wrote their first draft by May 4th and the film would end up being released exactly

145

# GAMERA VS. JIGER

HAVING HAD GAMERA FACE OFF AGAINST ALIEN MONSTERS TWICE IN A ROW, NIISAN TAKAHASHI APPARENTLY THOUGHT IT WISE TO SWITCH THINGS UP FOR *GAMERA VS. JIGER*. AS BOYS' MAGAZINES WITH STORIES ON ANCIENT CIVILIZATIONS WERE POPULAR, THE PLOT WAS CONSTRUCTED AROUND AN ANCIENT MONSTER FROM THE LOST CONTINENT OF MU. TAKAHASHI ALSO WANTED TO INCLUDE AN "OCCULT" ELEMENT WITH JIGER AND THE CURSED STATUE (TAKAHASHI'S IDEA PRECEDED THE OCCULT HORROR BOOM IN MOVIES THAT BEGAN WITH THE RELEASE OF 1973'S *THE EXORCIST*). DAIEI ALSO MANAGED TO SECURE A CROSS PROMOTION WITH EXPO '70, WHICH WAS ABOUT TO OPEN IN OSAKA. THEY WERE ABLE TO FILM EXTENSIVELY ON LOCATION AT THE EXPO'S FAIRGROUNDS. ON THE DOWNSIDE, THE EXPO '70 COMMITTEE WOULD NOT ALLOW DAIEI TO DESTROY ANY MINIATURES REPRESENTING THE EXPO.

two months later. Overall, the film isn't terribly well written. As a whole, it is paced decently enough but the ending is poorly handled and consists of a very lengthy piece of exposition. In the scene, a homicidal doctor explains how he hypnotized Yuko—the titular Vampire Doll—when she was at the point of death. The story then quickly wraps itself up by having Yuko kill the doctor—her biological father—by stabbing him in the neck, though the way Yamamoto shoots the action is unnerving. The imagery of the film is striking, particularly the gold contact lenses worn by Yuko (Yamamoto's idea). Two people heavily involved in this film, writer Ei Ogawa and actress Yukiko Kobayashi, would go on to work on Toho's next giant monster movie, *Space Amoeba*.

As covered in a previous chapter, *Space Amoeba* began life as *Giant Monster Assault* by Ogawa all the way back in 1966. Considered a potential co-production between Toho and UPA, it was shelved—possibly due to the behind the scenes drama surrounding *Hell in the Pacific*. In late 1969, Tanaka wanted to create a brand new special effects film to anchor another Champion Matsuri Festival—and for some reason, he didn't seem to want another Godzilla movie. Either liking what he remembered from *Giant Monster Assault* or perhaps just in a bind, Tanaka had Ogawa dust off his old script and tone it down to suit a lower budget.

The new script was submitted by Ogawa on December 22, 1969. In *Godzilla: Toho SPFX Films* (2014), the book explains, "Tomoyuki

Tanaka decided to rethink *Giant Monster Assault,* which he considered as a collaborative film in 1966. And on December 4, 1969, the second draft was made as *Giant Monster: Raid of the Sea* and the director Ishiro Honda and special effects supervisor Sadamasa Arikawa were decided upon."[2] For the sake of the budget, the initial *Gorath*-like globetrotting script was scaled down to be contained to a single tropical island named Sergio Island because, according to producer Fumio Tanaka, the films of spaghetti western director Sergio Leone were incredibly popular at the time.[3] Gezora is called Dodora (the name of the monster in *Giant Monster Assault*) in the second draft and it is unknown when the name was changed. Also, Gezora switched from the hot nature of the original Dodora to a freezing cold monster. Otherwise, the script is more or less like the finished film, though some scientific exposition was removed for the sake of the kiddies in the audience.

Though Toho had ideas of shooting in Guam as they had done with *Son of Godzilla*, this was deemed too expensive, so it was shot on Hachijo Island instead. There were also some last-minute change-ups with casting. Noriko Takahashi was supposed to play the female lead Ayako in this film but got married and decided to retire from acting.[4] The role eventually went to Atsuko Takahashi. Yoshio Tsuchiya says he was to play the alien-possessed Obata but let Kenji Sahara have the part as a sort of favor to him, telling Sahara, "You have to play this sort of role at least once."[5] Furthermore, in Ogawa's script, the alien "astro-quasars" leave Obata and he lives but Honda changed this so that Obata sacrifices himself to save the world. The production was soured when Eiji Tsuburaya died only two days into filming on January 25, 1970. "[*Space Amoeba*] is the last science fiction film that shows Mr. Tsuburaya's influence," Fumio Tanaka said.[6] The movie caused some bad blood between Honda, Arikawa, and Corporate Toho when they declined his request to put an "In Memoriam" card up for Tsuburaya. Fumio Tanaka explained why the in memoriam card wasn't included rather coldly: "It wasn't the property of the people who wanted to dedicate it to Mr. Tsuburaya."[7] The real reason was even colder. By the time Tsuburaya died, the business people who ran Toho hated him. When he discovered that Toho was using his name to sell their movies, Tsuburaya became unafraid to throw his weight around to get what he wanted for his special effects work and refused to tow the company line. Not only that, but the Toho bigwigs resented that Tsuburaya had gone off and created his own company. After

Tsuburaya died, Toho promptly turned his special effects studio into a gift shop.

Toho's refusal to extend even basic human decency ruined their relationship with Ishiro Honda and Sadamasa Arikawa. Honda left Toho to go help Eiji Tsuburaya's sons at Tsuburaya Productions where he would direct several TV series' episodes. Arikawa became so disgusted with Toho that he quit and retired from motion pictures altogether (however, he would come back to work on several non-Toho productions in the late 70s). At the same time, Toho disbanded their old studio system, which meant all the studio actors like Akira Takarada were no longer under contract. Toho divided itself into subsidiaries, one of which was Toho Eizo, Inc. (Toho Vision), formed in 1971, which produced the company's fantasy and special effects films. Tomoyuki Tanaka was made president of Toho Eizo and as a result, focused almost all his attention to rejuvenating the Godzilla series. In addition to all of the 1970s Godzilla movies, Toho Eizo also produced *Lake of Dracula* (1971), *Submersion of Japan* (1973), *Horror of the Wolf* (1973), *Prophecies of Nostradamus (Catastrophe 1999)* (1974), *ESPY* (1974) and *Conflagration* (1975). As a whole, Toho's output was drastically less; in the 1960s, Tanaka would produce several big features each year. Now, he would only do one or two, one of which was almost always a Godzilla film.

Chapter Notes

[1] In addition, the crew also screened *Goke, Body Snatcher from Hell* (1968), *The Fearless Vampire Killers* (1967), and *Rosemary's Baby* (1968).
[2] *Godzilla: Toho SPFX Films*, pp.116.
[3] In the Japanese dialogue, the characters pronounce it "Selgio Island" and it became "Selga Island" in the two English dubs.
[4] Takahashi was originally cast as Daiyo in *Ebirah, Horror of the Deep* (1966) before she got appendicitis and was replaced by Kumi Mizuno. Takahashi shot footage as Daiyo and at least one behind the scenes image of her in costume exists.
[5] Tsuchiya had played alien possessed scientists already in *Battle in Outer Space* and *Destroy All Monsters*.
[6] www.davmil.org/www.kaijuconversations.com/tanak.htm
[7] Ibid.

 **PROFILE: EI OGAWA**

Ei Ogawa was born March 10, 1930, and graduated from Chuo University of Law School. He studied under famous scriptwriter Keiichiro Ryu and soon began writing action movies for Toho (though his first film was 1959's *The Rambling Guitarist* for Nikkatsu). Ogawa's first project for Toho was to work on *International Secret Police: Directive No. 8* (1963), an entry in their James Bond-inspired series. In 1966, Ogawa tried his hand at writing his first monster movie for Toho, *Giant Monster Assault*. The story was essentially a much more ambitious version of *Space Amoeba* (1970) meant to be co-produced with Henry G. Saperstein and UPA. However, problems with other projects lead to its collapse and it was shelved until 1970. In the meantime, Ogawa wrote for quite a few TV series as well, starting with *Tokyo Combat* (1968) for Fuji Television. Fumio Tanaka said, "Mr. Ogawa mainly worked on television series. He is the one who made an industry out of script writing." [www.davmil.org/www.kaiju-conversations.com/tanak.htm] In 1968, Ogawa also wrote the sequel for *100 Shot/100 Killed*, *Golden Eye*. Scrambling for a new effects feature for their summertime Champion Matsuri Festival for 1970, Tomoyuki Tanaka decided to dust off *Giant Monster Assault*, with the understanding that Ogawa relocate it to a tropical isle and cut down on the global action. *Space Amoeba* was not particularly popular, though Ogawa continued to write for Toho, notably the same year's *The Vampire Doll*, which was enough of a hit to spawn a trilogy. The same director and composer returned with Ogawa for each film in what is today referred to as "the Bloodthirsty Trilogy." These were the only feature film screenplays Ogawa wrote throughout the rest of the 1970s aside from *ESPY* (1974), which was a huge hit (though the source material's author Sakyo Komatsu was disappointed in Ogawa's script). In 1982, Ogawa returned to film from his busy TV schedule for Toei's *Ninja Wars*. Ogawa's last screenwriting credit was for a direct-to-video Toei film, *Order of the Underworld Metropolitan War* (1992). Ogawa passed away two years later on April 27, 1994.

Selected Filmography
The Rambling Guitarist (1959) (story)
Man Against Man (1960) (writer)
International Secret Police: Directive No. 8 (1963) (writer)
Giant Monster Assault (1965) (writer) [unproduced, turned into Space Amoeba]
Epoch of Murder Madness (1967) (writer)
100 Shot/100 Killed: Golden Eye (1968) (writer)
Resurrection of the Beast (1969) (writer)
The Vampire Doll (1970) (writer)
Terror in the Streets (1970) (writer)
Space Amoeba (1970) (writer)
Lake of Dracula (1971) (writer)
Mako, the Mermaid (1971) (writer) [TV series]
Evil of Dracula (1974) (writer)
ESPY (1974) (writer)
Ninja Wars (1982) (writer)
Choshichiro's Edo Diaries: The Yagyu Conspiracy (1984) (writer)

24.
POLLUTION MONSTERS
ZIGRA VS. HEDORAH

The year 1971 would see the last Gamera film from Daiei before they went bankrupt, and also the first Godzilla movie of the new decade. Both films, *Gamera vs. Zigra* and *Godzilla vs. Hedorah*, came out within one week of each other in July of 1971 and dealt heavily with ecology and pollution.

Gamera vs. Zigra reportedly began as *Gamera vs. Leoman*.[1] How the story differed from *Gamera vs. Zigra* is unknown. What is known is that a recent shark attack in the news inspired Noriaki Yuasa to create a shark monster as Gamera's next opponent. "...we wanted to situate a story in the sea. Also, at that time in the news, someone had been attacked by a shark in Japan. And children are scared of sharks," Yuasa later explained at G-Fest X in 2003.[2] The sentient shark monster came from outer space and, in many ways, was similar to Viras, another space monster inspired by a deep-sea creature. However, Zigra took Viras' trait as an intelligent monster to the next level: Zigra speaks to humanity throughout the entire film. As a result, he becomes one of the more interesting villains in the Gamera series. The space shark hailed from a planet ruined by pollution. In fact, the film was supposed to begin with the destruction of Zigra's home planet (also drearily named Zigra). Noriaki Yuasa said, "The opening sequence of *Gamera vs. Zigra* was originally going to be a very long one showing disasters occurring on Zigra's home planet, but Mr. Nagata insisted that the sequence be deleted because it would have cost too much to shoot."[3]

As had been done on *Gamera vs. Jiger* with Expo 70, Daiei made a cross-promotional deal with Kamogawa Sea World and the storyline was written around that location. Though a miniature of Kamogawa Sea World was built for the film, Daiei was not allowed to destroy it in accordance with their agreement with the park. Reportedly, scenes of Lady X/Chikako in a bikini were included to appeal to fathers in the audience.

Overall, the film is one of the weaker entries in the series. Though interesting on an intellectual level, Zigra—voiced by Keiichi Noda[4]—was rather uninteresting on a physical level. When

151

 **SPECTREMAN**

ANOTHER TOKUSATSU FRANCHISE TO FOCUS ON THE EVILS OF POLLUTION WAS P-PRODUCTIONS' TV SERIES *SPECTREMAN*, WHICH WAS INCREDIBLY POPULAR IN 1971. THE SHOW BEGAN LIFE AS *ELEMENTMAN* AND FOCUSED ON A HERO WHO COULD CHANGE HIS FORM INTO LIQUID, GAS, AND SOLID STATES. A PILOT WITH THIS VERSION WAS FILMED. ELEMENTMAN SPORTED A SHODDY DESIGN COMPARED TO SPECTREMAN, AND HAD A RED AND BLACK COLOR SCHEME WITH A SILLY-LOOKING SILVER HELMET. ELEMENTMAN'S HUMAN HOST, JOJI GAMO, WAS PLAYED BY FUTURE *RETURN OF ULTRAMAN* STAR JIRO DAN IN THIS PILOT. ALSO, JOJI RAN A SPORTS STORE IN THIS ITERATION. THE COSTUME USED FOR DR. GORI LACKED THE BLONDE WIG OF THE FINISHED VERSION AND THIS SUIT WOULD PLAY THE CHARACTER OF LLA 2/KAH IN THE SERIES. THE PILOT EVEN HAD TWO DIFFERENT NAMES, *SPACE APEMAN GORI* AND *SUPERMAN ELEMENTMAN*. THE ORIGINAL INTENT WAS TO FOCUS ON THE VILLAINOUS DR. GORI OVER THE TITULAR HERO HIMSELF.

Gamera is incapacitated by his foe during a fight, Zigra causes Gamera to fall into a death-like coma by stopping the cellular activity in his body. This is rather mundane when compared to the previous film where Gamera was more or less impregnated by his opponent. Perhaps the most engrossing thing about *Gamera vs. Zigra*'s script is that it was the first giant monster movie to emphasize the dangers of environmental pollution over that of nuclear testing. The film—already rife with heavy-handed ecological messages—manages to squeeze one more in when Kenichi throws a pop bottle on the beach, giving his father an excuse to go into a lecture to close the film. *Gamera vs. Zigra*'s box office take is relatively unknown, but what is known is that Daiei was already bankrupt and had been since 1970, but were not telling the public or their employees. As a result, *Gamera vs. Zigra* was released by another company, Dainichi Eihai Company, LTD. The Gamera staff were told to plan the next year's film, but it is unknown if Daiei felt they could continue coasting by on fumes or if this was just a ploy to keep the truth from their filmmakers.[5] At any rate, even if the film somehow managed to be a blockbuster, it could not have saved Daiei, who were forced to finally officially declare bankruptcy in December of 1971.

Back at Toho, dissatisfied with *Space Amoeba*'s box office numbers, Tomoyuki Tanaka decided to bring back Godzilla once again. Initially, Ishiro Honda was announced to come back and helm Godzilla #11, but still sore over Toho's treatment of Eiji Tsuburaya, Honda turned them down flat. Tanaka then went to 40-year-old Yoshimitsu Banno, who had just completed the Expo '70 film *The Birth of the Japanese Islands*, which had impressed Tanaka greatly. The producer reportedly told Banno to reinvent Godzilla for a new generation. Banno's idea, inspired in part by the book *Silent Spring*, revolved around pollution. Its core concept was always the same: an unknown lifeform crashes on earth and feeds off of pollution until Godzilla must battle it. Kaoru Mabuchi wrote the first draft screenplay based on Banno's idea. Banno supposedly showed Tanaka the first draft just as the Osaka expo was winding down. Both men agreed Mabuchi's first treatment was lackluster (or so Banno implied in his autobiography, *The Man Who Made Godzilla Fly*).

Tanaka also gave Banno strict budgetary guidelines to adhere to when writing the script. Knowing his budget would be small, Banno claimed he wrote the first draft with these four principles in mind:

1. Reduce the set of drama parts.
2. Few characters. Do not use stars.
3. Drop any wasteful scenes of dialogue.
4. Shorten the finished scale as much as possible.[6]

The writing situation with Mabuchi was tense. His treatment, which was too simplistic for Banno's tastes, centered around a fisherman and his grandson. Banno said, "For this script, what they brought to me was basically junk. It was no good at the beginning. So I rewrote the whole thing." Banno and Mabuchi wrote the first draft, then called *Godzilla vs. Hedoron*, together in the mountains in Nagano Prefecture and had it completed September 17, 1970. Banno explained, "Most of the ideas for this movie came from me. I would fight with Mr. Kimura an awful lot. He became very diligent in what he was doing, but more of the environment and other themes were more of my idea."[7] According to Banno in his autobiography, Mabuchi shouted at him when Banno added a scene of Dr. Yano scuba diving without consulting him first. "If you write by yourself, I will go home!" Mabuchi declared.[8]

Several of the scenes Banno wrote, such as Mrs. Yano's aerobics class collapsing, were inspired by real events. "That incident at the Sunigami School in which girls collapsed from smog happened in July [1970] and we incorporated it into the film immediately,"

 **LAKE OF DRACULA**

WHEN *THE VAMPIRE DOLL* PROVED TO BE A BIG HIT WITH THE FEMALE CROWD IN JAPAN, FUMIO TANAKA COMMISSIONED MICHIO YAMAMOTO TO DO A SEQUEL. THIS TIME, IT WAS NON-NEGOTIABLE THAT YAMAMOTO WAS TO INCLUDE A DRACULA-TYPE CHARACTER. TITLED *PHANTOM VAMPIRE*, MASUMI OKADA (*LATITUDE ZERO*) WAS TO PLAY THE VAMPIRE BUT A SCHEDULING CONFLICT PREVENTED THIS. YAMAMOTO SUGGESTED HIS FRIEND SHIN KISHIDA FOR THE DRACULA ROLE AND TOHO EVENTUALLY AGREED (INITIALLY THEY ARGUED HE WAS TOO SHORT AND YAMAMOTO GAVE KISHIDA LIFTS!). ONCE AGAIN, YAMAMOTO HAD AN UNCREDITED HAND IN THE STORY, WHICH WAS INSPIRED BY KAZUO OKUMA'S "RUPO SPIRIT WARD." THAT STORY WAS SERIALIZED IN THE *ASAHI SHIMBUN EVENING SOCIETY* IN 1970 AND YAMAMOTO LONGED TO MAKE A FILM ADAPTATION. WHEN SUCH A FILM DIDN'T COME TO FRUITION, YAMAMOTO TRANSPLANTED IDEAS FROM IT INTO *LAKE OF DRACULA*, NAMELY THE DISBELIEF THAT LEAD CHARACTER AKIKO HAS SEEN A VAMPIRE. LIKE *THE VAMPIRE DOLL*, THE SCRIPT WAS ADAPTED AS WRITTEN WITH VERY FEW CHANGES DURING THE WRITING PROCESS OR FILMING. THOUGH THERE IS NO CONTINUITY BETWEEN THIS FILM AND *THE VAMPIRE DOLL*, THE STRIKING GOLD CONTACT LENSES RETURN, EXPLAINING THE FILM'S JAPANESE TITLE *CURSED HOUSE: BLOODSUCKING EYES*.

Banno revealed.[9] "Toho didn't tell us to change anything in the screenplay and for me, it was only natural [that people would die]," he said about the carnage that goes on in Tokyo, such as people dissolving in sludge and being skeletonized by Hedorah's sulfuric acid mist.[10] The visuals of polluted water were inspired by a visit the director took to a beach near Yokkaichi, which was polluted with strange bubbles in the water that smelled of sulfur.

The famous club sequence was inspired by both a nightclub in Akasaka and a gay bar in Chicago that someone in the art department had visited. "Crowds of young people would dance jammed together in a heaving, swirling mass," Banno said of the Akasaka club. "There was a platform up front, on which girls in miniskirts would be writhing to the music. I modeled the set on that club. But having the girl wear body paint was my idea."[11] The Mt. Fuji youth rally was Kaoru Mabuchi's idea and was influenced by his old ties to the Japanese communist party.

Other differences in early drafts included the character of Miki being the daughter of a Fuji City paper mill owner who badly pollutes the city. Also, Hedorah is listed as originating from "Exploded M87 Nebula," which isn't identified in the finished film. Though the early portions of the shooting script are basically the same, some of the animated vignettes are shuffled around in different spots. Initially, Banno approached legendary manga artist Yoshiharu Tsuge to do the animation for the film. Banno said he was inspired by a manga Tsuge drew where various objects floated down a river of sewage. However, when Tsuge was approached, he said he wasn't interested in movies and shied away from crowds and declined the offer. As for Banno's talent with split-screen sequences, this was honed at the Expo '70 in the Hall of the Future display he helped create.

As for the climactic battle, tanks were supposed to attack Hedorah at Mt. Fuji in the script. Though Haruo Nakajima has said *Godzilla vs. Gigan* was the first script to thoroughly explain the fight choreography, the battle is fully written out just as it is in the final film right down to Godzilla's *Ultraman* pose, which is explicitly mentioned.[12] Many American fans are confused by the white orbs Godzilla pulls from Hedorah's body until Teruyoshi Nakano clarified those were Hedorah's eyes. The script is more explicit as to what Godzilla holds in his hands, reading "white chunks of eyeballs, also connective nerve tissues and crystals appear."

In *Tokusatsu Hihou* Vol. 4, Banno revealed that *Matango* writer Masami Fukushima actually helped contribute ideas. "The idea of the electrode plate is that of science fiction writer Mr. Masami Fukushima. Tomoyuki-san set up a seat to listen to Mr. Fukushima to discuss the dried rice fields in Hokkaido done with electrode plates."[13] In the final draft script, the electrode plates fail and Godzilla doesn't use them to destroy Hedorah. As the Smog Monster flies away, a series of images were to play demonstrating the danger of the monster's continued existence, such as the dead bodies of the young people at Mt. Fuji, polluted rivers, and dead sea beds.[14] Originally, instead of flying, Godzilla simply ran after Hedorah, and nor does he return Hedorah to the electrode towers once he catches him. When Godzilla tears the monster apart on Mt. Fuji, the chunks of Hedorah's body then dry out in natural sunlight—perhaps to show nature triumphing over pollution. The end would have had two title cards: "And Yet, Another One?" and "Godzilla vs. Hedorah Part I. The End."[15]

The design process behind Hedorah itself was interesting, to say the least. Teruyoshi Nakano said, "Hedorah came from the

 **RETURN OF ULTRAMAN**

HAVING GIVEN THE ULTRA FRANCHISE A BREAK SINCE 1968, TSUBURAYA PRODUCTIONS DECIDED TO REVIVE ULTRAMAN IN 1971. AS THE TITLE SUGGESTS, THIS SERIES WAS ORIGINALLY MEANT TO BE THE RETURN OF THE ULTRAMAN FROM THE 1966-1967 SERIES, ALBEIT PRESUMABLY WITH A NEW HUMAN HOST. FURTHERMORE, IT WOULD BE SET 30 YEARS AFTER THE ORIGINAL SERIES! IN THE ORIGINAL OPENING SCENE, THE JAPANESE SELF DEFENSE FORCES ARE UNABLE TO DEFEND JAPAN FROM GIANT MONSTERS (RECENTLY AWAKENED DUE TO VOLCANIC ACTIVITY). AN ELDERLY CAPTAIN MURAMATSU LAMENTS, "I WISH ULTRAMAN WERE HERE." RIGHT ON CUE ULTRAMAN RETURNS, BEATS THE MONSTER, AND DISAPPEARS. IN THE NEXT EPISODE, ULTRAMAN JOINS WITH HIDEKI GOH AND IF JAPANESE TRANSLATIONS ARE CORRECT, A RETIRED SHIN HAYATA WOULD APPEAR TO HAND OFF THE BETA CAPSULE TO GOH. HOWEVER, IT WAS DECIDED THIS WAS DISRESPECTFUL TO EIJI TSUBURAYA'S MEMORY, AND THE ULTRAMAN BECAME SHIN ULTRAMAN (NEW ULTRAMAN). OTHER SOURCES SAY THAT SPONSORS VETOED THIS IDEA AND FELT A NEW ULTRAMAN WOULD SELL BETTER FOR TIE-IN MERCHANDISE.

Japanese word *hedoro*, which means sludge. It's a chunk of junk, but if we just used a chunk of junk, it wouldn't be appealing visually, so we put eyes and the nose on it."[16] Early storyboards by Yasuyuki Inoue show Hedorah to be an eye-less, almost yokai-like monster, lapping pollution from the water with a long tongue. The drawings also show Hedorah spewing poison gas from its eye, rather than the red laser of the finished film. In another storyboard, when Godzilla punches the eye, it explodes into poison gas. Banno stated, "Hedorah's eyes were modeled on female genitalia."[17] Nakano explained at a G-Fest panel in the late 1990s that, "I created the gory scenes where Hedorah destroys Godzilla's eye and melts his arm with its sulfuric acid. Around that time, there was a trend in the movie industry to show things they never had shown before."[18]

When filming started, Tomoyuki Tanaka soon began to regret his decision to hire Banno as he walked in on the nightclub hallucination scene. Shortly afterward, Tanaka fell ill forcing him to be hospitalized and his assistant to approve of things in his absence. One of the matters approved by Tanaka's assistant was Godzilla's notorious flying scene—which wasn't necessarily outrageous in the eyes of the children who saw it at the time.

Banno wrote in his autobiography, "The children who saw Godzilla flying in the sky for the first time in the theater applauded. Elementary school students played toys in the form of Godzilla's flying pose during the holidays."[19]

As to the inspiration for Godzilla's method of flying, Banno explained, "We got the idea from seahorses: blow air from the mouth, and move backwards."[20] And though that may be what Banno says, there was actually a more practical reason behind this "seahorse" idea. During the shooting of the ending, the production ran out of money. This is why the eyeballs Godzilla yanks out of Hedorah have no pupils—no one could be paid to paint them on. [21] There was also no money to make a flying Godzilla model. Therefore the old Godzilla model used in *Invasion of Astro-Monster* was brought out for the scene, which was positioned the way that it was because it had been curled up in a force-field bubble, not necessarily because Banno modeled it after a seahorse.

Nakano's comments are also somewhat dubious, as he claims that he wanted to make a socially-conscious movie about pollution while Banno was more conscious of the fact the film was for children. In all likelihood, the opposite was true. As filming progressed, Nakano came to feel somewhat guilty about all the doom and gloom. According to him, for the sake of the child audience, he pushed for a few humorous scenes such as Godzilla flying. The original script's version of the scene was also shot which had Godzilla running to catch Hedorah instead. Banno said, "As Mr. Tanaka was in the hospital, we were worried that he might not like it that Godzilla was flying. So we made others scenes of Godzilla's running and catching Hedorah."[22]

Even before the flying scene was invented, the original script had a scene that gave Godzilla a "power-jump" of sorts. The original script implied that Godzilla accomplished this jump by blasting his ray at the ground. Sharp eyed fans will notice publicity stills representing the scene, where Godzilla is jumping over Hedorah. The scene was never actually filmed that we know of, however.

During shooting in January of 1971, the film went through a name change from *Godzilla vs. Hedoron* to *Godzilla vs. Hedorah*. The impetus was the airing of *Spectreman,* which featured a sludge monster named Hedoron in its premiere episode on January 2, 1971. The similarities didn't end there, however. Though Hedoron didn't look like Toho's Hedorah (it had tentacles and emitted yellow, sulturous vapors), it did emerge from Fuji Bay and headed straight for Mt. Fuji. Also, when a young boy lost his father to the monster, he shouted his sorrow over the ocean—bringing to mind Ken Yano yelling to his missing father under the waves in *Godzilla vs. Hedorah*.

After the initial 35-day filming schedule was completed (sources claim production was shut down by Corporate Toho when Banno blew his budget), Ishiro Honda was called in to watch a rough cut of the film at the behest of Tomoyuki Tanaka. Banno claimed, "...we invited Ishiro Honda... to view the rushes, and with a word from Honda-san, we were able to shoot some additional material." [23] Banno felt his film needed more time and he persuaded Honda to go to Tanaka to ask for an extension of filming on his behalf, to which Tanaka obliged!

According to Banno, Tomoyuki Tanaka's infamous reaction to *Godzilla vs. Hedorah* may have been greatly exaggerated over the years. The director says Tanaka never yelled at him but seemed disappointed in *Godzilla vs. Hedorah*, looking at the film and saying, "Well, I guess there's no way we change that." Though Tanaka disliked what Banno did with Godzilla, he appreciated his ideas enough that he set him to work on the ecologically-minded *Prophecies of Nostradamus (Catastrophe 1999)* in 1974 (which he co-directed and mostly wrote, but received little credit for), and he was also present at the 1978 Godzilla Revival Meeting.

At the time of its release, *Godzilla vs. Hedorah* was a polarizing film in Japan, despite going on to become the second most successful Toho movie that year. Ostensibly a children's movie, it apparently frightened its target audience with its imagery and tone. In America, known as *Godzilla vs. the Smog Monster*, the film was ranked as an entry in the book *The Fifty Worst Films of All Time*. In the early 2000s, the film received something of a reappraisal as a classic relevant for its social commentary on the pollution era of the 1970s. Perhaps part of the film's divisiveness comes down to the fact that the Godzilla films of the late 1960s, like *Destroy All Monsters*, had more or less been light adventure films. *Godzilla vs. Hedorah* has a dark atmosphere with scenes of death and violence that one would typically find in a horror film—or, one could argue, the original 1954 *Godzilla* which Banno wished to emulate. Many people die in the film and nearly all of the main characters—even the child protagonist Ken—are injured by Hedorah in some way. Notably, a group of Mahjong players are drowned in Hedorah's sludge—thrown off the creature's body during the first battle with Godzilla. In a strange juxtaposition in the same scene, a kitten is also coated with the sludge but survives the encounter unscathed! These dark scenes, coupled with the film's "art house" touches, are likely what turned some off from the film. Today, however, these same touches are exactly what makes *Godzilla vs. Hedorah* a true classic of the 1970s.

Chapter Notes

[1] If Leoman was also two-headed is unknown, but in the U.S. Leoman was reported as a two headed-foe. It was also erroneously believed to be the film following *Gamera vs. Zigra*. Basically, the report confused the Leoman idea with *Gamera vs. Two Headed Monster W* which was for certain the next planned Gamera movie.
[2] "Mr. Yuasa's G-Fest", *G-Fan* #65 (Nov/Dec 2003), pp.14.
[3] http://www.davmil.org/www.kaijuconversations.com/yuasa.htm
[4] The voice of the titular character in *Goke, Body Snatcher from Hell*.
[5] The next film was actually planned in direct competition with Toho's *Return of King Ghidorah* (later *Godzilla vs. Gigan*). Daiei was going to have Gamera battle a two-headed, winged monster in *Gamera vs. Two Headed Monster W*. A deal was already in play with the Miyazaki City Phoenix Natural Zoo to serve as the film's main setting.
[6] Banno, *The Man Who Made Godzilla Fly*, pp.137.
[7] https://vantagepointinterviews.com/2017/05/09/making-godzilla-fly-an-interview-with-godzilla-director-yoshimitsu-banno/
[8] Banno, *The Man Who Made Godzilla Fly*, pp.136.
[9] Macias, *Tokyo Scope*, pp.34.
[10] Ibid.
[11] Ibid, pp. 32.
[12] While shooting the movie, Haruo Nakajima did not understand the story at all and "had no idea what he was doing" when performing as Godzilla.
[13] *Tokusatsu Hihou*, Vol. 4, pp.121-124.
[14] Perhaps these were meant to be thoughts Godzilla was having of a future if he failed to stop Hedorah?
[15] If that isn't a set-up for a sequel, then what is?
[16] Galbraith, *Monsters Are Attacking Tokyo*, pp.113.
[17] Macias, *Tokyo Scope*, pp.34.
[18] Ryfle and Galbraith IV, "Interview with Teruyoshi Nakano", *G-Fan* #27 (May/Jun 1997), pp.22.
[19] Banno, *The Man Who Made Godzilla Fly*, pp.136.
[20] Macias, *Tokyo Scope*, pp.35.
[21] Some of you, like me, were probably curious for years why, if Godzilla had yanked out Hedorah's eyes, does he still have eyes after that scene? That's because multiple Hedorah's joined together, so there was a second, smaller Hedorah living inside the bigger one. That is the Hedorah that escapes which Godzilla then chases down.
[22] https://vantagepointinterviews.com/2017/05/09/making-godzilla-fly-an-interview-with-godzilla-director-yoshimitsu-banno/
[23] Macias, *Tokyo Scope*, pp.34.

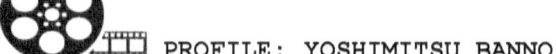

PROFILE: YOSHIMITSU BANNO

Yoshimitsu Banno, one of the most talented and divisive directors of the Godzilla series, was born on March 30, 1931. Banno recalled, "In my high school days, I did some plays in theaters and I established one team of drama performance but it was very difficult to live in the theater world. I had a chance to be employed by the Toho company, one of the biggest companies in Japan for motion pictures." [vantagepointinterviews.com/2017/05/09/making-godzilla-fly-an-interview-with-godzilla-director-yoshimitsu-banno/] Banno attended college at the University of Tokyo of Arts and History and graduated in 1955 after which he joined the Toho Photographer's Literature Department. In 1956, he became an assistant director. Having a scuba diving license, he was also assigned to Toho's underwater photography team in 1961. He served as an Assistant Director on close to twenty films, many of which were those of Japan's famed director, Akira Kurosawa. When Toho dismantled their studio system in 1970, Tomoyuki Tanaka took note of Banno's very successful film, *The Birth of the Japanese Islands*, created for Expo '70. Tanaka then tasked Banno with making the first new Godzilla movie in two years. Banno had hoped to reinvent Godzilla for a new generation along with Teruyoshi Nakano and took great care in writing the film's script (though he didn't get along well with co-writer Kaoru Mabuchi). Not only did Banno direct the movie, but he actually did the scuba diving scenes, portraying Dr. Yano (lead actor Akira Yamaguchi was cast due to his superficial resemblance to the director in stature). Tomoyuki Tanaka reportedly walked in on Banno's strange nightclub sequence and was very puzzled by what he saw. The producer became ill not long after and was hospitalized for the rest of the production. After *Godzilla vs. Hedorah's* release, Banno wrote a treatment for a sequel that was never made. Despite being disappointed in *Godzilla vs. Hedorah*, Tanaka suspected Banno would be well suited for the gloomy disaster film *Prophecies of Nostradamus (Catastrophe 1999)* in 1974. The film was a huge hit, coming in at the #1 spot for the highest-grossing Japanese film of 1974. Banno and Tanaka talked about a *Prophecies of Nostradamus* sequel, which was ultimately never produced. In the mid-1970s, Banno filmed a bevy of underwater documentaries and remembers the time fondly. "For four years, I visited many places, including Baja California to film gray whales, sea otters, and sharks… But Toho asked me to be the director of the planning section, and I changed my course to them."[Ibid] In 1978, Yoshimitsu Banno sat in on the Godzilla Revival Meeting, though so far as anyone knows, he contributed no story ideas. In 1983, he developed the large image "JAPANEX SYSTEM" using 70 mm film and in 1984, he became the Toho Image and Art Managing Executive Director, a position he held for ten years. In

2000, he established the Advanced Image Research Institute and assumed office as Representative Director. In 2004, Banno made plans to produce a 3-D Godzilla IMAX movie. The project lingered in "development hell" for 6 years until it morphed into Legendary Pictures' *Godzilla* (2014) initially announced in 2010. From there, the director opted to turn his aborted *Godzilla 3-D to the MAX* into *Gamera 3-D*. Likewise, another 3-D film called *Jewelers 3-D* was presumably based on alien creatures originally set to appear in Banno's unmade Godzilla movie, *Godzilla vs. Gezira*, which revolved around the impending Okinawan expo of 1975. There was one other aborted 3-D film, *Follow the Whales 3-D*. In 2017, Banno announced plans to make a new Hedorah movie, where the smog monster would be born of the Fukushima nuclear accident. On May 7th that same year, Yoshimitsu Banno died of a subarachnoid hemorrhage.

Selected Filmography
The Birth of the Japanese Islands (1970) (director)
Godzilla vs. Hedorah (1971) (writer, director)
Prophecies of Nostradamus (Catastrophe 1999) (1974) (writer, co-director)
Hedorah's Counterattack (1975) (writer) [unproduced]
Godzilla vs. Gezira (1975) (writer) [unproduced]
The Wizard of Oz (1982) (writer)
Techno Police 21C (1982) (writer)
Godzilla 3-D to the Max (2004) (writer, producer) [unproduced]
Gamera 3-D (2010) (writer, producer) [unproduced]
Godzilla (2014) (executive producer)
Jewellers 3-D (2014) (writer, producer) [unproduced]
Hedorah vs. Midora (2014-2017) (writer, producer) [unproduced]

25.
DUELING DRAFTS: THE DEVELOPMENT OF
GODZILLA VS. GIGAN

1972 was apparently the year of King Ghidorah.[1] Toho's recent Champion Matsuri Festival reissue of *Invasion of Astro-Monster* (retitled *Great Monster War: King Ghidorah vs. Godzilla*) drew in a strong attendance of 1,350,000 people—whereas the brand new *Godzilla vs. Hedorah* beat those numbers by only 400,000 people. The winter 1971 re-release of *Ghidorah, the Three-Headed Monster* (retitled *Godzilla, Mothra, King Ghidorah: The Greatest Battle on Earth*) also drew in sizeable numbers for a reissue. Tomoyuki Tanaka felt that a new King Ghidorah film was just what Toho needed to boost their numbers.

Not one but two scriptwriters were tasked with writing the next Godzilla film. Tanaka felt Yoshimitsu Banno's extreme approach in *Godzilla vs. Hedorah* had taken the series in the wrong direction and wanted to steer the series back into more traditional waters. To do so, Tanaka had Kaoru Mabuchi and Shinichi Sekizawa come up with separate concepts.[2] Both writers were given stipulations from Tanaka though to include King Ghidorah and a new monster, Gigan. Presumably, someone at the studio also insisted upon the Godzilla Tower, as it appears in both writers' drafts as well.

However, Tanaka was not the only one steering the project; Teruyoshi Nakano was allowed a great deal of input as well. In *Monsters Are Attacking Tokyo,* Nakano said, "I was involved with writing the script also, because the system at Toho was like that—the special effects team had the right to present its opinions during development and screenwriting."[3] Nakano, who said he wanted to "create a monster that was completely different from the previous film" ordered his effects team to create the unique new monster, Gigan. The effects director elaborated that, "Hedorah was a liquidy monster, so we wanted to make something solid, harder. We decided to work on the new monster in every detail, such as the size of the hands, and we wanted to add a mechanical feel to it. That's how we invented Gigan, whose hand was a sickle and stomach was a big knife [sic]. It was a very new and different design..."[4] Nakano thought it would be interesting to give Gigan a laser that could be shot from its "third eye" (the thing sticking out of Gigan's forehead above his single, red eye). However, in the middle of shooting, he decided the monster could do enough feats already and didn't need it.

But, onto the scripts, Mabuchi's treatment was titled *Godzilla vs. the Space Monsters* and featured a giant, disembodied brain named Miko invading the earth. Unlike the alien invaders of previous films, Miko is a single invader with no underlings aside from the giant monsters. To break the earth peoples' spirits, Miko hijacks TV broadcasts to send out propaganda, an interesting technique that only Mabuchi could have come up with. Miko's arsenal includes King Ghidorah, Gigan, and Megalon—a monster created by Shinichi Sekizawa for 1969's *All Monsters Attack*.[5] Though described as an "insect monster" for *All Monsters Attack*, Mabuchi's version of Megalon is only described as having an eye on the end of its antenna, what characteristics it had beyond that are hard to determine. In this draft, King Ghidorah was the central antagonist,[6] lording over the other two monsters and also serving as Miko's "chariot" at one point—a giant brain alien riding King Ghidorah? Now that's a visual!

Either a fan of Daiei's Majin films or just ripping it off wholesale, Mabuchi created the new character Majin Tuol as an ally for Godzilla and Anguirus.[7] Majin Tuol is a gigantic statue transported from South America to Science Land, a research center—the centerpiece of which is a Godzilla Tower—rather than an amusement park. However, Miko never uses the tower for nefarious purposes and has his black heart set upon possessing the stone body of Majin Tuol as a new body. When Gigan cuts into the body with his buzz saw, it comes to life and Majin Tuol defeats all three alien monsters with its sword while Godzilla, who has been distracted by Ghidorah, is left with little more to do than incinerate Miko.

Both Mabuchi and Sekizawa's first drafts were turned in by July of 1971. Sekizawa's first treatment had Godzilla, Rodan, and Varan teaming up for the earth to battle Ghidorah, Gigan, and an unproduced monster called Mogu. The *Encyclopedia of Godzilla (Mechagodzilla Edition),* lists the following outline: "Operating from the Godzilla Tower, an alien brain named Miko sends King Ghidorah, Gigan, and Mogu to destroy Tokyo. Godzilla and Rodan intercept them, sending them retreating to space. But they return, and Godzilla and Rodan team up with Varan to combat them once again. Godzilla destroys the Godzilla Tower and kills Miko, and the three Earth monsters are able to defeat the space monsters once again and force them back into outer space."[8] Upon seeing this draft, Tanaka probably reminded Sekizawa that there was no Varan suit and to cut the monster. Also, the Rodan suit needed some repairs and the Anguirus suit was in much better condition. In the next draft, Anguirus and the Mothra larva had replaced Rodan and Varan. Likewise, Mogu was replaced with Megalon.

Sekizawa turned in the second draft of his story, *The Return of King Ghidorah*, in August and Mabuchi turned in his second draft for *Godzilla vs. the Space Monsters* on September 18, 1971. Which of the two selections were better? Mabuchi's script might be superior to Sekizawa's final script for *Godzilla vs. Gigan*. The problem, as usual, came down to money. It's a shame too, because Mabuchi's script was full of exciting twists. At one point, we are lead to believe one of the main characters is being held hostage by Miko. He is actually being bribed—and happily at that—by the alien brain to be his spokesperson on TV. Another twist comes when parts of Tokyo are destroyed when Godzilla and the military show up to defend it from Miko's monsters. Miko orders his monsters to flee and then televises footage of Godzilla in the middle of a burning Tokyo as if it were all his fault! Miko's use of Gigan to destroy earth's satellites was also innovative as was Miko's human-android form that the human protagonists battle inside Godzilla Tower during the climax.

Seeing that Sekizawa's version was more straightforward and easier to film, Tanaka chose it and a third draft was commissioned which plays out very much like the finished film aside from including Mothra and Megalon. Another similarity shared by both drafts is that the monsters pop up frequently for the sake of the child audience. Teruyoshi Nakano explained:

> "Since Godzilla movies were showing at the Toho Champion Festival, we had to make them fairly easy to understand for kids. Kids complained if there was some slow human drama or confusing scene, and they started to eat candy bars or run around in the theater. But once a special effects scene came up, they sat quietly and concentrated on the screen. So we had to show Godzilla every few minutes. But we couldn't just throw Godzilla in without any reason, so we had to make the mystery linger throughout the movie to keep the kids at the edge of their seats."[9]

In the final screenplay, this is accomplished by having Anguirus swim from Monster Island to mainland Japan and back again. In other versions, the monster had far more to do. For instance, in

Mabuchi's story, Anguirus battles Gigan and Megalon on a tropical island while in Sekizawa's draft, he confronts Godzilla Tower rather than the self-defense forces.

Like most Toho scripts, the third draft of what would eventually become *Godzilla vs. Gigan* is a grander version of the final film as there are more monsters and the battles are much more energetic. Sekizawa's new version of Megalon is more akin to Hedorah, and is described as a pollution monster that emits smog. It can also roll up to do a "pinball" attack.

Sekizawa continued *Godzilla vs. Hedorah's* anti-pollution stance in this draft. There is an additional scene in the Chairman's office between Fumio and Gengo where a pollution alarm goes off, informing them that photochemical smog in the Kawasaki district got so bad around noon that people outdoors suffered from burning eyes. There was even to be inserted shots of children holding their eyes in irritation from the smog. In the final scene of the script, after the battle is over, Godzilla walks away flanked by Mothra and Anguirus. As the camera cuts back and forth between the monsters in motion, images of smokestacks, traffic jams, etc. would play. The final scripted line is "Godzilla continues silently walking."[10]

Shosaku, who looks a bit too old to be a hippie in the finished film, is here described as a "youth" before being given a name. Also in *Godzilla vs. Gigan*, Kubota mentions plans to destroy Monster Island which are never mentioned again. In this script, in scene #31 where Gengo and Machiko discuss Children's Land's strange activities, Tomoko brings in a recent newspaper that states Monster Island has just suffered some sort of disaster![11] In this version, Machiko and Shosaku go to the rural village to learn Kubota and Fumio's true identities while Gengo goes to Godzilla Tower again. Fumio is younger in this script, having only been in junior high rather than high school when he died. In this version, after Tomoko dispels Kubota and his men with her karate skills, Gengo jokingly calls her, "Mamagon, ally of justice!"

The third draft also starts off just like the finished film, with some of the first shots being described as the panels of a manga comic. Even more emphasis is placed on Gengo's life as an artist and some scenes shows him adapting his real-life adventures into a manga as the story progresses. Other differences include the scene where Gengo first goes to look for Shima in Godzilla Tower. Just when he thinks he's found Shima, Kubota catches him—and then the tower suddenly shakes! Anguirus has shown up to confront Godzilla Tower, which he strikes with several body blows until, for no apparent reason, he leaves.[12] During the chaos, Kubota is knocked unconscious. Anguirus returns to terrorize the tower again in a later scene and this time, is brutally driven away by the tower's laser beams. At the end of act two, Mothra's presence is announced when Gengo and his friends go to warn the military about the aliens as the caterpillar goddess is reported making landfall in Japan.[13] During the scene where the heroes are captured by the aliens, Mothra knocks out the power to Godzilla Tower then she and Anguirus both get blasted by the tower's rays, though the duo bravely continue their attack. Another scene has the ground defense forces attacking Godzilla Tower, after which the aliens obliterate them with their laser beams.

In the end battle, Megalon is the first to attack Mothra and blows smog at her, causing her to choke badly. Anguirus and Mothra fare rather well in the fight until King Ghidorah finally intervenes. The three-headed dragon seems to be in charge of Megalon and Gigan and mostly floats in the air as the other two monsters do the dirty work. It is even suggested that Megalon and Gigan work as a pair and that Gigan moves slowly due to being a cyborg/"future" monster while Megalon moves quickly. It also appears that this version of Megalon can roll into a ball and perform a rolling attack. In fact, the chimneys of an industrial area are described as being knocked over like bowling pins during one such scene.

When a harbor is set on fire, Mothra and Anguirus look forlorn since there is nothing they can do until Godzilla finally emerges. This battle is more energetic than the one in *Godzilla vs. Gigan* where Godzilla literally walks into King Ghidorah to start the fight. In this version, Godzilla and King Ghidorah roar at one another and Godzilla fires his ray at the flying King Ghidorah to get the fight going. As in the finished film, Godzilla is pushed towards the tower by wind gusts from Ghidorah's wings and is blasted by its rays. Rather than Gigan giving Godzilla a thorough beating after the tower's lasers have weakened him, here King Ghidorah does the job himself. But as in the film, Godzilla quickly regains his strength and turns the tables on the alien monsters. Though the translation is difficult to discern, it would appear that Mothra takes a brutal beating herself from Gigan, though eventually, she gains the upper hand by spraying her webbing over him.

Tomoyuki Tanaka obviously liked this script and gave it the go-ahead, though the Mothra larva and Megalon were removed for budgetary reasons. Megalon probably caused Mothra to get the ax. While the Mothra larva marionette last used in *Destroy All*

Monsters was likely still available, Megalon was a new monster that would require the creation of another new suit. Anguirus would require no wireworks, but Mothra would, so the big bug was the good kaiju to get the ax to even out the monster tag team match. Fans will notice Toho was trying to spend as little as possible on this film since the Godzilla suit seems to literally be falling apart on screen.[14] The suit, however, had been refurbished as best it could. The head was slightly changed and Godzilla's left eye was back, though his bone hand was still healing. The monster king takes a horrendous beating during the middle of the fight and it's also notable for being the first time Godzilla had ever bled on screen. Teruyoshi Nakano explained that,

"Godzilla was an innocent at first, but by now he had become something of a "tainted hero." Tainted heroes, or heroes with weaknesses, were "in" at the beginning of the 1970s, so maybe Godzilla was influenced by that... I had many meetings with the screenwriters... It might have been fun if we had made a movie where Godzilla did lose."[15]

In Shinichi Sekizawa's finished script, his underlying theme would seem to be rampant commercialism of the monsters. The film was written during a second giant monster boom of sorts and Sekizawa makes his statement on commercialism with the M-Space Hunter Nebula aliens, who plan to kill the denizens of Monster Island and then replace them with giant mockups within their amusement park, Children's Land. [16] By this time, the monster toys (first introduced in 1967) were becoming more and more lucrative. In fact, the grosses of the Godzilla films themselves were not as important as the tie-in toys, and merchandising was beginning to become Toho's main driving force in producing the films.

Godzilla vs. Gigan certainly offers the child audience what it wants, monster action and lots of it. However, whereas *Godzilla vs. Hedorah* had multiple battles spaced out throughout the film, *Godzilla vs. Gigan* begins the end battle midway through the film and never lets up! The big contention with this long battle is that there is quite a bit of jarring stock footage from *Ghidorah, the Three-Headed Monster* (1964), *Invasion of Astro Monster* (1965) and *Destroy All Monsters* (1968). Not only that, the entire score is made from old music from various Akira Ifukube movies (the "new" theme music was written for Yoshimitsu Banno's *The Birth of the Japanese Islands*, and was even already used in Toho's trailer for

Godzilla vs. Hedorah!). When Tomoyuki Tanaka asked Ifukube about using his old tracks to score the film, Ifukube felt his themes were ill-suited for a cyborg monster but apparently gave Tanaka the go-ahead anyways.

Though the film was shot under the title *Earth Destruction Directive: Godzilla vs. King Ghidorah*, sometime in early 1972, new monster Gigan would be given title billing and the film became *Earth Destruction Directive: Godzilla vs. Gigan*. Indeed, the "space dinosaur" Gigan turned out to be a very popular monster and *Godzilla vs. Gigan* would go on to become the most successful Godzilla film of the 1970s. This surely cemented Gigan's return engagement for the next film in the series, *Godzilla vs. Megalon*, which would take the influence of the superhero/monster boom of 1972 to an even greater extreme...

Chapter Notes

[1] Gamera director Noriaki Yuasa was aware of this fact and even stated in the 1991 featurette *Remembering the Gamera Series*, "When I was working on [*Gamera vs.*] *Zigra*, the next project and storyline was already being planned for the following year. Though we didn't have a big budget, this time we had to compete with Toho's King Ghidorah, so we all agreed to come up with a monster that could compete with Ghidorah." As covered in the previous chapter, that film would have seen Gamera battle a two-headed winged menace named Wyvern but Daiei finally declared bankruptcy.
[2] Some sources imply Mabuchi went first, and then Sekizawa refined his ideas. If one goes based off the script dates, it would seem they were competing projects.
[3] Galbraith, *Monsters Are Attacking Tokyo*, pp.114-115.
[4] Ibid.
[5] This is strange because Sekizawa didn't use the monster in his own treatment initially.
[6] Notably, in the 1980s Toho gave Ghidorah the new nickname "King of the Enemy Monsters."
[7] It is worth noting that "majin" is a real word in Japanese that means "demon god" and not a distinct name like most monsters have. Early throughout *King Kong vs. Godzilla*, the ape monster is referred to as "majin".
[8] wikizilla.org/wiki/The_Return_of_King_Ghidorah_(Showa)
[9] Galbraith, *Monsters Are Attacking Tokyo*, pp.114-115.
[10] This scene may have been shot and left unused. This book's editor has in his collection several stills of a morose-looking Godzilla and Anguirus walking around Japan, some of which feature electrical miniatures not seen elsewhere in the film. Also, was this perhaps an explicit continuity tie with *Godzilla vs. Hedorah*, showing Godzilla is disappointed mankind has done nothing about their pollution problems since then?
[11] The translation is vague, but it would seem the newspaper is questioning whether it was a natural disaster or not.
[12] In this version, the tape does not summon Anguirus to shore. He shows up inexplicably for no known reason.
[13] It is not said in this draft if she hails from Infant Island or Monster Island, but the latter is more likely as the Shobijin are again absent.
[14] Supposedly, the Toho Godzilla publicity suit was modeled after the Godzilla Tower, and indeed, the swimming Godzilla from *Godzilla vs. Megalon* looks just like the tower. I would even go so far as to speculate that perhaps Toho desired to make a new Godzilla suit for this movie that resembled the tower but time and money ran out.
[15] Galbraith, *Monsters Are Attacking Tokyo*, pp.114-115.
[16] Unfortunately, this idea on destroying Monster Island is never fully realized in the final script even if Godzilla himself almost bites the dust.

26.
ATTACK OF THE AUTOMATONS

By 1972, automatons (or a robot in the image of a human) seemed to be all the rage on Japanese television. There was *Android Kikaider, Mazinger Z, Iron King,* and many more that aired during that year. It all started in 1971 with the launch of P-Production's *Spectreman*. In December, Toho and Tsuburaya joined together for a joint publicity contest with department store chain Seiyu. The competition, a part of Seiyu's Kiddie Kaiju Campus, would solicit entries from children to design a new robot superhero. Things start to get murky regarding just what the winning entry would be: featured in either a Toho monster movie or a Tsuburaya TV series.

The winning entry, Red Arone, was announced on live TV during the program *Chibikko Special* (broadcast Sunday night at 7 pm on Tokyo Channel 12). The monster's creator, Masaaki Sano, was there to watch as his creation walked on stage in a newly-constructed monster suit. The boy, by most reports, looked none too pleased with the realization of his creation, which resembled both Ultraman and Tranzor-Z, albeit with wings and an insect-like head.

Oddly enough, Red Arone (as in Red Arrow) would eventually morph into *Godzilla vs. Megalon's* Jet Jaguar. Toho's intentions with Red Arone are somewhat unclear but considering Toho began producing *Zone Fighter* in spring of 1973, one has to wonder if they intended *Godzilla vs. Megalon* as a backdoor pilot for a Red Arone TV series at some point. This would seem to be the case as the book *Godzilla: Toho Special Effects Movies* states that "[*Godzilla vs. Megalon*] was a project mainly focused on debuting Red Arone, a new television character that was recruited jointly with Tsuburaya Productions in the summer, and Godzilla's central title change was insurance in terms of sales."[1] Notice that this text identifies Red Arone as a "new television character." And for the record, the film was always a Godzilla feature so far as anyone seems to know. Rumors that it began as "Red Arone/Jet Jaguar vs. Megalon" turned out to be false as Teruyoshi Nakano has stated several times that it was always a Godzilla movie.

170

Series stalwart Shinichi Sekizawa, now very tired of working on the Godzilla series, was approached in the latter half of 1972 to come up with the next story. Sekizawa was busy writing song lyrics and only offered Toho a concept wherein an undersea kingdom angered by nuclear testing attacks the surface world.[2] He titled his idea *Godzilla vs. the Megalon Brothers: Undersea Kingdom's Annihilation Strategy*. From the title, one might think that Megalon originally was a pair of twin monsters or perhaps there were two Megalon species. However, due to Gigan's immense popularity, he was likely the other "Megalon brother"—probably meaning teammate in this instance.[3] Even Japanese sources say Sekizawa's brief treatment is unknown to the general public.

With Sekizawa unavailable, writing duties fell to director Jun Fukuda himself. Though Fukuda obviously inserted ideas into his previous three Godzilla movies, this is the first one where he is credited as a writer. His story treatment—which identifies the giant robot as Red Arone and was submitted on September 5, 1972—was titled *Insect Monster Megalon vs. Godzilla: Undersea Kingdom's Annihilation Strategy*. Obviously, Megalon, a smog-emitting alien in *Return of King Ghidorah*, was back to being an insectoid monster (it had originated as such in the *All Monsters Attack* script in 1969) as bugs were becoming trendy among Japanese children at the time.

Another treatment was submitted on September 27th with the same title. In this version, Jet Jaguar is still called Red Arone and when he finds Godzilla on Monster Island, the friendly kaiju is doing what is called "Godzilla Exercises" in the preparatory draft. In the final draft, it would change to Godzilla engaging in samurai-like exercises with a tree he holds in his hands.[4] Many publicity photos exist of Godzilla brandishing a tree-like a sword on the battlefield set in a spoof of the TV/movie franchise *Kogarashi Monjiro* (*Cold Wind Monjiro*). In these stills, Godzilla can also be seen munching on a telephone pole like a toothpick just as the central character Monjiro does. This idea even made it into the film's manga adaptation. According to Eiichi Asada in *Toho Champion Matsuri Perfection*, the idea was that of Jun Fukuda's. When Tomoyuki Tanaka found out about the scene he vetoed it though it had already been shot and Fukuda apologized to the special effects staff for wasting their time.

Fukuda originally envisioned Goro and Jinkawa as being friends from the same university. Goro was an electronics engineer and Jinkawa was studying to be a geologist—likely a way to tie into examining the red Seatopian sand. It was eventually decided that

 **ULTRAMAN ACE**

THE FIRST CONCEPT FOR WHAT TURNED INTO *ULTRAMAN ACE* WAS ALTERNATIVELY KNOWN AS *ULTRA TOUCH* (BECAUSE A MAN AND A WOMAN WOULD TOUCH TO BECOME THE ULTRAMAN) AND *ULTRA V* (AS THE FIFTH ULTRA SERIES) DURING PRE-PRODUCTION. THREE WRITERS (MORIICHI ICHIKAWA, SHOZO UEHARA, AND SHIGEHARU TAGUCHI) WORKED ON THE SERIES, EACH WITH THEIR OWN PITCH THEY EVENTUALLY STREAMLINED TOGETHER. UEHARA'S PITCH HAD AN EARTH SCIENTIST WHO HATES HUMANITY CREATING A MACHINE THAT CONTROLLED MONSTERS. FIGHTER JUN AMUNO WOULD JOIN WITH AN ULTRAMAN TO BATTLE THEM. ICHIKAWA'S IDEA HAD A MAN AND WOMAN UNITING TO BECOME THE NEW ULTRAMAN WHEN AN ARMY OF SPACE MONSTERS ATTACK FROM THE ANDROMEDA NEBULA (THE IDEA OF A MAN AND A WOMAN UNITING WAS PARTIALLY DONE TO DIFFERENTIATE IT FROM MALE-ONLY SENTAI). LITTLE IS KNOWN OF TAGUCHI'S IDEA OTHER THAN SATAN STAR WOULD BE A REOCCURRING ALIEN. ALSO, YAPOOL, THE FRANCHISE'S FIRST SEASON-SPANNING MAIN VILLAIN, INITIALLY CREATED THE SUPER BEASTS BY FUSING CREATURES ON EARTH WITH SPACE MONSTERS.

Jinkawa would be more exciting as a race car driver, and the college aspect was dropped. Also, Goro was meant to be testing an R.C. mini-plane rather than the dolphin paddleboat in his introductory scene.[5]

Though an advance poster for the film still identified the robot as Red Arone, at the last minute Toho changed his name to Jet Arone and finally Jet Jaguar. Designer Akihiko Iguchi (of *Ultraman Ace*) had already streamlined Red Arone to the point that all that remained of the original was the red, yellow, and blue color scheme. The finished design still retained some arrow-like elements.[6] It's likely the reason the name changed to Jet Jaguar was to avoid any possible legal disputes with Seiyu (or an adult Masaaki Sano down the line) so that way Jet Jaguar would exclusively be a Toho creation.

Despite having scripts completed in the fall, production for the film ended up being very rushed in the end. "That movie seemed to take forever to develop, then it went into production without enough preparation," Teruyoshi Nakano recalled.[7] It was eventually filmed in only three weeks time, with the new special effects scenes shot in one of those weeks. A reason for the shooting's delayed nature could have been that the same year,

Toho almost loaned out Godzilla to be in a Tsuburaya Productions feature film entitled *Godzilla, Red Moon, Erabus, Halfon: No Man's Land of the Monsters* (better known stateside as *Godzilla vs. Redmoon*) that never came to be. Toho may have been waiting to see whether or not that film would happen before they produced a Godzilla movie of their own.

The finished version of *Godzilla vs. Megalon* more or less emulates the many TV series that it was inspired by. The movie barely has enough story to fill an hour plus film and could have easily been compressed into a 30-minute TV episode. This is why the film is padded with several car chase scenes (there was reportedly a tie in with Honda Motor Company).[8] However, the film is possibly better paced than *Godzilla vs. Gigan*. Though short on story, *Godzilla vs. Megalon* has some intriguing subtext concerning Seatopia being devastated by underground nuclear testing. What little subtext existed was basically obliterated when a scene near the end was cut. Having admitted defeat, Emperor Antonio muses that perhaps he was no better than the surface dwellers for sending Megalon to attack them. Not only does this give the one dimensional villain some depth but also implies Seatopia isn't as bad as we think. Furthermore, another line was deleted where Goro was supposed to remark how ironic it was that Godzilla and the Seatopians were both victims of nuclear tests. In any case, Sekizawa is to be commended for using invaders that come from under the ground rather than the stars for a change. Considering the M-Space Hunter Nebula aliens are wrapped up with the Seatopians somehow, every Godzilla film of the 1970s revolved around an alien invasion of some sort.[9]

Though a fun, colorful children's film, *Godzilla vs. Megalon* debuted with a record series low attendance selling under 1 million tickets. It's unknown whether or not this is what scrapped a possible Jet Jaguar TV series. Jet Jaguar's Japanese Wikipedia page cryptically states, "Activities in video works other than *Godzilla vs. Megalon* were planned." It's also worth noting that Sci-fi Japan's Keith Aiken has also heard that Red Arone/Jet Jaguar was briefly considered for a spin-off television series.

Instead, Toho decided to cook up a new Super Sentai for their planned TV series which was eventually entitled *Meteor Man Zone* (known as *Zone Fighter* to American fans). Guest stars Godzilla, Gigan, and King Ghidorah were not last second additions for the sake of ratings and were always slated to appear in the series. Toho once again pre-dates the Marvel Cinematic Universe in that it had a television series that ran concurrently with their top movie franchise. Unlike *Marvel's Agents of S.H.I.E.L.D.* which never featured an actual Avenger, *Zone Fighter* does feature Godzilla no less than five times over the course of the series run. On top of this, there was a well done two-part episode with King Ghidorah.

This program began life as *Toho Special Effects Terror-Beast Series: Meteor Man Zone.* The pilot episode was written by none other than Jun Fukuda himself.[10] Originally, Godzilla and Gigan were both scripted to debut here ("Please Blast the Terror-Beast Missiles!") and the end battle would have seen Godzilla and Zone Fighter vs. Red Spark, Jikiro, and Gigan. For whatever reason, Gigan and Godzilla's appearances were held over until later.

While many sentai series of the time featured only one or two giant heroes and/or heroic aliens, *Zone Fighter* featured an entire family of alien refugees, the Sakimori family, that comes to earth when their home planet Peaceland is destroyed by the evil Baron Garoga and his army called Terror-Beasts. In each episode, Hikaru Sakimori, the eldest son of the Zone Family, transforms into the towering superhero Zone Fighter to battle one of the beasts. Like Ultraman, Zone Fighter could only fight for a set amount of time before his power ran out. However, just as with the Godzilla films, many ideas planned for the series were scrapped and early versions were somewhat different.

One such revision—likely due to budgeting—occurred with the Hotaru/Zone Angel character, who was originally scripted as being able to transform into a giant as well. If she had, she would've been the first giant female superheroine. Pre-production art also shows her to have a "Meteor Missile Might" weapon on her arm similar to Zone Fighter's. Also axed was a small pet panda monster "Pandaran" (to be brought to life via puppetry) that could grow to human size (brought to life in suitmation in this form) when needed and protect Hotaru while she was in human form. At this point in the creative process, Akira was unable to transform into Zone Jr. Also, Hikaru and Hotaru could not transform on their own and had to shake hands with a member of the Zone family in order to do so. The family's backstory was also different as Peaceland hadn't been destroyed by the Garoga aliens but had simply perished because it had come to the end of its natural life cycle just like Superman's home planet Krypton. The Jo Takeru character—the Zone family's human ally—wasn't created until the second planning phase of the series.

Godzilla arrived in the fourth episode, *Attack! Great Garoga Corps - Godzilla Enters,* airing on April 23, 1973. Apparently having cooled down with Toho since 1970, none other than Ishiro

Honda directed the episode (he would direct a fair amount of the series' episodes, though not as many as Fukuda) with special effects directed by Koichi Kawakita! The action is rough and tumble and Godzilla's breath is brought life via a smoke sprayer instead of an optical effect as it would be in the remaining episodes. The next week, King Ghidorah appeared in a two-part story comprised of Episode Five: *Shoot King Ghidorah Point Blank!* and Episode Six: *King Ghidorah's Counterattack!*, both directed by Jun Fukuda with special effects directed by Teruyoshi Nakano. Of all the monsters to appear on the series, it is Ghidorah who fares the best and the three-headed beast—now missing his manes—is operated better here than he was in *Godzilla vs. Gigan*! Furthermore, though Ghidorah's rays were always called "gravity beams" in Japan, it is here that Ghidorah actually displays his gravity-altering abilities—something he never does in the films. Godzilla returned along with Gigan in Episode 11: *Hair's Breadth: Roar of Godzilla!* The battle with Gigan is one of Godzilla's wackiest fights ever as he sticks his tail in Gigan's mouth and then lifts him off the ground and drops him multiple times.[11] Adding insult to injury, after Godzilla leaves, Gigan gets back up and prepares to battle again (hardly a cowardly gesture) then puts up a magnificent fight against Zone Fighter. Then Gigan is killed by the hero's Meteor Missile Might (King Ghidorah was able to survive said attack because he had to still be alive for the 1999-set *Destroy All Monsters*).[12]

Godzilla was back by Episode 15: *Sinking! Godzilla, Save Tokyo*. During the battle, Godzilla literally rips the enemy monster Zandora's tail off and proceeds to beat him with it. This episode is also notable for a scene where Zone Jr. is shown playing with Bullmark's 1972 Tin Godzilla released to tie in with *Godzilla vs. Gigan*. This was also the first episode where Godzilla and Zone Fighter shake hands (a recreation of the scene with he and Jet Jaguar from *Godzilla vs. Megalon*), much to Zone Jr. and Angel's amusement. Episode 21: *Invincible! Great Godzilla Rampage* opens with Zone Fighter and Godzilla involved in a friendly sparring match. After the match is over, Godzilla retires to his very own Batcave-like hideout with retractable doors! Later in the episode, when Zone calls for Godzilla's help, the monster emerges from his cave and does the fastest running of his career.[13] During the battle, Godzilla and Zone fight a pair of creatures reminiscent of Hedorah.

In what would've served as a proper series finale, Godzilla appears in Episode 25: *Terrible! Zone and Godzilla vs. the Allied*

 **ULTRAMAN TARO**

THOUGH SOME AT TBS FELT THE ULTRA FRANCHISE SHOULD END WITH *ULTRAMAN ACE*, IN THE FALL OF 1972, PLANNING BEGAN FOR THE NEXT ULTRA SERIES AT TSUBURAYA, THEN CALLED "ULTRAMAN JACK" (*RETURN OF ULTRAMAN'S* ULTRA HAD NOT YET BEEN GIVEN THE DESIGNATION ULTRAMAN JACK AT THIS TIME). HOWEVER, DUE TO RECENT USE OF THE WORD HIJACKING, THAT NAME WAS DECIDED AGAINST IN FAVOR OF TARO (OTHER CONSIDERED NAMES INCLUDED ULTRAMAN FIGHTER, STAR, AND Z). RATHER THAN THE ORIGINAL ULTRAMAN, THIS NEW ULTRA WOULD BE BASED MORE ON ULTRASEVEN. THE TWO HORNS CAME FROM THE ULTRA FATHER, HERE, TARO'S ACTUAL FATHER.

Terror-Beast Army, where, as the title suggests, he and Zone battle a virtual army of monsters. Oddly, Episode 26: *Crush! Garoga Gamma X Strategy*, which aired as the series finale on September 24, 1973, fails to wrap up the story of the Zone family and the Garoga aliens. This is unusual because Japanese television series are typically produced for only one season and always includes a series finale to tie up loose ends.

Why other existing monster suits (notably Anguirus and Megalon) weren't also utilized like Gigan and King Ghidorah is anyone's guess. Furthermore, the series' Japanese Wikipedia page implies that Godzilla's role was originally to be even larger: that of the star! However, this could just be an error in translation. On the other hand, why wouldn't Toho consider making a live-action Godzilla TV series?

In any case, the *Zone Fighter* series is much better than people give it credit for and had writing that was on par and sometimes better than its contemporaries like *Ultraman Taro*. The action-packed series, which included both human-sized and monster-sized superhero fighting—a rarity at the time—premiered on Monday, April 2, 1973, at 7PM on the Nippon Television Network (NTV). The series drew a 10% ratings share, only about half of what *Ultraman Taro* was drawing that same year.

Chapter Notes

[1] *Godzilla: Toho Special Effects Movies,* pp.117.
[2] That, and Sekizawa wrote the lyrics for the Jet Jaguar theme song, "Godzilla and Jaguar Punch, Punch, Punch!"
[3] Gigan was not written in just to reuse the suit. He was included due to the monster's popularity and a brand new suit had to be constructed for the rigors of the extensive monster wrestling.
[4] Could this have been an attempt to explain that all these new moves Godzilla has are the result of practice and tests on Monster Island rather than him just making them up as he goes along?
[5] Perhaps it's just a coincidence but *Godzilla vs. the Space Monsters* was to open with the main character playing with an A.C. helicopter.
[6] Be sure to notice that Jet Jaguar has an arrow emblem on his abdominal region, and the design of his chest area is also arrow-like.
[7] Galbraith, *Monsters Are Attacking Tokyo,* pp. 115.
[8] Goro even takes the Seatopian sand sample to the Honda Motor Industrial Technology Research Institute.
[9] Even Hedorah came to earth from space.
[10] Writer/Director Fukuda was not fond at all of this series, for when David Milner asked him about it his response was, "You don't have to mention that show!"
[11] Or is Gigan trying to fly away? Gigan's backstory here is that he was so weakened by the battle in *Godzilla vs. Megalon,* that he can no longer fly and has to be air-ballooned into the battle by the Garogas. You hear Gigan's flying noise and when he disconnects from Godzilla's tail, he zooms off a little ways before crashing down again.
[12] Though Gigan dies here, supposedly Tomoyuki Tanaka suggested bringing him back for *Godzilla vs. Mechagodzilla* (1974).
[13] Perhaps inspired by the alternate, unused running take in *Godzilla vs. Hedorah*?

27.
HORROR OF THE WOLF (GUY)

In 1973, one of Toho's more interesting productions that year included an adaptation of Kazumasa Hirai's beloved novel *Wolf Guy* (1969). In 1970, the book was adapted, and also greatly altered, for an even more popular manga release. Toho, however, chose to adapt the more downbeat version of the novel for their movie version, *Horror of the Wolf*. Toho acquired the film rights in the early 1970s around the time the great studio shakeup was going on. As a result, it seemed that Toho Eizo and Toho Eiga, both separate divisions of Toho Co. Ltd., vied to produce the film. As Toho Eizo typically produced the company's special effects films, it became something of a co-production between the two. Three drafts of the script were written and according to *Toho Special Effects Movie Complete Works*, very few changes were made from one version to the next.[1] One of the primary writers was Jun Fukuda himself, though why he wasn't considered to direct is unknown. Shiro Ishimori and Masashi Matsumoto—the latter, the film's director—worked on the script with him.

The story in both the film and the book concerns Akira Inugami (secretly a werewolf) transferring to a new school. On the eve of his first day, he is attacked by a gang that stabs him in the stomach. A woman on the street, Akiko, sees this happen but is shocked to see the boy remove the knife and walk away. The next day, Inugami discovers the woman to be his teacher. Also, Inugami is singled out by another vicious gang, led by Do Haguro, who run the school. A special bond develops between Inugami and Akiko, while at the same time, Do's hatred for Inugami grows. It all leads to a showdown at the mansion of Do's rich father when he kidnaps Akiko to entice the werewolf into a fight. On Inugami's trail all the while is a mysterious reporter named Shinmei[2] who will have a surprising effect on the story's ending...

Fundamentally, the finished film follows the novel very closely.[3] Chief among the differences is Akira is very quiet in the movie while in the book he is much, much mouthier. The film wisely moves the setting up to high school. In the novel, Akira is a 9th Grader at Hakutoku Gakuen Middle School. Also, the film begins with the assassination of Akira's family in the Alaskan tundra. The book lets the mystery of Akira's origins linger and we don't get this flashback until the novel's ending.

The book's first major deleted piece not to make it on film concerns Do (the son of a gangster) and one of his cronies (nicknamed "Rabbit Face") beating up some men in a bar to show Do's physical prowess despite being only middle school-aged. Typical of most novel-to-film adaptations, *Horror of the Wolf* speeds up the action. In the novel, on Akira's first day of school, the teacher instructs him to write his name on the chalkboard. "Rabbit Face" throws a knife into the board as Akira writes. The new student casually removes it and places it into his pocket to keep for himself. The teacher does not reprimand "Rabbit Face" for fear it will only give him the attention he wants. Throughout the day, the tension mounts as the gang members study Akira and Ryuko, Do's girlfriend, who continuously flirts with him. Finally, at the end of the school day, the gang fights Akira on the school's rooftop.

In the film, the action is condensed. When the punk student throws the knife, Akiko scolds "Rabbit Face" and Akira marches up to him to brazenly return his knife. This escalates into a confrontation inside the class (rather than stretching it out for the whole day). As the fight defuses, the film cuts to the next scene where Akiko inspects a shirtless Akira for the knife wound she saw him receive the night before. In the book, this part preceded the knife throwing scene. This is followed by a scene not in the book where two of Do's gang members assault a woman. After this, we finally get to the confrontation on the roof between Akira and the Haguro gang which is very similar to the book, right down to Do carving the symbol for 'dog' into Akira's back.

In both the film and the book, Akiko goes to Akira's apartment in a high rise condo. When she sees Akira's wolf-like visage, he tells her that it is a mask. When he refuses to remove it, the two wrestle around the floor as she tries to remove it herself. The movie has a huge difference where, as this happens, Akira begins to think of his Alaskan home in the summer with Akiko in tow. The scene seems to convey that Akira feels happy and at ease with the older woman. This was an addition made to the final shooting script and it appears in neither the novel nor the early drafts. When Akiko walks home from the apartment feeling dejected, she is assaulted by two rapists on motorcycles. Akira rescues her in his wolf form. In the book, Akira only hospitalizes the men but in the film he kills them.

In the book as Akiko recovers at home, she is visited by a teacher colleague, Tadokoro, who informs her that Akira has been beaten up regularly for the past three days by the Haguro gang but shows no signs of injury! He also relates how passionate Akira is regarding wolves and how he chastised the teacher for comparing a wolf to a dog. The movie retains this scene but has a different character, the enigmatic reporter Shinmei, go visit Akiko.[4] In both the film and the source material, the school's anti-violence committee of students approaches Akira to represent them at an assembly. Akira chastises them for being so naïve to think it will make a difference—though in the book he is more loquacious. There, the school staff has a meeting about whether or not they should allow the rally (for fear of retaliation by the Haguro gang). It is revealed (only to the reader) that the principal has a deal with Do's father that Do can be absent as much as he likes and graduate so long as he doesn't cause "undue" trouble at school. The principal, a calculating individual, sees the powerful Akira as his way out of this problem and asks Akiko to make sure Akira goes to the rally. The principal's secret hope is that it will take attention away from the students and place it on the new boy. Akiko does as she's told and asks Akira to attend after class. He begrudgingly agrees. When Akiko goes inside to tell the principal that Akira will be there, she is introduced to reporter Shinmei, there to interview her about her rescue the other night by a wolf that injured the two would-be rapists.

In the movie, Shinmei was introduced much earlier and the debate amongst the school staff is not present. Also in the book, the anti-violence rally takes place within an indoor gymnasium but in the film, it's an outdoor stadium. In the book, the rally has 1/3rd of the student body show up while in the movie, hardly anyone comes to the stadium and a live band plays as the Haguro gang attacks Akira.[5]

A follow-up scene between Akiko and Tadokoro about how the principal likely put Akira in Akiko's class just to disassemble the Haguro Gang was not utilized in the film.[6] Soon after, Shinmei pulls up beside Akiko in his car and she tells him to quit following her because she gets a bad vibe from him. As soon as she arrives home, she receives a phone call from Shinmei. She then hears a wolf baying at the moon which entices her to go out for a walk (by now, she suspects Inugami as a werewolf). On her walk, she spots a wolf but it runs away. Shinmei then comes out of the shadows, noting how a wolf shouldn't be in Tokyo. This whole sequence is not in the film.

In the book, the School Unity club offers to escort Akira to and from school as a show of support. There is a scene where one of the girls from the club follows him to his condominium but in the movie, it is Akiko that does this. Around this same time, Akira walks into his room to find a naked Ryuko waiting for him. This also happens in the book but has bigger ramifications to the plot. In the book, Akiko goes to see Do to try to persuade him not to kill Akira. Do decides to hold her hostage to entice Akira into a fight. It is after this has occurred in the book that Akira finds Ryuko waiting for him in bed and it is she who informs Akira that Akiko is with Do. The placement of the bit with Ryuko in the movie just ends up being a throwaway scene.

In both the book and movie, Akira goes to Akiko's apartment to verify that she is missing (why he does so in the film is a mystery). In the book, Akira fights with his own conscience about trying to stay away from human emotion and to not rescue Akiko. In the movie, Shinmei shows up at Akiko's apartment. It would seem to be he who tells Inugami that Akiko has been kidnapped (in the film, he watches as Akiko goes to Do's mansion).

In both adaptations, Akira eventually does go to Do's home though the book has an additional scene where he fights a Doberman pincher in his human form. From that point on, the movie follows the novel closely regarding the ending; though the book is bloodier (and the film itself is already very bloody). In both versions, a badly wounded Akira is impaled on Do's sword. He then stabs Do with the same sword killing him. Do's father and his goons then come in to continue the fight. In the book, this fight is slightly glossed over but the movie stretches it out. Also, in the novel there is a scene where Do cuts off some of Akira's fingers and a hand. In the film, Do's father slices off some of Akira's fingers, but not his hand.

In the novel, when the severely wounded Akira is in his death throes after the battle, the boy has a flashback[7] to his youth on the tundra which is what opens the film version.[8] This lengthy flashback gives additional information not found in the film. The book implies that Akira's father is entirely human and his mother is likely another werewolf. In the film adaptation, the father figure is never seen, only the mother. Also, the book has an airplane, not a helicopter, massacre both his parents. The novel also reveals that Akira's first transformation occurred on that night, something not explicitly shown in the movie.

In both versions, Shinmei comes to Akira and Akiko's rescue (by this point, Akira has managed to kill Do's father and all his men) and takes them away in his car. There, Akiko holds a bloody, dying Akira in her arms. The film shows a wolf running away into the tundra and up into the sky—probably a metaphor for Akira's death. The book confirms Akira's death, however, with a lengthy epilogue that initially teases the reader into believing he survived.

The book continues with Akira's body on the operating table and the doctors eventually declare him dead. This is followed by Akiko having a dream of her chasing Akira through the snow. He turns into a wolf and she understands he has decided to leave the world of man behind no matter how much he loves her. When she awakens, Akira's aunt (never seen in the film) is there to see her. Feeling Akiko is too weak to talk, she leaves. That night, Akiko goes to the rooftop to kill herself but just as she is about to jump, the howl of a wolf pierces the night—Akira's cry, somehow, someway. This is enough to get her to back away. Shinmei soon pops up and does his best to talk her down and back into her room. Afterward, the reporter makes a phone call to Akira's aunt, who implies Akiko needs to believe Akira is alive so that she won't harm herself. Shinmei then flashes a grin described with "well developed canines"—the first and only clue that he is also a werewolf.

All is revealed when Akiko goes to visit Akira's aunt who tells her Akira's backstory, born as a hairy werewolf boy. This is why his parents (the aunt believes they were both human, though the book's narration implies the mother is a werewolf) took him to the tundra. Why they were killed is never explained. As Akiko leaves the mansion, it is finally confirmed that Shinmei is a werewolf. It was he who howled to get Akiko to climb down from the ledge. He drives her home and the two are attacked by surviving members of the Haguro gang. Shinmei scares them off with his werewolf prowess. He then convinces Akiko to go on living and to move to Alaska, where some other "wolf men" live.

Toho's *Horror of the Wolf* turned out to be very popular with the young adult audience it was made for, though it's interesting that the studio never bothered with a sequel. Toei, however, did produce *Wolf Guy* (1975), an adaptation of their own starring Sonny Chiba as an adult Akira Inugami which some might argue is a sequel of sorts. *Horror of the Wolf* has never been released in any form in the U.S., nor does it appear that Toho ever commissioned an English dub for it in Hong Kong. The only way for non-Japanese speakers to understand the film is to read the English translation of the novel (which is what this author did).

Chapter Notes

[1] The only major difference was initially Inugami had more dialogue about his dead mother but in the finished film, his feelings are illustrated through the numerous flashbacks to her death. Likewise, Do was supposed to have an intense hatred of his father that was apparently glossed over in the finished product.
[2] In the book his name is Akira (yes, the same first name as the main character), though we will keep with the movie version's name, Shinmei, to avoid confusion with the main character, Akira Inugami.
[3] Though the author doesn't outline the plots for the other films, this one is an exception as no English subtitled print of *Horror of the Wolf* exists. Therefore, many English speaking fans are unaware of the plot, even if they have seen the film.
[4] This would be Toshio Kurosawa's character. In the book he doesn't emerge until later and, again, is named Akira.
[5] It's conspicuous enough to make one wonder if Toho had difficulty obtaining extras.
[6] In the book, it is explained that Akira has a long history of non-violence despite being constantly tormented. Stranger still, most of Akira's tormentors end up dead or injured while trying to fight him. The principal sees this in the boy's records and hopes the same will happen with the Haguro gang.
[7] Supposedly, future *Godzilla vs. Space Godzilla* director Kensho Yamashita plays an unnamed character in one of the flashbacks.
[8] The movie can be rather confusing, but in the book it is revealed the wolves are normal wolves, not werewolves. Furthermore, in the scene where they are massacred in the film, this is not meant to represent the same people who killed Akira's parents, just normal hunters. This explains Akira's hatred for humans.

PROFILE: JUN FUKUDA

Though known primarily as an action film and Godzilla series director, Jun Fukuda was also heavily involved in the writing process of several films. Fukuda was born on February 17, 1923, in Manshu, Korea. Fukuda joined Toho in 1946 as an assistant director working under Hiroshi Inagaki. Later Fukuda served as the assistant director on *Rodan* (1956) under Ishiro Honda. Fukuda caught his big break when Honda was unable to direct *The Secret of the Telegian* (1960) as originally planned, and so Fukuda did it. It would end up being the lone favorite for Fukuda among his science fiction films—Fukuda doesn't have the best of things to say about his Godzilla movies, which he began working on in 1966. Working on *Ebirah, Horror of the Deep*, he told David Milner that he had to cut a great deal of scenes from the movie. When Milner asked what scenes Fukuda responded, "My memories about *Godzilla vs. the Sea Monster* are not very clear because I was working on a script for a television drama while we were shooting the film. As soon as we completed it, I went to the NHK studios and confined myself so I could finish the script. Toho sent me a copy of the VHS tape edition of *Godzilla vs. the Sea Monster* when it was released. It was like opening up an old wound."[www.davmil.org/www.kaijuconversations.com/fukuda.htm] Fukuda returned for *Son of Godzilla* in 1967 and wasn't asked back to the series until 1972's *Godzilla vs. Gigan*. In the 1970s, Toho began to lean on Jun Fukuda heavily in terms of not just directing, but also writing—and this didn't always include films that he was slated to direct, like *Horror of the Wolf* (1973). When Shinichi Sekizawa was too busy to flesh out a screenplay for *Godzilla vs. Megalon,* it was Fukuda who ended up writing the shooting script for it. The same thing happened again on the next Godzilla film. Even though Sekizawa had authored a screenplay, Fukuda was called in to polish it into the final script for *Godzilla vs. Mechagodzilla*. Fukuda also wrote the pilot for the *Zone Fighter* TV series which initially contained Godzilla and Gigan in that episode. In the end, Fukuda wrote three episodes of the series and directed six. Though Fukuda talked of a Mechagodzilla sequel in interviews in mid-to-late 1974, he ultimately didn't return for 1975's *Terror of Mechagodzilla*. After this, Fukuda and Toei writer Masahiro Kakefuda teamed to write *Invisible Man vs. the Human Torch*. Though some call it a sequel to *The Secret of the Telegian*, it is only a spiritual sequel and has no continuity ties. The fun cops and robbers meets sci-fi script was meant to relaunch Toho's mutant films that had been popular in the late 1950s and early 1960s. It sadly went unproduced. Fukuda was chosen to direct Toho's *Star Wars*-inspired *The War in Space* in 1977, his final feature film. After that, Fukuda was eyed to direct a potential Godzilla reboot in 1978 which never came to be. Fukuda's last directorial effort occurred on the TV series *Monkey* in 1979. After that Fukuda retired...or so one would think due to his IMBD page. In fact, Fukuda transitioned to working on documentaries, which he continued to do as late as 1998. Fukuda passed away two years later on December 3, 2000, in Setagaya, Tokyo.

Selected Filmography
Secret of the Telegian (1960) (director)
Ankokugai no kiba (1962) (writer, director)
Ebirah, Horror of the Deep (1966) (director)
Son of Godzilla (1967) (director)
100 Shot/100 Killed: Golden Eye (1968) (writer, director)
Operation Mystery (1968) (writer, director)
Zone Fighter [TV series, episodes 1, 2, 5, 6, 11, 13] (writer, director)
Godzilla vs. Megalon (1973) (writer, director)
Horror of the Wolf (1973) (writer)
Invisible Man vs. the Human Torch (1974) (writer, proposed director) [unproduced]
Godzilla vs. Mechagodzilla (1974) (writer, director)
Kigeki damashi no jingi (1974) (writer)
ESPY (1974) (director)
The War in Space (1977) (director)

28.
JAPAN SINKS!

Horror of the Wolf wasn't the only popular novel adapted by Toho in 1973. For their New Year's blockbuster in December of that same year, Toho unleashed *Submersion of Japan,* based on the hit novel by Sakyo Komatsu. The film was Toho's seminal success of the 1970s, drawing a crowd of nearly 9 million people, making it Toho's biggest moneymaker of the decade. However, the movie was almost made by Daiei instead.

Sakyo Komatsu began work on the novel all the way back in 1964. "Let me discuss why I wrote that novel," Komatsu told *G-Fan* magazine.

> "I started to write *Nippon Chinbotsu* in 1964, and it took 9 years to complete. Until 15th of August 1945, when the Showa Emperor officially declared the end of the war to the Japanese nation, all the Japanese, especially a teenager like me, believed in governmental slogans such as "honorable death for all hundred million Japanese nations" or "decisive battle is when Americans landed on mainland Japan." We all made up our mind for the coming death. However, once the war was over, Japanese overcame the consequence of defeat so easily, and by the 1960s, people were happy about the rapid economical growth of the country. When I saw those circumstances, I wanted to reconsider the meaning of what "Japan" is and what "Japanese" are. That is why I wrote *Nippon Chinbotsu.*"[1]

Komatsu had a good relationship with Toho as they had optioned one of his first novels for a film all the way back in 1964. Though the story, *The Japanese Apache,* went unproduced, Komatsu felt gratitude towards the studio. Toho had also optioned Komatsu's manga *ESPY* for a film in 1967, though it went unproduced until 1974. Komatsu's *Japan Sinks* was published on March 20, 1973, by Kobunsha and became a runaway hit, selling over 3 million copies and raking in ¥120,000,000 (around $1,099,923). However, even before it was published, the novel was being considered for a movie adaptation. Specifically in early 1971, Daiei was toying with making a film about the Great Tokyo Earthquake. Then in the fall of 1971, Daiei caught wind of Komatsu's novel. Without a written agreement with Komatsu, Daiei president Masaichi Nagata announced that the company would produce *The Sinking of the Japanese Archipelago*! However, Daiei officially admitted bankruptcy soon afterward. Komatsu stated in an interview with *Science Fiction Studies* that, "When I wrote *Japan Sinks*, I had no expectation that it would become a movie."[2]

One account states that Tomoyuki Tanaka optioned the novel even before it was published, but the book *Japan Sinks 1973 Complete Documentation* would make it seem that Tanaka read it the very day of publication and called Komatsu on the phone that evening. "I felt so obligated that in 1973 when we were discussing a film version of *Japan Sinks*, I gave them the movie rights with almost no conditions. I think they paid 1.5 million yen," Komatsu told *Science Fiction Studies*.[3] Toho fast-tracked the film for production, initially eyeing March of 1974 for release until bumping it up to become the New Year's Blockbuster for 1973. Akira Kurosawa was even discussed as director, though Shiro Moritani was chosen instead. Four script drafts were written, all of which followed the novel closely. A great deal of research also went into the film with consultation by geophysics expert Professor Hitoshi Takeuchi, seismic engineering professor Yorihiko Osaki, oceanography expert Professor Noriyuki Nasu, and volcanologist Akira Suwa, director of the Meteorological and Earthquake Research Institute. Special effects director Teruyoshi Nakano studied earthquakes as well. "I became sort of an expert on earthquakes, and read more than seventy books on the subject," he said in a 1997 *G-Fan* interview.[4]

Of the adaptation, Komatsu later said, "I was quite surprised when Toho had completed the film just after the book was published. The movie was quite faithful to the original story, and I was quite satisfied."[5] That said, there are naturally plenty of differences between the novel, the four scripts, and the finished film. For those that haven't seen *Submersion of Japan*, the general outline of the film is this:

When an island mysteriously sinks into the ocean overnight, Dr. Tadokoro is sent to investigate. In a submarine piloted by Onodera, Tadokoro makes a startling discovery in the Japan Trench. The doctor hypothesis that within a matter of years Japan will sink into the ocean. However, it becomes apparent the submersion will happen much sooner than that when an earthquake devastates Kanto, killing millions. Preparations are made to evacuate as many Japanese to other nations as possible. As Japan continues to sink into the sea, Dr. Tadokoro decides to die with the nation he loves, while Onodera searches for his missing fiancé, Reiko, in an unknown country.[6]

The book begins with Onodera walking through a sweaty mass of people on the street. He is on his way to take the train to his next assignment when he has a chance meeting with Rokuro Go, a worker on the Super Express Line—a character that didn't make it into the movie. The two share a beer on the train and Onodera tells him about the island that recently sank. The film, on the other hand, begins with Onodera looking over the Wadatsumi, where he is soon introduced to Dr. Tadokoro—described in the book as a portly man, not the dignified figure cut by actor Keiji Kobayashi in the film. Author Komatsu has a cameo in this very scene!

Another significant scene in the book had Onodera and the others witnessing a volcanic eruption at sea while on the way to their diving point. This sequence was included in the first draft of the script and was removed with rewrites. In another scene from the book, Onodera and the crew also receive testimony from the Japanese and Polynesian fishermen who were on the island when it sunk. Naturally, the movie has to condense the action and there are only two trips down below in the Wadatsumi but in the book, there are three. In one trip, the men see a quasi-kaiju: a 100-foot long stingray!

One of the bigger subplots in the book and the movie has Onodera's boss Yoshimura setting him up with a wealthy heiress, Reiko Abe, in the hopes that he can then promote Onodera within the company. In the novel, Yoshimura takes Onodera to a club and informs him of these plans while in the movie, he simply does so in his office. Also at the club, Onodera meets a hostess named Mako. Though this character wasn't included in the film, she has a significant impact on the book's final scene. After informing him of his plans, Yoshimura drives Onodera to Reiko's house to meet her. In the movie, this also happens and once we see Yoshimura pull up to the house, we immediately cut to Reiko and Onodera having a solo dinner getting to know one another.

 **JAPAN SINKS (THE SERIES)**

A TV SERIES ADAPTATION OF KOMATSU'S BOOK WAS PRODUCED IN CONJUNCTION WITH THE FILM, ALSO OVERSEEN BY TOMOYUKI TANAKA. IT WAS A TELEVISION RETELLING OF THE CONCEPT AND DIFFERENT ACTORS PORTRAYED THE ROLES. NATURALLY, THE STORYTELLING WAS MORE EPISODIC, SOMETHING KOMATSU EVEN JOKED ABOUT WITH *SCIENCE FICTION STUDIES*. HE TOLD HIS INTERVIEWERS, "THE NOVEL DESCRIBED THIS GRADUAL SUBMERGENCE OF JAPAN BY FOCUSING ON A FEW DIFFERENT AREAS, BUT IN THE TELEVISION SERIES, DIFFERENT LOCALES WOULD GO UNDER EVERY WEEK. AS IF THEY WERE TELLING PEOPLE, 'STAY TUNED FOR THE DESTRUCTION OF YOUR CITY!' (LAUGHS)."
[WWW.DEPAUW.EDU/SFS/BACKISSUES/88/KOMATSU-INTERVIEW.HTM] THE TV SERIES HAD SEVERAL NOTABLE DIFFERENCES FROM BOTH THE NOVEL AND THE FILM. WHILE IN THE FILM ONODERA AND REIKO ARE SEPARATED, IN THE TV SERIES IT IS REVEALED THEY BOTH ESCAPE TO AUSTRALIA. ALSO, THE BIG TOKYO EARTHQUAKE THAT TAKES PLACE IN THE MIDDLE OF THE FILM SERVES AS THE SERIES FINALE. THE FINAL SCENE OF THE SERIES SAW A PAIR OF LOVERS CLASPING HANDS FOR THE LAST TIME INSIDE A CHRISTIAN CHURCH, THE ONLY STRUCTURE IN JAPAN STILL STANDING AS THE LAST OF THE ISLAND NATION SINKS BENEATH THE WAVES. SAKYO KOMATSU HAD WANTED KAORU YUMI TO PLAY REIKO IN THE FILM. PERHAPS AS A CONSOLATION TO THE AUTHOR, SHE WAS GIVEN THE ROLE IN THE TV SERIES.

In the book, Reiko is having a party. Onodera mingles with various industrial types, one of which wants to create an underwater amusement park. In the book and movie alike, Reiko and Onodera go off alone for a swim in the ocean where Reiko reveals she knows of Yoshimura's plan. The two have a civil but somewhat awkward conversation but Reiko is actually interested in Onodera. In the book, it is stated that the two make love on the beach while the film only hints at this. In the book, as they lay on the beach, Onodera hears a radio report on the death of his friend Go, an apparent suicide because of his failure working on the Super Express line. After this revelation, the earthquake occurs. Onodera takes the party guests back to Tokyo via hovercraft in Sagami Bay. Onodera soon receives a phone call from Dr. Tadokoro requesting he come to his lab immediately. Furthermore, Tadokoro is funded by a mysterious, unseen group called The Church of the Seven Seas. In the film, the BAC World Oceanic Foundation is his sponsor.

189

Another significant scene exclusive to the book has Onodera enduring an earthquake in Kyoto at Go's funeral. From this point forward, the book and movie are quite similar up to the great Tokyo earthquake. In the book, the earthquake scene is told through the eyes of a character that only appears in the book, Yamazaki. Tadokoro and Onodera's ship then sails into Tokyo to help with rescue efforts in the water, something that doesn't happen in the film. The movie deals more with the aftermath of the earthquake while the book jumps ahead in time. As investigations into the Japan Trench continue, the book has an exciting scene not in the movie where Onodera is picked up from his research ship after doing a dive in unstable volcanic waters. While flying above the ship, a character named Katoaka informs Onodera that a submarine, likely from a foreign power, is spying on them (Japan's sinking has not yet been made public).

When Dr. Tadokoro confirms Japan's impending doom aboard the ship he states, "Even a child can figure out what will happen next." That line was scripted to take place inside the ship's control room in the final draft. During shooting, they decided the scene would work better on the deck. The movie also has Dr. Tadokoro prematurely release the dreadful news on live TV. When a reporter makes light of the situation, Tadokoro even attacks him! The scientist is labeled a quack and not everyone takes his prediction seriously. No such thing happens in the book.

After Onodera reconnects with Reiko, both plan to leave Japan for Switzerland. However, they are separated when Mt. Fuji erupts. In the book, Reiko disappears after her phone call to Onodera and for all we know, she may have died. In one draft of the script, the last we see of Reiko is her fainting during the Mt. Fuji eruption and there is no reveal that she is still alive in the final scene. Later drafts inserted Reiko into the tsunami scene where she is seen overlooking the shore and about to board a boat bound illegally for Korea. Onodera trying to warn the people going out to sea at the fishing port is not in the book either nor was it in early script drafts.

Though the movie has a montage of Onodera's efforts to rescue as many Japanese as possible, the book has a notable scene not in the film. Onodera and his chopper crew come across some stranded hikers who wish to climb the Japanese Alps one last time before they sink. Onodera gives up his spot on the chopper so that as many as possible can be flown to safety. Among the hikers who must stay are Mako, the hostess from earlier in the book. An eruption occurs, and this is the last we see of Onodera until the last few pages of the book...

The film ends with Dr. Tadokoro and Prime Minister Yamamoto sharing a lengthy talk about why Tadokoro wishes to die with Japan rather than be saved. It occurs right outside of Prince Watari's home after he has passed. In the book, the Prime Minister[7]—who doesn't have the presence that actor Tetsuro Tamba brings to the onscreen character—has already evacuated. Instead, this scene takes place between Tadokoro and Watari, simply known as "the old man" in the book. Watari compares the Japanese to infants who are losing their mother. In the movie, this dialogue is given to Tadokoro in his talk to the Prime Minister. This section of the book, before the old man dies, also includes one of Komatsu's most lamented deleted scenes. As the old man's youthful servant, Hanai, tells him that she wishes to stay by his side, he begs her to leave and have a life of her own. When he insists that she also change clothes for her journey, he asks if he may see her naked body and she obliges. "I wanted that in the movie, even if they had to film it from behind," Komatsu told *Science Fiction Studies*.

The movie famously ends with Reiko and Onodera on different trains, possibly on different sides of the world or even rolling past one another. This ending wasn't given to the film until late in the game and it's certainly not how the book ends. The book has something of a surprise ending, albeit an unhappy one. Onodera wakes up on what he thinks is a ship. He is in a foggy state of mind and the girl attending to him reminds him that she is his wife. We, as the reader, wonder if this is Reiko that he's finally been reunited with. Onodera asks her several times if Japan has sunk and to look out the port window and see. In the last two paragraphs, Komatsu reveals Onodera's fate: he's not on a ship with Reiko. He's on a train in Siberia with Mako, whom he has apparently married. We never learn what happened to Reiko and the book ends.

The film was a huge hit that perfectly captured the fears of the Japanese people. Author Stuart Galbraith summarized it best in his book *Japanese Science Fiction, Fantasy, and Horror Films* where he wrote, "it dramatized one of the most innate fears among Japanese citizens: the disastrous annihilation, natural or otherwise, of their vulnerable nation."[8]

Chapter Notes

[1] Homenick, "Universal Vision", *G-Fan* #80 (Spring 2007), pp.56.
[2] *Science Fiction Studies* #88, Volume 29, Part 3, November 2002. www.depauw.edu/sfs/backissues/88/komatsu%20interview.htm)
[3] Ibid.
[4] Ryfle and Galbraith IV, "Teruyoshi Nakano", *G-Fan* #27 (May/Jun 1997), pp.24.
[5] Homenick, "Universal Vision", *G-Fan* #80 (Spring 2007), pp.56.
[6] LeMay, *Big Book of Japanese Giant Monster Movies Vol.1*, pp. 226.
[7] Originally, we were to be introduced to the Prime Minister out on the golf course but there seemed to be trouble with the location so a new scene of the Prime Minister arriving at his private residence was substituted in its place (the scene on the golf course worked its way into 1980's *Deathquake* from Toho).
[8] Galbraith, *Japanese Science Fiction, Fantasy and Horror Films* pp. 214.

PROFILE: SAKYO KOMATSU

Of all the Japanese science fiction writers, Sakyo Komatsu is the best known outside of Japan. This is in large part because several of his epics were adapted into films released in America, like *Submersion of Japan* (1973, in the U.S. as *Tidal Wave* in 1975) and *Day of Resurrection* (1980, as *Virus* in the U.S.). Komatsu was born Minoru "Sakyo" Komatsu in Osaka on January 28, 1931. He studied Italian literature at Kyoto University and was a fan of writers like Kobo Abe, author of *Inter Ice Age 4*, a novel with a few of the same ideas as *Submersion of Japan*. Before striking it big as an author, Komatsu worked as a reporter and even wrote material for some stand-up comics. In 1961 he entered his short story, "Pacem in Terris", in a contest in *SF Magazine*. Though he didn't win, he received an honorable mention and ¥5,000 from Toho Studios (the sponsor). In 1962, his story "Memoirs of an Eccentric Time Traveler" was published in *SF Magazine*. Sometime after this, he also helped in the planning stages of Tsuburaya Productions burgeoning sci-fi series, later to be known as *Ultra Q*. In 1964 his first novel, *Japanese Apache*, sold a remarkable 50,000 copies and was almost adapted into a film by Toho. That same year, Komatsu also published *Day of Resurrection* which one day would be made as a movie, albeit 16 years later. Komatsu's next near-miss with motion pictures came when Toho planned on adapting his manga *ESPY* in 1967. That film too would eventually be made some years later after the success of the movie adaptation of *Submersion of Japan* (1973). The novel was a huge hit in Japan and was even released in the U.S. in 1975 at the same time that the U.S. version, *Tidal Wave*, was released. Komatsu was impressed by the fact that his novel had been translated into English, but not by the translation itself, which not only omitted scenes but also misinterpreted them. Komatsu told Science Fiction Studies that, "One [mistake] I noticed right away is in the part where the old man Watari is staying with Dr. Tadokoro at the villa on Lake Ashinoko. The translator mistook Ashinoko for the name of a woman. [Laughs] The scene is supposed to take place on a lake in the mountains of Hakone, but suddenly it was as if we had been transported to a hostess bar in Ginza!"[www.depauw.edu/sfs/backissues/-88/komatsuinterview.htm] After the success of *Submersion of Japan*, in 1974, Komatsu's *ESPY* was dusted off by Toho and finally put to film. That same year, Komatsu also worked as a writer for Tsuburaya Productions TV series *The Monkey Army* (released as a compilation movie in the U.S. called *Time of the Apes* in 1987). Around this time Komatsu also worked with Toho in trying to come up with a sequel to *Submersion of Japan*, though the film never happened (the sequel, *Japan Sinks, Part II*, in novel form, was finally published in 2006). Komatsu's next film adaptation was *Day of Resurrection* in 1980, released in the U.S. and starring the likes of George Kennedy, Glenn Ford, and other well-known Hollywood stars. Before that, in lieu of the success of *Star Wars*, Tomoyuki Tanaka had asked Komatsu to come up with a space opera for him. The fruits of this labor weren't published until 1982 as *Sayonara Jupiter*, which was filmed by Komatsu himself for Toho in 1984. Like Steven King on *Maximum Overdrive*, Komatsu more or less helped to direct *Sayonara Jupiter* and had almost complete creative control on the project (except for the budget that is). The film was a flop, as was the next Komatsu-inspired film: *Tokyo Blackout* (1987). Komatsu lived long enough to see *Submersion of Japan* remade by Shinji Higuchi in 2006 as *Japan Sinks*. Komatsu also ironically lived to see the Tohoku earthquake and tsunami of 2011 which he quasi-predicted in *Submersion of Japan*. On July 21st of that year, *Sakyo Komatsu Magazine* quoted its namesake's thoughts on the disaster. Komatsu said, "I had thought I wouldn't mind dying any day ... but now I'm feeling like living a little bit longer and seeing how Japan will go on hereafter." Komatsu died five days later on July 26, 2011, in Osaka aged 80. The cause was complications from pneumonia.

Selected Filmography/Bibliography
Matango (1963) (uncredited ideas)
Japanese Apache (1964) [novel] (writer)
Day of Resurrection (1964) [novel] (writer)
ESPY (1965) [manga] (writer)
Ultra Q (1966) [TV series] (development work)
Japan Sinks (1973) [novel]
Submersion of Japan (1973) (based upon the novel)
ESPY (1974) (based upon the manga)
The Monkey Army (1974) [TV series] (writer)
Japan Sinks (1974) [TV series]
(based upon the novel)
Tidal Wave (1975) (based upon the novel)
Day of Resurrection/Virus (1980)
(based upon the novel)
Sayonara Jupiter (1982) [novel] (writer)
Sayonara Jupiter (1984) (writer, producer, director)
Tokyo Blackout (1985) [novel] (writer)
Tokyo Blackout (1987) (based upon the novel)
Japan Sinks (2006) (based upon the novel)
Japan Sinks, Part II (2006) [novel] (writer)
Japan Sinks, Part III [concept, uncompleted]

29.
ENTER THE (MECHANICAL) DRAGON

With the Godzilla suit having survived its five beatings on *Zone Fighter*, Tomoyuki Tanaka decided to produce another film adventure for 1974 to celebrate the series' 20th anniversary.[1] Tanaka's own idea for the film was unique. Nuclear testing from the U.S. and China inadvertently creates two new, evil Godzillas. With Japan stuck in the middle, Godzilla must face off against the bad Godzillas. Though fascinating, Tanaka likely knew that by demonizing the U.S. and China, this might sully the film's appeal in those two markets so it was dropped.

In 1972 during construction on the Okinawa expo (to commence in 1975), Tanaka had run into sci-fi writer Masami Fukushima. It is thought that Tanaka asked Fukushima, who had previously worked on *Matango*, to come up with ideas for a Godzilla movie set around Okinawa to capitalize on the 1975 Expo.[2] Fukushima then came up with an idea for a mechanical monster, as he felt there were "too many dinosaur monsters" already.[3] Tanaka also asked Shinichi Sekizawa to come up with a plan for the next entry in the series. Sekizawa's response: "But there aren't any monsters left!"[4] Tanaka put Sekizawa and Fukushima together to come up with the new storyline. The result was a treatment entitled *Monsters Converge on Okinawa: Showdown in Cape Zanpa* that combined Okinawan folklore with space-age machinery. Oddly enough, this treatment featured neither King Seesar nor Mechagodzilla. In their place were Mothra and a robot named Garugan. Rather than the King Seesar statue, the heroes play keep away from the alien invaders with a "Secret Sword," which unlocks a hidden cave in Okinawa.

The treatment by Sekizawa and Fukushima was likely completed in the spring of 1973 and was then handed over to Jun Fukuda to be fleshed out into a full shooting script. Not wanting to write the whole thing himself, Fukuda called TV writer Hiroyasu Yamaura to help with the task. Yamaura remembers being surprised by the call (the writer wondered if it was because he had worked with Fukuda on the TV series *Operation Mystery* in 1968). In an interview in *Toho Champion Matsuri Perfection*, Yamaura said he considered it an honor to work on the Godzilla series, though he was completely unaware at this time that it was to be the 20th Anniversary Godzilla movie!

Yamaura remembered he and Fukuda wrote the screenplay with a small budget in mind and decided that setting the final battle along the exotic Okinawan shoreline would make up for the fact that there was no city to destroy in *Monsters Converge on Okinawa*. When the script evolved into *Godzilla vs. Mechagodzilla*, the oil field battle was added as a way to reuse footage from 1973's *Submersion of Japan*, the success of which Teruyoshi Nakano claimed enabled this film to have a slightly higher budget than the last three Godzilla films. Of his script, Yamaura said in *Toho Champion Matsuri Perfection*, "I had a desire to make a scintillatingly beautiful movie with a strong, fancy color pallet."[5]

Monsters Converge on Okinawa is similar to the finished film from a narrative perspective. It even has an opening akin to the one in the film. There, Anguirus witnesses an explosion in a snowy wasteland that goes completely unexplained. In the first draft, it is Godzilla that witnesses the explosion (also unexplained) on a glacier.[6] As for characters, this script focuses on a lead not unlike Masahiko Shimizu from the finished film. In this case, the character is a reporter for a TV series, *Folklore and Travel*, named Kan Futoshi who teams up with Nami, a ceremonial dancer from Okinawa, to transport a relic known as the Secret Sword back to Okinawa.[7] They travel via cruise ship which has a near-miss with Anguirus at sea.[8] Also on board are a whole group of Yakuza-like aliens intent on capturing the sword as well as two INTERPOL agents that intervene to save the heroes. When the parties reach Okinawa, it is learned the aliens—known as the Garuga—have constructed an 80-meter robot called Garugan. Interestingly, their plan is not to conquer earth for themselves, but to auction it off in a bidding war to other aliens (a unique idea that was laid aside in the finished draft)![9] Godzilla, Anguirus, and an adult Mothra (again sans Shobijin) appear to confront the robot and save the day by defeating Garugan. Futoshi, Nami, and the INTERPOL agents place a bomb on the low-budget aliens' Cessna, killing them. When the plane crashes, it is revealed that the aliens were really ape-like creatures when their charred remains hit the ground.

A scene where Mothra shows up to menace Cape Zanpa could be a precursor of sorts to the scene in the finished film where the characters puzzle over Godzilla ("Fake Godzilla," the disguised Mechagodzilla) going bad. Like Godzilla, Mothra's "attack" is shown on the news. There is also a precursor to the scalding chamber in the finished film. Here, the aliens trap the heroes in Garugan's silo as the machine is about to take off and they barely escape being incinerated. During the finale, Godzilla's ray notably collides with Garugan's just as his ray does with Mechagodzilla's. Also, Garugan was to battle the U.S. military in Okinawa.[10]

Tomoyuki Tanaka took issue with certain elements of the script—one of which was apparently Mothra's inclusion. Though she got the boot (likely due to wireworks issues and lack of a usable marionette), Tanaka actually came in with a bigger budget and advised Fukuda to change the script to better utilize this. Whereas the first script contained only one battle, the next would have three total. And though the 80-meter Garugan was interesting, Tanaka had other ideas. *King Kong Escapes* was to be the anchor for the 1973 Winter Champion Matsuri Festival, so robotic doppelgangers were on the minds of he and special effects director Teruyoshi Nakano.[11] One of the two suggested that Garugan become Mechagodzilla.

In *Monsters Are Attacking Tokyo* Nakano said:

"In the movies before it, Godzilla's opponents looked just like a costume, so I wanted to make something more unique. There was this robot called Mechani-Kong in *King Kong Escapes*, so I was wondering if I could make something like that in a Godzilla movie. Actually producer Tanaka thought about it. Mechagodzilla reminded people of the bad Godzilla of the 1960s. We couldn't have made Godzilla the bad guy, because children wouldn't have liked it, so we created Mechagodzilla and acted out our feelings through it—we transposed our feelings of going back to the origins of the Godzilla series on to Mechagodzilla. The only way to bring Godzilla back to the original point was to have Mechagodzilla act as the greatest evil."[12]

Nakano added about the creation of the new foe, "We used medieval armor for Mechagodzilla's inspiration; I went to the museum a lot to study armors from medieval times."[13] A translated interview with Nakano that appears in Peter Brothers' *Sons of Godzilla* is also illuminating:

"First of all, I got a tin plate Godzilla toy and said I wanted to smash it. Because making curved lines is difficult with

 **ULTRAMAN LEO**

ULTRAMAN LEO'S CONCEPT REMAINED MOSTLY THE SAME FOR THE DURATION OF ITS DEVELOPMENT. THE LAST MINUTE ADDITION WAS THAT OF ACTOR KOJI MORITSUGU RETURNING AS DAN MOROBOSHI. ORIGINALLY, THE CAPTAIN OF THE MONSTER ATTACKING CREW WAS TO BE TERUTARO KAWAKAMI, AN EARTHMAN WHO KNEW THE IDENTITY OF GEN AND TRAINED HIM. ALTERNATELY, IN ANOTHER ARTICLE TETSUTARO KAWAKAMI IS LISTED AS AN ALIEN WHO TRAINS GEN. IN EITHER CASE, THIS ROLE WAS ALWAYS OFFERED TO MORITSUGU WHO TURNED IT DOWN UNTIL THEY MADE THE CHARACTER A RETURNING DAN MOROBOSHI INSTEAD (REPORTEDLY EVEN THEN, MORITSUGU WAS VERY RELUCTANT TO RETURN TO THE ROLE). AS A RESULT, ULTRASEVEN APPEARS IN THE PILOT EPISODE AND IS INJURED TO THE EXTENT THAT HE CAN NO LONGER TRANSFORM. OTHERWISE, ONE COULD HAVE EXPECTED ULTRASEVEN TO POP UP SEMI-FREQUENTLY IN THE SERIES. THE ORIGINAL LEO SUIT HAD A SILVER LINE PATTERN THAT CLOSELY RESEMBLED ULTRASEVEN AND TARO'S RUNNING DOWN THE TORSO BUT IT WAS ERASED. AS ULTRAMAN LEO WAS BEING DEVELOPED AS ULTRAMAN TARO WAS STILL BEING PRODUCED, AN EARLY DESIGN FOR LEO BECAME THE FINAL ENEMY ALIEN ON *ULTRAMAN TARO* AND APPEARED IN THE 53RD EPISODE/SERIES FINALE AS ALIEN VALKIE. EPISODES 38 AND 39 (THE MAIN CROSSOVER EPISODE WITH PAST ULTRAS) OF *ULTRAMAN LEO* WAS ORIGINALLY TO BE EVEN MORE AMBITIOUS THAN IT ALREADY WAS AND WOULD HAVE INVOLVED SOME SORT OF ALL-OUT WAR INVOLVING THE LAND OF LIGHT. THIS STORYLINE WAS INSTEAD ADAPTED INTO THE 1979 ANIMATED *ULTRAMAN.*

metal work, we used as many sharp angles as we could, which is good, because it gave it a feeling of sharpness... so I gave the instructions to design something on the basis of this smashed-in shape."[14]

With these stipulations in mind, Fukuda and Yamaura created *Showdown in Zanpamisaki: Godzilla vs. Mechagodzilla* (though the duo decided against Tanaka's request that Gigan serve as Mechagodzilla's teammate).[15] More characters were changed and added. Futoshi Kan became Masahiko Shimizu and was demoted to being the kid brother of new lead character, Keisuke Shimizu. For whatever reason, Nami was downgraded to a minor character and was replaced by the character of Saeko, the head of an archeology department. Agent Tamura became Agent Nanbara and his partner was named Tamura and has a much smaller role. Roles were then written for Akihiko Hirata and Hiroshi Koizumi, to play Professor Miyajima and Professor Wagura, respectively, to further play into the celebratory 20th anniversary aspect of the film.

The aliens evolved from the Garuga into the ape aliens from the Third Planet of the Black Hole. Fans have long speculated that the alien's ape-like design stemmed from the *Planet of the Apes* films (which were very popular in Japan), the last of which, *Battle for the Planet of the Apes,* was released in Japan on July 21, 1973. However, equally to blame for the designs were the ape villains lead by Dr. Gori on *Spectreman*, a popular super Sentai program in Japan at the time.[16]

This script also featured a precursor to King Seesar, which was alternately called both King Barugan and King Vulcan.[17] The monster was bronze colored with "huge horns" said to deliver the killing blow to his enemies. Otherwise, the beast is basically King Seesar—statue, song, reflective eyes, and all—only with large horns and a different name.[18]

The script for *Showdown in Zanpamisaki: Godzilla vs. Mechagodzilla*, which Yamaura implies was written in ten days, contains 219 scenes, while the final draft contains 205. It begins like the finished film with Anguirus kicking off the story, only in this case, it would seem Anguirus is at a foggy seaside setting rather than a snowy one.[19] The script progresses as normal, but when Nami has her vision it is not of King Ghidorah and the script simply has the visual "monster wolf."[20]

The first additional scene in this draft was a superfluous one—likely later cut by Fukuda—of Keisuke Shimizu sitting inside his office when an on-site supervisor bursts in to tell him that a cave has been discovered. Keisuke and the supervisor go to inspect the cave, covered in red dirt. At first, the two wonder if it is an old WWII dugout/shelter. As they go inside they discover an ancient mural with "primitive monsters" and a statue that looks familiar to Keisuke. He then remembers that he saw it when Nami was doing her folk dance. The next additional scene has Saeko and Keisuke getting off the plane at Haneda Airport.

This script doesn't have Mechagodzilla being catapulted out of Mt. Fuji encased within a rock. It has Mechagodzilla rise from some smoke with lava splashing in the background. Also, the Fake Godzilla was to be confronted by jet fighters after it causes destruction. Shortly after this, Anguirus surfaces to confront the imposter. The battle is similar to the one in the film except the script says that when Anguirus bites Mechagodzilla, the metal breaks his teeth! In an even wilder departure, in this version Mechagodzilla doesn't reveal its true form during the oil refinery battle with Godzilla. In the scene, the real Godzilla emerges from the water rather than through a building built on a pier over the water as in the finished film (the latter was an idea by Teruyoshi Nakano to try to make Godzilla's entrance more interesting). The disguised Godzilla then takes flight and attacks the real Godzilla from the air! After landing and fighting Godzilla a bit, Mechagodzilla takes to the air a second time and knocks Godzilla over from behind. From there, the battle plays out as in the finished film.[21]

In another deleted scene, Professor Miyajima, Masahiko Shimizu, and Miyajima's daughter board a flight out of Tokyo for Okinawa. Following this is an additional bit between Keisuke and Professor Wagura where they continue to discuss the location of King Barugan. Once Wagura has figured out the spot to place the statue, Keisuke and Saeko get into a car and drive to the port where they will travel to Okinawa by boat. An alien operative tails them and a very brief car chase ensues where Keisuke loses the alien in traffic. On the cruise ship, Nanbara point blank asks Keisuke about the Barugan statue after he shoots the ape alien off the side of the ship. The agent then laughs and walks away, leaving Keisuke to wonder how he knows what the statue is.

The red sunrise is more elaborate in this version, with it making the sea and the hotel swimming pool appear red as well. In the film, when trying to escape the aliens' cavernous base, Keisuke's orange car is destroyed by a bomb planted by the aliens. If anyone wondered how Keisuke and Saeko made it to the beach where the Seesar Shrine is located, this script has a scene of Keisuke running down the road at night until he flags down a passing truck that gives him a lift.

The end battle has some significant differences. Firstly, Mechagodzilla never revealed its true form during the oil refinery attack.[22] So when the robot is launched from Okinawa, it still looks like Godzilla. Also, Mechagodzilla fires upon King Barugan as he is sleeping, waking the monster when Nami's song seems to have failed. The battle between the two progresses as it does in the finished film, only King Barugan head-butts Mechagodzilla with his horns. As the battle goes on, it is much more violent and physical, with more grappling than what is seen in the final film. Once Godzilla shows up[23] and starts blasting Mechagodzilla with his ray is when the monster's fake skin begins to gradually melt away (there is test footage in the film's trailer that shows Mechagodzilla transforming in Okinawa, but this is coincidental). This happens fairly late in the battle, and not long after the mechanical menace's real form is revealed Godzilla uses magnetic powers to draw the monster to him. After the machine explodes, there is another scene deleted from the final script where Miyajima explains his pipe to Nanbara. Masahiko asks Miyajima if he'll make a pipe made of space titanium next and the trio shares a laugh.

For whatever reason, in the final draft, King Barugan became King Shisa/Seesar (who lost his horns) and it was decided that Mechagodzilla would reveal its true form earlier during the oil refinery battle. Overall, Fukuda's last foray into the director's chair also ends up being one of his best as the film moves along at a brisk, exciting pace, much like *Ebirah, Horror of the Deep* (1966). While the last movie indulged in mad-cap car chases, here Fukuda's actors engage in gritty Sonny Chiba *Street Fighter*-like brawls. The monsters even get into the Chiba-style action with Mechagodzilla causing blood to squirt from Anguirus' jaws and Godzilla's neck. And it would seem that when he turns himself into a magnet, Godzilla's pose emulates the distinctive "redistributing his chi" poses Chiba strikes throughout *The Street Fighter*. Elements from the James Bond series and even spaghetti westerns popular at the time were also added into the mix. Most of these influences materialized in the form of Shin Kishida's cool INTERPOL agent character, Nanbara.

The finished film proved to be popular with fans (in large part, thanks to Mechagodzilla), increasing attendance from *Godzilla vs. Megalon* and inspiring another sequel—even if it would be the last for some time.

Chapter Notes

[1] At a talk at Takashimaya in 2004, Teruyoshi Nakano claimed that the fourteenth film was planned be the final entry in the Godzilla series until Mechagodzilla turned out so popular.
[2] Yoshimitsu Banno also had an idea for a story called *Godzilla vs. Gezira* (NOT Gezora, the Kanji are different) which would have had Godzilla fight an underwater alien at the Expo though Tanaka shot it down for budgetary reasons.
[3] *Toho Special Effects Movie Complete Works*, pp.170.
[4] As quoted in Guy Tucker's *Age of the Gods*.
[5] "Interview with Hiroyasu Yamaura", *Toho Champion Matsuri Perfection*, pp.118.

[6] This would be followed by shots of Mothra taking flight off of Infant Island and Anguirus departing Monster Island.
[7] Nami's grandfather, much less cantankerous here, also plays into *Monsters Converge on Okinawa*.
[8] The cruise ship and a stay at the Naha hotel were both givens due to a pre-arranged cross promotion agreement with Japan High-Speed Ferry, All-Japan Airways, Okinawa Tamaizunihora, and Teruken Yusen.
[9] The M-Space Hunter Nebula aliens from *Godzilla vs. Gigan* are mentioned specifically as candidates to buy the earth!
[10] Some sources claim Mechagodzilla was to attack U.S. forces in the draft entitled *Showdown in Zanpamisaki: Godzilla vs. Mechagodzilla*. However, this scene is not in the script that the author read.
[11] Mechagodzilla was created before the re-release, as the Champion Matsuri cut of *King Kong Escapes* ends with a teaser (text only) for *Godzilla vs. Mechagodzilla*!
[12] Galbraith, *Monsters Are Attacking Tokyo*, pp.116.
[13] Ryfle and Galbraith IV, "Teruyoshi Nakano", *G-Fan* #27 (May/Jun 1997), pp.24.
[14] Brothers, *Sons of Godzilla*, pp.158.
[15] Adding in Gigan is mentioned in *Toho Special Effects Movie Complete Works* on page 170 so the information would seem to be legitimate.
[16] Not coincidentally, one of the fully masked ape aliens (the one shot by Shin Kishida's character) in *Godzilla vs. Mechagodzilla* was portrayed by Takanobu Toya, who played the ape alien Dr. Gori on *Spectreman*.
[17] It would seem *Famous Monsters of Filmland* picked up on this early name. In his article "Monster Movie Memories" in *G-Fan* #69, Ronnie Burton remembers that *Famous Monsters of Filmland* described King Seesar as "a revamped version of Baragon".
[18] The book *Toho Special Effects Movie Complete Works* also made mention of King Barugan spewing a golden lava from his mouth, though this author saw no such ability displayed in the script.
[19] The film's opening scene with Anguirus is said to be set in Siberia. The reason for this hails all the way back to Japanese dialogue in *Godzilla Raids Again* (1955) which stated Anguirus originated from Siberia. However, Yamaura states in an interview in *Toho Champion Matsuri* that the location is actually Nemuro in Japan.
[20] The script denotes Mechagodzilla as a wolf in sheep's clothing when it is disguised as Godzilla, so perhaps this is a reference to that?
[21] Actually, the brutal beating Godzilla receives during the course of the film is reportedly because Jun Fukuda was beginning to hate Godzilla! Fukuda said he explicitly wanted Mechagodzilla to "beat the hell out of him", a line more or less spoken by the alien leader Kuronuma in the finished film!
[22] This is also the case in the manga, where Mechagodzilla isn't unveiled until the final battle.
[23] Godzilla's head rising over the hill in Okinawa was meant to emulate his introduction on Oto Island from the original *Godzilla* (1954).

PROFILE: HIROYASU YAMAURA

Hiroyasu Yamaura's introduction into the world of Godzilla is an interesting one in that before co-writing *Monsters Converge on Okinawa/Godzilla vs. Mechagodzilla* with Jun Fukuda, Yamaura was primarily a screenwriter for television. He was born on January 28, 1938, and attended college at Waseda University for a time before dropping out. In 1961, while studying under the university, he won the grand prize at the 16th Artistic Festival Publicly-Awarded Screenplay contest with his entry "Battle". His screenplay made its debut during the TV series *Toshiba Sunday Theater* that same year. From then on, Yamaura wrote steadily for television, and eventually became a writer for *Ultra Q* (1966). From there he went on to work on a number of other Tokusatsu themed TV series, notably *Ambassador Magma* (1967), *Ultraseven* (1967), and *Fight! Mighty Jack* (1968) to name a few. In 1971 he began writing for *Mirror Man*, and this led to him also writing for other Tsuburaya TV series like *Jumborg Ace* (1973). In 1973 he wrote *Godzilla vs. Mechagodzilla* with Jun Fukuda. Furthermore, either after this, or maybe before it, Yamaura wrote an additional Godzilla screenplay: *Japan S.O.S.: Godzilla's Suicide Strategy!* Considering Yamaura says in *Toho Champion Matsuri Perfection* that he was surprised to receive a call from Jun Fukuda to work on his first ever G-film in 1974, this would seem to imply Yamaura would have had to have written *Godzilla's Suicide Strategy* after *Godzilla vs. Mechagodzilla*. *Suicide Strategy* doesn't bear Fukuda's name, only Yamaura's, so it could be a sequel to *Godzilla vs. Mechagodzilla* or even *Terror of Mechagodzilla* (1975). Another possibility is that Yamaura submitted it for the 1978 Godzilla Revival, but this is unlikely as Tomoyuki Tanaka was dead-set on getting away from Godzilla's heroic image. In any case, the success of *Godzilla vs. Mechagodzilla* oddly didn't prompt more movie screenplays from Yamaura, who went back to writing for many TV series like *Lupin the Third* (1977-1980), *Star Wolf* (1978), and two of Tsuburaya's dinosaur series. In the 1980s, he contributed to *Ultraman 80*, and this was his last contribution to the giant monster genre. In 1987, Yamaura co-wrote the film adaptation of Sakyo Komatsu's novel *Disappearance of the Capital* (aka *Tokyo Blackout*) about alien clouds in Tokyo. In addition to his works in film and television, Yamaura is also a prolific novelist as the author of the Hoshiko series of the Cobalt Library.

Selected Filmography
Toshiba Sunday Theater ["Battle" episode] (1961) (writer)
Seven Detectives (1961) (writer)
Ultra Q (1966) (writer)
Ambassador Magma (1967) (writer)
Ultraseven (1967) (writer)
Monster Prince (1967) (writer)
Mighty Jack (1968) (writer)
Fight! Mighty Jack (1968) (writer)
Operation Mystery (1968) (writer)
Mirror Man (1971) (writer)
Mazinger Z (1972-1974) (writer)
Jumborg Ace (1973) (writer)
Unbalance: Horror Theater (1973) (writer)
Monsters Converge on Okinawa: Showdown in Cape Zanpimasaki (1973) (writer) [unproduced, developed into Godzilla vs. Mechagodzilla]
Godzilla vs. Mechagodzilla [feature film] (1974) (writer)
White Fang (1974) (writer)
Japan S.O.S.: Godzilla's Suicide Strategy (date unknown) (writer) [unproduced]
Dinosaur War Izenborg (1977) (writer)
Lupin the Third (1977-1980) (writer)
Star Wolf (1978) (writer)
Dinosaur Task Force Koseidon (1978-1979) (writer)
Galaxy Express 999 (1978-1981) (writer)
Ultraman 80 (1980-1981) (writer)
Adieu Galaxy Express 999 [feature film] (1981) (writer)
Tokyo Blackout [feature film] (1987) (writer)

30.
IN THE WAKE OF JAPAN SINKS:
ESPY AND CATASTROPHE 1999

Submersion of Japan was a game changer for the Japanese film industry and heralded the success of the "panic movie"—the Japanese equivalent of the U.S. disaster movie. It also made Sakyo Komatsu a very hot commodity. Before *Submersion of Japan* had even been released, Tomoyuki Tanaka optioned the rights to another hit disaster book, Tsutomu "Ben" Goto's *Great Prophecies of Nostradamus*, published in November of 1973. Toho optioned the book in early December and newspapers reported on the production in January.

Perhaps proving that Tanaka's dislike of *Godzilla vs. Hedorah* writer/director Yoshimitsu Banno was over-exaggerated, the producer approached Banno about converting Goto's book into a movie. In fact, it was probably *Hedorah's* ecological horror motif that convinced Tanaka that Banno was just the man for the job![1] Goto's book seemed to be more of a hypothetical scenario about what would happen to Japan if Nostradamus's predictions were to actually happen rather than a character-driven story as the film would turn out to be. The script for 1961's *The Last War* was used as a jumping off point and indeed, elements of that film are easy to spot in the main characters: a patriarch with a sick wife, his daughter, and her fiancé. Banno spent two weeks writing the film at the Shibuya Inn (with occasional input from director Toshio Masuda, who would go on to receive top writing billing) and gave the scenarios from Goto's book a more ecological slant.

"I did a lot of research to write that screenplay," Banno later told *Tokyscope*. "...so I was seeing data like, one out of every four babies born in the Niigata Prefecture at the time was deformed. When that's all you're reading every day, you really start to think the world is going down the tubes, that tomorrow it will all be over."[2] A scene featuring a red, polluted ocean (known as a red tide) and another where children that drink from a contaminated zinc mine develop strange abilities was based on the real-life Minamata Disaster. Experts on abnormal weather, food ecology, ultra-scientific phenomena, and plant sociology were also consulted on the film.

Remarkably, only two drafts rather than the usual four were written. It seems Toho had cold feet regarding the cannibalistic natives from the get go. The scene was in the first script but was removed from the second and final shooting script. When it came time to actually shoot, the scene was reinstated. Also, the Prime Minister's speech was twice as long in the first draft!

The resultant film, *Prophecies of Nostradamus (Catastrophe 1999)*, is a rather amazing feat as it manages to include a diverse array of disasters and phenomena in a coherent—if not slightly episodic—narrative. Climate change, cannibalism, nuclear war, giant animals, and zombies are all covered without the film feeling bloated or overloaded. Perhaps that's because at the backbone of the film is the same basic structure and emotional core of *The Last War* with the family that anchors the film. The ending of *The Last War* packs a bit more of an emotional punch, though, because there all but one of the main characters do actually die (and he knows he will soon die when he's subjected to the radioactivity in what used to be Tokyo). *Prophecies of Nostradamus (Catastrophe 1999)* ends with a simulation of the world being destroyed in a nuclear war. This is followed by an impassioned speech by the Japanese prime minister that gives some hope for the future. Though darker overall than *The Last War*, it does have a more upbeat ending (at least the original Japanese version does, some of the re-edits are a different story).

Two of the film's most shocking scenes (the cannibalistic natives in New Guinea and the post-apocalyptic 'soft-bodied' humans) would result in this picture's eventual fade into obscurity—after it rocked the Japanese box office, that is. It was Toho's #1 moneymaker in 1974. Trouble came for the film when a Bomb Sufferers Organizations Council and the No Nukes Group from Osaka Prefecture went to the Eirin Board (the Japanese equivalent of the MPAA) and demanded Toho stop screening the film. One week after release, Toho ran newspaper ads apologizing for the content of the film. They pulled the movie and recut it down to 90 minutes to remove the offensive footage. As was done with *Submersion of Japan*, a TV version was set to follow but was cancelled as was a planned sequel.[3]

Due to *Submersion of Japan's* success, Toho was hot to adapt another Sakyo Komatsu property. In this case, Toho turned to a film they had planned to produce seven years ago but had abandoned: *ESPY*. Komatsu's *Esupai* (or a spy with ESP) had

 **EVIL OF DRACULA**

WHEN *LAKE OF DRACULA* PROVED TO BE ANOTHER BIG HIT IN THE SUMMER OF 1971, FUMIO TANAKA WANTED DIRECTOR MICHIO YAMAMOTO TO PRODUCE ANOTHER. YAMAMOTO DIDN'T WANT TO AND THE TWO MEN WERE THEN TRANSFERRED TO TOHO'S TV DEPARTMENT ANYWAY. THREE YEARS LATER, AFTER THE CINEMATIC OCCULT HORROR BOOM HAD BEGUN, TANAKA AGAIN PITCHED A SEQUEL. WRITER EI OGAWA AT FIRST TURNED IN A SCRIPT CALLED *THE BLOODSUCKING CLAW* (THE FINAL VERSION IS CALLED *BLOODSUCKING ROSE* IN JAPAN AND *EVIL OF DRACULA* INTERNATIONALLY) ITS OVERALL CONTENTS ARE UNKNOWN AND THIS ITERATION OF THE SCRIPT WAS DIFFERENT ENOUGH THAT SEVERAL TOHO BOOKS CONSIDER IT A 'LOST PROJECT.' THOUGH YAMAMOTO FOUGHT TANAKA'S ATTEMPT TO MAKE THE PREVIOUS TWO FILMS INTO FULL BLOWN HAMMER HORROR COPIES, THE DIRECTOR FINALLY RELENTED ON THIS ENTRY AS THE FILM PULLS HEAVILY FROM HAMMER IN A NUMBER OF WAYS. IT REVOLVES AROUND THE PRINCIPAL OF AN ALL GIRL'S SCHOOL WHO IS REALLY A VAMPIRE. HE WAS ORIGINALLY A CAUCASIAN PRIEST WHO BECAME SHIPWRECKED IN JAPAN. THE PRIEST BECOMES A VAMPIRE WHO GAINS THE ABILITY TO WEAR THE FACES OF HIS DEAD VICTIMS. DURING THE ENDING, THE VAMPIRE WAS SUPPOSED TO REVERT BACK TO THE FORM OF THE CAUCASIAN PRIEST AS HIS BODY DECOMPOSED BUT THIS ASPECT WAS DROPPED. THOUGH SKILLFULLY MADE, *EVIL OF DRACULA* WAS NOT A SUCCESS LIKE THE OTHER TWO FILMS, CONCLUDING THE BLOODTHIRSTY SERIES.

begun as a manga in *Weekly Manga Sunday* in 1964. The film rights had been acquired by Toho in February of 1966 and was announced for production soon after. Even back then, Jun Fukuda was to direct the movie based upon a script written by Ei Ogawa.

It seems the 1966 iteration of *ESPY* (eyed for a 1967 release) was in part inspired by the huge James Bond/spy craze of the late 1960s. In fact, the original *ESPY* was to have starred Akiko Wakabayashi (Aki, the ill-fated Bond girl in *You Only Live Twice*), along with Tatsuya Mihashi (1970's *Tora! Tora! Tora!* and "Phil Moscowitz" in Woody Allen's *What's Up Tiger Lily?*), Makoto Sato (Uchida in *The H-Man*), and Mie Hama (Madame Piranha in *King Kong Escapes* and Kissy Suzuki in *You Only Live Twice*). However, Wakabayashi left Toho, which already had a busy year in 1967, and they shelved the film. The final nail in the coffin came with the launching of the U.S./Japanese co-production of *Latitude Zero*, which turned into a disaster from start to finish.

Submersion's massive success reminded Toho that they already owned the rights to another Komatsu story, but this wasn't the only reason the script was revived. "There was a great deal of interest in E.S.P. in the early 1970s. That also prompted Toho to produce *ESPY* when it did," Fumio Tanaka explained. A visit to Japan by famed psychic Uri Geller in 1974 also ignited a fire under Toho. "I remember that the pages of the screenplay were already beginning to turn yellow when I read [the script]," Tanaka said. [4]

Toei's Masahiro Kakefuda (author of Toho's soon-to-be-aborted *The Human Torch*) was commissioned to update the script in 1974. Whatever Kakefuda's update entailed, it was apparently unsatisfactory as original writer Ei Ogawa was called in to overhaul Kakefuda's take.[5] Fumio Tanaka revealed that budgetary constraints forced the following change to be made: "...The hideout of the villain originally was going to be a satellite in orbit instead of a mansion in the mountains." Oddly, this satellite remains on the release poster! Furthermore, in the original script from 1967, the villain Ulrov was an alien that lived on a satellite which lead ESPY Tamura would teleport himself to for the end showdown. Tomoyuki Tanaka himself stepped in to cut this aspect. Yet, there's an odd, throwaway line at the end of the finished film that alludes to Ulrov being possessed by some evil power "not of this earth"! An alternative story says that in one draft of the script Ulrov's base was located on the moon—an idea that Teruyoshi Nakano nixed himself.

Some of the character names were changed from the manga with Maria Tosti becoming Maria Harada. Added into the film version was a character that didn't appear in the manga or the 1967 script: Jiro Miki—a race car driver. Originally the character was to be a college student but someone decided race car driver would be more interesting. Ulrov transitioned from an alien to an ESP-enhanced human bent on avenging the death of his father by causing WWIII. Originally, Ulrov was named Linz (who claimed to have the abilities of Buddha) and came from Armenia. The prime minister in Ulrov's crosshairs was not from the fictional country of Baltonia but China. The final draft was reportedly very close to the finished film and the only notable scene cut was Ulrov executing one of his operatives, Judy, inside his western-style estate. This tracks since in the finished film, Judy just mysteriously disappears. Another cut scene would have featured actress Linda Blair. While promoting *The Exorcist* in Japan in July of 1974, Toho reached out to her with an offer to appear in the film. Blair was interested, but her agent advised her against it.[6]

It's possible Masahiro Kakefuda recycled some elements from his abandoned script, *The Human Torch*, when it came time to bring Ulrov's outer space lair down to earth. Much of *The Human Torch* revolves around a large, western-gothic style estate where a pyrotechnic being runs amok. Considering Ulrov resides in what is more or less a medieval mansion and meets his death by catching fire, the odds favor *Human Torch* inspiring the revised climax of *ESPY*.[7]

ESPY was another hit for Toho, coming in at #2 behind *Prophecies of Nostradamus (Catastrophe 1999)* for the title of top-grossing Japanese film of 1974. The film's success wasn't surprising at all; *ESPY* is a fast-paced action thriller clearly modeled after the James Bond series. Like the Bond films, locations for the story were global and ranged from Istanbul to Paris and Switzerland in addition to Japan. Overall, the idea of spies with psychic powers is utilized quite well throughout the film. However, even though Japanese audiences enjoyed the film, Sakyo Komatsu himself was reportedly not pleased with it.

Chapter Notes

[1] Though credited as an Assistant Director in addition to a writer, Banno's role on the film was almost closer to that of a co-director.
[2] Macias, *Tokyoscope*, pp.36.
[3] Fuji TV was to air the series, which was pitched in March of 1974 and written by May of that same year. Ishiro Honda and Jun Fukuda were slated to direct some of the episodes. The canned sequel, *Great Prophecies of Nostradamus II: Fear of the Great Devil*, was to concern spirit mediums contacting the dead spirit of Nostradamus. A huge U.F.O. then shows up in the skies of Japan as the world is consumed in WWIII. Instead of destroying the Japanese, the U.F.O. rescues the war-resistant nation and takes them away into space.
[4] http://www.davmil.org/www.kaijuconversations.com/tanak.htm
[5] There was hope Komatsu would author the script but he did not.
[6] *The Japanese Fantasy Film Journal* #11.
[7] To say *The Human Torch* was shelved isn't entirely accurate since it evolved into a second iteration called *Invisible Man vs. the Human Torch*. This script was never filmed either, though it came close.

31.
CLASH OF THE TITANS
TERROR OF MECHAGODZILLA

Inspired by the modest success of *Godzilla vs. Mechagodzilla*, Tomoyuki Tanaka decided to ride the momentum by issuing a story contest for a sequel featuring a return engagement with Mechagodzilla. Even the usually stoic Jun Fukuda appeared enthusiastic about the project, stating in an uncharacteristically positive interview conducted after the release of *Godzilla vs. Mechagodzilla* that, "a great second Mechagodzilla will attack again." When the interviewer asked him, "Well, what kind of weapon do you see the second Mechagodzilla as?" Fukuda responded, "I think that the second Mechagodzilla will be born of your ideas. Everyone please, send us an interesting idea."[1] From this intriguing comment, one can infer that Fukuda was aware of Tanaka's story contest and, at that time, thought he would end up directing the sequel. Conversely, Teruyoshi Nakano said of the production, "If I remember correctly, we did not have a major reason why we featured Mechagodzilla again in *Terror of Mechagodzilla*."[2]

It is unknown how many scripts Tanaka considered for the sequel contest but he seemed to take a liking to Yukiko Takayama's submission right away. Takayama was a young student at the Scenario Center, an independent school in Tokyo for aspiring scriptwriters.[3] "After completing the standard curriculum, I entered an advanced class in which plot development was covered. Two or three months after that class had started, I heard that Toho was holding a story contest for a sequel to *Godzilla vs. Mechagodzilla*. So, I sent in an entry," Takayama explained.[4] She remembered that Kenji Tokoro, an associate producer at Toho, came to her class in the spring of 1974 to speak about Toho producing a sequel to be called *Mechagodzilla's Counterattack* and that there would be an open story contest among the class. The story's only stipulation was that it feature Mechagodzilla. Tokoro was also careful to mention that production of the script wasn't a 100% guarantee. This would gel with comments from Nakano who stated, "Before production of *Terror of Mechagodzilla* began, there was talk within Toho that we

 **CONFLAGRATION**

HAD THERE NOT BEEN A GREAT CONTROVERSY REGARDING *PROPHECIES OF NOSTRADAMUS (CATASTROPHE 1999)*, TOHO'S BIG SUMMER PANIC FILM FOR 1975 WOULD HAVE LIKELY BEEN *GREAT PROPHECIES OF NOSTRADAMUS II: FEAR OF THE GREAT DEVIL*. INSTEAD, A NEW IDEA WOULD HAVE TO BE UTILIZED. LIKE THE PREVIOUS TWO PANIC FILMS, A NOVEL WAS AGAIN CHOSEN AS SOURCE MATERIAL: *CRITICAL EXPLOSION*—WHICH THE FILM FOLLOWS CLOSELY. THE BOOK WAS BY KOJI TANAKA, A PROLIFIC JAPANESE WRITER WHO WAS JUST STARTING HIS CAREER. ALSO, THE TALE OF TERRORISTS HIJACKING A JAPANESE OIL TANKER WITH IDEAS OF DETONATING IT IN TOKYO BAY WAS BASED ON A REAL LIFE INCIDENT FROM NOVEMBER OF 1974 WHEN AN OIL TANKER AND A CARGO SHIP ACCIDENTALLY COLLIDED IN TOKYO BAY.

should take a break and suspend the Godzilla series after that... We were also carefully thinking about the future course of the Godzilla series. We discussed which direction we should take for the Godzilla series."[5] Takayama also later said, "...actually, at that time, Toho did not know if they would really start production on the movie. So they said I could write anything I like."[6]

It was Kenji Tokoro who actually selected Takayama's script as the winner and passed it along to Tanaka, who approved of his choice. "[Tokoro] told me that Tomoyuki Tanaka was interested in my entry, and wanted to meet me. So, I went to see him, and he told me to go ahead and write a script," Takayama said.[7] When writing the story, Takayama said that since Mechagodzilla was already a cyborg, she immediately came up with a cyborg girl, Katsura Mafune. Apparently, Takayama came up with the last scene (suicide and all) first, in which the cyborg girl sheds a tear, and she wrote her story around that end goal.[8]

Tanaka gave Takayama free reign on the first draft of the script, only requesting one thing, that Godzilla land in Shinagawa—a district of Tokyo—just as the first Godzilla had in 1954.[9] Tanaka's requested changes would only come after the first draft and these were all for the sake of the budget. Initially, Titanosaurus was comprised of two separate male and female plesiosaur-like monsters, the Titans, who fused together into one monster. Yukiko Takayama described the monsters as "becoming enraged when their necks wreath together" in a *G-Fan* interview, while in *Toho Special Effects Movie Complete Works*, it said that the two animals created a strong magnetic field when spinning together. Takayama noted that she took the name from Greek mythology and that, "Titans are usually very friendly, but, once their necks got together, they become very violent. In those days, Godzilla movies always had a new kaiju, so I came up with an idea of Titans."[10]

"We had traditionally designed kaiju in Godzilla movies based on dinosaurs. But we had never designed Plesiosaura, so we tried it with Titanosaurus," Nakano said.[11] No design sketches exist for the Titans, but if they were inspired by plesiosaurs then they would have had to have been quadrupedal, and likely would have had flippers.[12] Ishiro Honda also remarked on the original idea, stating that the concept was "psychological—you could even call it poetic—but not terribly cinematic."[13] Such creatures would have been very clumsy to animate via suitmation, not to mention this would have necessitated the construction of three suits in all: two for the individual male and female Titans, and one suit for their combined form. It's presumable that the finished film's Titanosaurus was what the final, combined form of the two monsters would have looked like, though this isn't certain.

Originally, Mechagodzilla II was to be disguised as Godzilla with fake skin again for the attack on Tokyo with the Titans/Titanosaurus. A child would see Godzilla, shed tears, and cry out, "What happened Godzilla? You're supposed to help us!" At that, the real Godzilla would appear by bursting out from beneath the ground like Anguirus did in the previous film! Though repetitive of the last film—Mechagodzilla in disguise, a heroic monster bursting from the ground—it's a fantastic intro. And all of Tokyo was to be completely obliterated for once during the end battle, though this had to be scaled down for the budget (necessitating the monsters move to the mostly building-less countryside). Takayama said, "I came up with the idea that the city of Tokyo was destroyed completely. Mechagodzilla and Titanosaurus were to enter Shinagawa from Tokyo Bay, and the whole of Tokyo was going to be trampled by them..."[14] Apparently, Takayama specifically had her eyes set on destroying Tokyo Tower and the Kasumigaseki Building—a 36 story skyscraper. Takayama joked about the times in retrospect saying, "But the Godzilla movies in the '70s had a limitation of budget. So kaiju were always well behaved. They appeared in undeveloped land without buildings." [15]

It would seem Tanaka tried to get Takayama to cut the Tokyo scene entirely (his idea—make the third act about preventing the two monsters from reaching Tokyo altogether), but she argued against it strongly feeling the audience expected such a scene in a

Godzilla film. "Toho Studios said they could not destroy Tokyo. They wanted Godzilla to stop Mechagodzilla and Titanosaurus from invading Tokyo. They wanted the city of Tokyo to remain peaceful. But I told them it was the wrong idea. I told them, if Tokyo were not destroyed by kaiju in a Godzilla movie, the audience would not be happy. Only Toho people would be happy, as they could minimize the budget," Takayama said in *G-Fan*.[16] In the end, the studio compromised with Takayama and the monsters do destroy part of Tokyo. And, to get the most out of his budget, Nakano set up cameras at multiple angles to capture a city block exploding, then used the alternate and reverse angles to make the same city block appear multiple times. The copious miniatures of Tokyo were those left over from not being destroyed in the previous year's *Prophecies of Nostradamus (Catastrophe 1999)*.

Katsura and Ichinose's love story was more fleshed out in earlier drafts as was Katsura's rough childhood due to her family living in poverty and her mother's untimely death. It was also clearer that INTERPOL agent Yuri Yamamoto had romantic feelings for Ichinose. Though this element is still present in the finished film, Yuri had a bigger presence in the early scripts. These scenes remained up until the final fourth draft on December 20, 1974. According to Takayama, other changes over the course of the four drafts were minor. "I had a few meetings at Toho just for such small suggestions from them. And it was very unusual for a woman to write a Godzilla movie. So the Toho staff was making fun of me. They only gave me very small suggestions which would have made almost no difference."[17] It would seem Takayama had more influence than she let on. Fans may have noticed that the spacemen's uniforms are slightly different in this film compared to the preceding one, notably the somewhat silly helmets. Takayama described their costumes as "space samurai"—hence the somewhat awkward but vaguely samurai-like helmets they all wear.[18]

When it came time to choose a director, various stories float as to how Ishiro Honda returned. Honda felt production of the films should have ended after the death of Eiji Tsuburaya. According to Ed Godziszewski and Steve Ryfle in their Honda biography, Honda was approached by Tanaka about returning in mid-1974. Supposedly, Takayama herself had requested Honda and the director likewise took a liking to Takayama, who shared the same birthplace as he: Yamagata. Honda's wife Kimi remembered, "[Takayama] wanted [Honda], no matter what."[19] Honda also stated to Guy Tucker that he would have liked to have worked with Takayama again and that a "woman's perspective was especially fresh."[20]

Other rumors suggested that Jun Fukuda did not want to return and was hoping to start work on a film that would never take off, a restart of Toho's mutant films called *Invisible Man vs. the Human Torch*. Another rumor even said that Tanaka approached Yoshimitsu Banno about directing the film. Banno's stock had risen in Tanaka's book due to the success of *Prophecies of Nostradamus (Catastrophe 1999)*, though Banno denied he was ever discussed. Despite Banno's comments to the contrary, Guy Tucker's *Age of the Gods* strongly implied Banno was considered and that this was when the unmade "Godzilla vs. Hedorah II" in Africa was thought of.[21]

With Ishiro Honda in the director's chair, a few more changes to the script came, though Takayama appreciated them. "He suggested that I change a few sequences. He also suggested that I cut the sequence at the very beginning in which the submarine sent to recover the remnants of Mechagodzilla was seen on the surface of the water being readied for diving. Mr. Honda thought that it would be better to begin with the submarine already underwater," Takayama said.[22] It was also Honda's idea to start the movie with a reprise of the last.

Recently, Takayama's second draft of the script was published in *Showa Mechagodzilla Steel Picture Book* (Yosensha 2019). This draft contains the aforementioned scene, which shows the Akatsuki (here called the "Barracuda") being lowered into the water from a ship above the surface.[23] As in the final film, the submersible is attacked by Titanosaurus—this meaning that the Titans were axed by Draft #2. Rather than cutting to the INTERPOL meeting, we cut to Chief Tagawa in his office receiving word that the submarine has disappeared. We would have then cut to helicopters scouring the surface of the ocean where the sub sent its distress signal. The script then progresses as we know it, but with another soon-to-be-deleted scene. As Ichinose, Yuri, and Murakoshi wait for an elevator, they discuss a strange journal Yuri saw some time ago with a "horrible dragon" in it. Ichinose then surmises it must be the notes of a certain Dr. Mafune. This scene precedes the meeting between Ichinose and Ota, of the Oceanographic Institute.

The scene where Katsura meets Ichinose and Murakoshi at her home is basically the same but features an additional shot of Katsura watching the duo drive away in their car. As she does, her eyes glisten in an odd way. The next difference with this script concerns the escape of one of the aliens' prisoners: Kusakari (the one played by Masaaki Daimon in the film). In the movie, Kusakari gives the piece of space titanium to an adult working in a manhole but in this draft, he hands it off to a boy working in a field to cut grass.

Rather than on a seaport, Katsura and Ichinose's second scene together takes place along a beach. There, Ichinose picks up a piece of seaweed and says, "If you look at this seaweed, you will find dozens of tiny creatures. The sea is endless. We still don't know its limits." From here, the conversation plays out as in the finished film, except that it's the "Barracuda 2" that Ichinose reveals is being built rather than the Akatsuki 2. When Katsura returns home she is berated by her father for speaking with Ichinose, just like in the final draft. However, this draft features a flashback of Katsura's mother trying to buy groceries. The clerk tells her she is already behind by three months and he will give her no more credit. He walks away while Katsura's mother cries in shame and Katsura calls to her mother as people pass them by in the store.

Next up we get an alternate scene of what played out in the final draft. In the film, a man named Yamashita (the manhole worker) delivers the space titanium to Chief Tagawa in person. In this version, Tagawa receives an envelope in the mail containing the space titanium, which came from the local police station near the Amagi Mountains. During the scene where Katsura beseeches her father not to unleash Titanosaurus on Japan, rather than comparing the monster to King Ghidorah, Rodan, and Manda, here she compares him to King Ghidorah, King Kong, and Gorosaurus![24] The mention of Kong was interesting, as King Kong hadn't been name-dropped in a Godzilla film since 1962's *King Kong vs. Godzilla*.[25]

The initial confrontation between Godzilla and Titanosaurus is different. While Godzilla has an excellent entry in the movie (his silhouette revealed behind the Tokyo skyline), here he merely emerges from the water as usual. Back when Titanosaurus was two monsters, the Titans would intertwine their bodies to create a magnetic vortex. That element is retained here with Titanosaurus creating a magnetic vortex to deter Godzilla. As this happens, jet fighters also attack Titanosaurus. After Katsura is shot by Murakoshi and falls into the water, there is a scene between Murakoshi and Tagawa. Murakoshi confirms that Titanosaurus is under alien control and the duo wonder if the aliens are now using Titanosaurus in place of Mechagodzilla.

When the two monsters march on Tokyo, Mechagodzilla specifically destroys Tokyo Tower. Notably, Mechagodzilla is not wearing a Godzilla disguise, so that was apparently unique to the first draft. Godzilla does, however, still seem to emerge from underground to make his entrance! Or, specifically, it would seem Godzilla bursts out of a building that he tunneled under. Takayama's choreography for the battle is slightly different than what was filmed. Godzilla is never buried underground, though he does save the helicopter with the supersonic wave oscillator at the last second by attacking Mechagodzilla, who tries to take to the air.[26] This second draft also lacks the excellent scene where, after Godzilla twists off Mechagodzilla's head, the machine keeps fighting (this was Nakano's idea later). Godzilla was to defeat Titanosaurus at sunset and wade into the ocean. Though Ichinose still stands with the dead Katsura, the final scene was to be an exchange between Chief Tagawa and Ota from the Oceanographic Institute. Ota would state that there is still much that they do not know about the ocean. Tagawa agrees and Takayama writes that the final shot should be of the ocean waves crashing against the rocky shore.

Of the finished film, Takayama said, "I generally was pleased with the way it turned out. However, I was a little disappointed because the scenes showing Tokyo being destroyed were so limited in scope in comparison to what I'd originally envisioned."[27] Fans may also be surprised to know that in Japanese interviews Takayama has said that she views Titanosaurus as a female monster! Specifically, when she first saw Akihiko Iguchi's drawing of Titanosaurus she said, "I thought when I first saw this monster, this is a female."[28] Toho Kingdom also wrote, "When fused into the single 'Titan' monster, Takayama wrote the form as being predominately female. This tidbit can be found in the 2014 publication *Ishiro Honda: Uncrowned Master.*"[29] Nevertheless, the monster in the film has an obviously mammalian male chest and Toho considers Titanosaurus to be male.[30]

The preceding Godzilla movies of the 1970s had predominantly been children's films. 1974's *Godzilla vs. Mechagodzilla* shifted away from that element, but *Terror of Mechagodzilla* in no way seems to be a film aimed at children other than the fact that it features Godzilla and a bunch of especially oddball fighting maneuvers. The atmosphere is grim and moody, made all the more so by Akira Ifukube's excellent score. The film's signature scene is

Katsura's self-sacrifice. Though many fans would say Namikawa sacrificed herself in *Invasion of Astro-Monster*, this isn't necessarily the case. Namikawa didn't know for a fact she would die, though she certainly knew she was risking her life. Katsura, on the other hand, literally pulls the trigger and kills herself to save the day—making her Honda's first female character to truly commit self-sacrifice.[31] Though this will be heresy to some fans, her suicide scene is arguably more touching than Serizawa's powerful death scene in *Godzilla* (1954). Overall, while Takayama may have lacked the experience of Shinichi Sekizawa and Jun Fukuda, her script far outshines Sekizawa's final script, *Godzilla vs. Gigan*, and also Fukuda's two previous scripts for *Godzilla vs. Megalon* and *Godzilla vs. Mechagodzilla*. Though the aforementioned films were certainly fun, they lacked the pathos that Takayama managed to pack into *Terror of Mechagodzilla*.

Though undeniably one of the better Godzilla films of the Showa Era—and arguably the best G-film of the 1970s—*Terror of Mechagodzilla* was not a hit and sold even fewer tickets than *Godzilla vs. Megalon*. It would remain the box office failure champion of the series until finally dethroned by 2004's *Godzilla: Final Wars*. If the film had been a success, it's presumable Toho would have gone on producing more Godzilla movies.[32]

Chapter Notes

[1] *Toho Champion Matsuri Perfection*, pp. 114.
[2] "*Terror of Mechagodzilla*: The Ultimate Commentary", *G-Fan* #90 (Winter 2010), pp. 30.
[3] Attending the school with her was future *Godzilla vs. Space Godzilla* writer Hiroshi Kashiwabara. Coincidentally, that film's future director, Kensho Yamashita, was an assistant director on *Terror of Mechagodzilla*.
[4] www.davmil.org/www.kaijuconversations.com/takaya.htm
[5] "*Terror of Mechagodzilla*: The Ultimate Commentary", *G-Fan* #90 (Winter 2010), pp.30.
[6] Ibid.
[7] www.davmil.org/www.kaijuconversations.com/takaya.htm
[8] It's very well possible that Yukiko Takayama's storyline for *Terror of Mechagodzilla* was partially inspired by the TV series *Super Robot Red Baron* (1973), about a heroic robot that saves earth from aliens. In episode 11: *The Beautiful Plot of Evil*, a human girl sides with the evil aliens, called the Iron Alliance, and uses her disgraced father's robot, Magma Wolf, to exert revenge on the people of Japan who mocked him. The series' villain, Dr. Deviler even resembles Dr. Mafune with unruly gray hair and a mustache. To top it off, the girl (who is from Manazuru no less) switches to the good guys' side in the end but is shot by Dr. Deviler for her betrayal. Although not a cyborg herself, she could've been an inspiration for Katsura Mafune. Or perhaps it was all coincidence?

[9] Teruyoshi Nakano told David Milner that, regarding this film, "Toho wanted to revise the Godzilla series. So, Mr. Tanaka decided to portray Godzilla the way he had been in 1954." This is an odd comment considering Godzilla's actions in the film, where he does a lot of running compared to the plodding Shodai Godzilla. It should be noted there was a running craze in Japan at the time of the movie's production.
[10] "Words from the Heart", *G-Fan* #91 (Spring 2010), pp.12.
[11] *Terror of Mechagodzilla*: The Ultimate Commentary", *G-Fan* #90 (Winter 2010), pp.30.
[12] At the time, Japan was experiencing something of a dinosaur boom, see the next chapter for more details.
[13] Tucker, *Age of the Gods,* retrieved from www.tohokingdom.com/cutting_room/tomg_1st.htm
[14] "Words from the Heart", *G-Fan* #91 (Spring 2010), pp.12.
[15] Ibid.
[16] Ibid.
[17] Ibid.
[18] Though she said that, the helmets are suspiciously similar to those seen in *Gatchaman*, which was popular at the time.
[19] Ryfle and Godziszewski, *Ishiro Honda*, pp.266.
[20] Tucker, *Age of the Gods* retrieved from www.tohokingdom.com/movies/terror_of_mechagodzilla.htm
[21] Banno's other idea for a Godzilla movie, "Godzilla vs. Gezilla", revolved around the Okinawan Expo of 1975. In this script Godzilla would have battled an underwater alien (rumored to be inspired by a starfish) at the Expo.
[22] www.davmil.org/www.kaijuconversations.com/takaya.htm
[23] For those wondering, the script notes show the sub preparing to look for the remains in Okinawa.
[24] Presumably, had these monsters been kept, footage of Gorosaurus destroying the Arc de Triumph would have been used.
[25] Someone at Toho likely stepped in to cut Kong for fear that showing his image would cost Toho money. Ironically, in Germany this film was released as *Konga, Godzilla, King Kong: The Devil's Brood*!
[26] It's possible that this scene was shot as a very strange still exists in *Toho All Monsters Encyclopedia* which features Godzilla leaping through the air at Mechagodzilla.
[27] www.davmil.org/www.kaijuconversations.com/takaya.htm
[28] *Tokusatsu Hihou* Vol.5, pp.94.
[29] https://www.tohokingdom.com/cutting_room/tomg_1st.htm
[30] While we're still on the subject, it's worth mentioning that Tomoyuki Tanaka had also decreed that Titanosaurus was defeated, but not killed by Godzilla.
[31] No, Chika from *Abominable Snowman* doesn't count either. Though her death was heroic, Chika didn't know for a fact she was meeting her doom when she confronted the Snowman, who previous to the death of his son, had been gentle.
[32] Interestingly, the film's release poster noted the film as the "second entry of the Mechagodzilla" series. However, this probably was just done to emphasize the new monster's popularity and not to hint that Toho had plans for a "Mechagodzilla series."

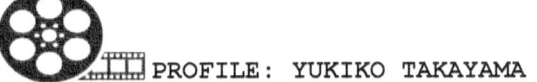

PROFILE: YUKIKO TAKAYAMA

Born April 4, 1945, not only was Yukiko Takayama the first woman to ever write a (produced) G-film on her own (Kazue Shiba wrote *Two Godzillas: Japan S.O.S.* and gets a screenplay credit for *Son of Godzilla*) she was also one of the youngest at the age of thirty. Her father, Tatsuo Takayama, was a famous painter who often took Yukiko with him to the cinema. As such, she had a love for movies and this included Ishiro Honda's Godzilla films. After graduating from the literature department of Keio University, Takayama moved on to the Scenario School for screenwriters. It was there that she became aware of and submitted the winning entry to a *Godzilla vs. Mechagodzilla* sequel contest in the spring of 1974. The same year that *Terror of Mechagodzilla* was produced in 1975, one of her other scripts was also adapted on a Fuji TV series, *A Dog of Flanders*. Ever since then, Takayama has worked sporadically writing scripts for TV, film, and even novels. Another of Takayama's theatrical works, *Gassan*, debuted in 1978 and was submitted as the official Japanese submission for Best Foreign Language Film at the 1979 Academy Awards, though it didn't get a nomination. In 1982, another of her works was adapted and again in 1988. Overall, Takayama has nine screenplay credits for feature films, and she even directed two of them: *Kaze no Katami* (1996) and *Musume Dojoji—jyaen no koi* (2004). Her novel, *Tale of Genji, Prince of Sorrow*, published in 2010, was made into a movie in 2011 titled *The Tales of Genji Mystery*. In a 2010 interview with totorom in *G-Fan* #91, she was asked what scenario she would create for a new Godzilla film. Though she said she thought it was best to leave Godzilla to the new generation, she did say, "If I had a chance, I would like to go back to the ancient time." [Totorom, "Words from the Heart," *G-Fan* pp.14] When asked to elaborate, she explained, "Truly the ancient time. People always look at the future. But why don't we look back? For example, imagine the armored warriors' fight with Godzilla." Totorom asked, "Do you mean Godzilla appears in the age of the samurai or early Japanese legend?" Takayama replied, "Yes. This is just a casual idea that popped into my head... A story like *The Tale of the Heike* would be good. The movie could have a princess from the Heian period and armored warriors. Godzilla could destroy the ancient palace or castle."[Ibid] In 2016, Takayama wrote a follow-up/Titanosaurus spin-off to *Terror of Mechagodzilla* in short story form for the magazine *Tokusatsu Hihou* (vol.5). Set 100 years after the events of *Terror of Mechagodzilla* in 2075, Katsura (here called "L・K"—or Lady K) is revived by a deep-sea mining corporation. The corporation uses thousands of human androids with A.I. to do their bidding and in their midst is a revived cyborg version of Titanosaurus (simply called Titano here). When the robots, led by the Mecha-

Titanosaurus, revolt and attack Tokyo, Katsura is called in to deal with the situation.

Selected Filmography
Flanders the Dog (1975) [TV series] (writer)
Terror of Mechagodzilla (1975) (writer)
Gassan (1979) (writer)
Tokugawa no Jotei: Ôoku (1988) (writer)
Kaze no Katami (1996) (writer, director)
Musume Dojoji—jyaen no koi (2004) (writer, director)
The Tales of Genji Mystery (2011) (writer)

32.
THE LAST DINOSAUR(S)

With the Godzilla series in hibernation, 1976 saw the release of no kaiju eiga. American films like *Jaws* (1975) and *King Kong* (1976) had changed the game for giant monster movies and coined the term "blockbuster."[1] To compete with those films, new monster films were expected to aim for realism with serious tones—if they didn't, they were considered mere 'B-movies' and Japanese studios took note. Toho teamed with Hammer Films in England to produce the eventually-aborted *Nessie* about the Loch Ness Monster. Toei had a similar agreement with Amicus—also of England—to produce a movie called *Kongorilla* which also ended up being cancelled.[2]

At the same time, the late 1970s also saw something of a dinosaur boom in Japan. Coupled with a fascination with U.F.O.s, the occult, and cryptozoology, the idea of remnant dinosaurs also became popular at this time. Various lake monsters similar to Nessie were even sighted in Japan, such as "Kussie" from Hokkaido's Lake Kussharo and also "Issie" from Lake Ikeda in Kyushu.

It should be no surprise that a Japanese studio would eventually concoct a remnant dinosaur horror movie. That the studio ended up being Toei, who mostly stayed away from giant monster movies, was something of a surprise. It's most likely that Toei had become excited by their *Kongorilla* prospect, which collapsed when Amicus went bankrupt. The constant reports that Toho was working on *Nessie* probably also inspired Toei to craft their own plesiosaur movie, *Legend of Dinosaurs and Monster Birds*.[3]

Though *Nessie* was to be a global epic with a giant-sized Loch Ness Monster[4] (mutated by a nuclear steroid spilled in the loch), Toei decided to use *Jaws* as a blueprint and basically replaced the shark with a prehistoric aquatic reptile: the plesiosaur.[5] It would seem, though, that the plesiosaur's real origin was the Japanese sea dragon deity Ryūjin. The first story concept dreamed up in the spring of 1976 was called "Great Monster Bird vs. Great Dragon". Apparently, this was the idea of Toei president Shigeru Okada.

221

 **HANNA-BARBERA'S GODZILLA**

IN LIGHT OF THE SUCCESS OF NBC'S PRIMETIME BROADCAST OF *GODZILLA VS. MEGALON* IN 1978, HANNA-BARBERA BOUGHT THE RIGHTS FROM TOHO TO DO AN ANIMATED GODZILLA SERIES. THERE ARE EVEN RUMBLINGS THAT THE SERIES WAS INITIALLY SET IN THE CONTINUITY OF THE TOHO FILMS BUT THIS IS UNCONFIRMED. STANDARDS FOR CHILDREN'S SERIES REGARDING WHAT THE PRODUCERS COULD AND COULDN'T SHOW, ALONG WITH NOT HAVING RIGHTS TO OTHER TOHO MONSTERS, PROBABLY SANK THIS IDEA. THERE WERE ALSO MANDATES FROM AN EXECUTIVE TO "LIGHTEN UP" THE MATERIAL. SPECIFICALLY, IN *JAPAN'S FAVORITE MON-STAR*, JOSEPH BARBERA SAID, "MY JOB BACK THEN WAS TO DIG UP NEW CHARACTERS, NEW IDEAS, NEW SHOWS, AND I HAD WANTED TO DO GODZILLA FOR A WHILE. I LIKED THE MONSTER THING, AND THE WAY IT LOOKED, AND I THOUGHT WE COULD DO A LOT WITH IT. SO I CONTACTED HENRY SAPERSTEIN, WHO WAS A VERY GOOD FRIEND AND WE GOT TALKING ABOUT IT. THEN THERE WAS AN EXECUTIVE AT THE NETWORK WHO WANTED TO GET INTO THE ACT, AND URGED US TO LIGHTEN THE STORYLINE UP. SO, I CAME UP WITH THE CHARACTER GODZOOKY, WHO WAS LIKE HIS SON." [RYFLE, *MON-STAR*, PP.209] IN NOTES, GODZOOKY IS SAID TO BE GODZILLA'S NEPHEW WHO THE CALICO RESCUED WHEN HE WAS STUCK IN BETWEEN SOME CORAL. HANNA-BARBERA WERE ALSO FORBIDDEN (I.E. WOULD HAVE BEEN CHARGED EXTRA) TO USE GODZILLA'S TRADEMARK ROAR, NECESSITATING A NEW ROAR CREATED BY TED CASSIDY (LURCH IN *THE ADDAMS FAMILY*). THE SERIES RAN SUCCESSFULLY FOR TWO SEASONS AND IF NOT FOR LICENSING FEES, PRESUMABLY THERE WOULD HAVE BEEN A THIRD SEASON.

Three Toei screenwriters, Masaru Igami, Isao Matsumoto, and Ichiro Otsu, were then tasked to come up with Toei's aquatic monster thriller. Despite the finished film's less than stellar reputation, the fault of the film certainly wasn't on the hands of the writers, who did a very good job. Had their scary screenplay been realized with better special effects, the film would likely have a very different reputation.

The most prolific of the writers was Masaru Igami, whose debut screenplay was *Prince of Space* (1959). He also penned Toei's other monster film, *Grand Duel in Magic* (*The Magic Serpent* in America), from 1966. After *Grand Duel in Magic,* Igami wrote teleplays for many tokusatsu TV series including *Johnny Sokko and His Flying Robot* and was the primary writer on Toei's *Kamen Rider* and its many sequels throughout the 1970s. *Legend of Dinosaurs and Monster Birds* was one of his few feature film screenplays and he followed it up with more work on *Kamen Rider* and the *Message from Space* TV series. Igami's co-writer was Isao Matsumoto, who was best known for writing screenplays for several Sonny Chiba action films (these do not include the *Street Fighter* films, though).

The man who fleshed out the full shooting script was apparently Ichiro Otsu, who had the smallest filmography of the three and like Matsumoto, mostly stuck to action pictures, specifically Shogun films—a few of which featured Sonny Chiba. It would appear work on the story treatments and scripts were done quickly as a first draft was completed on August 18, 1976, and the second (and presumably final) draft only a few weeks later on September 03, 1976. The film's Japanese Wikipedia page implies that Ichiro Otsu was instructed to come up with a treatment for the idea by Takao Oka (either the original director or a producer) overnight! Perhaps to better emulate *Jaws*, the initial setting was to be seaside rather than lakeside, Kisogashima in the Satsunan Islands. The Wikipedia page also claims, "...the dinosaurs and Archaeopteryx were changed to a plesiosaur and a Rhamphorynchus." We shall not let speculation run wild as to just what the "dinosaurs" might have been, but the fact the Rhamphorynchus began as an Archaeopteryx is interesting indeed.

It's possible the writers and director Junji Kurata had a few things to say about commercialism and tourism used to keep small villages alive (a theme also touched upon in *Jaws*). Even after six people have been killed by the plesiosaur in the lake, new signage featuring the dinosaur is excitedly created—the implication being that when things blow over, the town will have more tourists than ever. Actually, it should be noted that the town was promoting the lake monster even before all the killings occurred, which coincidentally began on the day of their annual Dragon Festival. Before the plesiosaur appears for real, two men swim into the lake with a huge shark fin which is quickly exposed as a hoax—another element lifted from *Jaws*. City officials berate one of the monster fin hoaxers for not doing a better job. It may even be ever so slightly implied that the city may have paid the youths under the table to perpetrate the hoax and are disappointed with the results. The two men with the fin in the lake end up eaten by the dinosaur shortly after.

The main character, Ashizawa, has an interesting if ambiguous arc. It's not entirely clear whether Ashizawa is searching out the dinosaur to prove his father's theory (who believed there was a dinosaur living in the lake and was mocked by the scientific community as a result) or to make a fortune, as he goes on about both throughout the film. In the end, when there is no more money to be made, Ashizawa tells Akiko that he has to see the animal with his own eyes, even if it costs him his life. And at the end of the film it possibly does, though it's not the plesiosaur that gets him. Instead, it's likely the eruption of Mt. Fuji that kills him (though we end the film with he and Akiko still alive, their fate uncertain). The third act of the film is just as much about Mt. Fuji erupting as it is about dinosaurs, cementing its status as a panic film (something that the Japanese trailer also makes explicit).

Legend of Dinosaurs and Monster Birds had something in its favor leading up to its release and the timing couldn't have been better. On April 25, 1977 (only four days before the film opened), the Japanese fishing trawler Zuiyo-maru dredged up what looked to be a plesiosaur carcass from the Pacific Ocean! Though this incident went on to become a highly celebrated mystery, particularly in Japan, whatever excitement it generated didn't carry over into *Legend of Dinosaurs and Monster Birds,* which was a failure at the box office (and upon seeing the film for the first time, the president of Toei called the film "an embarrassment")...

Legend of Dinosaurs and Monster Birds wasn't the only dinosaur flop in Japan in 1977. That same year, Tsuburaya Productions teamed with Rankin/Bass to produce a dinosaur film. The story's inception began in 1975 with cartoonist William Thomas Overgard (famous for the "Steve Roper" comic strip running since 1952). Overguard pitched a TV movie about a hunter who travels back in time to kill a dinosaur to ABC. The channel rejected the project based on Overgard's lack of credentials, planning to do a TV remake of *King Kong* instead. When the Dino De Laurentiis film derailed that idea, ABC came back to Overgard and accepted his idea, which eventually turned into *The Last Dinosaur.* The time travel element was discarded, the script was rewritten, and the film as we know it today was born.

There were some minor differences during development, the biggest of which was that Rankin/Bass had hoped the dinosaurs would be brought to life with stop-motion animation. Originally, Candace Bergen was offered the lead female role because she was also a photographer in real life like the character, Frankie (eventually portrayed by Joan Van Ark of *Knots Landing* fame). Basketball star Luther Rackley (of the New York Knicks), who was cast as Bunta, didn't read the screenplay until he was already on

 **DINOSAUR CORPS**

THE LAST DINOSAUR WASN'T TSUBURAYA'S ONLY RECENT DINOSAUR PROJECT. THE PREVIOUS YEAR, THE STUDIO HAD CREATED *BORN FREE* (*DINOSAUR EXPEDITION: BORN FREE* IN JAPAN). THE SERIES EVOLVED FROM THREE DIFFERENT CONCEPTS PITCHED IN 1976. THE FIRST WAS *GREAT PLANET*. NOT MUCH IS KNOWN OF THE PROJECT, BUT A THREE-MINUTE TEST PILOT WAS CREATED. PRESUMABLY, THE SERIES WAS TO BE LIKE A TV VERSION OF *GORATH* (1962). THIS TEST FOOTAGE, AND THE IDEA OF THE ASTEROID PASSING BY EARTH AND CAUSING HAVOC, WAS INSTEAD USED IN *BORN FREE*. THE NEXT CONCEPT WAS *DINOSAUR SPECIAL EXPLORATION CORPS DC-8*. THIS EARLY VERSION OF *BORN FREE* WOULD HAVE BEEN FILMED IN LIVE ACTION. NEXT WAS *SAURUS ADVENTURE*, WHICH WOULD HAVE BEEN FILMED USING PUPPETS INSTEAD OF ANIME. *BORN FREE* PROVED TO BE A HIT, SO A SEQUEL SERIES WAS PLANNED FOR 1977: *DINOSAUR EXPEDITION: BORN FREE II*. TSUBURAYA WAS FACED WITH SOMETHING OF A CHALLENGE BECAUSE THE TV NETWORK WANTED THE TASK FORCE TO FIGHT THE DINOSAURS THIS TIME. BEFORE COMING UP WITH THE COMPLETED, ALL-ORIGINAL *AIZENBORG* (*GREAT DINOSAUR WAR: AIZENBORG* IN JAPAN), THIS VERSION WAS A SEQUEL WHERE THE DINOSAURS TURN VIOLENT AND THE TASK FORCE TURNS INTO A DEFENSE ORGANIZATION. ORIGINALLY, *AIZENBORG* WAS JUST A GIANT HERO SIMILAR TO ULTRAMAN RATHER THAN A GIANT MECH. URURU, THE FIRST VILLAIN OF THIS SERIES, WAS BROUGHT TO LIFE USING THE LEFTOVER TYRANNOSAURUS COSTUME FROM *THE LAST DINOSAUR*. THE SAME SUIT WOULD ALSO BE UTILIZED AS "TYRANNOSAURUS JACKIE" IN *DINOSAUR CORPS KOSEIDON* (1978).

the way to Japan. According to Joan Van Ark, he was shocked to learn that he had no lines and would have walked from the project had he not already been on the plane halfway there. Also, reportedly it was the U.S. co-director, Alex Grasshoff's idea for the Tyrannosaurus Rex to appear in the reflection of water according to Japanese director Tom Kotani in *G-Fan*.[6] The film's dialogue may illuminate a change that occurred during filming. It seems likely that the scene involving the Uintatherium was originally meant for the Triceratops, as the Chuck Wade character identifies it as a "ceratopsian" when it's not even a dinosaur, but a prehistoric mammal that lived after the dinosaurs.

The premise of *The Last Dinosaur* is that it is essentially a TV movie[7] version of *The Land That Time Forgot*. Like the film and novel of the same name, a land of dinosaurs is found hidden in a volcanic crater in the Arctic. Naturally, the expedition party becomes stranded there when their craft, the Polar Borer, becomes damaged.[8] The story differentiates itself from similar "lost world" films by having the main character be a millionaire/big game hunter, Masten Thrust (Richard Boone, star of many popular western films and television series). Of course, Thrust is actually the last dinosaur of the title, something the catchy theme song makes clear. A good portion of the story and conflict isn't so much Thrust's obsession with killing the land's Tyrannosaurus Rex, but a love triangle between Boone, Van Ark, and the character of Chuck, played by Steven Keats (*Death Wish*). Though Frankie is smitten with Thrust, she chooses to leave the lost land with Chuck while Thrust wishes to stay there so that he can finally kill the Tyrannosaurus—even if it means never returning to the modern world. Even without the song, this ending more than anything hits home that Thrust is himself the true last dinosaur.

Chapter Notes

[1] Ironically, Steven Spielberg originally wanted to make *Jaws* like a Japanese monster movie before the shark didn't work properly and he stumbled onto that whole "less is more" thing that made the film work so well.
[2] Amicus was best known for its horror output like *Dr. Terror's House of Horrors* and *The House That Dripped Blood*. They also produced the 1970s fantasy films *The Land That Time Forgot*, *At the Earth's Core*, and *Warlords of Atlantis*. The teaming of two separate Japanese and English studios, specifically in regard to the fact that Toei was now Toho's main rival and Amicus was Hammer's, is certainly ironic, if not eyebrow raising.
[3] It's possible that Toei's next planned project after this was a kaiju eiga called *Devil Manta* scripted in 1976, which they hoped to be a U.S./Japanese co-production. When foreign investors failed to materialize on *Devil Manta*, Toei let the project sit on the backburner.
[4] Years later, when being interviewed by the magazine *Tokusatsu Hihou* about *Nessie*, the interviewer asked Teruyoshi Nakano to comment on any connections between *Nessie* and Toei's film. Nakano's simple answer was that he hadn't seen the film, and he quickly changed the subject back to the collapse of *Nessie*.
[5] *Jaws* was released in Japan in December of 1975.
[6] Homenick, "Chasing the Last Dinosaur", *G-Fan* #90 (Winter 2010), pp.58.
[7] *The Last Dinosaur* was meant to be a theatrical film until Rankin/Bass took a look at it. It was still released to theaters in Japan and Germany.
[8] The Japanese title is *Polar Probe Ship Polar Borer*.

33.
THE INFLUENCE OF STAR WARS IN JAPAN

In 1977, Tomoyuki Tanaka happened to catch a screening of *Star Wars* while in Hawaii. He, like many other executives, realized that not only was a boom of space-themed movies soon to be upon them, but that the old special effects B-Movie was essentially dead. Tanaka was also aware that 20th Century Fox had such little faith in *Star Wars* that they didn't even bother trying to release it in Japan. When they eventually did, all Japanese theaters were booked until the summer of 1978. This gave Tanaka ample time to beat *Star Wars* to Japan screens with his own film that could not only ride the hype wave but also serve as Toho's farewell to their own brand of special effects films. The first person Tanaka approached was his then-favorite hit-maker, Sakyo Komatsu (author of *ESPY* and *Submersion of Japan*).[1] Komatsu was interested but his ideas differed from Tanaka's. "When I was asked by Tomoyuki Tanaka, the producer of *Godzilla* and *Submersion of Japan*, to make a story like *Star Wars* for his movie, I had a feeling that I did not want to do a rip-off," Komatsu told *G-Fan*.[2]

Furthermore, Komatsu wanted to take some time to properly realize his idea and he did just that, creating *Bye-Bye Jupiter* (1984) some years later. Meanwhile, Tanaka was planning was to do a sequel to 1959's *Battle in Outer Space* which also served a space-based remake of *Atragon* (1963). The working title was even *Uchu Daisenso 2!*[3] However, any continuity ties to *Battle in Outer Space* were dropped—if there were any to begin with. The film being a remake of *Atragon* is very evident. The featured ships share the same name, the Gohten. The Gohten even looks similar to the one from *Atragon* and still somewhat resembles a seagoing vessel (though this idea was also inspired by the immensely popular anime *Space Battleship Yamato*). The interior set of the alien ship, the Daimakan, is somewhat reminiscent of the ancient yet advanced Mu Empire from *Atragon*, and also has a golden serpent near the Hell Commander's throne.

The human-sized "Space Beastman" Chewbacca clone was originally just a taller, bigger humanoid alien to contend with. Early drafts also supposedly contained giant, slug-like monsters on Venus.[4] Additionally, the planet was to be covered in lush jungle life[5] with moving plants and vines that attack like the one in *Mothra* (1961). The characters all had different names in early drafts as well, including the Hell Commander who hailed from "Hercules Zero." Takigawa's secret bomb weapon was not present in the first draft either. Though the translation could be wrong, it would seem the aliens had a fortress on Venus. However, said fortress could just be the same as the ship in the finished film.

Overall, Toho's *The War in Space* followed *Atragon* more closely than it did *Star Wars*. The only major tip of the hat to *Star Wars* was the Space Beastman and the laser show the movie tends to put on. For the most part, *The War in Space* is another fun Jun Fukuda popcorn flick written by relatively new talent Shuichi Nagahara (with a story credited to "Hachiro Jinguji," the captain's name from *Atragon*, but actually a pseudonym for Tomoyuki Tanaka).

The film is well-paced and like *Battle in Outer Space*, the first half of the story takes place on earth while the second half takes place in space.[6] The lead character is Professor Takagawa (played by *Gorath* and *Battle in Outer Space's* Ryo Ikebe), essentially this film's Jinguji. Takagawa lacks the prior captain's embittered streak and is a much less interesting character. He does do one thing that Jinguji never did in *Atragon*, however, and sacrifices himself Serizawa-style to detonate a deadly secret weapon he'd accidentally discovered to kill the aliens.

Toei would follow Toho with their own *Star Wars* rip-off, *Message from Space*. Before that project, however, Toei had another strange, space-inspired movie in the works: *Space Monster Devil Manta*. The story concerned a gigantic manta ray from the "void of outer space" who descends upon earth and causes chaos. A treatment was written sometime in early 1976 by Shotaro Ishimori followed by a screenplay by Susumu Takaku and Hajime Sato. Before production could begin, Toei hoped to get some money from foreign investors and make it a co-production as they had tried earlier with the aborted *Kongorilla*. August Ragone postulated that *Devil Manta* was scrapped after *Star Wars* hit screens in 1977 in favor of a space adventure rather than a space monster—not to mention their last monster movie, *Legend of Dinosaurs and Monster Birds*, was a disastrous flop.

Message from Space's storyline is actually an adaptation of *Nanso Satomi Hakkenden*, a Japanese fairy tale concerning eight samurai half-brothers, all of whom descended from a dog. Though

 **ULTRAMAN 80**

IN 1980, SIX YEARS SINCE THE LAST ULTRAMAN SHOW, TSUBURAYA PRODUCTIONS DECIDED TO PRODUCE ANOTHER LIVE ACTION ENTRY IN THE SERIES TITLED *ULTRAMAN 80*. GAMERA DIRECTOR NORIAKI YUASA WAS PART OF THE PLANNING PHASE FOR *ULTRAMAN 80*. YUASA SAID, "TSUBURAYA PRODUCTIONS WANTED TO JUST REMAKE THE ORIGINAL ULTRAMAN TELEVISION SERIES, BUT THE TOKYO BROADCASTING SYSTEM (TBS) WANTED TO PRODUCE SOMETHING A LITTLE DIFFERENT." IN *G-FAN*, YUASA IS QUOTED AS SAYING, "MY OPINION WAS THAT WE HAD TO CREATE A BRAND NEW TYPE OF ULTRAMAN. THE HERO, TAKESHI YAMANO, WAS TO BE A TEACHER, AND THEREFORE HE'S BUSY AT HIS SCHOOL DURING THE DAYTIME. SO WHAT WOULD HE DO IF A MONSTER ATTACKS WHILE HE'S AT WORK? THIS CONFLICT WOULD GENERATE A LOT OF DRAMA FOR THE NEW ULTRAMAN." [ISHIZUKA, "GAMERA'S GODFATHER: NORIAKI YUASA" *G-FAN* #59 (NOV/DEC 2002), PP.54]

the movie apes *Star Wars* with reckless abandon (such as featuring a character named Meia and having a giant planet weapon similar to the Death Star), some scenes that may seem inspired by *Star Wars* are actually taken from other Japanese movies (*Star Wars* itself had been heavily inspired by Japanese films). The final battle between Prince Han (Sonny Chiba) and Rockseia XII (Mikio Narita) was inspired by a similar scene from Kinji Fukusaku's *Battles Without Honor and Humanity: Deadly Fight in Hiroshima* (1973) in which Chiba and Narita had dueled.

The film began as *The Planet Fortress* though it was also announced as "*Star Wars* in Japan." *Grand Duel in Magic* (1966) and *Legend of Dinosaurs and Monster Birds* writer Masaru Igami teamed with Toei producer Toru Hirayama to cook up the story. After this was done, a second team was assembled to flesh out the full script. The group consisted of writers Masahiro Noda, Hiroo Matsuda and *Cyborg 009* manga creator Shotaro Ishinomori.

There is only one real significant difference between the screenplay and the finished film. Though the ending of the film was fantastic, it had one special effects scene that had to be cut. After the battle seems won, a giant flaming claw piloted by Grandmother Dark (Hideyo Amamoto) gives chase to the main characters. The scene proved so difficult during filming not enough usable takes were available to include the sequence.[7]

 **BLUE CHRISTMAS**

IN THE MIDST OF THE SPACE OPERA CRAZE, TOHO PRODUCED A TRULY UNIQUE FILM ABOUT ALIEN ABDUCTION WHICH NEVER SHOWS THE ALIENS OR EVEN THEIR SHIPS. TOMOYUKI TANAKA SAW A STORY ENTITLED *BLOOD TYPE BLUE* BY SO KURAMOTO IN *KINEMA JUNPO* AND DECIDED TO ADAPT IT. IF ADAPTED FAITHFULLY, THE SCRIPT WOULD HAVE BEEN "AS THICK AS A PHONEBOOK" ACCORDING TO DIRECTOR KIHACHI OKAMOTO, WHO FELT THE MOVIE WOULD BE BETTER SUITED AS A TV SERIES. TO MAKE MATTERS MORE CHALLENGING, KURAMOTO INSISTED THAT HIS SCRIPT BE UNALTERED. THIS DIDN'T HAPPEN AND SEVERAL SCENES DID HAVE TO BE CUT. ONE TOOK PLACE AT THE WHITE HOUSE IN AMERICA. AN OUTTAKE FROM THIS SCENE APPEARS IN THE MOVIE'S TRAILER WITH AN ACTOR PLAYING THE U.S. PRESIDENT, WHO OTHERWISE DOES NOT APPEAR IN THE FILM, REMARKING "MUST I DO WHAT HITLER DID?" ANOTHER DELETED SCENE SHOWED THE SPECIAL FORCES ATTACKING A LARGE GROUP OF PEOPLE IN HOKKAIDO AND SUPPOSEDLY STILLS OF THIS SCENE EXISTED IN AN ISSUE OF *KINEMA JUNPO*.

Meanwhile, Sakyo Komatsu continued work on his own space epic. "I felt, if I could make a movie set in space, I wanted to make something which can make the audience feel the theme of 'Universe and mankind' visually," Komatsu told *G-Fan*. Komatsu eventually took his idea to Hollywood rather than Toho and made sure that his second draft contained space battles similar to *Star Wars*. However, none of the U.S. studios were interested and Komatsu eventually realized he didn't wish to compete with *Star Wars*, so he cut the space battles and created a more introspective story which he also turned into a novel serialized in the *Weekly Sankei* in May of 1980.

Like many films, *Bye-Bye Jupiter* started out with a much more ambitious script than what could be realized onscreen (at one point, Toho even told Komatsu his third draft script was unfilmable on a technical level). In fact, had the film been shot as scripted, it would have run nearly four hours long! As a result, characters were compressed and combined and numerous scenes were removed entirely. Sakyo Komatsu reported, "Due to the limited time and budget, the scenes which were set on the moon were all cut out [though, the film opens with a scene on the moon]. Also scenes on Earth were cut out except for the Jupiter Beach sequence. As for the story, the past of Eiji and Maria, political struggles, were all cut out."[8] When Komatsu handed over the script to director Koji Hashimoto—who drastically cut it—Hashimoto changed the character of Carlos from a grown man into a teenage boy, and the final version of the story was complete.

The finished film was a dud critically and financially and Komatsu's own fans hit it the hardest. One wrote that "Komatsu revealed that his talent is limited to novels." Today, *Bye-Bye Jupiter* is remembered as something of an oddity and one of Toho's most ambitious failures. This is not entirely surprising as even today, the film isn't held in very high regard by fans. Part of the film's problem is that it has far too many characters—each of whom either experiences something tragic or has a tragic past. The tragedies mount until they finally become tiresome and trite.

Set in the distant future, the story revolves around the dubiously-named space scientist Eiji Honda who is working to ignite the planet Jupiter into a new sun, despite the efforts of a terrorist group (of which his old flame Maria Basehart is a member) that vows to stop the project. When a black hole comes hurtling into the solar system, it is discovered that the only way to divert it from destroying earth is to let it hit Jupiter instead, which will change the black hole's trajectory but destroy the gas giant in the process. With subplots involving extraterrestrial petroglyphs on the moon and Mars, alien spaceships hiding in Jupiter, and some earthbound hippies and their pet dolphin named Jupiter, the story is just too convoluted for its own good.

Chapter Notes

[1] An alternative to this tale says that Komatsu was already thinking about a space-based sci-fi film in 1976 before Tanaka ever saw *Star Wars*. This comes from *Toho Special Effects Movie Complete Works* and the book states it was planned to be an animated TV movie or series.
[2] Homenick, "Universal Vision", *G-Fan* #80 (Spring 2007) pp.57.
[3] Like *Battle in Outer Space*, which began as a sequel to *The Mysterians* and even carried over some of the same characters if not the continuity, *The War in Space* would seem to exist in a world with a rich backstory. In a scene between Miyoshi and Takagawa, Miyoshi seems to imply that the earth has suffered a previous alien invasion. Furthermore, some fans like to point out that the moon is never glimpsed in *The War in Space*. And, considering the space station from *Gorath* (1962) is used, some fans theorize this film is a sequel to *Gorath*, in which the moon was destroyed.
[4] Perhaps these would have been created by leftover props from *Prophecies of Nostradamus (Catastrophe 1999)* (1974)?
[5] This could have come from Edgar Rice Burroughs' Carson Napier of Venus Series, which portrayed Venus as a jungle planet.
[6] In the interest of being thorough, *Battle in Outer Space's* final scenes do take place on earth, but most of Act II and III do take place in space.
[7] Perhaps this was because they had a problem with the VistaVision filming technique, which also plagued the new Gamera footage in *Super Monster* (1980).
[8] Homenick, "Universal Vision", *G-Fan* #80 (Spring 2007) pp.56-57.

34.
THE LONG ROAD TO
THE RETURN OF GODZILLA

Godzilla's return to the silver screen in 1984 was truly one of the strangest behind-the-scenes cinematic journeys of all time. His planned return may have actually begun not long after *Terror of Mechagodzilla* with a mysterious script by Hiroyasu Yamaura titled *Japan S.O.S.: Godzilla's Suicide Strategy*. In it, a blinded Godzilla defends Japan from a resurrected Gigan and invisible metal monster Chamelegon in what was surely a continuation of the Showa series.[1] Whatever may or may not have been planned, official talk of reviving Godzilla began on February 4, 1978 with the Godzilla Revival Meeting.

In a bizarre move, Tomoyuki Tanaka had *The War in Space* writer Shuichi Nagahara take a look at the old aborted script *Bride of Godzilla?* from 1955 for inspiration for a new film.[2] From there, Nagahara scripted three story treatments based on Hideo Unagami's old idea. Each was a far cry from the original and mostly carried over the concept of the bloodsucking sea louse and underground cavern. The first draft had Godzilla become enamored with a female robot Godzilla (it's not as humorous as it sounds) and in the next two drafts, the "Bride of Godzilla" was a flesh and blood member of the same species as Godzilla a la *King Kong Lives* (1986). Amazingly enough, these three treatments eventually evolved into *King of Monsters: Godzilla Resurrected*, which itself eventually turned into *The Return of Godzilla* six years later—but the development would take several uncanny detours before that.

The strangest detour of all came from the mind of Nobuhiko Obayashi, director of *House*, who came up with "A Space Godzilla."[3] In it, a pregnant Godzilla dying of diabetes washes up on a beach in Japan and is revealed to be an alien named Rozan. Japan turns Rozan into a rocket and launches her back to the Planet Godzilla where her baby finds his father and overthrows an evil alien dictatorship there. This beyond wild story was published in two issues of *Starlog Magazine* in 1979. Obayashi had hoped to produce it with stop-motion, though in all likelihood Tanaka never even considered it. Almost equally as strange were a set of *Chariots*

 **SUPER MONSTER**

IN 1980, GAMERA DIRECTOR NORIAKI YUASA WAS TASKED BY TOKUMA PUBLISHING WITH REVIVING THE GAMERA SERIES. YUASA SAID, "I REMEMBER THAT WHEN I MET WITH YASUYOSHI TOKUMA AND ASKED HIM HOW LARGE THE PRODUCTION BUDGET WOULD BE, HE TOLD ME THAT IT WOULD BE VERY SMALL BECAUSE HE DIDN'T WANT TO RISK A LARGE AMOUNT OF MONEY." [WWW.DAVMIL.ORG/WWW.KAIJUCONVERSATIONS.COM/YUASA.HTM] TO HIS DISAPPOINTMENT, YUASA WAS INSTRUCTED TO SOMEHOW COBBLE A STORY TOGETHER OUT OF GAMERA'S PAST MONSTER BATTLES, AS ONLY A MINIMUM OF NEW MONSTER FOOTAGE WOULD BE SHOT. "I WAS GIVEN FOUR MONTHS TO DO THE EDITING. IT WAS A VERY PAINSTAKING JOB," YUASA EXPLAINED. [IBID] YUASA ALSO DECIDED THAT THIS WOULD BE THE LAST GAMERA MOVIE. "MR. TAKAHASHI AND I NEVER IMAGINED THAT THERE WOULD BE A NEW GAMERA SERIES. THAT'S WHY WE DECIDED TO GO AHEAD AND KILL GAMERA." [IBID] CONSEQUENTLY, THE FILM ENDS WITH GAMERA COLLIDING HEAD ON WITH SPACESHIP ZANON, A *STAR WARS*-INSPIRED SPACECRAFT, IN A HUGE EXPLOSION VIEWED FROM EARTH. BUT, IT DIDN'T ALWAYS END THIS WAY; IN THE SCRIPT THAT NIISAN TAKAHASHI WROTE, GAMERA WAS TO SURVIVE THE ENCOUNTER WITH ZANON, BUT WHEN YUASA SAW HOW THE FILM WAS TURNING OUT, THAT'S WHEN HE DECIDED TO CHANGE THE ENDING. "I GRIEVED FOR MY SON, GAMERA," YUASA SAID. "IT WAS A VERY STRANGE FATE." [GALBRAITH, *MONSTERS ARE ATTACKING TOKYO*, PP.114]

of the Gods-inspired Godzilla stories. These were the result of a 1979 meeting with several famous Japanese sci-fi writers, all of whom came up with various stories that retconned Godzilla's origin to be that of a bioweapon created by ancient aliens!

Tanaka tasked the other *War in Space* writer, Ryuzo Nakanishi, to come up with a Godzilla relaunch that featured only the Big G and no other supporting monsters (aside from the sea louse, eventually named Shokilas). Called *King of Monsters: Godzilla Resurrected*, the resultant story begins in the middle of an intense storm near Bikini Atoll. A ship, the Fuku-maru, is sucked into a swirling vortex. The lone survivor awakens in an underwater cavern. There he escapes a giant sea louse and swims to the surface where he is rescued by a fishing vessel. A scientist named Tachibana is put in charge of an expedition to explore the cave at Bikini Atoll. He soon suspects that the cave was the hiding place of Godzilla (revealing this story was not a remake, but a sequel to the 1954 *Godzilla*).

Back in Japan, extremists have stolen plutonium from a nuclear power plant that attracts Godzilla. The monster marches through Tokyo and soon resurfaces to attack the Nankai Nuclear Power Plant. A plan is hatched and carried out to lure Godzilla into an erupting Mt. Mihara with plutonium. The plan works and Godzilla is badly burned by the lava but retreats back to the sea. The world superpowers declare war on Godzilla and confront him in a massive naval battle that culminates in a nuclear explosion at Bikini Atoll. Though Godzilla is thought dead, he later resurfaces alive and hungry for radiation along the coastline of North America.

This story has some major similarities to *The Return of Godzilla*. The monster is first glimpsed in some Russian film footage, comparable to the Russian satellite photo in *The Return of Godzilla*. In an interesting departure, the destruction of Tokyo doesn't serve as the film's climax and actually precedes Godzilla's attack on a nuclear power plant, the exact opposite of *The Return of Godzilla*. Then comes the idea to artificially induce an eruption at Mt. Mihara and lure Godzilla into the crater, the biggest carryover into *The Return of Godzilla*.

Despite *King of Monsters: Godzilla Resurrected* being a fairly solid story, Toho brass wanted to see Godzilla fight other monsters—so it was back to the drawing board. Fumio Tanaka said, "A number of Toho's executives... felt that the film would have a greater chance of success if it featured Godzilla doing battle with another monster instead of Godzilla alone."[4] As a result, 1980's *Godzilla Resurrected*, by Akira Murao, would have seen Godzilla fight a transforming monster known as Bagan. The story outline is rather odd, as the conflict with Bagan is not the center of the plot and Godzilla defeats his opponent for good around the end of Act II. Act III is then about defeating Godzilla, similar to *Godzilla Raids Again* (1955).

Many familiar scenes and elements from *King of Monsters: Godzilla Resurrected* carryover such as a freighter illegally dumping nuclear waste coming into contact with Godzilla and a strange cave filled with the Shokilas. Even the terrorists from *King of Monsters: Godzilla Resurrected* return, who try to kidnap a scientist on the verge of a nuclear breakthrough here. Godzilla yet again attacks a nuclear power plant and absorbs all its radiation. In the end, Godzilla is attacked with laser beams from satellites that ignite nuclear fission in his body.[5] The script's last scene is lifted directly from *King of Monsters: Godzilla Resurrected* with Godzilla again washing up in North America near a nuclear power

 **DEATHQUAKE**

IN 1978, JAPAN SUFFERED THE MIYAGI PREFECTURE OFFSHORE EARTHQUAKE WHICH REIGNITED A PARANOID INTEREST IN EARTHQUAKES IN JAPAN. TOMOYUKI TANAKA SOON BEGAN DEVELOPING AN EARTHQUAKE FEATURE FILM BASED UPON THE NOVEL *DAI JISHIN/GREAT EARTHQUAKE* BY JIRO KOITABASHI, SHIGEKI MANABE, AND HITOSHI CHIBA. THE SCREENPLAY WAS WRITTEN BY KANETO SHINDO, A PLAYWRIGHT AND FILM DIRECTOR BORN IN 1912. DUE TO HIS AGE, SHINDO WAS OLD ENOUGH TO WITNESS THE GREAT KANTO EARTHQUAKE OF 1923, AND THAT COULD HAVE BEEN PART OF THIS STORY'S INSPIRATION. IN FACT, THE MAIN CHARACTER IS THE GRANDSON OF THE MAN WHO PREDICTED THE KANTO EARTHQUAKE. THE SCRIPT WENT THROUGH FEW CHANGES WITH THE FIRST ACT CONCERNING PREDICTING THE EARTHQUAKE, ACT TWO SEES THE QUAKE HAPPEN, AND ACT THREE DEALS WITH THE MAIN CHARACTERS SURVIVING THE AFTERMATH. THE ONLY DIFFERENCES CONCERNED THE DEVELOPMENT OF THE MAIN CHARACTERS, A GEOLOGIST (ORIGINALLY KAWAZU WAS OLDER), HIS WIFE, HIS MISTRESS, AND A REPORTER. SEVERAL IDEAS FROM *DEATHQUAKE* WERE DISCARDED IDEAS FROM *SUBMERSION OF JAPAN* (1973). IN THE BOOK *JAPAN SINKS*, A PASSENGER AIRPLANE TAKES OFF JUST BEFORE THE QUAKE GOES INTO FULL EFFECT. NO SUCH SCENE OCCURS IN THE 1973 MOVIE, BUT IT PROBABLY INFLUENCED THE SCENE IN *DEATHQUAKE* WHEN A JUMBO JET LANDS JUST AS THE EARTHQUAKE OCCURS AND EXPLODES, KILLING ALL THE PASSENGERS (INCLUDING ONE OF THE FILM'S LEAD CHARACTERS!). FURTHERMORE, A TALK BETWEEN THE PRIME MINISTER AND HIS ADVISORS ON THE GOLF COURSE ABOUT THE ONCOMING CALAMITY IN *SUBMERSION OF JAPAN* THAT WAS NOT FILMED WAS RECYCLED INTO *DEATHQUAKE'S* SCRIPT.

plant before the credits would roll. For whatever reason, the script was shelved for three years.

The second draft by Shuichi Nagahara from late 1983 is basically similar to the first but contains a helicopter rescue of the romantic leads that may have also influenced the helicopter rescue gone-wrong scene in *The Return of Godzilla* (1984). There is also a smorgasbord of advanced weaponry possessed by the defense forces. Among them are the Super Beetle, a flying fortress which later inspired the Super X from 1984's *The Return of Godzilla*.

Before Toho got around to actually making the film, America was trying to get in on the Godzilla rebooting act with the aborted production of *Godzilla, King of the Monsters in 3-D*. It was pitched to Toho by director Steve Miner (*Friday the 13th, Part 2* and *III*) and writer Fred Dekker (*The Monster Squad*). In the story, which was more reminiscent of *Gorgo* than *Godzilla*, a baby Godzilla corpse draws the adult Godzilla into San Francisco where it is eventually killed. The script features satellites carrying nuclear warheads and the baby Godzilla sinks a Russian submarine early in the script which Toho eventually incorporated into *The Return of Godzilla*. Dekker's Godzilla even steps on a laughing wino[6] and picks up a cablecar and looks in at the passengers! As Toho would have certainly reviewed the script, there is every possibility that similar ideas in *The Return of Godzilla* came from *Godzilla, King of the Monsters in 3-D*.

When the year 1984 arrived, Toho knew for certain they wanted to take advantage of Godzilla's 30th anniversary. Again, Tanaka turned to Nagahara and finally a new script, simply called *Godzilla*—the film's Japanese release title—was written. It is close to the finished film with some deviations. In the first draft of *Godzilla*, Okamura is not a university student aboard a fishing boat. Instead, he works for the Japan Atomic Energy Public Works Corporation aboard the research vessel the *Taiyo-maru*. As in Nagahara's *Bride of Godzilla* scripts, the ship is sucked into a whirlpool. Okumura and three other men manage to survive and make it to Daikoku Island. There, within a cave, the men are besieged by the giant sea lice common to many other drafts. Only Okumura survives. He exits the cave onto the interior of the island at night. He begins to climb a strange rock formation with an odd texture until finally, he realizes that it is the foot of a huge creature. He runs away into the darkness, and as he looks behind him, glimpses a massive eye in the dark. This is obviously a much more elaborate version of the opening scene that played out in the finished film where Okumura merely witnesses Godzilla burst out of Daikoku Island. Reporter Goro Maki just happens to cruise by and see a panicked Okumura waving his arms on the beach. He picks him up and takes him to Hachiji Island. There, government men take Okumura and Maki was to chase them in an action scene.

In the second draft, Godzilla was to confront the military at the Ihama Nuclear Energy Plant. Actually, before even arriving at Ihama, Godzilla was to emerge in a fishing port and destroy a small village. Originally, when Goro, Naoko, and Professor Hayashida escape from the building several of Hayashida's staff are trapped with them. Goro, Naoko, and the staff would flee to the streets where the staff would presumably provide fodder for the giant Godzilla foot prop as Godzilla was to chase them. Other ideas didn't come until the last minute, such as the idea to drop the building onto the Super X. This wasn't in the script and was thought up by the effects staff.[7] During the last scene, Nagahara wanted Godzilla to slowly sink into the magma instead of falling into the crater of the volcano and out of sight as in the finished film. And instead of the Prime Minister, it was to be Hayashida who expressed sadness at Godzilla being consumed by Mt. Mihara. He was scripted to say, "Godzilla can't die. Surely his life continues, surely..."

Dr. Serizawa himself, Akihiko Hirata, was originally cast in the role of Professor Hayashida. Unfortunately, he was too ill at the time of casting to even agree to be in the film. Another classic Toho actor was approached, Yoshio Tsuchiya, who turned down the part. Yosuke Natsuki was then asked and he did agree to play the role (but was unaware that it was originally intended for two other Toho veterans). Akihiko Hirata passed away just days before shooting of the film began.

The Return of Godzilla opened to success in December of 1984. It is structured like a panic film and was the last Toho movie to be influenced by *Submersion of Japan* (1973). Much like a hurricane or earthquake, all of the characters know that Godzilla is coming. The main characters spend most of their time preparing for and dreading his arrival. They even figure out how to defeat Godzilla well before the third act, making Godzilla not unlike a passing storm, earthquake, or other force of nature. Like the original *Godzilla*, there is some excellent subtext concerning the danger of nuclear weapons. In this case, Cold War tensions are effectively utilized within the story when the U.S. and Russia both pressure Japan to let them use nuclear weapons on Godzilla. The Japanese prime minister manages to convince the two nations otherwise. However, when Godzilla passes a Russian freighter in Tokyo Bay that contains a secret missile control, a Soviet missile is launched at Tokyo. The U.S. is then called upon to launch their own missile to intercept the Soviet's.

Director Koji Hashimoto, who had a background in panic films, does a splendid job with the film and Reijiro Koroku composes an excellent score. Though some fans will be disappointed that Ishiro Honda and Akira Ifukube declined to work on the film (Honda was more interested in making films with his best friend Akira

Kurosawa and Ifukube strangely turned down the project sighting, "I write music for 50 meter monsters, not 80 meter monsters."), they really shouldn't be since Hashimoto and Koroku make an excellent team themselves. It's a shame this director, composer, and writing team couldn't have returned for the sequel which would take four years to gestate.

Chapter Notes

[1] It's actually altogether possible that *Terror of Mechagodzilla's* poor box office wasn't what officially killed the series, but rather a new distribution deal between Toho and Disney. Toho didn't need a new Godzilla film to anchor their Champion Festival thanks to distributing re-releases of old Disney cartoons.

[2] Remember, the script was about Godzilla being discovered within a hollow earth containing giant bloodsucking lice. Godzilla then fights a giant female robot on the surface.

[3] The U.S. fan-base's interpretation of the story was that Godzilla died of diabetes and then went on a metaphysical journey through the universe before doing battle with one last evil monster before passing on to the afterlife/Heaven. That storyline had promise, but Obayashi's actual story is too strange to hold any real promise.

[4] www.davmil.org/www.kaijuconversations.com/tanak.htm

[5] Ironically enough, it is believed that the final release poster by Noriyoshi Ohrai for *The Return of Godzilla* was influenced by this scene!

[6] In *The Return of Godzilla*, Godzilla almost steps on the humorous bum played by popular comedian Tetsuya Takeda.

[7] This was meant to be a cultural joke which revolved around Tokyo's new "earthquake proof" skyscrapers, which many people mocked by rhetorically asking "So the buildings will just fall over flat?" This is, of course, exactly what happens to the building Godzilla pushes over.

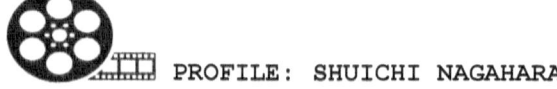
PROFILE: SHUICHI NAGAHARA

Born August 7, 1940, screenwriter Shuichi Nagahara began his career as the writer of hard-boiled crime thrillers. After graduating from college, he went to the Toho Literature Department as a research student. In 1967, he debuted at Nikkatsu writing the film *The Gun is My Passport*. After Nikkatsu's decline into the "pink genre" (soft-core porn), Nagahara switched over to television writing, penning scripts for detective shows such as *Angel Full of Scars* (1974). Nagahara was also known as an amateur baseball enthusiast and participated as a member of the amateur baseball team "JAWS" presided over by the screenwriter Kenji Kashiwabara. Nagahara later became independent from JAWS and founded his own team "Ragus". In the later 1970s, Nagahara came to Toho and wrote *Hakunetsu Dead Heat* in 1977. That same year, Tomoyuki Tanaka and Teruyoshi Nakano saw *Star Wars* while in Hawaii and immediately wanted to create the Japanese equivalent. At first, Tanaka approached Sakyo Komatsu, who said he would take years to develop his idea (1984's *Bye-Bye Jupiter*), so Tanaka gave Nagahara the task of adapting *Atragon* (1963) into a space fantasy. Happy with Nagahara's work on *The War in Space*, Tanaka immediately set him to work to revitalize the Godzilla series. As a reference, he gave him Hideo Unagami's *Bride of Godzilla?* script from 1955 and Nagahara eventually produced three drafts from the material. These drafts eventually morphed into *King of Monsters: Godzilla Resurrected* in 1978, which itself would eventually become *The Return of Godzilla* (1984). In 1978, Nagahara scored a big hit in the low-budgeted *The Most Dangerous Game*, which spawned a trilogy of crime thrillers. In 1983, Nagahara was given Akira Murao's 1980 to draft of *Godzilla Resurrected* to touch up before he was tasked to simply make a solo Godzilla movie. At the same time, helped polish Sakyo Komatsu's *Bye-Bye Jupiter* (1984). His last screenplay credit was 1990's Toei direct-to-video film *Beretta M92F Bullet*.

Selected Filmography
The Gun is My Passport (1967) (writer)
Hairpin Circus (1971) (writer)
The War in Space (1977) (writer)
The Most Dangerous Game (1978) (writer)
Bride of Godzilla (1978) (writer) [unproduced; developed into *King of Monsters: Godzilla Resurrected*]
King of Monsters: Godzilla Resurrected (1978) (writer) [developed into *The Return of Godzilla*]
Godzilla Resurrected (1983) (writer) [unproduced]
Sayonara Jupiter (1984) (consultant)
The Return of Godzilla (1984) (writer)
Beretta M92F Bullet (1990) (writer)

35.
"WONDER LIZARD IS DOWN FOR THE COUNT"
GODZILLA 1985

Before Raymond Burr became involved, the American version of *The Return of Godzilla* started out as an *Airplane!*-like spoof. Toho had trouble shopping the film around in the U.S. market, hoping to score a whopping $5 million for the rights! The highest they were offered was $2 million by Universal Pictures, but Toho passed and failed to garner a higher offer from any other American studio. Refusing to go back to Universal, all Toho eventually got was $500,000 from New World Pictures, the same company that had taken *Submersion of Japan* (1973) ten years earlier and turned it into *Tidal Wave* (1975) with new scenes featuring Lorne Greene. Though New World initially announced plans to release the film as *The Return of Godzilla*[1] (its official international title), the Americanization's original inception was as a comedy!

New World producer Anthony Randel was quoted as saying, "Because this was going to be dubbed from Japanese, there's no way it wasn't going to be funny."[2] The plan, specifically, was to dub the Japanese footage straight, but cut in newly-filmed American scenes that made light of the action.[3] "There was so much goofy stuff in it that we had to take a lighter approach, otherwise it wouldn't work," Randel told Steve Ryfle. Director R.J. Kizer explained that, "The thinking was that we would get someone like Leslie Nielsen to be the 'star', so to speak. There was all this silly dialogue, and it was very ambitious."[4]

Producer Straw Weisman was also asked about the Leslie Nielsen idea in *G-Fan* #80:

> **Brett Homenick:** We talked about this earlier, but you were not aware of any involvement that Leslie Nielsen was supposed to have as part of a parody that they were originally thinking about making?
> **Straw Weisman:** No, there may have been discussion about that. My involvement with it was, they were going to take this *Godzilla*, we are going to purchase the rights, we're going to add some American scenes, rewrite all the dialogue

in English, and release it as *Godzilla 1985*, an American picture.⁵

However, Kizer remembers reading the first draft of the script intended for Nielsen, stating that it was very "tongue in cheek, very lighthearted."⁶ Kizer said that Tony Randel told him that New World was actively pursuing Nielsen, though he was not going to be playing the older version of reporter Steve Martin—that came about only when Burr was cast. Kizer said that Nielsen would have simply been an American "super scientist" and that the role would have tonally mirrored what he had done in *Airplane!* Kizer also compared the Pentagon scenes to *Dr. Strangelove*.

In another contradiction amongst the producers of the film, Randel denied the Leslie Nielsen story. "Not to my recollection, no. We did hire Leslie Nielsen—everybody loved Leslie Nielsen—and we actually hired him to narrate a product reel once, but no, to my recollection—maybe we joked about it, but no, I always took it rather seriously." ⁷ Eventually, instead of Nielsen, someone suggested Lorne Greene, who had headlined New World's *Tidal Wave*. Randel then had the ingenious idea to go for Raymond Burr, star of *Godzilla, King of the Monsters!* (1956), instead. With that, the spoof version of the script evolved into something more serious. Kizer remembered, "Tony came in one day and said, 'We got Raymond Burr.' That started to change everything because now the tongue-in-cheek approach in the script had to be altered to accommodate Mr. Burr."⁸ This change solidified upon Kizer's meetings with his two main leads in the form of Burr and Warren Kemmerling, both of whom refused to make the film a comedic mockery. "I remember knocking on [Burr's] hotel room door, and he opened the door, fixed his eyes on me, and said, 'Godzilla is an allegory for the dilemma and madness of nuclear bombs in this world, and that is not something I will laugh at,'" said Kizer.⁹ Warren Kemmerling (who played a general in *Close Encounters of the Third Kind*), while sharing a drink with Kizer at Paramount Studios, also made his intentions known. Kizer continued, "The gist of the meeting was that [Kemmerling] was another one who took issue with the lighthearted tone of a lot of the scenes, and did not want to do it... That's why the poor lieutenant [Travis Swords] got stuck with all the stupid lines."¹⁰

From there, Kizer began to rework the comedic script. "So I wrote a draft, and Tony sent it to Straw, and Straw called back and said, 'Well, why don't you guys just go ahead and finish it.' And that was the last we saw of him. I got the clear impression that he was a little disappointed with how things were going, and he decided to absent himself."[11] From here, the "spoof script" faded into obscurity. In fact, one of the other writers, Lisa Tomei, even said she never saw a spoof version of the script. "I don't recall the whole parody debate. That must have happened before I was involved."[12]

In the end, many scenes in the shooting script played out differently onscreen. In Mr. Martin's room, there was to have been a photo of himself and Tomo (actor Frank Iwanagawa in *Godzilla, King of the Monsters!*). Kizer did have an excellent idea to include a memoir on Martin's desk entitled *Cairo via Tokyo*, though. Kizer said, "When I watched *Godzilla King of the Monsters*, I was struck by the route the Steve Martin character traveled to arrive in Tokyo. So I asked the props master to make up a dummy book cover with that route as the title and with Steve Martin as the author. I figured that would be a nice little reference for the fans."[13]

As for the strange carved serpent that Martin held throughout the film, when asked what the significance was, Kizer said that it was meant to be a memento from his first trip to Tokyo. In Kizer's mind, it represented a psychic link between Martin and Godzilla. And yet, in a separate interview, Kizer seemed to imply there was no thought behind the talisman and it simply looked interesting.

The scene where the military goes to collect Martin was originally longer, with an exterior shot of his home in Malibu Canyon at sundown. Kizer remembered in *G-Fan*, "Then the third day, we were supposed to spend a split day (half day, half night) shooting out at Malibu. We had daylight shots we wanted to do outside the house, but because the camera truck got lost, and didn't arrive until close to sunset, we had to abandon those."[14] Also in this scene, Martin's grandson Kyle was meant to run and jump into his arms at the sight of the imposing military man but this wasn't shot. Burr changed many of his lines for the control room scenes and there was supposed to be a shot of him looking saddened as he watched archive footage of Godzilla entering the ocean.[15] And for some reason, New World considered renaming the Super X the "S-R-X"!

Kizer also filmed an interesting deleted scene showing the aftermath of Godzilla stepping on the bum played by Tetsuya Takeda. The scene would have revealed the bum's bloodied hand sticking out of the rubble with an emphasis on his watch, stopped at precisely the time that the bomb was dropped on Hiroshima. "The idea was: after he screamed, and the screen went black for a moment, we were going to try to get a sense of the foot of Godzilla going away, and then we would zoom in on the bloodied hand of the homeless man lying in the rubble. On his hand would be a wristwatch with its crystal cracked, and the hands of the clock fixed at the time when the bomb was dropped on Hiroshima," Kizer said. However, shooting the scene didn't go as planned. "Neat idea, but our attempt at the shot didn't work. We didn't have the resources to really make it play, so we wound up taking it out," he explained.[16]

A few of Kizer's other ambitious ideas never made it into his scenes for the film. He told Steve Ryfle,

"We were going to have a sequence of a general arriving in a helicopter, landing on a heliport. We were trying to track down stock footage from the Air Force of B-52 planes being scrambled and fighter pilots reacting to a scramble horn and hopping in their jets, missiles being readied, all sorts of stuff. But all of that went by the wayside because of lack of time and money. We had a contact at the Department of Defense who was trying to push it through for us, but military channels take forever to push these things through. We were doing this in July, for a picture to be released at the end of August."[17]

Even a few ideas for the title sequence didn't pan out as originally planned. In an interview in *G-Fan* #76, title designer Ernest Farino (*Terminator's* title credits, among many others) told his idea for the original credits:

"The only component of that concept that was dropped was the idea of a blowtorch flame "cutting" the letters into a sheet of rusty steel (as if from Godzilla's incendiary breath). The basic animation reveal of the letters was kept, but the steel plate background didn't work. I had gone to a junkyard and found an interesting looking sheet of steel and shot some tests. Unfortunately, when I took it to the editing room and we all looked at the test, it became clear that the background wasn't recognizable as a piece of rusty steel and, out of context, several people even thought it was an aerial photo of countryside taken at 10,000 feet. Given the schedule and budget, we agreed to drop that element rather than struggle to make it work. So the final effect plays over a black background, which, in the end, is probably more dramatic."[18]

Some of the original version's comedic origins still remained in the finished film, mostly through observational "jokes" from Travis Swords' Major McDonough character. For instance, as Godzilla kicks through a railway track in Yurakucho, the stateside McDonough utters "That's quite an urban renewal program they got goin' over there." (cut to Steve Martin shaking his head with contempt). However, there were quite a few others that didn't make the cut which included: "Looks like an iguana with a pituitary problem." "Could make an awful lot of luggage outta of one of those." "Hate to see 'im during mating season."[19] There was even one humorous bit between Martin and Major McDonough that could have been funny without being offputting. When Godzilla is awakened by the nuclear fallout storm, McDonough demands to know, "Why didn't you tell us the electrical storm would revive him?!" to which Martin responds, "I didn't know it would. I only knew he wasn't dead."

Even though Warren Kemmerling had made it clear he wanted no funny business with his character, Kizer still tried to get the actor to make one joke regarding putting too much sugar in his coffee. "For the film, there was a wonderful dumb joke I wanted the general to do. But Warren refused to do it, and I was so unhappy about that... Admittedly, by this time the tongue-in-cheek aspect of the project had already started to evaporate. But I still felt we needed to put in a few lighthearted moments, or else we would be too dull," Kizer said.[20] There was also some contention regarding Burr and the infamous promotional tie-in with Dr. Pepper, who had partially funded the new footage. Fans will remember Travis Swords' character drinking Dr. Pepper near the end of the film, but the company itself wanted Burr to drink the soda onscreen! When the director asked Burr, Kizer said of the encounter, "[Burr] just fixed me with the most withering glare, so I just dropped it."[21]

Burr apparently also didn't entirely approve of his final lines. Writer Lisa Tomei said:

"Yes, he did not approve of his soliloquy. The analogies/metaphoric references were from my work (not saying my version was perfect, and not naming names), but some of my writing for his character had been seriously tampered with (to make it more combative) before Burr saw it—and I thought it was out of character, too. That lovely, fiery head credit I have leaves me the blame as well as the credit!"[22]

Here is what was written in the shooting script:

"In the modern age... in a world of innocence lost. Godzilla is a warning, a nightmare... escaped for a brief moment into the land of the living. A reminder that the reckless ambition of men... are often dwarfed by the dangerous consequences... and now... he's been summoned back to the earth, to slumber again. Whether he returns... remains for future generations to decide... for themselves."

Here is Burr's final version:

"Nature has a way sometimes of reminding man just how small he is. She occasionally throws up the terrible offsprings of our pride and carelessness to remind us how puny we really are in the face of a tornado, an earthquake, or a Godzilla. The reckless ambitions of man are often dwarfed by their dangerous consequences. For now, Godzilla, that strangely innocent and tragic monster has gone to earth. Rather he returns or not, or is never again seen by human eyes... The things he has taught us... remain."

Like *Godzilla, King of the Monsters!* before it, the U.S. version of the 1984 *Godzilla* isn't bad at all. In a few ways it even improves upon the original (one could argue that *Godzilla 1985* had better atmosphere than the Japanese version, where a lot of scenes went scoreless whereas creepy music plays over them in the U.S. cut). All that said, the original version is naturally far superior and the nuclear subtext is watered down in *Godzilla 1985* where the Cold War elements were tweaked for U.S. audiences. While in the Japanese cut, the Russian missile launches accidentally and the Russian captain dies trying to stop it, in *Godzilla 1985*, it is re-edited to make the launch intentional to negatively portray the Russians.[23] A new shot of a hand pushing a launch button was even added in. And what of Raymond Burr? Though he adds a great presence to the film, he's not as well integrated into the story as he was in *Godzilla, King of the Monsters!* In that film, he actually interacted with the original film's characters thanks to careful editing and body doubles. Here, Martin stays in the U.S. and literally just watches Godzilla trample Tokyo from the Pentagon. Though he was called on to be a consultant, most of his advice seems to go on deaf ears. If nothing else, Burr's end monologue is touching and caps off *Godzilla 1985* much better than *The Return of Godzilla*, which ends with a rather out of place pop song.

Chapter Notes

[1] The idea for the title *Godzilla 1985* came from producer Tony Randel who loved the title *Frankenstein 1970* (1958). However, New World Pictures also registered the film's title as "Godzilla is Alive" at the U.S. copyright office.
[2] Ryfle, *Japan's Favorite Mon-Star*, pp.237.
[3] Years later, Randel changed his tune and told *G-Fan* that "The idea of taking the film and joking it up is just not my thing. I would've found it disrespectful."
[4] Ryfle, *Japan's Favorite Mon-Star*, pp.237.
[5] Homenick, "Monster Script", *G-Fan* #80 (Summer 2007), pp.50.
[6] vantagepointinterviews.com/2018/06/26/urban-renewal-r-j-kizer-on-directing-godzillas-30th-anniversary-reboot-for-american-audiences/
[7] Homenick, "*Godzilla 1985*: Untold Tales", *G-Fan* #83 (Spring 2008), pp.45
[8] vantagepointinterviews.com/2018/06/26/urban-renewal-r-j-kizer-on-directing-godzillas-30th-anniversary-reboot-for-american-audiences/
[9] Ibid.
[10] Ibid.
[11] Ibid.
[12] Homenick, "Adapting *Godzilla 1985*: Easier Said Than Done," *G-Fan* #87 (Spring 2009), pp.28.
[13] vantagepointinterviews.com/2018/06/26/urban-renewal-r-j-kizer-on-directing-godzillas-30th-anniversary-reboot-for-american-audiences/
[14] Ibid.
[15] For a full side by side comparison of the shooting script to the finished film see *G-Fan* #101.
[16] vantagepointinterviews.com/2018/06/26/urban-renewal-r-j-kizer-on-directing-godzillas-30th-anniversary-reboot-for-american-audiences/
[17] Ryfle, *Japan's Favorite Mon-Star*, pp.237.
[18] Homenick, "'You can't choose what you're remembered for.' An interview with title designer Ernest Farino." *G-Fan* #76, pp.33.
[19] Shoemaker and Perkins, "*Godzilla 1985*: Screenplay Comparison", *G-Fan* #101 (June 2013).
[20] vantagepointinterviews.com/2018/06/26/urban-renewal-r-j-kizer-on-directing-godzillas-30th-anniversary-reboot-for-american-audiences/
[21] Ibid.
[22] Homenick, "Adapting *Godzilla 1985*: Easier Said Than Done," *G-Fan* #87 (Spring 2009), pp.28.
[23] Apparently, these changes came from the new conservative top of New World Pictures—Roger Corman had already sold the company several years prior. "This is the company we work for," director Kizer was told of the anti-Russian slant he was to give their version.

36.
"GODZILLA 2"
AND THE BIRTH OF BIOLLANTE

After the release of *The Return of Godzilla* (1984), Tomoyuki Tanaka decided to stir up some interest in Godzilla by holding an open screenplay writing contest for the film's sequel where the winner would be awarded ¥3,000,000. Toho announced the competition in April of 1985 and a whopping 5,025 entries were received. An overwhelming number of these treatments were written by fans who had grown up watching the films during the era of the Toho Champion Matsuri Festival, with most of the submissions from people in their twenties. The first review culled the submissions down to 202 entries, then 23 in the next, and ultimately, 13 finalists announced on October 25th that same year. Amazingly, among the storylines a sort of theme—or rather themes—clearly emerged. Ed Godziszewski explained it best in an interview with Scified: "[Toho] narrowed it down to fifteen different ideas and all of them fell into one of three categories. One category was Godzilla being used as a weapon controlled by a third party, of which there were several different 'third parties' to consider. One was a mad scientist, another was aliens, one was Godzilla being controlled by America and one even had Hitler involved with controlling Godzilla."[1]

The second category was, of course, Godzilla fighting another monster. The last category of the contest was Godzilla being cloned or Godzilla fighting himself or a variation of himself. At least one draft prominently featured a Godzilla egg and several utilized time travel. Many of the drafts were too ambitious to be filmed and called for exotic locations such as the Himalayas, the Antarctic, and even the Egyptian Tombs of the Pharaohs.[2] A notable number of drafts also contained elements of James Bond-like spy action. This story contest was rather prophetic of—or perhaps just downright influential on—the Heisei Godzilla series. Godzilla fought several clones of himself throughout the series, there was time travel in *Godzilla vs. King Ghidorah* (1991), a Godzilla egg in *Godzilla vs. Mechagodzilla* (1993), and the spy elements featured in the finished *Godzilla vs. Biollante*. An article in the Japanese

Starlog #28 in February of 1985 even mentioned these elements writing:

> Well, what kind of stories have you gotten a lot this time? It is said to be divided into roughly three types of stories total. 1: A pattern in which a third party attempts to control Godzilla and use Godzilla as a weapon including Hitler, mad scientists, aliens and so on... 2: Another monster to oppose Godzilla. 3: Instead of former nuclear fear, a cloned Godzilla with the development of genetic engineering replaces that fear in recent years. As a means to defeat Godzilla were the Oxygen Destroyer, freezing, the idea of letting Godzilla time-slip, and fantastic things such as launching it into space.[3]

Among the top scripts (or honorable mentions) were *The Blood of Godzilla* by Akira Ryusuke,[4] *The 80,000-Year-Old Grave* by Yoshinobu Sato, *Invisible Demon* by Naoki Mihara, *Godzilla II* by Ota Toshiaki, *NEW Godzilla 2* by Akio Asuka, and another by Tatsuo Kobayashi called *Godzilla vs. the Giant Robot Corps* (which eventually turned into Shinichi Sekizawa's *Godzilla: Legend of the Asuka Fortress*, and from there, supposedly, 1989's *Gunhed*). To pick a winner amongst these 13 scripts Tanaka, with Toho President Isao Matsuoka, assembled a panel comprising of science fiction critic Mitsutoshi Ishigami, famous Japanese comics artist Dr. Osamu Tezuka, and writers Baku Yumemakura and Chiaki Kawamata. Each panelist critiqued the scripts and Tezuka noted that *Godzilla vs. Biollante* had an interesting setting but thought a giant flower with a woman's face was too strange. On October 25th, *Godzilla vs. Biollante* was announced, along with the other finalists, as the "winner." Apparently, Toho didn't consider the story contest to have a clear-cut winner because none of the stories were good enough to be adapted as they were and the final result would be a combination of several of the top scripts with *Biollante* at the top of the heap.

As it turned out, *Godzilla vs. Biollante* had not been written by a novice writer. Author/dentist Shinichiro Kobayashi had previously written episodes of the 1972 TV series *Return of Ultraman*. Specifically, he wrote episode #34, "Unforgiving Life," about a scientist who combines the DNA of a plant and a lizard creating Leogon, a monster that fights Ultraman Jack in Lake Ashino. Furthermore, the kaiju was even designed by Kako Yodane, who would go on to help design Biollante for the new film!

Kobayashi's screenplay concerned two reporters, Sayaka and Ken. While investigating a mysterious ship sinking, the duo are lead to the lab of geneticist Dr. Shiranui. The doctor is being financed by the Adelia Republic to bioengineer a human-plant hybrid dubbed Biollante—which Shiranui uses the cells of his dead daughter Erica to create. As Sayaka has visions and dreams of human plants, the monster responsible for sinking the ship—an escaped giant rat-fish hybrid created by Shiranui named Deutalios—emerges in Tokyo Bay. Godzilla stirs in the sea near Oshima Island and comes to fight Deutalios, who retreats. The two monsters finally come to blows in Yokohama, while Sayaka confronts Shiranui regarding her visions. An agent of Adelia then chases Sayaka into the forest with plans to kill her. Godzilla kills Deutalios in Yokohama, devours him, then sets out for Shiranui's lab located in a dense forest that comes alive and begins attacking him. The form of Biollante erupts from the earth and battles Godzilla to the point he is so weakened that he retreats when the defense forces attack him. However, in a last act of hatred, he blasts Biollante in the face and the plant-human hybrid explodes into spores that drift skyward.

Overall, this more poetic rendition of *Godzilla vs. Biollante* is quite interesting, especially the extra monster Deutalios. Many of the characters in Kobayashi's version are archetypes for the characters in the finished film: Shiranui is a slightly more sinister precursor to Dr. Shiragami while Sayaka is a combination of Miki Saegusa and Asuka Okochi. Shiranui's protégé, Tachibana, became a precursor to Kirishima as Kobayashi's treatments progressed.

On November 9th, an awards ceremony was held at the main building of the Toho Photography Center in Tokyo for the winners of the "Godzilla 2" contest. Not only was Kobayashi in attendance but also many of the other runners up, all of whom were awarded and acknowledged by Isao Matsuoka. At this time, Kobayashi spoke to Tomoyuki Tanaka on the stairway inside the main building where Tanaka asked him, "What do you think of Kazuki Omori?" Little did Kobayashi know, not only would Omori direct his movie but also substantially alter his script.

Before Omori was called in to overhaul Kobayashi's concept, Toho gave the dentist a chance to do a second screenplay himself with a few guidelines set forth during a November 14th meeting with the two Tanakas: Fumio and Tomoyuki. At this meeting, the elder Tanaka reiterated that the story "needed conflict." At a later December meeting was when Tanaka instructed Kobayashi to change Biollante's origin to include Godzilla's cells. The idea to make Biollante a combination of not only Erica and a plant but also Godzilla's cells, gives the plant an excuse for growing to giant size. In the first screenplay, there is no logical reason why a plant produced by joining human and plant cells would grow to Godzilla-sized proportions (unless one is using Ultraman logic, that is). Tanaka also mandated the cutting of Deutalious as a way of lessening production costs.

On January 8, 1986, Kobayashi turned in his second story draft, which had many early elements that would find their way into the finished film. Chief among them was psychic girl Miki Saegusa, a college student who helps out in Shiranui's greenhouse. However, this Miki only communicates with Biollante and has no connections or intuitions regarding Godzilla at all.[5] The Middle Eastern element returns, though this time there is competition between the fictional Arabian country and the U.S.—not the fictional Bio-Major, but the actual CIA! Despite the inclusion of the real-life agency, somehow Kobayashi's second treatment seems less sophisticated than the first. Many outrageous ideas abound; and Shiranui now has more of a mad scientist vibe to him. Kobayashi even wrote a scene where as an early version of Biollante begins to die, Shiranui flashes a wicked smile at the thought of injecting the G-cells into the plant. The motivations of the Adelians (here called the Arabian Knights) are now a bit far out, as they believe Godzilla to be an incarnation of the Nile River crocodile god Sobek![6] It is their hope that Shiranui can regenerate Godzilla from his cells. Presumably, the Adelians then plan on controlling their Godzilla to rule the world.[7] Essentially, this plan all revolves around an ancient prophecy proclaiming that the resurrection of Sobek will lead to their country ruling the world.

Shiranui's guilt over Erica's death is more overt in this version. In this backstory, Erica died while she was on the verge of becoming a brilliant pianist. At one point, Shiranui watches an old film of her playing the piano during her birthday party. When standing up, she falls to the floor and becomes ill, blood splattering on the floor. Shiranui also has nightmares about taking his daughter off life-support in the hospital. All the while, the specter of the Arabian Knights looms over Shiranui's research. It seems likely that Kobayashi drew inspiration from *Terror of Mechagodzilla*, as the Middle Eastern backers and Shiranui with "surrogate daughter" Biollante all seem to parallel the Black Hole aliens, Dr. Mafune, and Katsura.

Kobayashi came up with the interesting idea of Biollante draining a forest of its life force to the point that the leaves begin to take on an autumnal hue in summer. The dentist/writer also introduced a prototype to the Super X2, the ZEUS (Zooming Electron Universal Shooter). Unlike the Super X2, it could not fly and had to be airlifted by choppers. Essentially, it was a maser tank that could reflect Godzilla's ray back at him.

The character of Tachibana was Erica's fiancé in the first draft, but that is removed by the second.[8] Here, the young man is Shiranui's colleague, and his reasons for wanting to create new life differ from Shiranui's. In Tachibana's case, after witnessing mass starvation in Africa, he has the idea to combine human and plant cells. In his mind, if humans could become hybridized with plants, all they would need to survive would be water, sunlight, and soil. This bizarre idea might fly in the world of Ultraman, but in the more grounded world established in *The Return of Godzilla*, it would have seemed out of place.

The hostage situation/tradeoff in the finished film may have descended from a similar concept in this story. Here, Dr. Shiranui is kidnapped by the Arabian Knights, angry that he never cloned Godzilla as promised (they don't count Biollante), and they offer to trade him back to Tachibana for his notes on the G-cells. When Tachibana relents with Miki tagging along, the CIA ambushes the trade to take out the Arabian Knights. One could also assume that the anti-nuclear energy bacteria element was inspired by a brief scene in this story where the CIA fires a massive tranquilizer into Godzilla by chopper, which Godzilla subsequently blasts from the skies. There is also an exciting sequence where the self-defense forces attack Biollante at Lake Ashino. Biollante crushes tanks into the ground with her vines and even swats planes from the sky. Also, while in the last treatment, Godzilla's escape from Mt. Mihara isn't explained or even addressed, here an earthquake in South America affects the tectonic plates all the way to Japan. As he would in *Godzilla vs. Mothra* (1992), the monster king swims through the earth's mantle until he pops out of the ground near Lake Ashino.

There is an exciting new layer to the relationship between Biollante and Godzilla—Godzilla's ray doesn't harm the monster. It only feeds her! Also, Biollante wants to use Godzilla as an incubator to grow even larger. The plant monster becomes a global threat that adds an element of excitement and suspense to the climax. Shinichiro Kobayashi seemed inspired by *Mothra vs. Godzilla* with his final battle—he compares Biollante's pollen spraying onto Godzilla as being similar to the Mothra larva's silken webbing in the script. Biollante is described here as having huge petals that act like a "butterfly's wings," and the plant blows the pollen all over Godzilla as she holds him in place with her vines. The battle ends as Biollante becomes so large that she appears to be preparing to eat Godzilla! At the last moment, as she drags Godzilla closer and closer to her mouth, she absorbs too much of his radiation and explodes into a pillar of fire. The mass of vines encompassing Godzilla begins to unravel and the monster king is free. One of the remaining Arabian Knights watches Godzilla and the pillar of fire with religious reverence. As Biollante dies, either one of the main characters or one of the vines plays one of Erica's favorite melodies on the piano (translation issues make it hard to tell who—or what—it is).

Tomoyuki Tanaka wasn't fully satisfied with this draft and gave Kobayashi one more try at another script. This third draft, the largest and most developed one yet, was turned in on January 30, 1986. Tanaka reportedly said of the third attempt: "It gets worse every time he changes it."[9] Kobayashi said that "The third manuscript I wrote was 320 pages. I handed it to Mr. Ishii at Yokohama Station on January 30th. Now, this manuscript is missing."[10] In February of 1986, Tomoyuki Tanaka approached up-and-coming filmmaker Kazuki Omori about taking over the writing for the new film. Not only did Tanaka give Omori Shinichiro Kobayashi's script, but also four other finalists' scripts as well. Omori explained, "[One of the scripts] was they were going to use the cells of Godzilla and reproduce them to make Godzillas all over the world or something like that. And the other was there was going to be a plant monster. And among the five left over, producer Tanaka liked these two, the one that had to do with the Godzilla cells and using them for something and the plant monster."[11] In addition to having Omori work on *Godzilla vs. Biollante*, as a sort of back-up plan, Tanaka had enlisted Shinichi Sekizawa to adapt *Godzilla vs. the Robot Corps*, the second runner-up, into another script that could be a potential "Godzilla 2" or "3".

However, Tanaka didn't cut Kobayashi out completely. On March 10, 1986, Omori and Kobayashi met in the Imperial Hotel Rainbow Lounge to exchange ideas. From there, the script entered into a period of what is today known as "development hell" for nearly three more years. This chiefly happened because Toho got cold feet on their "Godzilla 2" project after the failure of Dino DeLaurentiis' *King Kong Lives* (known as *King Kong 2*) in Japan. Toho took note that the usually popular King Kong had flopped and decided that "people aren't interested in giant monsters anymore." Soon after *Little Shop of Horrors* (1986, and also featured a plant monster) was released to success in Japan, and Toho's confidence in the Godzilla project was bolstered once again.

Omori's first drafts contain a milieu of strange changes such as making Miki Saegusa Erica Shiragami's sister! Omori's version of the character, he said, was inspired by the movie *Carrie* (1976). Tanaka didn't like the idea of the character at all. "Mr. Tanaka himself thought it was a bad idea at the beginning. He thought, 'No, (it must be) kaiju vs. kaiju. You're not supposed to have this young girl in this movie.'"[12]

The backbone of Omori's first treatment—just recently discovered and published for the first time in *Godzilla vs. Biollante Perfection*—is close enough to the structure of the finished film that a blow-by-blow of the story isn't needed.[13] Omori's opening scene doesn't place the battle between the Bio-Major agents in the aftermath of Godzilla's 1984 attack hours later but instead begins just as Godzilla is leaving the city. A man waiting in the subways receives a radio communication that Godzilla is leaving and that he is to commence "Operation G." These Bio-Major agents are then shot down by a Middle Eastern agent. English-speaking fans will be amused to know that before he was the notorious SSS9 (played by Manjot Beoi), he was named ASS9! Presumably, someone who spoke English at Toho eventually told Omori this would be a bad name to use.

Dr. Shiragami is a much more controversial figure here, having achieved human cloning 20 years ago through artificial insemination/gene manipulation with the frozen semen of Nobel Prize winners.[14] At one point, Erica mentions how she has been called the "daughter of Frankenstein." In this version, Erica is killed much later in the story and is introduced *after* the bombing of the Saradian lab, giving a lecture at the Godzilla Countermeasures Center. There, she speaks about the wonderful possibilities of biotechnology. Later, Erica views 19-year-old Miki Saegusa on the news in a segment detailing her ability to psychically communicate with flowers. This perks Erica's interest as she thinks that due to her age, Miki could be related to her father's experiments. And it is later discovered that Miki is the very "clone" child created by Shiragami 20 years ago!

At one point, Dr. Shiragami is kidnapped at a party where he is hit with a tranquilizer dart and then carted off in a wheelchair by SSS9. Shiragami is rescued by Erica and some of their compatriots, who evade SSS9 in a car chase through the streets of Tokyo. As Erica investigates the origins of Miki Saegusa as her father's experiment, she suddenly becomes gravely ill.[15] When the doctors tell Shiragami that Erica is brain dead, he asks for one last request before they pull the plug. Dr. Shiragami harvests Erica's cells before she dies and then injects them into Biollante, the mutant plant he has created from the cells of Godzilla and a rose.

When Godzilla is freed from Mt. Mihara by the terrorists, Dr. Shiragami confesses that Miki Saegusa has special abilities because he manipulated a mutation in her and that she could be used to defend Japan against Godzilla. Omori wisely utilizes the bird frequencies device[16] from *The Return of Godzilla* that lures Godzilla to a forest that emits an anti-bacterial mist, Omori's way of getting in the forest battle from Kobayashi's treatments. Godzilla soon revives from the ANEB forest and heads for the nearest nuclear power plant—in this case, Kawauchi Nuclear Power Station.

In this version, Biollante doesn't gestate in Lake Ashino, but Lake Biwa. There, Miki tells Shiragami that Biollante is calling him "father." At this point, a colleague named Kirishima realizes what Shiragami has done and calls him a monster. Elsewhere, Godzilla attacks the Ikata Nuclear Power Plant and absorbs its radiation. Through Miki, Erica berates her father for imprisoning her soul within the gigantic plant. Still, Miki and Shiragami ask Erica/Biollante if she will fight Godzilla to defend the country. In her anger, Erica shouts that Godzilla may as well destroy the whole country.

As Godzilla heads for nuclear power plants in the Osaka region, an emotional conversation takes place between Miki and Shiragami where it is learned that it was his own genetics he used to create Miki, making her his biological daughter and Erica's sister. Upon learning this, Erica/Biollante has a change of heart and says, "I do not want to fulfill my father's wish, but I will listen to my younger sister's wish." With that, Godzilla abruptly changes direction heading for Lake Biwa—apparently, Biollante has a psychic link with Godzilla because they share genetic material Godzilla is so determined to reach his clone that he completely ignores the military's efforts to stop him. Godzilla lumbers through Nara, destroying a huge bridge and the famous Buddha statue there.

Upon reaching Lake Biwa, some of the battle's choreography is like the Lake Ashino battle, but the ending differs wildly. In her final attack, Biollante emits deadly pollen which greatly irritates

Godzilla. Rose blossoms begin to float across the water and through the skies in an incredible show of beauty as Godzilla collapses. However, the monster quickly recovers with a vengeance, slapping Biollante with his tail. Biollante's rosebud head opens into a massive mouth and bites down onto Godzilla's head. Somehow, Biollante inexplicably begins to float into the sky taking Godzilla with her! Shiragami and Miki say goodbye to Erica and Biollante disappears out of sight with Godzilla. The two monsters crash into the sea, where Godzilla sinks into the depths.

Godzilla vs. Biollante Perfection contains a memo that contains many of Tanaka's requests for Omori in regards to his next revision. Among them are the removal of the ESP aspect and a mandate that Godzilla attack Osaka. This same memo also mentions that Shinichi Sekizawa had already successfully written his third draft of *Godzilla: Legend of the Asuka Fortress*.

Omori's first full screenplay was submitted on October 1, 1986, and was simply titled *Godzilla 2*, Toho's working title for the project. Its contents are virtually identical to the finished film in terms of the sequence of events such as Erica dying early in the bombing of the Saradian lab. The main difference is that certain scenes are much more ambitious. This draft begins with Godzilla's 1984 battle with the Super X in Tokyo as Bio-Major agents lay in wait in the subway system to collect G-cells.

In this version, Dr. Shiragami wears an eye patch over his right eye due to injuries sustained when the Saradian lab was bombed, an obvious reference to Dr. Serizawa. Actually, Omori wanted Akihiko Hirata to play the part but seemed to be unaware he had died in 1984,

"Akihiko Hirata is the name of one of the famous actors, and before *Biollante*, we wanted to work together, but he passed away before *Biollante* was in the process of being made, so we weren't able to work with him. In *Biollante*, there's a big role that I wanted him to play, and I wanted to ask him to do that role. But because he passed away, I found someone of equal quality to play that part. Yoshiko Kuga is the name of the actress in the movie. But Mr. Tanaka said having a woman do that kind of a role is not good, so I had to change it again. So I changed it to a man."[17]

Despite being written in 1986, this story still takes place five years after the events of *The Return of Godzilla* in 1989. Tokyo was meant to be shown still in the process of being rebuilt as glimpsed during a scene where Asuka and Kirishima share a drink. During an early scene where a helicopter flies over Mt. Mihara, Godzilla was supposed to get a close-up within the volcano showing his eyes moving menacingly and was also supposed to be glimpsed during the first tremor at Mt. Mihara. Here, there was to be another scene inside the volcano showing Godzilla's tail moving and another ominous shot of his eyes.

Some lengthy dialogue scenes were also cut for the final revision. This draft features a more in-depth, scientific discussion between Goro Gondo and Major Kuroki regarding the anti-nuclear energy bacteria. There is also an additional scene of Asuka and Kirishima sharing another drink before they get caught in the rainstorm. Kuroki has a few extra tricks up his sleeve in this version. Here, there is a scene of Kuroki watching the creation of a liquefied cadmium which is to be converted into a gas and then used on Godzilla—and it is when the monster emerges from the volcano.

Rather than having the Bio-Major agents break into Shiragami's home while he is absent, in this version, Kirishima and Shiragami are confronted in the latter's home by one such agent. The scene gets interesting when said agent threatens to burn the growing Biollante plant (then just a suspiciously large rose) to Shiragami's utter horror if he doesn't tell them where the G-cells are stored. When Shiragami tells them where the G-cells are kept in the Okochi Foundation, SSS9 shows up out of nowhere and begins shooting, prompting the Bio-Major agent to flee with the Saradian agent in pursuit. The Bio-Major agent takes the Biollante rose with him as he flees in his car. The plant then uses its vines to choke him to death, which sends his car crashing into Lake Ashino as SSS9 watches from afar. It's too bad this scene was so heavily altered. Not only is it more exciting, but it also makes better sense as to how the mostly immobile Biollante managed to get into Lake Ashino.

There is an interesting dream scene where Miki sees Erica's face submerged underwater. The dead girl's eyes open and she calls for Asuka to come help her. Miki awakens and realizes something is happening at Lake Ashino. Later, people aboard a pleasure craft react in horror as the glass sunroof begins to crack and the vines of a giant rose invade the boat. This sequence is problematic storywise because it turns Biollante into an aggressive villain. The rose monster doesn't just sink the ship, she absorbs its passengers into her body.

Godzilla's exit from Mt. Mihara is more ambitious in this version because Kuroki immediately sends a helicopter fleet to intercept him. The fleet sprays a yellow cadmium mist on Godzilla, who disappears within the yellow haze but is soon spotted heading out to sea. The Super X2 attacks Godzilla there, and in this version, the Fire Mirror is much more effective. Intelligently, Godzilla realizes the machine is reflecting his own ray and stops firing at it. The Big G retreats while the Super X2 is content to follow the monster from a distance now that he is heading away from Tokyo.

Around this same time, there is an elaborate car chase scene as SSS9 flees Tokyo, where all flights are grounded, to get to Osaka with the ANEB he has stolen from the Bio-Major agent. Passing through Odawara at the same time as Godzilla, SSS9 actually drives his Mustang underneath Godzilla's tail to get away from Colonel Gondo, who is in hot pursuit.[18] The Lake Ashino battle, this time set during the day, is livelier because the Super X2 fights Godzilla for a second time amid the fight with Biollante. The plant monster attacks the Super X2, catching it in her vines and tossing it into the lake where it becomes unresponsive.[19] Godzilla then approaches Biollante with some sense of admiration after she does away with the flying battleship, with no clear ill intent and seems to be merely curious. It is Biollante who attacks first when Godzilla gets too close and the fight begins in earnest. Biollante is mobile in this battle, even in her rose form, and runs away from Godzilla at one point. Most of the best bits of choreography from the film are present, including Biollante dragging Godzilla underwater. The battle ends with Biollante hiding underwater and when she surfaces, Godzilla tears her head off and then sets the body on fire with his ray.

After the battle, Dr. Shiragami and Okochi discuss harvesting more cells from the remains of the fight, though by this point, Shiragami is sickened by what he has done. Another scene has boats surrounding the floating Super X2 to prep it for repairs. The Super X2 confronts Godzilla at Naruto Bridge where it strikes his dorsal fin with a laser. Miki and Asuka drive out onto the bridge in a jeep against orders and in the midst of battling the Super X2, Godzilla turns around to face Miki. They have a brief staring contest and Miki faints. Godzilla proceeds to destroy the bridge as Asuka speeds off with Miki in tow just in the nick of time. Asuka and Miki are thrown from the vehicle. Miki lands safely on the ground, but Asuka hangs precariously from the destroyed bridge before somehow landing safely. SSS9 is about to escape Osaka by jumbo jet when Godzilla's arrival in the vicinity cancels all flights and in the terminal, Gondo quips to Kirishima, "This time, Godzilla is on our side." The duo spy the ANEB briefcase in the baggage claims and snatch it before SSS9 can.

The end battle is lacking compared to the final film in some ways yet more dramatic in others. Perhaps inspired by Kong's last stand in *King Kong Lives*, Omori has an ANEB-weakened Godzilla drop to his knees as Kuroki orders a final helicopter strike. Enraged by the attack and by sheer force of will, Godzilla stands and blasts the choppers from the sky (this scene happens in the film, just not with Godzilla on his knees). After this, Miki announces Biollante's return and a huge red rosebud descends from the sky. In this iteration, Biollante has yet to evolve into her fiercer, crocodilian design and is still more or less a giant flower.

Godzilla blasts Biollante with his ray repeatedly when suddenly a reptilian face emerges from beneath the rosebud on the trunk of the plant. This new, crocodile-like mouth then spews acidic sap upon Godzilla. Finally, because of the ANEB, Godzilla loses the ability to fire his ray and begins to sputter and choke. As Godzilla wretches in agony and Biollante's petals fall off, it is here that Dr. Shiragami observes both monsters in their suffering and states, "Godzilla and Biollante aren't monsters, but the men who made them." The rose monster wraps her thorny body around Godzilla and the bud tries to swallow Godzilla's head. Using her huge remaining petals like a butterfly's wings, Biollante succeeds in carrying Godzilla out to sea. This visual could have been beautiful or awkward depending on the techniques utilized at the time (though the latter is more likely). Not long after, Shiragami is shot and in this version, SSS9 gets away scot-free. Shiragami eloquently begs Kirishima not to experiment with the G-cells and then dies. The camera tilts up to reveal the massive Biollante bloom in orbit.

For the next two years, Kazuki Omori worked on the script and in 1988, new producer Shogo Tomiyama even created a new proposal for the film called *Godzilla: Godzilla vs. Biollante,* though little is known of Tomiyama's proposal or how it may have differed. Omori and new special effects director Koichi Kawakita had a meeting to decide what kind of special effects could be created for the final draft. Even this draft would feature a few ambitious scenes that would later be deleted and a few that were never filmed. To instill some suspense that perhaps Erica's spirit had been consumed by Biollante's nature, the plant monster was to intentionally go out of her way to destroy a self-defense force vehicle. However, the monster transforms only a moment later, ascending into the clouds and setting Erica's spirit free.

Godzilla was to destroy New Kansai International Airport, which was under construction at the time. The airport's owners felt having the airport demolished on film before its real-life counterpart was finished would give the building a bad reputation and vetoed the idea. The locale was switched to the Osaka Business Park, which was also under construction. In this case, the owner was all too happy to have his property destroyed by Godzilla on film.

Other ideas during development of the film can be found in storyboards. Such storyboards show a much more brutal battle between Godzilla and Biollante, where Godzilla rips Biollante right out of Lake Ashino with his mouth and throws her into the middle of a city. During the action, Biollante's radioactive blood kills the people underfoot. Even more intriguing are pre-production drawings of human-plant hybrids similar to the creatures from 1963's *Matango*—perhaps mutated by Biollante's blood? Another storyboard envisioned the end battle occurring on the streets of the endangered Takahama Nuclear Power Plant.

Biollante's reptilian form was also a relatively late addition to the script. She would have retained her rosebud head for the final battle and used her petals to glide across the landscape. One of Omori's stranger ideas (in a script full of strange ideas) had Miki Saegusa slightly lifting Godzilla into the air with telekinesis! Tomoyuki Tanaka was opposed to the idea and made sure it was cut. Omori said, "In my first script, she actually uses her power to raise Godzilla out of the ocean. If you've seen the movie, you can see that scene isn't in the movie because Mr. Tanaka got upset, thinking this little girl could take on Godzilla and float him out of the water."[20]

Omori turned in his third draft on January 17, 1987. The fourth and final draft was submitted on July 24, 1989. Overall, Omori's final script is superior to Kobayashi's original though it would have been nice had he been able to carry over a few of this script's more poetic elements and the monster Deutalios—axed as a cost-cutting measure to eliminate an additional monster suit. However, the studio ended up creating extra suits anyway when it was decided that Biollante should have two forms. [21] Reportedly, designs for the final stage were still being considered when the film was shooting in August! One of the early ideas—approved by Koichi Kawakita—was that Biollante would have a four-piece mouth, the idea of designer Shinji Nishikawa. Eventually the studio decided Biollante should better resemble Godzilla and was given a more reptilian look.

There were actually three Godzilla suits built for the new movie.[22] The first suit created proved unsatisfactory and is known as the "NG Suit" ("NG" is film jargon for "no good"). Ed Godziszewski told Scified, "They actually ended up making a preliminary suit which they decided not to use. It's got a wider face, a sort of ribbed chest and it was broader than the suit they actually used in the film. So they made this prototype suit and after judging it they decided it wasn't quite what they wanted. Then they modified it and eventually came up with the final design used in the film."[23] Koichi Kawakita said, "I think we took the 1984 Godzilla suit and redid the whole head, and a lot of the body was the same, but we ended up not using that."[24] However, Kawakita could not possibly have done that as the 1984 Godzilla suit had been transformed into the title character for *Pulgasari* (1985). Furthermore, pictures show that the "NG Suit" is its own thing and looks nothing like the 1984 suit. The "NG Suit" would eventually make it onscreen, cut in half and used for the sequence where Godzilla finally surfaces in the sea for the first time in *Godzilla vs. King Ghidorah* (1991).

The Super X2's designs were tweaked several times as well. Studio Nue submitted a design where the craft would change its appearance based upon land, water, and air modes. In Ed Godziszewski's coverage of the film in *Japanese Giants* #8 he described the three forms this way:

> "In its flying form, Super X2 resembled a jet fighter with a mazer [sic] cannon built into the nose, combined with a wide variety of superfluous surface detail. On land, Super X2 would be a streamlined Markalite clone, but replacing the parabolic mirror with four slim mirrored panels. In submarine form, Studio Nue's image of Super X2 bore resemblance to AAB Gamma, the spaceship from *X From Outer Space*."[25]

Ideas for the production changed even during shooting. For instance, the original ending—shot and then considered "NG"—had Biollante completely engulfing Godzilla. It was brought to life with a combination of live-action filming and Japanese animation. The idea wasn't that she was eating the monster king, however. It was that Biollante was taking away all of Godzilla's hatred so he would be at peace when he revived. Toho disliked this ending because they didn't want Godzilla to become a Showa-ish superhero again.

In its final form, *Godzilla vs. Biollante* contains some very interesting themes. As the Godzilla series had always done a good job of providing social commentary on the dangers of science, *Godzilla vs. Biollante* in particular breaks timely new ground by warning of the dangers of biotechnology rather than nuclear testing. In fact, *Godzilla vs. Biollante* may be one of the first sci-fi films to truly delve into the subject of biotechnology. David Kalat drew some significant parallels between Shiragami and Dr. Serizawa from the 1954 *Godzilla* in his *A Critical History and Filmography of Toho's Godzilla Series*. In the book, Kalat notes how both men have developed super weapons which could tip the balance of world power in Japan's favor. While both scientists die in their respective films, Serizawa commits suicide while Shiragami is assassinated. It's interesting to note that while Serizawa takes responsibility for his creation by taking his own life, Shiragami seems to feel far less guilty about his own research, which he selfishly pursues as a means of trying to preserve his dead daughter's essence. Only at the picture's end does Shiragami truly seem to comprehend the error of his ways when he concludes that Godzilla and Biollante aren't the real monsters so much as the men that made them.

Godzilla vs. Biollante was released on December 16, 1989— exactly five years and one day after the release of *The Return of Godzilla*—where it did poorly at the box office. For many years, the film was divisive for fans, with some loving its originality and others considering it too bloated with too many characters and subplots. However, in a Japanese poll conducted in 2016, *Godzilla vs. Biollante* was voted the best Godzilla movie in the series (though by 2017, it had fallen out of the top five in favor of the usual suspects for the same poll). Though done on a smaller scale, North American fans at a special panel at G-Fest XXV also concluded that *Godzilla vs. Biollante* was "Ostensibly the Best Godzilla Movie Ever."

Chapter Notes

---

[1]   www.scified.com/news/when-roses-attack-25-years-of-godzilla-vs-biollantewith-ed-godziszewski
[2] Though exotic locations weren't used in the Heisei series, it would seem this contest inspired Tanaka to push for exotic locations, including the Himalayas, in the cancelled *Mothra vs. Bagan*.
[3] *Godzilla vs. Biollante Perfection*, pp.83.
[4] Considering the title, it was likely one of the storylines dealing with cloning Godzilla.
[5] There was a psychic girl in Guy Tucker's "Godzilla 2" entry who had a psychic connection to the enemy monster. However, Miki was

more likely an evolution of Kobayashi's first treatment's Sayaka character.
[6] A real mythological figure for those no doubt wondering.
[7] This was a plot point common in the story contest, and one that Tanaka possibly mandated Kobayashi try to work into his revision.
[8] Amazingly, Kobayashi wanted actor Kunihiko Mitamura to play Tachibana, who was, in fact, cast as Kirishima in the produced film. For Miki, he indicated 20-year-old J-Pop star Yu Hayami and for Dr. Shiranui, he wanted Eiji Okada, star of films such as *The X from Outer Space*, *ESPY*, and *Blue Christmas*.
[9] *Godzilla vs. Biollante Perfection*, pp.85.
[10] Ibid, pp.80.
[11] https://vantagepointinterviews.com/2017/05/13/kazuki-omori-recalls-the-heisei-godzilla-series-tohos-writer-director-shares-his-memories-of-the-king-of-the-monsters/
[12] Ibid.
[13] In an interesting coincidence, as Kazuki Omori was working on the script for *Godzilla 2* in which Godzilla escapes Mt. Mihara, the volcano erupted for real on November 19, 1986. Toho acted quickly and arrived the next day to shoot footage of the lava. When the eruption became too intense on the 21st, they evacuated the island. These shots would finally appear in the finished film a full three years later.
[14] This aspect of the character is mentioned very briefly in the finished film, though in this case it was just an idea Shiragami had, not something he actually did.
[15] It was unclear to this author what caused Erica's sudden demise, but SSS9 likely played into this somehow.
[16] Also, one has to wonder why the frequency trick wasn't acknowledged in the finished film. In this script, Godzilla develops an immunity to the frequency and quits heeding its call, solving a rather nagging continuity question.
[17] https://vantagepointinterviews.com/2017/05/13/kazuki-omori-recalls-the-heisei-godzilla-series-tohos-writer-director-shares-his-memories-of-the-king-of-the-monsters/
[18] Ed Godiszewski's translation in *Japanese Giants* #8 is probably more accurate and states that what happens is Godzilla destroys the road before SSS9's car can pass. The agent abandons his car and runs into the woods.
[19] The Super X2 was likely cut from the finished battle because showing Biollante's vines wrapping around the ship with wireworks would have been very difficult.
[20] https://vantagepointinterviews.com/2017/05/13/kazuki-omori-recalls-the-heisei-godzilla-series-tohos-writer-director-shares-his-memories-of-the-king-of-the-monsters/
[21] Coincidentally, Biollante's first rose form is very similar to a plant monster from Toei's 1971 TV series *The Magic Teacher*.
[22] Curiously, script drafts of *Godzilla 2* featured the William Stout-designed Godzilla from Steve Miner's *Godzilla King of the Monsters in 3-D*!
[23] www.scified.com/news/when-roses-attack-25-years-of-godzilla-vsbiollantewith-ed-godziszewski
[24] Lees, "Godzilla's Godfather", *G-Fan* #59 (Nov/Dec 2002), pp.13.
[25] Godziszewski, *Japanese Giants* #8, pp.8.

PROFILE: SHINICHIRO KOBAYASHI

Shinichiro Kobayashi was born May 25, 1955, and is famous as the winner of a screenplay contest for "Godzilla 2." Before winning the competition, Kobayashi wrote episode 34 of 1971's *Return of Ultraman*, "Unforgiving Life," which concerned a plant/lizard hybrid named Leogon, whom Ultraman Jack battles in Lake Ashino! That same year, Kobayashi also wrote episode 3 of *Mirrorman*, entitled "The Disappearing Super Express." After this, the writer left tokusatsu behind to focus on becoming a dentist. In 1980, he graduated from the Kanagawa Dental University and then advanced to obtain his doctorate in 1984. In 1985, he caught wind of Toho's "Godzilla 2" script contest, though Kobayashi didn't have as much time as he had hoped to work on his treatment as he had to go to a doctor's conference. After it was over, he had only two days to write out his treatment, but did it anyway. The idea of a scientist trying to make his daughter immortal happened as Kobayashi looked upon his own six-month-old daughter wishing that he could grant her eternal life. He also thought of a monster that was both beautiful and fearful, one that could swallow Godzilla. Kobayashi won the contest and his script was adapted into the finished film by Kazuki Omori. Strangely enough, as the script continued to develop, it was Kobayashi who suggested that Godzilla have a double row of teeth! Omori had a good laugh about that in an interview stating, "He's probably the well-versed dentist in the world when it comes to Godzilla! And being a dentist, he was the one who came up with how to put Godzilla's teeth in the movie!"[vantagepointinterviews.com/2017/05/13/kazuki-omori-recalls-the-heiseigodzilla-series-tohos-writer-director-shares-his-memories-of-the-king-of-the-monsters/] In 1994, Kobayashi had some sort of involvement in the development of *Godzilla vs. Space Godzilla* as he submitted a design concept for the monster, technically introducing the crystal element of the character. In 1999, Kobayashi also had an unspecified role in the production of *Godzilla 2000*— it's possible Kobayashi even wrote a treatment for the film though this can't be confirmed. Kobayashi's Japanese Wikipedia page even says that he helped to put together the book *Toho Tokusatsu Unpublished Works* in 2010!

Selected Filmography
Return of Ultraman (1971) (writer)
Mirrorman (1971) (writer)
Godzilla vs. Biollante (1989) (writer)
Morphological Monster [Asahi Sonorama] (1993) (writer)
Godzilla vs. Space Godzilla (1994) (contributed ideas)
Godzilla 2000 (1999) (contributed ideas)

37.
BIG SCREEN
ULTRA Q

While Toho monsters were absent from silver screens in 1990 (no thanks to *Godzilla vs. Biollante*'s dismal failure), there was a movie incarnation of *Ultra Q* that year. Like many other films in this book, *Ultra Q: The Movie* began long before it was released. In the early 1980s, there was a great deal of interest concerning the possibility of producing a new Ultraman movie and Mamoru Sasaki, who wrote for the original *Ultraman*, had his own unique idea for such a movie. The story was called *Ultraman: Monster Bible* and was to be produced with ATG Productions[1] rather than just Tsuburaya Productions alone. Interestingly, the story was set during the original *Ultraman* series. Whether this was to be a reboot or not is unknown but since the original cast was too old at this point to reprise their 1966-era selves, new actors would be brought in to portray Shin Hayata and the rest.

Original series director Akio Jissoji was even supposed to direct the film. Story details are sparse but it would have centered around ancient aliens, secrets of the universe, and the titular ancient book that can somehow release monsters. Supposedly, even a "secret" of Ultraman would be revealed. Apparently, production collapsed due to friction between Mamoru Sasaki and ATG Productions. Elements of this script eventually evolved into *Ultra Q: The Movie;* the alien Kananga in *Ultraman: Monster Bible* evolved into Wadatsujin, who appears in the finished film.

This author has only seen small excerpts of the script and one involves Ultraman entering into a discussion with the Kananga alien, who pleads with the silver hero to stop defending the human race. Also predating *Ultra Q: The Movie* was *Ultra Q: Monster Concerto*. It was even announced in a newspaper article on May 11, 1985, complete with monster designs. One of these monsters later ended up being Monster King Myra in *Ultraman: The Adventure Begins*. As with *Monster Bible*, Akio Jissoji was attached to direct.

At some point, it was decided to produce an *Ultra Q* movie, and the structure was to have been that of an anthology film like *Twilight Zone: The Movie* (1983). It would have had three stories focusing around the monsters Kanegon, Garamon, and another mystery monster. This version was to have been directed by none other than Shusuke Kaneko, written by Kazunori Ito, and storyboarded by Shinji Higuchi of the not-yet-extant Heisei Gamera trilogy![2] Kaneko even mentioned the project in a *G-Fan* interview stating, "Once I wanted to make a movie version of *Ultra Q*, and I asked Mr. Ito to write the screenplay, but it never materialized."[3] In *Gamera Heisei Perfection,* Ito also spoke of the coincidence: "Since then, I did not realize it, but in Kaneko's film "Ultra Q", I was also writing a story about Garamon, so it is a type of Gamera in a way for that story. I wonder if my wavelength matched with Kaneko's at that time?"

Like many kaiju films, this film's storyline was affected dramatically due to issues regarding toy sales. Sega Enterprises (also a toy company) was a co-producer on the proposed film and they mandated that a new monster be created because if classic monsters were used then Bandai would be the only ones allowed to make figures to tie in with the movie. When the dispute arose over Bandai having sole marketing rights to the desired monsters, Kaneko, Ito, and Higuchi left and Akio Jissoji and Mamoru Sasaki were brought in to revive *Ultraman: Monster Bible* as an *Ultra Q* movie.

The (rarely seen in the U.S.) finished film is well done with a dark, *The X-Files* vibe and a storyline reminiscent of *The Day the Earth Stood Still* (1951). The story begins with a TV crew investigating a bizarre set of murders and earthquakes that plague the excavation site of newly discovered ancient ruins. Eventually, the crew connects with a mysterious woman named Hoshino whom they learn is an alien called Wadatsujin that came to earth in ancient times to investigate the earth's environment. Upset at mankind's polluting of the earth, she unleashes her monster Nagira on a small coastal town as a show of her power. In the end, she leaves Earth with a group of new followers but before that, warns the reporters that what Nagira did was only a preview of what she will do if the earth does not stop polluting the environment.

Chapter Notes

[1] ATG was the chosen abbreviation of the Japan Art Theater Guild which operated from 1961-1992.
[2] As Gamaron on the 1966 *Ultra Q* was semi-inspired by Gamera, it's an interesting coincidence that Ito chose to write about Gamaron with Kaneko!
[3] Ryfle, "Guardian of Gamera's Universe", *G-Fan* #40 (July/August 1999), pp.41.

PROFILE: MAMORU SASAKI

Of all the writers in this book, *Ultraman* writer Mamoru Sasaki is one of the most prolific with a very high volume of work in TV, books, and feature films. Sasaki was born on September 13, 1936 in Ishikawa Prefecture. He graduated from Meiji University, where he belonged to the Children's Literature Research Division. In 1960, he became employed by TBS writing radio dramas. In 1963, he made his TV debut when his screenplay for "Contemporary Child" was filmed. It was Sasaki's friendship with TBS writer and director Akio Jissoji that got him involved in Tsuburaya Productions' *Ultraman*, and from then on Sasaki would have a prolific career writing tokusatsu TV series like *Ultraseven*. Sasaki also wrote a script for *Mighty Jack* in 1968 which was never filmed. Sasaki even came up with the premise of offbeat shows such as *Iron King* in 1972. Sasaki also had film adaptations of his work occur sporadically, even after his death in 2006 when a *Silver Mask* movie was made based upon his writings.

Selected Filmography
Ultraman (1966-1967) (writer)
Ultraseven (1967-1968) (writer)
Mighty Jack (1968) (writer) [unproduced episode]
Operation Mystery (1968-1969) (writer)
Silver Mask (1971-1972) (writer)
Iron King (1972-1973)
Ultraman Taro (1973-1974) (writer)
Ultraman: Monster Bible [feature film script] (1980s) (writer) [unproduced]
Ultra Q: Monster Concerto [feature film script] (1985) (writer) [unproduced]
Ultra Q: The Movie (1990) (writer)
Ultraman: Fly Far Away Towards Border of Dreams [feature film script] (1990s) (writer) [unproduced]
Silver Mask [feature film] (2006) (concept) [based upon the works of Mamoru Sasaki]

38.
BACK TO THE FUTURIANS
MOTHRA AND KING GHIDORAH RETURN

In 1989, Tomoyuki Tanaka had a much grander approach to his burgeoning new Godzilla series. Rather than immediately following *Godzilla vs. Biollante* with "Godzilla 3", Tanaka wanted to produce a Mothra movie without Godzilla. Instead of tasking Kazuki Omori with a straight remake of *Mothra* (1961), the producer asked him to plot a film where Mothra fought the ancient Chinese beast Bagan—the name of the monster opponent for 1980's aborted *Godzilla Resurrected*. Omori obliged, and even as *Godzilla vs. Biollante* underperformed at the box office, continued working on the script until April of 1990.

The ambitious story took place across all of Asia and had a newly-discovered Mothra awakening to battle Bagan, a monster from Chinese mythology that destroys the environment. Miki Saegusa was included as a character in the script to let audiences know the new Mothra movie was connected to the new Godzilla movies. Her reveal towards the end of the second act would have served a similar function as Samuel L. Jackson's post-credits cameo as Nick Fury in *Iron Man* (2008). Several sources even claim that *Mothra vs. Bagan* would have ended with an ANEB-ridden Godzilla awakening at the bottom of the ocean.[1] From there, story elements and questions posed in *Mothra vs. Bagan*—namely, who created Bagan—would be answered in further Godzilla sequels and more non-Godzilla monster movies. According to Kazuki Omori, *Mothra vs. Bagan* would have begun a four-part story arc that would not only divulge the secret origin of Miki Saegusa but Bagan's alien creators as well. Sadly, this more diverse, alternate Heisei universe would never come to pass. But because *Godzilla vs. Biollante* performed so badly in theaters, the more Toho executives thought about it, the less they believed that Mothra could carry a film on her own without Godzilla.

With the Mothra/Bagan grudge match shelved, Omori reportedly began to develop *Mothra vs. Bagan* into *Mothra vs. Godzilla*, and possibly even a *Godzilla vs. Bagan*. The sequence of events is foggy but another story says Omori took note of the fact that *Back to the Future, Part II* was beating *Godzilla vs. Biollante* at the box office. "And as we were watching *Biollante*, we were wondering why there were so many more people at *Back to the Future, Part II*. We said it must be time slips or time warps, so we decided to work on the idea of finding the roots of Godzilla and King Ghidorah by taking time travel somewhere else, so that's how the movie came to be."[2] From those comments you can see where the next film's time travel antics gestated. However, the idea to bring back King Ghidorah was Toho's, not Omori's, who didn't want to do a movie about a "silly space monster."

The original version of *Godzilla vs. King Ghidorah* was more or less like the finished film, but with one major difference: the opening of the film would not be in the Sea of Okhotsk but on Venus! The Futurians would find King Ghidorah either sleeping or dead on the "gold planet" and take cellular material from him to create the Dorats, which they would in turn use to create their own King Ghidorah to destroy Japan in the 1990s. Reports have it that at this point, *The Return of Godzilla*'s Koji Hashimoto was attached to direct.[3] Despite the fact *Godzilla vs. Biollante* had done so badly, Toho Corporate wanted to stay with the youthful Kazuki Omori in hopes he would draw in a younger audience, so they assigned him to be the director of the new Godzilla movie. With Omori came the demand that King Ghidorah have no ties to outer space at all and so the opening Venus scene was struck—this also infers that the original story of *Godzilla vs. King Ghidorah* wasn't written by Omori at all. At any rate, the author of the film's Japanese novelization used Tanaka's original idea about Ghidorah being found on Venus.[4]

The previous film had begun a trend of having Godzilla's opponent go through two distinct forms. This not only added interest but doubled the possibility for toy sales. King Ghidorah would have two different forms for two different reasons. One was the fact that Tomoyuki Tanaka wanted there to be a monster battle of some kind every thirty minutes. So Godzilla wouldn't simply battle King Ghidorah twice, an idea was hatched that in the first battle, the audience would root for Godzilla to defeat King Ghidorah and the Futurians. However after this, Godzilla would go on to destroy Japan. Therefore, at the end, the tables would turn and a mechanized King Ghidorah would be the hero.

The idea to resurrect King Ghidorah in a mechanized form may actually have come from a story pitch written by Shinji Nishikawa for a remake of *King Kong vs. Godzilla*. Before King Ghidorah, Toho toyed with staging a rematch between Godzilla and Kong but it was determined it would be too expensive to get rights to the ape.

In Nishikawa's outline, when Kong becomes wounded, he is resurrected as a cyborg for the final round with Godzilla. It could all be a coincidence but it is rather interesting that the same thing happens to King Ghidorah in the finished film.

Tanaka's insistence that there be a monster battle every thirty minutes lead to the creation of a brand new monster—the Godzillasaurus, who wasn't even in the first draft of the script. In an interview, Omori said, "In the first draft of the script, with the time travel, Godzilla doesn't come out until the middle of the movie. 'Isn't there a big problem with that?' the producer said. So what we decided to do, since Godzilla wasn't going to come out until the middle of the movie, we came up with the Godzillasaurus." [5] Omori's first idea was that Godzilla would simply be mutated from a still-living Tyrannosaurus Rex. However, no one on the staff believed a Tyrannosaurus could transform into Godzilla, no matter how much radiation it absorbed, so the effects designers set about creating a dinosaur character with Godzilla's distinctive traits that conceivably could transform into the King of the Monsters.

Other differences from the finished film included designs for a battle-damaged Godzilla, scarred by King Ghidorah's ray blasts. Koichi Kawakita wanted the beam from each of Ghidorah's heads to be unique—some test footage of this idea even exists showing purple, yellow, and blue rays. The advance artwork poster (which often reflected early, unused concepts) had three different variations of the beam coming out of Ghidorah's mouths! Instead, this idea was integrated into Mecha-King Ghidorah's beams from the center, mechanical head. Mecha-King Ghidorah was also supposed to shoot an array of missiles from its chest that Godzilla would shoot from the sky.

The first battle between Godzilla and King Ghidorah was originally to have ended with both in the water. When Godzilla emerged victorious, he would have carried Ghidorah's severed middle head in his jaws back to shore. The Futurians' ship, Mother, emerged from Tokyo Bay at the beginning and there was no end twist that Emmy and Terasawa are related. Initially, rather than Godzilla attacking the Teiyo submarine, it shot a nuclear missile into an iceberg containing the Godzillasaurus (perhaps a nod to *King Kong vs. Godzilla*?). However, Tanaka didn't like the idea of Japan using nuclear weapons and insisted Godzilla attack the sub instead. And there was even to be a maser satellite that would attack Godzilla with laser blasts from the sky. The finished film pleased audiences and Toho executives both, as the movie sold more tickets than *Godzilla vs. Biollante* had and earned ¥1,450,000,000.

The storyline has a wonderful pace, never letting up enough to let the audience become bored. Only after the film is over does the audience have time to ponder the film's biggest plot hole: why, if Godzilla has been erased, does Japan still remember who Godzilla is, and why has nothing really changed if Godzilla never attacked?

The answer is simple: there is no plot hole. American fans often misinterpret the plot because the international dub doesn't address several important plot points in the movie. When the Futurians move the Godzillasaurus into the Bering Sea, this should have removed Godzilla from history, correct? But they didn't. The Futurians believed that the 1954 Godzilla and the 1984 Godzilla were the same monster (they are not). Their actions are what caused the creation of the second Godzilla, who appeared in *The Return of Godzilla*. What confirms this is when Terasawa finds a newspaper article that details a nuclear sub running aground in the Bering Sea in 1977. This accident is, of course, what irradiated the Godzillasaurus into the second Godzilla. The only thing this film doesn't address is how the 1954 Godzilla came to be and how the Heisei Godzilla became buried under Daikoku Island between 1977 and 1984. The Futurians are simply too egotistical to think they had done anything but succeed in their mission, despite the fact they and everyone else still knows who Godzilla is in this "new" 1992 (the year the movie takes place).

The film's time-traveling villains are not aliens by any stretch but they certainly provide the same function in the story. This author believes that some influence came from *The Mysterians* (1957), a favorite film of Koichi Kawakita. As in that film, the Futurians' ship appears at Mt. Fuji and the imagery in *Godzilla vs. King Ghidorah* is evocative of *The Mysterians*. Furthermore, an American named Mick Anger actually gave Kawakita a script entitled *Godzilla vs. the Mysterians* shortly after the release of *Godzilla vs. Biollante*, so that could have influenced elements of the Futurians as well. And like the Xians of *Invasion of Astro-Monster*, the Futurians appear to come in peace to aid mankind but instead wreak havoc with King Ghidorah. As for the android M-11, *Terminator 2: Judgment Day* (1991) had just came out in Japan and that inspired the Hollywood-loving Omori to create the character.

Kazuki Omori had something to say about Japan's bubble economy, which had begun in 1986. The bubble represented a time in which real estate and stock market prices were greatly inflated and people wondered when it would end.[6] Ironically, the bubble burst the year after *Godzilla vs. King Ghidorah* came out. In the film's storyline, it is revealed that in the future, Japan grows so prosperous that it buys up entire continents including South America and Africa. The Futurians are out to stop Japan's growth, because it has more or less taken over the world. Of the three Futurians, one is American, one is Russian, and the other is Japanese. The Japanese member, Emmy Kano, switches sides to defend Japan when the Futurians take things too far. Considering the Caucasian villains and the fact that the Godzillasaurus wipes out U.S. army troops on Lagos Island, some media outlets reported that the film had an intentional, anti-American slant. Kazuki Omori, however, denied this.

Ideas for the next Godzilla movie were free-flowing. Tanaka, both excited by the film's success and also disappointed with the monster's origin, proposed *Return of King Ghidorah*. In this story, the real King Ghidorah from outer space shows up. Koichi Kawakita had his sights set on reviving Mechani-Kong while the Toho brass were dead set on Mothra. This was thanks to a recent Toho poll which ranked the four favorite Godzilla monsters as follows: Mothra, King Ghidorah, Mechagodzilla and Rodan. As a result, Kawakita was tasked with submitting two new drafts: one that followed the Mechani-Kong idea (eventually discarded) and another that featured Mothra: *Godzilla vs. Gigamoth*.

In the treatment for the latter film, Mothra's egg is found on a South Pacific island. There, it is watched over by a lone Shobijin named Mana. The problem is that the egg has been infected by dumping of nuclear waste. The egg hatches twin larvae: the benevolent Mothra and the mutated, malevolent Gigamoth. The latter heads for Japan where it spins a cocoon around a nuclear power plant after battling Godzilla. A new form of anti-nuclear energy bacteria is created which manages to subdue the adult Gigamoth but not Godzilla. The adult Mothra comes along but is shot down by Godzilla. As she lay on the ground, Gigamoth stabs Mothra but both insects merge together into the true Mothra, who spins a cocoon around Godzilla and dumps him into the ocean.

From this treatment, one can discern the basic outline of the finished *Godzilla vs. Mothra* since Gigamoth is Battra with a different name. The idea of an island devastated by developers present in *Godzilla vs. Mothra* is also lifted from the *Gigamoth* treatment. The final communication between Mothra and Battra is also obviously taken from the *Gigamoth* treatment; only the matter is resolved peacefully rather than with violence. In the

Gigamoth treatment, the title character plunges a horn into Mothra, which causes a fusion of the two beings. The treatment by Kawakita, Yuji Yoshida, and Marie Teranuma was handed over to Kazuki Omori who combined *Godzilla vs. Gigamoth* with his *Mothra vs. Bagan* script. Essentially, Omori replaced Bagan with Gigamoth/Battra and Godzilla both.

Mothra vs. Bagan has Mothra's egg being discovered by a TV crew in Borneo at the same time that the ancient monster Bagan awakens in the Himalayas. As Bagan marches across Asia, the Shobijin are abducted by a greedy promoter named Joji who whisks them away to Asia in the path of the rampaging Bagan. The Shobijin are saved from the greedy promoter by the hero, only to have him turn around and try to sell the Shobijin himself! The man is confronted by Mothra while he is in a hotel where he has a change of heart. Eventually, Mothra and Bagan clash, the Shobijin are rescued, and Earth is saved. Sound familiar?

The big carryover from *Mothra vs. Bagan* would be the main characters (along with certain scenes from said script, but certainly not all of them). Masako Tezuka is even the name of the female lead in *Mothra vs. Bagan*, the same name given to the ex-wife character in *Godzilla vs. Mothra*. Her love interest is essentially the same as the Takuya Fujito character only here he's named Ando, the name given to the salaryman character in *Godzilla vs. Mothra*! One scene even involves Ando trying to sell the Shobijin after rescuing them from an evil entrepreneur just as Fujito does in the 1992 film. Masako and Miki Saegusa go to Ando's hotel where they find the Shobijin just as Mothra (in her adult form here) approaches. However, this scene takes place in Bangkok rather than Tokyo. The bridge collapse scene in the jungle is even present. Here, it takes place in Borneo and is even more inspired by *Indiana Jones and the Temple of Doom* due to the Shobijin's native guards throwing spears at Masako and Ando when the bridge collapses.

In only three months, Omori had managed to create the first draft of *Godzilla vs. Mothra*, which transplanted the characters (and a few of the ideas) from *Mothra vs. Bagan* into the basic structure of *Godzilla vs. Gigamoth*. Of course, even these drafts contained ideas that didn't make it into the finished film. Director Takao Okawara said that he originally wanted to have Mothra land at a seaport for her final scene and later, a stadium. The Cosmos were also supposed to be first introduced standing in front of Mothra's egg rather than behind a flower, as in the finished film. There was also going to be some banter about Mr. Ando exploring

Infant Island in a suit to provide comic relief. And Frankie Sakai, the lead in the original 1961 *Mothra*, was supposed to have either a cameo or small role, but a scheduling conflict did not allow him to do so.

Ryu Hariken's storyboards for *Godzilla vs. Mothra* also provide a look at some key details omitted from the final film. From his drawings, it would seem that in one draft Mothra's egg was to be airlifted from Infant Island rather than towed by boat. Battra (the name derived from "Batoru-Mosura/Battle Mothra") also changed into its adult form in Nagoya and then flew out to sea to battle Godzilla. The underwater battle between Godzilla and the adult Battra is even storyboarded as a high-speed chase! Some pre-production sketches of the Battra adult show it as a bipedal creature with much smaller wings, though these might actually be designs for Gigamoth. Yet another crazy *King Kong vs. Godzilla*-esque storyboard showed Godzilla balancing himself with his tail to perform a dropkick to Mothra's head in the final battle! There was also an idea considered where Mothra would drop Godzilla into an erupting Mt. Fuji.

Rather than simply dumping Godzilla at a random spot in the ocean, a piece of dialogue from the Cosmos would have explained it was not just some random spot. Takuya Fujito asks the Cosmos, "Where are [Mothra and Battra] taking [Godzilla]?" The Cosmos would answer, "To a point which emanates a special force that will neutralize Godzilla. A submerged area which used to be part of our land."[7] In this version of the scene, the water would glow to signal the spot before Mothra drops Godzilla and the dead Battra into the ocean. Battra and Godzilla were to be shown sinking into the ocean until they crash into an ancient structure similar to Stonehenge but shaped like Mothra's symbol. Both monsters are then engulfed in a tremendous light. It's unknown if this dialogue was filmed but Kawakita and his crew spent a whole day shooting a single scene where Godzilla and Battra hit the ocean floor. Whether any ancient ruins featured is unknown, but the scene was cut.[8]

While the previous film focused on Japan's bubble economy, *Godzilla vs. Mothra*'s story is themed around the environment. This theme actually stemmed back to the *Mothra vs. Bagan* script in which Bagan awakens due to climate change. In the film, it is Battra who awakens due to a combination of climate change and a meteorite that crashes into the ocean (which also wakes up Godzilla, who has been resting in the Ogasawara Trench since the events of *Godzilla vs. King Ghidorah* earlier that year). One could argue that perhaps the film's message would have come through stronger if the monsters were awakened only due to man's mistreatment of the earth as opposed to a meteorite—which really wasn't anyone on earth's fault. The idea of the meteor resurfaces in the finale, where it is revealed that Mothra will journey into space to destroy another one set to hit earth in 1999.[9] Though Omori was clearly setting up another story thread, it was never resolved in the Heisei series and we never do learn what happened to Mothra in space ...[10]

Godzilla vs. Mothra turned out to be the second highest-grossing Godzilla movie when released in 1992. It was extremely successful due in part to appealing to Japan's #1 movie audience demographic: young, single women. The feminine monster Mothra had always held appeal to women and lead actor Tetsuya Bessho was also a popular heartthrob at the time.

Chapter Notes

[1] This scene is not in the script the author read however.
[2] Homenick, "The Man Who Revived Godzilla", *G-Fan* #78 (Winter 2007) pp.35.
[3] This author would speculate that perhaps since Omori was working on *Mothra vs. Bagan*, they had Hashimoto working on the prep for "Godzilla 3". According to *Markalite* #3, Hashimoto left the project willingly upon the delivery of the second draft of the script.
[4] This is also why another King Ghidorah movie about the real monster from outer space was immediately considered after this one because Tanaka wanted to do right by the monster.
[5] Homenick, "The Man Who Revived Godzilla", *G-Fan* #78 (Winter 2007) pp.35.
[6] Omori also briefly touched upon this in his *Mothra vs. Bagan* script.
[7] Ragone, "The unused ending for *Godzilla vs. Mothra*", *G-Fan* #11 (Sep/Oct 1994), pp.41.
[8] On one final wild note, Koichi Kawakita also toyed with the idea of Mothra dying at the end so he could make a Mecha-Mothra! When David Milner asked Kenpachiro Satsuma about this, Satsuma replied, "Mothra originally was going to be killed... So, Koichi Kawakita thought of turning him into a cyborg called Mecha-Mothra. It was going to look more like a dragonfly than like Mothra." http://www.davmil.org/www.-kaijuconversations.com/satsum.htm
[9] The original treatment for 1961's *Mothra* ended with the big bug flying off into space, but not to destroy an asteroid.
[10] This plot point was attempted to be resolved in both *Godzilla vs. Astrogodzilla* (a precursor to *Godzilla vs. Space Godzilla*) and an early draft of *Godzilla vs. Destroyah*. Instead, we merely see Mothra traveling through space in *Godzilla vs. Space Godzilla*. This thread would presumably have been resolved in the Mothra trilogy until it was decided to set it in its own, distinct universe.

PROFILE: KAZUKI OMORI

Much of the style and direction of the Heisei Godzilla series is thanks to director/screenwriter Kazuki Omori, born March 3, 1952, in Osaka. Omori had a love for movies at a young age and told Brett Homenick, "The first movie I ever saw that had to do with Godzilla was when I was five years old, so I've known Godzilla for a very long time. Growing up, I saw a lot of kaiju movies. At 15 years old, I found out that 007, James Bond, was a lot more fun, so I forgot about Godzilla for a while and went into that area." Omori's "official" directorial debut was 1978's *Orange Road Express*, though before that, he had helmed several independent films. Omori developed something of a following in Osaka and presumably, one of his friends suggested Omori as the director of "Godzilla 2" to Tomoyuki Tanaka. While he worked on the script for "Godzilla 2" (adapting Shinichiro Kobayashi's *Godzilla vs. Biollante*), Omori wrote and directed *Women in Love* in 1986 and directed two more features by the time Toho finally got around to making *Godzilla vs. Biollante* in 1989. Omori then wrote *Mothra vs. Bagan* which was eventually cancelled in favor of a new Godzilla movie as Toho felt Mothra couldn't stand on her own. Omori directed *Godzilla vs. King Ghidorah* (1991) but chose not to return as the director for *Godzilla vs. Mothra* due to scheduling conflicts but did write the script, which he adapted from *Mothra vs. Bagan*. "One thing I thought myself was that *Godzilla vs. King Ghidorah* was the perfect movie and so after we'd done Mothra, I thought it was a little bit less than what I'd done in King Ghidorah, and so I just wanted to back away from it for a little while," Omori told Homenick [vantagepointinterviews.com] as to why he didn't return to write more Godzilla movies until 1995's *Godzilla vs. Destroyah*—though he kept writing and directing other projects. Though there have been rumors Omori wrote *Destroyah* only because his home had been destroyed in the devastating Kobe earthquake of January 1995, Omori was already working on the 1995 Godzilla project before this time. In 2005, Omori returned to the world of Toho special effects films when he directed *Sazer X: The Movie*.

Selected Filmography

Orange Road Express (1978) (writer, director)
Women in Love (1986) (writer, director)
Sayonara Women (1987) (writer, director)
Godzilla vs. Biollante (1989) (writer, director)
Mothra vs. Bagan (1990) (writer) [unproduced]
Godzilla vs. King Ghidorah (1991) (writer, director)
Godzilla vs. Mothra (1992) (writer)
Shoot! (1994) (director)
Godzilla vs. Destroyah (1995) (writer)
Sazer X the Movie: Fight! Star Soldiers (2005) (director)

39.
ATTACK OF THE (GODZILLA) CLONES

In 1993, Toho found themselves at a crossroads with their main cash cow, Godzilla. They were just coming off their most successful Godzilla film in decades and Tri-Star Pictures had just paid Toho for the rights to produce their own American version of Godzilla. This was where things started to become complicated as Toho would not produce a new Godzilla movie in 1994 since Tri-Star was planning to release their film that same year. Before the Tri-Star deal had been inked, Toho already knew they would be bringing back Mechagodzilla for the fifth entry in the Heisei series. But after the Tri-Star deal was set into motion, two new concepts entered the fray for "Godzilla 5": possibly killing Godzilla, and giving him an heir. The reasons for both were simple: killing Godzilla would give the story a dramatic lynchpin (and possibly make way for the Tri-Star version). Giving the king an heir—Toho hoped—could incite Tri-Star to use Godzilla's son in their own series. As for Mechagodzilla, Toho had polls taken with Japanese fans every year and the four top popular monsters were consistently Mothra, King Ghidorah, Mechagodzilla, and Rodan.[1] In *Toho Tokusatsu Unpublished Works*, Shogo Tomiyama half-jokingly said that if not for the Tri-Star film, "Godzilla 6" could have been *Godzilla vs. Rodan* but since Toho felt this may be the last Godzilla film, they decided to include Rodan here as well.

Rodan wasn't in every story treatment submitted initially, nor was the new Baby Godzilla. *Godzilla vs. Berserker,* a precursor to *Godzilla vs. Mechagodzilla*, had a virus from space crashing on earth in a meteorite and absorbing various metals into its body. Recognizing Godzilla as the dominant lifeform on the planet, it models its mechanical body after the King of the Monsters. To combat both monsters, the Teiyo company—introduced in *Godzilla vs. King Ghidorah* and now run by Yasuaki Shindo's son—builds a Super X-III. This fourteen-page treatment was submitted by anime designer Yutaka Izubuchi of *Gundam* fame. An alternate description says that Mechagodzilla was built by mankind until it was infected by a computer virus that made it go rogue. Godzilla then was to save mankind from the very robot they created to destroy him. Whatever the case, the concept art for Berserker shows both the typical bipedal Mechagodzilla and other versions which look like a towering mass of wires and machinery.

A story outline by monster designer Shinji Nishikawa was also submitted, entitled *Godzilla vs. Mechagodzilla: Metallic Battle*. Reports that Godzilla was to die (permanently) in this film may have come from this treatment, which again utilized the *Fantastic Voyage* idea first introduced in Koichi Kawakita's "Godzilla vs. Mechani-Kong" idea where scientists are injected into Godzilla's body. In this version, tampering with Godzilla's innards causes him to have a nuclear meltdown and explode. Baby Godzilla then absorbs his radiation and becomes the new Godzilla, and destroys Mechagodzilla in retaliation for his father's death.

Once Wataru Mimura was hired and began to write his version of the screenplay, changes were still rampant. Mimura's first draft began with a scene set in the prehistoric past and had a Godzillasaurus battling a Pteranodon to set up the rivalry between Godzilla and Rodan.[2] "A brief scene set in prehistoric times was deleted from the first draft. I was very fond of it," Mimura said.[3] The next scene would have actually shown Mecha-King Ghidorah being dragged from the ocean (this idea carried over from Shinji Nishikawa's aforementioned treatment).

In the first draft, Mechagodzilla was composed of seven separate armored units that could merge into one giant machine called "Union Mechagodzilla." Likewise, Garuda was a robot with legs and wings and was not one of the seven parts of Union Mechagodzilla.[4] In a nod to the original *Rodan*, there would be two pteranodons (male and female) discovered on Adonoa Island. In this draft, it was Mechagodzilla, not Godzilla, who battled the Rodans, electrocuting the male to death and crushing the female's eye. The female then plunges into the water and later mutates into a white Rodan when she attacks a Russian nuclear submarine.[5]

Godzilla's first battle with Mechagodzilla occurs at the Yokkaichi Complex in this draft and the machine escapes Godzilla by separating into its individual units. Though undeniably cool-sounding, this would have been a nightmare to film with practical effects. Also, during this battle, Baby Godzilla experiences an alarming six-meter growth spurt. When Godzilla approaches Baby Godzilla's vicinity, he becomes frightened and sends out a distress call that makes Godzilla go away. As in the finished film, the female Rodan absconds with Baby Godzilla and builds a nest on top of a skyscraper and obtains plants from Yumenoshima

Tropical Greenhouse Dome to feed the baby monster. Rodan is attacked by the seven separate Mechagodzilla vehicles and—to defend itself—the dinosaur creates a tornado by flying in circles. This effort, however, exhausts Rodan to the point of death and she crashes into the sea not to be seen again. So, instead of Rodan, once Godzilla dies, the nuclear reactor of Garuda goes critical and resurrects Godzilla's dead body when he absorbs the radiation. Miki Saegusa is not part of the Mechagodzilla crew here (Takao Okawara would add that later) and arrives on the scene in a helicopter only after the final battle is over.

In the second draft, Mechagodzilla was simplified into two separate crafts—a flying form (the lower body) and a boat/tank form (the upper body)—that join together into one robot and this idea was later used for MOGERA in *Godzilla vs. Space Godzilla* (1994). The tank/boat portion of Mechagodzilla kills the male Rodan on Adonoa Island with a heat beam while the female again survives to further mutate into a white Rodan. The female lead here is named Catherine and Aoki was to fly in on her while she was taking a bath—presumably in Baby Godzilla's enclosure as flying into a bathhouse would be a difficult feat! The pteranodon robot here is called the "Mini-Garuda." In their first battle, Mechagodzilla attacks Godzilla with something called Domyumu Missiles and separates into its two halves mid-battle. This backfires when the machines are unable to reform into Mechagodzilla because of a sudden computer glitch.

The G-Crusher—requiring a target lock in this version—gave director Okawara a better way of integrating Miki into the plot and had her join the Mechagodzilla crew. It sounds as if in this version, the machine's upper half is destroyed and Miki escapes in the bottom portion. If the other crew escape with her is unknown. As in the finished film, she telepathically encourages Baby Godzilla to leave with his father.

Rumors regarding Godzilla's demise were greatly exaggerated in the west. Toho may have considered killing Godzilla "for good" if not for Tri-Star's 1994 release date becoming less and less likely. Takao Okawara was apparently still keen on the idea though. "Godzilla was going to be killed by Mechagodzilla. I feel that Godzilla's death is what makes [the original Godzilla] so powerful. So, I wanted to kill Godzilla in *Godzilla vs. Mechagodzilla*. However, Toho would not permit it."[6]

In the final draft, it was decided that Rodan, rather than Garuda, would revive Godzilla to reinforce the movie's theme of life vs. artificial life. This also brought forth Godzilla's new red ray, which was not in the script and thought up during filming. "I decided to change the color of Godzilla's breath for two different reasons," Koichi Kawakita said. "One was the fact that Rodan changes color after Godzilla attacks him with his radioactive breath, and the other was my desire to show the power of nature."[7] Also, after destroying Mechagodzilla, Godzilla was to pick up Baby Godzilla in his mouth and head out to sea. The image was decided to be too unrealistic due to the two monsters' considerable differences in size and it was revised to have Baby follow Godzilla out to sea.

Godzilla vs. Mechagodzilla also featured the official debut of G-Force, a special military branch dedicated to battling Godzilla.[8] During an interview, Shusuke Kaneko explained how he got military cooperation for his Gamera films. He then began to speak of the Toho Godzilla films. "Do you know G-Force? The self-defense forces stopped cooperating on [the Heisei] films, so Toho created G-Force."[9] The reason is surprising; the Japanese self-defense forces had been criticized for attacking Mothra! "In (*Godzilla*) vs. *King Ghidorah* and vs. *Mothra*, the self-defense forces were there. But in *Mothra*, the self-defense forces attacked Mothra. The little girl asked the defense forces, 'Why did you attack the good monster, Mothra?' So the defense forces stopped cooperating with Godzilla films."[10]

Early concept art for the film showed a bevy of different monster and mech designs. A design for Garuda portrayed the mech as a sort of Mecha-Rodan, as it is very bird-like.[11] Yet another concept had Garuda as a combination of two separate vehicles. One of Shinji Nishikawa's designs for Baby Godzilla was startlingly similar to the design for Little Godzilla in *Godzilla vs. Space Godzilla* (actually, that is the design from *Space Godzilla* as it turns out). The reason for this, though, was because pretty much everyone but Okawara wanted to bring back Minilla. It was Okawara who insisted on a new character, Baby Godzilla.

Many of the early concept designs for Mechagodzilla had a red color scheme and one was green. These designs were also boxier compared to the final version's smooth contours. One design even resembled Kiryu, a future incarnation of the machine later seen in *Godzilla Against Mechagodzilla* (2002). A few others superficially resembled the original 1974 Mechagodzilla.

Even when shooting commenced, there was a bevy of deleted scenes, many of which were shot and a few that weren't. One such scene that made its way into the final shooting script involved Miki Saegusa helping Aoki hijack the Garuda but this was altered to

 **YAMATO TAKERU**

IN THE EARLY 1990S, TOHO DECIDED TO FINALLY BRANCH OUT FROM THEIR GODZILLA MOVIES TO TRY A GIANT MONSTER MOVIE IN THE SUMMER. THEY DECIDED TO REMAKE 1959'S *THE THREE TREASURES* AND HIRED WATARU MIMURA TO WRITE THE FILM. MIMURA TOLD BRETT HOMENICK THAT, "I HAD BEEN INTERESTED IN THE LEGENDS OF JAPAN FOR A LONG TIME... I WANTED TO WRITE SOMETHING LIKE JOHN MILIUS' *CONAN THE BARBARIAN*..." [HOMENICK, "SPINNING THE GODZILLA SAGA," *G-FAN* #88 (SUMMER 2009), PP.42] DAVID MILNER ASKED DIRECTOR TAKAO OKAWARA HOW MANY CHANGES THE FILM WENT THROUGH AND THE DIRECTOR RESPONDED, "A LARGE NUMBER OF CHANGES WERE MADE. YAMATO TAKERU ORIGINALLY WAS GOING TO BE A REMAKE OF *BIRTH OF JAPAN* (1959). HOWEVER, SINCE THE MOVIE WAS GOING TO BE THE FIRST OF THREE FILMS BASED ON KOJIKI, I FELT THAT IT WOULD BE BETTER TO FOCUS MORE ON THE RELATIONSHIP BETWEEN YAMATO TAKERU AND OTO TACHIBANA. SO, I OMITTED SEVERAL OF THE EVENTS THAT TAKE PLACE IN THE MYTH, AND INSERTED A NUMBER OF NEW EVENTS. FOR EXAMPLE, I DECIDED TO HAVE YAMATO TAKERU RETRIEVE THE MAGATAMA, THE CIRCULAR MIRROR, AND THE SWORD." [WWW.DAVMIL.ORG/WWW.KAIJUCONVERSATIONS.COM/MIMURA.HTM] SHINJI NISHIKAWA'S MONSTER DESIGNS WERE ALSO QUITE DIFFERENT IN SOME CASES. NOTABLY HIS DESIGN FOR MUBA WAS AN UNDERWATER VERSION OF BIOLLANTE WITH THE ORIGINAL FOUR-PIECE MOUTH. HIS EARLY DESIGN FOR OROCHI WAS THAT OF EIGHT GIANT SNAKES THAT HAD KNOTTED THEMSELVES TOGETHER IN THE MIDDLE. LIKEWISE, HIS DESIGN FOR KUMASOKAMI LOOKED TO BE A HALF MAN, HALF SPIDER. ALSO, A GIANT SALAMANDER WAS MEANT TO FIGHT OTO TACHIBANA, BUT NISHIKAWA DECIDED IT WAS REDUNDANT BECAUSE OF HER SCENES WITH THE SEA MONSTER MUBA. THE ORIGINAL END BATTLE WAS SUPPOSED TO BE MUCH LONGER, AND YAMATO TAKERU WAS TO HAVE JUMPED ON OROCHI'S HEADS NOT ONCE, BUT TWICE. THIS FOOTAGE WAS SHOT BUT CUT FOR PACING. MIMURA ALSO EXPLAINED THAT, "*YAMATO TAKERU* WAS ORIGINALLY GOING TO BE A TRILOGY. SO THIS MOVIE WAS THE FIRST PART OF THE TRILOGY, AND THAT IS WHY IT DID NOT HAVE A BOSS CHARACTER (HEAD VILLAIN)." [HOMENICK, "SPINNING THE GODZILLA SAGA," *G-FAN* #88 (SUMMER 2009), PP.42]

have Aoki knock out the pilot by himself in a scene that was later deleted. One enlightening deleted scene revealed that Shelley Sweeney's crew character was actually an android herself!

The finished film is considered by some fans to be one of the best entries in the Heisei series. The film is better-balanced and features fewer subplots and major characters than Omori's scripts. Writer Wataru Mimura, who turned in a draft for *Godzilla vs. Mothra*, said that,

> "The story of *Godzilla vs. Mechagodzilla II* was based on the plot I wrote earlier for *Godzilla vs. Mothra*. The theme was "Life." Godzillasaurus deposited an egg in the nest of the Pteranodon. I like this brood parasitism idea, which is quite original for the movie. Baby Godzilla and Rodan were tied with a brother-like bond. It is a bond between (two) lives."[12]

In the finished film, Mimura's theme went from "Life" to "Life vs. Artificial Life" in which the former triumphs. This idea is even expressed aloud by the character of Susan, a member of the Mechagodzilla crew. Considering that a deleted scene revealed her to be an android, this makes that line coming from her all the more interesting.

Upon release, *Godzilla vs. Mechagodzilla* came close to equaling the grosses from *Godzilla vs. Mothra*, but fell short. The film had even more tie-in merchandising that reaped enormous profits for Toho. The next Godzilla movie was practically guaranteed, especially in light of the constant delays on the Tri-Star Godzilla. Thanks to the overwhelming success of the tie-in merchandising, "Godzilla 6"—more so than any other in the series—was dictated by marketing and studio politics in terms of its development.

The initial foe for "Godzilla 6"[13] was a space-based incarnation of Ghidorah first pitched in the 1992 version of *The Return of King Ghidorah*. This Ghidorah, called Emperor Ghidorah, supposedly would have descended from the eight-headed Orochi from the upcoming 1994 *Yamato Takeru* film in some way. In all likelihood, someone decided that from a marketing perspective, it was a bad idea to use King Ghidorah again so soon and changed the space monster into a space version of Godzilla.[14] Even Shogo Tomiyama wrote in his autobiography that, "All the popular characters were used up in the previous work. So I had to start thinking about a new monster."[15] The lone holdover from the Ghidorah idea was that of gravity rays that Space Godzilla uses on the Big G—apparently, this ability would have been given to Emperor Ghidorah as a way of differentiating him from the 1991 version.

The first iteration of *Godzilla vs. Space Godzilla* was called *Godzilla vs. Astrogodzilla*. The ambitious, almost Showa-like narrative saw Godzilla's clone from space taking over the minds of both Miki Saegusa and Little Godzilla and turning them against the homegrown Godzilla. Also slated to appear in the seemingly overcrowded story was G-Force's new creation MOGERA (now an acronym for "Mobile Operations Godzilla Expert Robot Aerotype" in the Japanese version) and also Mothra, who would return to earth to aid Godzilla in battling his twisted clone.[16] In the end, Godzilla would team up with MOGERA, Mothra, and his son to battle Astrogodzilla. Though some concept art exists depicting the space-based Godzilla as being a hulking four-legged beast similar to a crystalized Biollante (sans tentacles) Astrogodzilla was envisioned as an albino Godzilla with wings, shoulder spikes, and two tails. The alien beast would have had an icy freezing ray that turns objects into crystal, plus the aforementioned psychic powers that possess Little Godzilla and Miki.

Unlike the finished Space Godzilla, which didn't have a concrete origin, Astrogodzilla was going to be a mutation of Biollante's cells. An article in *G-Force* #8 entitled "Godzilla's Next Foe" even stated, "Paul Roche reports that Biollante will reappear from orbit, but vastly mutated by solar radiation experienced while in space. The new movie is to be called *Godzilla vs. Space Godzilla*."[17] *G-Fan* #9 followed up on this writing, "The new monster will reportedly be white in color and, like King Ghidorah, have two tails. Instead of an atomic heat beam like Godzilla, one of the space mutant's principle weapons will be a freezing ray."[18]

Somewhere in this nebulous development period, *Godzilla vs. Biollante* writer Shinichiro Kobayashi submitted the idea for *Godzilla vs. Neo Godzilla*. Allegedly, this was where the aspect of living crystals first emerged so it's possible *Godzilla vs. Neo Godzilla* came first. Kobayashi even contributed a design sketch, which appears in *Godzilla Heisei Perfection*, that is fairly close to the final design of Space Godzilla.

However, when the mega-budgeted *Yamato Takeru* flopped hard at the box office, this hurt Toho enough financially to necessitate a budget cut on "Godzilla 6." Therefore, the potentially pricey storyline for *Godzilla vs. Astrogodzilla* would need to be overhauled to cut down on the budget. The first causality, ironically, was a monster that ended up in the finished film anyway: MOGERA. The logic was that being a giant robot, MOGERA could easily be replaced by the existing Mechagodzilla suit for a rebuilt "Mechagodzilla II."[19] Mothra's role was cut and she was replaced by Fairy Mothra—a creation that would go on to be an integral part of the Heisei Mothra trilogy.[20]

A new treatment (written by Shogo Tomiyama himself) entitled *Godzilla: Super Wars* was relatively close to the finished *Godzilla vs. Space Godzilla*. However, it is still far more interesting than the final film. It seems that Space Godzilla is the Heisei equivalent of the Showa King Ghidorah in this treatment as he has already destroyed several planets according to the Cosmos.[21] Fairy Mothra had an exciting expanded role; here, it is Fairy Mothra who leads Sakura, an early version of Shinjo, to the location of the kidnapped Miki Saegusa. That aspect of the plot is more interesting here too. Rather than the yakuza, it is a conspiracy within a corrupt corner of G-Force itself that is planning to counterfeit Miki's telepathy as a way of controlling Godzilla. The man behind the curtain was to be G-Force's Deputy Commander, in the translation named Hikoku. Commander Hikoku is close enough to Commander Hyodo, played by Koichi Udea in *Godzilla vs. Mechagodzilla* (1993) and *Godzilla vs. Space Godzilla* (1994), to assume the characters are one and the same. Though the translation was hard to discern, it would seem that Hyodo and his corrupt cohorts would decide what would be torn down and rebuilt in Japan through Godzilla's controlled rampages.

Unlike the final story, Miki Saegusa doesn't seem to be as much of a focus, and it's unclear whether or not she has a romance with the male lead. Here, the male lead is infatuated with a female character named Akiho Ishimaru. However, upon the story's conclusion, it is hinted that he is now attracted to Miki because she saves him during the conclusion. Prototypes of all the other characters exist with different names. In place of Shinjo and Sato are the slightly more rough and tumble Sakura and Hikaru. The two are described as trouble makers at G-Force who hang around the G-Force bar and love to fight. The Dr. Gondo character isn't related to Goro Gondo from *Godzilla vs. Biollante*, is male, and is named Dr. Yodobashi. It would seem that General Aso does not return in this storyline nor is there a Yuki character at all.[22]

The final fight between the monsters isn't described in great detail (as this was a fairly short treatment and not a full script) but mentions that Godzilla would fight Space Godzilla on the ground while Mechagodzilla II, joined with Garuda, would blast rays at Space Godzilla from the air. A special chemical fusion added to Mechagodzilla II gives the machine a powerful new self-destruct function that G-Force plans to use on Space Godzilla. After Sakura sets the self-destruct, like Yuki in the finished film, he has trouble getting out because of a hatch malfunction. Miki uses her telekinesis to open it, allowing him to escape at the last moment. Specifically, Mechagodzilla II grabs Space Godzilla from behind and flies him into the air. Godzilla then blasts them both, completely destroying his two doppelgangers.

This treatment does have the notorious outer space battle between Space Godzilla and Mechagodzilla II, here piloted by Sakura. Mechagodzilla II is also aided by another mech codenamed Mars, piloted by Hikaru. From the best the author can tell, Mars is just one of several superweapons descended from the lineage of the Super X—mentioned in the treatment. There are three in all, the other two named Taranis and Belenus, figures in Celtic mythology.[23]

There is no Birth Island battle or even a Birth Island for that matter. This film's island is Mikado Island in the East China Sea. Here, meteors crash on Mikado Island carrying eggs that hatch giant dragonflies. The giant dragonflies battle Baby Godzilla (not called Little Godzilla[24] and described as 20 meters tall) in the island's "primeval forest." This battle takes place while Godzilla is under Miki's control and Hikaru, feeling sorry for the infant, fights the dragonflies in his Belenus vehicle. In keeping with Miki's sympathetic feelings towards Godzilla, she lets the elder monster go from her control to defend his son. It is too late, however, and the dragonflies carry Baby Godzilla all the way to Mt. Aso in Kyushu where more dragonflies have constructed a "crystal altar" for the arriving Space Godzilla.

The demonic space monster, knowing it must defeat the strongest organism on earth to conquer it, wants to use Baby Godzilla to lure his father into combat. It works and Godzilla battles Space Godzilla at Mt. Aso. Needless to say, this is much more interesting than what plays out in the finished film with Baby Godzilla trapped inside the crystals on the island. The battle is described as being one of hand-to-hand combat, but eventually the two cross rays like in *Godzilla vs. Mechagodzilla* (1974 and 1993). Also, Godzilla has to battle the dragonflies in addition to Space Godzilla, who leaves Godzilla so badly beaten that he is near death.[25] It's also worth noting that Space Godzilla's wings carry over from the previous treatment (but only when he is in space), and his ray still has the ability to crystalize objects. Otherwise, the design for Space Godzilla in this treatment is presumably much closer to the one seen in the finished film.

In all likelihood, *Godzilla: Super Wars* was considered too pricy just like *Godzilla vs. Astrogodzilla* and was overhauled once again. Surprisingly, MOGERA was reinstated even though the reason he was cut was to save money by reusing the Mechagodzilla suit. Toy marketing was likely a factor as to why; a new MOGERA toy was more likely to sell over the same Mechagodzilla figure from last year. *Godzilla vs. Mechagodzilla* had reaped more profits from tie-in merchandising and toys than any Godzilla film before it. Furthermore, Koichi Kawakita held a decent amount of sway at Toho by this time and Mogera from 1957's *The Mysterians* was a favorite of his. Early concept art of MOGERA also gave it a huge chest drill. The mecha's ability to separate into two different crafts came from early drafts of *Godzilla vs. Mechagodzilla* where Mechagodzilla could do the same.[26] In addition to MOGERA, Mothra was also reinstated in a smaller capacity via some stock footage, though Fairy Mothra's role was reduced as well. Space Godzilla's final design is incredibly similar to the title character (a final form of Godzilla) from the Super Nintendo game *Super Godzilla* which might have played into the title *Godzilla: Super Wars*.

Other ideas in this script seem influenced by the video game. In the game (set in the year 199X), G-Force controls Godzilla from the Super X2 with a "control box" injected into his neck. In this version, Miki conducts Project T to control Godzilla from the Super X! This Super X is given no differentiation, simply the "Super X".

With the monster roster set, new (to Godzilla) writer Hiroshi Kashiwabara was brought in to write the script. Though Miki, like the monsters, was already set as the lead, Kashiwabara decided on many of the newer characters. Because he was a fan of Goro Gondo from *Godzilla vs. Biollante*, Kashiwabara created the role of Dr. Gondo, his sister. The character of Akira Yuki was also Kashiwabara's creation, though originally the role was set to be played by famed singer and actor Kenichi Hagiwara, whom Kashiwabara envisioned playing the part "like Rambo." A fan of John Wayne Westerns, Kashiwabara wrote Akira Emoto's version of Yuki to be reminiscent of John Wayne and scenes of Yuki trying to attack Godzilla on Birth Island were inspired by the John Wayne animal safari movie *Hatari!* "At first, I came up with the idea that they catch Godzilla with a (rocket) net as in *Hatari!* in which a lot of monkeys are caught with one. But it didn't work," Kashiwabara said.[27]

The in-production Gamera movie over at the newly-revived Daiei also gave Kashiwabara some problems since he wanted the end battle set in Fukuoka, a city Daiei had also chosen to have Gamera wreck. "I did want to use Fukuoka Dome, but it was decided to change it to Fukuoka Tower because Daiei had already set part of its Gamera movie there."[28] Furthermore, apparently Toho and

Daiei actually communicated about the process and decided between the two of them which locations within Fukuoka would be attacked!

Despite all the previously listed wild ideas, when asked how the first script differed from the final draft, director Kensho Yamashita hadn't much to say on any wild discarded concepts and offered up fairly mundane details such as, "There was a scene featuring two young men admiring a young woman at the beginning of the first draft, but it was not included in the final one. In addition, the battle in outer space between Space Godzilla and Mogera was much longer in the first draft." Of other deleted scenes he said, "We shot a scene in which a young man teases a waitress in a restaurant. It was going to be inserted at the beginning of the film. We also shot a scene in which the head of the mafia orders Dr. Okubo to send Godzilla to attack Tokyo."[29] He also stated that Akira Emoto improvised many of Yuki's final lines about showing Dr. Gondo around Fukuoka and leaving fighting Godzilla to the younger generation. Oddly, Yamashita didn't mention the movie's more prominent deleted scenes that were shot involving the yakuza subplot which was far more fleshed out. There were some notable cut monster scenes too, like Godzilla trying and failing to free Little Godzilla from the crystal prison, and Godzilla battling G-Force in the countryside of Kyushu. In fact, Yamashita's original cut was 2 1/2 hours long, but Toho cut it down to an hour and fifty minutes without his permission.

One person who didn't care for the final script was composer Akira Ifukube. The maestro told David Milner, "When I read the script for *Godzilla vs. Space Godzilla*, it reminded me of teenage idol films. In addition, the movie was going to have rap music in it. So, I thought, 'Well, this is not my world, so I better not score this one.'"[30] Ifukube wasn't wrong in his assessment as director Kensho Yamashita was best known for his teen idol film *Nineteen* (1987)[31] and *Godzilla vs. Space Godzilla* has some 'teen idol' aspects in it. This is because the human storyline focuses heavily on Miki Saegusa falling in love (writer Kashiwabara's idea). It's surprising it took so long for Miki to finally emerge as the main character considering she debuted four films ago![32] However, the love story between her and Shinjo is rather weak.[33] The two are meant to represent opposite ends of the spectrum and Miki argues with Shinjo about violence not always being the answer. More interesting is a subplot concerning Yuki, the G-Force operative out to avenge the death of his best friend, Colonel Gondo, killed in *Godzilla vs. Biollante*. In the end, after the Big G vanquishes his clone, Yuki decides to drop his grudge and hook up with Gondo's younger sister instead of trying to kill Godzilla.

Godzilla vs. Space Godzilla wound up being less successful than Godzilla vs. Mothra or Godzilla vs. Mechagodzilla, but still turned in a better profit than Godzilla vs. King Ghidorah had. Like the previous film, it made a great deal of profit from its tie-in merchandise. As with Godzilla vs. Mechagodzilla, before the film's release, early rumors circulated that Godzilla would die at the end of the movie. Those rumors, naturally, turned out to be false, though they certainly hinted at what was to come ...

Chapter Notes

[1] Anguirus had recently beaten Rodan, so why they didn't choose the ankylosaur which had appeared in the original Godzilla vs. Mechagodzilla in 1974 is curious.
[2] Ironically, in this particular draft, despite the set-up, Godzilla never meets either of the two Rodans in present day!
[3] www.davmil.org/www.kaijuconversations.com/mimura.htm
[4] The Garuda is not fully constructed until after Union Mechagodzilla is defeated by Godzilla.
[5] An early issue of G-Force/G-Fan reported on a similar story element that stated that Rodan would have been mutated by the same incident that created the new Godzilla in 1991's Godzilla vs. King Ghidorah.
[6] www.davmil.org/www.kaijuconversations.com/okawar.htm
[7] www.davmil.org/www.kaijuconversations.com/kawakit.htm
[8] The Maser helicopters that attack Godzilla at Mt. Fuji in Godzilla vs. Mothra have G-Force insignias on them, despite the group not being formally introduced into the series.
[9] vantagepointinterviews.com/2018/06/13/on-directing-godzilla-and-gamera-shusuke-kaneko-on-filmmaking-the-kaiju-way/
[10] Ibid.
[11] Aspects of these designs carried over into the White Bird of Heaven in 1994's Yamato Takeru.
[12] www.davmil.org/www.kaijuconversations.com/mimura.htm
[13] A letter from Japanese based fan Hikari Takeda of Okegawa City to J.D. Lees in G-Force #8 (March 1994) stated that the writer heard that King Kong and Gamera were both discussed as potential foes. In the same issue, Robert Biondi and Paul Roche also mentioned rumors of Kong being the desired opponent of "Godzilla 6."
[14] This, in turn, would lead to the cancellation of ghost Godzilla as an opponent in the next film as it would have made for three movies in a row with Godzilla based opponents.
[15] Tomiyama was referring to a poll that listed King Ghidorah, Mothra, Mechagodzilla and Rodan in that order.
[16] This is pure conjecture on the part of the author, but it's most likely the asteroid subplot from Godzilla vs. Mothra (1992), wherein Mothra leaves earth to destroy an asteroid in 1999, would have been resolved in some manner.
[17] G-Force #8, vol. 1 (March/April 1994).
[18] "Space Godzilla details revealed", G-Fan #9 (May 1994), pp.3.

[19] This theory doesn't hold up terribly well considering that *The Making of Godzilla vs. Mechagodzilla* special shows them blow the hell out of the Mechagodzilla suit. It does not look repairable by the time they're through with it.
[20] It should be noted it's possible Fairy Mothra also appeared in the Astrogodzilla draft too, though.
[21] In the treatment, the Cosmos aren't implied to appear, just their voice through Fairy Mothra. Also, the idea of psychic music from the previous film carries over here. The first scene was to have NASA discover the wreckage of an alien craft (covered in crystals) on an unspecified planet. They detect a strange signal, which we later learn to be the music of the Cosmos. The music warns that "the Great King of Darkness shall descend."
[22] On the note of General Aso, the film's eventual director said that after Aso's failure in the previous movie, he was supposed to be finished at G-Force. However, Mogera in this film is his attempt at redemption. Mogera is meant to be even more powerful than Mechagodzilla, but that never once seems the case. Additionally, both Yamashita and Akira Nakao agreed that Aso should no longer be "an angry person."
[23] A note in the treatment says, "Since Garuda, it was fashionable in G Force to name new creations after the gods of war."
[24] He's never referred to as "Little Godzilla" in *Space Godzilla* either. The characters all call him "Chibi Goji" and the only time he's called by a proper name is when Yuki refers to him as "Bebi Gojira/Baby Godzilla." Only in the end titles is the character referred to as "Little Godzilla".
[25] As Toho's CGI capabilities were in their infancy at this point, cutting the dragonflies was likely a wise decision.
[26] Originally the Star Falcon was called Garuda though, apparently a continuation of the machine from the last film.
[27] vantagepointinterviews.com/2019/05/03/godzilla-on-paper-screenwriter-hiroshi-kashiwabara-on-writing-the-godzilla-series/
[28] Ibid.
[29] www.davmil.org/www.kaijuconversations.com/yamash.htm
[30] www.davmil.org/www.kaijuconversations.com/ifukub3.htm
[31] Yamashita was also a second unit director on *Terror of Mechagodzilla* (1975).
[32] Megumi Odaka still doesn't get top billing though!
[33] In his interview with Brett Homenick, writer Hiroshi Kashiwabara said he felt the love story didn't go well because of the actor who played the love interest, Jun Hashizume, whom Kashiwabara felt was too serious.

40.
REBIRTH OF GAMERA

Supposedly, rumblings of Gamera's return began as far back as 1984, when Toho was prepping their new Godzilla movie. For certain, Niisan Takahashi submitted a script (possibly unsolicited) to Daiei in the early 1990s called *Armageddon: Gamera vs. Phoenix*. The story was not a reboot, but a continuation of the Showa series (though it certainly ignored *Gamera Super Monster*, which Takahashi and Yuasa both disliked). The story bore some interesting similarities to the eventually-produced *Gamera, Guardian of the Universe* (1995).

In Takahashi's story, a fiery mythical bird called the Phoenix emerges from the Nazca lines in Peru because of humanity's disregard for the environment. The next similarity is that the military now views Gamera as a threat. However, they have good reason; Gamera has recently begun attacking industrial factories during nighttime raids (it is later revealed that a hole has been punctured in the ozone layer and Gamera was trying to prevent any further damage by destroying heavily polluting factories—but only at night when the workers had gone home). The story, which is heavily steeped in mythology, ends with Gamera defeating the Phoenix and then flying towards the ozone hole to somehow fix it.

Whether Daiei seriously considered the script or not is unknown.[1] Certainly in 1990, they began discussing the revival with initial ideas being for a short, direct-to-video production.[2] In 1993, anime writer Kazunori Ito was commissioned to write a script revolving around Gamera and Gyaos with a stipulation that both monsters have ties to the lost continent of Atlantis (which only Gamera had in the Showa series). The script he turned in was titled simply *Gamera* and could be considered a precursor of both *Gamera, Guardian of the Universe* and *Gamera the Brave* (2005).

As in *Guardian of the Universe*, Gamera and Gyaos are both the creations of Atlantis, the ruins of which are actually explored in a submersible.[3] A baby Gyaos in a strange cocoon is discovered by scientists, while several young children discover a mysterious turtle that is growing larger at a rapid rate (similar to *Gamera the Brave*). As Gamera grows and becomes known to the military, he is attacked because he is viewed as a threat. Eventually, the military comes to their senses and aids Gamera in destroying Gyaos.

Once Shusuke Kaneko came on board, he and Daiei immediately began arguing about the child element of the film. According to Kaneko, there were two scripts before Ito's that were "terrible" and "completely for children."[4] Kaneko said, "I think the company probably really wanted to have something in between those two discarded scripts and Mr. Ito's script." Kaneko also said, "Ito disliked those children in the films who act like adults and boss all the stupid grownups around... But Daiei's people didn't feel the same way Mr. Ito did about it."[5] According to Kaneko, Daiei had done a great deal of research as to what an audience would expect from a Gamera movie and felt that Gamera helping children and vice versa should be included in the film. Instead, both parties came to a compromise: a teenage girl named Asagi Kusanagi.

The original script for *Guardian of the Universe* had a few minor differences from the finished film. One was that the floating atoll would be submerged underwater and brought to the surface with airbags. Naoya Kusanagi doesn't let Yonemori join the expedition either so Yonemori must blackmail his way onto the team. He does this by threatening to expose the scandal of the accident on the high seas that opens the film (where the ship briefly runs aground on the floating atoll). Of this development, Kaneko said, "In the original draft, there were too many scenes before Yonemori gets to Asagi's house. He had to go through all these obstacles to get there. And in the original story, when Yonemori got involved with doing research on the ship, originally Kusanagi didn't let him join."[6]

There were five Gyaos originally and the defense forces immediately attack Gamera upon his surfacing in Fukuoka. When Kaneko learned from the real self-defense forces that the monster wouldn't be attacked that quickly, he cut it for the sake of both the budget and added realism. Also cut was an aerial battle between Gamera the military, as well as another separate aerial military assault where fighter jets attack Gyaos. Special effects director Shinji Higuchi explained, "There was a battle between Gyaos and a number of F-15s in the first two drafts of the script. During the battle, one of the F-15s was going to be sliced apart by Gyaos' supersonic beam and debris from the plane was going to fall on the Yurakucho Mullion building. However, the scene was deleted because representatives of the self-defense force objected to it. They argued that it would never actually take place because self-defense force pilots are trained to minimize civilian casualties."[7] Instead of Tokyo Tower, the effects crew wanted to destroy the Riverside Mansion, a huge apartment building in Tokyo. Kaneko also mentioned that Gyaos was meant to nest atop a high rise building instead of Tokyo Tower. Gamera was to look more like a sea turtle and feature the flippers in flight that he does sport in the sequel. However, Daiei executives wanted Gamera to look as close to the original monster as possible.

The biggest surprise of all is that Mayumi Nagamine isn't even in the first draft and Kaneko created the character himself. Kaneko also added the bridge scene where Gamera saves Yonemori and Nagamine to make the story a bit more dramatic. "Mr. Ito felt a little uncomfortable about putting in a scene in which the hero saves the girl and the child on the bridge. He felt kind of embarrassed to include such a scene, it felt awkward."[8] Kaneko went on to explain that the writer felt such a scene was clichéd. When writing the scene, Kaneko and Ito both thought of the bridge rescue scene from the original *Mothra* (1961). Ito also likened this first encounter between Gamera and Gyaos between the first bout between the title characters of *King Kong vs. Godzilla* (1962).[9]

When the film was released in 1995, it was something of a shocker for many giant monster fans. Many agreed the film was better than Toho's *Godzilla vs. Space Godzilla*. The adult-geared film was comparable to going from the campy Batman TV series of the 1960s to the dark, serious Tim Burton *Batman* from 1989. Kaneko, Ito, and Higuchi had accomplished quite a feat doing that for Gamera. The creature was, after all, a flying turtle and a friend to children—which he is in this story, albeit in a much more believable manner.

Upon release, the film was critically praised in its home country and managed to see a limited theatrical run in the U.S. in 1997. It also received a fairly high profile home video release from A.D. Vision. Despite being well-received, the film was not a hit on the level that *Godzilla vs. Space Godzilla* was, even if *Gamera, Guardian of the Universe* was the superior monster movie.

Chapter Notes

[1] Daiei had managed to get back into the film game somehow by distributing movies, notably the mid-80s slasher movie *Cheerleader Camp*!
[2] *G-Fan* #9 reported how the project had grown from being a "short feature" to its present state, but falsely reported that it would still be aimed at children.
[3] Though in *Guardian*, it's heavily implied to be Mu in the Pacific.
[4] What they were is unknown, but one could have been *Gamera vs. Phoenix*.
[5] Ryfle, "Guardian of Gamera's Universe", *G-Fan* #40 (July/August 1999), pp.42.
[6] Ibid.
[7] www.davmil.org/www.kaijuconversations.com/higuchi.htm
[8] Ryfle, "Guardian of Gamera's Universe", *G-Fan* #40 (July/August 1999), pp.42.
[9] Ito interview in *Gamera Heisei Perfection*, pp.213. A separate interview also implies that *The War of the Gargantuas* (1966) served as inspiration.

PROFILE: KAZUNORI ITO

Kazunori Ito was born December 24, 1954, to parents who just happened to run a movie theater, the Tokiwa Pavilion, which operated up until the mid-1990s. Ito went to school at Waseda University and began writing manga in the very late 1970s working on *Cyborg 009*. Eventually, Ito began working on screenplays and began writing an *Ultra Q* anthology movie with Shusuke Kaneko in the mid-1980's. One of Ito's chosen monsters was even the turtle kaiju Gamaron (a semi-parody of Gamera from 1966)! Though the project was cancelled (due to a dispute with toy giant Bandai), it may have led to a similar anthology movie that Ito wrote called *Twilight Q* (1986). In 1993, he wrote for the Tsuburaya TV series *Ultraman Powered* (*Ultraman: The Ultimate Hero* in the west) which Shinji Higuchi was also involved in. That same year, Ito was approached by Daiei to reimagine the Gamera series for them, though Ito felt somewhat shackled by the "friend of all children" concept and wished to shed it. His first draft, simply titled *Gamera*, kept the kiddies but by the time Shusuke Kaneko came on board, he was able to trade them for teenage girl Asagi. When that film proved to be a success, Ito got to work on the sequel which became *Gamera 2: Advent of Legion*. Though Ito wrote the treatment for *Gamera 3*, Kaneko eventually stepped in and revised Ito's ideas into the final script. Ito still works steadily today and shows no signs of slowing down anytime soon.

Selected Filmography
Cyborg 009 [manga] (1979) (writer)
Ultra Q: The Movie (mid-1980s) (writer) [unproduced]
Twilight Q (1986) (writer)
Ultraman Powered [TV series] (1993) (writer)
Gamera (1993) (writer) [unproduced; developed into *Gamera, Guardian of the Universe*]
Gamera, Guardian of the Universe (1995) (writer)
Ghost in the Shell (1995) (writer)
Gamera 2: Advent of Legion (1996) (writer)
Ghost in the Shell 2 (1997) (writer)
Gamera 3: Revenge of Irys (1999) (writer)
Avalon (2001) (writer)
DIGITAL MONSTER X-Evolution (2005) (writer)

41.
LONG LIVE THE KING
DEVELOPING DESTROYAH

In 1993, rumors had surfaced that Toho planned to kill Godzilla in *Godzilla vs. Mechagodzilla* to make way for Tri-Star's Godzilla movie—then expected to come out as early as 1994. When the American film was delayed, Toho nixed those plans and produced another Godzilla movie in 1994 as their New Year's Blockbuster. By 1995, Toho decided to finally pull the trigger and kill the Big G. This would work as both a publicity stunt and also pave the way for Tri-Star's *Godzilla*, by now firmly expected for 1997.

Considering this was to be the final Godzilla film for some time (at the time, Godzilla's hiatus was announced as being until 1999), a plethora of concepts were pitched—from literally anyone at Toho who was interested. Assistant Director Yosuke Nakano pitched *Space Godzilla's Counterattack*. Another idea was *Godzilla vs. Varan*, oddly enough, which would have Godzilla and Little Godzilla battle Varan, now an embodiment of some sort of 1999 doomsday prophecy. Later this idea morphed into yet another version of *Godzilla vs. Bagan*.[1] This idea supposedly would have featured Mothra and also a revamped Gohten/Atragon while yet another rumor suggested the combined might of Godzilla, Mothra, and Rodan would defeat Bagan. However, none of these ideas really led into *Godzilla vs. Destroyah*.

What became the final Heisei Godzilla movie very nearly followed in the footsteps of the previous two films in having Godzilla fight another variation of himself. The early story concept being bandied about was *Godzilla vs. Ghost Godzilla*—an idea from Shogo Tomiyama. The first version of this story had Godzilla Junior being sent back in time to 1954 to battle the original Godzilla. Not much is known about this storyline other than its bizarre core concept, which was wisely discarded. After this, the treatments that followed involved the ghost of the 1954 Godzilla possessing Little Godzilla, who grows to match his father. Godzilla must then battle his son to exorcise the ghost. The next treatment had Godzilla die by the Oxygen Destroyer midway through the story. Godzilla Junior then defeats the Ghost Godzilla. Crazier still, the final treatment pitched utilizing Ghost Godzilla was called *Godzilla vs.*

Baraguirus. Here, updated versions of Baragon and Anguirus fuse into the single monster Baraguirus... who is then possessed by Ghost Godzilla.

Kazuki Omori's treatment for *Godzilla vs. Ghost Godzilla* contains some notable character precursors to those in *Godzilla vs. Destroyah*. There is a middle-aged scientist character similar to Professor Ijuin, a reporter named Yuriko who is a less sympathetic version of Yukari Yamane, and a young genius similar to Kenkichi Yamane. Here, the young man is named Hideki Ogata and is the son of Hideto Ogata and Emiko Yamane from the original *Godzilla* (1954). A few scenes in the treatment also foreshadow ideas from *Godzilla vs. Destroyah*, such as a Godzilla bone discovered during the construction of a tunnel in the Ariake Waterfront sub center where Destroyah is found. Also, Little Godzilla dies in front of Godzilla and Miki Saegusa before being resurrected later. Lastly, it is the Oxygen Destroyer that is the cause of the Ghost Godzilla's creation.

Takao Okawara explained why the Ghost Godzilla concept was rejected: "Godzilla was pitted against Mechagodzilla in *Godzilla vs. Mechagodzilla* and Space Godzilla in *Godzilla vs. Space Godzilla*. So, it was felt that it would not be a good idea to have him take on another incarnation of himself so soon."[2] Even some of the other unusual ideas discussed after *Godzilla vs. Ghost Godzilla* included elements that would make their way into the final film. *Godzilla vs. Biomonster*, which almost looked to be a new version of *Godzilla vs. Frankenstein*, would have had Godzilla and a humanoid opponent die in battle. *Godzilla vs. Deep Sea Life* would focus on Godzilla battling a strange sea monster, with G-Force using the Oxygen Destroyer on both monsters.

Supposedly, it was Koichi Kawakita who pushed for Godzilla to die and the effects director is quoted in *G-Fan* as saying, "Toho was against killing Godzilla, but I said no, we have to go through with this... we have to kill him. I pushed that through."[3] Kazuki Omori remembered the sequence of events like this:

> "Another producer named Tomiyama, he brought the idea of bringing something in like a Godzilla Predator that could disappear, Ghost Godzilla. So even though they brought that idea to me, I had no idea what they were talking about! After Ghost Godzilla, the next idea they brought to me was that Godzilla would die. So in December 1994, they brought the idea to me. I thought it was quite an interesting idea and a challenge to kill Godzilla and thinking how to do it."[4]

How to finally kill Godzilla had been thought up long ago by none other than designer Yoji Yoshida. The artist had come up with the 1991 story *Godzilla's Counterattack*, a variation of *Godzilla vs. Mechani-Kong*, where Godzilla is in the process of thermonuclear meltdown. However, even that pitch was pre-dated by an entry in Toho's "Godzilla 2" contest by none other than American fan Guy Tucker who also pictured Godzilla amidst a meltdown in his submission, *Godzilla vs. Ankyron*.

The first real early version of *Godzilla vs. Destroyah* was called *Godzilla vs. Barubaroi*. In it, Godzilla would battle a Hedorah-like transforming monster with ties to the Oxygen Destroyer. In addition to Barubaroi, there would be a bevy of potential mechanical foes for the Big G, among them a new Super X-III—more or less a new version of the Gohten piloted by General Aso. A mecha constructed from the remains of MOGERA was also sketched out by Shinji Nishikawa and called G-END.[5] There was even talk of a Neo Oxygen Destroyer to be used at the very end of the film, possibly via the Gohten.

The early conception of the enemy monster Barubaroi was similar to Hedorah. It began as a group of small tadpole-like monsters that would merge into a larger one. Like Destroyah, Barubaroi is found in Tokyo Bay, where the original Oxygen Destroyer was detonated, and taken to the Yamane Paleontology Research Laboratory where it preys upon other creatures. Barubaroi is later transported to a G-Force laboratory where it escapes and may have faced off with the military in a similar scene to the SWAT set-piece from *Godzilla vs. Destroyah*.

Eventually, Barubaroi was discarded for the much cooler sounding "Destroyer"—which evolved into Destroyah only when Toho learned the English word "Destroyer" could not actually be copyrighted. The first treatment with Destroyer as the main villain began with G-Force concerned with the possibility of Godzilla undergoing nuclear meltdown (there is no Burning Godzilla in this draft). They are worried that if Godzilla continues absorbing nuclear energy, he could potentially meltdown, or explode. Since an explosion by a living nuclear bomb would destroy Japan, G-Force decides to kill Godzilla.

G-Force determines to recreate the Oxygen Destroyer to kill Godzilla, but their experiments backfire on them when several sea creatures become mutated into "Destroyer" or "Destroyers." The man-sized monsters begin attacking humans and seem impervious to attacks. Godzilla soon arrives to wreak havoc in Japan once more. The self-defense forces begin attacking Godzilla but G-Force tries to get them to stop for fear of an explosion. The argument between the two agencies (G-Force lead by General Aso and the defense forces by Commander Hyodo) heats up and the two agencies wind up attacking each other instead. The result is G-Force's weapons are obliterated and after the battle, it is discovered that Godzilla has left the warring humans to their skirmish.

Destroyer has grown to a height of 10 meters (stage two in its development). After destroying a village in rural Japan, it reaches stage three, a massive, winged gargoyle-like super beast standing 120 meters tall. Destroyer then begins annihilating Tokyo. Godzilla and Godzilla Junior—now 50 meters tall—arrive to take on the malicious monster. A spectacular battle to the death is fought at Haneda Airport that ends with Destroyer triumphant, Godzilla mortally wounded, and Godzilla Junior dead. The defense forces are convinced the dying Godzilla will explode, so they launch their newly-constructed Oxygen Destroyer Missile into Godzilla, finally killing him. In his last act, Godzilla does for Junior what Rodan had done for him and donates his life-force to the child.[6] Junior resurrects and grows to a height of 80 meters, much to the defense forces' chagrin.[7] At the same time, Mothra has returned from outer space. Realizing what has happened, she allies herself with the new Godzilla, and they seek out Destroyer and work in tandem to kill him.

Bit by bit, the story evolved into the one seen in the finished film. The idea of Godzilla rampaging outside of Japan and into Hong Kong was first pushed in the *Barubaroi* treatment by Kawakita, though Shogo Tomiyama was initially reluctant to have Godzilla leave Japan. Alternate design choices for the "Burning Godzilla" included a glowing white version. "The original idea was to have Godzilla be luminescent. He was going to be white and red. We tried using both luminescent paint and light reflecting tape, but they didn't look sufficiently natural," Kawakita told David Milner.[8]

There were also multiple discarded ideas as to just why Godzilla was melting down. One of the ideas was that Godzilla's meltdown was caused by a space virus Godzilla had caught from being bitten by Space Godzilla. This virus would've made Godzilla unable to control his nuclear fission properly, causing it to run wild (*Space Godzilla's Counterattack*, indeed!). Another idea went that there were uranium deposits on Birth Island that nobody knew about. While wandering on the island with Little Godzilla, the uranium reacted with the radiation in Godzilla and caused a nuclear explosion. The sudden influx of nuclear energy absorbed into

Godzilla's body in a matter of seconds, caused him to begin meltdown and also radically mutated Little Godzilla into Godzilla Jr.

Eventually, the idea of Destroyah being a new life form mutated by G-Force's experiments was abandoned in favor of the creature being a prehistoric crustacean released after the usage of the Oxygen Destroyer in 1954. The idea that Godzilla caused Birth Island to be destroyed due to his impending meltdown was also introduced. As to the Oxygen Destroyer, Takao Okawara explained,

"There were a number of last minute changes to the screenplay. The Oxygen Destroyer, for example, was first mentioned at the beginning of the script, but I felt that the device should be treated as a forbidden subject. So, I delayed the first mention of it until the middle of *Godzilla vs. Destroyer*."[9]

Writer Kazuki Omori then started experimenting with yet more radical concepts. One idea he had was that because G-Force had built Mechagodzilla and MOGERA that were just destroyed by Godzilla, they were now broke and all they could afford to make was a Super X-III. Using the Gohten as a springboard from older ideas, Super X-III was outfitted with a freezing gun to slow Godzilla and cool his radioactive core. In another draft, Junior battled the stage two Destroyah (now, more or less, looking like what appeared in the final film) and lost but was not killed. The final battle was to have taken place in Tokyo Bay. The fight between Godzilla and the third stage Destroyah ended with a gigantic explosion which killed both monsters.

In Omori's nearly final draft of the script (which he seemed proud of in an interview with *G-Fan* magazine), the storyline was more or less the final movie, except Junior was killed by Destroyah, Miki Saegusa committed suicide out of grief (she had been compliant in leading Junior to Destroyah), Destroyah is killed, and Godzilla melts down. No new Godzilla, just a bitter 'The End.' Omori explained to *G-Fan*, "On the other hand, because this was the last movie Miki was in, we were thinking about having her die. We were thinking about having her killed off, but Tanaka said, 'Well, maybe we'll bring her back sometime, so maybe we better not kill her off,' so we didn't."[10] Tanaka also forbade the killing of Godzilla Junior without resurrection. Once these guidelines were laid down, the "final" Godzilla film was born—more or less.

There were still a few last-minute changes. Godzilla was initially supposed to destroy the jumbo jet taking off in Hong Kong, but none of the airlines would allow filming in their cockpits if the plane was to be destroyed on film. Takao Okawara added in the scene where one of the Destroyahs attacks Yukari Yamane, as well as the scene where Miki and Meru's helicopter is destroyed. Also, the end battle was originally to take place at the 1996 Tokyo World City Exposition.

Toho was uncertain of just how to film the ending right up to the very end. One of the final ideas had Godzilla embracing Destroyah during his meltdown as a way of killing the monster. In the end, Toho decided all the emphasis should be placed on Godzilla's death, and as such, Destroyah should be defeated before he melts down. Strangely enough, Toho finally elected to have Godzilla kill Destroyah through scientific means by superheating the ground while the self-defense forces froze him in mid-air. It's certainly not as satisfying as seeing Godzilla rip the monster apart, but the monster king does technically deal the killing blow. An alternate ending was shot where Godzilla grabs Destroyah by the horns and pummels the monster mercilessly as the self-defense forces shoots both monsters with freeze missiles. As Godzilla begins meltdown, Destroyah evaporates and dies. Toho felt the emphasis should be on Godzilla, though, and went with the other ending. Koichi Kawakita explained that, "Godzilla and Destroyer originally were both going to die when Godzilla melted down. We shot that version of the ending, but weren't very happy with it."[11]

Kenpachiro Satsuma himself wasn't given the script until late in the game for security reasons (he couldn't divulge what he didn't know). Satsuma imagined Godzilla's demise much differently:

"I was surprised that Godzilla was going to die on land instead of in the ocean, which was his cradle. I think it's natural for Godzilla to die because he is a living thing, but I envisioned his death differently. My idea was based on the legend of the tomb of elephants. According to the legend, when an elephant begins to feel that he is going to die, he secretly goes to the tomb. I envisioned Godzilla returning to the South Pacific when he began to feel that his end was coming. There then would have been some implication that Godzilla had died."[12]

The next subject of debate was whether or not Junior's resurrection would undercut Godzilla's death so Kawakita suggested making it a post-credits scene (Junior was to have turned around to face the camera, roared one last time, then blasted the screen with his ray in which a final "Owari" [The End] would have appeared). However, the crew felt most theatergoers would not stay to the very end and would miss the important development.

Ultimately, *Godzilla vs. Destroyah* serves not only as the culmination of the Heisei series but also as a direct sequel to the original film. Even the character of Emiko Yamane returns and is again played by Momoko Kochi. Two of the main characters are descendants of Shinkichi Yamane, the orphan boy from Oto Island adopted by Dr. Yamane. Miki Saegusa receives one of her better character arcs and her end scenes watching the deaths of both Godzilla Junior and his father are quite touching and serve as a fine cap for the series. Godzilla's death itself was no surprise to either the characters in the film or the audience watching it. The death was the lynchpin of the film's marketing campaign ("Gojira Shisu"/"Godzilla Dies" was plastered all over Japan and is even bigger on the poster than the title!) and the main characters learn early in the story that Godzilla's days are numbered. The question becomes not if Godzilla is going to die, but when and how... and will he take the world with him?

Upon release, Toho's ploy to kill Godzilla paid off, and *Godzilla vs. Destroyah* was nearly as profitable as 1992's *Godzilla vs. Mothra*, selling 4 million tickets. And though Godzilla Junior's post-credits resurrection was bumped up to happen before the credits, theatergoers who stayed through the end titles (which according to Akira Ifukube, were most people in the theater) were treated to another surprise: an advance trailer for a new *Mothra* film.

Chapter Notes

[1] *Godzilla vs. Bagan* was first considered back in 1991 as a continuation of the evolution that began with *Mothra vs. Bagan*.
[2] www.davmil.org/www.kaijuconversations.com/okawar3.htm
[3] Lees, "Godzilla's Godfather", *G-Fan* #18 (Jan/Feb 2015), pp.19.
[4] vantagepointinterviews.com/2017/05/13/kazuki-omori-recalls-the-heisei-godzilla-series-tohos-writer-director-shares-his-memories-of-the-king-of-the-monsters/
[5] It resembled the titular robot from 1989's *Gunhed* and was extremely top heavy. It could stand on the ground but not walk or fly. A version of this mecha, called Mogera II, appears in the video game *Godzilla Generations: Maximum Impact*.
[6] A storyboard for this sequence seems to have made its way onto Toho's making of "Special Disc" for *Godzilla vs. Destroyah*.
[7] Early designs for Godzilla Junior show him in the stance of a velociraptor and another, by Yosuke Nakano, even designed a Godzilla Junior shedding his skin to become a pure white Godzilla, presumably after absorbing the dead Godzilla's radiation.
[8] www.davmil.org/www.kaijuconversations.com/kawakit2.htm
[9] www.davmil.org/www.kaijuconversations.com/okawar3.htm
[10] vantagepointinterviews.com/2017/05/13/kazuki-omori-recalls-the-heisei-godzilla-series-tohos-writer-director-shares-his-memories-of-the-king-of-the-monsters/
[11] www.davmil.org/www.kaijuconversations.com/kawakit2.htm
[12] www.davmil.org/www.kaijuconversations.com/satsum3.htm

42.
MOTHRA FLIES SOLO

With Godzilla set to die in *Godzilla vs. Destroyah* as a way to make room for the Tri-Star Godzilla, rumblings began in 1995 that Toho would turn their attention to vehicles for Mothra and King Ghidorah. For the space dragon's film, King Ghidorah was to fulfill Nostradamus's prophecy about a King of Terror descending from the sky in 1999. Instead, King Ghidorah would be relegated to the villain for Mothra's trilogy swan song, but the series would kick off with a brand new type of Ghidorah, never before seen.

Audiences got their first glimpse at the new Mothra movie in a teaser trailer shown at the end of *Godzilla vs. Destroyah*. The trailer featured Mothra flying over New York City—if this was an abandoned concept from the film or just a cool visual for the teaser is unknown. Those moviegoers were promised that "she appears before those who believe." Some sources claimed that initially the *Mothra vs. Bagan* script was looked at as inspiration but was never seriously considered and Koichi Kawakita maintained that he pondered making Bagan the enemy monster for the new film.[1] Furthermore, some of Shinji Nishikawa's early drawings for the enemy monster resembled Bagan more than King Ghidorah. Other sources said that several discarded ideas from early *Godzilla vs. Destroyah* drafts influenced the storyline of what eventually became known as simply, *Mothra*. In all likelihood, these were the concepts of Godzilla dying when fighting alongside Godzilla Junior, who takes on the enemy monster in the climax in the same way the adult Mothra dies fighting alongside her larva who defeats Death Ghidorah as an adult for the climax.

Initially, *Mothra* was to take place within the Heisei continuity and Death Ghidorah would be the same Futurian-created King Ghidorah from 1991's *Godzilla vs. King Ghidorah*. The story would have seen Ghidorah resurrected by magic from the bottom of the Sea of Okhotsk (presumably by Belvera or a precursor). The monster would emerge with a skeletal middle head and wreck undead havoc until Mothra—having finally returned from space—steps in to stop him. This incarnation of the three headed dragon would be redubbed "Death Ghidorah." However, someone likely

 **GAMERA 2: ADVENT OF LEGION**

AFTER *GAMERA, GUARDIAN OF THE UNIVERSE'S* RAVE REVIEWS CAME IN, THE PRESIDENT OF DAIEI, YASUYOSHI TOKUMA, ENTHUSIASTICALLY STATED THERE WOULD BE A TRILOGY AND THAT *GAMERA 2* WOULD BE FILMED IN CANADA AND PART THREE WOULD BE "GAMERA VS. GODZILLA"! NEARLY ALL THE OLD GAMERA FOES WERE CONSIDERED FOR AN APPEARANCE IN *GAMERA 2*. THOUGH INITIALLY THE GYAOS WERE DISCUSSED TO RETURN (AS WERE VIRAS AND JIGER BRIEFLY; *GAMERA HEISEI PERFECTION* EVEN MENTIONS GUIRON), ALIENS WERE QUICKLY DECIDED UPON FOR THE SEQUEL. LEGION'S BIRTH CAME FROM SOMETHING VERY SIMPLE: KAZUNORI ITO HAVING LUNCH WITH SHINJI HIGUCHI. ITO SAYS HE LOOKED AT THE CRABS HE WAS EATING AND QUIPPED, "THESE GUYS ARE DEFINITELY NOT THE CREATURES OF THE EARTH." FROM THAT, THE IDEA OF INSECTOID ALIENS WITH EXOSKELETONS WAS BORN (KANEKO WANTED LEGION TO RESEMBLE A GIANT PRAYING MANTIS, BUT DAIEI FEARED THIS CREATION WOULD BE TOO CLOSE TO TOHO'S KAMACURAS). THE FIRST DRAFT FROM AUGUST OF 1995 WAS SIMILAR TO THE FINAL DRAFT EXCEPT THE FLOWER POD ELEMENT WAS DOWNPLAYED AS THE MAJOR THREAT OVER THE SOLDIER LEGIONS. THE FINAL DUEL BETWEEN GAMERA AND THE GIANT LEGION WAS SET TO BE AN AERIAL ONE AS OPPOSED TO THE FINISHED FILM'S LAND-BASED FIGHT (THIS AERIAL BATTLE WOULD BE USED IN *GAMERA 3: REVENGE OF IRYS*). ALSO IN THIS VERSION, HONAMI ESCAPES IN A HOT AIR BALLOON WITH ASAGI RATHER THAN BY HELICOPTER. KANEKO WAS ALSO PUTTING SOME THOUGHT INTO THE FUTURE OF GAMERA AS A CHARACTER. IN *G-FAN* #40, KANEKO SAID, "COMPARED TO THE PREVIOUS FILM, GAMERA'S CHARACTER ALSO SEEMS TO HAVE GROWN UP, SPIRITUALLY AND PHYSICALLY. BEFORE, IT WAS KIND OF OBVIOUS THAT GAMERA WAS FIGHTING FOR MANKIND, TO SAVE THE PEOPLE. BUT NOW, WHEN THE MONSTER FIGHTS, THE QUESTION ARISES AS TO WHY. I WANTED TO SHOW WHAT HE IS FIGHTING FOR." [RYFLE, "GUARDIAN OF GAMERA'S UNIVERSE", *G-FAN* #40 (JUL/AUG 1999), PP.43]

stepped in to mention how this would not fit in with *Godzilla vs. King Ghidorah*'s continuity and aspect of time travel regarding Mecha-King Ghidorah. Perhaps wanting to be free of continuity altogether, the new Mothra movie was then set within its own universe. This also allowed Toho to cast new, younger actresses as the Shobijin, now known as the Elias.

The monster's new name stuck, but the original concept was discarded altogether. When Death Ghidorah was reimagined, it became a one-headed creature until it sprouted another two heads along with wings for the finale (an idea similar to Bagan in *Mothra vs. Bagan*). Also like Bagan, Death Ghidorah became an alien monster that attacks the environment who was sealed away by Mothra millennia ago. To further differentiate it from King Ghidorah, Death Ghidorah became a quadruped. Mothra was to have had an additional "high speed flight" form in this film. However, this angular design was saved to become Aqua Mothra in the sequel the following year. The living room battle between the Elias and Belvera was apparently a late addition missing from early drafts of the script. And the new Mothra was to kill Death Ghidorah with a beam weapon that resembled the roots of a tree!

The finished film is unquestionably geared for children and as a child's film, it's not bad by any means. Like *Mothra vs. Bagan*, the overarching theme is the preservation of the environment. As this idea had also seeped into *Godzilla vs. Mothra* (1992), it's possible Toho wanted Mothra to take on the role of an environmental defender in the 1990s. The Shobijin/Elias also evolved interestingly and have a very proactive role in the film. The duo even engage in several well-staged action scenes.[2] While *Godzilla vs. Mothra* had invented an evil version of Mothra called Battra, here, we are introduced to a third, villainous fairy named Belvera. Unlike the Shobijin, the Elias are not identical twins, but three distinct sisters: Belvera (the oldest), Moll (the middle), and Lora (the youngest). While the Mothra design from 1992 returns for the mother, the child Mothra gets a makeover and unlike the Tri-Star Godzilla, it's actually well done. Dubbed Mothra Leo by Toho (though never called as such in any of the films), the new version sports a white, black and green color scheme (the green representing the environment). Toho had initially given their new Mothra movie the English title *Mothra, the Queen of Monsters*. However, when it came time for it (and its two sequels) to be dubbed in Hong Kong and sold for overseas markets in 1998, they retitled it *Rebirth of Mothra*.

Though it wasn't received well by much of Japan, the film was apparently profitable for Toho (it cost half the amount of *Godzilla vs. Destroyah* and also pulled in a little over half the money at the box office). Toho wasted no time developing a sequel as *Mothra* ended with a teaser trailer that had the new Mothra flying off to meet an asteroid in space—it's enough to make one wonder if an early story pitch was tied to *Godzilla vs. Mothra* (1992) where the asteroid thread from that movie would finally be resolved. The only thing known for sure is that Shogo Tomiyama said that the original story pitch was discarded for something totally new: an underwater battle. Adding to the mystery, in his *Drawing Book of Godzilla*, designer Shinji Nishikawa said he became involved very late in pre-production and the direction of the enemy monster had already changed, implying a major overhaul of some sort was done on the enemy monster, Dagarah—named for the Pagan god Dagon of the Bible.

Though the ocean off Okinawa would seem a prime location for *Mothra 2: Undersea Battle's* [3] story about underwater civilizations, the first draft was instead set around a lake! Also, Go-Go, the fluffy white creature from Nilai Kanai, was described as a "rain traveler." Eventually, the story was shifted to take place near Okinawa and revolved around starfish monsters called Barem. The creatures are a by-product of the long-lost civilization Nilai Kanai and the sea monster Dagarah. To defeat its opponent (and sell more toys) at the film's end, Mothra morphs into an Aqua Mothra (based off a discarded design from the previous Mothra movie).[4]

The bit where Aqua Mothra swims inside Dagarah was a last-minute idea and not in the script (so Mothra's original means of defeating Dagarah remain unknown). Koichi Kawakita was retiring and *Mothra 2* would be his last major motion picture for Toho as special effects director. An idea he had long lamented not using was the *Fantastic Voyage*-type action scene from his *Godzilla vs. Mechani-Kong* story. The idea was that a team of scientists would be shrunk down in a submarine and injected inside Godzilla. Inside, they would fight off starfish-like antibodies. It is by no means a coincidence that when Aqua Mothra splits itself into an army of mini-Mothras that swim inside Dagarah, it then uses its laser beams to attack the Barem starfish monsters that give Dagarah his power.

On paper, *Mothra 2* sounds fantastic and the core concept—Mothra coming into contact with an ancient, undersea civilization—is excellent. It simply isn't executed very well. The leading trio of child characters is likable enough, but the film isn't paced well and it's a little too nonsensical, even for a Japanese children's film. Likewise, Aqua Mothra looks great on the poster but isn't realized adequately on film. Dagarah had all the makings of a fine villain but in the film, the kaiju is constantly in the water and the rubber suit is made all the worse-looking for it (consequently, he seems far faker than he has any right to be at this point in Kawakita's career). The story's main moment of interest occurs when Belvera has a change of heart at the last minute and saves all the main characters—setting up her arc for the next film.

Mothra 2 was released to less fanfare than its predecessor and also ended with a teaser for a *Mothra 3*. Back in 1995, Toho had considered a King Ghidorah movie where the monster fulfills Nostradamus's prophecy about a prince of terror descending from the skies in 1999.[5] Instead, Toho would end up integrating this concept into *Mothra 3*. Before this decision was made, instead of fighting King Ghidorah in the prehistoric past, *Mothra 3* originally had the big bug facing off against another brand new monster as in the past two films. Here, Mothra would have flown back in time to the Edo period of feudal Japan to defeat a fire-themed monster. Because the beast was fire-themed, someone suggested using Fire Rodan and for a short time, the pteranodon was the opponent for *Mothra 3*.[6]

Fearing Rodan was not popular enough to carry the film, Fire Rodan was switched for King Ghidorah, and the Edo Period became the Cretaceous. Concepts for *Mothra 3* that were written for the final storyline but didn't make it into the finished film included the aforementioned King Ghidorah being the "prince of terror." All that remains of this in the finished film is the "prince of terror" nickname the Elias keep using for no discernible reason. There was also the idea that Death Ghidorah from the first movie was King Ghidorah's son and that Ghidorah came to finish his son's job after he'd been imprisoned on earth. The battle with Cretaceous King Ghidorah was originally to be more brutal with Mothra losing one leg and an eye! Likewise, the younger King Ghidorah would lose a head rather than a tail, though this was deemed too brutal for a children's film and changed. Though unspoken in the finished film, the Mt. Fuji dome is meant to be King Ghidorah's stomach and the blue fluid that comes from the ground its digestive fluids. When Mothra time travels back to the present for the end battle, its new form, Armor Mothra, seems like the idea of Koichi Kawakita. Even if he wasn't involved in the film, he may well have pitched ideas and back in 1992, he pushed for Mothra to die at the end of *Godzilla vs. Mothra* so that he could create a Mecha-Mothra for the next film!

Shinji Nishikawa said this about Grand King Ghidorah's design (named to differentiate it from the incarnation of the monster seen in *Godzilla vs. King Ghidorah*) in a 2019 interview:

> "Since he's said to be a Ghidorah who has been living since the age of the dinosaurs, I had this image of him being quite aged. Our nickname for Grand Ghidorah was Grand(father) Ghidorah.' I designed him with transforming wings that were

well suited for flight, and rather than having him be monochromatic, I added black specks to his scales, but unfortunately these weren't carried through in his molding."[7]

Though it suffers some of the same pacing problems as the previous two films, *Mothra 3* managed to emerge as the best entry of the trilogy. Like its predecessors, the Mothra mythos is expanded upon yet again when prehistoric Mothra larvae show up to spin a cocoon around the damaged Mothra from the future. The mythology of the Elias is also more expounded upon, with the film hinting they were destined to fight King Ghidorah. The three-headed space dragon is so feared, that Belvera—the villain in the previous two adventures—is terrified of his imminent arrival and doesn't have a villainous moment at all. As a result, Belvera, now an unabashed hero, walks away with the best story arc of the whole trilogy.

Chapter Notes

[1] Rumors also persist Bagan was considered for the enemy monster role in *Mothra 2* and *3* as well.
[2] The first example of a proactive, aggressive version of the Shobijin dates back to the original *Mothra* manga which shows them kick and karate chop their way through the vampire plant to save Chujo.
[3] Simply called *Rebirth of Mothra II* for overseas distribution.
[4] Aqua Mothra briefly returns in *Mothra 3's* time travel scene, one could argue the design as a high speed flight Mothra is finally being realized.
[5] Marc Cerasini also used this idea in his 1997 novel, *Godzilla 2000*.
[6] Some think the concept sprang from the fact that birds and insects were natural enemies since birds feed on insects.
[7] www.tohokingdom.com/blog/shinji-nishikawa-interview/

43.
TRI-STAR'S GODZILLA

In 1993, the news that Tri-Star Pictures had acquired the rights to make a big-budgeted, American version Toho's Godzilla franchise started trickling out of Hollywood. The project had its genesis in a 1992 meeting between Henry G. Saperstein and producers Cary Woods and Robert Fried of Sony about a possible Mr. Magoo movie! The Sony executives were uninterested in Mr. Magoo but jumped at the idea of a Godzilla movie, of which Saperstein could begin negotiations.

Tri-Star held a meeting of creative minds in early 1993 that included the likes of Tim Burton and Clive Barker. Despite the more high profile prospects, Tri-Star chose a relatively new screenwriting team, Ted Elliot and Terry Rossio, who had done rewrites for Disney's mega-successful *Aladdin* (1992). The pair came up with a scenario where Godzilla is an ancient guardian left behind by benevolent aliens who used dinosaur genes to create the monster. Godzilla had been left on earth to battle, the Gryphon, an alien doomsday beast who will eventually arrive to destroy the earth.[1] However, there's a problem: Godzilla awakens from his ancient tomb too early and the military doesn't understand he is an ally, not a threat. At the center of it all is a female protagonist, Jill Llewellyn, whose husband is killed when Godzilla awakens. Llewellyn was essentially an Ahab-type character who learns that Godzilla is well-meaning by the end of the film. Like most Godzilla movies, the two titans would clash in a major city (in this case New York City) for the end showdown. Godzilla kills the Gryphon and wades off into the sea to await a hoped-for sequel. Jan De Bont (fresh off the success of *Speed*) was attached to direct and all looked well for the King of the Monsters' first American outing. Then Sony balked at the proposed budget, De Bont walked, and this version of Godzilla was scrapped.

Because they were hot off *Independence Day* (1996)—not to mention the fact that they were usually good about coming in on budget—the producer/director duo of Dean Devlin and Roland Emmerich were brought in.[2] They threw out the original script immediately—in spite of a massive amount of pre-production work

309

already completed on the film (including Godzilla and Gryphon maquettes created by the renowned Stan Winston plus an entire set). In *G-Fan* #19, Dean Devlin was quoted as saying, "We're abandoning all the script work that's been done before and going back to the original Godzilla movie and remaking it, a complete page one rewrite. We came up with a whole different take on that first story, which actually gives us a reason to make this film." Terry Rossio said, "[Devlin and Emmerich] were complimentary of our draft, and said it showed them that a film could be made—but concluded 'It wasn't a story we wanted to tell.' They kept some elements, and changed most."[3] The aforementioned elements Rossio spoke of were a few simple scenes including Godzilla becoming entangled with fishing trawlers and an old Japanese man who mutters the word, "Gojira."[4]

Soon, rumors on the project began to fly and by 1997, it was reported that Jennifer Aniston was cast as the female lead and that she would develop an Ann Darrow-style relationship with Godzilla! Though this rumor was false, other rumors turned out to be true such as Godzilla having chameleon abilities. Though this ability didn't make it into the finished film, it is in the first draft script dated February 19, 1996. The first draft is remarkably similar to the finished film from start to finish (because Devlin and Emmerich wrote it over the course of a single weekend in Mexico!).

One of the first descriptions in the script is hilariously inept as it describes, "Kimono dragons [sic], Gila monsters and chameleons all in their natural tropical environment"! This is doubly funny as Gila monsters most certainly don't live on the same island as Komodo dragons (who, of course, do not wear Japanese robes). The sinking of the Japanese fishing trawler is a bit more detailed and elaborate in this version and the final shot was originally meant to be the lone survivor (the old man who mutters "Gojira") sliding off the ship and into the water as an obscured Godzilla tips it over.

In this first draft, Jean Reno's Philippe Roaché is named Phillip Raymond (a nod to Raymond Burr?). Likewise, Kevin Dunn's General Hicks is imagined as being a bit younger in this draft, his 30s (Dunn was in his 40s). Vicki Lewis' Elsie Chapman (the redheaded paleontologist) is described as heavyset in this draft, presumably an attempt at humor to make her attraction to Nick more awkward. And finally, Michael Lerner's Mayor Ebert was Mayor Faustino and he didn't have a berated assistant of any kind, Gene or otherwise. All the other characters were basically the same.

There's an unused scene as Nick inspects the Japanese trawler. When he dislodges the mysterious reptile flesh, a dead crewman slips from the ship, hanging upside down in front of him, scaring the young scientist. Following that, the sinking of the three fishing trawlers—the one scene taken from Rossio and Elliot's script—takes place during the day rather than a stormy night. The crewmen aren't playing poker when they come across Godzilla.

Surprisingly, the famous teaser trailer scene with the old man at the docks isn't present in this draft. After Godzilla attacks and then disappears, there are a few news interviews with people on the street. One man says, "What are we running from? A big lizard? I've got cockroaches in my building that could kick the crap out of it." During the scene where Mayor Faustino tries to calm some of his wealthy campaign donors, Donald Trump was among them! Obviously, he declined the cameo.

The initial attack on Godzilla is quite different from the finished film. As soon as Godzilla begins eating the fish, the military fires gas canisters at him. Annoyed, Godzilla wafts away the smoke with his tail then uses his "infamous POWER BREATH"—no, this isn't his beloved nuclear ray, just a huge gust of wind that he uses to blow away the gas. Godzilla's "gale force winds" shatter glass and even move tanks backward (really the scene is similar to Rodan's "shock wave" breath attack in his debut film). Godzilla was to run into the "famous lighted square (looking remarkable like Tokyo)" during the chopper attack, which doesn't occur in the final film. Also, Godzilla was to dismantle two choppers with one bite as he ambushes them from behind.[5] The script confirms the rumor of Godzilla's chameleon ability when he blends in with a building hiding from a chopper. Considering all the changes made to Godzilla anyway, it's a shame this power was removed.

Another aspect that was cut was vendors taking advantage of the situation, selling copies of Animal's famous videotape along with dinosaur toys and T-shirts with Godzilla's image on them. A few additional pregnancy jokes aside, Nick and Audrey's reunion is very much as it is in the final film, right down to her stealing the tape and then being scooped by Charles Caiman. Instead of intercepting Nick in the taxi, Philippe meets Nick in a bar at the airport as he prepares to leave town. The gist of the discussion is the same, just less exciting and in a different place.

In the film, Animal's wife Lucy walks into her apartment to find it filled with strangers. In the first draft, it is explained that in a preceding scene, Animal had interviewed people cut off from their homes in a tent city. Obviously, he felt sorry for them and invited them to stay in his apartment. The third act in Madison Square Garden and the ensuing cab chase are essentially the same with a few small alterations in choreography here and there.

When the film premiered Memorial Day weekend of 1998, diehard fans were mortified. Actually, diehard fans were already mortified because Godzilla's radical redesign (which Dean Devlin swore was a rejected concept) had leaked to the public. According to designer Patrick Tatopoulos, Devlin and Emmerich more or less told him to "go crazy" with the design and he did. Toho was shocked when the creature was unveiled and said something along the lines that the designers "went very far." Emmerich, who was in Japan without Devlin as he was sick, told Toho that's the design they would be going with (in other words, if you don't like it, too bad). Though aghast at the design (Shogo Tomiyama didn't even know how to describe it to Tomoyuki Tanaka) Toho was also afraid that if they vetoed the model after one false start already, the film might never get off the ground. With reluctance they eventually told Emmerich, "You can keep your Godzilla and we'll keep ours."

Not only had Godzilla's image been overhauled, but the monster's character had been changed as well. Wanting to make Godzilla more animal than monster, he runs from the military rather than confront their forces head-on. This aspect upset fans as much as the new look had. Even the monster's backstory was jettisoned. Instead of being a prehistoric animal awakened and mutated by atomic bomb tests, this Godzilla was just an iguana mutated by French nuclear tests. And only at the last minute was this Godzilla even given a fiery breath—this was done when the studio learned just how irate fans were about the lack of the nuclear ray on top of everything else. This Godzilla reproducing asexually and having hundreds of offspring makes for a fun third act, but is also quite out of character for Godzilla at the same time. Godzilla chasing a taxicab[6] carrying the main characters is fun, but the film's resolution—Godzilla simply being shot to death by six missiles—was so underwhelming that it was met with shock and disappointment by the extras during filming! From there, the film apes the closing moments of *King Kong* (1976) as Nick and the dying Godzilla have the exact same final exchange as Kong and Dwan do (right down to the audible heartbeat slowly coming to a stop)!

These rather major flaws aside, *Godzilla* is actually a fun film at times. A dumb movie for sure, but a fun, well-paced story nonetheless. The problem was that it just wasn't Godzilla. Many fans complained it could just as well have been a remake of *The Beast from 20,000 Fathoms* or any manner of 1950s "monster on the loose" movies—and they were right. Perhaps in damage control mode, Devlin claimed in a post-release interview that he felt it more respectful to leave the original Godzilla as he was, rather than inserting him into a new environment. "We felt it was much more respectful to do that," Devlin said in *G-Fan* a year later.[7] He continued, "We never wanted Godzilla 98 to replace the classic Godzilla. That's why we wanted the look to be so different."[8] In contrast to this statement, when Emmerich was interviewed in 2004 for the 50th anniversary of Godzilla he said that he still thought he'd made a great movie and he could not understand why people liked the Japanese movies at all!

In the annals of history—in large part thanks to Legendary Pictures' *Godzilla* movie of 2014—the Tri-Star *Godzilla* has gone down as an oddity. A sequel was planned for a few years until Sony eventually lost interest and let their rights lapse. However, this film's Godzilla managed to return six years later in 2004's *Godzilla: Final Wars*. Though that film was reviled by a large number of fans, most agreed that the scene where the real Godzilla kills his all-CGI American version[9] in all of about twelve seconds was something to cheer about!

Chapter Notes

[1] Originally this was King Ghidorah but Toho wanted a separate license for that monster and Sony decided to just create a new one.
[2] Devlin was reportedly the more passionate of the two, and Emmerich didn't want to do the project.
[3] http://www.wordplayer.com/archives/GODZILLA.intro.html
[4] Rossio and Elliot disapproved of the resultant film so much that they were ashamed to have their names attached to it.
[5] Perhaps Devlin originally imagined the monster being a little bigger.
[6] Ironically, at the same time that *Godzilla* was being developed, Peter Jackson was working on his *King Kong* script which featured a scene where Kong chases a taxi through New York. Jackson's *King Kong* was eyed to start production in 1998 until *Godzilla* proved to be a critical dud.
[7] Lees, "Interview with Dean Devlin", *G-Fan* #39 (May/Jun 1999) pp.10.
[8] Ibid, pp.12.
[9] Toho renamed the creature as "Jira/Zilla" because Toho felt the Americans had taken the "god" out of Godzilla.

44.
GAMERA 3:
INCOMPLETE SCREENPLAY

It was obvious in the epilogue of *Gamera 2: Advent of Legion* (1996) that writer Kazunori Ito was planting seeds for where he wanted to take the series for *Gamera 3*. Lead character Midori Honami makes mention of humanity potentially becoming Gamera's enemy one day if they continued mistreating the earth. Many fans assumed that the next film could concern Gamera vs. humanity rather than an enemy monster. Others even heard talk of Gamera fighting another evil Gamera. Instead, the trilogy's finale would again revolve around the grudge match between Gamera and the Gyaos. However, the return of the Gyaos wasn't necessarily a part of some grand story scheme on the creative team's part. Rather, it was partly because Gyaos toys sold better than Legion toys according to Daiei executives![1]

As script ideas moved toward the Irys/Gyaos story, Midori was originally slated to return from *Gamera 2* alongside Asagi Kusanagi and even Colonel Watarase. From *Gamera, Guardian of the Universe*, Mayumi Nagamine, Inspector Osako, Naoya Kusanagi, Masaaki Saito, and even Yoshinari Yonemori would return. This draft placed greater attention on Asagi, struggling with life after losing her link with Gamera in the previous movie, which was meant to parallel Ayana's relationship with Irys. In this story, there were also three monster battles: the first was Gamera and two Gyaos fighting over the ocean. The second battle occurred in Shibuya between Gamera and Irys. The final battle occurred in Kyoto. Shusuke Kaneko wisely requested that Kazunori Ito take out some of the excess characters so Kusanagi, Watarase, and Yonemori were removed. Kaneko wanted Midori to stay in the script but actress Miki Mizuno had a scheduling conflict and was subsequently written out as well.

Some of the battle maneuvers came from discarded ideas too ambitious for previous screenplays, in particularly Gamera and Irys's energetic mid-air fight. Such a scene had been scripted for *Gamera 2* between the turtle and Legion. There seemed to have also been talk of an ambitious underwater battle, so the aerial battle was given a few underwater qualities to it. It was Higuchi who desired to do an underwater scene in *Gamera 3*—that was until the release of *Mothra 2: Undersea Battle* in 1997 (*Gamera 3* started pre-production in 1996 right after the second movie was released) soured such an idea. According to Higuchi in a making-of feature for the film, he said, "There was a lot to begin with in Mr. Ito's screenplay, but I said, I'm sorry, we can only do about the same things we did the last time and if we can't do any better, hold off on it for now."

Ito's treatment—initially titled *Gamera 1999*—begins similarly to the finished film, set in early 1999 in Southeast Asia's rain forests. There, Mayumi Nagamine and an assistant discover a new Gyaos nest with freshly-hatched eggs. At the same time, a survey vessel of the Japanese Coast Guard (which includes Yoshinari Yonemori) is conducting a survey at the bottom of the sea where they discover a Gamera graveyard. This, too, happens in the finished *Gamera 3*, just not with Yonemori on hand. From there, the title would have appeared and cut to Tokyo, specifically the Yashima Marine Insurance Company. There, Naoya Kusanagi was to meet with Mito Asakura of the Kyoto Office of the Imperial Household Agency. Asakura is there to inspect the curved jewels found four years ago by the company but Naoya tells her that all of the jewels mysteriously cracked apart during the Legion attack when Gamera revived in Sendai. This scene also made it into the finished film, just minus Kusanagi.

Asagi pops up earlier in the treatment and is given greater emphasis, which is where this story deviates from the film. Asagi is struggling to come to grips with the fact that she has lost her connection with Gamera—the idea that Ito seems to be going for here is that Asagi feels like a jilted lover. This fact is not lost on her fiancé, a new character named Miyuki Uozumi.

After checking in on Asagi, we are introduced to Ayana and her young brother living with her extended family. Her backstory is the same as in the finished film and the same sequence of events play out as well—the tenuous relationship with Moribe,[2] Ayana being dared to move the sacred stone, and so on. Where we find more differences concerns Nagamine proposing to capture the new species of Gyaos at the government meeting. Nagamine's idea catches the attention of Asakura, who is in league with a Taoist mastermind named Kiyomori Kibi (who would become Shinya Kurata in the film). Soon afterward, Kibi pays a visit to the Sapporo Science Museum where he meets with Asagi. There, he asks her,

"What is Gamera? What will you do if Gamera becomes hostile to humans?"

The sequence of events plays out as in the film until a battle between Gamera and two Gyaos over the ocean. The corpse of one of the dead Gyaos drifts ashore in the Irako Cape near Aichi Prefecture. The recently-promoted Saito theorizes Gamera killed the Gyaos as evident by the huge tears and claw marks on its body. A new strategy group is formed within the defense agency. Among its numbers are Colonel Watarase, who helped to defeat Legion in the previous film. Watarase makes waves for disagreeing with a report that considers Gamera as a threat equal to or even greater than the Gyaos. Among those spearheading the plan to destroy Gamera in secret is Asakura and Kibi.

The basic outline continues to play out like the film but has an additional scene of Nagamine analyzing the Gyaos cadaver. Nagamine also uses radar reports to track the new Gyaos to a nest in Tanimura Prefecture where Ayana lives. In this story, when Ayana encounters the growing Ryuseicho in the forest, it grabs her when she tries to run away. Moribe, Nagamine, and Osako happen upon the location just as the monster takes flight. As they lose sight of the monster, Gamera flies overhead in pursuit. Gamera and Ryuseicho make landfall in Shibuya, where their battle causes tremendous casualties and damage, most of it caused by Gamera, just like in the finished film.

As in the film, Gamera becomes public enemy number one when the battle is over and Ryuseicho escapes. Asakura and Kibi's plan to turn Japan's military might against Gamera is sanctioned though Nagamine still contends that Gyaos is the bigger threat. Naoya Kusangai travels to Kyoto to meet with Asakura and reunites with Asagi along the way. Nagamine, meanwhile, has come to the realization that Kibi and Asakura want the Gyaos to prevail. The treatment, which seems to be unfinished, leaves off with an aerial battle between Gamera and Ryuseicho over Kyoto. As the treatment is unfinished, it's unknown if this version of Ayana switches sides or how Asagi's story ends. In the final screenplay,[3] Asagi comes to terms with the fact that Gamera has severed his ties to her and Ayana finally forgives Gamera.

Ultimately, as the screenplay progressed, three battles were condensed into two with the conflict between Gamera and the Gyaos at sea being cut and replaced with Gamera battling the Gyaos in Shibuya instead. His battle with the Ryuseicho, now named Irys, was saved for the end of the film in Kyoto only.

At the time of the film's release, some fans were quite disappointed by the conclusion where a one-armed Gamera wades into a sea of flames to battle a massive horde of Gyaos. There is some hope left when humanity's military forces decide to ally themselves with Gamera to battle an oncoming Gyaos swarm (of which their number is "impossible to say") heading straight for Gamera. Essentially, the ending is about the power of belief. And Kaneko does clue the audience in to Gamera's fate, it was simply lost on most American fans. Daiei's international title for the film was *GIII: Incomplete Struggle.* However, the film's end super reads "Gamera: 1999 - The Absolute Guardian of the Universe," which is meant to clue the audience in that Gamera will win.[4]

According to Kaneko, during the intricate development of *Gamera 3,* studio interference led to some interesting developments. Daiei president Yasuyoshi Tokuma didn't want Kaneko to use actress Ai Maeda and insisted he cast Nozomi Ando. To circumvent this, Kaneko created a new character for Ando to play and kept Maeda where he wanted her. Stranger still, after two consecutive films and proving a popular character in both, an unnamed Daiei producer who didn't like Ayako Fujitani wanted Asagi's character written out of the story. "Ayako's character is to connect emotionally with Gamera. That was her role," Kaneko said. "But Mr. Ito's idea was to create another role, for another character to hate Gamera. So I thought the concept needed Ayako, too. So if Ayako disappeared, the story would be unfair to Gamera."[5]

Gamera 3's themes delve even deeper into the mythological door opened in the first film. However, it asks more questions than it answers. Is Irys a new Gyaos mutation or an ancient guardian similar to Gamera that has gone bad due to Ayana's influence?[6] The movie tries to imply both, though when Kurata talks about Irys being a mutated Gyaos, he may be an unreliable narrator. Ayana and her arc make the film's most interesting twist on the mythos established in the previous two films. The idea of a girl with the power to connect to Gamera who instead hates him and fights against him with another monster was positively inspired.

Gamera 3: Revenge of Irys was lauded by American fans as one of the greatest giant monster movies of all time. Japanese fans, however, were less enthusiastic with how esoteric it was and the film did poorly at the box office as a result. It didn't help matters any that Daiei had gone bankrupt yet again but this time, the crew of the film were made aware and promised to complete the movie for no pay, in hopes the returns would be phenomenal. Though

Kaneko was happy with the way his trilogy ended, Daiei executives naturally wanted greater financial success to save the company. When this didn't happen, Gamera would remain absent until six years later when, much like Tokuma Publishing before it, Kadokawa Pictures (which began as a publishing company) would buy Daiei and bring Gamera back in the reboot *Gamera the Brave*.

Chapter Notes

[1] Never mind that the Gyaos toys were inexpensive when compared to the large, pricey Legion Bandai figures!
[2] In Kazunori Ito's early treatment, the Moribe family had periodically sacrificed some of their children to the Ryuseicho for the sake of prosperity!
[3] To be thorough, "final screenplay" is a misnomer in this case as Kaneko and Higuchi both shot their material from different drafts!
[4] Higuchi wanted to include a post-credits scene that would have shown Gamera still battling the Gyaos after humanity has gone extinct. Shusuke Kaneko disliked this idea though because it completely undercut the point of his ending. It's also worth noting that even though Kaneko wanted to end the series, Daiei planned to make a "Gamera 4" if the film grossed over ¥1 billion, which it did not.
[5] vantagepointinterviews.com/2018/06/13/on-directing-godzilla-and-gamera-shusuke-kaneko-on-filmmaking-the-kaiju-way/
[6] It is also implied that Irys is a phoenix, and some fans even take this to mean the monster was partially inspired by Niisan Takahashi's unproduced *Gamera vs. Phoenix* script.

PROFILE: SHUSUKE KANEKO

Though many directors dabbled in the world of kaiju during the Heisei era, none were quite as distinctive as Ishiro Honda had been during his day. Arguably, the only director to come close was Shusuke Kaneko. Though his output wasn't as great as Honda's, it was certainly distinctive. Kaneko grew up making 8mm movies and loved monsters. His success with his first student film lit a fire for Kaneko to become a director. He got his foot in the door with Nikkatsu, who were notoriously making Japanese 'pink films.' Kaneko eventually directed his own hit movie, 1988's *Summer Vacation 1999*. He soon began dreaming of making a kaiju movie and went to a video store and rented one to jog his memory. Not long after, he became involved in developing an *Ultra Q* anthology movie (*Ultraman* was one of his favorite series growing up). Ironically, the scriptwriter was none other than Kazunori Ito who would later work with Kaneko on the Gamera films. When the *Ultra Q* movie didn't pan out, Kaneko remembered watching *Godzilla vs. King Ghidorah* (1991) in theaters. When he saw the advance trailer for *Godzilla vs. Mothra,* he actually sent Shogo Tomiyama a New Year's greeting card asking if he could direct the film. Tomiyama wrote Kaneko back to inform him that Takao Okawara was already on board, which ironically begat a rumor that Kaneko was a legitimate contender to helm the film. This caught the attention of Daiei, who contacted Kaneko and asked if he would be interested in making either a Gamera or a Majin film. Kaneko asked about the budget and when he was told it was only $5 million, he actually suggested that they make it a comedy at first. History turned out differently and the film was critically very well-received and made enough money for Daiei to warrant two sequels. In 2001, in large part thanks to his success on the Gamera movies, Kaneko was approached by Shogo Tomiyama about doing a "Kaneko Godzilla movie." The film turned out to be the biggest hit of the Millennium Godzilla series. After that in 2005, Kaneko even got to fulfill his childhood dream of directing episodes of the current Ultraman series, *Ultraman Max*. Kaneko continues to work steadily to this day.

Selected Filmography
Galaxy Cyclone Braiger [TV series] (1982) (writer)
Ultra Q: The Movie (mid-1980s) (proposed director) [unproduced]
Summer Vacation 1999 (1988) (director)
My Soul is Slashed (1991) (writer)
Gamera: Guardian of the Universe (1995) (director)
Gamera 2: Advent of Legion (1996) (director)
Haunted School 3 (1997) (writer, director)
Gamera 3: Awakening of Irys (1999) (writer, director)
Crossfire (2000) (writer)
Godzilla, Mothra and King Ghidorah: Giant Monsters All-Out Attack (2001) (writer, director)
Ultraman Max [TV series] (2005) (director)
Death Note (2006) (director)

45.
GODZILLA 2000: (NEW) MILLENNIUM

July 1998, Tri-Star's *Godzilla* was released in Japan. The only people pleased with it were Toho's money men. Though Toho had been considering just when they may or may not revive Godzilla,[1] fan pressure in response to the Tri-Star film inspired the studio to prepare another Godzilla film right away.[2]

Before his death in 1997, Tomoyuki Tanaka had submitted his own idea for the next Godzilla movie to follow 1995's *Godzilla vs. Destroyah*. Rumors from Japan in late 1996 and 1997 suggested that the story revolved around G-Force creating its own monster from the remains and genetic material of Battra, Destroyah, and Godzilla. It was G-Force's hope to control the beast to defend themselves from monster attacks. Presumably, the monster would go out of control and Godzilla Junior would have to battle it.[3] But, as Tanaka had been dead for over a year when it came time to revitalize the series, Shogo Tomiyama wasn't interested in developing the *Bio Godzilla* idea.

The ever-entertaining—if dubious—rumor mill said the initial story concept for what became *Godzilla 2000* featured only Godzilla and no other monsters. The Big G would instead face a huge combined military force comprised of various nations,[4] somewhat like the ending of 1978's *King of Monsters: Godzilla Resurrected*. As had happened during the development of the aforementioned film, Toho insisted that Godzilla needed an opponent to face. Oddly, the top three candidates rumored—and I stress the word rumored—were Anguirus, King Seesar, and Kumonga in that order. Another more credible rumor suggested the new film would be a quasi-remake of 1957's *The Mysterians* with Godzilla Junior battling the aliens.[5]

While the eventual storyline didn't feature the Mysterians, it did involve aliens—the idea of Hiroshi Kashiwabara, returning from 1994's *Godzilla vs. Space Godzilla*. The first story was called *Godzilla Millennium* and the news coming out of Japan in 1999 was that Godzilla Junior had been missing since the end of *Godzilla vs. Destroyah*. When a search party is sent to determine his whereabouts, Junior is discovered sleeping on an island alongside a mysterious U.F.O. The U.F.O. suddenly comes back online and produces what was planned-to-be a fully-CGI monster that had characteristics akin to a bubble! Why such a strange concept? Toho may have guessed that a bubbly, possibly amorphous monster would be easier to animate than a solid creature. And in the final film, Orga itself begins in a somewhat amorphous state created by CGI.

In an interview, Kashiwabara said that three versions of the story were written by himself, Wataru Mimura,[6] and Shogo Tomiyama. "There were many opinions, so Mr. Mimura and I changed the story," Kashiwabara explained. Therefore the island concept—but not the U.F.O.— was discarded by Mimura and Kashiwabara for the first draft of the screenplay. The duo's writing process was unusual in its method which yielded lacking results, a fact Mimura later admitted in an interview:

"We divided the story into four parts. Mr. Kashiwabara wrote 'Part A' and 'Part C.' I did 'Part B' and 'Part D.' Then we put them together to complete the whole story. After the movie was completed, we realized this writing process did not work well. The finished scenario did not have consistency. It was as if the writers' minds in the story were scattered."[7]

In this version of the story (now titled *Godzilla 2000*), very much like the finished film, Godzilla Junior returns to Japan, where he mysteriously begins destroying its power supply stations. Though this happens in the movie as well, here there is actually a specific reason: the benevolent Godzilla Junior knows that the Millennian aliens are coming to use humanity's energy against itself. Oddly, it was Shogo Tomiyama who decided to give Junior the boot and create a new continuity. The producer repeatedly stated that he wanted to make "a Godzilla unique to Japan." Presumably, this was a remark directed towards the Tri-Star Godzilla. There could be another reason Tomiyama did this. Had the story concerned Godzilla Junior, the old Heisei design would have to be used and Toho was apparently itching to redesign Godzilla themselves.

Essentially, Toho decided to take Godzilla back to his Showa roots, scaling him down to 55 meters (180 feet). One plan was even to bring back the 1954 look! A design crew headed by Shinji Nishikawa was assembled and working with him were Hideo Okamoto, Yasushi Torisawa, and Shinichi Wakasa to design a new, though still-familiar Godzilla. The new Godzilla began with a smaller head with small dorsal fins. Eventually, both those features were enlarged and Godzilla's neck took on a flare similar to a cobra's. Early designs for the U.F.O. were even more rock-like, and one resembled a seashell. Initial designs for Godzilla's opponent, Orga, were more angular, much like the enemy monster from *Gamera 3: Revenge of Irys*. Orga could also fire spear-like projectiles from its arm at this time. In the final film, many fans were dumbstruck at a scene where Orga opens its massive mouth and Godzilla obliges by bending over and sticking his head into it! Or, at least, this is what some audience members assumed (Godzilla, in fact, realized the best way to destroy Orga would be from within, but this idea doesn't get across as well as it should). Storyboards made more sense and had tendrils coming out of the mouth to drag Godzilla inside.

Kashiwabara's influence for this movie's array of characters was the movie *Twister* (1996)—ironically, directed by Jan De Bont as a result of leaving his version of Tri-Star's *Godzilla*. *Twister's* influence is quite clear in that the main characters are essentially Godzilla storm chasers from an organization called the Godzilla Prediction Network (GPN). The team is led by a father and daughter (Mimura's idea) who are joined by a female reporter who goes on a ride-along with them when Godzilla appears in Hokkaido.[8] Like the team in *Twister*, there is also a former friend turned adversary, the machiavellian government official Katagiri.

Trouble arose when Toho brought back a proven director, Takao Okawara, who did not like the new script. Both writers had plenty to say about this in interviews. Kashiwabara said, "I didn't like the director's ideas. Mr. Mimura rewrote the final draft of the script. I tried to quit the production."[9] Wataru Mimura explained, "Mr. Okawara, the director of the movie, seemed not happy with our job, either, so he wrote the scenario himself. The final scenario had a lot of input from Mr. Okawara."[10] Mimura went on to say that he was so dissatisfied with the film himself that he novelized it into a version he liked much better.

As the film's release neared (now titled *Godzilla 2000 Millennium*), advertising proclaimed that a big secret about Godzilla would be revealed.[11] However, the "big secret" was something most fans already knew about the monster: that his cells could regenerate (disclosed way back in 1989's *Godzilla vs. Biollante*). The plot revolves heavily around Godzilla's cells and a component called Organizer G-1 (renamed Regenerator G-1 for no apparent reason in the U.S. dub) which the aliens discover when they run across Godzilla and wish to steal it for an unknown reason in order to walk the planet. This marked the first time since

 ## GODZILLA VS. MEGAGUIRUS

OF ALL THE MILLENNIUM-ERA GODZILLA FILMS, THE LEAST IS KNOWN ABOUT THE DEVELOPMENT BEHIND *GODZILLA VS. MEGAGUIRUS* (2000). ONE OF THE ONLY JUICY TIDBITS IS THAT ORIGINALLY IT WAS TO BE THE SECOND ENTRY OF A TRILOGY SET WITHIN THE CONTINUITY OF *GODZILLA 2000*. HOWEVER, AS SOME MAJOR "WORLD BUILDING" BEGAN, IT WAS DECIDED IT WOULD BE EASIER TO SET THE STORY IN ITS OWN UNIVERSE. THE FILM'S ENEMY MONSTER CAME FROM A RATHER UNLIKELY SOURCE: THE MEGANURONS FROM *RODAN* (1956), AN IDEA OF HIROSHI KASHIWABARA'S. AND, THOUGH NONE OF THE CREATURES TOOK FLIGHT IN THAT FILM, STORYBOARDS FOR *RODAN* SHOW SOME MEGANURONS WITH WINGS. SHINJI NISHIKAWA BEGAN DRAWING NEW VERSIONS OF THE CREATURES ALL THE WAY BACK IN 1991. HE TOLD TOHO KINGDOM THAT, "WITH KING GHIDORAH HAVING BEEN RESURRECTED, WE THOUGHT WE WERE GOING TO HAVE A POLICY OF BRINGING BACK MONSTERS OF THE PAST RATHER THAN CREATING NEW ONES. RATHER THAN SIMPLY PUTTING THESE MONSTERS INTO THE FILMS EXACTLY AS THEY HAD BEEN PORTRAYED ORIGINALLY, I DREW MEGANURON WITH THE INTENTION OF HAVING HIM BE A MONSTER WE KNEW FROM THE PAST BUT WHOSE APPEARANCE WAS LIKE SOMETHING WE HAD NEVER SEEN BEFORE, HOPING TO THUS COMBINE THE APPEAL OF NEWNESS WITH THAT OF NOSTALGIA." [WWW.TOHOKINGDOM.COM/BLOG/SHINJI-NISHIKAWA-INTERVIEW/] THE FILM'S OTHER UNIQUE ASPECT IS THE MEANS WITH WHICH GODZILLA IS DEFEATED: A BLACK HOLE CANNON! WRITER WATARU MIMURA EXPLAINED HIS IDEA FOR THE DEVICE, CALLED THE DIMENSION TIDE: "I WAS TRYING TO COME UP WITH A MOST UNEXPECTED WEAPON AGAINST GODZILLA. I THOUGHT IT WAS IMPOSSIBLE TO DESTROY GODZILLA WITH ANY WEAPON AVAILABLE TODAY. IT WAS AN INTERESTING IDEA TO SHOOT GODZILLA BEYOND THE ATMOSPHERE, WHICH WAS A LARGE-SCALE IDEA. THE IDEA JUST POPPED UP TO ME. OF COURSE, I HAD THE STRATEGIC DEFENSE INITIATIVE OF THE U.S. AIR FORCE IN MY MIND." [HOMENICK, "SPINNING THE GODZILLA SAGA", *G-FAN* #88, PP.43] MIMURA ALSO LEARNED FROM HIS MISTAKE IN THE DISJOINTED WRITING OF *GODZILLA 2000* WHEN WORKING ON *GODZILLA VS. MEGAGUIRUS*. "WE DIVIDED THE STORY INTO TWO PARTS. MR. KASHIWABARA WROTE THE FIRST HALF, AND I DID THE SECOND. THIS APPROACH WAS EASIER, AS I COULD WRITE WITH A CONSTANT MIND. COMPARING THOSE TWO MOVIES, *GODZILLA VS. MEGAGUIRUS* HAS A BETTER QUALITY," MIMURA SAID. [IBID] THE JAPANESE MOVIEGOERS DISAGREED, HATING THE RESULTING FILM AND CAUSING IT TO ALMOST BECOME THE BIGGEST BOMB OF THE SERIES (IT DID BECOME THE SECOND-BIGGEST BOMB OF THE SERIES AT THAT TIME). RATHER THAN THE WRITERS OR THE DIRECTOR, TOHO BLAMED SPECIAL EFFECTS DIRECTOR KENJI SUZUKI FOR THE FILM'S FAILURE AND FIRED HIM.

the 1970s that aliens were brought in as the villains. When rebooting the series in 1984, Tomoyuki Tanaka took a strong anti-aliens stance for the Heisei series. However, since he was gone now, the new guard was able to bring that concept back into the fold. The idea that the U.F.O. had been dormant on earth for millions of years is interesting and could even harken back to old storylines from the Godzilla Revival Meeting of 1978 which involved ancient aliens.

The end battle between Godzilla and the U.F.O. is fun and utilizes a fascinating idea where the alien craft uses Tokyo itself to attack Godzilla. Though the idea could have been realized better, it is intriguing to see Tokyo fight back against Godzilla for a change. Naturally, Godzilla defeats the U.F.O. and Orga—an alien from within the flying saucer who tried to use Organizer G-1 on itself but wound up being transformed into a horrible monster. After seemingly saving humanity, Godzilla then proceeds to torch Tokyo as the main characters ponder the true nature of the monster, and Shinoda cryptically remarks, "Godzilla is inside every one of us."

The film did middle of the road business grossing a few million less than *Godzilla vs. Destroyah* when released in Japan in December 1999. Godzilla's staunch fans were not enough to make the movie the huge success Toho had hoped for (it's possible the Japanese at large felt too burned by the American fiasco). As luck had it, a few executives from Sony were in Japan during the film's theatrical run. Knowing that Americans were dissatisfied with what they had done with the character, the execs decided to take a chance and lobby for a U.S. theatrical release of *Godzilla 2000 Millennium*. The King of the Monsters hadn't been seen on U.S. theater screens since the similarly-titled *Godzilla 1985*. Unfortunately, when released in America the following August as *Godzilla 2000*, it did far worse there than it did in Japan.

Chapter Notes

[1] Some rumors stated that Toho wouldn't do a new film until 2004, for the 50th Anniversary. More reputable reports stated that Toho would always resume the series, with Godzilla Junior, in 1999.
[2] The earliest reports of this new "trilogy" in *G-Fan* stated that Godzilla would be a supernatural avenger of sorts. Considering this was the case in 2001's *Godzilla, Mothra and King Ghidorah: Giant Monsters All-Out Attack*, perhaps Shusuke Kaneko was already in talks to helm a Godzilla movie?
[3] Another rumor suggested that the *Godzilla vs. Ghost Godzilla* storyline was also brought up again.
[4] This was Takao Okawara's idea.
[5] Koichi Kawakita had seen an American script by Mick Anger in 1989 for a *Godzilla vs. the Mysterians*. Kawakita had longed to remake *The Mysterians* and also claimed in 2001 that he was talking to Toho about doing just that on the DVD commentary for *The Mysterians*.
[6] In an interview with Toho Kingdom, Shinji Nishikawa mentioned how Mimura had the idea of a visual of a Godzilla skeleton showing up on the moon during the development of the film. He said, "I had drawn [Godzilla on the moon] based on a request from our producer, Shogo Tomiyama. He said it had come about as an idea from scriptwriter Wataru Mimura back during *Godzilla 2000 Millennium* (1999), but it seems Mimura hadn't thought up any further plot for it beyond just that one image." www.tohokingdom.com/blog/shinji-nishikawa-interview/
[7] Homenick, "Spinning the Godzilla Saga", *G-Fan* #88 (Summer 2009), pp.42.
[8] On the note of Godzilla's entrance, Kashiwabara wanted to introduce him via his footsteps. They would cause a urinating man to have difficulty aiming. Toho didn't like the scene, even though the gag appears in Shusuke Kaneko's *Godzilla, Mothra and King Ghidorah: Giant Monsters All-Out Attack* (2001).
[9] vantagepointinterviews.com/2019/05/03/godzilla-on-paper-screenwriter-hiroshi-kashiwabara-on-writing-the-godzilla-series/
[10] Homenick, "Spinning the Godzilla Saga", *G-Fan* #88 (Summer 2009), pp.42.
[11] Considering *Godzilla vs. Destroyah's* advertising revolved around the death of Godzilla, perhaps the marketing department decided that another ploy was needed to intrigue fans.

46.
GIANT (HOLY) MONSTERS ALL-OUT ATTACK

By this point, most fans know 2001's *Godzilla, Mothra and King Ghidorah: Giant Monsters All-Out Attack* started out with Godzilla battling Baragon, Varan, and Anguirus instead of Mothra and King Ghidorah, who replaced the latter two kaiju. [1] Many, including this author, assumed that the story outlines were identical aside from the monster swaps, though this isn't the case. Shusuke Kaneko's first treatment[2] was different from the one written with Keiichi Hasegawa and Masahiro Yokotani. The differences, though, are still minor compared to other scripts in this book.

The version featuring Varan and Anguirus would have played out like this:

> When communication is lost with an American submarine off the coast of Guam, a reconnaissance craft is sent to investigate but it too disappears. Before it sinks, it manages to report spotting a huge creature in the water which leads the Japanese government to believe that Godzilla may have revived. At the same time, strange supernatural events plague Japan in regions connected to the ancient record of the Guardian Monsters of Yamato. These Guardian Monsters comprise of the white wind monster Baradagi (located in Akita, at Lake Tazawa), red fire monster Baragora, and golden ice monster Angila (in Aokigahara forest). According to legend, the Royal Court had overcome these monsters thousands of years ago and sealed them away should Japan need protecting in the future. Various disturbances awaken all three monsters who eat their noisy victims, leaving no trace of them behind. Reporter Yuri Tachibana investigates the incidents, believing them to be perpetrated by the three Guardian Monsters. Before government investigations can reach any conclusions, Godzilla surfaces and marches on Japanese soil. The self-defense forces scramble to confront the monster with Maser tanks, which prove ineffective. Yuri figures out that the

Guardian Monsters revived because they mistook the loud noises they heard to be the roars of Godzilla and attacked. She passes on her findings to her father, Admiral Taizo Tachibana. He informs the defense forces, who rename the monsters Varan, Baragon and Anguirus. Baragon surfaces at the Fuji Speedway and then intercepts Godzilla at Owakudani. The battle ends with Baragon's defeat and Godzilla marches on to Yokohama where he is confronted by Varan and Anguirus. Lightning strikes revive Baragon, who joins the action and the three monsters use ice, wind, and fire to battle Godzilla. Baragon and Anguirus are the first to die, while a mortally wounded Varan catches Yuri who has fallen from the Yokohama Bridge before it dies as well. The defense force launches a secret weapon they constructed 50 years ago to battle Godzilla, the Gohten, piloted by Admiral Tachibana. The weapon is successful and Godzilla is killed.

To delve even deeper into the details, Varan surfaces from Lake Tazawa and rather than killing the hooligans who try to drown a dog with a rock, it is merely campers by the lakeside playing music too loud that causes the monster to awaken. Naturally, it would have been more fun to see Varan surfacing from a lake to terrorize the surface dwellers than what we get in the film: Mothra plucking the hoodlums one by one underwater in larval form in a very un-Mothra type manner. Rather than being awakened by a suicidal man (played by Heisei Gamera alum Yukijiro Hotaro in the final film) late in the game, Anguirus gets revived from his ice cave early in the story when cultists in the woods of Aokigahara—Japan's infamous suicide forest—disturb him. Only Baragon's awakening because of noisy motorcyclists is generally the same. These reptilian guardians eat their victims, leaving behind large traces of saliva in their wake. Hideyo Amamoto's character Isayama, who warns about the monsters, seems to be absent from this treatment.

The design concept for Varan (sepia colored in the original, but to be colored white here) looked virtually unchanged since his original 1958 outing and the first sculpt of Baragon looked similar to his Showa design as well. Anguirus was the only one of the bunch to have drastic redesign.[3] His tail, in particular, is more like that of an ankylosaur. Anguirus also had a rather regal pose, and his quadruped stance was different from Baragon's. The question at hand is how would suitmation have brought this stance to life? Reportedly, the main reason Koichi Kawakita never revived

Anguirus in the Heisei series was that the monster's quadruped stance was too hard to bring to life without simply having a man in a suit crawling around on their knees. Baragon, on the other hand, in the design process is still a knee-walker.

It always seemed strange that Baragon did not participate in the final battle of the finished film. In this treatment, after being defeated by Godzilla, lightning strikes revive the kaiju and he comes to the aid of Anguirus and Varan in Yokohama.[4] It's also said that Godzilla's biting and drawing blood from King Ghidorah's neck was a tribute to a similar scene from *Godzilla Raids Again*, so in all likelihood, Kaneko intended for Godzilla to bite Anguirus's neck in a similar manner before the monster switched to being Ghidorah. Anguirus, given a golden hue like Ghidorah, would have apparently gained the new ability to freeze objects, as the treatment mentions the three monsters using wind, fire and ice to battle Godzilla. As Varan can fly, and Baragon can breathe fire, it is easy to surmise Anguirus would be given an ice ray or something of that nature. However, Toho Kingdom lists the beast's powers as having an ice-cold body temperature; the ability to create strong turbulence when its freezing body is near Baragon's fiery ray and spikes on the monster's body can extend and regrow if broken off. Apparently, even Anguirus's spikes would resemble icicles and when the monster is defeated in battle, he melts until he turns to bones which themselves crumble and deteriorate into nothing. In what sounded like quite the showstopper, Anguirus and Baragon would have used their fire and ice powers together to create a strong wind turbulence for Varan to glide along!

The treatment, like the finished film, is strange in how it spends so much time setting up the guardian monsters only to have the technology of man defeat Godzilla in the end. Rather than the simple submersible Satsuma, Kaneko wanted to bring back the Gohten from *Atragon*![5] Or, this could have been Tomiyama's idea, as it was he who eventually brought the Gohten back for *Godzilla: Final Wars* (2004).

The concept was first turned into Toho on July 28, 2000. On November 30, 2000, a full script was submitted with the name: *Godzilla vs. Varan · Baragon · Anguirus: Giant Monsters All-Out Attack*. Shogo Tomiyama actually approved of Kaneko's original monster pairing, it was the upper bosses at Toho that feared the obscurity of Kaneko's choices and requested Mothra and King Ghidorah. Executives were particularly edgy as the last Godzilla film had done terribly at the box office.[6] Kaneko apparently didn't buck their decisions, though he did consult with friends first who apparently weren't terribly familiar with Baragon, Varan, and Anguirus either (which is odd considering Anguirus was still very popular in the 90s). Furthermore, Kaneko also found Mothra and King Ghidorah to be more festive choices for a New Year's movie. Kaneko then suggested that *Ultraman Cosmos* series writer Keiichi Hasegawa and Masahiro Yokotani join him for the next four drafts that swapped in Mothra and King Ghidorah—making for five drafts total.

Developing the final version, Tomiyama said he wanted to give Kaneko as much creative freedom as possible since the director had waited ten years to make a Godzilla movie (Kaneko had approached Tomiyama back in 1992). They had only slight points of contention, such as Kaneko wanting Godzilla's eyes to be all white. Tomiyama let him have his way but made the look less severe and blackened the area around the eyes to make them narrower. The monsters were not allowed to have beam weapons except for King Ghidorah. Kaneko felt the Heisei series end battles were too heavy on beam weapons and wanted to differentiate his film. However, Shogo Tomiyama intervened and stated that King Ghidorah should retain this ability so the monster's gravity beams were added in. Tomiyama also suggested the idea that this be a "young" King Ghidorah resulting in his less imposing stature in this film since Kaneko wanted Godzilla to be the big bad of the film.

Generally speaking, *Godzilla, Mothra and King Ghidorah: Giant Monsters All-Out Attack* is considered by most fans as the best of the Millennium Godzilla series. More than the previous two entries, Kaneko goes out of his way to remind the audience of Godzilla's ties to the atomic bomb and WWII. In this incarnation, Godzilla is the original 1954 Godzilla (or at least the same Godzilla that had attacked in 1954, as this version is 60 meters tall) reconstituted and possessed by the spirits of those who died in WWII, feeling that Japan has forgotten their sacrifice during the war and the atrocities they committed on other nations' soldiers. Godzilla even surfaces from the same port that the Lucky Dragon No. 5 came from. Perhaps Kaneko's best directorial touch is that he personalizes Godzilla's victims before they're killed. One of the more notable scenes has a poor woman who survived Godzilla's first appearance in the Bonin Islands trapped in a hospital bed and can't get away as she watches the monster approach. The monster walks past the hospital without causing any harm. As the woman sighs a breath of relief, Godzilla's tail comes into frame and smashes the building. At one point, Godzilla even singles out a woman in a crowd for screaming too loud while fleeing and blasts her with his ray for her trouble!

Like Kaneko's Gamera films and the previous Godzilla movie, a woman is the lead character and like the characters in the films of the 1960s, she is a reporter. Her father is a military man and instead of a forced romantic relationship, their father/daughter chemistry makes up the emotional core of the movie which is a refreshing change of pace. This idea likely bled over from Kaneko's original vision for his Godzilla storyline, which also centered around a father/daughter relationship (in this case an astronaut turned alien being who protects his daughter and all of Japan from Godzilla).

Placed on a double bill with a feature-length Hamtaro cartoon, *Godzilla, Mothra and King Ghidorah: Giant Monsters All-Out Attack* managed to be a hit at the box office. It wasn't a sudden overnight sensation, though. Positive word of mouth from moviegoers to others (the Japanese were telling each other "this one's actually good!") got more viewers in theaters, eventually making the film the most successful entry of the Millennium series. However, it still wasn't bringing in Heisei-era amounts of money. In 2000, leading up to the release of *Godzilla vs. Megaguirus*, Toho announced they had planned to only make three "alternate universe" Godzilla movies, but based on this film's performance, it kept the monster king on movie screens for a few more years.

U.S. Sony executives, also took note of the movie's staying power in Japan. During the 2002 American Film Market when Toho was shopping the film (and other properties) to international markets, those same Sony execs went to a screening of *Giant Monsters All-Out Attack* to consider possibly releasing the film theatrically in the United States. However, showing a marked—and considering their 1998 misfire, perhaps unsurprising—ignorance about Godzilla, they walked out during the Baragon fight, grumbling to each other, "they're still using men in rubber suits over there…"

Chapter Notes

[1] Contrary to some rumors, Manda was never considered as one of the guardian monsters for the film according to Kaneko. *G-Fan* #49 in February 2001 was already reporting rumors that Kaneko's film would feature Mothra, King Ghidorah, Rodan, and possibly Anguirus and Baragon as well.

[2] It should also be noted that before this storyline, Kaneko had an idea for Godzilla to battle a swarm of Kamacuras until he learned that Godzilla battles a swarm of Meganuron in *Godzilla vs. Megaguirus*. After this, Kaneko came up with another storyline called "Godzilla vs. M" by fans, which was heavily influenced by both an episode of *Ultra Q* and *Ultraman*.

[3] The designer, Fuyuki Shinada, drew influence from the Kirin, a mythical, hooved, unicorn-like creature from China, when designing Anguirus.

[4] In some drafts of *Godzilla, Mothra and King Ghidorah: Giant Monsters All-Out Attack*, it is believed he also participated in the final battle.

[5] Perhaps this is where rumors of Manda's inclusion sprang from?

[6] Apparently, a 15-minute meeting took place that almost ended the Godzilla series at the time. The Toho execs agreed to continue only if Kaneko chose Mothra and King Ghidorah to appear.

47.
BIRTH OF
THE KIRYU SAGA

The basic storyline of *Godzilla Against Mechagodzilla* was initially dreamed up by 26-year-old Masahiro Yokotani, a student of Wataru Mimura's who had apparently helped develop *Godzilla vs. Megaguirus*, even if he wasn't credited in the final film. At the time of *Megaguirus's* filming, Shogo Tomiyama wanted to continue that film's continuity. Yokotani was instructed to write a scenario with Mechagodzilla and did so on November 26, 2000.[1]

Yokotani's wild treatment imagined a world oversaturated with robotic machinery where Japanese scientists have secretly developed a new technology called "cyber-spheres" that have artificial intelligence. One day, Godzilla comes to the mainland and destroys the research institute containing this new technology. This has an unintended side-effect: the cyber-spheres scatter across Japan and begin to take on the characteristics of animals. They also start attacking people. The organization GROC (Get Rid of Creatures) is set up in conjunction with the self-defense forces. A new robot, remote controlled by human beings in a manner similar to *Pacific Rim* (2013), is created to battle these creatures. To deal with Godzilla, an idea is hatched to dredge the bones of the 1954 Godzilla from the ocean and build a mechanical exoskeleton over them.[2] It is equipped with a weapon that would evolve into the Absolute Zero Cannon. This version of Mechagodzilla is able to create a force field to block Godzilla's ray like the Showa incarnation. The mechanical monster is built in an underwater lab and, at one point, is stolen by spies! Though there are many differences, the story ultimately ends similarly to the finished film with Mechagodzilla driving Godzilla away.

Upon the greenlighting of Shusuke Kaneko's Godzilla film, the Mechagodzilla idea was put on the backburner, though it apparently gestated in the mind of Masaaki Tezuka for the rest of that year. Tezuka even said that the terrorist attacks of September 11, 2001 inspired part of his thought process for this film. "To fight poison make poison," he said. "To fight Godzilla, create another Godzilla."[3] When *Godzilla, Mothra and King Ghidorah:*

Giant Monsters All-Out Attack proved to be a hit in 2001, Tezuka got his wish to direct another Godzilla movie. Wataru Mimura was then brought in to work over his student's old treatment. However, the only major ideas that carried over were an A.I. named Becky and, of course, Mechagodzilla.

The first draft began in 1999. However, this version opens not with a typhoon, but the grand opening of the National Godzilla Museum, where the original Godzilla's skeleton is displayed upright within a huge tower. A conclusive statement is then issued saying that scientists have determined there is no threat of a second Godzilla existing. Naturally, this signals the entrance of the second Godzilla. We are then introduced to our female hero, Reiko Anzai. Instead of a Maser tank platoon in the Anti-Special Creature Self-Defense Forces, she is a fighter pilot in a squadron that attacks the new Godzilla. Needless to say, Godzilla decimates the squadron.

Shinzo Tonegawa, a character in his mid-60s who will later develop Mechagodzilla, watches as Godzilla approaches the bones of the 1954 Godzilla. He stares at them but does not attack. Godzilla strangely turns and walks back into the sea. Presumably the only survivor, Reiko emerges alive from her crashed jet and watches Godzilla with intense hatred. Shinzo shines a light inside the Godzilla skull as an idea hits him... Cut to the main title.

The story picks up three years later in the Godzilla Countermeasures Headquarters. There, a hardened Reiko trains in a program that uses a futuristic aircraft called the Hokage. Also part of the program are two A.I. units, Miki and Becky. The latter has the ability to fly and Miki is described as being like a fairy. It would seem these A.I.s were developed from the bones of the 1954 Godzilla as Becky says she is, "an artificial life, but it is actually an organic life born from air bubbles in the spinal nerve of Godzilla"! Just what precisely Mimura envisioned for Mechagodzilla is hard to imagine, but in his own words, "a huge skeleton with artificial muscles and armor plates."

Godzilla's second scene has him swim under a cruise ship. A married couple thinks the form they saw was a huge whale until Godzilla's tail slams into the boat and destroys it. The basic narrative structure is the same as in *Godzilla Against Mechagodzilla*. The self-defense forces try to get Mechagodzilla online before Godzilla makes landfall in Japan again. Reiko flies the Hokage, which controls Mechagodzilla from above, and confronts Godzilla along the Miura Peninsula. The mechanical dragon takes Godzilla by surprise from the air and knocks him down. It then beats Godzilla with its tail and fires missiles out its back onto the downed monster. Godzilla counters by swiping his robotic doppelganger off its feet with his tail. As the battle progresses, a blast to the neck disables Mechagodzilla's remote control system. With the machine down, Godzilla heads for Tokyo.

Mechagodzilla is repaired and brought to face Godzilla in Ginza where it unleashes the Zero Cannon on the monster. Godzilla is hurt—but not enough—and attacks the machine again. When Mechagodzilla is overwhelmed, it is given an electrical boost from a satellite. Said boost interferes with the controls and the bones of the original Godzilla take over.[4] To Godzilla and the defense force's confusion alike, the robot protector begins to destroy Tokyo itself. Godzilla then springs into action and the two kaiju destroy the city together!

To stop the out-of-control robot, a missile containing Becky is fired at Mechagodzilla's neck, allowing the A.I. access into its head. As Becky flies towards Mechagodzilla, Godzilla takes note and tries to destroy her in midair but his attempt is unsuccessful. Even Mechagodzilla tries to shake Becky off its neck when she lands to repair the remote control apparatus. Reiko commands the Hokage to distract Godzilla from Becky so she may continue her repairs. Quite the battle ensues between Godzilla and Reiko. Eventually, Godzilla catches the craft in his arms and tries to crush it. This essentially serves as the climactic moment of the script as Mechagodzilla comes back online just in time to save Reiko from being crushed. Once Reiko—or rather the craft she's in—is saved, the machine grabs Godzilla and flies him out to sea where it detonates the Zero Cannon again. Godzilla swims away as Reiko watches. Instead of slating the credits to roll here, there was to be an epilogue back at the Godzilla Countermeasures Headquarters and following this, a final shot of Godzilla's eye opening at the bottom of the sea.

The next version of the story was much closer to the final film, except two female heroes were to appear before they were simplified into one character. Prime Minister Tsuge was originally a man before Kumi Mizuno was cast and the new Prime Minister Igarashi was supposed to be played by Masahiko Tsugawa. Godzilla was still going to destroy Tokyo Tower in this film but construction on the tower prevented this, so it was destroyed in the next movie instead. Also, Makuhari was the proposed battle site for *Godzilla Against Mechagodzilla* until it was decided the buildings were too high for the below 60-meter-tall monsters. An idea where Anguirus battled Mechagodzilla was considered. Wilder still, suit designer Shinichi Wakasa wanted to put tiger stripes on Godzilla for this film (but director Masaaki Tezuka was having none of it)! In an interview with *Sci-Fi Japan TV*, Tezuka revealed that he wanted the film to end with Akane dying, the water would freeze, and no monsters would emerge at all.

Though it lacks the subtext of Kaneko's film, in many ways, Tezuka's second Godzilla movie might be the best of the Millennium series from a purely popcorn perspective. Considering that it has the same writer, the film's subtext is again Life vs. Artificial Life as it was in the 1993 *Godzilla vs. Mechagodzilla*. The twist here is that Mechagodzilla is actually just the first Godzilla, somehow spiritually resurrected through robotic technology. A RoboCop Godzilla, if you will. The ethical aspects of the situation would be better explored and resolved in the sequel.

Chapter Notes

[1] Only a few days later though a treatment had also been turned in for Shusuke Kaneko's Godzilla film involving Anguirus and Varan. If these were competing projects, or if Tomiyama knew he planned on the Mechagodzilla feature for 2002, is unknown.
[2] In a way, one could consider Kiryu to be a continuation of the Ghost Godzilla idea. Shogo Tomiyama would seem to have been long fascinated with having the modern Godzilla fight the 1954 original in some capacity. Kiryu finally realizes this concept.
[3] *Godzilla X Kiryu Perfection,* pp. 89.
[4] It's possible the manga adaptation of *Godzilla vs. Mechagodzilla* (1993) by Takayuki Sakai could have influenced this idea. In the manga adaptation, the programing of Mecha-King Ghidorah takes over the robot causing it to become more aggressive.

48.
FROM ROLISICA WITH LOVE
GODZILLA X MOTHRA

Satisfied with the path they were taking with *Godzilla Against Mechagodzilla*, Toho approved the next film being a direct sequel before *Mechagodzilla* was even released, but insisted that Mothra be brought into the main action. The first treatment, called *Godzilla vs. Mothra*[1] in some sources, and was written by director Tezuka and Wataru Mimura's understudy, Masahiro Yokotani. The story begins in the Ogasawara Islands, where two battle-damaged Mothra larvae come on land and are spotted by the Japanese self-defense forces. It is soon apparent what injured them when Godzilla shows up on their trail and the battle resumes. Kiryu is sent to battle Godzilla and their ensuing battle was to go into the ocean and then underwater where Kiryu has the advantage because here, Godzilla apparently cannot fire his ray underwater.[2] The machine then freezes Godzilla with the Zero Cannon but Godzilla breaks out of the ice and resumes his attack until he defeats Kiryu. Godzilla swims away and the defense forces are left to ponder their defeat.

Sometime later, it is revealed that one of the surviving Mothras was brought to a containment facility in Japan. Upon learning this, the public worries what will happen when it reaches maturity. Another main story point is the fact that the Zero Cannon seems to be ineffective, so the defense forces debate ways to make it more powerful. There is another problem as well: because of the close contact with Godzilla, Kiryu's brain cells are not only activating again but also multiplying.

One of the main characters gets the idea of implanting Mothra's cells into the mix as a way of soothing the wild Godzilla cells within Kiryu. As this character approaches Mothra's cocoon, he is initially frightened when a crack appears in the chrysalis—thinking that perhaps Mothra will emerge. Instead, two tiny fairies come out and offer their help in the matter of the Mothra cells (the character had asked the cocoon for help). The government proceeds to study the twin girls as well as a strange new type of flower found on their home island. Soon thereafter, Godzilla reappears.

As the defense forces struggle and fail to stop Godzilla from making landfall (Kiryu is still in repairs), Mothra emerges from her cocoon. The scientists and the military watch and wait in fear, worrying what side she will take. Naturally, Mothra takes to the skies to battle Godzilla. In this version, Mothra defeats Godzilla and drives him back to the ocean. Japanese media outlets rejoice and praise Mothra as a hero. In the interim before the final battle, the treatment again explores the strange flowers and their curious relationship to the DNA of both Godzilla and Mothra. Godzilla emerges again in Tokyo Bay. Mothra and the defense forces attack him in tandem but this time, Godzilla defeats Mothra, who falls to the ground. A new version of the Absolute Zero Cannon (not attached to Kiryu) is also used on Godzilla to no avail. Kiryu then arrives to do battle in a much more physical, close combat nature. The Zero Cannon is fired at Godzilla again and manages to freeze him into a chunk of ice... which quickly begins to crack.

The wounded Mothra springs to the air and carries the frozen Godzilla into the air just as he wakes. Similar to 1992's *Godzilla vs. Mothra*, he blasts her with his ray and the two monsters fall into the ocean. At the same time, the twin girls disappear. In an epilogue, a memorial service is held for Mothra and the girls on a naval vessel. The two main characters hear the voice of the fairies telling them that Mothra is not actually dead. The final scene would have shown Mothra stirring at the bottom of the ocean (instead of Godzilla, for once).

The story's next evolution became more like the outline for the final film, with a young male protagonist who is infatuated with Kiryu. His name is Daisuke and he is not related to Professor Chujo, nor is he an engineer. He is training to be a pilot. The story begins with Daisuke piloting Kiryu and fighting Godzilla. It turns out just to be a training simulation much like a deleted scene in *Godzilla vs. Mechagodzilla* (1993). Daisuke is chastised for his failure by his training officer.

Next, we cut to the discovery of a mysterious cocoon. The defense forces naturally think that it is Mothra. But upon firing at the cocoon, Godzilla mysteriously emerges! It would seem that the moth goddess must have trapped Godzilla within her cocoon recently. Had this great idea been utilized, it would have ranked as one of Godzilla's more surprising entrances.

Some digging is done by the defense forces, who eventually discover through satellite images shared by the U.S. military that Godzilla and a Mothra larva recently battled near a military research facility belonging to Rolisica—the same fictional country from 1961's *Mothra*! [3] Elsewhere, Daisuke's younger brother Takeshi is walking to school when he is approached by a tiny fairy. He takes it home to show his friends.

Other countries across the world want to make their own mechanical weapons similar to Kiryu. It is even discovered that the Rolisicans have G-cells in their possession—likely the reason Godzilla attacked their base. It is also thought that a Rolisican spy stole intel from the defense forces regarding Kiryu. However, this alleged spy appears to be only 30cm tall on camera. The "spy" seems to be one of Mothra's fairies—or is it?

When Takeshi meets up with Daisuke, the fairy reveals herself to him. Daisuke recognizes her as the Rolisican spy on the surveillance camera. He takes her back to the base and it is discovered that she is a cyborg clone of the original Shobijin created by Rolisica! This is why Mothra attacked the base at the same time as Godzilla; she was drawn to the DNA of the Shobijin.

Daisuke takes pity on the tiny machine, however. As she is comprised of living DNA, she has real thoughts and feelings. Daisuke takes it upon himself to steal the tiny girl before she can be dissected alive. At the same time, the Mothra larvae land in Japan. The populace panics because if Godzilla also shows up, Tokyo will be leveled. Back home, Daisuke shows the tiny girl to a Kiryu engineer named Sekiguchi. The two realize that Kiryu is the same as this poor girl in that it is a robotic organism with living cells forced to do a government's bidding. The two also discover that by removing a remote control bracelet on the girl's arm, she is freed from Rolisican control.

The girl confesses to Daisuke where the stolen intel is hidden. Daisuke and Sekiguchi leave Takeshi and the girl in a shelter to go find it. Naturally, Takeshi and the girl follow them. It's a good thing too because upon arriving at the location, Daisuke is attacked by another Rolisican agent. The Mecha-Shobijin demonstrates immense strength despite her tiny stature and defeats the agent, whom the girl identifies as Kamizaki. Godzilla emerges from Tokyo Bay and in the confusion, Kamizaki regains consciousness and escapes with the intel—containing Kiryu's controls! Kamizaki flies to Kiryu and hijacks the mechanical monster and begins using it to destroy Tokyo! Kiryu and Godzilla come to blows and Godzilla manages to knock the robot out (in the battle Kamizaki is also rendered unconscious). Daisuke climbs inside and takes back control of the machine to the shock of his superiors.

During the battle just as Daisuke loses control of the robot and is about to die from a fatal blast of Godzilla's ray, Kiryu activates a force field on its own saving itself and its pilot. Kiryu, seeming to sense Daisuke's compassionate nature towards it, begins communicating with him! The treatment then becomes strangely condensed and less detailed, giving only a basic outline of the end battle. An adult Mothra shows up to help Kiryu battle Godzilla. They succeed in driving the beast off and the mechanical Shobijin is accepted by Mothra as one of her own. Before the tiny girl departs on Mothra, she communicates to Daisuke that it's sad she and Kiryu are both machines forced to fight against their will.

From this, we can see the basic outline and character types emerging that would appear in the cumbersomely-titled *Godzilla vs. Mothra vs. Mechagodzilla: Tokyo S.O.S.* To better tie the siblings to Mothra, they were made the grandchildren of Professor Chujo from the original *Mothra* and that character himself was added into the next script as well. The next draft is closer to the final film but with a few more minor differences. The best-known difference is the identity of the monster carcass on the beach. Originally, a Liopleurodon—an obscure species of plesiosaur—was meant to be the corpse that washes up on the beach. Then, it became a cameo for Anguirus, but Shogo Tomiyama decided this would only anger fans so Anguirus was swapped with Kameba from *Space Amoeba* (1970).

The final script also contains several notable scenes that were never filmed. One had Godzilla battling naval destroyers with Maser cannons on them. Godzilla was to destroy one of the ships and then submerge underwater. Storyboards show some ambitious differences between Godzilla and Mothra's battle in Tokyo. After grabbing Godzilla by the neck, Mothra was meant to drag Godzilla through Tokyo by the tail and swing him into a building. Godzilla was then to swat Mothra with his tail and knock her into a building. As Godzilla corners her, Mothra would have used her legs to scratch at Godzilla's face. When Mothra becomes inflamed by Godzilla's ray she was to dive into the ocean. Also, Kiryu was meant to use several Tokyo buildings as cover during onslaughts of Godzilla's ray blasts. Several ideas were scrapped regarding the larvae (originally meant to cause more destruction as they travel through Tokyo) such as showing them strategizing together against Godzilla. The monster was also to pick up one larva and throw it into the other. Conversely, the scene where Kiryu tells Yoshito Chujo goodbye was not in the final shooting script and was thought up during shooting even though an earlier treatment had Kiryu communicating with Daisuke.

Initial designs for Mothra were more wasp-like before the Showa look was retained. Specifically, Shinichi Wakasa began with the Rainbow Mothra from *Rebirth of Mothra 3* and changed the wings to resemble Mothra's original patterns. As a way of differentiating Godzilla and Kiryu from the previous movie (and most likely to sell new toys), both were given battle scars. Godzilla has a chest scar from the Zero Cannon and Kiryu has a new drill hand.

The story structure where the monsters are concerned, is reminiscent of *Godzilla vs. Gigan*, of all things. In that film, the "final" monster battle began midway through the film and lasted until the end. Here it is the same. Whereas Godzilla or another monster usually have a fight early or midway into the film and then disappear until the climax, here once Godzilla emerges in Tokyo Bay, he stays in the picture until the end. Breathlessly, he battles the defense forces, the adult Mothra, Kiryu, and then Kiryu and the Mothra larvae in that order.

Masaaki Tezuka and Masahiro Yokotani continue Wataru Mimura's theme from the previous film of Life vs. Artificial Life. While the previous draft had a lone Shobijin clone created against her will, here there is the real Shobijin coming to Japan to warn scientists that it is wrong to resurrect the bones of the dead Godzilla. There isn't much more explanation than that, just that Mothra, a divine figure, knows that Godzilla's bones should be laid to rest. This is hard for the young Yoshito Chujo to hear as he loves machines, especially Kiryu. The final scene, where Yoshito must escape from Kiryu—who, at this point, has fully transformed spiritually into the 1954 Godzilla after he's ordered to kill off the current Godzilla—before he plummets into the ocean, is both touching and exciting. The Kiryu Saga is wrapped up nicely as Godzilla's bones and the gravely wounded Godzilla sink into the deepest recesses of the Pacific Ocean, back where they belong.

Chapter Notes

[1] In Japan, in terms of visual lettering on the posters, 'X' took the place of 'VS' from the Heisei series. However, if one were to pronounce the titles out loud they would still be "Gojira tai Megaguirus," etc.
[2] The manga adaptation of *Godzilla vs. Mechagodzilla* (1993) by Takayuki Sakai featured an underwater battle between Godzilla and Mechagodzilla.
[3] This would seem to confirm, in this continuity at least, that the U.S. and Rolisica are not the same country.

PROFILE: WATARU MIMURA

Wataru Mimura was born the same year as Godzilla in 1954 in Mie Prefecture. Mimura graduated from the College of Art of Nihon University. In 1982, Mimura won the Sanrio Screenwriter Award, which led to him working as a writer on Shochiku's *Green Boy*. Mimura's debut screenplay was *Freeter* about contract and temporary employees in Japan. In the early 1990s, his work shifted to direct-to-video movies from Toei. Through a connection with *The Return of Godzilla* director Koji Hashimoto, Mimura was introduced to Shogo Tomiyama. Mimura said that he and Hashimoto "were going to make a comedy movie (a kind of revival of the "Wakadaisho"/"Young Guy" series), but it did not work out. Then Mr. Hashimoto introduced me to Mr. Tomiyama." [Homenick, "Spinning the Godzilla Saga", *G-Fan* #88, pp.42] Tomiyama asked Mimura to write his own version (likely just a treatment) for the in-development *Godzilla vs. Mothra*. Mimura says that his theme for this unused scenario was that of "Life." Tomiyama apparently liked Mimura's idea even though it wasn't used, and tasked him with not only writing the next Godzilla movie but also *Yamato Takeru*. *Godzilla vs. Mechagodzilla* was a success, while Mimura's *Yamato Takeru* was not (Mimura was allowed to write a sequel which was never produced). Mimura didn't return to the Godzilla series until 1999 when he was paired with Hiroshi Kashiwabara. Mimura explained that, "I did not know Mr. Kashiwabara before. He was an open-minded person and we worked together well." [Ibid] After the relative success of *Godzilla 2000*, Mimura and Kashiwabara returned for the next Godzilla movie (which was not a success), and Mimura alone returned for *Godzilla Against Mechagodzilla* (2002). Mimura sat out the 2003 Godzilla movie to work on a film called *Round One*, but returned to the series for the 50th Anniversary film, *Godzilla: Final Wars*. Mimura continues to write to this day.

Selected Filmography
Freeter (1989) (writer)
Little Sinbad (1990) (writer)
Godzilla vs. Mothra (1992) (writer) [unproduced version of *Godzilla vs. Mothra*]
Godzilla vs. Mechagodzilla (1993) (writer)
Yamato Takeru (1994) (writer)
Yamato Takeru II (1995-1997) (writer) [unproduced]
Big Boss (1995) (writer)
Godzilla 2000 (1999) (writer)
Godzilla vs. Megaguirus (2000) (writer)
Godzilla Against Mechagodzilla (2002) (writer)
Round One (2003) (writer)
Godzilla: Final Wars (2004) (writer)
Sampo Shojo (2016) (writer)

49.
DON'T CALL IT A COMEBACK:
GODZILLA JUNIOR IN FINAL WARS?

In late 2003, based off of a post credits scene in that year's *Godzilla: Tokyo S.O.S.*, many fans thought that the next film would round out a Kiryu trilogy. In the post-credits stinger, viewers saw a lab full of kaiju DNA ready for experimentation. Production art from Japan appeared featuring a possible story where robotic versions of other monsters like Varan, Kameba, and Baragon existed.[1] This would have made sense for a 50th Anniversary film, after all.

However, Toho announced that not only would the 50th Anniversary film be the last one for at least ten years, but that Masaaki Tezuka would not return to the director's chair (unsurprising, considering *Tokyo S.O.S.* made about 11 million dollars on a roughly 12 million dollar budget).[2] Instead, a hot director popular in the United States named Ryuhei Kitamura (2000's *Versus*) was chosen to helm Godzilla's anniversary film. 2004's *Godzilla: Final Wars* was a wild, divisive film amongst the fandom. What most fans don't know, though, was that this film began as a sequel to *Godzilla vs. Destroyah*.

Though he had decided to break the Heisei continuity with 1999's *Godzilla 2000*, series producer Shogo Tomiyama hinted that he would like to return to the Heisei continuity in a *G-Fan* interview back in 2002. He and J.D. Lees were discussing the different continuities, or "streets", taken by the Millennium films. Tomiyama made the remark, "In [*Godzilla vs. Destroyah*] there was another street we were walking down. I want you to remember that."[3]

And indeed, according to several reports the first treatment for *Godzilla: Final Wars* was written by Shogo Tomiyama and Wataru Mimura and was set in the Heisei continuity.[4] Specifically, the Godzilla in this story was to be the fully-grown Godzilla Junior last seen in the closing moments of *Godzilla vs. Destroyah*. Tomiyama also wanted to insert some ideas that were cut from early versions of "Godzilla 7"—specifically the Gohten. In the opening scene of *Godzilla: Final Wars*, the Gohten battles Godzilla. It is notably commanded by signature actors from the Heisei series, Akira

Nakao and Koichi Ueda, who played General Aso (*Mechagodzilla* through *Destoroyah*) and Vice-Commander Hyodo (*Mechagodzilla* through *Space Godzilla*), respectively. While many assumed this was just a tip of the hat to the veteran actors, it was actually much more than that. In the first draft of what became *Final Wars*, that would have actually been Aso and Hyodo commanding the Gohten. In the unproduced *Godzilla vs. Barubaroi*, Aso was to pilot the Gohten, which would in some way tie into his past.

Fans took note of the fact that previous Millennium entries had shrunk Godzilla down to 55 meters (and 60 meters in *Giant Monsters All-Out Attack*), while in *Final Wars*, he was again 100 meters as in the Heisei continuity—again, because this originally was the Heisei continuity. Presumably, the story outline was basically the same with Godzilla Jr.—or now just Godzilla—being frozen in ice in the, ahem, cold open only to be freed to battle aliens later.

It's even highly likely that Keizer Ghidorah was also a leftover concept from the Heisei era. Back in 1994, Toho briefly flirted with producing *Godzilla vs. Emperor Ghidorah* as "Godzilla 6". In that story, the original Ghidorah (whose cells the Futurians used to create the Dorats in 1991's *Godzilla vs. King Ghidorah*) would come to earth. The monster was to have gravity beams that actually levitated objects—just like Keizer Ghidorah in *Final Wars*. Like Death Ghidorah [5] and Keizer Ghidorah, this Emperor Ghidorah was also very likely a quadruped (as a way of differentiating itself from the 1991 version). Furthermore, in German, the word "kaiser" means "emperor."[6] So, no matter how one looks at it, Keizer Ghidorah is Emperor Ghidorah.

Even Godzilla's bout with the Tri-Star Godzilla comes from another aborted Heisei era idea. In 1994, as *Godzilla vs. Space Godzilla* was shooting and the Jan De Bont *Godzilla* was in development, there was an idea to do a film where the Heisei Godzilla fought the Tri-Star Godzilla! This idea came from production assistant Shinichiro Arimasa. Of course, De Bont's version never happened and the battle between Godzillas in *Final Wars* could be coincidence.

The final scene of *Final Wars* is lifted from another aborted idea for "Godzilla 7". At one early point, the idea for that film was *Godzilla vs. Varan*! Varan awakens in 1999 and launches a campaign to destroy the world. Godzilla and Little Godzilla appear on the scene to fight back for humanity and emerge victorious. As the story was set close to New Year's Eve, the final scene was to be of Godzilla and Little Godzilla swimming off over the horizon as the sun rises. A clock would appear onscreen flipping over from 1999 to 2000. It would seem this aborted ending inspired the parting shot of Godzilla and Minilla used in *Godzilla: Final Wars*.

Apparently, all ties to Heisei continuity—aside from 100-meter scale monsters—were done away with upon the arrival of Ryuhei Kitamura and his writer, Isao Kiriyama. When asked about the writing process, Kitamura said, "First, we began with the synopsis, which was basically Godzilla versus everybody. Some (of the characters were) the Xiliens, this new breed of hybrid human. That was all there."[7] Taking those comments into account, it would seem the story did follow the same structure, only with Godzilla Junior and a few characters from the Heisei series like General Aso. This author would go so far as to presume that perhaps General Aso was originally, more or less, the Captain Gordon role played by UFC fighter Don Frye. While Kitamura admitted that Captain Gordon was his idea in the interview, he unfortunately couldn't confirm who the original character was in Gordon's place. "Some kind of captain was in the original idea, I think, but it wasn't as strong as [Captain Gordon]," Kitamura said.[8] And before Don Frye was cast, Kitamura originally wanted the Tri-Star *Godzilla's* Jean Reno in the role! Akira Takarada had also met Reno and the two had expressed a desire to work together. However, Reno was unavailable so Christopher Lambert (*The Highlander, Mortal Kombat*) was approached and then Don Johnson (*Miami Vice*)! Due to scheduling conflicts and expensive salaries, eventually UFC fighter Don Frye was approached and he made the new Captain Gordon character his own.

Kitamura went on to say that he basically liked Mimura and Tomiyama's ideas but wanted to bring in Isao Kiriyama, who wrote *Azumi* (2003), to help integrate new ideas. Wataru Mimura relayed his perspective on the process in *G-Fan* #88, which also mentioned Kitamura bringing in Kiriyama:

> "Toho decided it was going to be the last Godzilla movie, so my writing team joined the plot, planning about one year before the actual production. It was Mr. Tomiyama's idea. When the plot was completed, I wrote the first scenario. After that, Mr. Isao Kiriyama from the team of Mr. Ryuhei Kitamura, director of the movie, co-wrote the revised scenario together with Mr. Kitamura. The story line was not changed, but the nature of the characters and some words changed, according to Mr. Kitamura's taste."[9]

Even after Kitamura had re-written the screenplay, there were more changes. Originally, the film was also to feature Mechagodzilla, the Mothra larva, the Odako (the giant octopus), and, at Kitamura's request, Gorosaurus. King Ghidorah was also considered for the final monster "boss," but eventually a new creation was decided on instead. The final monster roster ended up consisting of some surprising choices. Among them were Godzilla (of course), Minilla, Gigan, Rodan, Anguirus, Mothra, Ebirah, King Seesar, Kumonga, Kamacuras, and Hedorah (who only has a one-scene cameo after the bulk of his footage was cut from the final movie). According to Kitamura, the lineup was literally decided by he, Tomiyama, and the two writers who sat around a table covered in Godzilla toys![10]

Many fans were upset by the fact that some monsters get little more than a cameo—namely Hedorah. Kitamura had bigger plans for the Smog Monster; he wanted the kaiju to attack the Japanese island of Odaiba in a scene that also would have spoofed *Bayside Shakedown*, a popular police comedy series at the time. Shogo Tomiyama vetoed this idea but as a consolation prize, apparently allowed extra footage of Hedorah to be shot destroying Tokyo which was shown during the end credits.[11]

The film also included a new creation, Monster X—who really turned out to be a smokescreen of sorts to keep Keizer Ghidorah's appearance a secret (who was also hidden from all publicity and behind-the-scenes materials). Last but not least, many fans love this movie solely because the computer-generated Tri-Star Godzilla (here renamed Jira/Zilla) makes an appearance and is unceremoniously killed by the real Godzilla. This was also Kitamura's idea, who was shocked when Tomiyama told him Toho had rights to use the monster. "I really wish now I would have made that scene much longer," Kitamura said in retrospect.[12]

The main drama of *Final Wars* focuses on Shinichi Ozaki (played by popular musician/actor Masahiro Matsuoka), a mutant human. Ozaki is one of many mutants to have emerged on earth. This element was seemingly inspired by Fox's *X-Men* franchise (and the costume design by *The Matrix* trilogy). The villains harken from the Showa Godzilla series and present an updated version of the Xians from *Invasion of Astro-Monster* (1965). Even non-Godzilla films like *Gorath* (1962) are represented in the film (the aliens claim a giant asteroid called Gorath is heading for earth and will destroy it which turns out to be fake) making the film as much of a celebration of Toho special effects films as it is a Godzilla 50th anniversary film. With so many characters and monsters, the film is a wild ride—some say too wild. Writer Wataru Mimura even admitted this in a *G-Fan* interview:

> "It was the last movie of the Godzilla series, so I wanted to make it something you can enjoy as 'party movie' with a lot of familiar kaiju characters. I am not sure if you could really enjoy it. I personally think that the kaiju could have been featured more in the movie. If I score the quality, it would be 50 points (out of 100)."[13]

The film's storyline moves at a breakneck pace and is structured mainly around the action scenes, for the humans and monsters alike. The story is simple and straightforward: aliens arrive proponing peace a la *Invasion of Astro-Monster* only to use earth's monsters to conquer the planet. After this has been established, the humans must go on a quest to free Godzilla. Upon his release, Godzilla simply travels to countries between the South Pole and Japan, beating up or killing the alien-controlled monsters. There is no subtext to speak of, though Kitamura's violent film would seem to end with an anti-violence message when Minilla convinces Godzilla to cease his squabble with mankind (in one of the few bits of characterization in the film, when Godzilla attacks a village in Japan, it is explained that the monster king hates mankind for creating the atomic bomb), while a child character convinces the adult humans to stop attacking Godzilla.

Kitamura even admitted that Minilla was the heart of the movie's main theme. According to Mimura, Minilla wasn't in the first script—which makes sense considering that it was set in the Heisei continuity. Kitamura said that as the story developed, he felt that it needed a message, though not as strong of a message as the original. The director explained that,

> "I just felt like we need that heart and soul for the movie because we knew this was more like a '70s Godzilla fun movie, which we were trying to make. We were not planning to do a reboot of the original Godzilla, which had that strong message. But still, I felt like we need to send out a message in our own way."[14]

Upon release, *Godzilla: Final Wars* was very divisive and it was not a money maker for Toho (it finally managed to dethrone 1975's *Terror of Mechagodzilla* as the biggest bomb of the series, pulling in a mere $13 million on an exuberant $18 million budget). Some fans found it vulgar and insulting while others thought it was a fun update for the franchise. Because so many fans were split, perhaps it is for the best that the film didn't take place in the Heisei continuity, which is rather beloved by many fans. True to their word, Toho would not produce another Godzilla movie for ten years. Instead, Godzilla's resurrection would come from the most unlikely of sources...

Chapter Notes

[1] Oddly, when asked about making another G-film, Tezuka never mentioned a Godzilla vs. Godzilla story but instead implied he would have enjoyed doing a Kiryu spinoff.
[2] It's worth mentioning there was a rumor Shusuke Kaneko was approached but this can't be confirmed.
[3] Lees, "Godzilla's Boss", *G-Fan* #55, (Mar/Apr 2002), pp.19.
[4] It's possible the title *Final Wars* is a new version of another Tomiyama treatment, *Godzilla: Super Wars*.
[5] This author very much believes that Death Ghidorah from *Mothra* (1996) was inspired by Emperor Ghidorah.
[6] However, because of Toho's bizarre official English practices, Kaisaa Gidora/Kaiser Ghidorah would become "Keizer Ghidorah".
[7] vantagepointinterviews.com/2019/01/02/godzillas-final-cut-director-ryuhei-kitamura-on-crafting-godzillas-50th-anniversary-film-godzilla-final-wars/
[8] Ibid.
[9] Homenick, "Spinning the Godzilla Saga", *G-Fan* #88 (Summer 2009), pp.44.
[10] In his interview with Brett Homenick, Kitamura himself even admitted that Ebirah was an odd choice and couldn't remember who chose the monster. Kitamura also mentioned a sizeable number of Japanese fans who voiced disappointment at Jet Jaguar not being in the story.
[11] Supposedly Kitamura had carte blanch on this movie, so that doesn't really add up, but the story is out there just the same.
[12] vantagepointinterviews.com/2019/01/02/godzillas-final-cut-director-ryuhei-kitamura-on-crafting-godzillas-50th-anniversary-film-godzilla-final-wars/
[13] Homenick, "Spinning the Godzilla Saga", *G-Fan* #88 (Summer 2009), pp.44.
[14] vantagepointinterviews.com/2019/01/02/godzillas-final-cut-director-ryuhei-kitamura-on-crafting-godzillas-50th-anniversary-film-godzilla-final-wars/

50.
LEGENDARY MONSTERS
GODZILLA

Almost immediately after *Godzilla: Final Wars* tanked in Japan, reports began coming in that Toho still wasn't done with Godzilla yet (one rumor even suggested Toho was entertaining direct-to-video Godzilla films, which would've been the modern-day equivalent of the Champion Matsuri-made 70s movies). Eventually, there came the shocking news that Toho would allow Yoshimitsu Banno, director of 1971's notorious *Godzilla vs. Hedorah*, to make an IMAX 3-D Godzilla movie for America! Though it wouldn't be a feature-length film, technically it would constitute itself as the "next" Godzilla movie. In its own odd way, *Godzilla 3-D to the MAX* was a quasi/ spiritual sequel to *Godzilla vs. Hedorah*. In this feature, Godzilla would awaken from underneath a waterfall in South America when the pollution monster Deathla arrives on the earth. Godzilla then battles the alien monster across the globe, eventually ending up in the U.S. The final battle alternated between New York City and also Las Vegas (depending on the story draft).

The project lingered in development hell for six years. In 2008, Banno's backers, Kerner Productions, approached Legendary Pictures about a potential partnership. What ended up happening instead was that Legendary took over the production completely and turned it into a feature-length reboot. Unlike Tri-Star, Legendary was smart enough to stay true to Godzilla's roots and traditional design. As for Banno, he was allowed to stay on board as an executive producer. The film was announced in 2010, with a projected release date of 2012. Eventually, director Gareth Edwards, who had impressed Legendary with his low-budget film *Monsters* (2010), was hired.

It could possibly be argued that the film's theme, Man vs. Nature, sprang from a lunch meeting between Banno and Edwards. As fans know, Banno was keen on the idea of Godzilla as an ecological defender. Furthermore, Edwards's introduction to Godzilla was through the Hanna-Barbera cartoon (itself inspired by a successful TV broadcast of *Godzilla vs. Megalon* in 1978). Perhaps it is no surprise that throughout the finished film,

Godzilla is nothing but heroic and any damage he causes is only at the expense of trying to kill the bad monsters.

The Man vs. Nature theme wasn't the only thing that Banno worked into Legendary's Godzilla film. The nuclear power plant disaster that opens the film was Banno's idea as a nod to the Fukushima Nuclear Power Plant disaster of 2011.[1] Edwards fully embraced Banno's ideas and ran with them. Edwards told Den of Geek that,

"[Godzilla] really represents nature in the world. And the MUTOs represent our abuse of nature. So Godzilla is here because of our sins and our misuse of the power of nature, and specifically the power of using nuclear weapons. Hopefully, you can watch this film and enjoy it as entertainment, but I personally like science fiction and fantasy when it has a little meaning behind it. So, there was the idea of man versus nature, which was this dominant theme throughout the movie."[2]

Rumors exist stating that King Ghidorah was the initial opponent for this film but was axed by Gareth Edwards himself who didn't want Godzilla fighting an alien monster since it wouldn't match the balance of nature theme. If so, this mirrors the 1994 axed Jan De Bont Godzilla movie, which also began with King Ghidorah as the villain before a new monster was created.

Ironically, this film has quite a few similarities to the aborted 1994 *Godzilla* scripted by Ted Elliot and Terry Rossio. Though Rossio and Elliot obviously get no screenwriting credits for legal reasons, it's not hard to speculate Gareth Edwards and Max Borenstein were aware of, if not secretly inspired by, the Rossio/Elliot script. In fact, this story's original beginning would've found Godzilla (or more specifically, the dead body of a Godzilla) frozen in ice, which is how he's found in the Rossio/Elliot script. *Godzilla: The Art of Destruction* claims the scene was scrapped because of a similar scene in Legendary's *Man of Steel* (2013), but could that merely be a cover story to avoid a potential lawsuit by Rossio/Elliot? Food for thought.

Furthermore, both stories open with an accident in which a member of a family unit is killed and then flash-forwards about 15 years (give or take a few) picking up with a parent and a child. In the case of *Godzilla '94*, it was a mother and daughter. In the new film, it's a father and son. Godzilla also wasn't scripted to get much screen-time in the De Bont film, and he certainly doesn't in the 2014 film either. In the Rossio/Elliot version before the final battle, Godzilla's only scenes scripted were his "birth" coming out of the ice, a brief encounter with a freighter at sea, his arrival in San Francisco, and his battle with the winged Gryphon in New York. While the flying MUTO Godzilla battles in San Francisco certainly isn't the Gryphon, they are similar in that both are weird, winged foes who are original monsters and not traditional Toho creations. The end battle of the De Bont film had Godzilla decapitating the Gryphon and here, he decapitates the female MUTO but doesn't spike its head on any buildings as in the '94 script.

The initial script for Legendary's *Godzilla*, written by David S. Goyer, David Callaham, and Max Borenstein, had quite a few differences from the finished film but follows the same basic story structure. Godzilla was initially set to be a whopping 600 feet high! The male and female MUTOs were differentiated in this script as the Hokmuto (male) and the Femuto (female).

The opening scene where the atomic bomb is detonated was longer and originally showed the U.S.S. Nautilus emerging from the water as a sort of fake out as though it was a monster itself. When we jump to 1999, the remains of the dead Godzilla and the MUTO were to be found in the ice of Krasnokamensk, Siberia until Legendary decided against it due to the similar icy excavation scene in *Man of Steel*. The character of Dr. Vivienne Graham is absent from the scene (and the entire script, actually) and Ishiro Serizawa is simply named Honda. Furthermore, Ford Brody is Ford Maddox in this draft and is an 18-year-old senior in high school in the opening scenes. In this draft, he has no wife, but a 13-year-old sister named Elle.[3] Joe Brody is not their father in this draft but a stepfather named Nathan Brody. Instead of Janjira, the parents work at the Jancorp Nuclear Power Plant in Hokkaido. The MUTO attack on the plant is shorter, and there is no tearful goodbye between Nathan Brody and his wife, here named Linda. After the accident, Nathan takes the fall for the event at work and at home as Ford blames him for his mother's death.

When we jump to the present day, Ford is still a military officer but is working at a Marine Reserves office. Nathan, who lives in an old trailer park in the U.S. rather than Japan, travels to San Francisco to tell Ford about a mysterious signal emanating from Jancorp. Apparently, Ford and Elle (who lives with Ford) don't believe their stepfather and he leaves. The children break into Nathan's mobile home to learn more and apparently become convinced that he is on to something because next, Ford is travelling to Japan. In a scene infamously cut from the final film, a customs official (a cameo for Akira Takarada during shooting) at the airport in Sapporo welcomes Ford to Japan. Ford is set to board a flight to Hokkaido where he can get to the remains of Jancorp, which Nathan explores alone in this script. Nathan discovers the remains of his home and witnesses the Hokmuto chrysalis generate a green energy aura in the sky. In this version, rather than Monarch there is the Special MUTO Unit (headed by a character named Professor Bayer) which is feeding the monster plutonium in an effort to figure out how it achieves cold fusion. When the MUTO hatches, Nathan Brody survives the attack. The monster then burrows underground rather than taking to the air.

Meanwhile, Ford's flight to Hokkaido is rerouted to Honolulu, where he witnesses Godzilla battle the Hokmuto (lacking wings and therefore incapable of flight). Here, Godzilla seemingly vanquishes the insect monster and leaves it for dead.[4] The MUTO Unit then plans on transporting the corpse to a special holding facility. In the aftermath, Ford manages to see to it that Nathan is transferred to a hospital in San Francisco where he will be under Elle's care. As in the finished film, following this we get some exposition aboard the Navy ship about Godzilla's origins and where he got his name. It's basically the same shtick used in Tri-Star's *Godzilla*. The monster is first recognized as Gojira, a creature from a legend on Oto Island, and Admiral Stenz mangles it into "Godzilla."

The female MUTO heads for San Francisco and, upon it and Godzilla's arrival in the city, Nate and Elle reunite. As Godzilla walks past Alcatraz, he is besieged by U.S. military forces who manage to injure him slightly. At the same time on the cargo ship transporting the Hokmuto to America, Honda realizes the big bug isn't dead. It's too late, however, and the creature breaks out of its chrysalis in a new, winged form and flies toward California.

Back in San Francisco Bay, marines transport an intercontinental ballistic missile to Alcatraz while Godzilla slips back into water. Elle takes part in an action scene at this time, as she must drive in reverse on a bridge to escape a falling jet fighter. Ford is part of the group to go on the HALO jump but here, Honda hands Ford a picture of him, Elle, and his mother and father. Honda tells Ford his parents would be proud of him. Meanwhile, Elle and Nathan take shelter inside the Transamerica Pyramid as Godzilla battles the MUTOs outside. When the battle collapses the building, Elle and Nathan take shelter inside a bank vault. Godzilla hits the Hokmuto with his atomic breath and then tears a wing off. The Femuto—who in this draft, has electromagnetic powers which makes Godzilla unable to fire his atomic ray in her presence—joins the fray. The Hokmuto then claps his remaining wings to make a shockwave which stuns Godzilla. Harkening back to *Godzilla vs. Destroyah*, Honda theorizes that Godzilla will "go into meltdown" if the MUTOs cause him to quit firing his ray long enough (a variation of this idea was used in the sequel).

Ford comes along to save Godzilla when he figures out that the Femuto responds to pressure placed on the egg sack that she has laid. Ford grabs a bolt cutter and somehow destroys it. Godzilla then delivers the killing blow to Hokmuto by crushing his skull in his jaws. Godzilla then decapitates the Femuto when he swings his claws across her throat. As Ford watches this, he declares Godzilla "King of the f---ing monsters."

This version would have offered the audience more screen time with Bryan Cranston,[5] who played Joe Brody, the character Nathan became, in the final film. One of the bigger complaints among fans of *Godzilla's* human storyline was the death of Joe Brody so early in the film. This iteration also gave Ken Watanabe's character, again, here called Honda, much more to do as well. For instance, he tells Stenz about what his father witnessed in the aftermath of Hiroshima in great detail.

Though 2014's *Godzilla* was everything that the Tri-Star version wasn't—Godzilla (sort of) retains his classic design, is a badass, and fights other monsters—many fans were still upset with the film. The reason why Edwards got the job was also the reason many fans didn't like the finished film: he emphasized the human characters over that of the monsters as he did in *Monsters* (2010). Truthfully, the two MUTOs get a significant amount of screen time and story focus, while it is Godzilla himself who is rarely glimpsed until the finale. Edwards cited the sparring use of the shark in *Jaws* (1975) as his inspiration, but it really wasn't necessary here. As far as screen time and story function go, the film is really no different from Godzilla's role in *Terror of Mechagodzilla* (1975). In that film, Godzilla pops up twice to battle the enemy monsters—the first match is very brief in both films—and has no real significant scenes outside of the battles.[6]

Overall, Legendary's Godzilla was received much better critically than the Tri-Star *Godzilla*. However, fans began to wonder if the film had been profitable enough for Legendary to produce a sequel. Luckily, *Godzilla* was launched in the aftermath of *Marvel's The Avengers* (2012), which officially made "Cinematic Universes" a thing. This, of course, was nothing new in the land of Godzilla, who had his own rich cinematic universe cemented with the release of *Mothra vs. Godzilla* way back in 1964 (which also came to a head with 1968's *Destroy All Monsters*). It's altogether possible that a sequel to Legendary's *Godzilla* would have never been announced if not for one thing: around the same time Legendary released *Godzilla*, they were beginning negotiations to do a King Kong movie with Universal. Like a lightbulb, it clicked that they could potentially have King Kong battle Godzilla. Therefore, *Kong: Skull Island* was written into the universe of Legendary's *Godzilla* and the "Monsterverse," as it is now called, was born.

Chapter Notes

[1] Before his death, Banno wished to make a Hedorah standalone movie that tied into the Fukushima disaster too.
[2] www.denofgeek.com/us/movies/godzilla/235640/interview-gareth-edwards-on-godzilla
[3] This author wonders if the characters were changed to husband and wife upon the casting of Aaron Taylor Johnson and Elizabeth Olson, who were set to play sibling superheroes in *Avengers: Age of Ultron* the next year.
[4] One has to wonder that if this script had been shot, would Godzilla have received more screen time in this version?
[5] Since this book is all about the creative process, it's worth noting that Cranston improvised many of his scenes and deviated fairly often from the script.
[6] One would be justified in arguing that Godzilla shouldn't have been sidelined in what was essentially a debut film/relaunch though!

APPENDIX I:
SCRIPT DEVELOPMENT DATES

*Scripts, treatments, and story proposals are listed under their developmental titles at the stage that they progressed (if the developmental title is totally unfamiliar to the release title, the latter is sometimes listed in parentheses for reference). For instance, many Showa Gamera films are noted as "Gamera vs. Monster X." This is because Daiei would often have contests to let the public name the monsters therefore in early drafts, the titular enemy monsters are always known as 'X' from *Gamera vs. Gyaos* on. Following the developmental title is the date of the proposal, treatment, or script followed by the writer. Proposed directors are also listed because occasionally they differed from the final choice such as Ishiro Honda on *Son of Godzilla*. In the tradition of Japanese vernacular, projects that didn't reach fruition will be noted as 'NG' for "No Good"—even though some of them were quite spectacular on paper and undeserving of the designation.

"Project G" 1954 (story proposal) by Shigeru Kayama (Toho)

"Project G" 06/1954 (treatment) by Shigeru Kayama **Proposed Director:** Senkichi Taniguchi **Proposed SPFX Director:** Eiji Tsuburaya (Toho)

Godzilla 06/10/1954 (third draft script) unknown/1954 (fourth draft script) by Takeo Murata & Ishiro Honda **Proposed Director:** Ishiro Honda **Proposed SPFX Director:** Eiji Tsuburaya (Toho)

Invisible Man 1954 (story proposal) by Hiroshi Beppu (Toho)

Invisible Man 1954 (first draft script) by Shigeaki Hidaka & Hiroshi Beppu **Proposed Director**: Motoyoshi Oda **Proposed SPFX Director**: Eiji Tsuburaya (Toho)

"Project S"/*Snowman of the Alps* 10/16/1954 (story proposal) by Shigeru Kayama **Proposed Director:** Ishiro Honda **Proposed SPFX Director:** Eiji Tsuburaya (Toho)

Godzilla's Counterattack 1955 (first draft script) by Shigeaki Hidaka & Takeo Murata with Shigeru Kayama **Proposed Director:** Motoyoshi Oda **Proposed SPFX Director**: Eiji Tsuburaya (Toho)

355

Abominable Snowman 1955 (final draft script) by Shigeru Kayama & Takeo Murata **Proposed Director:** Ishiro Honda **Proposed SPFX Director:** Eiji Tsuburaya (Toho)

Bride of Godzilla? 6/17/1955 (third draft script) by Hideo Unagami (Toho) NG

The Alien Appears in Tokyo (Warning from Space) 09/23/1955 (final draft script) by Hideo Ogukuni (based on Gentaro Nakajima's novel *Spiritual Reality*) **Proposed Director:** Koji Shima **Proposed SPFX Director**: Toru Togi (Daiei)

Cosmic Cross Earth Is Targeted! (Fearful Attack of the Flying Saucers) 1956 (screenplay) by Shinichi Sekizawa **Proposed Director:** Shinichi Sekizawa **Proposed SPFX Director:** Shintoho Special Technical Production/Kunko Film Corporation (Shintoho)

The Birth of Rodan 05/22/1956 (story proposal) by Ken Kuronuma (Toho)

Giant Monster of the Sky: Rodan 1956 (script drafts 1-2) 07/16/1956 (third draft script) by Takeshi Kimura & Takeo Murata **Proposed Director:** Ishiro Honda **Proposed SPFX Director:** Eiji Tsuburaya (Toho)

Earth Defense Forces 1957 (story proposal) by Jojiro Okami (Toho)

Earth Defense Forces 1957 (script drafts 1-4) by Takeshi Kimura **Proposed Director:** Ishiro Honda **Proposed SPFX Director:** Eiji Tsuburaya (Toho)

Transparent Human and Fly Man 1957 (first draft script) by Hajime Takasago **Proposed Director:** Mitsuo Murayama **Proposed SPFX Director:** Toru Masabu (Daiei)

Liquid Man Appears 1957 (story proposal) by Hideo Unagami (Toho)

Liquid Human 11/1957 (first draft script) by Takeshi Kimura (Toho)

Beauty and the Liquid People 02/1958 (second draft script) 03/1958 (third draft script) 03/1958 (fourth draft script) by Takeshi Kimura **Proposed Director:** Ishiro Honda **Proposed SPFX Director:** Eiji Tsuburaya (Toho)

Giant Monster Varan: Monster from the Orient 1958 (story proposal) by Ken Kuronuma (Toho)

Giant Monster Varan: Monster from the Orient 06/11/1958 (first draft script) 06/30/1958 (second draft script) by Shinichi Sekizawa **Proposed Director:** Ishiro Honda **Proposed SPFX Director:** Eiji Tsuburaya (Toho)

The Birth of Japan 1959 (script drafts 1-5) by Toshio Hachiju & Ryuzo Kikushima **Proposed Director:** Hiroshi Inagaki **Proposed SPFX Director:** Eiji Tsuburaya (Toho)

Great War of the Universe (Battle in Outer Space) 1959 (script drafts 1-4) by Shinichi Sekizawa **Proposed Director:** Ishiro Honda **Proposed SPFX Director:** Eiji Tsuburaya (Toho)

The Electrically-Transmitted Man (The Secret of the Telegian) 1959 (script drafts 1-2) by Shinichi Sekizawa **Proposed Director:** Ishiro Honda **Proposed SPFX Director:** Eiji Tsuburaya (Toho)

The Electrically-Transmitted Man 12/10/1959 (third draft script) by Shinichi Sekizawa **Proposed Director:** Jun Fukuda **Proposed SPFX Director:** Eiji Tsuburaya (Toho)

Gas Human Being No. 1 06/1959 (story proposal) *Gas Human Being No. 1* 06/14/1960 (second draft script) unknown/1960 (third draft script) by Takeshi Kimura **Proposed Director:** Ishiro Honda **Proposed SPFX Director:** Eiji Tsuburaya (Toho)

The Third World War: 41 Years of Fear 1960 (story proposal) by Shigeaki Hidaka **Proposed SPFX Director:** Shozo Konishi (Toei)

The Third World War: The Last Day of the World 07/29/1960 (first draft script) *The Third World War: Tokyo's Last Day* 08/11/1960 (second draft script) 09/02/1960 (third draft script) by Shinobu Hashimoto & Toshio Yasumi **Proposed SPFX Director:** Eiji Tsuburaya (Toho)

Great Earth Modification (Gorath) 1960 (story proposal) by Jojiro Okami (Toho)

Giant Monster Thing 01/1961 (first draft script) *Giant Monster Mothra* 01/14/1961 (second draft script) 02/05/1961 (third draft script) by Shinichi Sekizawa (based on *Mothra and Her Luminous Fairies* by Shinichiro Nakamura, Takehiko Fukunaga, & Yoshihiro Hotta) **Proposed SPFX Director:** Eiji Tsuburaya (Toho)

World War III (The Last War) unknown/1961 (fourth draft script) by Toshio Yasumi unknown/1961 (fifth draft script) 06/26/1961 (sixth draft script) by Toshio Yasumi & Takeshi Kimura **Proposed Director:** Shue Matsubayashi **Proposed SPFX Director:** Eiji Tsuburaya (Toho)

Great Earth Modification 1961 (first draft script) by Takeshi Kimura & Jojiro Okami ***Giant Star Gorath*** 10/26/1961 (second draft script) unknown/1961 (third draft script) 11/28/1961 (fourth draft script) by Takeshi Kimura **Proposed Director:** Ishiro Honda **Proposed SPFX Director:** Eiji Tsuburaya (Toho)

The Whale God 1962 (final draft script) by Kaneto Shindo (Daiei)

Space Monster (Space Monster Dogora) 1962 (story proposal) by Jojiro Okami

Space Monster 1962 (treatment) by Shinichi Sekizawa **Proposed Director:** Ishiro Honda **Proposed SPFX Director:** Eiji Tsuburaya (Toho)

King Kong vs. Godzilla 03/26/62 (first draft script) unknown/1962 (second draft script) unknown/1962 (third draft script) 04/29/1962 (fourth draft script) by Shinichi Sekizawa **Proposed Director:** Ishiro Honda **Proposed SPFX Director:** Eiji Tsuburaya (Toho)

Frankenstein vs. Gas Human Being No.1 02/20/1963 (first draft script) by Shinichi Sekizawa **Proposed Director:** Ishiro Honda **Proposed SPFX Director:** Eiji Tsuburaya (Toho) NG

Continuation: King Kong vs. Godzilla 1963 (treatment) by Shinichi Sekizawa (Toho) NG

Godzilla vs. Frankenstein 1963 (treatment) by Jerry Sohl (UPA) NG

Matango 1963 (story proposal) by Masami Fukushima (based on William Hope Hodgson's "A Voice in the Night") (Toho)

Matango 05/30/1963 (first draft script) unknown/1963 (script drafts 2-3) by Takeshi Kimura **Proposed Director:** Ishiro Honda **Proposed SPFX Director:** Eiji Tsuburaya (Toho)

Undersea Battleship 08/31/1963 (first draft script) 09/15/1963 (second draft script) unknown/1963 (third draft script) by Shinichi Sekizawa **Proposed Director:** Ishiro Honda **Proposed SPFX Director:** Eiji Tsuburaya (Toho)

Giant Horde Beast Nezura 9/30/1963 (final draft script) by Kimiyuki Hasegawa **Proposed Director:** Mitsuo Murayama **Proposed SPFX Director:** Yonesaburo Tsukiji (Daiei) NG

Mothra vs. Godzilla 12/31/1963 (first draft script) 01/28/1964 (second draft script) 02/10/1964 (third draft script) by Shinichi Sekizawa **Proposed Director:** Ishiro Honda **Proposed SPFX Director:** Eiji Tsuburaya (Toho)

Earth Martial Law 1964 (second draft script) ***Space Monster Dogora*** unknown/1964 (script drafts 3-4) by Shinichi Sekizawa **Proposed Director:** Ishiro Honda **Proposed SPFX Director:** Eiji Tsuburaya (Toho)

Frankenstein vs. Godzilla 07/03/1964 (first draft script) by Kaoru Mabuchi (based on Jerry Sohl's *Frankenstein vs. Godzilla*) (Toho) NG

Three Giant Monsters: The Greatest Battle on Earth 08/27/1964 (first draft script) 09/26/1964 (second draft script) 10/07/1964 (third draft script) by Shinichi Sekizawa **Proposed Director:** Ishiro Honda **Proposed SPFX Director:** Eiji Tsuburaya (Toho)

Frankenstein vs. Underground Monster 03/23/1965 (third draft script) 05/10/1965 (fourth draft script) by Kaoru Mabuchi (adapted from *Frankenstein vs. Godzilla*) **Proposed Director:** Ishiro Honda **Proposed SPFX Director:** Eiji Tsuburaya (Toho)

Giant Fire-Breathing Turtle Attacks Tokyo (treatment) by Niisan Takahashi (Daiei)

Giant Monster Gamera unknown/1965 (script drafts 1-2) by Niisan Takahashi **Proposed Director:** Noriaki Yuasa **Proposed SPFX Director:** Yonesaburo Tsukiji (Daiei)

Great Monster War 07/24/1965 (first draft script) 08/23/1965 (second draft script) 09/30/1965 (third draft script) by Shinichi Sekizawa **Proposed Director:** Ishiro Honda **Proposed SPFX Director:** Eiji Tsuburaya (Toho)

Fourth Interglacial Period 09/07/1965 (first draft script) by Kobo Abe based on his novel **Proposed Director:** Hiromichi Horikawa **Proposed SPFX Director:** Eiji Tsuburaya (Toho) NG

Batman vs. Godzilla 11/1965 (story proposal) ***Godzilla vs. Batman*** unknown/1965 (script drafts 1-2) by Shinichi Sekizawa (Toho) NG

Frankenstein's Sons 1965 (story proposal) by Kaoru Mabuchi (Toho)

Giant Monster Gamera vs. Space Ice Man unknown/1966 by Niisan Takahashi (Daiei) NG

Great Monster Duel: Gamera vs. Barugon unknown/1966 (first draft script-final shooting script) by Niisan Takahashi **Proposed Director:** Shigeo Tanaka **Proposed SPFX Director:** Noriaki Yuasa (Daiei)

Daimajin unknown/1966 (script drafts 1-3) by Tetsuro Yoshida **Proposed Director:** Kimiyoshi Yasuda **Proposed SPFX Director:** Yoshiyuki Kuroda (Daiei)

The Frankenstein Brothers 01/26/1966 (first draft script) 03/22/1966 (second draft script) *Battle of the Frankensteins* 04/29/1966 (third draft script) *Frankenstein's Monsters: Sanda vs. Gaira* 05/1965 (fourth draft script) by Kaoru Mabuchi & Ishiro Honda **Proposed Director:** Ishiro Honda **Proposed SPFX Director:** Eiji Tsuburaya (Toho)

Continuation: Daimajin 1966 (film proposal) by producer Hisashi Okuda (Daiei)

Daimajin Grows Angry 1966 (script drafts 1-2) by Tetsuro Yoshida **Proposed Director:** Kenji Misumi **Proposed SPFX Director:** Yoshiyuki Kuroda (Daiei)

Daimajin Strikes Back 1966 (film proposal) by producer Hisashi Okuda (Daiei)

Daimajin's Counterattack 1966 (script drafts 1-3) by Tetsuro Yoshida **Proposed Director:** Kazuo Mori **Proposed SPFX Director:** Yoshiyuki Kuroda (Daiei)

Giant Monster Assault 05/09/1966 (first draft script) by Ei Ogawa (Toho/UPA) NG

Operation Robinson Crusoe: King Kong vs. Ebirah 07/13/1966 (first draft script) by Shinichi Sekizawa **Proposed Director:** Jun Fukuda **Proposed SPFX Director:** Sadamasa Arikawa (Toho/Rankin-Bass) NG

Godzilla, Ebirah, Mothra: Big Duel in the South Seas 08/09/1966 (second draft script) 08/24/1966 (third draft script) by Shinichi Sekizawa (adapted from *Operation Robinson Crusoe: King Kong vs. Ebirah*) **Proposed Director:** Jun Fukuda **Proposed SPFX Director:** Sadamasa Arikawa (Toho)

Ultraman: Operation Giant 09/27/1966 (first draft script) by Toshihiro Iijima (Tsuburaya Productions) NG

Flying Fighting Battleship 1966 (story proposal) 10/03/1966 (first draft script) by Shinichi Sekizawa **Proposed Director:** Ishiro Honda **Proposed SPFX Director:** Eiji Tsuburaya (Toho) NG

Jiraiya & Orochimaru (Grand Duel in Magic) 1966 (first draft script) by Masaru Igami **Proposed Director:** Tetsuya Yamauchi (Toei)

Giant Monster Gigant 1966 (story proposal) by Hideo Kodama (Nikkatsu) NG

Giant Squid Akitiusu 1966 (story proposal) by Hideo Kodama (Nikkatsu) NG

Magical Monster Momonra 1966 (story proposal) by Hideo Kodama (Nikkatsu) NG

Reigon: Devil of the Seabed 1966 (story proposal) by Hideo Kodama unknown/1966 (first draft script) by Shunichi Yukimuro & Ryuzo Nakanishi (Nikkatsu) NG

Colossal Beast Gappa 07/19/1966 (final draft script) by Iwao Yamazaki & Ryuzo Nakanishi **Proposed Director:** Haruyasu Noguchi **Proposed SPFX Director:** Akira Watanabe (Nikkatsu)

SPFX Space Monster 1966 (story proposal) by Akihiko Shimada & Ryu Mitsuru unknown/1966 (script drafts 1-2) *SPFX Giant Space Monster Guilala* (third draft script) by Kazui Nihonmatsu, Eibi Motoshomi, & Moriyoshi Ishida **Proposed Director:** Kazui Nihonmatsu (Shochiku)

Gamera vs. Vampire 1966 (story proposal) *Gamera vs. Gyaos* 1967 (first draft script) *Giant Monster Mid-Air Battle: Gamera vs. Gyaos* unknown/1967 (final draft) by Niisan Takahashi **Proposed Director:** Noriaki Yuasa (Daiei)

King Kong Escapes 1966 (story proposal) by William J. Keenan & Kaoru Mabuchi *King Kong's Counterattack* 02/04/1967 (first draft script) 03/31/1967 (second draft script) by Kaoru Mabuchi **Proposed Director:** Ishiro Honda **Proposed SPFX Director:** Eiji Tsuburaya (Toho)

Two Godzillas: Japan S.O.S. 1967 (first draft script) by Kazue Shiba *Monster Island Showdown: Godzilla's Son* 08/22/1967 (first draft script) by Shinichi Sekizawa & Kazue Shiba **Proposed Director:** Ishiro Honda **Proposed SPFX Director:** Sadamasa Arikawa (Toho)

Monster Island's Decisive Battle: Son of Godzilla 08/29/1967 (second draft script) by Shinichi Sekizawa & Kazue Shiba **Proposed Director:** Jun Fukuda **Proposed SPFX Director:** Sadamasa Arikawa (Toho)

Monster Total Progress Order (Destroy All Monsters) 11/22/1967 (first draft script) by Kaoru Mabuchi **Proposed Director:** Ishiro Honda **Proposed SPFX Director:** Eiji Tsuburaya & Sadamasa Arikawa (Toho)

Gokemidoro 1967 (script for TV pilot) by unknown (P-Productions) NG

Gokemidoro 1967 (first draft script) by Susumu Takaku Planning (P-Productions/Shochiku)

Gamera vs. Giant Space Monster X 1967-1968 (first draft script) *Gamera vs. Outer Space Monster Viras* unknown/1968 (final draft script) by Niisan Takahashi **Proposed Director:** Noriaki Yuasa (Daiei)

100 Ghost Stories 1968 (first draft script) by Tetsuro Yoshida **Proposed Director:** Kimiyoshi Yasuda (Daiei)

Attack of the Marching Monsters 01/09/1968 (third draft script) by Kaoru Mabuchi & Ishiro Honda **Proposed Director:** Ishiro Honda **Proposed SPFX Director:** Eiji Tsuburaya & Sadamasa Arikawa (Toho)

Vampire Gokemidoro unknown/1968 (final draft script) by Susumu Takaku & Kyuzo Kobayashi **Proposed Director:** Hajime Sato (P-Productions/Shochiku)

Insect Human (Genocide) 1968 (first draft script) ***Great Insect War*** 09/19/1968 (second draft script) by Susumu Takaku **Proposed Director:** Kazui Nihonmatsu **Proposed SPFX Director:** Kenji Kawakami (Shochiku)

Battle Beyond the Stars (The Green Slime) 1968 (first draft script) by Tom Rowe, Charles Sinclair, & William Finger (MGM/Toei)

Great Sea War (Latitude Zero) 1968 (first draft script) by Ted Sherdeman (Toho)

Great Sea War: Latitude Zero May/1968 (second draft script) ***Latitude Zero Campaign*** unknown/1968 (third draft script) 10/25/1968 (fourth draft script) by Ted Sherdeman & Shinichi Sekizawa (based on "Latitude Zero" by Ted Sherdeman) **Proposed Director:** Ishiro Honda **Proposed SPFX Director:** Eiji Tsuburaya (Toho)

Spook Warfare 1968 (script drafts 1-2) by Tetsuro Yoshida **Proposed Director:** Yoshiyuki Kuroda (Daiei)

Star of Adam 12/09/1968 (first draft script) by James Miki **Proposed Director:** Hiki Onika (Toho) NG

Gamera vs. Giant Beast X unknown/1968-1969 (script drafts 1-3) by Niisan Takahashi **Proposed Director:** Noriaki Yuasa (Daiei)

Godzilla • Minilla • Gebara: All Monsters Attack 09/17/1969 (first draft script) ***Godzilla • Minilla • Gabara: All Monsters Attack*** 09/29/1969 (second/final draft script) by Shinichi Sekizawa **Proposed Director:** Ishiro Honda **Proposed SPFX Director:** Eiji Tsuburaya (Toho)

Giant Sea Monster Raid (Space Amoeba) 12/04/1969 (second draft script) by Ei Ogawa **Proposed Director:** Ishiro Honda **Proposed SPFX Director:** Eiji Tsuburaya & Sadamasa Arikawa (Toho)

Myth of Man and Woman 12/10/1969 (second draft script) by James Miki (from *Star of Adam*) **Proposed Director:** Minoru Tokoro **Proposed SPFX Director:** Eiji Tsuburaya (Toho) NG

Gezora, Ganime, Kameba: Decisive Battle! Giant Monsters of the South Seas 12/28/1969 (third draft script) 01/07/1970 (fourth draft script) by Ei Ogawa **Proposed Director:** Ishiro Honda **Proposed SPFX Director:** Sadamasa Arikawa (Toho)

Fear of the Ghost House: Bloodsucking Doll 04/06/1970 (first draft script) 05/04/1970 (second draft script) by Ei Ogawa & Hiroshi Nagano **Proposed Director:** Michio Yamamoto

Gamera vs. Demon Beast X 1969-1970 (script drafts 1-2) by Niisan Takahashi **Proposed Director:** Noriaki Yuasa (Daiei)

Godzilla vs. Hedoron 09/17/1970 (first draft script) by Kaoru Mabuchi & Yoshimitsu Banno **Proposed Director:** Yoshimitsu Banno **Proposed SPFX Director:** Teruyoshi Nakano (Toho)

Phantom Vampire (***Lake of Dracula***) 1970 (first draft script) (Toho)

Godzilla vs. Hedoron 10/21/1970 (second draft script) by Yoshimitsu Banno & Kaoru Mabuchi **Proposed Director:** Yoshimitsu Banno **Proposed SPFX Director:** Teruyoshi Nakano (Toho)

Phantom Vampire 11/21/1970 (second draft script) 12/12/1970 (third draft script) by Ei Ogawa & Masaru Takesue **Proposed Director:** Michio Yamamoto (Toho)

Godzilla vs. Hedoron 12/17/1970 (third draft script) ***Godzilla vs. Hedorah*** unknown/1970-1971 (fourth draft script) by Yoshimitsu Banno & Kaoru Mabuchi **Proposed Director:** Yoshimitsu Banno **Proposed SPFX Director:** Teruyoshi Nakano (Toho)

Cursed House: Bloodsucking Eyes 01/08/1971 (fourth draft script) by Ei Ogawa & Masaru Takesue **Proposed Director:** Michio Yamamoto (Toho)

Earth Crisis: Gamera vs. Deep Sea Monster X 02/10/1971 (story proposal) unknown/1971 (script drafts 1-2) by Niisan Takahashi **Proposed Director:** Noriaki Yuasa (Daiei)

Godzilla vs. the Space Monsters 1971 (first draft script) 09/18/1971 (second draft script) by Kaoru Mabuchi (Toho) NG

King Ghidorah's Counterattack unknown/1971 (first draft script) ***Earth Destruction Directive: Godzilla vs. King Ghidorah*** 08/1971

(second draft script) 10/06/1971 (third draft script) unknown/1971 (fourth/final draft script) by Shinichi Sekizawa **Proposed Director:** Jun Fukuda **Proposed SPFX Director:** Teruyoshi Nakano (Toho)

Gamera vs. Two-Headed Monster W 11/1971 (production announcement) (Daiei) NG

Japan Archipelago Sinks 11/1971 (production announcement) (Daiei) NG

Tsuburaya Productions' Modern Fairy Tale Extravaganza unknown/1972 (first draft script) by Kitao Chiba & Toshihiro Iijima *Tsuburaya Productions' Modern Fairy Tale: Daigoro vs. Goliath* unknown/1972 (script drafts 2-3) by Kitao Chiba **Proposed Director:** Toshihiro Iijima **Proposed SPFX Director:** Jun Oki and Minoru Nakano (Tsuburaya Productions/Toho Eizo)

Godzilla vs. the Megalon Brothers: Undersea Kingdom Annihilation Strategy unknown/1972 (story proposal) by Shinichi Sekizawa *Insect Monster Megalon vs. Godzilla: Undersea Kingdom Annihilation Strategy* 09/05/1972 (second draft script) 09/27/1972 (third draft script) by Jun Fukuda (based on a story pitch by Shinichi Sekizawa) **Proposed Director:** Jun Fukuda **Proposed SPFX Director:** Teruyoshi Nakano (Toho Eizo)

New World Raiders 1973 (story proposal) by Toru Yano (Toho Eizo) NG

Godzilla, Redmoon, Erabus, Halfon: No Man's Land of the Monsters unknown/1973 (first draft script) by Tetsuo Kinjō & Kazuho Mitsuda **Proposed Director:** Shokei Tojo **Proposed SPFX Director:** Kazuo Sagawa (Tsuburaya Productions) NG

Japan Sinks 1973 (script drafts 1-3) 09/05/1973 (fourth draft script) by Shinobu Hashimoto & Sakyo Komatsu **Proposed Director:** Shiro Moritani **Proposed SPFX Director:** Teruyoshi Nakano (Toho Eizo)

Continuation: Sinking of Japan 1974 (story proposal) by Sakyo Komatsu **Proposed Director:** Shiro Moritani **Proposed SPFX Director:** Teruyoshi Nakano (Toho Eizo) NG

Monsters Converge on Okinawa: Showdown in Cape Zanpa! 1973 (story proposal) by Shinichi Sekizawa & Masami Fukushima unknown/1973 (first draft script) by Hiroyasu Yamaura & Jun Fukuda (based on the story proposal by Shinichi Sekizawa & Masami Fukushima) *Showdown in Cape Zanpa: Godzilla vs. Mechagodzilla* unknown/1973 (first draft script) *Godzilla vs. Mechagodzilla* unknown/1973 (script drafts 2-3) by Hiroyasu Yamaura & Jun Fukuda

Proposed Director: Jun Fukuda **Proposed SPFX Director:** Teruyoshi Nakano (Toho Eizo)

Flame Human 01/31/1974 (first draft script) by Makoto Masahiro **Proposed Director:** Jun Fukuda (Toho Eizo) NG

"Godzilla vs. Gezila" (real title unknown) unknown/1975 (story proposal) by Yoshimitsu Banno (Toho) NG

Hedorah's Counterattack unknown/1975 (story proposal) by Yoshimitsu Banno (Toho) NG

Nourishing Blood (Evil of Dracula) 1974 (story proposal) *The Bloodsucking Thorn* unknown/1974 (first draft script) by Ei Ogawa **Proposed Director:** Michio Yamamoto (Toho Eizo) NG

Bloodsucking Rose 02/04/1974 (first draft script) 03/04/1974 (second draft script) by Ei Ogawa & Masaru Takesue **Proposed Director:** Michio Yamamoto (Toho Eizo)

Great Prophecies of Nostradamus 04/15/1974 (first draft script) 04/30/1974 (second draft script) by Yoshimitsu Banno & Toshio Masuda (based on the book by Tsutomu Goto and *The Last War* by Toshio Yasumi) **Proposed Director:** Toshio Masuda **Proposed SPFX Director:** Teruyoshi Nakano (Toho Eizo)

Mechagodzilla's Counterattack 07/01/1974 (first draft script) by Yukiko Takayama (Toho Eizo)

ESPY 08/05/1974 (first draft script) 08/24/1974 (second draft script) 09/05/1974 (third draft script) by Ei Ogawa & Jun Fukuda (based on the works of Sakyo Komatsu) 10/01/1974 (fourth draft script) by Ei Ogawa **Proposed Director:** Jun Fukuda **Proposed SPFX Director:** Teruyoshi Nakano (Toho Eizo)

Mechagodzilla's Counterattack 10/14/1974 (second draft script) 12/05/1974 (third draft script) 12/28/1974 (fourth draft script) by Yukiko Takayama **Proposed Director:** Ishiro Honda **Proposed SPFX Director:** Teruyoshi Nakano (Toho Eizo)

Great Prophecies of Nostradamus II: Fear of the Great Devil 1974 (concept) by Tomoyuki Tanaka unknown/1975 (story proposal) by Masato Ide, Toshio Masuda, & Yoshimitsu Banno **Proposed Director:** Toshio Masuda **Proposed SPFX Director:** Teruyoshi Nakano (Toho Eizo) NG

Transparent Human vs. Flame Human 1975 (first draft script) 05/30/1975 (second draft script) by Masahiro Makoto 10/24/1975 (third draft script) by Jun Fukuda & Masahiro Makoto **Proposed Director:** Jun Fukuda (Toho Eizo) NG

Nessie 1976 (script drafts 1-3) by Christopher Wicking **Proposed Director:** Brian Forbes **Proposed SPFX Director:** Teruyoshi Nakano (Hammer/Toho) NG

Space Monster Devil Manta 1976 (story proposal) by Shotaro Ishimori (first draft script) by Susumu Takaku & Hajime Sato **Proposed Director:** Hajime Sato **Proposed SPFX Director:** Nobuo Yajima (Toei) NG

Birth of the Monster Neston 1976 (first draft script) by Hisao Okawa **Proposed Director:** Masaharu Segawa (Shochiku) NG

House 06/01/1976 (first draft script) **Proposed Director:** Nobuhiko Obayashi (Toho)

Great Monster Bird vs. Great Dragon 1976 (story proposal) by Shigeru Okada (Toei)

Legend of Dinosaurs and Ominous Birds 1976 (first draft script) 08/18/1976 (second draft script) 09/03/1976 (third draft script) by Masaru Igami, Isao Matsumoto, & Ichiro Otsu **Proposed Director:** Junji Kurata **Proposed SPFX Director:** Fuminori Ohashi (Toei)

House 12/10/1976 (second draft script) 01/31/1977 (third draft script) by Chiho Katsura & Nobuhiko Obayashi **Proposed Director:** Nobuhiko Obayashi (Toho Eizo)

Molk: Dictator of 2051 unknown/1977 (story proposal) by Yoshimitsu Banno & Kenichiro Kakuda (from Angus MacVicar's *Frozen Human*) (Toho Eizo) NG

Great Planet War 1977 (story pitch for review) by Hachiro Jinguji (Tomoyuki Tanaka) 09/13/1977 (first draft script) 10/03/1977 (second draft script) 10/12/1977 (third draft script) by Ryuzo Nakanishi & Shuichi Nagahara **Proposed Director:** Jun Fukuda **Proposed SPFX Director:** Teruyoshi Nakano (Toho Eizo)

Great Planetary Fortress 1977 (story proposal) by Shotaro Ishimori (first script draft) by Masaru Ino **Proposed Director:** Hajime Sato (Toei)

Message from Space unknown/1977 (first draft script) by Hiroo Matsuda & Kinji Fukasaku with ideas from Shotaro Ishimori & Masahiro Noda unknown/1978 (second draft script) 02/02/1978 (third draft script) by Hiroo Matsuda & Kinji Fukasaku **Proposed Director:** Kinji Fukasaku **Proposed SPFX Director:** Nobuo Yajima (Toei)

Battle of the Galactic Empire 1978 (story proposal) by Sakyo Komatsu, Yasunaga Toyoda, Tadashi Taka, & Koji Tanaka (Toho/TBC) NG

Martian Army/Mars Corps 1978 (story proposal) by Mitsutoshi Ishigami, Junichi Unno, & Santsushi Ishigami (Toho) NG

UFO Blue Christmas 1978 (first draft script) ***Blue Christmas*** 01/07/1978 (second draft script) 01/07/1978 (third draft script) by So Kuramoto & Kihachi Okamoto (Toho)

King of Monsters: Godzilla Resurrected 06/22/1978 (story proposal) by Ryuzo Nakanishi 10/22/1978 (first draft script) by Ryuzo Nakanishi & Akira Murao **Proposed Director:** Jun Fukuda **Proposed SPFX Director:** Teruyoshi Nakano (Toho) NG

Sayonara Jupiter 1979 (first draft script) by Sakyo Komatsu (unknown)

Earthquake Archipelago 02/24/1980 (third draft script) 03/27/1980 (fourth draft script) 04/14/1980 (fifth draft script) by Kaneto Shindo **Proposed Director:** Kenjiro Omori **Proposed SPFX Director:** Teruyoshi Nakano (Toho)

Godzilla Resurrected 1980 (first draft script) by Akira Murao (from a concept by Ryuzo Nakanishi) (Toho) NG

Sayonara Jupiter unknown (second draft script) 05/19/1982 (third draft script) 11/17/1982 (fourth draft script) 03/08/1983 (fifth draft script) by Sakyo Komatsu **Proposed Director:** Koji Hashimoto **Proposed SPFX Director:** Koichi Kawakita (Toho)

Godzilla Resurrected 02/17/1984 (first draft script) ***Godzilla*** 04/02/1984 (second draft script) 05/30/1984 (third draft script A) 05/31/1984 (third draft script B) 07/16/1984 (fourth draft script A) 07/16/1984 (fourth draft script B) by Shuichi Nagahara **Proposed Director:** Koji Hashimoto **Proposed SPFX Director:** Teruyoshi Nakano (Toho)

Godzilla vs. Biollante 06/10/1985 (story proposal) by Shinichiro Kobayashi (Toho)

Godzilla vs. the Robot Corps 06/1985 (story proposal) by Tatsuo Kobayashi ***Godzilla: Legend of the Asuka Fortress*** 1985 (script drafts 1-3) by Shinichi Sekizawa (Toho) NG

Godzilla vs. Biollante 01/10/1986 (first draft script) 01/30/1986 (second draft script) by Shinichiro Kobayashi (Toho)

Godzilla 2 10/01/1986 (first draft script) unknown/1987 (second draft script) ***Godzilla 2: Godzilla vs. Biollante*** 01/17/1987 (third draft script) 05/10/1988 (fourth draft script) by Kazuki Omori (from Shinichiro Kobayashi's story pitch *Godzilla vs. Biollante*) **Proposed Director:** Kazuki Omori (Toho)

Gunhed unknown (script drafts 1-3) 12/12/1988 (fourth script draft) by Masato Harada & James Bannon **Proposed Director:** Masato Harada **Proposed SPFX Director:** Koichi Kawakita (Toho/Sunrise/Kadokawa/Bandai)

Godzilla vs. Biollante 07/07/1989 (fourth draft script B) 07/24/1989 (final draft script) by Kazuki Omori **Proposed Director:** Kazuki Omori **Proposed SPFX Director:** Koichi Kawakita (Toho)

Mothra vs. Bagan 04/04/1990 (first draft script) by Kazuki Omori **Proposed Director:** Kazuki Omori **Proposed SPFX Director:** Koichi Kawakita (Toho) NG

Godzilla vs. King Kong 1991 (story proposal) by Shinji Nishikawa (Toho) NG

King Ghidorah vs. Godzilla 10/17/1990 (story proposal) by Kazuki Omori (Toho)

Godzilla vs. King Ghidorah 1991 (script drafts 1-2) 05/01/1991(third draft script) by Kazuki Omori **Proposed Director:** Kazuki Omori **Proposed SPFX Director:** Koichi Kawakita (Toho)

King Ghidorah's Counterattack 1991 (concept) by Tomoyuki Tanaka (Toho) NG

Micro Super Battle: Godzilla vs. Gigamoth 11/07/1991 (story proposal) by Koichi Kawakita & Yuji Yoshida (Toho) NG

Godzilla vs. Gigamoth (story proposal) 11/12/1991 by Koichi Kawakita & Yuji Yoshida (Toho) NG

Godzilla's Counterattack 11/12/1991 (story proposal) by Yuji Yoshida (Toho) NG

Godzilla vs. Mechani-Kong: Micro Universe in Godzilla 11/25/1991 (story proposal) by Koichi Kawakita (Toho) NG

Godzilla vs. Mothra 1991 (story proposal) by Wataru Mimura (Toho) NG

Yamato Takeru 1992 (story proposal) by Wataru Mimura (Toho)

Mothra vs. Godzilla 01/15/1992 (first draft script) by Kazuki Omori (adapted from *Mothra vs. Bagan*) (Toho)

Godzilla vs. Mothra 03/10/1993 (first draft script) 04/11/1992 (second draft script) by Kazuki Omori (Toho)

Godzilla vs. Mothra 05/16/1992 (third draft script) by Kazuki Omori **Proposed Director:** Takao Okawara **Proposed SPFX Director:** Koichi Kawakita (Toho)

Yamato Takeru 07/11/1992 (first draft script) by Wataru Mimura (Toho)

Godzilla vs. Berserk 1992 (story proposal) by Yutaka Izubuchi (Toho) NG

Godzilla vs. Mechagodzilla 12/1992 (story proposal) 01/1993 (first draft script) 03/08/19993 (second draft script) 04/08/1993 (third draft script) by Wataru Mimura (Toho)

Godzilla vs. Mechagodzilla 04/12/1993 (final draft script) by Wataru Mimura **Proposed Director:** Takao Okawara **Proposed SPFX Director:** Koichi Kawakita (Toho)

Armageddon: Gamera vs. Phoenix 1993 by Niisan Takahashi (Daiei) NG

Gamera 1993 (first draft script) by Kazunori Ito (Daiei) NG

Yamato Takeru 07/30/1993 (second draft script) by Wataru Mimura (Toho)

Gamera: Giant Monster Mid Air Battle 12/1993 (first draft script) unknown/1994 (second draft script) by Kazunori Ito (Daiei)

Yamato Takeru 01/14/1994 (third draft script) by Wataru Mimura **Proposed Director:** Takao Okawara **Proposed SPFX Director:** Koichi Kawakita (Toho)

Gamera: Giant Monster Mid Air Battle 03/1994 (third draft script) by Kazunori Ito (Daiei)

Gamera, Guardian of the Universe unknown/1994 (fourth draft script) by Kazunori Ito **Proposed Director:** Shusuke Kaneko **Proposed SPFX Director:** Shinji Higuchi (Daiei)

Godzilla vs. Astrogodzilla 03/10/1994 (story proposal) by Kanji Kashiwa (Toho)

Godzilla: Super Wars unknown/1994 (treatment) by Shogo Tomiyama (Toho)

Godzilla vs. Space Godzilla unknown (script drafts 1-2) 06/27/1994 (third draft script) by Hiroshi Kashiwabara **Proposed Director:** Kensho Yamashita **Proposed SPFX Director:** Koichi Kawakita (Toho)

Giant Space Monster Guilala 1995 (first draft script) by Moriichi Ichikawa & Kazuyuki Izutsu (Shochiku) NG

Godzilla 7 01/25/1995 (story proposal) by Shogo Tomiyama (Toho)

Godzilla vs. Destroyer 03/04/1995 (first draft script) 05/27/1995 (second draft script) by Kazuki Omori (Toho)

Godzilla vs. Destroyer 06/30/1995 (final draft script) by Kazuki Omori **Proposed Director:** Takao Okawara **Proposed SPFX Director:** Koichi Kawakita (Toho)

Gamera 2: The Real Guardian of the Universe 1995 (script drafts 1-3) *Gamera 2: Advent of Legion* 10/19/1995 (fourth draft script) by Kazunori Ito **Proposed Director:** Shusuke Kaneko **Proposed SPFX Director:** Shinji Higuchi (Daiei)

Mothra unknown (story proposal) by Tomoyuki Tanaka (Toho)

Mothra 02/23/1996 (second draft script) by Masumi Suetani (Toho)

Mothra 04/20/1996 (third/final draft script) by Masumi Suetani **Proposed Director:** Okihiro Yoneda **Proposed SPFX Director:** Koichi Kawakita (Toho)

Mothra 2 03/24/1997 (first draft script) *Mothra 2: Undersea Battle* unknown/1997 (second draft script) 06/11/1997 (third draft script) by Masumi Suetani (from a story concept by Tomoyuki Tanaka) **Proposed Director:** Kunio Miyoshi **Proposed SPFX Director:** Koichi Kawakita (Toho)

Mothra 3 1998 (first draft script) by Masumi Suetani (from a story concept by Tomoyuki Tanaka) (Toho)

Japan Sinking 1999 1998 (first draft script) by Kazuki Omori (based on the book by Sakyo Komatsu) (Shochiku) NG

Gamera 1999 02/10/1998 (first draft script) by Kazunori Ito (Daiei)

Mothra 3: King Ghidorah Attacks 03/31/1998 (second draft script) by Masumi Suetani (Toho)

Gamera 1999 04/27/1998 (second draft script) by Kazunori Ito (Daiei)

Mothra 3: King Ghidorah Attacks 04/30/1998 (third/final draft script) by Masumi Suetani **Proposed Director:** Okihiro Yoneda **Proposed SPFX Director:** Kenji Suzuki (Toho)

Gamera 1999 05/11/1998 (third draft script) 05/25/ 1998 (fourth/final draft script) by Kazunori Ito & Shusuke Kaneko **Proposed Director:** Shusuke Kaneko **Proposed SPFX Director:** Shinji Higuchi (Daiei)

G 12/25/1998 (first draft script) *Godzilla 2000* 03/29/1999 (second draft script) by Hiroshi Kashiwabara & Wataru Mimura (Toho)

Godzilla 2000: Millennium 05/06/1999 (third/final draft script) by Hiroshi Kashiwabara & Wataru Mimura **Proposed Director:** Takao Okawara **Proposed SPFX Director:** Kenji Suzuki (Toho)

G 2001 03/02/2000 (second draft script) by Hiroshi Kashiwabara & Wataru Mimura (Toho)

Godzilla vs. Megaguirus: G Eradication Strategy 04/07/2000 (third draft script) by Hiroshi Kashiwabara & Wataru Mimura **Proposed Director:** Masaaki Tezuka **Proposed SPFX Director:** Kenji Suzuki (Toho)

Godzilla vs. Mechagodzilla 11/26/2000 (story proposal) by Masahiro Yokotani (Toho)

Godzilla vs. Varan, Baragon, Anguirus: All Monster Attack Godzilla 07/28/2000 (story proposal) by Shusuke Kaneko (Toho)

Godzilla vs. Varan, Baragon, Anguirus: Giant Monsters Attack 11/30/2000 (first draft script) by Keiichi Hasegawa, Masahiro Yokotani & Shusuke Kaneko **Proposed Director:** Shusuke Kaneko (Toho)

Godzilla vs. Mothra, Baragon, King Ghidorah: Giant Monsters All-Out Attack 01/19/2001 (second draft script) *Godzilla, Mothra, King Ghidorah: Giant Monsters All-Out Attack* 02/09/2001 (third draft script) 03/03/2001 (fourth draft script) 04/20/2001 (fifth/final draft script) by Keiichi Hasegawa, Masahiro Yokotani, & Shusuke Kaneko **Proposed Director:** Shusuke Kaneko **Proposed SPFX Director:** Makoto Kamiya (Toho)

Godzilla vs. Mechagodzilla 12/25/01 (first draft script) 03/12/2002 (second draft script) 04/19/2002 (third draft script) 05/13/2002 (fourth draft script) by Wataru Mimura **Proposed Director:** Masaaki Tezuka **Proposed SPFX Director:** Yuichi Kikuchi (Toho)

Godzilla, Mothra, Mechagodzilla 12/10/2002 (first draft script) 03/20/2003 (second draft script) *Godzilla vs. Mothra vs. Mechagodzilla: Tokyo S.O.S.* 05/12/2003 (third/final draft script) by Masahiro Yokotani & Masaaki Tezuka **Proposed Director:** Masaaki Tezuka **Proposed SPFX Director:** Eiichi Asada (Toho)

GODZILLA 50th Godzilla: FINAL WARS 3/31/2004 (story proposal) by Wataru Mimura & Isao Kiriyama (Toho)

Godzilla: Final Wars unknown/2004 (final draft script) by Wataru Mimura & Isao Kiriyama **Proposed Director:** Ryuhei Kitamura **Proposed SPFX Director:** Eiichi Asada (Toho)

Little Braves: Gamera 2005 (first draft script) by Yukari Tatsuri **Proposed Director:** Ryuta Tazaki (Kadokawa)

Guilala's Counterattack: Lake Toyo Summit Crisis 2008 (final draft script) by Masakazu Migita **Proposed Director:** Minoru Kawasaki (Shochiku)

APPENDIX II:
PROJECT HIERARCHY

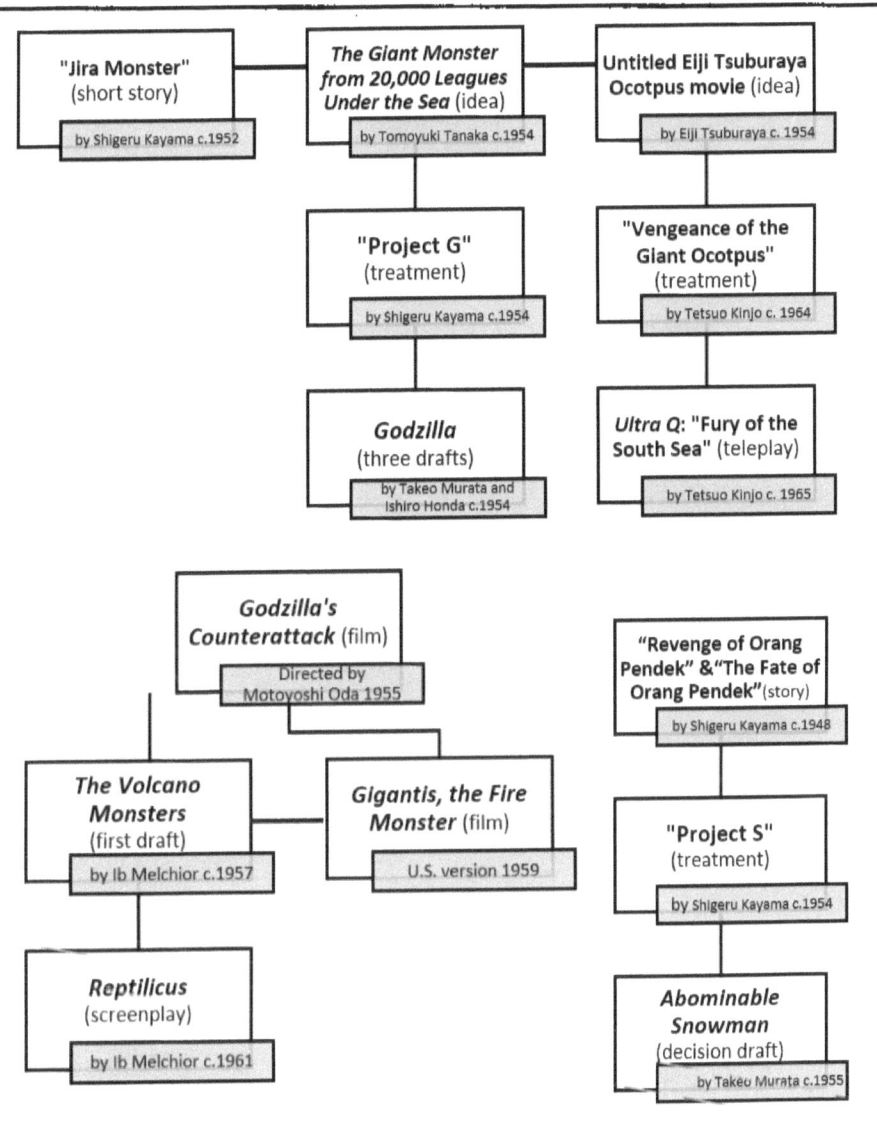

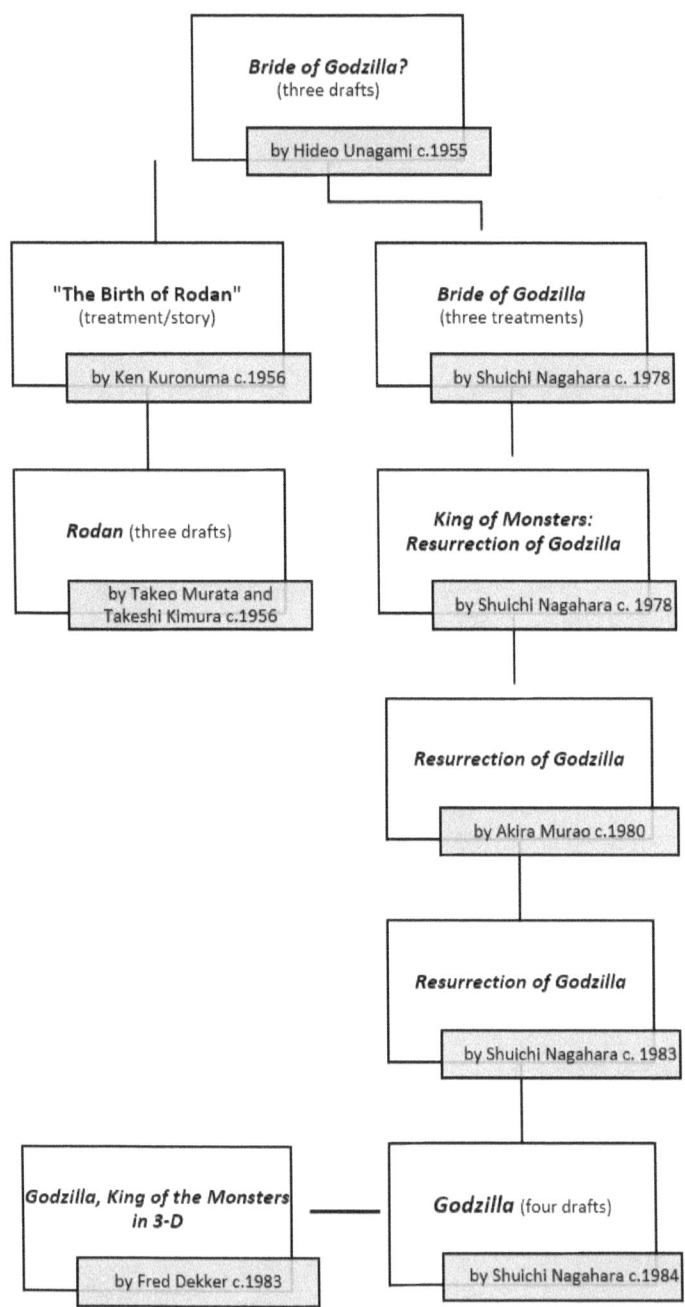

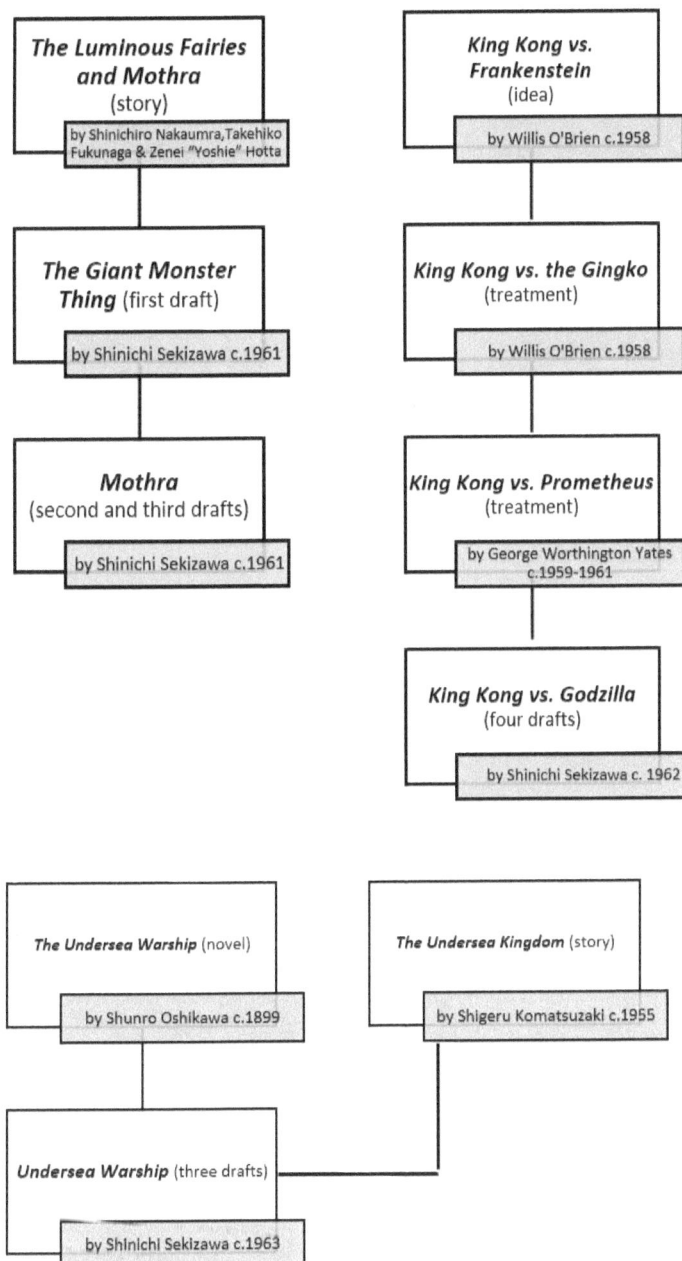

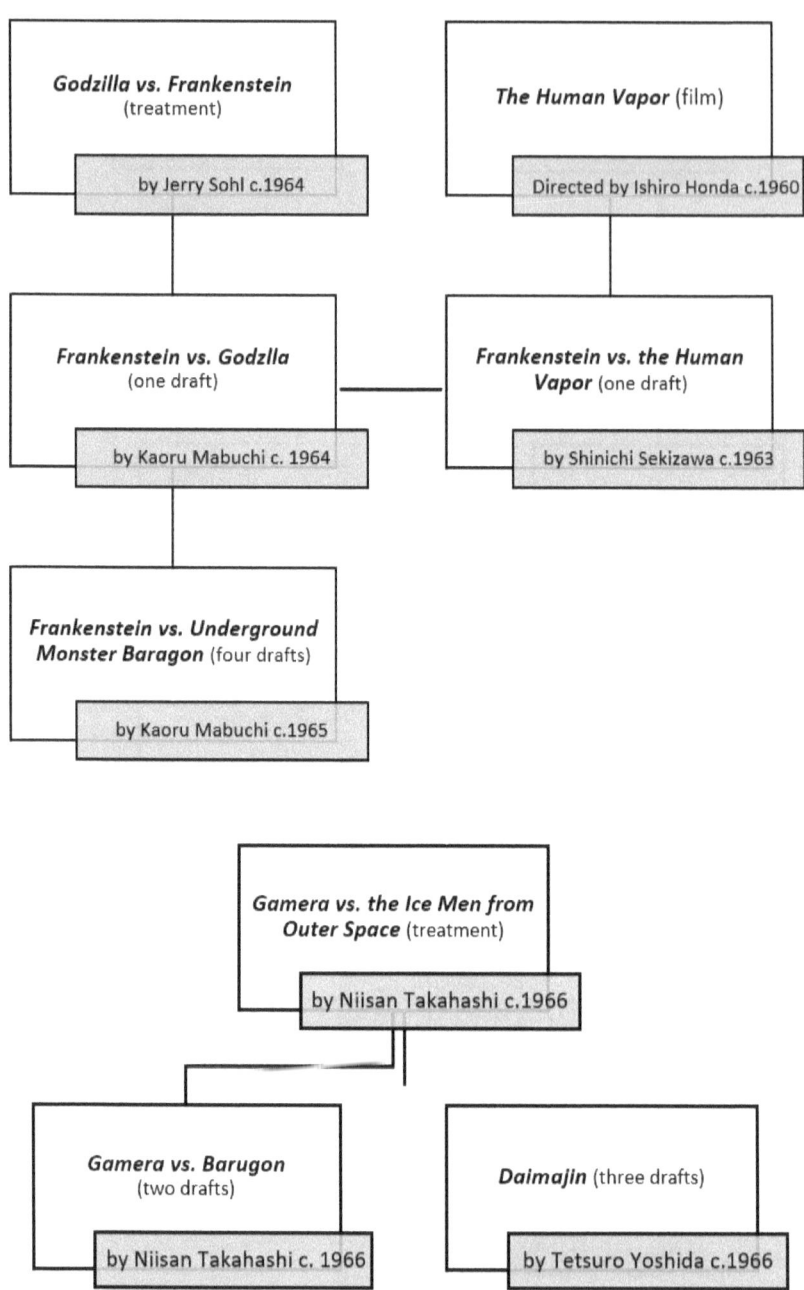

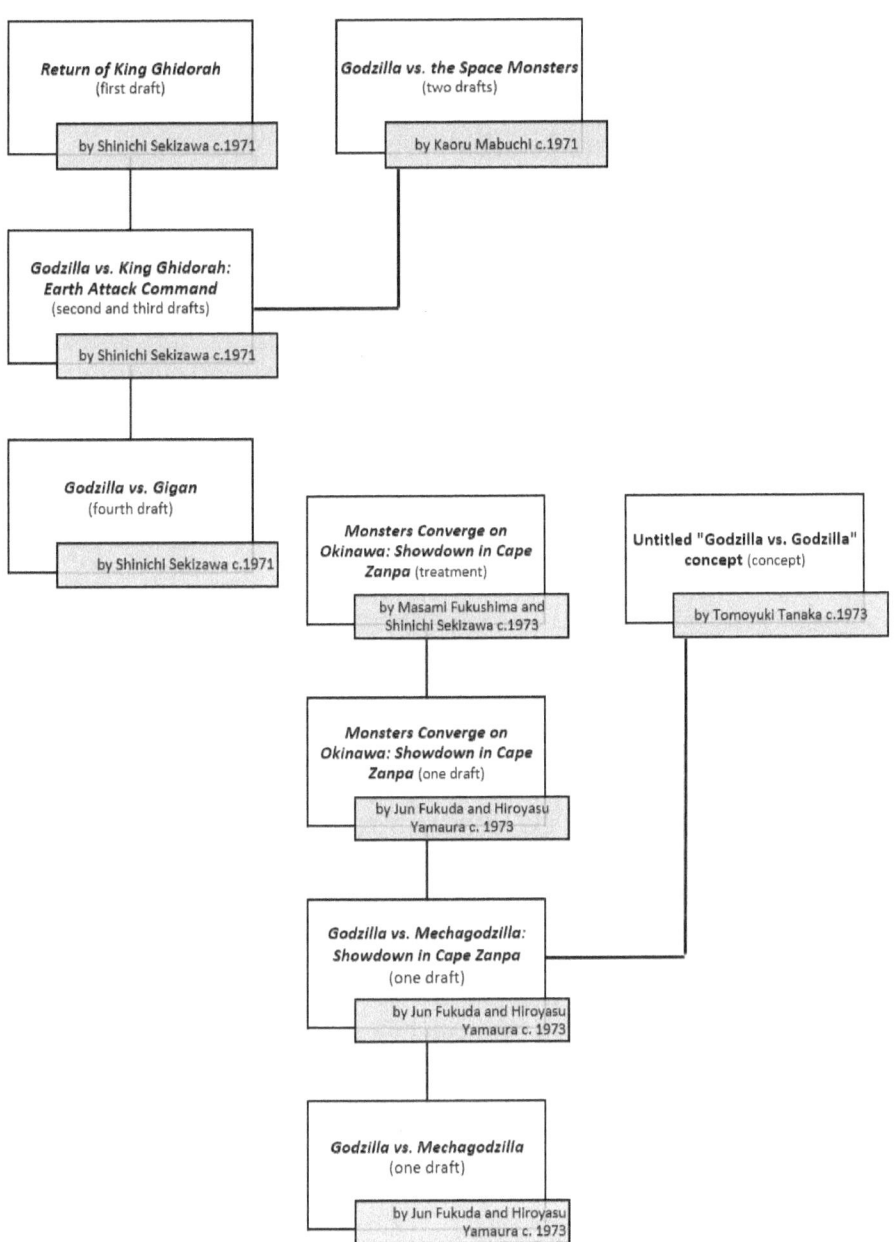

APPENDIX III:
TOHO MANGA ADAPTATIONS

Every so often, the manga adaptation of a kaiju movie uses a few discarded ideas from the script. In fact, some mangas are even based on early scripts. Listed below are notable differences between films and their manga adaptations. I should also note that this Appendix is not exhaustive and comprises only of mangas that I have seen myself. For instance, I have never seen the manga adaptation of *Godzilla vs. Destroyah* (1995), which is why it is absent.

GODZILLA Believe it or not, *Godzilla*'s first manga adaptation happened concurrently with his first film in October of 1954, published in *Omoshiro Book*. The adaptation was by Wasuke Abe and called "Science Adventure Picture Story Godzilla." Abe helped design Godzilla, though his manga version presents Godzilla as a straight dinosaur and lacks the monster's signature dorsal plates. It follows the film closely and also includes a few deleted scenes either shot for the film or planned for the film that didn't make the final cut.

Abe's story features a scene where Emiko mistakes Godzilla for some boulders in the ocean until they begin to move. A similar scene was shot for the film where Ogata and Emiko mistake Godzilla's tail for a boulder in the surf. Emiko is a child in this version of the story so there is no love triangle between her, Ogata, and Serizawa (the latter two are old school friends here, by the way). Oto Island orphan Shinkichi has a more prominent role (which was also the case in one of Shigeru Kayama's early treatments). Shinkichi is elementary school-aged learning to be a fisherman. He is also on one of the vessels Godzilla sinks and has a deep-seated hatred for the monster throughout the story. The manga ends utilizing another deleted scene depicted in storyboards: Serizawa using his flashlight to lure Godzilla to him underwater.

Obviously, without the love triangle, the manga versions lacks some punch when it comes to Serizawa's death. The fact that Godzilla is more or less just a giant, fire-breathing dinosaur here also lessens interest a bit. Overall, there's really no improvements that the manga makes over the film aside from the slightly more suspenseful climax where Godzilla must be lured to the Oxygen Destroyer.

MONSTER PICTURE STORY: GODZILLA This manga adaptation of *Godzilla* comes directly from Shigeru Kayama and follows the film fairly well except for one major detail. This iteration of the story is told through the eyes of Hagiwara, the journalist who plays only a minor role in the film. Here, he is also the older brother of Shinkichi, the orphaned Oto Island boy from the film that is adopted by the Yamanes. In this version, it would appear that the Yamane's are just babysitting Shinkichi for Hagiwara. Furthermore, there is no Emiko Yamane, but instead, a younger Yamane daughter named Fumiko.

Hagiwara goes to Yamane after the ships are lost at sea and asks him if a monster could be the culprit. Yamane identifies a prehistoric creature called a *pleurotomaria* as a candidate. Fumiko, Dr. Yamane, Shinichi, and Hagiwara go to Oto Island to investigate. There, Fumiko sees Godzilla emerge from a volcanic crater and when Yamane snaps a picture of the beast, it fires its atomic ray.

Returning to the mainland, Yamane reveals to the public that Godzilla soaks in the hot volcanic waters of Oto Island in between sinking ships. Godzilla comes to Japan, where he briefly battles the self-defense forces at sea, then disappears before emerging off Shinagawa. For some reason, Hagiwara is the one who devises a way to defend Japan from the monster by means of electrical high tension towers. A military man also mentions Dr. Serizawa and his deadly weapon the Oxygento.

The story climaxes with Hagiwara sacrificing himself to detonate some dynamite in the sewers below Godzilla when he marches on Tokyo. This drives Godzilla back into the sea, where Serizawa also sacrifices himself by using the Oxygento. Notably, Shinkichi accompanies Serizawa to the seafloor but does not perish. A deleted scene planned to be shot is also in the manga where a wreath is dropped in Tokyo Bay in honor of Serizawa.

GODZILLA RAIDS AGAIN In this version, Tsukioka flies a radically different plane more in line with a military bomber to find Kobayashi. As in storyboards for the film, Godzilla spies on the two men before they see the beast themselves. Also as in the storyboards, Godzilla reaches for the two men before he begins fighting Anguirus. Later in the story, Godzilla destroys a lighthouse. Again, in keeping with storyboards, the battle between Godzilla and Anguirus begins in the waters of Osaka Bay. Godzilla's foot dramatically destroys a tank too—so this panel all but confirms that this manga used the storyboards as its influence. Anguirus even breathes fire himself to roast a tank.

MOTHRA The manga for *Mothra* comes in two parts. The first deviation in Part I shows the survivors of the shipwreck climbing the ladder of a helicopter to get off the island. In the film, we simply see a helicopter fly over the island and we never do see just how the survivors are rescued. The manga's next big difference is that it makes Shinji Chujo, Professor Chujo's kid brother, more of a main character, if not the main character. In fact, the film version's two leads, Senichiro and Michi, are introduced to Professor Chujo by way of Shinji in this version. As for Clark Nelson, he is even more villainous here, wearing some sort of hypnotic jewel embedded in his necktie! In one scene, he uses it to distract a man while his henchman knocks him over the head. To top it off, the man's chair was on top of a trick hatch that drops the poor man to his doom! Why, this author doesn't know since he can't read Japanese, but it looks as though a business deal between the man and Nelson didn't go as planned.
   During the Infant Island scenes, Chujo is saved from the grasp of the vampire plant by a much more aggressive version of the Shobijin who karate chop their way through its vines! They prove much more difficult for Nelson to capture and one panel shows them taking long leaps and bounds to evade him. As this happens, Senichiro and other sympathetic members of the expedition try to fight Nelson. To condense the story, in this version, Nelson does manage to steal the Shobijin on this trip by catching them in a cage (in the film, he has to capture them on a second, secret visit). The islanders, who look like cavemen (some have beards, while in the film none do), run off the expedition and then go to the temple where Mothra's egg rests atop a large pillar. The egg hatches, Mothra sets out to sea, and Part I of the manga ends.
   Part II of the manga begins with Mothra (who has luminescent eyes here) swimming into a ship at sea and later, a lighthouse. Around the same time, Shinji sneaks in to rescue the Shobijin but is blinded by Nelson's strange trick necktie. Shinji is then forced at gunpoint to walk out onto a pier (to jump into the water) by Nelson's goons when Mothra suddenly emerges. Shinji is saved and the larva eats one of the goons! As Mothra tears through

Tokyo, Nelson chases after Shinji in a helicopter and scoops him up. This all ties into a revised version of the *Mothra* script which at one point had Nelson kidnapping Shinji during the ending. Elsewhere, Mothra has spun her cocoon and survived the heat ray attack, bursting out of her chrysalis accompanied by a bright ray of light. In keeping with *Mothra's* revised ending set in the Japanese Alps, the manga has Nelson's helicopter land there with Shinji and the Shobijin as hostages. When one of the goons trips, Shinji grabs his gun and manages to hold the men at gunpoint and get back the fairies. Shinji runs off with them and is met by the police, who somehow found him in the mountains. However, Mothra shows up causing enough confusion to allow Nelson to grab the Shobijin again and abscond with them in a nearby truck. Mothra chases the truck and causes it to careen off a cliff. The truck crashes, Nelson dies, and the unharmed Shobijin levitate into the air and fly back to Mothra. Mothra then flies off as the main characters wave goodbye.

Overall, the Shobijin are the most interesting departure in the manga with their more proactive nature and advanced powers, namely that of great strength (despite their small size) and flight. Toho may have wanted the fairies to fly in the 1961 film but it may have been too tricky to pull off. The fairies did take flight at the end of 1992's *Godzilla vs. Mothra* and before that, they appeared to fly in *Ghidorah, the Three-Headed Monster* (1964) when they appear on a television program. Mothra's bright eyes and other luminescent qualities were also rather interesting and one has to wonder if those were attributes that were hoped to be brought to life on film. Also, the Japanese Alps ending suits the manga version better as it is slightly more engaging from a character perspective even though the destruction of New Kirk City suits the film version better.

MOTHRA VS. GODZILLA This manga adaptation for *Mothra vs. Godzilla* seems to have a comical slant to it. This is first evident upon the portrayal of Professor Murai as a portly, balding man who tries various Looney Tunes-like methods to crack open Mothra's egg. When Godzilla is attacked by the Artificial Lightning System, the towers look much more futuristic and are similar to the heat rays from the original *Mothra* (1961). When Godzilla arrives at Happy Enterprises, he plucks the Kumayama character out of a window. That would have been a great visual for the film! In this version, the egg hatches immediately after the adult Mothra dies and the battle with the twin larvae takes place right there on the spot as a way of speeding up the action. Otherwise, there are no other noteworthy additions to discuss.

GHIDORAH, THE THREE-HEADED MONSTER All that's known of this manga is that Godzilla defeats Ghidorah by ripping out his middle head, so the monster ends the manga as "Ghidorah the Two-Headed Monster."

FRANKENSTEIN VS. BARAGON As *Frankenstein vs. Baragon* always had a rather complicated backstory, perhaps it should come as no surprise that it was condensed for its manga version. Similar to the film, the manga begins with the heart in a box being delivered to the Japanese by the Nazis. After we see the mushroom cloud over Hiroshima, we jump straight to Dr. Bowen (an older version with a beard) tending to Frankenstein—the introduction of the mysterious boy, his growth rate, etc. are done away with to jump straight to the giant Frankenstein who Bowen somehow found. The monster becomes agitated when a spectator throws a bottle at his head prompting the monster's angry escape—though he doesn't lose a hand. Soon after Baragon emerges from a lake within a forest. He attacks some campers and roasts them rather graphically when they try to flee. As in the film, Frankenstein is blamed and the military sets out to look for him. In the forest, Bowen stands before the military and claims Frankenstein would do no such thing. At that moment, Baragon bursts from the ground to grab Bowen (Sueko isn't even in the story, by the way). Frankenstein himself then emerges from nowhere to save the doctor. The two monsters fight (this more caveman-like version of Frankenstein even has a club) and the battle causes an earthquake that swallows both into the ground. Bowen says that Frankenstein is immortal and will likely emerge again one day.

SON OF GODZILLA The *Son of Godzilla* manga opens with a shot of flying fish leaping out of the water in front of Sollgel Island. From there, it goes to the scene from the film where Morio and Furukawa investigate one of the weather control towers and hearing a strange noise they can't explain. From there, it cuts to an odd variation of first scene in the film: Godzilla's reveal at sea. Here, it's an ocean liner instead of an airplane. The captain and first mate look below at something under the surface. As the ship sails away, Godzilla surfaces behind it but doesn't give chase. He then begins heading in the direction of Sollgel Island.

From there, events are basically the same: Goro arrives, the test occurs, and the baby Godzilla hatches. The deviations begin when Furukawa goes berserk and wants to leave the island. While in the film, he was crazy enough to run into the ocean as though he was going to swim home, here he steals a speedboat. The boat runs headfirst into Godzilla, dumping Furukawa into the ocean. The man swims back to the island in fear as Godzilla comes ashore. Again events play out the same, only Godzilla actually climbs a rock wall (in a very lizard-like fashion) to get to Minilla. Surprisingly, the fire-breathing lesson goes on for about three pages in the manga and is more detailed than the one in the movie! Godzilla is also meaner, knocking Minilla in the head with his fist and even blasting his tail with his atomic ray!

The manga has an additional scene where Minilla comes across the scientific team members, who point their rifles at him until Saeko convinces them that he's friendly. There is no jungle fever sequence, and Kumonga seems to just randomly appear to attack the expedition. Minilla tries to defend the humans, but he is captured in Kumonga's web. The expedition tries to help Minilla by shooting Kumonga with machine guns. Godzilla shows up and the choreography for the end battle is better in the manga than it is in the film. For instance, Godzilla begins the fight by bashing Kumonga over the head with his tail. This is followed by a beautiful panel of Godzilla keeping Kumonga from biting him by grabbing the spider's two front legs.

The story's final moments deviate from the film. After Godzilla kills Kumonga, it appears that Furukawa needlessly detonates the freezing device (in the film, this is done as a way of keeping the monsters at bay). Goro then pounces on top of Furukawa in retaliation. It would seem he and Saeko are angry at Furukawa for needlessly freezing Godzilla and his son on the island and Saeko's final appearance has her crying. The very final panel doesn't feature Godzilla and his son covered in snow but has them simply watching the rescue ship sail away as the snow falls around them.

ALL MONSTERS ATTACK The *All Monsters Attack* manga opens with a beautiful shot of all the monsters on Monster Island: Godzilla, Minilla (on Godzilla's shoulders), Rodan (absent from the film), Gorosaurus, Anguirus, Manda, Mothra larva (absent from the film), Kumonga, Ebirah, Kamacuras, and Baragon (absent from the film). A group of children—including Ichiro and a burlier version of bully Sanko/Gabara—fly over the island in a helicopter as part of a tour like in *Jurassic World*. Below, they watch Godzilla fry Ebirah. In the chopper, Sanko says he has heard of a new monster that is even more powerful than Godzilla. He is referring to Gabara the monster, which he mentions is a mutated toad—a detail the film neglects to reveal even though that is Gabara's official backstory. Gabara appears and then begins to trounce on Minilla. As the action amps up, Ichiro wakes up. He was daydreaming in class and now he is being scolded by his teacher.

As Ichiro walks home from school with a female friend, he is accosted by Sanko (without his gang, who never appear at all). The confrontation is a bit rougher than what appears in the film with the bully slapping both Ichiro and his female friend! Upon arriving back at his apartment building, Ichiro goes to see Minami. Interestingly, the character is portrayed as a young man in his twenties or thirties as opposed to the older portrayal by actor Hideyo Amamoto. Ichiro also refers to Minami as "Old man Kamacuras" here. This is interesting as Ichiro is more or less a stand-in for Minilla, Gabara is the name of the bully and the monster, and now Minami is for some reason likened to Kamacuras!

The Monster Island dream scenes present the thing fans wish they could have seen in the movie such as Manda coiling around Gorosaurus as Kumonga squares off against Kamacuras. In the manga, Ichiro is not a fan of Minilla and is repulsed by the fact Sanko compares him to Minilla in the real world. When Minilla (always giant sized in the manga, by the way) saves Ichiro, the boy is at first terrified that the young monster will eat him. Eventually, the two become friends and begin to speak (because Ichiro is a monster otaku he understands monster talk, according to the manga). In what would have made a great scene in the movie, Gabara the monster shows up with Gabara the bully riding on top of his head! Both Gabaras taunt Minilla and Ichiro, who both run away only to run into Godzilla. At this point, Ichiro is woken up by a knock on his door. It turns out to be the two robbers, posing as men interested in buying Minami's car. Ichiro later follows the two men to their abandoned warehouse hideout and is accidentally spotted by them. Ichiro runs back home and falls asleep, heralding the next dream scene.

While the film had mostly all stock footage battles, the manga creates brand new battles for the reader. Godzilla battles Gorosaurus and considering the Gorosaurus suit was in relatively good condition in 1969, this author thinks a fight between the two was a very real possibility. In any case, Kumonga joins in on the fight against Godzilla and Minilla jumps in to help his father blowing smoke rings at the giant spider. Godzilla roasts Kumonga with his ray and then tosses Gorosaurus onto the flaming spider. New footage of Kumonga was planned to be shot for the film so perhaps the manga battle really does present an idea originally scripted. Anyhow, the two Gabaras show up again and the monster blasts Minilla with an electric ray from his fingertips. Much like Gigan's laser beam featured in publicity photos and several mangas, Gabara's electric fingertip ray was also featured in publicity photos. This implies that Gabara was meant to show this ability on film as well before it was scrapped.

The next scene shows a disappointed Godzilla giving his son a lesson in fire breathing after his defeat at the hands of Gabara. As in the film, a plant monster awakens Ichiro, which turns out to be the bank robbers in real life. They stuff Ichiro into the back of Minami's car and take off. In the backseat, Ichiro falls asleep again! In his dream, he witnesses Minilla battle Gabara and the choreography is basically the same as the film's. Though Minilla basically wins the fight, Godzilla lands the last blow to Gabara, who it should be noted is a bit smaller than Godzilla here. Ichiro wakes up inspired by Minilla's victory and decides to take proactive measures against the robbers. Though the film's depiction of these events are fun in their own *Home Alone*-like way, the manga is a bit more ambitious. In the speeding car, Ichiro opens up the briefcase full of money, causing it to go flying out the window. This causes the robbers to stop the car, giving Ichiro a chance to flee. As in the film, Ichiro's maneuvers against the robbers are accompanied by flashbacks to Minilla's battle with Gabara.

The epilogue of the manga is truncated compared to the film. We don't see Ichiro's parents, there's no incident with the sign painter's bicycle, etc. Instead Ichiro has a one-on-one showdown with Sanko and knocks him out with one punch. Ichiro's girlfriend kisses him and the two run off into the city of Kawasaki together.

Other than the new monster battles, the main benefit that the manga has over the finished film is that Sanko the bully occasionally shows up in Ichiro's nightmares. Nicholas Driscoll summed up the situation best in his review of the manga on Toho Kingdom, in which he states:

> By bringing Gabara the bully to the dream world, and having him deliberately look for (and ultimately befriend and actually ride upon!) the monster Gabara, the manga sets up an even more obvious dynamic in which Gabara IS the

monster, and in which the monster defeated in the dream equates to the bully being overcome in real life as well.
[www.tohokingdom.com/comics/all_monsters_attack_kodansha17.html]

SPACE AMOEBA Like the film's opening credits, the manga for *Space Amoeba* begins with the monsters battling each other. The story progresses as normal, but the plans that we see for the island resort are rather futuristic. A bullet train system and also what appear to be flying saucers supported by wires can be seen. Visually speaking, this was the only difference the author could spot and the 54-page manga appears to be remarkably faithful to the film.

GODZILLA VS. HEDORAH The opening for the manga is rather intriguing and one has to wonder if such a scene was ever in one of the various script drafts of the script. The first scene has a policeman find what he thinks to be a drunk passed out under a statue in a park. The policeman helps the man up and begins to walk him elsewhere. As this happens, the man begins to decompose until nothing but bones remain. Soon afterward, the policeman notices that smokestacks are beginning to rapidly decay and collapse. Had this occurred in the movie, it could have made for an amazing pre-credits scene.

Following that, there are various glimpses of a polluted Japan. This is followed by Ken Yano's poem about how Godzilla hates pollution. In his first scene, we see Ken with a Godzilla action figure which the boy talks to as though it's the real Godzilla. The manga here features something only hinted at in the film: Ken has a psychic connection with Godzilla. As Ken holds the doll in the air, he tells it that he can feel Godzilla's own feelings. And as the manga progresses, this is expounded upon.

The next scene, set at the Yano dinner table, is similar to the film as the family watches the first news report of Hedorah. It differs when Ken tells his father that he has a smaller version of the creature, which he found swimming in the ocean, in a tank in his room. This prompts Dr. Yano and Ken to go to the docks, where they see multiple tadpoles of large size swimming below. In an interesting visual, they watch the tadpoles swim towards the horizon where they form the giant Hedorah. The monster surfaces next to a group of men at the pier, startling them before it jumps out of the water and immediately morphs into its flying form— something that didn't happen until much later in the film. Hedorah goes on a rampage, causing graphic death just as he does in the film (even the infamous scene of the construction worker decomposing before he can hit the ground is present).

Dr. Yano prompts Ken to run but his son claims there is no need because Godzilla is coming to fight the monster. Yano pulls him along until Ken trips on a rock, accidentally throwing his Godzilla toy into the air in the process... as the real Godzilla appears. Godzilla battles Hedorah in various methods seen in the finished film except that it is during the first manga battle here that Hedorah blinds Godzilla in one eye rather than the last. Unlike the film, Godzilla loses the fight and tumbles into the water. The next scene has Ken and his father in their lab discussing how to kill Hedorah, which Dr. Yano figures out how to do using electrodes. The scene is more or less the same except Yano makes the comment that Hedorah could reduce Godzilla to a pile of bones. The film would have benefited from such a line, which would have given the proceedings some added suspense.

The next portion of the manga is the climactic battle at Mt. Fuji, though more time seems to be spent showing Hedorah battling the military than Godzilla. Like in early drafts of the script, Hedorah battles a tank platoon at Mt. Fuji. After Hedorah's sludge destroys an electrical line to the grid and all hope seems lost, a military officer throws his gun into the air in anger. Ken copies him and throws his Godzilla toy. Through the panels, the toy seems to either morph into the real Godzilla or just foreshadow his arrival. Whatever the case, Godzilla begins the battle by flying onto the scene whereas in the film this doesn't happen until towards the battle's end. During his flight, Godzilla delivers a flying drop kick to Hedorah (promotional photos for the film showed Godzilla drop kicking his opponent). The battle resumes and Ken frets that Godzilla is on a suicide mission to kill Hedorah. The Smog Monster picks Godzilla up and flies him through the air. Hedorah drops Godzilla from such a height that it creates a crater. This is where the infamous sludge pit scene occurs in the manga. In this iteration, Hedorah takes aim for Godzilla's remaining eye, but the kaiju king ducks out of the way and in retaliation, rips out both of Hedorah's eyes! In the process, both of Godzilla's hands become skeletonized (in the film this only happens to one hand). Godzilla fights the eyeless Hedorah (a very creepy visual) in between the grid and uses his breath to jumpstart it.

Oddly enough, the comic's epilogue contains more subtext than the film itself. As Godzilla—visibly damaged, walks away—the characters comment on the irony that mankind's atom bomb testing had awakened Godzilla, and now mankind's pollution has nearly killed the poor monster. As in the film, the last panel shows another potential Hedorah emerging from the ocean...

GODZILLA VS. GIGAN The manga for the manga-influenced *Godzilla vs. Gigan* is one of the longer adaptations of the entire series. The first interesting addition is that Gengo meets a construction worker at Children's Land who has no pupils. His hardhat seems to have the emblem of a cockroach on it. Also, Children's Land is bigger and more elaborate here than in the film. The next deviation has a burlier version of Shosaku and Machiko Shima following Gengo to his apartment to get back the tape Gengo picked up. When the tape is played, we see a panel of Anguirus, Minilla, Kumonga, and an adult Mothra reacting to it (in the film, the latter three only appear via stock footage, and Mothra is a larva). When the tape is played a second time, we get a panel featuring Mothra, Kumonga, and Kamacuras reacting along with two brand new monsters. The kaiju are both reptilian, with the one to the panel's left having a large frill around its neck (it's possibly the Ultra monster Gabora). The kaiju to the right is spiky and has two small horns on its head plus a nasal horn, like a triceratops minus the head crest (it's possibly Kingsaurus III). For those no doubt wondering, this actually wasn't the first time that Toho had depicted new monsters living on Monster Island. A map of Monster Island produced for *All Monsters Attack* featured a new monster that resembled a plesiosaur living in a lake.

During the scene where Gengo goes to Godzilla Tower to look for Shima, he sees a creepy line of construction workers that lack pupils. Moments later as he enters the tower, a swarm of cockroaches rushes past his feet (this creepy scene would have made an interesting visual in the film). When it comes time to rescue Shima, rather than take the stairs, the main characters climb up the tower by rope. Also, Tomoko engages in a second karate brawl with the aliens before being captured. In another exciting addition, King Ghidorah and Gigan battle a fleet of jet fighters upon entering the earth's atmosphere, which they easily destroy. The scene where Godzilla Tower blows up the heroes' car is absent. Instead, the aliens shoot machine guns as Shosaku drives them away to safety. After this, the end monster battle is basically the same except Gigan uses his eye laser on Godzilla once.

Ultimately, the manga doesn't really improve upon the film though it would have been nice if Toho had the ability and the budget to add in some of the manga's alterations. Chief among these would have been new footage of the monsters on Monster Island, the space monsters' battle with jet fighters, and also the creepy construction workers seen by Gengo. Though these additions wouldn't have altered the somewhat slow story pace, it would have at least added some more interesting details.

GODZILLA VS. MEGALON The manga adaptation for *Godzilla vs. Megalon* starts with the first scene on Monster Island. While in the film, there is new footage of Godzilla and Anguirus (Rodan is stock footage), in the manga, we see Godzilla, Anguirus (in bipedal stance), and Kumonga react to the earthquake. Next up, there is Goro, Jinkawa, and Rokuro at the lake eating some rice cakes (a detail not present in the film). After witnessing the lake dry up, as they drive home, they discuss how Mu and Lemuria sank beneath the ocean waves three million years ago. Unlike the film, we get a nice visual aid of the continents sinking amidst volcanic earthquakes. The manga adds a minor character to the story when Goro takes the Seatopian sand samples to a friend who is a geologist (in the original script, Jinkawa was himself a geologist and in the film, all we see is a brief montage of the sand being studied).

The subterranean Seatopian Square depicted in the comic is similar to the one in the film only a bit more elaborate. Antonio stands over a high ledge to address the other Seatopians, whose garb somewhat resembles the people of Mu from *Atragon* (1963). In the manga, Megalon emerges from a volcano rather than a rocky enclosure, bursting dramatically out of molten rock and magma. The Seatopian agent that holds Jinkawa captive also confirms that Seatopia was a part of Lemuria rather than Mu. He further explains that when their city sank, it was encased in a huge air bubble, which is how they survived. This manga answers a question that neither *Godzilla vs. Megalon*—nor *Atragon*, for that matter—bother to address: just how the underwater nations survived. Soon after Jinkawa escapes, Megalon bursts from the dried lakebed spewing lava into the air—a fun visual to say the least. Unlike the film, Megalon never does attack a city (nor does he ever use his napalm balls).

When Jet Jaguar goes to fetch Godzilla, the comic confirms that Godzilla and the robot understand one another through sign language. Also, there are no scenes on Monster Island here, and we only see Godzilla swimming in the ocean with the robot overhead. Around this same time, Megalon kills the Seatopian agent. While in the film he does so with a boulder, in the manga he knocks a tree onto him. When Jet Jaguar grows in size, the scene is much more dynamic and it's too bad the film wasn't able to pull off this particular version of the scene. Here, Jet Jaguar grows to full size under Megalon and punches him under the mandible as his stature rises. Megalon and the robot battle for a few panels and here, we see that Megalon's ray doesn't resemble King Ghidorah's, but is fuller like Godzilla's.

As in promotional photos from the film, Godzilla shows up munching on a telephone pole and brandishing a tree sword, making quite the entrance. This is one of the greatest examples of a Godzilla manga showcasing a confirmed deleted scene from one of the films. Godzilla spits the telephone pole onto the back of Megalon's head and then blasts him in the face with his ray. He then knocks Gigan and Megalon to the ground with his tree sword and after this, Megalon incinerates it with his ray.

The manga's epilogue is a bit more elaborate than the film's. In this version, a great crowd cheers for Godzilla as he swims away. They also cheer on Jet Jaguar as he shrinks back down to normal size amongst them. The closing panels are similar to the final shots in the film with Goro, Jinkawa, and Rokuro walking alone with Jet Jaguar—the crowd has mysteriously disappeared. This is one of the only areas where the manga truly improves upon the film. While the film has a strangely desolate feel to it in that there aren't a lot of extras running around, the manga has a greater volume of Seatopians and final spectators for the final battle. Yet, in other ways, the manga is even less grand than the film, like lacking the destruction of Tokyo.

GODZILLA VS. MECHAGODZILLA Like the manga for *Godzilla vs. Megalon*, ideas abandoned from script drafts were integrated into the manga for *Godzilla vs. Mechagodzilla*. Specifically, the first draft of the film had Mechagodzilla retain his Godzilla skin throughout the oil refinery battle and partially into the final battle. The same happens here. Other changes were made to the manga to better appeal to children, however. For instance, the adult Masahiko Shimizu is now Keisuke Shimizu's kid brother in the manga. However, his function in the story is still the same in that he finds the space titanium in Gyokusen Cave. The action is condensed so that when Keisuke finds the hidden cave, Nami and her grandfather walk in to teach him the history of King Seesar and the prophecy foretelling of a monster that will destroy the world. Oddly, Nami and her grandfather willingly give Keisuke the King Seesar statue to take away to study. The manga also includes a nice panel representing a flashback of King Seesar (in profile) rising out of the ocean. It appears that the monster has split some ocean-going vessel in half! Perhaps the ship belonged to an enemy of the royal Azumi family.

The story proceeds with business as usual, with the fake Godzilla emerging from Mt. Fuji to literally "trample the people who try to run away"—there is actually a panel of the monster squishing some people! As in the first draft script, Godzilla shows up to battle his doppelganger who never sheds his fake skin. Instead, both monsters tumble into the ocean and disappear (by contrast, in the first draft script the fake Godzilla flies but in the manga, it does not). As in the film, Keisuke battles an alien invader (here, named M2) who tries to steal the King Seesar statue. This scene is essentially a combination of the house fight and the Corral Queen fight. Here, the alien ape's face is revealed. It is at this point that Miyajima figures out aliens are afoot and they must have constructed the second Godzilla seen at the oil refinery. From here, the manga cuts to the underground alien base where the manga's version of Kuronuma, the alien leader, is introduced. Here, he wears a cape and resembles Dr. Gori from TV's *Spectreman*.

During the finale, King Seesar is more of a force to be reckoned with compared to his activity in the finished film where Godzilla leads the fight. Here, Keisuke reaches Okinawa just as the fake Godzilla reemerges and marches to destroy King Seesar before he can awaken. Laser beams shoot out of the statue's eyes and free the real King Seesar from his rocky tomb. He doesn't awaken, however, and just as Mechagodzilla is about to blast him, Godzilla shows up to fire upon his counterpart. This melts the fake skin revealing Mechagodzilla's true form. The machine then gives Godzilla a thorough beating as Nami beseeches Seesar to wake up. The lion monster literally springs into action on all fours and runs to join the battle, biting Mechagodzilla's tail. Godzilla smashes the machine's head, destroying it in only one blow. The more powerful version of Seesar then runs to the alien base and plunges his paw underground to smash the aliens. The final panels show Seesar sitting on a ledge watching Godzilla swim into the sunset, as if to imply Seesar will remain free.

Having now discussed the additions, this is what was lost along the way: Anguirus makes no appearance whatsoever and nor does King Seesar ever use his reflective eyes. Professor Miyajima's pipe never comes into play and the INTERPOL agents and Saeko don't appear at all. Other than the fact that King Seesar—who received a lot of buildup in the film—is better portrayed, the manga offers no improvements over the film version.

TERROR OF MECHAGODZILLA Like the film, the manga begins with a flashback to the previous battle between Godzilla and his metal doppelganger—only here, their climactic duel takes place in a city rather than Okinawa. From there, the basic outline is similar to the film only sped up. The first major scene is Titanosaurus attacking the Akatsuki—only here, the sub learns that supersonic waves are the dinosaur's weakness (in the film, this happens during the second encounter). From there, it goes to the INTERPOL meeting which is quickly followed by the history of Dr. Mafune (a panel in the comic shows him walking away from his burning home while holding a baby Katsura). Soon after, we see Mafune with the Black Hole Aliens, who in the manga, look like hairless apes dressed in Nazi-like attire (Mugal even has a monocle).

Titanosaurus is quickly unleashed upon Japan, bursting from under an ocean liner in Tokyo Bay. The monster then goes on a spectacular rampage and turns over a monorail among other things. This is where the story gets weird. In the chaos amidst the city is when the male lead, a self-defense force officer (presumably this story's version of Ichinose), meets Katsura. What makes the scene so odd is that the defense force wears the aliens' costumes from the movie, weird helmets and all! Katsura seems to bond with the man who saved her as Godzilla shows up to battle Titanosaurus. Then, a Maser cannon-like vehicle shows up with the Supersonic Wave Oscillator attached to it. This drives away Titanosaurus here rather than Mafune himself. Learning of her dinosaur's weakness, Katsura plants a bomb on the tank causing it to explode. The defense force officers chase her to a cliff over the ocean. There, she blasts away one man with laser eyes before being shot and falling off the edge into the sea. After this, Katsura's notorious breast shot is recreated in the manga in not one but two panels!

Later as Katsura recovers and walks around Tokyo, she is spotted by the male lead who follows her back to the alien base. He is captured and forced to watch as Mechagodzilla II and Titanosaurus destroy Tokyo. Godzilla shows up to fight his enemies, and in an interesting deviation from the film's choreography, Mechagodzilla lands on top of Godzilla, burning him with his jets as he descends. Titanosaurus is shown to be as strong as he is in the film, knocking Godzilla far away with a single punch. The defense force officer, meanwhile, frees himself and just as one of the aliens is about to blast him with a ray gun, Katsura shoots the alien from behind to save the officer. This begins Katsura's turn to the light side and a battle ensues between her, the defense force officer, and the aliens. She is mortally wounded during the battle and in her last act, flips a switch on a control panel that deactivates both herself and Mechagodzilla. This happens just as the machine is about to jam a handful of missiles down Godzilla's throat. Godzilla punches Mechagodzilla to the ground and then turns his attention to Titanosaurus (he repeats his notorious tail slide from Godzilla vs. Megalon). Godzilla's atomic breath combined with the repaired Supersonic Wave Oscillator causes Titanosaurus to explode in a huge mushroom cloud. The defense force officer weeps in a field of flowers as the mushroom cloud blooms into the sky.

GODZILLA VS. BIOLLANTE The manga adaptation of Godzilla vs. Biollante was reportedly based on an early version of the script. The first notable example has Biollante attack some approaching defense force boats, a scene in the shooting script that wasn't shot. Biollante even eats one of the men! The next alteration occurs when Biollante completely submerges beneath the lake to attack Godzilla. The ending of the manga uses an alternative ending that was shot for the film. Here, Godzilla collapses mid-battle because of the anti-nuclear energy bacteria. Biollante then swallows Godzilla and morphs into a giant rose! However, the monster doesn't eat Godzilla; she is actually removing the hate from Godzilla's spirit! Biollante then disintegrates and drifts into the sky. This version begins in 1984 and has a young Miki Saegusa predicting Godzilla's resurgence to her teacher. Believing Miki to be disturbed, she is taken by her parents to a psychologist in Tokyo—at the same time that Godzilla makes landfall. Miki's parents are then killed in the rampage that follows.

GODZILLA VS. KING GHIDORAH This manga has fewer characters than in the film, lacking Mr. Shindo, Miki Saegusa, Professor Masaki, and Yuzo Tsuchiashi. The U.F.O. lands in the middle of Tokyo rather than in the countryside and when they go back in time, Terasawa is attacked by the Godzillasaurus, who picks him up in his hand! Rather than jet fighters, King Ghidorah battles MBT-92 Maser tanks. During the end battle, Godzilla slams Mecha-King Ghidorah's head into the Tokyo City Hall Complex. At the very end, as the cyborg carries Godzilla over the ocean, Godzilla blasts off Mecha-King Ghidorah's middle head. In a rather anti-climactic move, Godzilla also blasts at Emmy in KIDS from the ocean floor in a furious counterattack and appears to destroy her. The last panel is of Godzilla surrounded by the remains of Mecha-King Ghidorah on the ocean floor.

GODZILLA VS. MOTHRA (VERSION A) Some fans think this manga was better than the film itself. As a way of condensing the action, Takuya's jail stint is done away with. It opens with him in full Indiana Jones regalia raiding the temple. When he almost falls to his death, he is caught by the hand of his ex-wife Masako, who has just arrived to offer him the Infant Island job. Upon arriving on the island, they study an ancient temple before it is destroyed by a construction team that Masako works for. In the process, the egg is unearthed.

Meanwhile, Battra gets an additional scene attacking a ship at sea with some energy sphere weapons. After Godzilla and Battra destroy the ship transporting Mothra's egg, Masako is rescued by Takeshi Tomokane, the head of the company she works for. Takuya is meant to be left behind but like Indiana Jones, grabs onto the plane before it takes off and rides on the outside. The Thunder Control System from *Godzilla vs. Biollante* is used on Mothra as she crawls through Tokyo and it appears that Major Kuroki is the one in charge of the operation. Godzilla and the larval Battra have a second battle in Yokohama harbor. During the battle, Battra somehow encases himself in a giant cocoon that also acts as a shield and quickly bursts out in his adult form. In order to bring Battra over to her side, Mothra literally takes a hit of Godzilla's atomic blast. As the battle rages, in a nearby building, Tomokane confronts Masaeko and Takuya in an effort to steal the Cosmos. During the skirmish, Masako is shot so badly that it would appear she dies. Tomokane manages to make it outside to a getaway vehicle, which is crushed by Godzilla.

GODZILLA VS. MOTHRA (VERSION B) There is another manga version of the film which has Masako and Takuya as a happily married couple hired to investigate Infant Island. Daughter Midori stows away on the ship to go with them along with a very special guest: Miki Saegusa's younger brother Koji! This version of Infant Island has the giant egg and ancient ruins to go along with it. Ando accompanies the family but he is separated from them when the suspension bridge they cross is destroyed in an earthquake. Things progress normally enough that it doesn't warrant discussion until Mothra hatches. In this case, during her and Godzilla's ocean-based battle, everyone but Ando falls out of the boat. He tosses them a life raft and then speeds away with the Cosmos! After Godzilla and Battra are sucked into an underwater fissure, Mothra pushes the heroes all the way to Tokyo in the life raft. There, she begins looking for the Cosmos. She is badly wounded by Maser tanks until Koji Saegusa speaks with the general on her behalf, giving the caterpillar time to spin a cocoon. Miki shows up to back her little brother and reinforces that Mothra is only here to get the Cosmos. Godzilla emerges from Mt. Fuji and makes his way to Tokyo, where he attacks Mothra's cocoon. Ando speeds away in a getaway car with Takuya and Koji on his tail. Ando's car crashes into Battra's seemingly dead body—in reality, a discarded husk. The adult Battra makes his presence known and joins the battle. From there, things more or less progress as in the finished film.

GODZILLA VS. MECHAGODZILLA One of the ideas in this manga can possibly be traced back to *Godzilla vs. Berserk* and also predates ideas used in *Godzilla Against Mechagodzilla* (2002). In this version, Mecha-King Ghidorah's programming causes Mechagodzilla to occasionally take on a mind of its own, which is the manga's first alteration with a test run scene. One idea that does seem to be taken from one of Wataru Mimura's early drafts is that Garuda goes to Adonoa Island though it's merely to transport the researchers there, not to fight Rodan. That kaiju gets a great reveal when he plunges his giant beak into the tent of one of the researchers in an effort to get at the egg. The battle between Godzilla and Rodan is the same, except after Rodan is defeated, Godzilla grabs hold of Garuda. The ship lifts Godzilla into the sky and then drops him into the ocean.

The theme of "Life" plays into Rodan's resurrection. Here, he is found dead on the surface of the island's beach. Animals all around him are also dying because Rodan is absorbing their life force! The manga's first battle between Godzilla and his double is wildly different as Godzilla grabs Mechagodzilla and drags him underwater. On a seafloor covered with volcanic holes, the machine must battle Godzilla and try to prevent the volcanoes from erupting. Also, a lone pilot controls Mechagodzilla *Pacific Rim*-style. The battle is brutal and leaves Mechagodzilla missing a few limbs.

The next significant alteration comes when Major Kuroki from *Godzilla vs. Biollante* steps in to assume control of operations pertaining to the egg, which still has yet to hatch. The egg—rather than the baby—and Ms. Gojo are transported via helicopter, which is attacked by Rodan. The flying monster takes Gojo and the egg to the top of a skyscraper where Rodan sits on the egg in order to hatch it. Gojo realizes Rodan isn't out to harm anyone and only wants what's best for the egg. During the ending, Gojo fights against Mechagodzilla in Garuda to protect Rodan! Specifically, Gojo is rescued by Garuda and once inside, manages to grab the controls from the pilot so Garuda takes a blast of Mechagodzilla's ray to protect Rodan.

The end battle is incredibly violent. Merged with the robot to become Super-Mechagodzilla, Garuda blasts out Godzilla's eyes. When the monster is down on his knees and clearly defeated, G-Force decides to capture the monster. But then, the programming of Mecha-King Ghidorah—still wanting revenge—again takes over and Mechagodzilla proceeds to blast Godzilla to pieces, culminating in the robot blowing Godzilla's head off his neck!!!

The baby Godzilla hatches around this time and the machine, still controlled by Mecha-King Ghidorah's programing, marches on the baby monster to kill it too. As in the film, Rodan's life force resurrects Godzilla (here, reconstituting him as well), who attacks his doppelganger just in time to save his adopted son. Finally, Super-Mechagodzilla latches onto Godzilla to self destruct—with Aoki and Gojo still trapped inside Garuda. The two make it out in an escape pod at the last second as the mechanical monster detonates in a huge explosion.

This new ending has pros and cons. On one hand, it is more suspenseful. On the other, the film was interesting because it was somewhat ambiguous as to who you should be rooting for. In *Godzilla vs. Mechagodzilla,* Godzilla only comes to Japan to retrieve his young and really isn't out to harm anyone. Godzilla has, however, attacked Japan in the past and the Japanese government is entitled to defend their nation. The manga, on the other hand, makes it clear that the villain is Mechagodzilla.

So, even though the manga certainly has some interesting ideas from a pure "popcorn perspective," like Mecha-King Ghidorah's programing taking over, the film's subtext is better. Essentially, man is the villain in *Godzilla vs. Mechagodzilla.* One could argue the simple message is this: God created man. Man created atomic bombs. Atomic bombs created Godzilla. Man's punishment for creating Godzilla is that he must live alongside him. Therefore, when man creates Mechagodzilla it ends in defeat for man.

GODZILLA 2000 The last great Godzilla manga adaptation to wildly alter the source material was that of *Godzilla 2000*. For instance, the ghostly tentacles of the Millennian aliens capture Io (Shinoda's daughter) and create a clone of her! Through the clone, they explain to Shinoda and Yuki the history of their race.

During the battle, as the Millennian aliens harness Godzilla's life force, they begin to take on humanoid shapes before shrieking in pain. To destroy the UFO, Godzilla jumps backward into the air, destroying it with his dorsal plates. The biggest departure is Orga's size. Much like the oversized "final bosses" in the Heisei Ultraman films, Orga dwarfs Godzilla (think King Kong compared to Ann Darrow)! It's a wild visual that I wish could've been in the film itself. Orga grabs Godzilla in his mouth and proceeds to eat him—before Godzilla blows him up, of course.

APPENDIX IV:
DAIEI MANGA ADAPTATIONS

Starting with 1967's *Giant Monster Midair Battle: Gamera vs. Gyaos* and running through 1971's *Gamera vs. Deep-Sea Monster Zigra*, a series of five contemporary manga adaptations of the Gamera films were produced. These manga drew upon the treatments and shooting scripts for each film; examining these comics provides an interesting exercise in how things changed across the two types of media to better serve their particular art form and intended audience. Characters were dropped or combined, scenes reshuffled, cut, and blended, and aspects of the scripts that never made it to production (usually due to budgetary reasons) were included. There was later an eight volume set of manga adapting each of the Showa Gamera films (released in conjunction with the Heisei Gamera trilogy) as well as individual/multiple adaptations of *Giant Monster Gamera* and *Great Monster Duel: Gamera vs. Barugon*. There were adaptations of the four Heisei films and all-new stories as well. However, for the purposes of this appendix, we'll just be looking at the five contemporary manga adaptations.

GIANT MONSTER MIDAIR BATTLE: GAMERA VS. GYAOS Out of the five manga, this is probably the one that deviates the most from the source material, sometimes in totally unexpected directions. It uses the same characters as the film and most of the same basic set pieces and plot points, but does away with the crowds of villagers refusing to sell their property and the construction crew. Rather, the focus is on the Kanamaru family- grandfather Tatsuemon and his grandchildren Eiichi and Sumiko. As in most manga, the character models bear little resemblance to how they looked on screen—rather, they were exaggerated portrayals to make the characters easier to differentiate in print. In particular Eiichi was upgraded from the kid who rode on Gamera's back to a tougher version wearing a Meiji style student peaked cap. Sumiko regressed from being a girl in her late teens to be closer to Eiichi's age so as not to overshadow him, and also to appeal to the age range of girls of the manga's readership.

The manga opens very early in the morning with Tatsuemon (henceforth referred to as 'Gramps') raging against Foreman Shiro

Tsutsumi, yelling in no uncertain terms he wasn't selling his property on Mt. Momiji to the government so a road could go through. While Shiro attempts to sway him by outlining the benefits to society and quality of life, Gramps taunts him with a ladle full of the foul-smelling brew produced on the farm. This brings Eiichi and Sumiko out to see what all the fuss is about—and things come to an explosive head when nearby Mt. Fuji erupts. Attracted by the flames and heat, Gamera enters the picture (first in saucer form and then using his rear-leg thrusters only). He enters the lava and begins to feed on the energy. While our cast watches this tableau, Shiro's assistant finds himself levitating off the ground—with the next panel showing him in the grip of the bat-like Gyaos! It seems Gyaos had been released from its abode in Mt. Momiji by the eruption of Mt. Fuji.

Gyaos wastes no time making a snack out of the terrified assistant (not shown but implied as the assistant's helmet is shown hitting the ground). As one might expect it's every man for himself as our terrified heroes scatter for cover. Shockingly, Sumiko is picked up by Gyaos and is shown ready to be popped into his gaping maw. At this point one would think Sumiko is going to take Eiichi's role from the film of being saved by Gamera and getting to ride on his back. But, in a stunning turn of events, she too is eaten, again implied rather than shown by having her hair ribbon hit the ground. Gramps immediately is overcome with grief, shouting her name over and over. Gyaos reaches for Eiichi and Gamera finally intervenes! The dramatic impact of the scene would have been amazing to see on screen, but no doubt having a child gobbled up by Gyaos would have traumatized many a child.

The battle plays out, combining two of the fights between Gamera and Gyaos in the film. Gamera roasts Gyaos with his fire breath but Gyaos almost cuts off Gamera's foot with a shot of his sonic beam. The sun rises and Gyaos attempts to flee, but is restrained by Gamera. The tug-of-war ends with Gamera chewing through Gyaos's left leg, allowing the murder bird to escape. Combining the scenes from the film into one makes for a nice juxtaposition as each combatant lost (or almost lost) a foot. Shiro watches Gyaos's severed foot shrink in the sun and makes the connection that sunlight is anathema to Gyaos. Gramps continues to mourn his lost Sumiko.

We move on to the Hotel Fuji, now the headquarters of the JSDF as tanks and jet planes arrive. Mt. Momiji glows with an unearthly aura, heralding the emergence of Gyaos. The military opens fire on Gyaos to no avail, and all the hardware is cut to ribbons by

Gyaos's sonic beam. After destroying the army, Gyaos takes out his anger on nearby Nagoya, culminating in cleanly cutting Nagoya Castle in half. While the TV news reports the carnage, the JSDF and Shiro try to come up with a new plan. Frustrated and angry about the death of his sister, Eiichi smacks an office chair, sending it spinning around rapidly. Seeing this, Shiro believes that using centrifugal force against Gyaos would make it dizzy and give the sun a chance to destroy it—and that they need a compound of artificial blood with a strong scent to attract him (hearkening back to when Gramps was taunting them with his smelly brew). Just as in the film, the trap is set up on top of the hotel, and people believe this is really going to work.

While this is going on, Gramps mourns Sumiko, looking upon her favorite doll and in a series of flashbacks remembering how happy she was and so full of life. He resolves to take the life of Gyaos himself.

Back at the hotel, against all odds, the plan is actually working! Gyaos has arrived, is being spun around like a top, and the sun rises. Suddenly, one of the soldiers spots Gramps, armed with a spear, clambering up on top of the platform. Gramps flings aside his headband, signaling his resolve and readiness to do battle with the creature that killed his granddaughter! He stabs Gyaos repeatedly in the eye, and things look bad for the evil creature...

...until the platform he is spinning upon begins to catch fire from the friction. It's now a race against time—will the platform last long enough to allow the sun to cook Gyaos, or will the hungry demon's good luck rule the day? Well, you've probably guessed that the machinery breaks apart long before Gyaos's will does. In a final desperate effort, Gramps plunges his spear into Gyaos's eye, angering the beast, who swats Gramps from his perch on the platform to the ground many stories below. Gyaos then makes his escape. Gramps lives long enough to give an extended 'deathbed speech', telling Shiro to set fire to the trees on Mt. Momiji, both to flush out Gyaos and attract Gamera to do battle again. Gramps then enters the Pure Land, with Sumiko's little hair ribbon fluttering out of his robe as he dies. Eiichi is now an orphan.

Mt. Momiji is set afire and as expected causes Gyaos to flee his lair. Gamera, never late for a barbecue, arrives moments later. The battle is short and brutal: a flying Gamera slices off both of Gyaos's wings and dodges his sonic beam. Once Gyaos is properly grounded, Gamera lands and unloads with all the fire he can muster and Gyaos is burned to ashes, much like Zigra was in the

1971 film. There is no need to drag him into Mt. Fuji as in the film version. Gamera flies off into a setting sun.

By focusing the story on the Kanamaru family and downplaying the conflict on the sale of the land to the government, the film carries a much greater emotional impact. The death of a child, the deep grief of the grandfather, and the sacrifice he makes while trying to avenge her would have made the film much more serious. In tone, it would have been like the prior entry in the series, *Great Monster Duel: Gamera vs. Barugon*. However, to appeal to the kids in the audience, the film took a far more family friendly route-a route that was to become more pronounced as the series progressed.

GAMERA VS. OUTER SPACE MONSTER VIRAS Unlike *Gamera vs. Gyaos*, the manga for *Gamera vs. Viras* follows the film virtually scene by scene-up to a point. It's also the longest of the mangas. While the others ran about 30 pages each, the Viras manga was about 50. Up until Viras becomes kaiju-sized, it recaps the action in the film, including having 'stock footage'.

Just as a refresher, we open with Gamera in space destroying the Viran spaceship. The action cuts to the Boy Scout Jamboree where Masao and Jim miss roll call because they're off gleefully sabotaging the sub being used by the Marine Institute. As in the film this results in the adults failing to be able to control the sub (and getting WAY more shaken up than in the film), with Masao and Jim 'volunteering' to show them how it's done. They of course know just how to control it, and eventually see Gamera resting on the ocean floor. While investigating, a second Viran saucer arrives and shoots its Super Catch Ray at Gamera, inadvertently capturing the boys as well. With a supreme effort Gamera manages to dead lift the dome formed by the ray, allowing the two scouts to escape. The aliens probe Gamera's mind (with 'manga stock footage' of his previous battles) and just as in the film discover his one weakness is his love for children and desire to protect them. Jim and Masao have just made it onto shore again when the Virans beam them on board the ship. Gamera has by this time escaped (the Super Catch Ray is only good for 15 minutes) and is rocketing to attack their ship. The Virans stop him by threatening to harm the two kids. A mind control device is attached to Gamera, and he rampages through Tokyo and destroys a dam (in effect again using 'manga stock footage' of the first two Gamera films). The Virans give Earth an ultimatum: the usual 'surrender, or we kill the two boys'. The military is on the verge of surrendering but after speaking to Masao and Jim encourage the boys to try to attack the Virans from within their ship using the same tactics they used on the sub. They do, reversing the mind control on Gamera and also allowing them to beam down into the center of the city. This is where the manga breaks from the film and has a much more elaborate climax, one that appears to have been excised from the film due to budgetary reasons.

Viras spends some time yelling at his subordinates, letting them know what idiots they are for being bested by children. Gamera, seeing the boys safe near his position and free of mind control, immediately attacks the Viran saucer, hitting it with his spinning shell attack and forcing it to the ground. Viras informs his subordinates they need to sacrifice themselves and combine in order to fight Gamera. Unlike the film where he decapitates them, they do so willingly here with their limbs, heads, and torsos simply falling off (they appear to be hollow artificial shells rather than actual human bodies as in the film). They merge with Viras and the real fun begins.

One of the theatrical posters for this movie features Gamera throwing Viras into a building, a scene that never appears in the film. But it does in the manga, indicating at one point the entire end battle was meant to take place in the city, not on the beach where it actually did. Viras strikes first, blasting Gamera with a force ray emanating from the tip of his head, a power he didn't have in the film. Gamera charges relentlessly and gorilla press slams Viras into a building. He unloads on his squid-like foe with his fire breath. Viras manages to knock Gamera on his back using his thrashing tentacles. He then impales Gamera with the point of his head, rearing up and powerlifting Gamera upward. From here things are just like in the film: Gamera begins to spin like crazy, lifting Viras higher and higher into the air. He then dislodges him from a great height, smashing Viras to pieces when he hits the surface of the water beneath. Once again Gamera flies off into the sunset, another job well done.

For the most part, the manga follows the finished film faithfully. What would have been expensive effects shots at the end were written out and replaced with a battle on the barren beach and the ocean. But they remained in the manga! Other than that, the only real changes were to character models. For example, the Virans are all dressed as scientists with lab coats and the scouts are all wearing the Japanese Boy Scout uniform whether they're American or Japanese. Perhaps the oddest rendition is the Scout

Master, dressed in what appears to be an old school Buck Rodgers/Space Ranger type of uniform and at times appears to be carrying a blaster!

GAMERA VS. GIANT EVIL BEAST GUIRON This manga adaptation also sticks fairly closely to the film, although it eliminates most of the comic relief (no Kon-chan) and makes the three main characters much older—Tom, Akio, and Tomoko all appear to be high school age. It also consolidates the Gamera-Guiron battles into one and has a longer Space Gyaos scene. The Space Women Barbella and Florbella are much more direct and to the point.

The action starts off just as in the film, with the three teens stargazing and seeing an alien ship streaking from the sky and landing nearby (the ship appears just as it does in the film). They run out to investigate (no bike riding, sorry) and find the ship in a clearing. Tom and Akio enter the ship and Tom decides that pushing that CONSPICUOUS BUTTON is a good idea. Naturally, this launches the ship into space and not only that, but straight into an asteroid field. The two boys are thrown around by the impact of small asteroids hitting the ship, and it looks to be all over when the mother of all asteroids moves into view. Of course, this just give Gamera the perfect place to appear and play hero, which he does magnificently by effortlessly moving the asteroid out of the boy's path. Their joy at being rescued is cut short when they realize they still can't control the ship, and even Gamera can't keep pace with them.

Meanwhile, back on Earth, Tomoko finds that no one believes her story of the two boys being spirited away by the spaceship. As the ship lands on the planet Tera, the boys leave the ship and in a humorous scene it appears as if a giant bird has defecated on their heads. The scene quickly becomes terrifying when they look up and see that it is actually drool from a Space Gyaos rising up behind them! They tear off with the winged beast in hot pursuit, and their luck seems to have run out when they come to the edge of a deep cliff. Two eyes hover in the darkness from that direction as well, and reveal themselves to belong to the knife-headed Guiron! Ignoring the boys for now, the two kaiju engage in battle. Space Gyaos hits Guiron on his bladed prow but it bounces off harmlessly. Guiron displays a power he lacked in the film (but that Jiger had in the next one) when he activates a suction beam on his palm and inexorably draws in Space Gyaos. Once Gyaos is caught, Guiron unceremoniously decapitates him and turns his attention to the boys. Tom and Akio flee into a building and come face to face with the two Spacewomen, Barbella and Florbella. The two women greet the boys and relate the history of Tera (as in the film, Earth's sister planet on the other side of the sun), explain how they can speak Japanese (advanced machinery), and explain how Guiron is their protector against the flocks of Space Gyaos that have decimated their planet. Now, in the film, this is where they would try to ply the boys and win their trust with milk and donuts, but this time it's 'why bother'—they offer the boys seats which immediately clamp metal restraints around them. Akio gets his head shaved and when a laser gun is pointed at his head for some impromptu brain surgery, you figure it's about time for Gamera to show up—which he does, right on schedule as always.

The two Spacewomen shoot a missile at Gamera, which he easily catches and sets aside. That missile will likely show up later. At that point Guiron bursts through the ground dramatically to challenge Gamera. The giant turtle socks Guiron with a roundhouse left, sending him spinning into the building our heroes are in, coincidentally smashing the machine that controls the restraints on their chairs, setting them free. Now it's a free-for-all as Gamera and Guiron battle it out with the two boys being chased by the Spacewomen. Before long Tom and Akio are cornered. But again, it's Gamera to the rescue-in the manga he has a ridiculously long tail, longer than Godzilla's, which he uses to great effect by smashing the Spacewomen into a wall of rock, burying them in a landslide, never to be seen again. He then does his famous 'gymnastics' move, this time spinning around on a rock outcropping to knock down Guiron.

Up to now the fight has been all Gamera, but Guiron has had enough. He almost cuts off Gamera's right arm, slashes Gamera right below the throat, fires off half a dozen shuriken that bury themselves into Gamera's body and eye, and then leaps upon Gamera, digging into his chest for the final blow. But as luck and the script would have it, Gamera lands directly next to the missile he had put aside earlier. He chucks it into Guiron's head, sets it afire, blowing up Guiron into multiple chunks, much more satisfyingly than the film. As the boys cry about being stuck on Tera, Gamera sets them down next to the damaged spaceship, prompts them to enter, and then flies the ship back to Earth in his mouth.

The Guiron manga combines techniques and elements of the two earlier *Gyaos* and *Viras* ones. It keeps scenes that were probably cut from filming for being too expensive. It eliminates much of the comedy that was used for filler. This also gives the manga a chance to have Gamera interact with and directly destroy the 'human' foes. The comic doesn't change as much as *Gyaos*, or stick to the film as faithfully as *Viras*—it falls somewhere in the middle. The next manga was to take a more radical and creative approach.

GAMERA VS. GIANT DEVIL BEAST JIGER The manga opens with a scene out of the middle of the film, plunging right into the action. As the Kitayama and Williams family watch TV, they see a room full of Expo 70 big shots, government officials, and scientists viewing a film of a clash between Gamera and Jiger. Onscreen is the eldest son, Keisuke, who is in an obvious state of distress. As the film plays, Gamera and Jiger are shown facing each other down in the ocean. Jiger (here bipedal, not quadrupedal) shoots spikes from her fingers (not her face as in the movie) and impales Gamera. Gamera's entire body (not just his head and left arm like the film) turns translucent, glowing and showing his skeletal structure inside. Jiger then turns her attention to the military onshore, shooting her finger spikes at the tanks attacking him. The spikes embed themselves into the ground and Jiger's Super Ultra Wave shoots from each, crisscrossing the area with a huge wave of energy that disintegrates everything in its blast zone.

The film ends and EXPO-sition is given. It seems the Expo 70 site had removed the Devil's Whistle statue from Wester Island for display at the Expo-the statue had been an object of worship by the natives for years and as it turned out, was the artifact that had kept Jiger confined over the decades. Although not shown, Jiger makes his way to Japan and lays waste to everything around him. As often happens, the lowest level employee gets blamed for the decisions of the higher ranked ones, and in this case it's Keisuke. Keisuke is being roughed up and harangued by an extremely unhinged official and is only saved when a cooler headed official intervenes. Watching this on TV, Keisuke's family relaxes. A chance remark by Susan Williams about space seems to trigger an idea in Hiroshi. He envisions a spaceman floating in the void. He, Susan, and her brother Tommy rush off.

The action returns to the Expo 70 meeting, where the official that saved Keisuke is going over the threat to the Expo—and humanity at large—by Jiger. Suddenly Hiroshi, Susan, and Tommy burst into the room. Despite being restrained by guards, Hiroshi manages to convey his idea to the assemblage to enter Gamera's body with a mini sub and resuscitate him (the vision of the spaceman he had reminded him of a scuba diver swimming in water...like Gamera's bloodstream). His idea is dismissed at first but undaunted he continues to push it. At this point, Jiger returns to finish off the disabled Gamera and humanity realizes this might be their last chance. Hiroshi enters Gamera's bloodstream ala Fantastic Voyage and attaches an electric stimulator to Gamera's heart. As Jiger closes in, it's unsure if Hiroshi will be able to escape Gamera's body in time for the stimulator to be turned on (if it's turned on while he's in there, the sub will short out, and he'll die). The unhinged official from before panics and pushes the activation button to the horror of the others, but Hiroshi escapes from Gamera's mouth just in time!

Gamera is revived and he and Jiger grapple. Jiger impales Gamera with her hand spikes but for the time being the giant turtle is immune. Gamera retreats into his shell, flies above in his spinning form, and creates a vortex that draws Jiger into it. Gamera races off, grabs the Devil's Whistle, returns, and drives the statue into Jiger's chest, killing her. All is well once again and Keisuke thanks his brother for his brains and bravery.

This manga took a wonderfully creative approach by picking up in the middle of the movie via a film, then giving the background, and connecting the action in the Expo with the goings-on at Hiroshi's home (who were watching the Expo meeting on TV). It's like there're several layers of time and levels of viewing. The manga also does something none of the others did—subtly changing one of the characters and their relationship to the others. In the film, Keisuke Sawada (an Expo 70 official) was the boyfriend of Miko Kitayama. In the manga, Miko no longer exists and Keisuke is now one of the Kitayama family! This makes the characters more straightforward and connected and adds to the drama of the proceedings.

There were a lot of changes made to Jiger and her powers. As already mentioned, she walks upright now instead of all fours. She shoots paralysis spikes from her hands, and the spikes also activate her Super Ultra Wave (instead of coming from her horn). Gone is her impregnating stinger and baby Jiger. Gone are her hand suction cups, her neck jet boosters, and her face stingers. No doubt this was done so as not to overwhelm the reader and keep the focus on one special attack for the story.

Much of the beginning of the story was jettisoned (with the initial battle between Jiger and Gamera), and the sonic aspect of the Devil's Whistle was left out as well. The statue was also shown to be just like one of the statues on Easter Island and not resembling the one from the film. The sub used by Hiroshi was more like a futuristic submersible car, and he swam around in Gamera's bloodstream like a scuba diver. Rather than being revived by electric lines to the lung as in the movie, here it's Gamera's heart. All of these changes made the manga less predictable and more interesting.

The *Viras* manga included virtually all the story, but *Guiron* and *Jiger* increasingly began to eliminate whole chunks of what was in the finished film. This trend was to culminate in *Gamera vs. Zigra*, where most of the beginning and middle were eliminated.

GAMERA VS. DEEP-SEA MONSTER ZIGRA Drs. Yosuke Ishikawa and Tom Wallace are on their research vessel in the ocean, listening to a radio broadcast as it describes a massive earthquake in Arabia. With thousands killed and hundreds of thousands injured, the two talk over the situation when all of a sudden their children Helen and Kenichi emerge from hiding. While the two children are being scolded, a flaming object streaks from the sky and smashes into the ocean. Being researchers, Yosuke and Tom decide to investigate even with the two children on board. Their trip is cut short as their ship is hit with a 4th Dimensional Ray from the Zigran spaceship (looking more like a submerged Science Patrol VTOL than the candy bowl full of Skittles seen in the film) lying on the ocean floor, having just crashed into the ocean. The ship is transported on board the spaceship.

There they are met by Woman X, Zigra's second in command. She tells them of the Zigran plan to conquer the Earth. When the researchers seem unconvinced, she sets the spaceship's vibration generator to hit Tokyo with a high magnitude earthquake. With an evil "Fu fu fu" she pulls the switch, and we are given two pages of building destruction (something not shown in the film). Woman X explains how the Planet Zigra was made uninhabitable by polluted waters, much like what is happening on Earth now. When Yosuke and Tom try to overpower her, she paralyzes them with a snap of her fingers. This sets the two kids into action with Helen and Kenichi blindly flailing away at every button and switch in the ship. Three full pages of button flailing! They manage to freeze Woman X in her tracks and get their boat to rematerialize. They load up their fathers and themselves before the vessel reappears in the water. As luck would have it, Gamera swings by, picks up their ship, and drops them off at Sea World.

While there, Yosuke and Tom are reanimated when it's figured out that sound waves are the key to breaking the state of hypnosis Zigra and Woman X can incapacitate someone with. Unlike the movie, Woman X doesn't come to her senses by the same method later. Here, Woman X casually strolls onto the scene and announces she's actually Chikako Sugawara 'moon researcher' and has no clue what's going on—she has completely recovered with no explanation.

Then it's on to the bottom of the ocean floor. Gamera looms over Zigra's ship and blows it up with his flame breath, leaving Zigra in his kaiju form. There's an extremely short battle—Zigra shoots his 4th Dimensional Ray (from the curve in his head, not from a point just above his beak like in the movie) at Gamera but misses. Gamera picks up Zigra, rockets into the sky, drops him, and reduces him to ashes with his flame breath. Zigra, we hardly knew ye.

Just as in the film, there's a final scene where Kenichi is scolded by his dad for starting to throw an empty bottle into the ocean and continuing the cycle of pollution that destroyed Planet Zigra and that now threatens Earth.

This is all just as abrupt, arbitrary, and random as it sounds. Huge chunks of the story are omitted from the manga as well as much of the monster action. Three pages of button flailing! Granted, we get some earthquake destruction not seen in the film, but otherwise it's just a straight rehash of the least interesting parts of the film with nothing creative or original to offset it. It seems both the film and manga ended at creative low points for the franchise.

BIBLIOGRAPHY

Articles

Brothers, Peter. "Moon with a View: The Making of 'The Great War in Space." *G-Fan* #74 (Winter 2005)

Godziszewski, Ed. "*Atragon*: A Toho Classic Revisited." *G-Fan* #21 (May/June 1996)

---------------- "*Godzilla vs. Biollante.*" *Japanese Giants* #8 (Spring 1994)

---------------- "Godzilla Speaks! A Conversation with Haruo Nakajima." *G-Fan* #22 (July/August 1996)

Homenick, Brett. "Lovely Lady from Latitude Zero." *G-Fan* #82 (Winter 2008)

-------------------- "The Man Who Revived Godzilla." *G-Fan* #78 (Winter 2007)

-------------------- "Chasing the Last Dinosaur." *G-Fan* #90 (Winter 2010)

-------------------- "Universal Vision." *G-Fan* #80 (Spring 2007)

-------------------- "Monster Script." *G-Fan* #80 (Summer 2007)

-------------------- "*Godzilla 1985*: Untold Tales." *G-Fan* #83 (Spring 2008)

-------------------- "Adapting *Godzilla 1985*: Easier Said Than Done." *G-Fan* #87 (Spring 2009)

-------------------- "'You can't choose what you're remembered for.' An interview with title designer Ernest Farino." *G-Fan* #76 (Summer 2006)

-------------------- "Spinning the Godzilla Saga." *G-Fan* #88 (Summer 2009)

Ishida, Hajime. "Memories of Ishiro Honda." *Famous Monsters Ack-ives* (Volume 1, May 2019)

Ishizuka, Daisuke and Yoshikazu Ishii. "Gamera's Godfather: Noriaki Yuasa." *G-Fan* #59 (Nov/Dec 2002)

Lees, J.D. "Bigger than Life! An Interview with Henry G-Saperstein." *G-Fan* #15 (May/Jun 1995)

----------- "*Terror of Mechagodzilla*: The Ultimate Commentary." *G-Fan* #90 (Winter, 2010)
----------- "Godzilla's Godfather." *G-Fan* #59 (Nov/Dec 2002)

----------- "Interview with Dean Devlin." *G-Fan* #39 (May/Jun 1999)

----------- "Godzilla's Boss." *G-Fan* #55 (Mar/Apr 2002)

Ragone, August. "*Godzilla vs. Megalon*: Love It or Hate It, Jet Jaguar Rocks!" *Famous Monsters of Filmland.* (September/October 2013)

------------------ "The unused ending for *Godzilla vs. Mothra*." *G-Fan* #11 (Sep/Oct 1994)

Ryfle, Steve. "Guardian of Gamera's Universe." *G-Fan* #40 (July/August 1999)

Ryfle, Steve and Stuart Galbraith IV. "Interview with Teruyoshi Nakano." *G-Fan* #27 (May/Jun 1997)

Szczepanski, Michael. "The Return of the King!" *G-Fan* #60 (Jan/Feb 2003)

Shoemaker, Greg and Allen Perkins. "*Godzilla 1985*: Screenplay Comparison." *G-Fan* #101 (June 2013)

Totorom. "Words from the Heart." *G-Fan* #91 (Spring 2010)

"G-Fan Kaiju Scrapbook", *G-Fan* #120 (Summer 2018)

"Information Explosion: Teruyoshi Nakano talks of Godzilla past, present and future." *G-Fan* #71 (Spring 2005)

"Mr. Yuasa's G-Fest." *G-Fan* #65 (Nov/Dec 2003)

Books
Brothers, Peter. *Atomic Dreams and the Nuclear Nightmare: The Making of Godzilla (1954)*. Createspace, 2015.

-------------------*Sons of Godzilla*. Createspace, 2018.

Cooke, Bill. *Gorgo*. Bear Manor Media, 2014.

Derendorf, Kevin. *Kaiju For Hipsters: 101 "Alternative" Giant Monster Movies*. Maser Press, 2018.

Dunning, John. *On the Air: The Encyclopedia of Old-Time Radio*, Oxford University Press, 1998.

Galbraith, Stuart IV. *Monsters Are Attacking Tokyo*. Venice, CA: Feral House, 1998.

Godziszewski, Ed. *The Illustrated Encyclopedia of Godzilla*. By the Author, 1998.

Hirai, Kazumasa and Edward Lipsett (translator). *Wolf Guy*. LUNATECH, 2015.

Kalat, David. *A Critical History and Filmography of Toho's Godzilla Series*. London: McFarland, 1997.

Komatsu, Sakyo and Michael Gallagher (translator). *Japan Sinks*. NY, Dover Publications, Inc.: 2015.

Macias, Patrick. *TokyoScope: The Japanese Cult Film Companion*. San Francisco: Cadence Books, 2001.

Ragone, August. *Eiji Tsuburaya: Master of Monsters*. San Francisco: Chronicle Books, 2007.

Ryfle, Steve. *Japan's Favorite Mon-Star: The Unauthorized Biography of "The Big G"*. Chicago: ECW Press, 1998.

Ryfle, Steve & Ed Godziszewski. *Ishiro Honda: A Life in Film, From Godzilla to Kurosawa*. Middletown: Wesleyan University Press, 2017.

Scheimer, Lou & Andy Mangels. *Lou Scheimer: Creating the Filmation Generation*. TwoMorrows Publishing, 2012

Takahashi, Niisan. *Gamera vs. Phoenix: Monster War of Love and Emotion*. Bunko, 1995.

Terrace, Vincent. *Radio Programs, 1924–1984: A Catalog of More Than 1800 Shows*. London: McFarland, 1998.

Warren, Bill. *Keep Watching the Skies!* London: McFarland, 2016.

Japanese Language Books
Banno, Yoshimitsu. *The Man Who Made Godzilla Fly*. Tankobon: 2016.

Tomio Tomii, Editor. *1973 "Japan Sinking" Complete Documentation (Film Hidden Collection)* (Yosensha, 2018)

All Toho Monster Large Picture Book (Yosensha, 2014)

Gamera Heisei Perfection (Kadokawa, 2014)

Godzilla Heisei Perfection (Kadokawa, 2012)

Godzilla Special Effects Making Photograph Collection (Kodansha, 2018)

Godzilla: Toho SPFX Films (Kodansha, 2014)

Godzilla: Toho Tokusatsu Unpublished Material Archive: The Era of Producer Tomoyuki Tanaka. Shinichiro Kobayashi, Editor. (Kadokawa Shoten, 2010)

Godzilla vs. Biollante Perfection (Kadokawa, 2015)

Godzilla X Kiryu Perfection (Kadokawa, 2016)

Mothra/Mothra vs. Godzilla Toho SPFX Movies (Toho, 1985)

Showa Mechagodzilla 2019 Movie Treasures (Yosensha, 2019)

Toho Champion Matsuri Perfection (Kadokawa, 2014)

Toho Special Effects Movie Complete Works (Village Books, 2012)

Tokusatsu Hihou Vol. 2 (Yosensha, 2015)

Tokusatsu Hihou Vol. 4 (Yosensha, 2016)

Tokusatsu Hihou Vol. 5 (Yosensha, 2017)

Tokusatsu Hihou Vol. 6 (Yosensha, 2017)

Websites
www.cyberkids1954.com

www.tohokingdom.com/cutting_room.htm

Homenick, Brett. "Vantage Point Interviews." https://vantagepointinterviews.com

GMAN. "When Roses Attack: 25 Years of Godzilla vs. Biollante with Ed Godziszewski." https://www.scified.com/news/when-roses-attack-25-years-of-godzilla-vs-biollante-with-ed-godziszewski

Milner, David. "Kaiju Conversations."
www.davmil.org/www.kaijuconversations.com

Mirjahangir, Chris. "Interview: Keizo Murase."
https://www.tohokingdom.com/interviews/keizo_murase_12-2017.html

Napier, Susan and Tatsumi Takayuki, Kotani Mari, and Otobe Junko. "An Interview with Sakyo Komatsu." *Science Fiction Studies* #88 Volume 29, Part 3 (November 2002)
https://www.depauw.edu/sfs/backissues/88/komatsu%20interview.htm

wikizilla.org/wiki/The_Return_of_King_Ghidorah_(Showa)

Godzilla All Movies DVD Collector's Box (Kodansha, 2018)
Vol. 15 *Son of Godzilla*

Vol. 19 *Godzilla vs. Megalon*

INDEX

Abe, Kobo, 193
Abominable Snowman, 15-17, **19-20**, 21, 29, 218, 356
AB-PT Pictures, 29-31, 40
Adams, Nick, 78
Agon the Atomic Dragon, 75, 77, **114-115**
All Monsters Attack, 77, 97, 99, 113, 128, **139-144**, 163, 171, 362, 383
American International Pictures, 105, 107, 109-110, 119
Arikawa, Sadamasa, 19, 96, 113, 123, 126, 147-148, 360-363
Atragon, 6, **58-63**, 64, 77, 133, 138, 227-228, 240, 329, 336, 389, 409
Bandai, 266, 294, 368
Banno, Yoshimitsu, 153-159, **160-161**, 162, 167, 201, 205, 214, 363, 365, 366
Battle in Outer Space, **32**, 46, 49, 60, 64, 75, 77, 148, 227-228, 232, 357
Beast from 20,000 Fathoms, The, 8-9, 35, 313
Beck, John, 51-52
Bercovitch, Reuben, **85**
Bio Planet WoO, 103
Birth of Rodan, The, 23, 34, 356
Birth of the Japanese Islands, The, 153, 160-161, 167
Bloodthirsty Trilogy, The, 56, 149
Blue Christmas, **230**
Borenstein, Max, 351
Bride of Godzilla, 22, 24, 27-28, 34, 233, 237, 240, 356
Burr, Raymond, 241-246, 310
Callaham, David, 351
Chiba, Sonny, 182, 201, 223
Chibikko Special, 170
Cold Wind Monjiro, 171
Columbia Pictures, 43, 46

Conflagration, 148, **211**
Continuation: King Kong vs. Godzilla, 65
Cooper, Merian C., 53
Creature from the Black Lagoon, 94
Cyborg 009, 229, 294
Daimajin (1966), **87**
Day of Resurrection, 193
De Bont, Jan, 309, 323
Deathquake, **236**
Dekker, Fred, 237
Destroy All Monsters, 7, 25, 111, **123-129**, 139-140, 144, 148, 158, 167, 175, 361
Devlin, Dean, 309, 313
Dunham, Robert, 70
Ebirah, Horror of the Deep, 77, **96-98**, 99, 112, 127-128, 142, 148, 184-185, 201
Edwards, Gareth, 349-354
Elliot, Ted, 309
Emmerich, Roland, 309, 313
ESPY, 128, 133, 148, 149-150, 185-186, 193, **206-209**, 227, 263, 365
Evil of Dracula, **207**
Facts in the Case of M. Valdemar, The, 145
Fearful Attack of the Flying Saucers, 31, 75, 356
Final War, The, 47-48
First 41 Hours of World War III, The, 47-48
Flying Battleship, The, 64, 133, 137
Frankenstein Conquers the World, 80
Frankenstein vs. Baragon, 7, 13, **78-84**, 85, 93, 99, 125, 128-130, 132, 382
Frankenstein vs. Godzilla, 70, 74, 78, 80, 128, 359
Fujitani, Ayako, 317
Fujuki, Yu, 52

414

Fukuda, Jun, 42, 44, 96-99, 110, 127, 171, 174-175, 178, **184-185**, 195, 202-203, 207, 209-210, 214, 217, 228, 357, 360-361, 364-367
Fukusaku, Kinji, 229
Fukushima, Masami, 55, **57**, 155, 195, 358, 364
Gamera (1965), **86-87**, 90, 110, 119
Gamera 2: Advent of Legion, 294, **304**, 314
Gamera 3: Revenge of Irys, **314-318**, 320, 323
Gamera Super Monster, 232, **234**, 290
Gamera the Brave, 290, 318
Gamera vs. Barugon, **87-88**, 104-105, 119, 359, 398, 401
Gamera vs. Giant Beast Garasharp, 91
Gamera vs. Guiron, 7, 92, **141**
Gamera vs. Gyaos, 90, **104-105**, 106, 119-121, 355, 361, 398, 401
Gamera vs. Jiger, **146**, 151
Gamera vs. Leoman, 151
Gamera vs. Phoenix, 91, 113, 290, 293, 318, 369, 411
Gamera vs. Two-Headed Monster W, 90, 159, 364
Gamera vs. Viras, **119-122**, 140, 355, 401
Gamera vs. Zigra, **151-152**, 159, 407
Gamera, Guardian of the Universe, 91, **290-293**, 314
Gappa, the Triphibian Monster, 7, 40, 103, **106-108**
Ghidorah, the Three-Headed Monster, **71-74**, 78, 99, 114, 162, 167, 381
Ghostly Whale That Came from the Sea to Attack Tokyo, The, 13
Giant Behemoth, The, 35
Giant Horde Beast Nezura, 86, 90
Giant Monster Assault, 95-96, 146
Giant Monster Gamera vs. the Ice Men from Outer Space, 87
Gigantis, the Fire Monster, 30
Go! Greenman, 113, 142
Godzilla (1954), **8-14**, 15-17, 19, 21, 29, 202, 217, 234, 410
Godzilla (1998), 295, 303, 305, **309-313**, 321, 323
Godzilla (2014), 313, **349-354**
Godzilla (Filmation series), 140
Godzilla (Hanna-Barbera series), **222**
Godzilla 1985, **241-247**, 325, 409-410
Godzilla 2000, 4, 264, 308, **321-326**, 342-343, 371
Godzilla 3-D to the MAX, 161, 349
Godzilla Against Mechagodzilla, 280, **333-336**, 337, 341-343, 395
Godzilla Raids Again, 15-16, **17-19**, 20-21, 27, 29-30, 34, 202, 235, 329, 379
Godzilla Resurrected, 235
Godzilla vs. Astrogodzilla, 275, 282-283, 285
Godzilla vs. Barubaroi, 344
Godzilla vs. Biollante, **248-263**, 264-265, 268-269, 271, 276, 283-284, 286-287, 323, 367-368, 393-394, 396, 409, 412
Godzilla vs. Destroyah, 275-276, **295-302**, 303, 305, 321, 325-326, 343
Godzilla vs. Frankenstein, 70, 74, 78, 358
Godzilla vs. Gigamoth, 272-273, 368
Godzilla vs. Gigan, 74, 76-77, 113, 129, 155, 159, **162-169**, 170, 173, 175, 184, 202, 217, 341, 388
Godzilla vs. Hedorah, 57, 68, 129, 131, 132, **152-159**,

415

160-162, 165, 167, 169, 177, 205, 214, 349, 363, 386
Godzilla vs. King Ghidorah, 116, 168, 248, 261, **268-272**, 273, 277, 288, 303, 307, 319, 363, 368, 394
Godzilla vs. Mechagodzilla (1974), 7, 57, 76, 177, 184-185, **195-202**, 203-204, 210, 216, 288
Godzilla vs. Mechagodzilla (1993), 248, **277-282**, 284, 288, 295, 338, 395
Godzilla vs. Megaguirus, **324**, 331-333, 342
Godzilla vs. Megalon, 7, 76-77, 129, 144, 168, 169, **170-173**, 174-175, 184-185, 201, 217, 349, 389-391, 393, 410, 413
Godzilla vs. Mothra, 46, 252, **272-275**, 276, 282, 288, 301, 305, 319, 338, 342, 368-369, 381, 394-395, 410
Godzilla vs. Space Godzilla, 14, 26, 183, 217, 264, 275, 279-280, **282-288**, 289, 292, 321, 344, 370
Godzilla vs. the Devil, 85
Godzilla vs. the Space Monsters, 163-164, 177, 363
Godzilla, King of the Monsters in 3-D, 237
Godzilla, King of the Monsters!, 29, 40, 242-243, 246
Godzilla, Mothra and King Ghidorah: Giant Monsters All-Out Attack, 14, **327-332**
Godzilla, Red Moon, Erabus, Halfon: No Man's Land of the Monsters, 173
Godzilla: Final Wars, 14, 313, 329, **343-348**, 349
Godzilla: Legend of the Asuka Fortress, 75, 249
Godzilla: Super Wars, 285
Godzilla: Tokyo S.O.S., **337-343**

Gorath, 7, 47, **49-50**, 52, 61, 69, 128, 130, 132, 147, 228, 232, 347, 357-358
Gorgo, **35-40**, 107, 237, 410
Goto, Tsutomu, 205
Goyer, David S., 351
Grand Duel in Magic, 104, 222, 229
Great Thief, The, **60**
Gulliver's Travels Beyond the Moon, 75
Gunhed, 249, 302, 368
Half Human, 20
Hashimoto, Koji, 231, 238, 269, 367
Hashimoto, Shinobu, 48
Haynes, Lynda, 137
Hell in the Pacific, 85, 95, 146
Hidaka, Shigeaki, 17
Higuchi, Shinji, 194, 266, 291, 294, 369-371
Hirai, Kazumasa, 178
Hirata, Akihiko, 99, 199, 238, 256
Hirose, Shoichi, 94
Hitchcock, Alfred, 55
H-Man, The, 22, 27-28, **30**, 46, 128, 132, 207
Hodgson, William Hope, 54-57, 358
Honda, Ishiro, 6, 10-15, 19-25, 31, 33, 38, 44-46, 49-56, 62, 65, 67-68, 70, 73-74, 83-84, 90, 94, 96, 99, 105, 113,123, 126-131, 136-137, 140-144, 147-148, 152-153, 158, 173-177, 184, 209, 212-219, 231, 238, 351, 355-365, 409, 411
Horror of Dracula, 145
Horror of the Wolf, 148, **178-183**
Hoshi, Shinichi, 55
Hoshi, Yuriko, 47
Human Torch, The, 208
Human Vapor, The, **44**
Ifukube, Akira, 167, 238, 287, 301
Igami, Masaru, 222, 229

In the Shadow of Glory, 8, 10, 86
Inoue, Yasoyuke, 142
Inter Ice Age 4, 193
Invasion of Astro-Monster, 77, **82**, 85, 98, 99, 102, 126-127, 157, 162, 217, 271
Invisible Avenger, **18**
Invisible Man vs. the Human Torch, 184-185, 209, 214
Ito, Jerry, 44
Ito, Kazunori, 266, 290, 292-293, **294**, 314-315, 369-371
Ito, Yumi and Emi, 43
Japan S.O.S.: Godzilla's Suicide Strategy!, 203, 233
Japan Sinks (TV series), **190**
Japan Sinks, Part II, 193
Japanese Apache, The, 186, 193
Jaws, 221, 223
Jira Monster (short story), 9, 15
Jissoji, Akio, 265-267
Johnny Sokko and His Flying Robot, 222
Journey to the West, 21
Kaiju Gojira (novel), 13
Kaiju Gojira (radio serial), 13
Kajita, Koji, 60, 62
Kakefuda, Masahiro, 208
Kamen Rider, 222
Kaneko, Shusuke, 266, 280, 291, 294, 314, 317-318, **319-320**, 326, 369-371
Kashiwabara, Hiroshi, 217, 286, 289, 321, 323, 370-371
Kawakita, Koichi, 26, 175, 259-261, 270-272, 275, 278, 280, 286, 296, 298, 300, 306, 326, 328, 367-370
Kayama, Shigeru, 8, 13, **15-16**, 17, 21, 25, 34, 41, 84, 355-356, 378-379
Kemmerling, Warren, 242, 245
Kimura, Takeshi, 23, 26-27, 30, 48-49, 55, 70, 79, 83, **130-132**, 356-358
King Brothers, The, 29, 35-40

King Kong (1933), 13, 108
King Kong (1976), 221, 312
King Kong Escapes, 79, **108-109**, 139, 197, 202, 207, 361
King Kong Lives, 233, 253, 259
King Kong Show, The, 96-99, 108, 139
King Kong vs. Frankenstein, 51
King Kong vs. Godzilla, 13, 40, **51-53**, 65, 66, 68, 75, 77, 80, 83, 97, 107, 169, 215, 269-270, 274, 292, 358, 368
King of Monsters: Godzilla Resurrected, 234-235, 240
Kinjo, Tetsuo, 13, 100-101, 115-116, **117-118**
Kitamura, Ryuhei, 343-348, 372
Kizer, R.J., 241-247
Kobayashi, Shinichiro, 249, 252-253, **264**, 276, 283, 367-368, 412
Kochi, Momoko, 20
Koizumi, Hiroshi, 20, 45, 68, 99, 199
Komatsu, Sakyo, 100, 133, 149, 186, 191-192, **193-194**, 203, 205, 206, 209, 227, 230, 240, 364-367, 370, 413
Komatsuzaki, Shigeru, 60-61, **64**, 69, 100
Kubo, Akira, 50, 55
Kuronuma, Ken, 23-24, 31, **34**, 41, 356
Kurosawa, Akira, 24, 71, 160, 187, 239
Kurosawa, Toshio, 183
Kuru Island, 35-39
Lake of Dracula, 148, 150, **154**
Last Dinosaur, The, 14, **224-226**, 409
Last Godzilla, The (manga), 39, 46
Last War, The, 7, **47-50**, 94, 130, 132, 205-206, 357, 365
Latitude Zero, 77, **133-138**, 139, 140, 208, 362, 409

Legend of Dinosaurs and Monster Birds, **221-224**, 228-229, 366
Lourié, Eugene, 35-40
Luminous Fairies and Mothra, The, 41-43
Mabuchi, Kaoru, 83, 93-94, 108, 123, **130-132**, 153-154, 160, 162, 359-363
Madame White Snake, 27
Maeda, Ai, 317
Masuda, Toshio, 205, 365
Matango, **54-56**, 57, 62, 64, 128, 130, 132, 155, 194-195, 260, 358
Matsubayashi, Shue, 48, 357
Melchior, Ib, 29
Message from Space, 223, 228, 366
Mifune, Toshiro, 60-61, 95
Mighty Jack, 64, 77, **136**, 203-204, 267
Mimura, Wataru, 278, 282, 322-323, 326, 333-337, 341, **342**, 343, 345-347, 368-369, 371-372, 396
Miner, Steve, 237
Mirror Man, 203
Mizuno, Kumi, 72, 93, 97-98, 148
Monkey Army, The, 193
Monster King Godzilla, 39
Monsters Converge on Okinawa Showdown in Cape Zanpa, 195-199
Mori, Iwao, 8, 13, 17, 27, 41, 45, 48, 109
Moritani, Shiro, 187
Mothra (1961), **41-46**, 48, 52, 65, 68, 107, 268, 292, 338
Mothra vs. Bagan, 262, 268, 273-276, 302-303, 305, 368
Mothra vs. Godzilla, 45-46, **65-68**, 69-70, 73, 77, 88, 99, 102, 252, 268, 354, 358, 368, 381, 412
Murao, Akira, 235, 240, 367
Murase, Keizo, 52, 73, 413

Murata, Takeo, 10, 17-18, **21**, 23, 84, 130, 355, 356
Mysterians, The, 15-16, **25-26**, 27-28, 33, 49, 51, 60, 64, 69, 115, 132, 232, 271, 286, 321, 326
Nagahara, Shuichi, 233, 236, **240**
Nagata, Masaichi, 86-90, 119, 187
Nakajima, Haruo, 63, 125-126, 155, 159, 409
Nakamura, Shinichiro, 41
Nakanishi, Ryuzo, 40, 107, 234, 361, 366-367
Nakano, Teruyoshi, 7, 13, 53, 73, 80, 97, 135, 155-157, 159-160, 162-164, 167, 170-172, 175, 187, 192, 196-197, 200-202, 208, 210, 218, 226, 240, 363-367, 410
Natsuki, Yosuke, 70, 238
Negishi, Akemi, 19
Nessie, 221, 226, 366
New World Pictures, 241-247
Nielsen, Leslie, 241-242
Nishikawa, Shinji, 260, 269, 278, 280, 297, 303, 306-307, 322, 326, 368
Noda, Keiichi, 151
O'Brien, Willis, 51-52
Obayashi, Nobuhiko, 233
Ogawa, Ei, 95, 145-146, **149-150**, 207-208, 360, 362-363, 365
Okami, Jojiro, 25, 49, 69, 356-358
Okawara, Takao, 273, 279, 296, 299, 300, 323, 369-371
Omori, Kazuki, 46, 250, 253-256, 259-260, 263-264, 268-273, 275, **276**, 282, 296, 299, 367-370
Operation Robinson Crusoe: King Kong vs. Ebirah, 95-96
Orang Pendek's Revenge, 15
Oshikawa, Shunro, 58
Overgard, William, 224

Prophecies of Nostradamus (Catastrophe 1999), 49, 148, 158, 160-161, **205-206**, 209, 213-214, 232
Pulgasari, 261
Randel, Anthony, 241-247
Rankin/Bass, 96, 99, 108-109, 224, 226, 360
Rebirth of Mothra, 45, **301-303**, 305, 308
Rebirth of Mothra II, **306-307**, 315
Rebirth of Mothra III, **307-308**
Red Beard, 71-72
Reno, Jean, 310, 345
Reptilicus, 29-30
Resurrection of the Beast, 145
Return of Godzilla, The, 22, 114, **233-240**, 241, 247-248, 252, 255-256, 262, 269, 271, 342
Return of King Ghidorah, The, 164
Return of Ultraman, **156**, 249, 264
RKO, 51-53, 96
Rodan (1956), 21, **22-25**, 27-28, 34-35, 38, 130, 132, 184, 278, 336
Rossio, Terry, 309-310
Rybnick, Harry, 29
Sagisu, Tomio, 100
Sahara, Kenji, 30, 52, 147
Sakai, Frankie, 47, 52, 274
Sano, Shiro, 14
Saperstein, Henry G., 7, 70, 81, 83, 85, 93-95, 99, 139, 149, 309, 410
Sasaki, Mamoru, 265-266, **267**
Satsuma, Kenpachiro, 300
Sayonara Jupiter, 194, 227, **230-231**, 240, 367
Schreibman, Paul, 29, 30
Scientific Investigation Agency Bemular, 101-102
Secret of the Telegian, The, **42**, 184-185, 357
Sekita, Hiroshi, 94, 99

Sekizawa, Shinichi, 6-7, 31-34, 42-44, 52, 57, 59-74, **75-77**, 96-98, 109, 110-117, 130-131, 135-137, 140-144, 162-173, 177, 184, 195, 217, 249, 253, 256, 356-362, 364, 367
Sharpe, Don, 133-138
Sherdeman, Ted, 133-138, 362
Shiba, Kazue, 110
Shin Godzilla, 9-10
Shintoho, 31, 75, 356
Sohl, Jerry, 70, 74, 78-79, 81, 84, 358-359
Son of Godzilla, 77, **110-112**, 123, 128-129, 139, 142, 147, 184-185, 219, 355, 361, 382, 413
Son of Kong, 20
Space Amoeba, 95, **146-148**, 150, 152, 340, 362, 386
Space Battleship Yamato, 62, 227
Space Monster Devil Manta, 228, 366
Space Monster Dogora, 7, 64, **69-70**, 74, 77, 114, 359
Space Monster Guilala, **105-106**, 361, 370
Spectreman, 89, **152**, 157, 170, 199, 202, 391
Star Wars, 184, 194, 227-232, 240
Street Fighter, The, 201, 223
Submersion of Japan, 47, 100, 148, **186-192**, 193-196, 205-206, 227, 238, 241
Super Godzilla (video game), 286
Super Robot Red Baron, 217
Sword and the Dragon, The, 71
Takahashi, Niisan, 86-87, **90-92**, 104-105, 119, 290, 318, 359, 361-363, 369
Takahashi, Noriko, 97, 147
Takarada, Akira, 47, 49, 99, 148, 345, 352
Takashima, Tadao, 52

Takayama, Yukiko, 110, 210-211, 217, **219-220**, 365
Tamba, Tetsuro, 191
Tanaka, Fumio, 76, 145, 147, 149, 208, 235, 363
Tanaka, Tomoyuki, 6, 8, 13-17, 20-27, 31, 34, 41, 47, 57, 59, 61, 71, 86, 94, 96, 110-112, 123, 130-131, 139-140, 147-149, 152, 156, 158, 160, 162, 166, 168, 171, 177, 187, 194-195, 197, 203, 205, 208, 210-211, 218, 227-228, 233, 240, 248, 250, 253, 260, 268-269, 276, 299, 312, 321, 365, 368, 370, 412
Tani, Seji, 123
Taniguchi, Senkichi, 10, 355
Tatopoulos, Patrick, 312
Terror Beneath the Sea, 57
Terror of Mechagodzilla, 110, 184, 203, **210-218**, 233, 239, 251, 289, 392, 410
Tezuka, Masaaki, 249, 273, 333-337, 341, 343, 348, 371-372
Tezuka, Osamu, 75
The Fate of Orang Pendek, 16-17
Them!, 24
Three Treasures, The, 13, 33, 46, 61, 63, 130
Tidal Wave, 193, 241
Toho Champion Matsuri Festival, 248
Tokyo Blackout, 194, 203
Tomei, Lisa, 243, 245
Tomiyama, Shogo, 6, 259, 277, 282, 284, 288, 295-298, 305, 312, 319, 321-322, 326, 329, 333, 336, 340, 342-348, 369-370
Toshimitsu, Teizo, 11
Tsuburaya Productions, 100, 103, 107, 115, 125, 148, 170, 173, 193, 224, 265, 267, 360, 364

Tsuburaya, Eiji, 6, 8, 13-15, 21, 25, 33, 49, 73, 84, 94-98, 100-102, 109, 117, 126, 147-148, 153, 213, 355-363, 411
Tsuchiya, Yoshio, 18, 20, 26-27, 56, 71-72, 74, 79, 147-148, 238
Two Godzillas: Japan S.O.S., 110, 219
Ultra Q, 13, 21, 95, 98, **100-101**, 102-104, 115, 117-118, 125, 193-194, 203-204, 265-267, 294, 320
Ultra Q: The Movie, **265-266**
Ultraman (1966), 21, 75, 100, **101-103**, 104, 115, 125, 155, 265
Ultraman 80, **229**
Ultraman Ace, **172**
Ultraman Leo, **198**
Ultraman Powered, 294
Ultraman Taro, **176**
Ultraman: Monster Bible, 265
Ultraman: The Adventure Begins, 265
Ultraseven, **115-116**, 121, 203, 267
Unagami, Hideo, 22-24, **27-28**, 30, 34, 233, 240, 356
UPA, 70-71, 80, 83, 85, 94, 96, 139, 146, 149, 358, 360
Vampire Doll, The, **145-146**, 147-150
Varan (1958), **31-33**, 34, 40-41
Varan, the Unbelievable, 33
Voice in the Night, The, 54-57, 358
Volcano Monsters, The, 29-30, 40
Wakabayashi, Akiko, 72, 207
War in Space, The, 128, 184-185, **227-228**, 232-234, 240, 409
War of the Gargantuas, The, 64, 82-85, **93-94**, 104, 132, 293, 336
Watanabe, Akira, 72, 103, 361
Weisman, Straw, 241-242

Woo, 21, 100-101, 115
Worthington Yates, George, 51
X From Outer Space, The, **105-106**, 261
Yamamoto, Michio, 145, 363, 365
Yamashita, Kensho, 183, 217, 287, 370
Yamato Takeru, **281**, 282-283, 288, 368, 369
Yamaura, Hiroyasu, 195, 201, **203-204**, 233, 364
Yamazaki, Gan, 40, 106
Yashiro, Miki, 55
Yasumi, Toshio, 48, 130-131, 357, 365
Yokotani, Masahiro, 327, 330, 333, 337, 371
Yongary, Monster from the Deep, **109-110**
Yoshida, Yuji, 297
Yuasa, Noriaki, 86-90, 104, 119, 121, 151, 169, 359, 361-363, 410
Zatoichi, 91
Zero Fighter, 63, 75, 77, 110
Zone Fighter, 129, 170, **173-176**, 184-185, 195

About the Author

John LeMay is the Rondo Award nominated author of such film histories as *The Big Book of Japanese Giant Monster Movies: The Lost Films; Kong Unmade: The Lost Films of Skull Island;* and *Deadly Spaghetti: The Goodest, the Baddest & the Ugliest Italian Westerns Ever Made*. LeMay also writes on Fortean subjects such as cryptozoology and ufology in the *Cowboys & Saurians* series and *The Real Cowboys & Aliens* series with Noe Torres. LeMay is also a contributor to magazines *G-Fan, Mad Scientist, Xenorama,* and *Cinema Retro*.

SPECIAL PREVIEW
A Chapter from the upcoming book
EDITING JAPANESE MONSTERS
A comprehensive reference book that covers the differences between the original Japanese versions vs. overseas versions such as *Godzilla Raids Again* vs. *Gigantis, the Fire Monster*; *Varan* vs. *Varan, the Unbelievable*; *Gamera* vs. *Gammera the Invincible*; *Great Monster War* vs. *Monster Zero*; *Submersion of Japan* vs. *Tidal Wave*; *Conflagration* vs. *High Seas Hijack*; *Legend of Dinosaurs and Monster Birds* vs. *The "Legend of Dinosaurs,"* and many more!!!
Available in 2021

GIANT MONSTER VARAN vs. TELEVISION

Giant Monster Varan	Part I: "Varan Appears"; Part II: "Varan's Counterattack"
October 14, 1958	Never Broadcast, DVD release 2005
87 minutes	54 minutes
Cut Scenes: 35 minutes	Added Scenes: 2 ½ minutes

*(differences between the different versions are represented via **emboldened** text)

GIANT MONSTER VARAN actually began life as a U.S. TV movie, presumably requested by AP-TV to Toho. Eventually, the American end of the production backed out, and Toho decided to change *Varan* into a theatrical feature right in the middle of filming. This explains why *Varan* was shot in black and white in the Academy ratio when Toho had previously made the jump to color and widescreen with *Earth Defense Force* in 1957. Though it was too late to switch to color, Toho did "convert" it into Tohoscope, or rather Toho-Panscope" in which they cropped the existing footage from the top and bottom into widescreen.

Actually, even after making the jump to a feature film, Toho wanted to keep the TV export option open for overseas distribution. As such, Akira Ifukube would compose two different soundtracks, one for television and one for the film with a larger orchestra to greater dramatic effect. Shooting finished in August and the TV score was recorded for three days at the end of that month from the 27th to the 29th. From there, Toho prepped the Japanese theatrical release and the hoped for American TV deal at the same time. *Toho Special Effects Movies Complete Works* even stated that Toho shipped off the TV miniseries version of *Varan* in two parts: "Varan Appears" and "Varan's Counterattack" (each 27 minute segment consisting of three film reels), to their international office in Los Angeles.[1] If these reels were in the original "un-cut" Academy Ratio is unknown but they probably were. What is known is that when Toho released *Varan* on DVD in 2005, as a special feature, they recreated the lost TV version as an extra.[2] Naturally, this version is reconstructed using the theatrical widescreen footage and is incomplete with missing footage (though the TV soundtrack is complete) running 54 minutes, or two 27 minute episodes.[3]

Watching the TV version is an interesting experience due to the fact that it more or less has the same score by Ifukube, just recorded in a less grand manner. Essentially the TV version is similar to the original but excises most of the opening and also the interlude of Varan battling the military at sea. This is not at all surprising, as the original teleplay didn't include the sequence set at sea—that was added in purely to pad out the running time to feature length. To a lesser degree, some—but not all—of the opening scenes were added in only when the teleplay became a screenplay. For certain, the butterfly hunting scene was not in the teleplay, though some of Kenji and Yuriko's scenes in the Iwaya Village may have been.

The TV version begins with the same theatrical credits, and opens with the same narration (and rocket scene) only extended to fit a **prologue**. The extra narration, with the visuals in brackets, goes thusly: **"There is an area called the Tibet of Japan [zoom in on map of Tohoku region]…about 40 km in diameter in the Tohoku region [the two university students in their jeep driving through the forest]. People have believed that there is a mountain god [stone marker in the village]…called Baradagi living in the area [the jeep drives through the village]. Baradagi suddenly emerged in front of a scholar [the two university men recoil in fear]…who had entered the area to**

---

[1] *Toho Special Effects Film Ultimate Collection*, pp.33-36
[2] This author can find no mention that the TV version aired anywhere, and it may have been constructed the same year as the DVD based off of old notes and the timing of the TV score and audio.
[3] As to even more alternate Japanese versions of Varan, at one time, there reportedly existed a VHS version of Varan that ran one minute shorter than the original. Toho cut out about a minute's worth of footage concerning the Iwaya villagers. As the current DVD runs a full 86 minutes rather than 85, it's presumable these scenes were kept in for the DVD release.

425

solve the mystery [Varan emerges from the lake]." The narration notably does not contain the line, **"We are now about to reveal the most mysterious story ever told,"** and ends on the shot of **Varan emerging from the lake. Varan walking through the countryside, causing an avalanche, and destroying the native village is shown in an abbreviated form.** We then cut to the Anti-Varan Headquarters (which the narrator explains to us briefly) and get one line of dialogue from an authority announcing that "there's nothing we can do against Varan." From here we cut to Professor Sugimoto's lab and the episode finally begins in earnest. The scene is slightly abbreviated and is the one where Sugimoto explains that the monster is a Varanapode and the JSDF asks for his help.

The next sequence, where the JSDF arrives at the lake and prepares to attack is actually extended, not cut! The extensions are easy to spot because they are audio only. This would have to mean a decent amount of footage was edited out of the film's theatrical cut. Most of these "scenes" appear to just be extended shots, as they offer only sound effects or music but no dialogue. As for bits that do contain dialogue, one of the more notable extra bits includes the following exchange between two onlookers:

Onlooker 1: Did you hear a strange sound?
Onlooker 2: A strange sound?
Onlooker 1: Like tick tock, tick tock…see yeah…
Onlooker 2: I hear that too!
Onlooker 1: Sounds like a heartbeat!
Onlooker 2: Don't scare me like that!

Later, more of this cut dialogue from the same men can be heard again:

Onlooker 1: How long do we have to wait?
Onlooker 2: Hmm…

After this, Varan finally emerges. Though there are many extended scenes, there are no deleted scenes per say. **Kenji does have one extra piece of dialogue in the cave when he tells Yuriko, "Hang on!"** It's pretty obvious in the theatrical cut that Varan's flight scene represents a huge turning point in the film based upon how the music hits a high note and it fades to black. Here this does indeed signal the end of the episode "Varan Appears."

Though it's not designated as such, it is obvious that the second half is "Varan's Counterattack" as it begins with the credit scene all over again plus another recap. The narration goes, **"Varan suddenly emerged in the area called the Tibet of Japan. Despite the attack by the Self Defense Force, Varan disappeared into the sky. And now, Varan is approaching Tokyo after it evaded the attack of the Maritime Self Defense Forces [Shots of the sea attack on Varan]. Can we let Varan destroy Tokyo? It means our abandonment of the rights of Man and blasphemy against the gods who created us. We must annihilate this evil monster."**

From here the episode begins with the mobilization of military forces in Tokyo and basically plays out like the climax of the finished film with the extended take here and there. Both the episode and the theatrical film end exactly the same way with the same closing line from the narrator, "Thus, Varan has vanished into a veil of mystery. After a desperate struggle, man has now won another victory."

Worth Watching? For historical value, yes? For that matter, *Varan* is one of the more boring, padded out monster movies from Toho. As such, those looking for a quick *Varan* fix may find this version preferable to the full cut.

Overview (differences in bold)

Original Version	TV Version
Toho Panscope Logo/ Opening Credits (0:00-1:45)	Part I Opening Credits (0:00-1:26)
Rocket Launch (1:46-2:46)	Rocket Launch/**Prologue** (1:27-2:09)
Prof. Sugimoto's lab (2:47-3:40)	
Butterfly hunting/ Killed by Baradagi (3:41-7:44)	
Meeting in Prof. Sugimoto's lab/Meet Yuriko (7:45-9:48)	
Journey to Iwaya/Meet Gen (9:49-13:08)	
Village of Iwaya (13:09-16:45)	
Searching for Gen (16:46-20:46)	
Varan surfaces	

(20:47-23:26) **Varan destroys the village** (23:27-26:04)	
The JSDF meets with Sugimoto (26:05-27:32)	Anti-Varan HQ/The JSDF meets with Sugimoto (3:16-4:36)
Military arrives at the lake (27:33-31:59)	Military arrives at the lake (4:37-9:15) **[0:12 longer]**
Launching the attack/ Varan emerges/Military retreats (32:00-40:04)	Launching the attack/ Varan emerges/Military retreats (9:16-18:52) **[1:32 longer]**
Varan attacks Kenji and Yuriko/Varan takes flight (40:05-47:27)	Varan attacks Kenji and Yuriko/Varan takes flight (18:53-27:00) **[0:45 longer]**
Anti-Varan HQ discussion (47:28-50:26)	**Part II Opening Credits** (27:01-28:33)
Varan battles JSDF at sea (50:27-59:13)	**Part II Recap** (28:34-29:57)
Depth charges used on Varan (59:14-1:02:34)	
Evacuating Tokyo/ Fujiyama's new explosives (1:02:35-1:06:21)	Evacuating Tokyo/ Fujiyama's new explosives (29:58-33:44)
Attacking Varan at Haneda Airport/Kenji drives the truck under Varan (1:06:22-1:17:09)	Attacking Varan at Haneda Airport/Kenji drives the truck under Varan (33:45-44:36) **[0:04 longer]**
New plan of attack/Varan explodes (1:17:10-1:26:39)	New plan of attack/Varan explodes (44:37-54:06)

Other Books in the
Big Book of Japanese Giant Monster Movies Series

Similar Books by this Author

www.ingramcontent.com/pod-product-compliance
Lightning Source LLC
Chambersburg PA
CBHW031054080526
44587CB00011B/675